D0208442

Postcolonial African Writers

Postcolonial African Writers

A BIO-BIBLIOGRAPHICAL CRITICAL SOURCEBOOK

Edited by
Pushpa Naidu Parekh and
Siga Fatima Jagne

Foreword by **Carole Boyce Davies**
Emmanuel S. Nelson, Advisory Editor

Greenwood Press

Westport, Connecticut

Library of Congress Cataloging-in-Publication Data

Postcolonial African writers : a bio-bibliographical critical
  sourcebook / edited by Pushpa Naidu Parekh and Siga Fatima Jagne ;
  foreword by Carole Boyce Davies.
       p.   cm.
  Includes bibliographical references and index.
  ISBN 0–313–29056–3 (alk. paper)
    1. African literature—Bio-bibliography.   2. Authors,
African—20th century—Bio-bibliography.   I. Parekh, Pushpa Naidu.
II. Jagne, Siga Fatima.
PL8010.P585   1998
809'.8896'0904—dc21
  [B]   97–5856

British Library Cataloguing in Publication Data is available.

Library of Congress Catalog Card Number: 97–5856
ISBN: 0–313–29056–3

First published in 1998

Greenwood Press, 88 Post Road West, Westport, CT 06881
An imprint of Greenwood Publishing Group, Inc.

Printed in the United States of America

The paper used in this book complies with the
Permanent Paper Standard issued by the National
Information Standards Organization (Z39.48–1984).

10 9 8 7 6 5 4 3 2 1

CONTENTS

FOREWORD

The post-colonial theoretical project has been to identify a contextual paradigm for cultural and intellectual production, and to identify economic, social, and political realities in the wake of European colonialism and in light of the continuing condition of what has now been defined as post-coloniality. Those located within this theoretical sphere, who are then defined variously as colonial or post-colonial subjects occupy a range of geographical and historical locations united by their relation to European (largely British commonwealth) colonialism. In this particular, here literary, context, African writers constitute the subject of a specific (post) coloniality and are therefore brought within a singular analytic frame based on the internal logics of this discourse.

Postcolonial theory has made tremendous strides into becoming a respectable academic discourse. The assertions and critiques of the conceptualization of post-coloniality have been variously articulated. A recent collection of essays, *Contemporary Post-Colonial Theory, A Reader* edited by Padmini Mongia presents a fair range of positions.[1] My own particular critique has supported those of Shohat, McLintock, Mukerjee, and Suleri and includes the fact that along with its totalizing approach, post-colonial theory continues to turn on the same masculinist assumptions of coloniality even as it claims to speak for the entire population.[2] Additionally, while one may recognize the post-colonial condition as a descriptor of the conditions of both the colonized and the colonizers in the wake of colonialism, the formulation of post-colonialism so far has taken more account of the experience of the (formerly) colonized and their perpetuated condition of coloniality and has been short on analyses which bring into play questions of global/late capitalism and American imperialism which more accurately describes the colonial condition today.

Further clarifying their position on postcoloniality, editors Chris Tiffin and

Alan Lawson, in their concluding comments to their collection *De-Scribing Empire: Post-Colonialism and Textuality* titled "Reading Difference," argue that the "(post-) colonial subjects—races as well as individuals—continue to be interpellated by a range of imperial mechanisms just as effectively as they were previously coerced by the overt and formal institutions of Empire (230)."[3] They assert further that imperialism and its practices continue although not necessarily in the same form. Thus, for them, the practice of postcoloniality moves in two interrelated directions: (1) it interrogates imperial texts to expose the founding ideologies of imperialism and (2) it accounts for the texts of those postcolonial subjects in order to recognize the numerous voices of those affected by Empire and thereby to resituate the former. Thus, a kind of relationality between the two discourses is put into play.

We come then to this particular text and its contributions. *Postcolonial African Writers: A Bio-Bibliographical Critical Sourcebook* works with the second level of this postcolonial project by putting forward the works of a wide range of "postcolonial" writers. This collection becomes a particular intervention in the field of postcolonial studies. Its primary and most important contribution is that it accounts concretely for a range of writers of a specific geographic specificity within the larger field of postcolonial studies. One of the concerns of those critical of postcolonial studies is that it often erases the specificity of a number of groups of writers and instead accounts for writers as they relate to colonialism. Thus African literary production, with its various valences, can easily get subordinated under this larger formulation. This text intervenes in an important way here by providing, within the rubric of postcolonial studies, a body of writers emanating from the African cultural experience.

Another significant contribution of this collection is that it consciously produces a gender balance in terms of its selection of writers and critics. Few texts have even bothered to sustain this balance. The fact that it is edited by two conscious women scholars from the "postcolonial" world is not to be dismissed. And while texts like *Into the Nineties, Post-Colonial Women's Writing* now exist, their existence often means that work dealing with the literature of specific geographic areas can avoid the task of full representation.[4] In the Preface to this book, Pushpa Naidu Parekh states, "the central organizing principle of the volume is postcoloniality as it is reflected in the novels, poetry, prose, and drama of major, minor, and emerging writers from diverse countries of Africa, including representative North and South African writers and writers of the Indian diaspora born in Africa, both male and female." The reach of *Postcolonial African Writers: A Bio-Bibliographical Critical Sourcebook* is towards broad representation at a variety of levels.

Each anthology struggles with its own question of inclusiveness. It is to this collection's credit that in its very structuring, representation of a variety of identities within the larger metanarrative of "postcoloniality" has been addressed. But even further, while the editors are definite about making sure that women's voices are heard, they are as clear that women's subject positions be recognized, "not as simply women's concerns, but as contentious, often desta-bilizing interventions that are located at all nodes of spatiality and temporality of postcolonial African writing" (preface). And this sense of inclusivity in terms of gender is not achieved at the expense of male writers and is mirrored as well in terms of geography, language, region, generation.

As postcolonial theory enters the academy more firmly as a recognized dis-course, texts previously studied under a range of rubrics are relocated within the larger definition of postcoloniality. A variety of texts studied as specific national literatures—African literature or Caribbean literature, or Australian lit-erature—now have another identity as postcolonial literatures just as they may have identity as women's literature or occupy some other category. *Postcolonial African Writers: A Bio-Bibliographical Critical Sourcebook* makes sure that African writers are not left behind as this discourse expands and clarifies itself. Instead it provides a wide range of authors and their texts, biographical and bibliographical information written by well-respected scholars in the field. Its existence makes the study of this literature much more accessible. For me, as a teacher of some of these literatures, it means an important addition, a necessary research tool, and a text which fills a variety of spaces in the existing body of critical materials.

NOTES

1. Padmini Mongia, ed., *Contemporary Post-Colonial Theory, A Reader* (London: New York: St. Martin's Press, 1996).

2. Carole Boyce Davies, *Black Women, Writing and Identity: Migrations of the Subject* (London: Routledge, 1994), 80–112.

3. Chris Tiffin and Alan Lawson, eds., *De-Scribing Empire: Post-Colonialism and Textuality* (London and New York: Routledge, 1994), 230–231.

4. Anna Rutherford, Lars Jensen, and Shirley Chew, eds., *Into the Nineties, Post-Colonial Women's Writing* (Australia, U.K. and Denmark: Dangaroo Press, 1994).

—*Carole Boyce Davies*
Florida International University

PREFACE

Postcolonial African writers have been, and currently are, engaging a major intervention in counterdiscursive and revisionist projects impacting the academic world since the fifties. Grasping the multiple coordinates of their intense investigations, deliberations, and debates underlying their literary productions involves an equally challenging, often overwhelming, but increasingly gratifying task. As editors of this reference sourcebook, Siga Jagne and I are passionately involved in making a commitment to effecting this task while recognizing that any grasping is also a letting go and any understanding is also a concession to the irreducibilities of mind and spirit. In a world where claims of global transnationalism are muted within the folds of neoimperialism and neocolonialism, a number of us who have traversed time and space and contentious borderlines are still imbricated in the ambivalences and contradictions of our realities.

In response to these realities, we bring together in this systematic reference volume over fifty bio-bibliographical and critical entries on selected known and emerging writers from diverse African countries, writing mainly in English and French. The selection of Anglophone and Francophone and a couple of Lusophone writers is not intended to reinscribe the notion that indigenous African languages are lost and forgotten or that important and significant literature is not produced in them. On the contrary, we acknowledge that in many instances, more artistically powerful and sociopolitically relevant material is being produced in the indigenous languages. Karin Barber discusses these issues very effectively in "African-Language Literature and Postcolonial Criticism."[1] We believe, however, that work in these diverse language areas should be undertaken and is being undertaken by scholars specialized in these languages. Albert S. Gérard in *African Language Literatures* undertook, as he stated, "to embark upon the task of gathering as many relevant historical facts within [his] scope of knowledge in languages that are known to [him] and ordering them into some sort of coherent pattern covering the fifteen-odd centuries that have elapsed since written composition began in Ethiopia.''[2] Other scholars, such as Mugyabuse M. Mulokozi, Randall L. Pauwels, Flora Veit-Wild, and C. F. Swanepoel, have undertaken useful and much-needed study of indigenous African-language literatures.[3] We have therefore limited our selections and wish to clarify that we do not claim to represent all postcolonial African writers, only a selective sample of writings mainly in English and French, with a glimpse into two Lusophone writers. I believe that ideally these writers should be read in conjunction with indigenous African and Arabic writers writing in Africa in order for us to understand the various trajectories of postcoloniality in African writing. As Gayatri Chakravorty Spivak put it, we must learn to become ''inter-literary.''[4] Moreover, in light of Gérard's cautionary warning that European-language writing in Africa may not last forever, even as Latin did not in Europe, since its producers are themselves dissatisfied with addressing only ''a tiny privileged minority,'' one can make no naïve assertions of future trends.[5]

Many of the writers we have included in this sourcebook are being studied in some undergraduate and several graduate programs in institutions across the world. Increasing interest in postcolonial studies, we know, does not reflect a readiness in academia to include hitherto-neglected area studies, or if they are included, to study them in ways that would destabilize the privileged grounding of a Western critical discourse of all literary productions. But it does begin to pose questions regarding what our students as well as faculty need to know and research before introducing courses on aspects of African literature. In fact, a sourcebook like ours hopefully will challenge academicians to think in terms of particular regional, cultural, social, political, and economic contexts and to research bio-bibliographical details. A major component of each entry, ''Major Works and Themes,'' provides a concise, interpretive summary of the writer's works in chronological sequence and a clear sense of the writer's primary themes and strategies. The central organizing principle of the volume is postcoloniality as it is reflected in the novels, poetry, prose, and drama of major, minor, and emerging writers from diverse countries of Africa, including representative North and South African writers and writers of the Indian diaspora born in Africa, both male and female. The contributors to this volume directly address the impact of the writer's experience and consciousness of postcoloniality, such as concerns with the issues of emerging identities in the postcolonial climate, neocolonialism and new forms of oppression, cultural and political hegemonies, neoelitism, language appropriation, economic instability, or the politics of publication and distribution, on his or her artistic imagination. The analysis of the works in most entries is also focused within the framework of postcolonial cultural and critical ideologies and theories. The ''Critical Reception'' section in each entry provides a summary of the critical reactions to the writer's work. A crucial objective of this section is to locate the significance of the writer in the postcolonial African literary context as well as the larger context of postcolonial literatures. The "Bibliography" consists of two sections—works by the writer and studies (or selected studies) of the writer. The selective secondary sources include significant critical studies that address in some way the postcolonialist aspects of the writer's life and works.

In this volume, we as editors have included several entries that discuss African women's subject positions in the context of colonizing and neocolonizing processes, not simply as women's concerns, but as contentious, often destabilizing interventions that are located at all nodes of spatiality and temporality of postcolonial African writing. While volumes specifically on African women serve their purpose, we hope, by placing several known and emerging women and men writers alongside each other, to expose, question, and often dispel the center-versus-margin construction of identities and ideologies as they are reflected in literary discourses. Many of the entries in this volume will locate African women in their own contexts, identifying both possibilities and problematics in their own realities, their concerns, and their issues. However, the critics' and theorists' insights, whether in this volume or outside, should not go unchallenged. It is the "subaltern" women's voices that need to be heard. Whether directly challenging Western feminists' colonization of the female experience or questioning their own authority in articulating all the problems of the subaltern women, these voices give shape and meaning to their own theoretical preoccupations.

Having said this, I would like to emphasize that I see our contributors as polyphonic voices. Their entries provide not only information regarding the life and works of the selected African writers but also divergent intellectual frameworks that define or emerge from the differences in colonial and post-colonial experiences within the various African states across the continent. Many entries illuminate thematic, structural, and narrative patterns as they embody multiple configurations of literature as intersections of specific aesthetic, political, sociohistorical, cultural, and economic forces created and sustained within colonial and post-colonial realities. Samuel A. Dseagu, Emmanuel S. Nelson, Emevwo Biakolo, Hema Chari, Vanessa Everson, Harold Barratt, and Brinda Bose, among others, provide insight into specific expressions of these intersections.

Samuel A. Dseagu elucidates the central concerns in Ayi Kwei Armah's novels by a careful examination of the symbolic representation of their characters within the context of postcolonial Ghana. The encroachment of Western materialism, the vacuum in leadership as a result of political instability and economic malaise, and the irony of who gains social status in postcolonial Ghana are imposing reflections of "larger national and international forces at work." Dseagu notes that Armah in his works, ranging from *The Beautyful Ones Are Not Yet Born* to *Two Thousand Seasons*, deals with Africa's "identity and predicament" in the context of "Africa's progression from independence, 'so woefully assimilated' to the West." Dseagu also raises the question of publication as crucial in Armah's critique of colonial and neocolonial politics. After having his first three novels published by American companies, Armah went to East

African Publishing House in order to support "the dissemination of local texts for the populations." With the publication of *Two Thousand Seasons*, Armah is committed, as Dseagu notes, to Africa as "the center of his reading public."

Emmanuel Nelson evaluates Chinua Achebe as a postcolonial writer who, through his engagement and "constant dialogue" with the history of the Igbo people of Nigeria, reconstructs an "oppositional," sometimes "subversive," version of "official," "authorized" history, even as he records the "private dilemmas of an individual post-colonial." Nelson illustrates, through a close analysis of the novels, that Achebe provides a "benevolent counterpoint" to the violence and madness of postcolonial realities, whether it be through women's "tasks of national renewal and the return to political sanity" (as in *Anthills of the Savannah*) or the emergence of "self-knowledge" and an "understanding of the daunting complexities of his nation's politics" (as in *A Man of the People*). Nelson combines a finely balanced interplay of close analysis and application of postcolonial theoretical framework in his criticism.

Emevwo Biakolo analyzes J. P. Clark-Bekederemo's poetry and plays in terms of two related concerns: "the celebration of African cultural experience and achievements, as exemplified among the Ijaw and Urhobo people of the Niger Delta, as well as lamentation and criticism of European colonialist exploitation, along with the psychological crisis produced in modern Africans by the European encounter." He also discusses Clark-Bekederemo's criticism of "American social and political life" in his prose travelogue.

Hema Chari's engagement in her entry on Nuruddin Farah is with "the postcolonial nature of his writings" and the concerns that "underlie his unyielding criticism of neocolonial practices in contemporary Somali politics." She focuses on two thematic concerns in his novels, "the ethics of human freedom and the oppression of women in postcolonial Somaliland." In order to clarify these themes, Chari explores, with compelling force, Farah's investigation of "other related sociopolitical issues that regulate the nature of freedom in Somali culture," such as patriarchy, kinship practices, "public and private sites of negotiation available for women," family structures, "the metaphorical relationship between political and domestic power," "Somalia's political independence," and the "vacuity of the country's nationalist agenda," as well as "Somalia's complex relationships with foreign powers."

Vanessa Everson evaluates Ferdinand Oyono's limited but significant literary production of three novels in the light of Cameroonian colonial politics and its baggage of "religious hypocrisy, physical brutality, and moral turpitude." Everson characterizes Oyono's writing, marked by "acid wit" and incisive satire, as "a melody in counterpoint." She further observes, "His fellow countrymen do not escape his critical gaze, for they allow themselves to be duped."

Harold Barratt delineates the "sociopolitical and ideologically charged nature of Alex La Guma's fiction" through an analysis of the recurring theme of "the dehumanizing process that South Africa's apartheid system inflicts upon both oppressor and oppressed.'' He examines La Guma's language and symbols as powerful strategies to unveil the violence and horror of the apartheid regime.

Another South African writer, Lewis Nkosi, and his sociopolitical commitment are studied by Brinda Bose. Examining his literary criticism, his play *The Rhythm of Violence*, his novel *Mating Birds*, and short stories, Bose articulates Nkosi's concern with the impact of colonialism and its ''repercussions on the country's social and literary life.''

Several contributors discuss themes and issues related to the location and construction of the postcolonial female subject. Marie Umeh, Eleni Coundouriotis, Hildegard Hoeller, Juliana Makuchi Nfah-Abbenyi, Mary Vogl, Siga Fatima Jagne, Elaine Savory, Christine Loflin, Lisa McNee, Maxine Beahan, and Lindsay Pentolfe Aegerter consider various explorations of the female self and space and of the contours of her social, political, and cultural realities.

Marie Umeh's detailed study of Buchi Emecheta identifies her literary achievement as marking ''a turning point in Nigerian literary history.'' Umeh analyzes the major theme in Emecheta's works as ''the extirpation of retrogressive Igbo cultural norms that prevent women from participation in a wide range of activities said to be the preserve of men.'' Umeh appraises Emecheta's engagement with compelling issues, such as raising ''the political consciousness of all women,'' challenging ''the marginalization of women in all social systems,'' depicting ''the woes of Igbo women due to repressive patriarchal norms that condemn them to prescribed fates of subsistence and subjugation,'' and exposing the conflicts between the values and precepts of Igbo traditional culture and the Western colonial culture. Emecheta also deals with the heroic and leadership roles of women in the Biafran war, the neocolonial evils of Nigerian society, and even the ''potential evil of polygamous relationships,'' as well as sexual abuse of children. Umeh further evaluates Emecheta's ''revolutionary imperative'' as resting on the ''need for 'balance,' 'equalization,' and 'alliance' in male-female relationships within the Igbo sociocultural framework.'' She critiques this imperative as sometimes leading to overstatement and depiction of males as one-dimensional. Umeh also notes Emecheta's artistic development in terms of moving from ''episodic'' plot narration to ''technically mature creations.'' Umeh's entry also provides insight into the various scholarly studies that involve a reevaluation of feminist studies in the context of African women and the complexity of postcolonial Igbo life and culture.

Eleni Coundouriotis examines Tsitsi Dangarembga's two published works in the context of Zimbabwe's colonial history and traditional practices. She suggests that the novel *Nervous Conditions* can be seen as a ''rewriting of the male education novel'' in which a woman's ''possibilities of selfhood'' are ''enabled only by the active negotiation of conflicting cultural codes.'' Coundouriotis further unravels the class-gender-colonization nexus within which the ''politicization'' of the native self, especially the female native self, is constructed.

Hildegard Hoeller identifies Ama Ata Aidoo's major focus to be the ''psychological impact of the colonial and post-colonial experience on her male and particularly her female characters.'' She notes Aidoo's representation of the diverse African women's struggle through challenging ''the concept of marriage, the role of other women in the oppression and liberation of her heroines, the concept of sanity, and finally language and literary forms themselves, as they in their traditional forms seem unable to represent a woman's truth accurately.''

Juliana Nfah-Abbenyi discusses Calixthe Beyala's vision of the postcolonial female subject's self-liberatory act within the constraints of poverty, violence, exploitation, and degradation. ''What we see consistently is Beyala's ability to portray tragic conditions that Africans in the post-colonial era have created or have to live with, but she also leaves the post-colonial subject with a potential for change.''

Mary Vogl's entry on Assia Djebar explores how ''Algerian women have faced a double colonization, colonial and patriarchal, and have had to fight to redefine their role in postcolonial Algerian society.'' Vogl discusses, with penetrating insight, Djebar's understanding of ''the politics of language'' and postcolonial Algerian women's experiences as they become manifest significantly in ''related themes of voice, body language, aphasia, sound, and silence.'' Vogl also assesses the value of the coexistence of French and Arabic in Djebar.

Siga Fatima Jagne situates her detailed and textured analysis of Mariama Bâ's two major novels in ''the oral tradition of the Senegalese griot women,'' writing a ''speakerly text.'' She unravels the multiple ''positionings'' of Bâ—''a postcolonial position she has been assigned to by a conflicting tradition and Islam'' besides the impact of French colonization, shaped by ''the Wolof view of fatalism,'' informed by Islam, as well as one located within the traditional practices of the caste system: ''Her positionings as female, Muslim, *guer*, Western educated, orphaned, mother, and a divorcée inform her experiences and the different tensions in these multiple positionings.'' Jagne's final argument rests on the observation that the oppositions and tensions in the lives of Bâ's women characters are ''not always negative,'' as ''Bâ seems to leave space for transformation. . . . At the same time, this does not absolve her from reinscribing caste in ways that can be read as acquiescence.''

Elaine Savory's essay on Bessie Head examines the multiple and conflicted identity layers of the biracial, colored African woman within the context of South Africa and later as an exile in Botswana. She analyzes the several ''hybrid'' and ''exiled'' cultural spaces from which Head's women protagonists articulate their critique of ideological and political containment. Savory considers the specific ways in which Bessie Head questions the systems of domination, as they define her reality, in order to resist them. She envisions Head as a writer whose concerns include the whole of humankind: ''She decided to opt for 'mankind as a whole.' ''

Christine Loflin examines the women's ''dialogue'' motif in Flora Nwapa's novels and short stories as an affirmation of indigenous African feminism evolving from the ''community of women.'' Nwapa dismantles not only imposed

Western values but also outmoded traditional beliefs such as the glorification of motherhood in both *Efuru* and *Idu*. Loflin also assesses the recent critical attention and reevaluation devoted to Nwapa's works. These readings resist placing Nwapa's works "within preexisting frameworks of Western feminism or cultural studies." Loflin then accounts for the relevance of recent postcolonial feminist studies to African women writer's works.

The entry on Nafissatou Diallo by Lisa McNee focuses on the intersection of private and public spheres in Diallo's works. Her autobiography, historical romances, and the juvenile novel all reflect and critique aspects of contemporary social practices. McNee examines Diallo's works as addressing "issues of women's representation and roles in public life." Diallo critiques, in the process, as McNee notes, the "depredations of the ruling classes" as well as "the caste system that continues to influence Senegalese society in light of Muslim values."

Maxine Beahan points out Muthoni Likimani's role as one of the first Kenyan women to become "a program producer at the Kenyan Broadcasting Commission, now the Voice of Kenya," and a writer who promotes women's issues. Beahan analyzes Likimani's works for their expression of political activism. She also discusses the wide-ranging social themes in Likimani's novel *They Shall Be Chastised*, a verse collection, *What Does a Man Want?*, and a document titled *Women of Kenya: In the Decade of Development*, published for the United Nations Women's Conference held in Nairobi in 1985. These themes encompass the problems of increasing Westernization, particularly through the impact of Christianity, on "traditional Kikuyu social structures"; images and roles of women; pressures of traditional practices in a changing society; and "divisions between women who work in the country while their husbands work in the city."

Lindsay Pentolfe Aegerter analyzes Ellen Kuzwayo's contribution to rewriting "autobiography" as "autoethnography" in order to "educate her audience about the politics of African women's identities." Grounding Kuzwayo's work in the oral tradition, Aegerter explores the connections among the structure, style, function, message, and method of storytelling in both works, *Call Me Woman* and *Sit Down and Listen*. Aegerter points out, "For Kuzwayo, the combination of fiction and nonfiction, of symbolic and 'realistic' suggestibility, works to create a womanist vision of wholeness." In Aegerter's view, within the South African apartheid context, Kuzwayo creates the "miracle" of retaining and continuing "traditional values" and engaging dialogically the contentious politics of colonial exploitation and collective efforts at "personal and cultural wholeness."

Femi Euba, Iyunolu Osagie, Elaine Savory, Jo Nel, and Adaku Ankumah examine the place of African playwrights whose plays can be viewed as a forum for the exploration of postcolonial concerns and issues. Femi Euba, a founding member of the 1960s Masks, a "theatre laboratory" founded by Wole Soyinka, analyzes Soyinka's life experiences and works with scholarly insight and personal knowledge. Clarifying the centrality of the Yoruba Ifa-oracle corpus in Soyinka's works, Euba also addresses its links to postcolonial realities—the ruptures and antinomies in the postcolonial corrupt Nigerian state are played out against the restorative creative-destructive potential embodied in the Ogunian tragic hero figure.

Iyunolu Osagie identifies Femi Euba's concern with the "theoretical and performative ritual role . . . of the black dramatist as bearer of tradition and conscience of society." His plays of satire, as Osagie points out, reflect his political commitment as well as a "social vision for the postmodern realities of our times." In "Euba's search for a definition of black diasporic theater," Osagie captures "a unifying concept of identity through a physical and metaphysical journey of fate as controlled and directed by Esu-Elegbara, the god of fate, the messenger god who distributes both good and evil to the human race."

Elaine Savory focuses on how Femi Osofisan "utilizes Yoruba tradition but in the service of opening up political dialogue." She also traces Osofisan's connections with and departures from Soyinka. Most significantly, Osofisan rejected the "mythopoetic style of Soyinka" in order to express his "radical socialism." Savory also illuminates Osofisan's unique blend of theatrical styles.

Jo Nel reflects upon the postcolonial themes and techniques in Athol Fugard's plays and novel, such as the relationship of past and present and the exposure of the apartheid victim's conditions of "confinement, poverty, and deprivation." Nel also discusses Fugard's use of drama as "an autobiographical vehicle."

Jo Nel in his examination of Fugard's novel, *Tsotsi*, analyzes the impact of racial separation of the white man's city from the township of the black community, resulting in violence and suffering. Nel also discusses the theme of time and its associations with "mutability, with change, and with decay."

Focusing on Efua Sutherland's various contributions as playwright and theatre director in Ghana, Adaku T. Ankumah highlights her role in founding the Experimental Theatre Players, the Ghana Society of Writers, a community theatre, and a touring theatre group at the School of Drama, University of Ghana, Legon. Ankumah notes that Sutherland combines "relevant European dramatic forms and the traditional Akan storytelling art called *Anansesem* and its dramatic techniques, including audience participation." Her plays also examine "the role of women in contemporary society." Ankumah, in her close analysis of plays such as *Foriwa* and *Edufu*, discusses these roles as those of nation and community building.

A preoccupation with identity underlies a number of postcolonial African writers and is reflected in issues of racial, sexual, class, caste, language, ethnic, and national identity in the literary texts. Through direct and indirect confrontation of these issues, thematically, stylistically, or rhetorically, the writers either question, subvert, or dismantle certain inscribed codes regarding identity designations as they inform the "political unconscious" of the colonial texts. John C. Hawley, Chinyere Grace Okafor, Christine Loflin, Soraya Mékerta, J. Roger

Kurtz, and Pushpa Naidu Parekh address these preoccupations in writers with varying agendas and methods.

John C. Hawley and Chinyere Grace Okafor note the impact of class structure on the neocolonial African state. Hawley assesses Ngugi wa Thiong'o's commitment to "the struggle of the common people of Kenya to come to terms with the effects on their culture of colonialism and the neocolonialism that followed." Hawley observes that Ngugi's shift to writing in Gikuyu and "translating the work—often into Kiswahili first, and then into English," as well as his chronicling of the Mau Mau revolution in his fiction, is clear evidence of his commitment to nationalist literature through linguistic indigenization and class alignment. His works, often progressively, show an increasing "understanding of the postcolonial situation and the politics and economics of exploitation." In Hawley's analysis, these complexities are reflected in Ngugi's "interior search for the various motives of those who participated in the [Mau Mau] war. . . . His is an organic view of group interchange." Hawley demonstrates in his analysis and critique that Ngugi brought "the newer politics of responsibility" to writing. Ngugi's responses to the "challenges of national independence" are investigated within the ideology of Marxism embodied in decolonization theorists like Frantz Fanon.

Writing in response to and against the ideological constructions of identity within colonial and neocolonial frames of reference, postcolonial writing often constitutes an uneasy engagement. It implies revolutionary change but also participates in the dubious project of displacement. Scholars note the multiple ways in which postcolonial African writers envision the configurations of this revolution and displacement in rewriting the new social order.

Chinyere Grace Okafor identifies Vincent Chukwuemeka Ike's concern with the complex nature of postindependence social order. Okafor identifies this new drive as a conflicting one of breaking the boundaries of ethnicity while affirming ones "attachment to [one's] roots," as illustrated in the issue of interethnic marriage in Ike's novels *Toads for Supper* and *Sunset at Dawn*. Okafor also discusses Ike's allegorical envisioning of neocolonial political intrigues in *The Naked Gods* by focusing on the choice of leadership, in this case of a vice-chancellor for Songhai University. Other issues central to Ike's works are a critique of the colonial education system, widespread corruption as exemplified in the leakage of examination papers, the class structure of the Nigerian-Biafran "war experience," and the "pretensions of the intellectual community," as well as the conflict between the old and the new generation in the modern African society. Okafor observes that Ike places his faith in the young to draw all "segments of the society" to revamp the "precarious situation of neocolonial Africa."

Chinyere Grace Okafor also examines Festus Iyayi's representation of neocolonialism in Africa through a focus on Benin City, where "juxtaposition of traditional African and modern, Westernized cultures" provides an exposition of "the injustices and suffering of the masses." The system of neocolonialism fosters violence, poverty, depravity, alienation, and corruption. Okafor notes Iyayi's portrayal of these realities as a critique of "the class structure of the post-colonial system" so clearly exemplified in the life of the modern city (as in the novels *Violence* and *The Contract*). Okafor discusses Iyayi's examination of this issue in *Heroes* in relation to the "exploitation of the ordinary soldier and civilian in the Nigeria-Biafra war" and his emphasis on "the class structure of the war" as he delineates how the "Biafran and Nigerian upper classes contrived the war as a result of their conflict and implicated the lower class to fight the war for them while their own children are protected from the war."

Christine Loflin examines Zaynab Alkali's *The Stillborn* to note how, in the postcolonial experience of migration, not only the city but also the village has been influenced by Western modernization and the missionary work: "Thus Alkali disturbs and undoes the dichotomy of the village and traditional life versus the city and modernity." Loflin addresses Li's "fluidity of identity" as she moves from "daughter to wife to educated single parent to 'the man of the house' to, prospectively, matriarch of her family" in the context of Homi Bhabha's salutary warning in *The Location of Culture* that migration creates a need "to think beyond narratives of originary and initial subjectivities."[6] Alkali does not therefore promote the modern woman as simply one kind; she could combine economic independence with a solidarity with men "to build a new society." Loflin further illuminates the implications of stylistic innovation in postcolonial writers; she argues that the use of dreams in Alkali's novels reflects a "move away from the standards of Western realism."

Soraya Mékerta's entry on Tahar Ben Jelloun explores what she calls the "very real and concrete situations" that he writes about. She also points out that he ventures into the depth of memory of the Maghrebian people and the Maghreb. Mékerta's observations rest on Tahar Ben Jelloun as a writer, critic, and activist who understands, questions, and critiques "all forms of abuse, specifically those inherent in colonialism and neocolonialism; cultural and linguistic impositions; racial and ethnic intolerance; [and] class, gender, and sexual oppression." Jelloun's writing, Mékerta tells us, is wide and varied in scope, forcing an interdisciplinary reading of his works. Mékerta characterizes his work: "Deeply rooted in the Maghreb, in France, and in between, Tahar Ben Jelloun's voice is forceful and passionate; it demands to be listened to."

J. Roger Kurtz reads Francis Imbuga's plays and novels as providing an indirect criticism of postcolonial East African politics and society. He evaluates Imbuga's *Shrine of Tears*, for example, as an examination of "the contradictory roles of politicians, of the police forces, of the universities, of expatriate 'experts,' and of traditional cultural forms." Kurtz identifies in Imbuga's indirect criticism not only survivalist motives but an effectual deterrent to volatile silencing of artists by corrupt government machinery. He points out, "Imbuga's texts allow the targets of his criticism to save face and provide them room to reform themselves by avoiding direct confrontation."

Pushpa Naidu Parekh's entry on Gabriel Okara examines his radical aesthetics of revolutionary change in colonial and postcolonial phases of Nigerian history. Parekh observes that the discursive and ideological reconstruction of the historical, political, and spiritual self is effected through linguistic and structural innovations. The speaking voices in Okara's poetry and particularly Okolo in *The Voice* search for and find an inner, self-generated aesthetics in which the seeds of a transformative vision and revolutionary activism are engendered. By the end of *The Voice*, the individual leader moves the communal masses to defy the anxiety, fear, materialism, and hatred of the colonized mentality through stages that correspond to those that Fanon delineates in *The Wretched of the Earth*.

Samba Diop, Ode S. Ogede, Alma Jean Billingslea-Brown, Dominic Thomas, Judith Imali Abala, and Norman Weinstein propose shifts in approaching the writers and their works, keeping in mind the various sociopolitical influences that determined their artistic choices. Samba Diop provides a clear understanding of Léopold Sédar Senghor's stature, his contributions to the philosophy of Negritude, and the shifts in Senghor's poetic development, as well as his political engagements and commitments and his prominence with regard to pan-Africanism and diaspora issues. Diop's entry critically reevaluates, beyond the advocacy/censure divide, the significance of the Negritude movement as a much-needed amd timely response to colonial constructions of African culture and people. He further notes how the movement was critiqued and provides both sides of the debate, while acknowledging the relevance of moving beyond the dialectics of Africa and Europe.

Ode S. Ogede locates David Mandessi Diop's poetry within the Negritude school, his main decolonization project being the advocacy of using African languages in literature. Ogede observes that Diop's style, his "assertive, defiant tone," and "his angry response to the evils of colonialism" influenced the work of exiled writers like Mazisi Kunene and Ngugi was Thiong'o, as well as the Black Consciousness poets of South Africa such as Mafika Gwala and Don Mattera and the West African poet Kofi Awoonor. Ogede notes how, as a conscious expression of his political commitment, Diop adopted African oral forms, such as praise-names, in his celebration of the African woman.

Ogede assesses Molara Ogundipe-Leslie's poetry as setting "a new standard for Nigerian women's poetry." He notes Ogundipe-Leslie's use of African rhetorical devices, such as the "adynation symbol," to convey feminist messages. He clarifies how Ogundipe-Leslie formulates her sense of "commitment" as one that goes beyond literary resistance to "tell about being a woman."

Alma Jean Billingslea-Brown identifies the themes of "death, grief, and loss" in Kofi Awoonor's works as closely connected to Anlo-Ewe oral tradition— "the Ewe dirge, a traditional verse form of loss and lament." Billingslea-Brown notes that the grieving in Awoonor's poetry is for the loss of traditional culture through the imposition of Christianity. By abandoning his own Christian name,

George Awoonor Williams, he reclaims his own identity through a "ritualistic process."

Dominic Thomas observes the complex use of French in Sony Labou Tansi's works and connects it to his "historical relationship to it," that is, one of colonization and linguistic "rape." This connection impacts Tansi's "radical syntactic and lexical reform," "a modification of traditional narrative linearity," and "extensive use of neologisms." Violence in language reflects, as Thomas notes, the "extravagance of the political regimes and the horrors perpetrated by a number of post-colonial dictatorships." Thomas also explores Aminata Sow Fall's works, revealing their concern with the question of "political power" in a postcolonial society, as well as with the "aesthetic aspects of literary production."

Judith Imali Abala examines Micere M. Githae Mugo's role in the "battle against the hegemony of Eurocentrism" through her questioning of "the 'authenticity' and 'accuracy' of Kenyan historical accounts written from a European point of view" (in *The Trial of Dedan Kimathi*, coauthored with Ngugi wa Thiong'o). Abala cites Mugo's use of songs and affirmation of dance and recitation as a celebration of her "own culture and modes of expression."

Norman Weinstein explores Amos Tutuola's works in the mode of the quest romance but also connects his repeated use of the motif of "trial by fire" to revealing the "present political, social, and economic realities of postcolonial Africa." Discussing the critical reception of Tutuola, Weinstein assesses two currents: critics who see stylistic innovations, especially his use of "Yoruba English," and critics like Chinua Achebe who focus on Tutuola's moral dimension.

Several postcolonial African writers express themselves out of a specific ethnic culture and draw their perceptions from that particular worldview. As noted earlier, Mariama Bâ as much as Wole Soyinka and Kofi Awoonor, among other writers, shape their literary world out of these perceptions. In analyzing Okot p'Bitek's writings as they emerge out of Acoli culture and its traditions, Awuor Ayodo notes that with colonialism and later independence, p'Bitek was "faced with the urgent question of whether to define the emergent post-colonial societies, the African, and the African worldview in terms of an ethnic group . . . ; in terms of Western culture; or as a symbiosis of both." P'Bitek's belief in "the primacy and value of ethnic culture" is reflected in his works, both in Acoli (or Luo) and those translated by himself into English.

Brian Evenson and David Beus's collaborative essay on Camara Laye focuses on his celebration of traditional African cultures, particularly the Malinké culture in *L'enfant noir*. The contributors note that while other writers delineate the impact of clashing cultures, Laye celebrates "a single culture." Although the book was critiqued as "idyllic and insufficiently engaged," Evenson and Beus point out Laye's perceptions of Africa as other than a Western-defined, appropriated, and constructed realm.

Nalini Iyer and Anne E. Lessick-Xiao delineate the multilayered African identity by focusing on the multicultural influences on particular writers. Iyer, in her analysis of Christopher Okigbo, attests to his envisioning of the African poet as "a product of a complex culture who gives voice to its values." His poetry draws from "Ibo myth and beliefs, Christianity, Virgil, Nigerian music and rhythms, and English and American modernist poets." Iyer also comments on the poet's political themes in his last sequence of poems, *Path of Thunder*. Anne E. Lessick-Xiao unravels the multiple interests in Emmanuel Dongala's life—music, mathematics, science, drama, and the novel. Attesting to his "multiculturalism," Lessick-Xiao notes that his troup has performed works of varied playwrights, including Yukio Mishima and Jean-Paul Sartre. She also notes the influence of Asian literature and philosophy, Latin American writers, and, most significantly, African-American music, particularly jazz, on Dongala's writings.

Craig McLuckie's entry on Dennis Brutus highlights the "balance of the poetic with the political" in his writings. McLuckie notes the movement and progression in Brutus's poetic output, in particular the specific validation of occasional poems as well as committed ones, within the context of South Africa's politics of apartheid, Brutus's phases of activism, and his present concerns regarding a growing transnational "society dominated by mass media."

Carol Marsh-Lockett, Christine Sizemore, Jo Nel, and Nicholas Birns examine the complexities of identity construction from the standpoint of white settler writing in South Africa. Marsh-Lockett traces the development of Nadine Gordimer's works in the context of South Africa's apartheid and colonialist politics and ideology. The moral failure of colonialism and the consequent spiritual and psychological destruction is confronted in various areas: "sexual adventurism," "miscegenation," and "narcissistic liberalism." Marsh-Lockett observes that Gordimer raises an important issue regarding the place of whites in a changing Africa; she underscores the moral issues at stake and her conviction that the whites who wish to stay in postapartheid Africa must do so on the terms of the African peoples (*None to Accompany Me*).

Christine Sizemore begins her analysis of Doris Lessing by pointing out her "ambiguous relationship" to the colonial "English literary tradition" as well as to "the landscape of Africa." Observing that all of Lessing's writings "focus on the issue of difference," Sizemore examines racial, national, class, gender, and age as well as species differences in relation to the "issues of power, control, and exploitation that she [Lessing] saw as a child in colonial Rhodesia."

Jo Nel anchors his discussion of Alan Paton's works on certain prevailing themes, "the disintegration of traditional influences on African youth, especially as they migrate from the rural areas toward the cities," "obsession with racial purity," "the effect of apartheid laws on the citizens of the country" and "the inexorable erosion of the human soul in the enactment of racialist ideology," and "the challenge posed to Christian principles by the political aberration called 'apartheid.' "

Nicholas Birns elucidates Olive Schreiner's "awareness of the political and moral tragedies afflicting her native South Africa" through an examination of what he calls her "visionary style." He examines Schreiner's novels and short stories for their depiction of the condition where personal events have political parallels and implications.

Several scholars discuss the politics of identity as a concern of the writers they examine. Moving away from essentialist notions of identity to an engagement with historical moments and geopolitical locations in subject formation, several post-colonial African writers reexamine the colonialist and imperialist paradigms of "otherness," "difference," and "authority" in terms of cross-cultural mobility. Postcolonial and culture studies theorists like Gayatri Spivak, Homi Bhabha, Carole Boyce Davies, bell hooks, Audre Lorde, Gloria Anzaldua, Kwame Anthony Appiah, and Trinh T. Minh-ha have articulated their critique of essentialism in the context of their specific theoretical terrains. Notions of "hybridity," "diaspora," "memory," and "mestiza consciousness" therefore shape the works of many writers. Ama Ata Aidoo in *Our Sister Killjoy* poses these contested articulations as constant displacements of cultural codes within the combative space of transglobal movement. So do other writers, as examined by Robert Bennett, J. Roger Kurtz, Jogamaya Bayer, and Moredewun Adejunmobi.

Robert Bennett notes Ben Okri's "remarkable sense of formal experimentation" evidenced in his reinterpretation of the European novelistic conventions from a "postcolonial perspective." Noting the necessity of "aesthetic responses to colonialism," Bennett focuses on Okri's experimentation with African narrative techniques, extending the scope of the novel to include "mythical journeys, intense dreams, and other African rituals or rites of passage." Commenting on Okri's later fiction, Bennett identifies Bhabha's concept of the postcolonial aesthetic of hybridity as central to Okri's exploration of "the liminal border between diverse cultural traditions." Bennett notes the need for critics to explore further Okri's development of a "uniquely African sense of postmodernism that derives from a creative extension of African folklore."

J. Roger Kurtz explores Peter Nazareth's interest in the complexities of genealogy as arising from his own personal history of Goan identity in an East African setting, culturally distinct from both African and Asian groups. This preoccupation "constitutes a classic example of the rootlessness, border crossing, fragmented identity, and cultural hybridity that typify what has come to be described as the 'postcolonial condition.' " In this process, Nazareth incorporates, in Kurtz's view, "an examination of how traditions are modified for new contexts" through the figure of "the trickster, a stock character in various African literary traditions." Kurtz examines Nazareth's interest "in how entire texts function as tricksters, making subversive readings available. . . . The Trickster Tradition, by Nazareth's account, offers an alternative to the Great Tradition."

Jogamaya Bayer examines the impact of the colonial construct of racial hierarchy on Essop Patel, whose grandfather came from India to South Africa when he was thirteen. Several of Essop Patel's poems express an idealized "solidarity among people all over the world," while exposing the racist laws of South Africa's apartheid government, such as the Immorality Act, which prohibited racial intermixing. He examines the limitations of racial categorization and compartmentalization.

Moradewun Adejunmobi provides an insight into Jean-Joseph Rabearivelo, whose competency in French and Malagasy confirmed his "role of mediator between cultures." Adejunmobi places Rabearivelo in the context of Madagascar's literary climate, where a "thriving written literary culture flourished" long before the British introduced "roman script in the nineteenth century." With the French colonization, the status of the Malagasy language became uncertain, while French was adopted as the only recognized language for any kind of literature. Rabearivelo, as noted by Adejunmobi, "sought to give expression to the henceforth inevitably hybrid and multicultural character of colonized culture."

Maghrebian Francophone literature is explored through entries by Lynne Dumont Rogers, S. D. Ménager, Mary Vogl, and Soraya Mékerta. While I have discussed Vogl's and Mékerta's pieces in an earlier section of this Preface, I will specifically look at the other two scholars here. Lynne Rogers examines Moroccan writers Driss Chraïbi and Mohammed Khaïr-Eddine. Considering Driss Chraïbi's novels, both realistic and symbolic, Rogers focuses on his range of themes from an indictment of Islamic society imbued in certain hypocritical traditions (as in *Le passé simple* and *La civilisation, ma mère!*) and the imperialist French constantly displacing and devastating the Arab immigrants in France (*Les Boucs*) to the "role of the individual caught in a historical whirlwind of modernization" (as in *L'âne* and *Un ami viendre vous voir*), "the illusion of leadership and the role of political discourse in the creation of both a communal reality and the future," the epic Berber trilogy covering the Arab conquest of North Africa to the present, and the Inspector Ali adventure novel. Rogers emphasizes the appeal Chraïbi has for the "second generation of modern Moroccan writers" and Arab feminists because while never presuming to speak for women, Chraïbi depicts them with "warmth and understanding."

Similarly, Rogers finds in Khaïr-Eddine a rejection of "the assimilation offered by Europe" and a refusal "to find refuge in the comfort of ethnic nativism." His writing, she notes, is informed by his political commitments expressed as "complex allegories that draw on the oral traditions of southern Morocco and on Sufi mysticism, as well as the Western literary canons."

S. D. Ménager's study of the Algerian writer Leïla Sebbar explores her early interest in Jean-Paul Sartre and Simone de Beauvoir and her "interpretation of aspects of the African colonial myth" as well as her later preoccupation with "the condition of the immigrant North African family." Ménager clarifies that Sebbar has been cited as a Beur writer, although she was born in Algeria and not in France (Ménager explains that the name "Beur" refers to "the slang talked by the new generation descending from immigrant parents, born in France, educated there, ignorant of their parent's culture," "Beur" itself being an "approximate reversal" of the word "Arab"), because she deals with the "Beur" culture in her works, particularly the *Shérazade* trilogy. Cultural crossing and racial mixing as themes dominate the novel *Le Chinois vert d'Afrique*. Ménager reads Sebbar's latest novel *Le silence des rives* as "a parable on exile and memory" in which women continue to play a central role.

Brian Evenson studies the contentious spaces that some African writers occupy in the historical and cultural map of postcolonial Africa. Viewing Dambudzo Marechera as a "controversial and irreverent" writer of Zimbabwe, Evenson focuses on biographical elements in his writing, such as rootlessness, nihilism, violence, poverty, and turmoil, even as he draws on political themes, as in *The House of Hunger, Black Sunlight*, and *Mindblast*. Evenson notes the influence of American beat writers on Marechera's work as well as his need to transform language expressed in his unique style, combining sharpness and eccentricity, for example, the " 'drugged' narrative style" in *Black Sunlight*. Referring to Marechera as "an odd sort of postcolonialist," Evenson identifies his "inverted postcolonialism, the negative equivalent of other writers' affirmation."

Jared Banks's entries on Mia Couto and Ungulani Ba Ka Khosa, both writers from Mozambique, depart from others in that they exemplify certain currents in Lusophone writing, an area that is not the main focus of this volume. His entries on a privileged white, Mia Couto, and the black writer Ungulani Ba Ka Khosa within the parameters of Portuguese colonization are therefore merely a slim reflection of the peculiarities and preoccupations of Lusophone writers of Africa. However, they invite further in-depth study of individual Lusophone writers.

Musa Dube addresses an important concern with regard to postcolonial studies in the West. Through her analysis of the emerging writer Mositi Torontle, she illustrates the politics of publication and distribution as a major obstacle in the dissemination of postcolonial writers' expressions. These politics are major deterrents to the decolonizing agenda and seem to suggest the implacable ways in which postcolonial critical discourse co-opts or reifies the silencing of some African writers by naming only those readily available in the Western market, as well as those who seem to fit into the Western-defined theoretical models of resistance to colonialism.

Each of the scholars in this volume contributes to the ongoing discussion regarding the theory and practice of postcolonial literatures in Africa. The groupings I have conceived are only some of the ways in which the connections among them could reveal certain preoccupations within the postcolonial critical discourse. This volume, we hope, will provide the groundwork on which more critically focused work can begin. However, even this process of preparing the groundwork has required each one of us to investigate, research, and discover both the quality and quantity of available resources. The fact that technology, like the Internet and multimedia, will make it possible to reach across continents to locate an article or an ongoing work and to communicate with the actual authors and researchers in ways inconceivable even today is exhilarating. Yet it should also make us wary of possible ethical transgressions through the retrenchment of the mentality that the world, especially the so-called Third World, is a marketable consumption for the armchair, electronic-geared intellectual tourist in the so-called First World. However, I also see the other side of the picture. It is in fact the so-called Third World, with its extremely well trained high-tech computer specialists, software programmers, electronic engineers, and the large masses of educated people (besides Western-educated), that is increasingly becoming the consumer for this technology. For them, it displaces the hierarchies of writing over oral forms and European languages over non-European ones, even as it becomes the best medium for interdisciplinary studies. Whatever the new technology does, I envision that sourcebooks, whether in print or electronic form, will always be an asset for the further research and serious study that African literatures, like other literatures of the world, invite.

NOTES

1. Karin Barber, "African-Language Literature and Postcolonial Criticism," *Research in African Literatures* 26.4 (Winter 1995): 3–30.

2. Albert S. Gérard, "Foreword," *African Language Literatures: An Introduction to the Literary History of Sub-Saharan Africa* (Washington, D.C.: Three Continents Press, 1981), x.

3. Mugyabuse M. Mulokozi, "A Survey of Swahili Literature: 1970–1988," *Africa Focus* 8.1 (1992): 49–61; Randall L. Pauwels, "Swahili Literature and History in the Post-structuralist Era," *International Journal of African Historical Studies* 25.2 (1992): 261–283; Flora Veit-Wild, *Teachers, Preachers, Non-Believers: A Social History of Zimbabwean Literature* (London: Zell, 1992); C. F. Swanepoel, ed., *Comparative Literature and African Literatures* (Pretoria: Via Afrika, 1993).

4. Gayatri Chakravorty Spivak, "The Burden of English," *Orientalism and the Postcolonial Predicament*, ed. Carol A. Breckenridge and Peter van der Veer (Philadelphia: University of Pennsylvania Press, 1993), 153.

5. Gérard, "Foreword," xiv–xv.

6. Homi Bhabha, *The Location of Culture* (London: Routledge, 1994), 1.

—Pushpa Naidu Parekh

ACKNOWLEDGMENTS

We would like to express our sincere gratitude and appreciation to several of our well-wishers and supporters in this project. Our sincere thanks go to Dr. Emmanuel S. Nelson, Greenwood Advisory Editor, for his editorial guidance and unwavering assistance, and Dr. George Butler, Associate Acquisitions Editor of Greenwood Press, for his professional expertise and patience during the preparation of this manuscript. We are highly indebted to Professor Carole Boyce Davies for taking time out of her very busy schedule to write the Foreword for our sourcebook. We are grateful to Dan Bascelli, Assistant Director of the Spelman Writing Center, for all his computer assistance and good humor in times of technological crises. We have also been supported by the Spelman institution in several other ways; a Bush Faculty Grant in the summer of 1995 supported this project. We appreciate Dr. Glenda Price, the Provost of Spelman College, for providing several avenues for research support. We are also indebted to the assistance provided by our Spelman student research associates and volunteers, Kelesha Fowler, Alana Wyke, Fatou Joof, Jasmine Palmer, Princess Tate, Ava Williams, Heather Crocker, Maisha Wynn, Aeva Gaymon, Peggy Madkins, Maia Hunt, Karimah Lamar, Aurora Anderson, Naima Abdul-Halim, Jamila Wade, Becca Thompson, Meca Coote, and Margaret Johnson, each one of whom has cared deeply enough to engage in bibliographic research with sincerity and diligence. Dr. Johnetta Cole, the President of Spelman College, our chairs and colleagues in the English Department and in interdisciplinary studies, the African Diaspora and the World, as well as the Ford Diversity Project, and the Spelman community have also extended their warm support of our project. We thank our friends and associates, with their various helpful comments, criticisms, and suggestions, for making this project possible. Most of all, we thank our families for their constant encouragement, enthusiasm, and interest in our project and for their willingness to be an integral part of our struggle, strife, and achievement.

I, Pushpa, would like to give special thanks to my husband, Bharat, for his unflagging support, encouragement, and willingness to help in every way possible, and my daughter, Shruti, for her unconditional love, delightful playfulness, and superb understanding. I am ever grateful to my parents for their prayers and blessings, and my sisters and their families for their warm affection and sincere interest in all my pursuits. In particular, I thank my parents-in-law for their encouragement of and pride in my professional engagements.

I, Siga Fatima, would also like to give special thanks to my family, my parents (deceased) for molding me, my brothers and sisters and their families for their support—and last, but not least, Soraya Mékerta and Yama Jallow for their unconditional friendship.

INTRODUCTION

This Introduction aims at raising various compelling and significant issues related to the expression, production, publication, and distribution of African literary writing and to critical discourses that have constructed models for interpretive approaches to and/or theoretical frameworks for these writings. In the first section, Pushpa Naidu Parekh considers the viability of applying emerging critical concepts and theoretical models being discussed and debated within the field of postcolonial theory to postcolonial African writers. Reconsidering the tendencies to reinscribe the separation of theory and practice and to privilege critical discourse, Parekh provides a detailed look at the ways in which theory informs practice and practice directs or even determines theory. In order to do this, she identifies certain conceptual paradigms constructed at specific moments of colonial and postcolonial sociohistorical and political climates in specific postindependence African states, as discussed in the various scholarly entries of the sourcebook. She also raises crucial issues related to the theory and practice of postcolonial African writing as evidenced in the collected entries. In the second section, Siga Fatima Jagne provides critical reflections on certain definitions regarding the category "woman" in feminist theory and its relation to African women. By calling into question the simplified conflation of various issues such as class, race, and sexual orientation, as well as nationality, Jagne begins her arguments regarding the category "woman" in the African context by identifying the specific and often contradictory locations occupied by specific women in and outside the literary field.

POSTCOLONIAL CRITICISM AND AFRICAN WRITING

Pushpa Naidu Parekh

The colonial world is a Manichean world. It is not enough for the settler to delimit physically, that is to say with the help of the army and the police force, the place of the native. As if to show the totalitarian character of colonial exploitation the settler paints the native as a sort of quintessence of evil.

—Frantz Fanon
The Wretched of the Earth

Babamukuru was God, therefore I had arrived in Heaven. I was in danger of becoming an angel, or at the very least a saint, and forgetting how ordinary humans existed—from minute to minute and from hand to mouth.

—Tsitsi Dangarembga
Nervous Conditions

Struggle. Struggle makes history. Struggle makes us. In struggle is our history, our language and our being. That struggle begins wherever we are; in whatever we do: then we become part of those millions whom Martin Carter once saw sleeping not to dream but dreaming to change the world.

—Ngugi wa Thiong'o
Decolonising the Mind

I think that many writers, in reaction against the humiliation of the colonial era, would like to build up an image of Africa, other than the humble humility of the sparsely furnished hut.

Some of one's work is like reclaiming that humility that has been trampled on and abused.

—Bessie Head
A Woman Alone[1]

Several historical events and shifts of political and socioeconomic significance have propelled the institutionalizing project of African, Asian, and postcolonial studies in the wake of African-American studies in the United States. While a steady growth of African studies programs at the graduate level indicates one direction of this project, the paucity of undergraduate courses on African or African diaspora studies, especially in U.S. colleges and universities, as well as the politics of "ghettoizing" certain area studies and the equally problematic labeling of these studies as "minority" or "multicultural," has constantly undermined the potential for effective transformation of hegemonic agendas both within and outside the academia. Gayatri Chakravorty Spivak in "Marginality and the Teaching Machine" identified the contentious nature of "the difference and the relationship between academic and 'revolutionary' practices in the interest of social change":

If there is a buzzword in cultural critique now, it is "marginality." Every academic knows that one cannot do without labels. To this particular label, however, Foucault's caution must be applied and we must attend to its *Herkunft* or descent. When a cultural identity is thrust upon one because the center wants an identifiable margin, claims for marginality assure validation from the center. It should then be pointed out that what is being negotiated here is not even a "race or a social type" . . . but an economic principle of identification through separation.[2]

At this juncture, it would be useful to consider the term "post-colonial" as indicative of chronological historicity and "postcolonial" as an ideological con-ceptualization. In most countries that gained independence from European col-onizers and could be considered "post-colonial," the persistence of imperialist and neocolonialist agendas and infrastructures, as well as ineffectual attempts to dismantle the Eurocentric and Western paradigms, makes the term take on ironic inflections. Often the term "decolonization" seems to imply the serious ques-tioning and dismantling of these paradigms. At the same time, "postcolonial" evokes the very spatial split (West and non-West are no longer self-exclusive entities) and temporal deferral (separation of past, present, and future are con-stantly ruptured by liminality and memory transference) at the heart of the emer-gence and identification of the human subject within the context of what Homi Bhabha calls "the colonial space of consciousness and society."[3] Stephen Sle-mon, in "The Scramble for Post-Colonialism," points out the heterogeneity of the concept as an "apparatus of institutional power":

"Post-colonialism," as it is now used in its various fields, describes a remarkably het-erogeneous set of subject positions, professional fields, and critical enterprises. It has been used as a way of ordering a critique of totalizing forms of Western historicism; as a portmanteau term for a retooled notion of "class," as a subset of both postmodernism and post-structuralism . . . ; as the name for a condition of nativist longing in post-independence national groupings; as a cultural marker of non-residency for a Third World intellectual cadre; as the inevitable underside of a fractured and ambivalent discourse of colonialist power; as an oppositional form of "reading practice"; and . . . as the name for a category of "literary" activity which sprang from a new and welcome political energy going on within what used to be called "Commonwealth" literary studies.[4]

Karin Barber in "African-Language Literature and Postcolonial Criticism" provides an incisive second look at the so-called oppositional form of postco-lonial criticism, granting that while "postcolonial criticism is a field of enquiry rather than a unified theory—and a field, moreover, within which people have taken up heterogenous and contradictory positions—it does nevertheless produce a predominant theoretical effect."[5] Barber's critique not only exposes the lim-itations of postcolonial criticism as it is being formulated and reformulated by a largely Western-educated elite intelligentsia, but also elucidates its complicity with the colonial project: "Nonetheless, postcolonial criticism shares with Com-monwealth criticism its effacement of modern indigenous-language expression in colonized countries."[6] Barber critiques postcolonial criticism for "consign[ing] indigenous-language expression to the background, paradoxically by an inflation of its role as source and resource to the anglophone written tradition."[7] The politics of postcolonial criticism thus traverses a precarious terrain in both exaggerating and simplifying "the effects of the colonial imposition of European languages" and turning "the colonizing countries into unchanging monoliths, and the colonized subject into a homogenized token."[8] Barber proceeds to unveil the elisions and contradictions emanating from this model: "Modern expression in indigenous languages is not considered to exist: as in Commonwealth criticism, African languages in this model are strongly yoked to orality and to the pre-colonial order."[9] Barber claims that theorists like Ashcroft, Griffiths, and Tiffin (*The Empire Writes Back*) and Chantal Zabus (*The African Palimpsest: Indigenization of Language in the West African Europhone Novel*) reinscribe these elisions and contradictions through adopting the paradigm of binary opposition in which "the columns get glued into permanent sets, resulting in a picture of two separate worlds of experience, one of which is in the process of superseding the other."[10]

Barber's arguments are helpful in assessing the viability of postcolonial criticism as it exists as well as its reformulations to evaluate postcolonial African writers. A close look at groups of essays in the latter part of this section will also illuminate ways in which Barber's analysis tends to homogenize postcolonial criticism as one unified methodology while denying it to be so. In the process of utilizing the postcolonial concepts and ideas, the scholars in this sourcebook redefine the various implications of these theories in relation to actual practice. Perhaps theory aligned more closely to practice would dismantle the privileging of European models even within postcolonial criticism.

Barber's position that postcolonial criticism tends to reify the perceptions of the monolithic colonizer and colonized can, to some extent, be supported and contested by the increasing articulation of varying positions by "Third World" feminists. Chandra Talpade Mohanty in "Under Western Eyes: Feminist Scholarship and Colonial Discourse," Carole Boyce Davies in *Black Women, Writing, and Identity: Migrations of the Subject*, Trinh Minh-ha in *Woman, Native, Other: Writing Postcoloniality and Feminism*, and Sara Suleri in "Woman Skin Deep: Feminism and the Postcolonial Condition" provide serious examinations of the concept "postcolonialism" in the context of feminism and "the Third World woman."[11] Mohanty critiques the Western feminist reinscription of the "colonialist move" in assumptions of "Third World women" as an oppressed group: "Western feminists alone become the true 'subjects' of this counterhistory. Third-World women, on the other hand, never rise above the debilitating generality of their 'object' status."[12] Boyce Davies resists the "totalizing" posture and "re-male-ing" discourse of "post-coloniality."[13] She challenges the "macro-discourse of postcoloniality" by offering black/Third World women's "migration narratives" and "horror stories" that constantly resist being obscured, managed, elided, or "post-poned."[14] Through "multiple ways of voicing that reside in Black women's textualities,'' located outside the master discursive field of ''post-coloniality,'' these stories create '' 'elsewhere' worlds and places and consciousness.''[15] While Minh-ha queries the representation of the categories of gender, race, and nativism within feminist discourse, Suleri examines the ''iconicity'' that is granted to the ''imbrications of race and gender'' in the voice of the ''postcolonial Woman'' and seeks to ''dismantle the iconic status of postcolonial feminism.''[16]

Moreover, criticism of attempts to formulate a homogenizing, ''comprehensive postcolonial theory,'' as in *The Empire Writes Back*,[17] attests to the multiple forms of postcolonialisms, ''viewed as ideological orientations rather than as a historical stage,'' as discussed by Vijay Mishra and Bob Hodge in ''What Is Post(-) Colonialism?'': ''We are really talking about not one 'post-colonialism' but many postcolonialisms.''[18] Distinguishing between ''oppositional postcolonialism'' (''found in its most overt form in post-independent colonies at the historical phase of 'post-colonialism' '') and ''complicit postcolonialism'' (''as always present 'underside' within colonization itself''), Mishra and Hodge identify ''postcolonial women's writing'' as requiring ''a different order of theorizing'' that would take into account the ''twice disabling discourse'' that burdens the postcolonial women.[19] They also discuss the need ''to recognize the different histories of White settler colonies which, as fragments of the metropolitan centre, were treated very differently by Britain'' and of ''non-White colonies.''[20] Contending with the elisions of racism and the politics of second language and of violent forms of colonial oppression in nonsettler colonies, Mishra and Hodge expose the ''pan-textualist bias'' and ''seamless theorizing'' in works like *The Empire Writes Back* that reduce all forms of postcolonialism to ''the liberal Australian version of multiculturalism,'' validating pluralist notions of ''syncretism/hybridization'' over ''any claims of indigineity.''[21] Mishra and Hodge's essay is particularly relevant to identify the specific ''material conditions which give rise to post-colonial difference,'' especially since the colonial policy and treatment of the white settler colonies were similar whereas they varied in the nonsettler colonies.[22] These different experiences of colonialism define the different forms of postcolonialism that exist:

In the Indian subcontinent the colonial experience seems to have affected the cities only, in Africa it worked hand in hand with Evangelical Christianity, in Southeast Asia the use of migrant labour—notably Chinese and Indian—mediated between the British and the Malays. In the West Indies slave labour, and later indentured Indian labour, again made the relationship less combative and more accommodating.[23]

Mishra and Hodge's essay also warns that the ''complicit postcolonialism'' of white settler colonies and now of global capitalism ''is on the way of becoming the literary dominant of 'postcolonialism' ''; it is therefore important to ''acknowledge difference and insist on a strongly theorized oppositional postcolonialism as crucial to the debate'' without conflating it to one type.[24]

THEORIZING AFRICAN WOMEN

Siga Fatima Jagne

African women, specifically, have been in the Western classroom for centuries, but always as objects of speculation and subjects of inquiry with little or no agency afforded to them. Their existence as historical subjects, inhabiting multiple locations and positionings, is hardly, if ever, mentioned. That is, in these representations they have existed in a vacuum, suspended in time. This construction and image of the African woman, exoticized and misrepresented, became the standard way in which images of the African woman were sifted and scrutinized through the centuries.[25]

Ifi Amadiume and Christine Obbo observe the fact that generally African women are portrayed as victims and powerless human beings. This stance, they argue, shows a total misunderstanding of the complexities of African women and their lives. Amadiume goes on to explain why Third World women should take their research seriously, especially in the context of the generalizing tone that the studies on these women take on in the West. She writes, "It was, of course, from my knowledge of my own people that I recognized that a great deal of what anthropologists and Western feminists were saying about African women's lack of power was incorrect."[26]

This questioning of the category of woman and women becomes particularly relevant when one talks about African feminist writing and criticism. African women's discourse continually challenges notions of womanhood and femaleness that have been inscribed and prescribed in the discursive practices in which they have been "represented." The whole notion of the inscription of the subject as being ahistorical and apolitical is, therefore, challenged in their works. Spivak, in "The Politics of Interpretations," posits the fact that it is not only problematic, but "difficult to speak of a politics of interpretation without a working notion of ideology as larger than the concepts of individual consciousness and will."[27] African women occupy unique spots that complicate a definition of homogeneity. Filomina Chioma Steady, Carole Boyce Davies, Molara Ogundipe-Leslie, and others have questioned these definitions in their discussions of African women.[28]

This rejection of essentialist categories and definitions leads to the question of the African woman writer. What are her concerns and issues? Molara Ogundipe-Leslie offers her view of what Third World writers should be concerned about:

That the female writer should be committed to her third-world reality and status may lead to disagreements. Being aware of oneself as a third-world person implies being politically conscious, offering readers perspectives on and perceptions of colonialism, imperialism and neo-colonialism as they affect and shape our lives and historical destinies.[29]

Here Ogundipe-Leslie is arguing that a political commitment to the realities of the African women writers, as colonized and decolonizing subjects, should be evident in their work. That is to say, these women, even when writing what moves them personally, should have an awareness of the society in which they live and that has shaped their experiences.

But it may well be important to juxtapose Gayatri Spivak's other view of this critique, not specifically of the writer, but of the subaltern woman all the same. Spivak explains how the Third World woman cannot be accommodated in the First World discourse because she has been doubly displaced and it would be difficult to place her in a "psychoanalytic allegory."[30] I think that the Third World "woman" experiences a triple displacement: as a woman in patriarchal discourse, as the feminine that undoes the whole in deconstructional discourse, and as a colonized woman.

DISCOURSE ON FEMINISM: VOICE AND AGENCY

Therefore, the question to be raised is the discourse on language and voice. How do Western women's theories include infibulation without condescension— "we know better"?[31] When Hélène Cixous, an African by geographical location (a fact that is never factored into her identity in Euro-American academe), talks about women's sexuality, using the metaphor of the dark continent, does she remember her sisters who have to deal with the problem of "double displacement"?[32] Is she also celebrating them too?

This is not to say that African women are not feminists, because if anything the term "feminist" fits these women well. The reason for disavowal by many African women is the connotations associated with the word. To most of these women, the colonial ties between feminism and multinational capitalism make them suspicious of this kind of political movement. Mariama Bâ, even though an avowed feminist, is quick to point out that she is not a feminist in the Western sense of the word, because she understands the contradictions between Western feminism and traditional African customs. As she says: "Politically organized women may be able to influence the progress of a country. The plain women's organizations do not aspire to that. . . . We have no illusions that we, by ourselves, can change the fate of Sénégal's women."[33] This African feminism Bâ is talking about can only be understood within the confines of the culture Bâ is writing about.

What then is involved in the subaltern woman speaking for herself and telling her own story? Is this another way to shut up voices and intellectuals from the rest of the world? Claims about original native voices can also be used to question the authority of intellectuals and writers in the Third World. Writing is as much an act of exclusion as it is an act of inclusion. As an act of creating knowledge, one writes from a position of power and privilege.[34]

When the writer sits to write, there are factors that come into play, such as her own history, location, gender, class, and the different spots she inhabits.

Taking these factors into consideration, what makes the writer representative of her or his group or people?

However, questions about "authentic" voices in the West come up too. Are all Western feminists defined in the same terms Luce Irigaray sets?[35] In recent years there has been a substantial amount of literature written by the subaltern woman. Rather than having Westerners and the subaltern male tell their story, subaltern women have decided to break their silence and let their voices be heard. Perhaps this is a misleading way, because subaltern women until recently have been voices in the wilderness, screaming but not heard—but now Westerners are willing to listen. What does this listening entail? Are these listeners actually hearing, or are they doing their own interpretation of what they think they hear?

This newly found voice of subaltern women poses direct challenges to Western feminism, as it questions the Western feminists' colonization of the female experience and exclusionary practices and challenges its exclusivity. These new voices also create problems for the subaltern female writer. Is she an authority? Can she articulate all the problems of the subaltern woman? Does writing not privilege presence as truth?

Critics and theorists in their quest to provide insight into authors' works do not leave space for the authors' own theoretical preoccupations. Critics and theorists are quick to judge authors without totally exploring the author's right to do what she or he wants with her or his creativity and experience. Sometimes the relationship between critic and author becomes one of envy and disdain. Even more problematic are the new theorists (poststructuralists and deconstructionists), who feign the death of the author and do a coup d'état on the text.[36]

THE "COMMITMENT" DEBATE

Ogundipe-Leslie's questioning of the African woman writer's commitment regarding the status of her womanhood, though valid, takes us back to that whole question of whether the writer can really address everything of concern to his or her society. There is a need to put Ogundipe-Leslie's concerns in perspective and historicize them. Her perspective on the African woman writer and her commitment was part of a set of ongoing discourses in Nigeria on commitment and the writer that is in a way tied to some form of activism. This discourse emerges from social and anticolonial critics (some Marxists, others not). Chinua Achebe's article "The Role of the Writer in a New Nation" places the role of the writer within the framework of a commitment to representing society.[37] Biodun Jeyifo, Onoge, Fatunde, and Darah, writing in Georg Gugelberger's collection of essays on Marxism in African literature, explore these concerns.[38] Onoge's premise is that there is a crisis of consciousness in modern African literature. This crisis, he argues, is a problem of definition: "African writers have phrased the problem under the conceptual rubric of 'role', 'responsibility' or 'commitment' of the writer to his [sic] society. While critics, African and foreign, have generally posed it in terms of the validity of the sociological character of the contents of the bulk of the literature.''[39] Onoge sees the foreign prescriptives as perpetuating the master/slave dichotomy and continuing with the exoticism of the Other. He cites critics such as Kesteloot and Blair as upholding ''cultural liberalism'' and ''authentic exoticism.'' Biodun Jeyifo's sustained work on Marxism and African literature sees the relationship of the writer to the critic as one based on what the writer is concerned about and what the critics think he or she should be doing, but he sees some problems in this relationship:

Some of these parallel or competing discourses are either incorporated into the ''dominant'' discourse or neutralized, marginalized. At this level where one discourse achieves relative dominance over other discourses, we are beyond the power of individual scholars, critics or theorists to serve as arbiters of opinion, knowledge or value, no matter how gifted or influential they might be.[40]

This is further complicated by the division into the camps of the local versus foreign critics. ''The real danger,'' Jeyifo contends, of ''a dichotomization of the two camps is located elsewhere: in recent times, 'Africanists' have come to hold sway over the discipline in an especially problematic manner, and their narrowly formulated agenda increasingly dominates perceptions of 'what is to be done' at the present time in the field.''[41] This concern over the control of African literature, especially at this juncture in academe, when it is being appropriated for Western theories, is justified. In another essay, Onoge concludes on the note that ''the very sociality of the literature requires that criticism go beyond the literary text to include the many structures of its manufacture.''[42] Most of these writers are coming out of the Fanonian base that enacts a coming together of praxis and theory. This is an act that Fanon thought that the new African intellectual was capable of in the decolonizing project. Sekou Touré, in his address to the Second Congress of Black Writers and Artists, had noted:

To take part in the African revolution it is not enough to write a revolutionary song; you must fashion the revolution with the people. And if you fashion it with the people, the songs will come by themselves. In order to achieve real action, you must yourself be a living part of Africa and of her thought; you must be an element of that popular energy which is entirely called forth for the freeing, the progress, and the happiness of Africa. There is no place outside that fight for the artist or for the intellectual who is not himself concerned with and completely with the people in the great battle of Africa and suffering humanity.[43]

The intellectual then becomes the creative balancer in this decolonization and neocolonial sequence. For Touré, one cannot be a writer and not show some political awareness of the human condition that surrounds one.

Fanon, on the other hand, sees the role of the intellectual as retrogressive in the colonial structure because of his or her displacement from his or her culture to that of Western culture. The geographical equation here becomes important but problematic. The term "West" automatically assumes a dominant position, and any geographical area that is situated in opposition to the West is automatically subordinated in Western discourse and Western discursive practices. This subordination is inherent in colonialism, and Fanon states that as long as the West posits itself as the center and the rest of the world as a marginalized periphery, there will always be reason for production of counterdiscourses—even if it means using the theories of the West and stretching or subverting them.[44]

Amilcar Cabral, another Marxist revolutionary, makes the same point as he points out that in a subordinated subject position, such as that of a colonial subject, which is fixed, subversion has to take place because the subordination of the subject is oppressive.[45] So the revolutionary movements of the colonized countries as they move toward decolonization (a term Fanon prefers over post-colonialism) "express antagonisms that emerged" (in the case of Africa) in response to the hegemonic formation installed since the 1500s.[46] Therefore, in this new discourse of decolonization, in which the base and superstructure of the West do not work, new alternatives are to be found, and at the forefront will be the new intellectual who will lead with the masses of the different colonized countries.

The "counterhegemonic" project of the new intellectual will necessarily include a conscious African bourgeoisie who can articulate the nature of "multileveled oppression" in which the African peoples find themselves and resist its impulses. This is the major point with which some African critics are concerned. This counterhegemonic project becomes even more urgent when one looks at the homogenizing and dismissal of Africans. Africans have been lumped into one category—that of race, regardless of class and culture. The new African intellectual, I argue, should be able to recognize that the cultural, political, and social formations of each group in the different countries take on different dimensions (some horizontal, some vertical formations) and should be sensitive to these differences. The formation of superstructures by the colonial elite from the West, being perpetuated by a few trained African elite, should be destroyed by these new intellectual and indigenous structures put in their place. These elites (traditional intellectuals, Antonio Gramsci calls them) were put in place to serve the interest of the colonizing group; they need to reorient themselves to the interest of their people.

Moving from the critics back to the writer, one finds a view that is more sympathetic to a bourgeois analysis. The women writers, specifically, discuss and situate their writings in both a personal and a universal context that has been attacked by male critics as being Western and that is a total misunderstanding of African traditions.[47]

Ogundipe-Leslie situates herself within this Marxism debate on this issue of commitment, but adds feminist commitment to it.[48] However, what is problematic in her presentation is the lack of transformation of the male ideas to the specific politics of location of the female writer.

The whole question of truth in regard to African women writers raises the question of how a truth claims to operate on writers of fiction that is not truth to begin with. It is understood that Ogundipe-Leslie is working in a specific theoretical framework—a framework that is very male and mainstream, rendering it problematic when applied to African women writers. This in no way detracts from the excellent points she makes. Perhaps a different way of reading the Marxist "commitment," by putting the women's work in context, would have helped. As it is, it is easy to take Ogundipe-Leslie out of her context and see her as assuming the stance that the African woman writer should be the authority and articulate all the problems of African women.

Both Tsitsi Dangarembga and Aminata Sow Fall contest Ogundipe-Leslie's point that only Ama Ata Aidoo and Micere Mugo show political consciousness in their writing. Just being aware of oneself as a female writer is a political act in itself, and, as Aimé Césaire said in an interview, the act of writing is a political act.[49] Whenever a writer puts pen to paper, it is political.

Ogundipe-Leslie's reference to the female writers resisting the title of feminists is equally true for the purveyors of *écriture feminine*: Cixous, Irigaray, and Julia Kristeva, who see the rejection of maternity by some feminists as an incapacity to transcend a phallocratic attitude toward women.[50] For these subaltern women writers, I argue against Ogundipe-Leslie: the reason they refuse to accept the label feminist is because, as Dangarembga argues, "white Western feminism" does not name African women's experience. African women's writing reflects concerns they have as women, as Ogundipe-Leslie rightly points out.

The problem with the term "feminist," I argue, rests on its location within an imperialistic, racial language and other discourses. In recent years, feminists from the West have taken on the imperial project of teaching African women about the horrible things associated with clitoridectomy, which they have renamed "genital mutilation." This, of course, is a presupposition that African women have no concern over their welfare and need to be guided, somehow, into an understanding of what is good or bad for them. The fact that there has been, on the continent, a grass-roots women's organization for years to fight this practice is voided by the "discovery" of the West of this "mutilation." (This attitude brings to mind the "discovery" of America by Columbus and what I term the Kipling complex.)

Filomina Steady discusses the position of the black woman as a view of history being the enemy of the black woman. Steady explains that the black woman, especially the African woman, is the "original feminist," because she always had to take on roles that Western women never thought of taking up. The African woman has to be self-reliant, resourceful, and intensely involved in production and is not afraid to lose her femininity in the process. Steady argues the fact that the nature of oppression for the black woman is complex because her experiences "represent multiple forms of oppression rather than simple sexual oppression."[51]

The major point of contention, then, between Western feminists and some African women rests on the concept of individualism versus communalism, that is, individualism, as the desired goal in Western culture, versus communalism in most African cultures—a concept that takes precedence over the needs of the individual. Toni Morrison, writing about this point in black literatures, notes:

These community values (I call them village values) are uppermost in the minds of the Black writers, and it may be this feeling of village values as opposed to Gopher Prairie despair that causes so much misadventure in white criticism of Black writers: such critics tend not to trust or respect a hero who prefers the village and its tribal values to heroic loneliness and alienation. When a character defies a village law or shows contempt for its values, it may be seen as a triumph to white readers, while Blacks may see it as an outrage.[52]

"SANI BAAT"—THROWING VOICE

When one looks at the works of some African women writers, this conflict of the individual versus the community, especially in the creation of a voice, becomes problematic. So far, we have seen the different prescriptions of commitment and some writers' responses to them. The question now is how the writer gets to a voice and one with agency. How does one create a fictional world and remain true to one's experiences?

Ama Ata Aidoo, in an interview with Adeola James, explains the fact that the question with the muted writer's voice is a reflection of the position of women in society. "Women writers," she asserts, "are just receiving the writers' version of the general neglect and disregard that women in the larger society receive."[53] The intellectual production mirrors the notion that women, like children, can be seen, but not heard. This silencing of the female writers goes on even as critics include them in their analysis, an act Aidoo defines as appropriation. She alludes to the state of the criticism of African literature today as "meat out there in the market place, with everybody dragging it, including people who do not care for Africans or what they are writing. But they see that it is a way of making a name for themselves as critics of African Literature."[54]

Consequently, Spivak suggests that "in seeking to learn to speak to (rather than listen to or speak for) the historically muted subject of the 'subaltern' woman, the postcolonial intellectual [writer] systematically unlearns female privilege." This unlearning process, Spivak further explains, necessarily involves "learning to critique postcolonial discourse with the best tools it can provide" and not "simply substituting the lost figure of the colonized."[55]

What does this "looking to the past" in recovering one's voice and agency mean to the African woman? Adrienne Rich, in the following passage, offers a reading of the re-visioning that she believes women writers are doing when they write:

Re-vision—the act of looking back, of seeing with fresh eyes, of entering an old text from a new critical direction—is for us more than a chapter in cultural history: it is an act of survival. Until we can understand the assumptions in which we are drenched we cannot know ourselves. And this drive to self-knowledge, for woman, is more than a search for identity: it is part of her refusal of the self-destructiveness of male-dominated society. A radical critique of literature, feminist in its impulse, would take the work first of all as a clue to how we live, how we have been living, how we have been led to imagine ourselves, how our language has trapped as well as liberated us; and how we can begin to see—and therefore live—afresh.[56]

The African women writers, I point out, indicate the commonalities between internal patriarchy and external colonialism in their texts. They seem to have an understanding of their femaleness, since their female characters inhabit the center of their work. Gayatri Spivak maintains that "between patriarchy and imperialism, subject-constitution and object-formation, the figure of the woman disappears ... displaced ... caught between tradition and modernization."[57] When the subaltern woman is placed in this position, she is rendered mute. Spivak places this lack of agency within what she defines as "the other side of the international division of labour": "the subject of exploitation cannot know and speak the text of female exploitation, even if the absurdity of the nonrepresenting intellectual making space for her to speak is achieved."[58]

I would like to offer an alternate reading and locate myself within the concept of "voice throwing." I believe that by "throwing" in one's voice, a disruption of discourse can take place. The act of "throwing" one's voice can create an epistemic violence to discourse that will create a space for hitherto-unheard voices. The problem that will arise from such an action will be the appropriation of this voice within the particular discourse it interrupts, an act that may or may not render it mute.

Margaret Walker explains these "truths" further by mentioning that it is hard for the black female writer to deal with racism, with its denial of a creative black mind, because to white people blacks lack intelligence and emotion and creativity. Facing these kinds of repressions, both economic and political, it is a marvel that these subaltern women learn to speak. Gayatri Spivak concludes at the end of her article "Can the subaltern speak?" that the subaltern cannot speak, within the prescribed Western parameters of discourse, because "there is no space from which the sexed 'subaltern' can speak."[59] But the subaltern can speak through human agency, despite discursive determinants. The subaltern sees then through different eyes and critiques the practices around her. She can speak in her own language and has started to speak. She needs to be listened to and not attacked ferociously to be rendered mute again. As Margaret Walker puts it:

Everyday, I have lived, however, I have discovered that the value system with which I was raised is of no value in the society in which I must live. This clash of my ideal with the real, of my dream world with the practical, and the mystical inner life with the sordid and ugly world outside—this clash keeps me on the battlefield, at war, and struggling, even tilting windmills. Always I am determined to overcome adversity, determined to win, determined to be me, myself at my best, always female, always black, and ever-lastingly free.[60]

Revising Spivak, however, or as a pretext of Spivak, I would like to again evoke the Wolof concept of "throwing voice" in my subsection on agency. I believe, as the Wolof people do, that the best way to interrupt discourse, albeit a negative way, is by throwing one's voice into it. No apologies are needed for this type of disruptive speech that brings the speaker into the center of the discourse. Because of the plurality of positions and spots that African women inhabit, mostly in the margins, it is important for them to "throw" their voices into the established discourse. Only then will they be heard.

NOTES

1. Frantz Fanon, *The Wretched of the Earth* (New York: Grove Press, 1968), 41; Tsitsi Dangarembga, *Nervous Conditions* (London: Women's Press, 1988; Seattle: Seal Press, 1989), 70; Ngugi wa Thiong'o, *Decolonising the Mind: The Politics of Language in African Literature* (Portsmouth, N.H.: Heinemann, 1986), 108; Bessie Head, *A Woman Alone: Autobiographical Writings*, ed. Craig MacKenzie (Portsmouth, N.H.: Heinemann, 1990), 79.

2. Gayatri Chakravorty Spivak, "Marginality and the Teaching Machine," *Outside in the Teaching Machine* (New York: Routledge, 1993), 53, 55.

3. Homi Bhabha, "Remembering Fanon: Self, Psyche, and the Colonial Condition," *Colonial Discourse and Postcolonial Theory: A Reader*, ed. Patrick Williams and Laura Chrisman (New York: Columbia University Press, 1994), 116. The article originally appeared as the Foreword to Frantz Fanon's *Black Skin, White Masks* (London: Pluto Press, 1986), vii–xxi.

4. Stephen Slemon, "The Scramble for Post-Colonialism," *De-Scribing Empire: Postcolonialism and Textuality*, ed. Chris Tiffin and Alan Lawson (London and New York: Routledge, 1994), 16–17.

5. Karin Barber, "African-Language Literature and Postcolonial Criticism," *Research in African Literatures* 26 (Winter 1995): 4.

6. Ibid.

7. Ibid., 7.

8. Ibid., 3.

9. Ibid., 9.

10. Ibid., 11.

11. Chandra Talpade Mohanty, "Under Western Eyes: Feminist Scholarship and Colonial Discourse," *Third World Women and the Politics of Feminism*, ed. Chandra Talpade Mohanty, Ann Russo, and Lourdes Torres (Bloomington: Indiana University Press, 1991) (first published in *Boundary 2* 12.3–13.1 [Spring/Fall 1984]: 333–358); Carole

Boyce Davies, *Black Women, Writing, and Identity: Migrations of the Subject* (London: Routledge, 1994); Trinh T. Minh-ha, *Woman, Native, Other: Writing Postcoloniality and Feminism* (Bloomington: Indiana University Press, 1989); Sara Suleri, "Woman Skin Deep: Feminism and the Postcolonial Condition," *Colonial Discourse and Post-Colonial Theory: A Reader*, ed. Patrick Williams and Laura Chrisman (New York: Columbia University Press, 1994), 244–256.

12. Mohanty, "Under Western Eyes," 71.

13. Davies, *Black Women, Writing, and Identity*, 80.

14. Ibid., 82–83.

15. Ibid., 82, 89.

16. Suleri, "Woman Skin Deep," 244.

17. Bill Ashcroft, Gareth Griffiths, and Helen Tiffin, *The Empire Writes Back: Theory and Practice in Post-colonial Literatures* (London: Routledge, 1989).

18. Vijay Mishra and Bob Hodge, "What Is Postcolonialism?" *Colonial Discourse and Post-Colonial Theory: A Reader*, ed. Patrick Williams and Laura Chrisman (New York: Columbia University Press, 1994), 284.

19. Ibid., 284.

20. Ibid., 285.

21. Ibid., 287.

22. Ibid., 287, 289.

23. Ibid., 289.

24. Ibid.

25. For a more detailed treatment of this theme, see Aimé Césaire, *Discourse on Colonialism* (New York: Monthly Review Press, 1972); Frantz Fanon, *Black Skin, White Masks* (New York: Grove Press, 1967); Christopher Miller, *Blank Darkness: Africanist Discourse in French* (Chicago: University of Chicago Press, 1985); and V. Y. Mudimbe, *The Invention of Africa: Gnosis, Philosophy, and the Order of Knowledge* (Bloomington: Indiana University Press, 1988).

26. Ifi Amadiume, *Male Daughters, Female Husbands: Gender and Sex in an African Society* (London and New Jersey: Zed Books, 1987), 9. See also Christine Obbo, *African Women: Their Struggle for Independence* (London: Zed Books, 1980).

27. Gayatri Chakravorty Spivak, "The Politics of Interpretations," *In Other Worlds: Essays in Cultural Politics* (London: Routledge, 1988), 118.

28. Carole Boyce Davies, "Introduction: Feminist Consciousness and African Literary Criticism," *Ngambika: Studies of Women in African Literature*, ed. Carole Boyce Davies and Anne Adams Graves (New Jersey: Africa World Press, 1986); Molara Ogundipe-Leslie, "African Women, Culture, and Another Development," *Theorizing Black Feminisms: The Visionary Pragmatism of Black Women*, ed. Stanlie M. James and Abena P. A. Busia (London: Routledge, 1993); Filomina Chioma Steady, Introduction to *The Black Woman Cross-Culturally* (Cambridge, Mass.: Schenkman, 1981).

29. Molara Ogundipe-Leslie, "The Female Writer and Her Commitment," *Women in African Literature Today*, ed. Eldred Durosimi Jones, Eustace Palmer, and Marjorie Jones (London: James Currey, 1987), 11.

30. Spivak, "Can the Subaltern Speak?" *Marxism and the Interpretation of Culture*, ed. Carey Nelson and Lawrence Crossberg (Urbana: University of Illinois Press, 1988), 271–313.

31. There is an ongoing debate in gender and human-rights studies on the issue of clitoridectomy. The arguments are complex and cannot be summarized here. See Nawal

El Saadawi, *The Hidden Face of Eve: Women in the Arab World* (London: Zed Press, 1980); Awa Thiam, *Speak Out, Black Sisters: Feminism and Oppression in Black Africa* (London: Pluto, 1986); Alice Walker and Pratibha Parmar, *Warrior Marks: A Documentary* (New York: Harcourt Brace, 1993), and *Possessing the Secret of Joy* (New York: Harcourt Brace Jovanovich, 1992).

32. Hélène Cixous, "The Laugh of the Medusa," *New French Feminisms*, ed. Elaine Marks and Isabelle de Courtivran (Amherst: University of Mass. Press, 1980).

33. Mariama Bâ, interview in Barbara Arnhold's "The Long Road to Emancipation," *Afrika* (1980): 24.

34. Minh-ha, *Woman, Native, Other.*

35. Luce Irigaray, *Je, Tu, Nous: Toward a Culture of Difference*, translated from French by Alison Martin (London: Routledge, 1992).

36. This is only of interest for a canonized writer. For a critique of this in regard to women, see Nancy Miller, "Changing the Subject . . . ," *Feminist Studies/Critical Studies*, ed. Teresa de Lauretis (Bloomington: Indiana University Press, 1986), 104.

37. Chinua Achebe, "The Role of the Writer in a New Nation" in *Morning Yet on Creation Day* (London: Heinemann, 1975).

38. Georg Gugelberger, ed. *Marxism and African Literature* (Trenton, N.J.: Africa World Press, 1985), 21.

39. Onoge, "The Crisis of Consciousness in Modern African Literature."

40. Biodun Jeyifo, "The Nature of Things: Arrested Decolonization and Critical Theory," *Research in African Literatures* 21 (1990): 34.

41. Ibid., 44.

42. Onoge, "Towards a Marxist Sociology of African Literature," 62.

43. Sekou Touré, from the speech "The Political Leader as the Representative of a Culture," Rome, Italy, 1959.

44. Fanon, *Wretched of the Earth*, 40.

45. Ernesto Laclau and Chantal Mouffe discuss this issue in their work *Hegemony and Socialist Strategy: Towards a Radical Democratic Politics* (London: Verso, 1985).

46. Frantz Fanon, *Wretched of the Earth.*

47. In particular, Femi Ojo-Ade's problematic "Female Writers, Male Critics," *African Literature Today* 13 (London: Heinemann, 1982), 158–179.

48. Ogundipe-Leslie, "African Women, Culture, and Another Development." At this point I would like to assert that my counterpoints to Ogundipe-Leslie's articulations are by no means an attack on her ideas. She is one of our pioneers in writing about African women. I respect her work, and the arguments that follow in no way detract from her contributions, but are my attempts to try and understand what she is attempting to do for my own clarification.

49. Siga Fatima Jagne, unpublished interview with Aimé Césaire, October 1985.

50. Cixous, "The Laugh of the Medusa"; Irigaray, *"This Sex Which Is Not One"*; and Kristeva, "Woman Can Never Be Defined."

51. Steady, *Black Woman Cross-Culturally*, 33.

52. Toni Morrison, "City Limit, Village Values: Concepts of the Neighborhood in Black Fiction," 1981, 38.

53. Ama Ata Aidoo, interview in *In Their Own Voices: African Women Writers Talk*, ed. Adeola James (London: James Currey, 1990), 11.

54. Ibid., 13.

55. Spivak, "Can the Subaltern Speak?" 295.

56. Adrienne Rich, *Of Woman Born: Motherhood as Experience and Institution* (New York: Norton, 1976), 48.

57. Spivak, ''Can the Subaltern Speak?'' 306.

58. Ibid., 287.

59. Ibid., 295.

60. Margaret Walker, ''Being Female, Black, and Free,'' *The Writer on Her Work*, ed. Janet Sternburg (New York: W. W. Norton and Co., 1980), 101.

CHINUA ACHEBE (1930–   )

BIOGRAPHY

Chinua Achebe was born in Ogidi in eastern Nigeria on November 16, 1930, to Isaiah Okafor Achebe and Janet Achebe. His parents, though they instilled in him many of the values of their traditional Igbo culture, were devout evangelical Protestants; his childhood, therefore, was marked by the rich ambivalence of a complex inheritance. He attended mission schools, for example, but remained emotionally close to many of his relatives who were not Christians. These early negotiations of cultural duality would later enable him to develop a necessary distance from the competing and conflicting forces that had shaped his sense of self and formed his worldview—a distance that he now affirms as a prerequisite to see the totality of life "steadily and fully" (*Morning Yet on Creation Day*, 68).

In 1944 Achebe enrolled at the prestigious Government College in Umuahia. Four years later he entered the London-affiliated University College at Ibadan to study medicine, but soon abandoned medicine in favor of literature, philosophy, and history. He became involved in a variety of political and cultural activities on campus. He edited, for example, Ibadan's *University Herald*, to which he also contributed essays and short fiction, and wrote occasional commentaries for student publications such as the *Bug* and *Eagle*.

After his graduation in 1953 Achebe joined the Nigerian Broadcasting Corporation. He first served as talks producer (1954–57), then became controller (1958–61), and finally assumed the directorship of the corporation's External Broadcasting (1961–66).

In 1958 Achebe published his first novel, *Things Fall Apart*. Heinemann Educational Books published it rather reluctantly—the editors were unsure if Western readers would buy a novel by an African—and printed only 2,000 copies. But the novel became a stunning success: since its first publication, it has been translated into nearly fifty languages and has sold millions of copies internationally. Though it was not the first novel published in English by an African author, its spectacular worldwide success inaugurated a new era in African literary history and helped secure a firm foundation for an emerging tradition. Achebe has published four other novels, two collections of essays, a book of short fiction, a volume of poetry, and numerous miscellaneous pieces, but *Things Fall Apart* remains his most widely read work.

One of Africa's most outspoken intellectuals, Achebe has been and continues to be a public figure deeply involved in the political life of his nation. During the Nigerian Civil War (1967–70), precipitated in part by Biafra's attempt to secede from the Nigerian federation, Achebe—a staunch supporter of Biafran independence—became the province's most committed and eloquent spokesperson. In 1983, upon the death of Mallan Aminu Kano, Achebe was elected the deputy national president of the People's Redemption Party. He remains a keen observer of Nigeria's turbulent politics and continues to be a fearless critic of the military dictators whose coups and countercoups have profoundly destabilized his nation's democratic foundations.

Achebe has also played a pivotal personal role in the emergence of postcolonial Anglophone literature in Nigeria and elsewhere in Africa. As the director of Heinemann Educational Books in Nigeria, he has encouraged and published the work of dozens of African writers. *Okike: An African Journal of New Writing*, which he founded in 1971, has provided a forum for a generation of young African artists. *Uwa ndi Igbo: A Journal of Igbo Life and Culture*, a bilingual periodical that he established in 1984, is an invaluable source for students of Igbo civilization.

Achebe is a superb storyteller, a gifted poet, an insightful literary critic, and a brilliant cultural commentator; his phenomenal career as a professional writer spans five decades. Among the numerous honors he has received are the Jock Campbell Award for Literature (1964), the Commonwealth Poetry Prize (1972), the Nigerian National Merit Award (1979), and over a dozen honorary doctorates. He has held professorships at numerous African as well as North American universities. Achebe and his wife, Dr. Christie Okoli Achebe, until recently lived in Nsukka, where he was associated with the Institute for Africa Studies at the University of Nigeria. Currently he is at Bard College in upstate New York. They have four children: Chinelo, Ikechukwu, Chidi, and Nwando.

To appreciate fully the achievement of Chinua Achebe, one must understand his artistic credo, which he has eloquently articulated in "The Novelist as Teacher"—an essay that first appeared in London's *New Statesman* (1965) and was subsequently reprinted in his *Morning Yet on Creation Day* (1975). Achebe views himself, first and foremost, as a teacher who reflects as well as shapes the communal visions and values of his people. He summarily rejects the modern Western notion of the artist as an alienated individual who projects a private vision forged in isolation. To Achebe, the artist is an integral part of his or her community; what he or she creates, therefore, must have functional value and relevance to those individuals who make up the community. He also rejects the pseudo-universalist precepts and apolitical pretensions of the Western aesthetic orthodoxy. To Achebe, art and political concerns, be they local or global, are not mutually exclusive. Indeed, he insists that the artist has an obligation to remain committed to the well-being of his or her people: the most compelling duty of the current generation of African intellectuals, according to Achebe, is to help their fellow Africans regain the dignity and self-esteem lost during the colonial years. He defines himself as a cultural nationalist with a revolutionary mission: "to help my society regain belief in itself and put away the complexes of the years of denigration and self-abasement" (*Morning Yet on Creation Day*, 44). His artistic objective, then, is explicitly political: the achievement of psychosocial rehabilitation through cultural literacy. This educational intent is manifest in much of Achebe's work.

MAJOR WORKS AND THEMES

History—and the struggle to come to terms with it—is an obsessive theme in virtually all post-colonial literatures. Our coming to terms with our problematic historical inheritance, after all, is essential for racial self-retrieval, for forging an authentic and liberating sense of personal and cultural wholeness. Indeed, our meaningful reconnection with our history is indispensable for healing the cultural fracture caused by the catastrophic impact of colonial intrusion; it is a prerequisite for cultural reclamation, for continued resistance. It is precisely this vital and fundamental nexus between establishing a valid connection with the past and achieving a wholesome sense of self that prompts the post-colonial writer to engage in constant dialogue with history.

Inevitably, then, the post-colonial writer runs into intellectual conflict with European-generated imperialist historical discourses. She is faced with the need to reappropriate her past from colonialist historical narratives; she has to salvage her past from distortions and denigrations; and she must revise her history to redefine her past. Her dialogue with the authorized versions of history, therefore, assumes a subversive character. Chinua Achebe's *Things Fall Apart* is one of the most celebrated imaginative attempts to subvert official history by constructing an oppositional version of it.

A landmark piece of post-colonial fiction, *Things Fall Apart* is set in the Igbo village of Umuofia in eastern Nigeria; the action takes place during the closing decades of the nineteenth century. The narrative, divided into three parts, focuses on the rise and fall of its strong-willed protagonist, Okonkwo. While mapping the course of Okonkwo's life, Achebe manages to provide a memorable re-creation of Igbo life before, during, and immediately after the British colonial intrusion.

Part 1 tracks the social ascendancy of Okonkwo in the tribal setting. Haunted by the memory of his father, whom he regards as a failure, Okonkwo—through sheer hard work and determination—emerges as a key figure in the village's power structure, but his ruthlessness renders his hard-won status rather precarious. When he accidentally murders a son of Ezeudu, a priest, Okonkwo is banished to the nearby Igbo village of Mbtana for seven years. In this section of the narrative Achebe also reconstructs precolonial Igbo society: it is a stable, functional, cohesive community that promotes the work ethic and rewards personal achievement; it has an elaborate judicial system and a flexible mode of government; its elaborate rituals and ceremonies help reinforce the people's shared ontological sense. Achebe, however, resolutely avoids romanticizing the Igbo past: he refers to many culturally sanctioned cruelties—ritualized sexism, abandonment of twins, routine sacrificial murders. But he also makes it obvious through reform-minded characters such as Obierika that the precolonial Igbo culture was a dynamic one with the capacity for internally generated progressive change.

Part 2 of the novel documents Okonkwo's difficult exile, his incremental awareness of the perils of excessive individualism, and his growing appreciation of kinship and community. This section also reveals ominous signs of the encroaching colonialism and indications of Okonkwo's resistance to it.

Part 3 chronicles Okonkwo's return to Umuofia, where he hopes to reintegrate himself into the village life. But Umuofia, during his absence, has changed drastically. Things have begun to fall apart: colonial administrative structures, now securely in place, have radically altered traditional life; aggressive proselytization by British missionaries has injected new values that have undermined tribal cohesion. Okonkwo's own son, Nwoye, adopts the Christian faith and rejects his father. Okonkwo's violent resistance to change lands him in jail; his kinsmen, afraid of the colonial administrators, offer him little support. Unwilling to come to terms with the new realities, Okonkwo commits suicide.

The novel ends with a marvelously ironic paragraph. The narrative point of view, which until now has sympathetically presented the complex world of Okonkwo, now abruptly shifts to the arrogant and shallow imperialist perspective of the District Commissioner. His limited vision reduces Africa to stale colonialist stereotypes—the very stereotypes the novel had earlier successfully disrupted. David Carroll, in his *Chinua Achebe: Novelist, Poet, Critic*, correctly identifies the function of this narrative tactic: "The author is recovering an area of experience from stereotype, and the final ironic shift is to challenge the reader to apply the stereotype if he [*sic*] dare" (61).

A modern classic, *Things Fall Apart* is Achebe's calculated response to the imperialist versions of the colonial encounter. Here he offers a contestory rearticulation of history that is explicitly designed to destabilize European discursive constructions of Africa's past. Such a reinscription of African history, of course, fits neatly into his larger project of educating his audience: "I would be quite satisfied if my novels (especially the ones I set in the past) did no more than teach my readers that their past—with all its imperfections—was not one long night of savagery from which the first Europeans acting on God's behalf delivered them'' (*Morning Yet on Creation Day*, 45).

No Longer at Ease, Achebe's second novel, was published in 1960. At the center of the action is Obi, the son of Nwoye and grandson of Okonkwo; here, as in *Things Fall Apart*, the narrative records the rise and fall of its protagonist. But the fictional milieu, however, is radically different: the work is set in the Nigeria of the 1950s, on the eve of the nation's political independence. As its title suggests, the novel explores the malaise of modern Nigeria: the uneasy coexistence of traditional ethos and European values and the absence of a coherent cultural framework that can give a firm direction to the country in general and to its educated elite in particular.

The novel begins with the trial of Obi, a promising young official in the Nigerian Civil Service, who has been arrested on charges of bribery. A brilliant student in his village, Obi is sponsored by the Umuofia Progressive Union to study at an English university; upon his return he enters the prestigious Civil Service. Unable to integrate his anglicized attitudes and indigenous values, he increasingly finds himself rootless and alienated. He rejects certain Igbo cultural practices, such as the caste system that ostracizes the *osu*; yet he does not have the moral courage to marry his girlfriend Clara, because his parents violently object to having an *osu* daughter-in-law. His failure to formulate a coherent set of moral values to live by ultimately destroys him. He begins to accept bribes—a pervasive practice among government officials—but does so ineptly and gets caught. The novel ends with Obi's conviction.

Here, as in *Things Fall Apart*, Achebe is concerned with the debilitating impact of colonialism on the individual as well as on the national psyche. But in *No Longer at Ease* the theme of cultural dislocation—a recurrent theme in post-colonial writing in general—is particularized even more poignantly: the focus is not on a community in disarray but on the private dilemmas of an individual post-colonial. The gently ironic tone of the authorial voice, however, suggests that Achebe is not entirely sympathetic to his alienated, culturally schizophrenic protagonist. Indeed, the novel could be read as a cautionary tale: the post-colonial failure to achieve the necessary synthesis of indigenous traditions and the imposed Western values into a coherent and functional system could be a formula not only for individual tragedies but national disasters as well.

Published in 1964, *Arrow of God* is Achebe's third novel. Here he returns to Nigeria's past and, as in *Things Fall Apart*, explores the impact of change— profound and traumatic change—on individuals and communities. *Arrow of God* is set in the Igbo territory of Umuaro in eastern Nigeria; it narrates the story of Ezeulu, a tribal priest, who is faced with the gradual loss of his authority because of the advent of Christianity, the encroachment of colonialism, and the emergence of intratribal rivalries. When Captain Winterbottom, the District Commissioner, appoints him as a chief warrant officer—as part of the new British effort to decentralize political power and impose indirect rule—Ezeulu rejects the patronizing offer. He is jailed for disobeying imperial authority, but he is

released when Winterbottom becomes ill. Now seemingly triumphant over colonial power, Ezeulu returns to his village. But he refuses to perform the Feast
of the New Yam, which authorizes each new harvest, because he had not eaten
the ritual yams to mark each new moon while he was in jail. The people go
hungry. Sensing a fine opportunity to gain more converts, the local missionaries
offer a Christian version of the Feast of the New Yam. The people respond by
abandoning their traditional faith and by adopting the new religion. Stunned by
the dramatic erosion of his priestly authority, Ezeulu sinks into madness, and
the Christian conquest of Umuaro is now complete.

Like Okonkwo in *Things Fall Apart*, Ezeulu resists change and defies the
inexorable flow of history. Predictably, and tragically, he fails. Here, as in his
first novel, Achebe assesses the disruptive nature of Africa's encounter with
Europe, but the much more elaborate anthropological information that he has
integrated into *Arrow of God* makes it less entertaining as a work of fiction.
Nevertheless, the novel is a powerful meditation on the nature of individual
authority and the question of political power—the issues that will dominate his
next two novels.

A Man of the People, Achebe's fourth novel, generated considerable interest
and curiosity, for it seemed to predict, at the time of its publication in 1966,
Nigeria's first military coup. The novel, set in an unnamed African country that
resembles Nigeria, ends on a grim description of a military takeover; within
weeks of the book's publication, there was in fact a coup that overthrew the
civilian government. Most Nigerian readers were hardly surprised by the coincidence; many, in fact, had anticipated the coup for months. But some critics
of Achebe speculated, without any evidence, that the author might have been
part of the conspiracy that culminated in the coup.

Narrated by Odili, an idealistic university-educated young man, *A Man of the
People* dramatizes a complex set of political events that push his country to the
brink of anarchy. The central conflict in the novel is between Odili and Chief
Nanga, a corrupt and ruthless but widely popular politician who views himself
as a man of the people. The anglicized narrator considers himself superior to a
majority of his fellow citizens and finds their cultural institutions and practices
odious and uncouth. In contrast, Nanga, though corrupt and opportunistic, has
finely honed political instincts that allow him to connect with the people and
earn their affection. Ironically, Nanga is indeed the man of the people while
Odili, despite his idealism, is a mere misfit.

Though Odili and Nanga are friendly to each other in the beginning, Odili
gradually begins to view Nanga's political indecencies with distaste. He becomes hostile when Nanga, with little effort, seduces Elsie, Odili's girlfriend.
Seeking revenge, Odili joins his friend, Max, to found a new political party—
the Common People's Convention—to challenge Nanga's reelection. The campaign becomes violent. Odili is severely beaten by Nanga's hired thugs. While
he is recovering at a hospital, Max is killed by a campaign vehicle that belongs
to Chief Koko, one of Nanga's colleagues; Koko, in turn, is shot dead by Max's

girlfriend, Eunice. Nanga's vicious thugs inflict havoc, the country slips into political chaos, and the army responds by staging a coup.

A Man of the People reflects Achebe's deep personal disappointment with what Nigeria has become since its independence. It is also a brilliant political satire. While Achebe's contempt for Chief Nanga is obvious, he also implicates the narrator, Odili, in the general malaise: even as Odili reports on the corruption around him, he unwittingly reveals his own naïveté, insularity, and crassness. What redeems the novel from total pessimism is Odili's emerging self-knowledge—his evolving new consciousness of himself and his increasingly sharper understanding of the daunting complexities of his nation's politics. Such growth holds out new possibilities and hopes.

Achebe's fifth and most recent novel, *Anthills of the Savannah*, appeared in 1987, almost twenty-one years after the publication of *A Man of the People*. Here again Achebe explores the psychology of power in an attempt to understand the political nightmare that Nigeria has turned into. A polyvocal text with multiple narrators, *Anthills of the Savannah* focuses on the convergence of the lives of four major characters: Sam, a Sandhurst-trained military officer, who has become President of Kangan, an imaginary West African state, by orchestrating a coup; Chris Oriko, Sam's boyhood friend and member of his cabinet; Ikem Osodi, a poet and journalist and also a friend of the President's; and Beatrice Okah, Chris's London-educated girlfriend and a top government official. Beatrice, the novel's most compelling character, serves as an agent of Chris's and Ikem's moral transformation. Both men, in different ways, begin to defy Sam's mad authoritarianism; their loss of political power becomes a measure of their increasing identification with the dispossessed millions of their country. Both die resisting brutal abuse of power, and there is yet another military coup that eliminates Sam. In the end it is Beatrice and the community of women she has created that seem to embody the benevolent counterpoint to the mindless violence of male power. The women, it appears, are now entrusted with the tasks of national renewal and the return to political sanity.

Anthills of the Savannah reveals Achebe's ongoing engagement with Nigeria's unstable politics. His anger and pain are obvious; however, as Nadine Gordimer points out, Achebe is "a writer who has no illusions but is not disillusioned" (1). Though his deep sorrow at the betrayal of the Nigerian people by their irresponsible, self-appointed political leaders informs *Anthills of the Savannah*, the novel ends on a gently defiant note of hope: the people still have the potential to redirect the course of their nation.

Though Achebe is most widely known for his novels, he is also a distinguished poet. His only collection of published poetry, *Beware, Soul Brother* (1971), won the first Commonwealth Poetry Prize and has assured him a secure place in the Anglophone African tradition in poetry. Divided into five sections—"Prologue," "Poems about War," "Poems Not about War," "Gods, Men, and Others," and "Epilogue"—the thirty poems in the volume, often autobiographical, are anguished commentaries on the Nigerian Civil War and its lingering consequences. The mood of the poems, in general, is elegiac: the poet mourns the loss and longs for the grace of even momentary hope. Clearly grounded in the Igbo traditions of songmaking, each of the poems is meticulously crafted and startling in the freshness of its imagery. Among the most powerful poems are "Mango Seedling," which memorializes Christopher Okigbo, a fellow Nigerian poet who was killed in the conflict, and "Christmas in Biafra," which testifies to the monumental courage of ordinary people in the face of terror and hopelessness caused by war.

The Nigerian Civil War is also the setting for the title story in Achebe's collection of short fiction, *Girls at War and Other Stories* (1972). The most substantial piece in the volume, "Girls at War," effortlessly evokes the horrors of war by focusing on the relationship between self-deluded Gerald Nwanko, a government official, and Gladys, once an idealistic volunteer fighter who is now a desperate yet defiant survivor. Other stories, such as "The Voter" and "Vengeful Creditor," satirize corruption and abuse of power. But the volume also includes some of the earliest sketches that Achebe wrote as an undergraduate student at Ibadan; these early works suggest the thematic concerns and narrative styles that characterize his later, major publications.

A significant text among Achebe's nonfiction prose works is *The Trouble with Nigeria*. Published in 1983, this booklet helps clarify the trenchant political criticism inscribed in his two most recent novels. In *The Trouble with Nigeria* Achebe lists a variety of social evils that he believes are endangering the very survival of Nigeria as a modern nation-state: violent tribalism, pervasive corruption, widespread inefficiency, and endemic apathy. These ills, he argues, make Nigeria one of "the most unpleasant places on earth" (9–10). But Achebe does not believe that Nigeria is irredeemable; in fact, he is convinced that there are enough talented and committed women and men in Nigeria who can save their nation from sinking into anarchy. What Nigeria badly needs and has never had an adequate supply of is responsible political leadership. In other words, the trouble with Nigeria is its arrogant, selfish, misguided, power-hungry politicians who have led the nation to the abyss of chaos and destruction. Achebe's relentless criticism is devastating; yet lurking beneath the scathing attack is his enduring conviction that Nigerians still have the capacity to rescue their country from its dictators.

Achebe's other two major nonfiction prose works—*Morning Yet on Creation Day* (1975) and *Hopes and Impediments* (1988)—are collections of essays. "The Writer as Teacher," which appears in the first volume, is indispensable for an understanding of Achebe's art. "The African Writer and the Biafran War" formulates a bold definition of the artist's political responsibilities. "The African Writer and the English Language" engages one of the vexing issues in postcolonial literature: the employment of imperial language to articulate indigenous reality. A most notable essay that appears in both volumes is "Colonialist Criticism." A classic piece of postcolonial critical theory, it engages the politics of literary reception and offers a cogent attack on the pseudo-universalist, ethnocentric, and even racist assumptions that often underlie European assessment of non-European art. The second volume includes Achebe's controversial reading of Conrad's *Heart of Darkness*; here Achebe convincingly exposes the vulgar racism that informs Conrad's text—a text that is widely taught and canonized in the West. Other essays, such as "Language and Destiny of Man" and "Thoughts on the African Novel," not only exemplify his critical shrewdness, but also offer a theoretical framework to locate and understand Achebe's own artistic productions. The second volume ends with his poignant eulogy for his friend, the great African-American writer James Baldwin.

Achebe has also published three short, delightful children's books: *Chike and the River* (1966), *The Drum* (1977), and *The Flute* (1977). In contrast to the countless children's books about Africa written by Westerners for Western consumption, these narratives are written with Achebe's own and other African children in mind. His mission here, explicitly, is to educate: to create culturally affirming images of Africa and its people for Africa's children. These texts are a moving testament of Achebe's transcendent commitment to the present and future generations of Nigerian as well as other African children.

CRITICAL RECEPTION

Achebe's art has elicited considerable critical attention. In addition to over 200 scholarly articles, there are several book-length studies devoted to his work. Among the critics there is a general consensus that Achebe's work has earned him a significant place in the contemporary world of literature and canonical centrality in African Anglophone writing. Many have acknowledged Achebe's status as a literary pioneer. John Povey, for example, finds him "very clearly the best novelist in that group of writers who at Ibadan in the fifties contrived the birth of West African Literature in English" because "his work has a structural strength and architectural coherence unmatched by other novelists" (97). C. L. Innes concurs: acknowledging the considerable influence that Achebe's work has had on a generation of African writers, she endorses the view that he is "the father of the African novel" (19). T. A. Hale considers him "Africa's most significant black novelist" (1924). Nadine Gordimer, herself a superb African novelist, enthusiastically asserts that Achebe "is gloriously gifted with the magic of an ebullient, generous, great talent" (1).

But Achebe has not always been the recipient of such adoring praise. His early novels have in fact sometimes provoked crude and condescending responses from a few Western reviewers who were clearly ill equipped to assess his work. For example, a reviewer identified only with the initials J. H. calls *Things Fall Apart* a novel about "primitive rites, the witchcraft, and superstitious savagery as well as the more acceptable facets of heathen existence" (9). While J. H. only primitivizes Achebe's art, R. C. Healy infantalizes it as well; to Healy, *Things Fall Apart* is an "authentic native document, guileless and unsophisticated . . . [devoid of any] sense of plot or development. . . . This is plain and unvarnished storytelling in the best primitive tradition'' (8).

Healy's reaction to Achebe's second novel, *No Longer at Ease*, is remarkably similar. Unable to discern the novel's many complex layers of signification, he finds it "disarmingly ingenious" and "bare of rhetorical subtlety," which he considers to be signs of "artlessness" and "primitive storytelling" (28). M. S. Byam agrees; he finds the plot of *No Longer at Ease* "almost juvenile in its simplicity" (2118). Achebe's essay "Colonialist Criticism," of course, articulates a brilliant retort to such Eurocentric critical inanities.

In general, however, critics are enthusiastic about Achebe's work. Many praise his smooth blending of fiction and anthropology. Others note his inventive use of language—manipulation of idioms, use of pidgin, incorporation of Igbo proverbs—to give his narrative a distinct African lilt. A number of critics admire his wit, humor, and deft handling of the tools of satire. His poetry, praised for its clarity, grace, and technical sophistication, receives substantial and favorable attention in C. L. Innes's *Chinua Achebe* and in David Carroll's *Chinua Achebe: Novelist, Poet, Critic*. His two major collections of essays, *Morning Yet on Creation Day* and *Hopes and Impediments*, which demonstrate his skills as a literary and critical theorist, have been widely praised for their intellectual agility and polemic liveliness. His children's books, however, have received very little scholarly attention so far.

A commanding figure in post-colonial African literature, Achebe has played an enormously significant role in reappropriating Africa from the self-serving fictions and fantasies of Europe. Resistant counternarratives, his novels collectively offer a sustained intellectual challenge to European constructions of Africa and its people. His works, in the words of Biodun Jeyifo, are "powerful exemplary texts of nationalist contestation of colonialist myths and distortions of Africa and Africans" (51). Such a contestation has been the defining project of Achebe's career as a writer. His successful reclamation of Africa from the heart of European darkness remains the central achievement of his life and art.

BIBLIOGRAPHY

Selected Works by Chinua Achebe

Things Fall Apart. London: Heinemann, 1958.
No Longer at Ease. London: Heinemann, 1960.
Arrow of God. London: Heinemann, 1964.
Chike and the River. Cambridge: Cambridge University Press, 1966.
A Man of the People. London: Heinemann, 1966.
Beware, Soul Brother. London: Heinemann, 1971.
Girls at War and Other Stories. London: Heinemann, 1972.
Morning Yet on Creation Day. London: Heinemann, 1975.
The Drum. Enugu, Nigeria: Fourth Dimension, 1977.

The Flute. Enugu, Nigeria: Fourth Dimension, 1977.
The Trouble with Nigeria. London: Heinemann, 1983.
Anthills of the Savannah. London: Heinemann, 1987.
Hopes and Impediments. London: Heinemann, 1988.

Selected Studies of Chinua Achebe

Abrahams, Cecil A. "George Lamming and Chinua Achebe: Tradition and the Literary Chroniclers." *Awakened Conscience: Studies in Commonwealth Literature.* Ed. C. D. Narasimhaiah. New Delhi: Sterling, 1978. 294–306.

Ackley, Donald. "The Male-Female Motif in *Things Fall Apart.*" *Studies in Black Literature* 5.1 (1974): 1–6.

Adebayo, Tunji. "The Past and the Present in Chinua Achebe's Novels." *Ife African Studies* 1.1 (1974): 66–84.

Babalola, C. A. "A Reconsideration of Achebe's *No Longer at Ease.*" *Phylon* 47 (1986): 139–47.

Bottcher, Karl H. "Narrative Technique in Achebe's Novels." *Journal of the New African Literature and the Arts* 13/14 (1972): 1–12.

Brown, H. R. "Igbo Words for the Non-Igbo: Achebe's Artistry in *Arrow of God.*" *Research in African Literatures* 12 (Spring 1981): 69–85.

Bruchac, Joseph. "Achebe as Poet." *New Letters* 40.1 (1973): 23–31.

Byam, M. S. Review of *No Longer at Ease. Library Journal* 86 (June 1961): 2118.

Carroll, David. *Chinua Achebe: Novelist, Poet, Critic.* London: Macmillian, 1990.

Cobham, Rhonda. "Problems of Gender and History in the Teaching of *Things Fall Apart.*" *Matatu: Journal for African Culture and Society* 7 (1990): 25–39.

Cott, Jonathan. "Chinua Achebe: At the Crossroads." *Parabola: The Magazine of Myth and Tradition* 6.2 (May 1981): 30–39.

Egudu, R. N. "Achebe and the Igbo Narrative Tradition." *Research in African Literatures* 12 (Spring 1981): 43–54.

Ehling, Holger, ed. *Critical Approaches to Anthills of the Savannah.* Amsterdam: Rodopi, 1991.

Emenyonu, Ernest. "Ezeulu: The Night Mask Caught Abroad by Day." *Pan-African Journal* 4 (1971): 407–19.

Gakwandi, Shatto Arthur. *The Novel and Contemporary Experience in Africa.* London: Heinemann, 1977.

Gikandi, Simon. "Chinua Achebe and the Post-Colonial Esthetic: Writing, Identity, and National Formation." *Studies in Twentieth Century Literature* 15.1 (Winter 1991): 29–41.

———. *Reading Chinua Achebe: Language and Ideology in Fiction.* London: James Currey, 1991.

———. *Reading the African Novel.* London: James Currey, 1987.

Gleen, Ian. *Achebe and the Dilemma of the Nigerian Intellectual.* Cape Town: Centre of African Studies, 1983.

Gordimer, Nadine. Review of *Anthills of the Savannah. New York Herald Tribune Book Review* February 21, 1988: 1, 26.

H. J. Review of *Things Fall Apart. Christian Science Monitor* June 11, 1959: 9.

Hale, T. A. Review of *Morning Yet on Creation Day. Library Journal* 100 (October 1975): 1924.

Healy, R. C. Review of *No Longer at Ease*. *New York Herald Tribune* April 30, 1961: 28.

———. Review of *Things Fall Apart*. *New York Herald Tribune Book Review* April 12, 1959: 8.

Ikegami, Robin. "Knowledge and Power, the Story and the Storyteller: Achebe's *Anthills of the Savannah*." *Modern Fiction Studies* 37.3 (1991): 493–507.

Innes, C. L. *Chinua Achebe*. Cambridge: Cambridge University Press, 1990.

Innes, C. L., and Bernth Lindfors, eds. *Critical Perspectives on Chinua Achebe*. Washington, D.C.: Three Continents Press, 1978; London: Heinemann, 1979.

Iyasere, Solomon. "Narrative Techniques in *Things Fall Apart*." *New Letters* 40 (1974): 73–93.

———. "Okonkwo's Participation in the Killing of His 'Son' in Chinua Achebe's *Things Fall Apart*." *College Language Association Journal* 35.3 (1992): 303–15.

JanMohamed, Abdul. *Manichean Aesthetics: The Politics of Literature in Colonial Africa*. Amherst: University of Massachusetts Press, 1983.

———. "Sophisticated Primitivism: The Syncretism of Oral and Literate Modes in Achebe's *Things Fall Apart*." *Ariel* 15.4 (1984): 19–39.

Jeyifo, Biodun. "For Chinua Achebe: The Resilience and the Predicament of Obierika." *Chinua Achebe: A Celebration*. Ed. Kirsten Holst Petersen and Anna Rutherford. Sydney: Dangaroo Press, 1990. 51–70.

Kalu, Anthonia. "The Priest/Artist Tradition in Achebe's *Arrow of God*." *Africa Today* 41.2 (1994): 51–62.

Killam, G. D. *The Writings of Chinua Achebe*. London: Heinemann, 1977.

Kuesgen, Reinhardt. "Conrad and Achebe: Aspects of the Novel." *World Literature Written in English* 24 (Summer 1984): 27–33.

Leslie, Omolara. "Chinua Achebe: His Vision and His Craft." *Black Orpheus* 2.7 (1972): 34–41.

Lewis, Mary Ellen. "Beyond Content in the Analysis of Folklore in Literature: Chinua Achebe's *Arrow of God*." *Research in African Literatures* 7 (1976): 44–52.

Lindfors, Bernth, ed. *Approaches to Teaching Things Fall Apart*. New York: Modern Language Association of America, 1991.

Melamu, M. J. "The Quest for Power in Achebe's *Arrow of God*." *English Studies in Africa* 14 (1971): 225–40.

Moore, Gerald. "Chinua Achebe: Nostalgia and Realism." *Twelve African Writers*. London: Hutchinson University Press, 1980.

Niven, Alastair. "Another Look at *Arrow of God*." *Literary Half-Yearly* 16.2 (1975): 53–68.

Nnolim, C. E. "The Form and Function of the Folk Tradition in Achebe's Novels." *Ariel* 14 (1983): 35–47.

Obiechina, Emmanuel. *Culture, Tradition, and Society in the West African Novel*. Cambridge: Cambridge University Press, 1975.

Petersen, Kirsten Holst and Anna Rutherford, eds. *Chinua Achebe: A Celebration*. Sydney: Dangaroo Press, 1990.

Povey, John. "The Novels of Chinua Achebe." *Introduction to Nigerian Literature*. Ed. Bruce King. Lagos: Africana Publishing Corporation, 1972. 97–112.

Quayson, Ato. "Realism, Criticism, and the Disguises of Both: A Reading of Chinua Achebe's *Things Fall Apart* with an Evaluation of the Criticism Relating to It." *Research in African Literatures* 25.4 (1994): 117–36.

Ravenscroft, Arthur. *Chinua Achebe*. Harlow, England: Longmans, 1977.

Robson, Andrew. "The Use of English in Achebe's *Anthills of the Savannah*." *College Language Association Journal* 37.4 (1994): 365–76.

Sanchez, Sonia. "Nigerian Bard Tells His Own Story." *Emerge* 6.5 (March 1995): 60–61.

Swados, Harvey. "Chinua Achebe and the Writers of Biafra." *New Letters* 40.1 (1973): 5–13.

Swann, Joseph. "From *Things Fall Apart* to *Anthills of the Savannah*: The Changing Face of History in Chinua Achebe's Novels." *Crisis and Creativity in the New Literatures in English*. Ed. Geoffrey Davis and Hena Maes-Jelinek. Amsterdam: Rodopi, 1990.

ten Kortenaar, Neil. "Beyond Authenticity and Creolization: Reading Achebe Writing Culture." *PMLA* 110.1 (January 1995): 30–42.

Turkington, Kate. *Chinua Achebe: Things Fall Apart*. London: Edward Arnold, 1977.

Watts, Cedric. " 'A Blood Racist': About Achebe's View of Conrad." *Yearbook of English Studies* 13 (1983): 196–209.

Winkler, Karen J. "An African Writer at a Crossroads: Now at Bard College, Chinua Achebe Has Become an Influential Figure in Western Literary Circles." *Chronicle of Higher Education* 40.19 (January 12, 1994): A9, A12.

Winters, Marjorie. "Morning Yet on Judgment Day: The Critics of Chinua Achebe." *When the Drumbeat Changes*. Ed. Carolyn A. Parker and Stephen H. Arnold. Washington, D.C.: Three Continents Press, 1981.

———. "An Objective Approach to Achebe's Style." *Research in African Literatures* 12 (Spring 1981): 55–68.

Wren, Robert. *Achebe's World: The Historical and Cultural Context of the Novels of Chinua Achebe*. Washington, D.C.: Three Continents Press, 1980; Harlow, England: Longman, 1981.

Yankson, Kofi. "The Use of Pidgin in *No Longer at Ease* and *A Man of the People*." *Asemka* 1.2 (1974): 68–79.

EMMANUEL S. NELSON

AMA ATA AIDOO (1942–   )

BIOGRAPHY

Ama Ata Aidoo was born on March 23, 1942, in the Fanti town Abeadzi Kyakor in central Ghana. As a child of Nana Yaw Fama, a chief of Abeadzi Kyakor, and her mother Maame Abba Abasema, Aidoo grew up with a clear sense of African traditions and a Western education. Aidoo describes her father as a "highly politicized individual and an artist" and regards her mother as politicized in her own way (James, 13). Looking back to her parents and her grandfather, who was imprisoned, tortured, and killed by the British, Aidoo sees herself as "coming from a long line of fighters" (James, 13).

Aidoo attended Wesley Girls' High School in Cape Coast and received her bachelor's degree (a B.A. in English with honors) in 1964 from the University of Ghana, Legon. During the same year Aidoo completed her first play, *The Dilemma of a Ghost*, which was performed by the Students' Theatre in Legon in March 1964. At the beginning of her career as a writer, Aidoo won a prize in a short-story competition organized by Ibadan's Mbari club. Aidoo's major work includes two plays, *The Dilemma of a Ghost* (1965) and *Anowa* (1970), a short-story collection, *No Sweetness Here* (1970), two novels, *Our Sister Killjoy* (1977) and *Changes* (1991), and a volume of poetry, *Someone Talking to Sometime* (1985).

Aidoo has taught, lectured, and studied at numerous universities in West and central Africa and in the United States. She has been a professor of English at the University of Ghana, Cape Coast, was a fellow at the Institute for African Studies at the University of Ghana, where she wrote and researched Fanti drama, has served as a consulting professor to the Washington bureau of the Phelps-Stokes Fund's Ethnic Studies Program (1974–75), has attended an advanced creative writing course at Stanford University, and has been at the Harvard International Seminar. Aidoo also held the position of Minister of Education under the government of Jerry Rawlings in 1983–84. Aidoo explains that she sought this position because she believes in the crucial importance of education and because she wanted direct access to political influence and power.

What characterizes Aidoo as much as her heroines is a strong historical and political awareness of Africa's colonial past and post-colonial present, and particularly a powerful sense of the problems facing an African woman in and outside of Africa. This "hypersensitivity," as Aidoo calls it, to the pains and confusions common to Africans, and particularly to African women, accounts both for the focus on human suffering and the stylistic and linguistic concerns of Aidoo's work.

To Aidoo, being a writer and being a mother have been two important and enriching aspects of her life. Most recently, Aidoo has been living in Harare, Zimbabwe, where she writes. She is the mother of one daughter, Kinna Likimani.

MAJOR WORKS AND THEMES

In an interview, Aidoo once said: "You come to literature or things like that, and it's then that you really understand a term like neo-colonialism. . . . It's beautiful to have independence, but it's what has happened to our minds that is to me the most frightening thing about the colonial experience" (McGregor, 26). Aidoo's entire work speaks powerfully to this issue. Her writing focuses on the psychological impact of the colonial and post-colonial experience on her male and particularly her female characters; her writing is not about overt political action but about the individual pains, struggles, and confusions of her heroines and heroes as they are striving to create meaningful lives in and outside of Africa in the psychological, cultural, linguistic, and political chaos of a post-colonial reality. Aidoo particularly focuses on the often hopeless search of her female characters to find happiness in marriage and to find solidarity in other women.

Aidoo's first play, *The Dilemma of a Ghost* (1965), tells the story of the marriage between Ato Yawson, a young Ghanaian studying in America, and Eulalie, an African-American who meets Ato in the United States. As a married couple, both return to Ghana to Ato's family. The play articulates the difficulties that arise from the clash of the traditional family values of Ato's family and Eulalie's often naïve hopes and preconceptions about "coming home" to Africa; the play particularly highlights Ato's failure to negotiate both sides or even to be sensitive to them and his own role as interpreter. While this play accentuates the almost unsurmountable problems of the educated African male returning to his home country, Aidoo suggests in the final reconciliation between Eulalie and her Ghanaian mother-in-law a female solidarity that may resolve some of the conflicts inside the African diaspora.

The play *Anowa* (1970) retells an old legend of a woman marrying a man against the will of her parents. Anowa, like Aidoo's other heroines, is a woman whose historical awareness and determination to choose her own destiny and husband lead to her tragic end. In this play, Aidoo revises a legend told to her by her mother and gives it a tragic, "pseudo-Freudian" (McGregor, 23) ending. Set in the 1870s on the Gold Coast, the play presents the story of Anowa's marriage to Kofi and its eventual failure. Anowa and Kofi become increasingly alienated when Kofi begins to buy slaves in order to obtain riches. Anowa's sense of slavery as an unethical institution that connects the black slaveholder with the white colonists isolates her more and more from her husband Kofi. While Anowa's and Kofi's business flourishes, their marriage fails. Anowa is driven almost into insanity because nobody will back her in her "hypersensitive" reaction to her husband's role as slaveowner. The play ends tragically with the suicide of both Anowa and Kofi when Anowa reveals that Kofi's power as a slaveowner masks his impotence as a man. Aidoo shows that the slow disintegration of her heroine's mind and social position is a result of Anowa's insistence on her own moral and political standards. In this play, Aidoo further suggests that the people in Anowa's environment, her husband but also her family and her neighbors, are partially responsible for Anowa's unhappiness and death because they judge before they think. It is Anowa's insistence on her historical perspective and her individualized decisions that make her an outcast and that render her unable to find a meaningful and sane life for herself, or even just to survive. It is this insistence also that reveals the underlying sexual and moral insecurities that define her husband's and neighbors' inability to face history and their own position and responsibilities in it.

Aidoo's short-story collection *No Sweetness Here* (1970) once again illustrates that Aidoo is interested in the impact of the post-colonial situation on all people, urban and rural, old and young, men and women. The title of the first story of the collection, "Everything Counts," alludes to Aidoo's comprehensive and touchingly human vision in these well-crafted stories. For example, in "The Cutting of a Drink" and "Two Sisters" Aidoo tackles the issue of prostitution in the city; in the story "For Whom Things Did Not Change" she depicts the consciousness of an African who remains, despite independence, the "slave" of his young master; the story "Everything Counts" deals with the troubling issues of a black female character and her struggle with white beauty ideals. Aidoo depicts the many different confusions and dilemmas her African characters face in post-colonial Africa: the dilemma between Western and African values, the country and the city and the individual urge to succeed in Western terms, and the traditional values sacrificed on the way.

Our Sister Killjoy (1977) is Aidoo's most radically experimental book. Written in a mixture of verse and prose, this novel depicts the vexed consciousness of Sissie, who cannot experience joy but relives the colonial past when visiting England and venturing into the "heart of darkness" of Bavaria, Germany. It is the radical style of this novel that makes it perhaps Aidoo's most programmatic book; with dramatic irony that distances the writer from her character, Aidoo is able to express her main concerns through the troubled consciousness of her character Sissie—a character who feels uncomfortable about the use of a language that "enslaved" her, who looks at a German castle as symbolizing the tyrannical and exploitative system that enabled its construction, who speaks about organ donors and medical advances in terms of the inherent racism in such a system (blacks giving organs for whites), who urges her male compatriots to return to Ghana, who experiences racism and ignorance about Africa throughout her journeys, and who finally accepts that her former lover and the person sitting next to her in the plane may consider her crazy; she does not care about being considered crazy because she realizes that her concerns are crucial to her return to Africa. Aidoo's experimental mixture of genres and her stylized use of language (sometimes one word covers an entire page) expresses the discomfort of the consciousness of Sister Killjoy and the ways in which Sissie's vision destabilizes our own sense of a narrative and challenges our expectations. It also places Sissie's consciousness at the verge of sanity, at a place of "hypersensitivity" that, like Anowa's, comes along with a strong and strongly expressed historical and political consciousness. Aidoo's uncomfortable novel is a particularly successful and challenging artistic rendering of the psychological consequences of political and historical awareness in the post-colonial era.

Aidoo's volume of poems *Someone Talking to Sometime* (1985) allows her to make many voices heard. The poems range from dramatic monologues of mothers and lovers to satirical representations of political speech. In these poems, as in *Our Sister Killjoy*, Aidoo can mix the representation of an individual consciousness with the programmatic, the personal with the political. It is in her satire as well as in the urgency and the troubled nature of the voices she represents that Aidoo once again provides a comprehensive picture of human suffering, political injustice, the problems of neocolonialism, and some faint glimmers of hope.

It is well known that Aidoo once claimed that she would never write a story about two lovers in Accra, and it is a sign of her changing perspective of what constitutes the political that she, after all, decided to write about just that in her latest novel. Commenting on her latest love story set in Accra, Aidoo says that she "is beginning to say that love or the workings of love is [sic] also political" (James, 14). In *Changes* (1991) Aidoo aptly portrays the search of her heroine Esi, an urban professional young woman working in the Department of Urban Statistics, for a "truth" that can capture her experience as a woman in post-colonial Accra. While less experimental in style than her earlier novel, this latest piece shares Aidoo's concern with language and its inability to adequately describe a woman's experience. Like Sissie, Esi comes to the verge of hysteria trying to find a language that can capture her dilemmas and confusions. It is neither the language of feminist, sociological discourse, nor that of her mother, nor that of her friend and "sister" Opokuya that can capture the truth of her experience, her confusions, resistances, and decisions. After divorcing her first husband, who raped her and confined her with his possessiveness, Esi later becomes the second wife of the handsome Ali; while she hopes to find in the polygamous marriage the kind of freedom she needs to pursue her career, such a modern redefinition of polygamy remains impossible, and Esi's marriage to Ali fails to satisfy her. Torn between traditional and modern demands, desires, and restrictions, Esi's search for a truth remains unsuccessful. She concludes that there is no "fashion of loving" (*Changes*, 166) adequate to her needs.

What pervades Aidoo's work, then, is a particular sensitivity to the plight of the African woman as she struggles for an emotional, political, and moral independence—before and after Ghana's independence. Representing this struggle, Aidoo challenges the concept of marriage, the role of other women in the oppression and liberation of her heroines, the concept of sanity, and finally language and literary forms themselves, as they in their traditional forms seem unable to represent a woman's truth accurately.

CRITICAL RECEPTION

Aidoo criticism has mostly centered around three interrelated issues: her style or form, her feminism, and her concern with the African diaspora and the construction of an African selfhood. Formal studies have emphasized Aidoo's use of the oral and written tradition. For example, Arlene Elder's article concentrates on "Aidoo's paradoxical role as an artist attempting to continue the moral function of the communal oral performer in an individualistic, materialistic present" (117). Elder concludes that "one may revitalize the forms of traditional culture as Aidoo demonstrates so skillfully in all of her work, but history has guaranteed that the substance, the ethical bond between artist and audience, will probably never return" (117). Mildred A. Hill-Lubin shows that Aidoo's texts are "talking stories" that make us into "readers/listeners/audience" and that show that much of the oral tradition is still "alive and effective" ("Storyteller and Audience," 245). Dapo Adelugba examines Aidoo's use of language in her dramas and shows that Aidoo uses many different linguistic registers to "portray with veracity and accuracy the different generations and levels of education in present-day Africa" (83).

Typical for a feminist approach is Chimalum Nwanko's article, which stresses the feminist achievements of Aidoo's writings and stands in a telling tension to Elder's formal study. To Nwanko, Aidoo does not face a paradox but takes "the lead among other African women in search for social justice through creative literature" (159). The experimental nature of Aidoo's writing becomes a "defiant artistic form in which prose and poetry freely blend with each other. That posture takes care of the feminist campaign for women's freedom" (155) and, according to Nwanko, other issues, such as racism. Caroline Rooney discusses Aidoo's feminism inside a larger theoretical frame of "white feminism" versus "black womanism." To Kofi Owusu, who also sees Aidoo's feminism within the context of "womanism," *Our Sister Killjoy* gives a sense of "structural and linguistic anarchy'' that serves to ''challenge 'canonized literature' that tends to black out Black and blanch out Woman'' (361). Sara Chetin sees *Our Sister Killjoy* as a feminist text that ''both structurally and thematically, resists identification with Western male literary traditions [. . .] and implicitly [questions] the ways in which the First World feminist reader can enter African female-centered realities and interpret the unfamiliar codes produced by the text'' (147). She concludes that ''as First World feminists, we 'listen-in' from an unprivileged position in an attempt to understand the parameters that determine African women's writing'' (159).

Kwaku-Larbi Korang and Gay Wilentz concentrate on *Our Sister Killjoy*'s renegotiations of central and marginal positions. Wilentz discusses ''how the novel exposes a rarely heard viewpoint in literature in English—that of the African woman exile'' (''Politics of Exile,'' 161), which works to dispel the myth surrounding the position of the male exile. Korang also sees the novel as ''an *other* traveler's tale'' (51); with Sissie's return to Africa, according to Korang, Aidoo ''underlines the commitment of the woman novelist to an Africanist project of collective self-discovery'' (59).

As the single book-length study of Aidoo's writings, Vincent Odamtten's *The Art of Ama Ata Aidoo* (1994) presents a ''polylectic'' reading of Aidoo's entire work—a ''self-interpellative'' reading that attempts to ''account for as many of the complexities of the specific (con)text of the literary/cultural product as possible'' (5). Odamtten tries to encompass the various critical voices (feminist, formalist, and so on) and even to challenge their ''reductive'' emphasis on one angle of Aidoo's work over another. His ''recuperative feminist reading'' considers literary form, feminist concerns, and specific historical contents of Aidoo's writing.

Aidoo herself believes in the importance of the literary critics to create through their attention ''female Achebes,'' to make female writers known and canonized. The increasing amount of criticism written on Aidoo's work gives me hope that Aidoo is right when she states about women writers: ''Sooner or later, somebody will have to notice that we've been around.''

BIBLIOGRAPHY

Works by Ama Ata Aidoo

The Dilemma of a Ghost. Accra: Longmans, 1965.
Anowa. London: Longman Group, 1970.
No Sweetness Here. London: Longman Group, 1970.
Our Sister Killjoy. 1977. Hong Kong: Longman African Classics, 1988.
Someone Talking to Sometime. Harare: College Press, 1985.
The Eagle and the Chickens and Other Stories. Enugu: Tana, 1986.
Birds and Other Poems. Harare: College Press, 1987.
Changes. London: Women's Press, 1991.

Selected Studies of Ama Ata Aidoo

Adelugba, Dapo. "Language and Drama: Ama Ata Aidoo." *African Literature Today* 8 (1976): 72–84.

Amankulor, J. "Ama Ata Aidoo: *The Dilemma of a Ghost.*" *Okike Educational Supplement* 3 (1982): 137–150.

Berrian, Brenda. "African Women as Seen in the Works of Flora Nwapa and Ama Ata Aidoo." *College Language Association Journal* 25.3 (March 1982): 331–339.

Booth, James. "Sexual Politics in the Fiction of Ama Ata Aidoo." *Commonwealth Essays and Studies* 15.2 (Spring 1993): 80–96.

Brown, Lloyd. "Ama Ata Aidoo." *Women Writers in Black Africa*. Westport, Conn.: Greenwood Press, 1981. 84–121.

———. "Ama Ata Aidoo: The Art of the Short Story and Sexual Roles in Africa." *World Literature Written in English* 13 (November 1974): 172–183.

Bruner, Charlotte. "Child Africa as Depicted by Bessie Head and Ama Ata Aidoo." *Studies in the Humanities* 7.2 (1979): 5–12.

Chetin, Sara. "Reading from a Distance: Ama Ata Aidoo's *Our Sister Killjoy.*" *Black Women's Writing*. Ed. Gina Wisker. New York: St. Martin's Press, 1993. 146–159.

Coussy, Denise. "Is Life Sweet? The Short Stories of Ama Ata Aidoo." *Short Fiction in the New Literatures in English*. Ed. Jacqueline Bardolph. Nice: Faculté des Lettres et Sciences Humaines de Nice, 1989. 285–290.

Elder, Arlene. "Ama Ata Aidoo and the Oral Tradition: A Paradox of Form and Substance." *African Literature Today* 15 (1987): 109–119.

Hill-Lubin, Mildred. "The Relationship of African-Americans and Africans: A Recurring Theme in the Works of Ama Ata Aidoo." *Présence Africaine* 124 (1982): 190–201.

———. "The Storyteller and the Audience in the Works of Ama Ata Aidoo." *Neohelicon* 16.2 (1989): 221–245.

James, Adeola. "Ama Ata Aidoo." *In Their Own Voices*. Ed. Adeola James. London: Heinemann, 1990. 8–27.

Jones, Eldred. "Ama Ata Aidoo: *Anowa.*" *African Literature Today* 8 (1976): 142–144.

Korang, Kwaku-Larbi. "Ama Ata Aidoo's Voyage Out: Mapping the Coordinates of Modernity and African Selfhood in *Our Sister Killjoy.*" *Kunapipi* 14.3 (1992): 50–61.

Mackenzie, Clayton G. "The Discourse of Sweetness in Ama Ata Aidoo's *No Sweetness Here.*" *Studies in Short Fiction* 32.2 (Spring 1995): 161–170.

McGregor, Maxine Lautre. "Ama Ata Aidoo." *African Writers Talking*. Ed. Cosmo Pieterse and Dennis Duerden. New York: Africana, 1972. 19–27.

Needham, Anuradha Dingwaney. "An Interview with Ama Ata Aidoo." *Massachusetts Review* 36.1 (Spring 1995): 123–133.

Nwanko, Chimalum. "The Feminist Impulse and Social Realism in Ama Ata Aidoo's *No Sweetness Here* and *Our Sister Killjoy.*" *Ngambika: Studies of Women in African Literature*. Ed. Carole Boyce Davies and Anne Adams Graves. Trenton: Africa World Press. 1986. 151–159.

Odamtten, Vincent O. *The Art of Ama Ata Aidoo*. Gainesville: University Press of Florida, 1994.

Ogede, Ode. "The Defense of Culture in Ama Ata Aidoo's *No Sweetness Here*: The Use of Orality as a Textual Strategy." *International Fiction Review* 21 (1994): 76–84.

Owusu, Kofi. "Canons under Siege: Blackness, Femaleness, and Ama Ata Aidoo's *Our Sister Killjoy*." *Callaloo* 13 (Spring 1990): 341–363.

Ridden, Geoffrey. "Language and Social Status in Ama Ata Aidoo." *Style* 8 (Fall 1974): 452–461.

Rooney, Caroline. "Are We in the Company of Feminists? A Preface for Bessie Head and Ama Ata Aidoo." *Diverse Voices*. Ed. Harriet Devine Jump. New York: St. Martin's Press, 1991. 214–247.

Wilentz, Gay. "Ama Ata Aidoo's *The Dilemma of a Ghost*." *Binding Cultures: Black Women Writers in Africa and the Diaspora*. Bloomington: Indiana University Press, 1992. 38–57.

———. "The Politics of Exile: Ama Ata Aidoo's *Our Sister Killjoy*." *Studies in Twentieth Century Literature* 15.1 (Winter 1991): 159–173.

HILDEGARD HOELLER

ZAYNAB ALKALI (1950–   )

BIOGRAPHY

Zaynab Alkali was born in the Tura-Wazila community of Borno State, Nigeria. She was educated at Queen Elizabeth Secondary School in Ilorin, Nigeria, Ahmadu Bello University, Zaria, and Bayero University, Kano. She was the principal of Shekara Girls' Boarding School, Kano, an assistant lecturer at Bayero University, lecturer in English and African literature, University of Maiduguri and senior lecturer in English and coordinator of English and general studies, Modibbo Adama College, University of Maiduguri. She is currently engaged in research at Bayero University. In his forties Alkali's father converted to Christianity. In the early 1960s Alkali herself became a Muslim, yet she feels that both Christianity and Islam have influenced her. In 1971 she married Dr. Mohammed Nur Alkali, director-general of the Nigerian Institute of Political and Strategic Studies, Jos, Nigeria. They have six children.

MAJOR WORKS AND THEMES

Zaynab Alkali's first novel, *The Stillborn*, was published by Longman in its Drumbeat series in 1984. It won the Association of Nigerian Authors (ANA) prize for prose fiction in 1985. The novel is set in northern Nigeria and explores the challenges facing Li, a young Nigerian woman, as she tries to balance the claims of her family and her own need for economic and emotional independence. Li's father, Baba, is overbearing, abusing his traditional authority to completely control the lives of his children. Li's grandfather warns, ''Children shouldn't be caged . . . for if the cage got broken by accident or design, they would find the world too big to live in'' (25). This warning is prophetic; as the household breaks up, Li's brother runs away, and her sister Awa marries an alcoholic. Li herself marries Habu, who has dreams of leading a luxurious, European-style life in the city, but is unable to make enough money even to support himself and his wife. Alkali uses the theme of the classic division between the traditional country village and the modern city in her novel, but with a twist; when Li returns to her father's village for the last time, she sees that the village has been modernized and altered. The missionaries in the village have influenced the rhythms of village life throughout Li's childhood through the sound of their electric generator turning off and on and the glare of their electric lights at the hospital and in the missionary compound. Now the villagers themselves have zinc roofs, kerosene lamps, and gas generators: all segments of Nigerian society have been affected by Westernization.

The novel builds itself around Li's movements between the village and the city. Rather than following the classic linear movement from the traditional village to the modern city, Li's journey repeats and returns; at each return, she discovers a new mode of being for herself. At the end of the novel, she prepares to return to the city, but this is not simply a move toward the modern: Li's movement to the city is also a return to her husband. Thus Alkali disturbs and undoes the dichotomy of the village and traditional life versus the city and modernity. As Homi K. Bhabha emphasizes in his study *The Location of Culture* (New York: Routledge, 1994), migration creates a need ''to think beyond narratives of originary and initial subjectivities'' (1). Li's movement from daughter to wife to educated single parent to ''the man of the house'' to, prospectively, matriarch of her family shows the fluidity of identity; the integration of modern technology in the life of the village itself by the end of the novel also reflects the novel's undoing of traditional dichotomies.

Alkali incorporates dreams as part of the structure of the novel, influencing action and presaging events. This innovation gives the novel a superficial similarity to the ''magic realism'' of Latin American fiction, but more significantly is part of a trend among younger African writers to move away from the standards of Western realism to reflect the lived realities of African people. The dream images help the reader accept the outcome of events as peculiarly suited to the heroine. When Li dreams of her life as an old woman, dozing on the day of her great-granddaughter's wedding, it reveals Li's devotion to her family and presages her role as a matriarch, both of which make Li's self-sacrifice and her determination to make her marriage work more understandable. In *The Stillborn*, Li supports her family from her earnings and at the end of the novel returns to her husband, determined to rebuild their relationship. Thus Alkali emphasizes women's need for economic independence, but also the need for women to work with men to build a new society.

Dreams are also used as a structural device in her second novel, *The Virtuous Woman*, a novel for adolescents published in 1987. This novel is a shorter, morally pointed work, describing the perils of two young women returning to school by public transportation without an escort. Nana, careful and conservative, finds a serious young man, while Leila, more impulsive, is still mistaking affection for romance at the end of the novel. Alkali has also published three short stories in German, "Salzlose Asche" (Saltless Ash), "Das eigene Lieben" (The Survivor), and "Haus des Schreckens" (House of Horror), one of which, "Saltless Ash," has also been published in *The Heinemann Book of African Women Writers* (1993). Her third novel, *The Cobwebs*, is soon to be published. *The Cobwebs* reveals the maturing of the Nigerian woman and touches on "the evil of child-brides, the ill consequences of unemployment and child abuse" (Nwamuo interview, *West Africa*). As compared to her earlier work, *The Cobwebs* is broader and more mature; Alkali feels that it is her most important work to date.

Many African women writers disdain the term "feminist," which has come to be narrowly defined as a Western idea of strict gender equality, or even a synonym for an anti-male stance. Alkali also rejects the term, as she distrusts any labels or "isms." In her essay "Feminism, a Radical Theme in West African Literature," Alkali calls for the development of a new feminism that would emphasize improving the socioeconomic and political status of women. Feminism would not focus on gender equality alone, but would struggle against cultural traditions, class privileges, and "mental colonialism" (the residue of Western sexism) that have prevented women's progress. "Such a movement," Alkali claims, "should involve everybody." If the term "feminist" were redefined in this way, Alkali asserts that African women writers, including herself, would be proud to declare themselves feminists.

CRITICAL RECEPTION

Seiyefa Koroye's "The Ascetic Feminist Vision of Zaynab Alkali" is one of the few studies of Alkali's works. Focusing exclusively on *The Stillborn*, Koroye emphasizes the self-sacrifice Alkali demands of her heroine, calling Li "a model of the heroic and truly liberated woman." Alkali has been interviewed several times about her work; the most accessible interview is in Adeola James's *In Their Own Voices: African Women Writers Talk*. In this interview, she mentions possible influences on her work from Chinua Achebe, Ngugi wa Thiong'o, Catherine Cookson, and Ernest Hemingway. She also discusses the difficulties of writing in English about characters who are speaking another language. Further critical studies of her work are needed, particularly comparisons with other Nigerian writers and with other writers from Muslim West Africa. Recently, Marie Umeh described Zaynab Alkali as one of Flora Nwapa's "literary followers" (Umeh, 121) and also included her in a list of womanist writers, suggesting that her works will soon receive the critical attention they deserve.

In all of her work, Alkali offers a rare insight into life for Muslim women in northern Nigeria. Not content with simply showing how things are, Alkali also builds a vision of a better life based on economic independence, self-sacrifice, and solidarity between men and women.

BIBLIOGRAPHY

Works by Zaynab Alkali

The Stillborn. Harlow, Essex: Longman Drumbeat Series, 1984. Republished in Longman African Classics, 1988.

The Virtuous Woman. Ikeja: Longman, 1987.

"Salzlose Asche" (Saltless Ash), "Das eigene Leben" (The Survivor), and "Haus des Schreckens" (House of Horror). *Salzlose Asche: Kurzgeschichten aus Nigeria*. Ed. Lotta Suter. Zurich: Stechapfel Verlag, 1989. "Haus des Schreckens" is also included in *A Voyage Around: Literatur aus Kamerun, Nigeria, Simbabwe*. Berlin: Andenbuch: Arabische Buch, 1990.

"The Nightmare," "Saltless Ash," and "Feminism: A Radical Theme in West African Literature." *Touchstone* 15, *African Women Write*. Ed. Guida Jackson. Houston: Touchstone, 1990.

"Landlicher Markt in Nigeria." *NZZ-Folio* October 1992: 71–73.

"Saltless Ash." *The Heinemann Book of African Women's Writing*. Ed. Charlotte Bruner. Portsmouth, NH: Heinemann, 1993.

The Cobwebs. Unpublished manuscript.

Interviews

Ibeleme, Emmanuel. "Women Writers Bag Top Fiction Prizes." *New African* 222 (March 1986): 49. Also interviews Tess Onwueme, on winning ANA awards (ANA fiction award for 1985 for *The Stillborn*).

James, Adeola. "Zaynab Alkali." *In Their Own Voices: African Women Writers Talk*. Portsmouth, NH: Heinemann, 1990. 28–32.

Nwamuo, Chris. "Important . . . But Not the Same." *West Africa* 3700 (July 11, 1988): 1256.

Ofeimun, Odia. Interview. *Guardian* (Lagos, Nigeria) March 27, 1985:9.

Studies of Zaynab Alkali

Bürgi, Chidi. "Träume werde empfangen wie Kinder: Porträt der nigerianischen Schriftstellerin Zaynab Alkali." *WoZ* 35.28 (August 1992): 17–18.

Galle, Etienne. "The Probable Young African Hero." *Commonwealth Essays and Studies* 15.1 (Autumn 1992): 29–35.

Koroye, Seiyefa. "The Ascetic Feminist Vision of Zaynab Alkali." *Nigerian Female Writers: A Critical Perspective*. Ed. Henrietta Otokunefor and Obiageli Nwodo. Ikeja, Nigeria: Malthouse Press, 1989.

Umeh, Marie. "Finale: Signifyin' the Griottes: Flora Nwapa's Legacy of (Re)Vision and
    Voice." *Research in African Literatures* 26.2 (Summer 1995): 114–123.

Book Reviews

Obradovic, Nadezda. Review of *The Stillborn*. *World Literature Today* 64 (Spring 1990):
    354.
Review of *The Stillborn*. *Choice* 29 (September 1991): 46.
Review of *The Stillborn*. *Sunday New Nigerian* January 12, 1986: 2.

CHRISTINE LOFLIN

AYI KWEI ARMAH (1939–)

BIOGRAPHY

Ayi Kwei Armah was born in 1939 in Takoradi, then the only deep-sea harbor on the Gold Coast. He is descended on his father's side from a royal family in the Ga tribe inhabiting the environs of the present capital of Ghana. During the nineteenth century there arose a conflict within the royal family over succession to the royal stool as a result of which the ancestral family withdrew into exile to settle in Dahomey.

When the Takoradi harbor was built and the town became the hub of international trade on the Gold Coast, many people, including the father and relatives of Ayi Kwei Armah, moved there in search of a job. The father must have been prosperous, because he married into the Fante tribe inhabiting the western section of the country where Takoradi is located. Aspects of the family life are presented in the semibiographical *Fragments*.

Ayi Kwei Armah had his secondary education from 1953 to 1958 at the Prince of Wales's College, now better known as Achimota School, the most prestigious secondary school in Ghana, established by the colonial administration to provide education for the middle class. On account of his outstanding academic performance he was awarded a scholarship for further studies in the United States, where he studied between 1959 and 1963 and obtained a degree cum laude in social studies from Harvard. Later, between 1968 and 1969, he went to Columbia and obtained a graduate degree in fine arts, a feat that was unusual in those days and is rare in Africa today.

From his parentage, upbringing, and education, Ayi Kwei Armah was well marked for a comfortable situation in life as an establishment figure. However, his exposure as a teenager from Africa to the liberal culture of America and also to the radical politics of African Americans, culminating in the street and campus riots of the late 1960s, must have profoundly affected his temperament. The 1966 Ghanaian coup d'état that toppled Kwame Nkrumah from power must also have confirmed him in his views about the corruption of privilege and power. As is shown in *Fragments*, he therefore opted out of the privilege that would have been his into an austere way of life as a writer living by his pen.

Upon graduating from Harvard, he went to work as a translator in Algeria, then, thanks to the polemical writings of Frantz Fanon, one of the most progressive decolonized countries. He soon returned to Ghana, where from late 1964 until September 1967 he worked first at the then newly established Ghana Television as a scriptwriter under the authority of George Awoonor Williams, now known as Kofi Awoonor. After the 1966 coup d'état, he became a teacher at Navrongo Secondary School in the far north of the country, as if to go as far as he could away from the capital of the country.

He left Ghana in 1967 for France, where he worked briefly on the staff of *Jeune Afrique*. From there he returned to the United States, where between September 1968 and June 1970 he remained at Columbia as a student and later as a lecturer of fine arts. From August 1970 to June 1976 he taught at the Tanzanian College of National Education of Chang'ombe. He went south in 1976 to teach for the next two years in the Department of English of the National University of Lesotho. In the first half of 1979 he taught as a visiting professor in the Department of African Languages and Literature of the University of Wisconsin at Madison. Since then he has been living in Dakar, Senegal, where he has been working as a French and English translator, a job with which he started his working life.

It would appear from his sojourns that Ayi Kwei Armah has planned to live and work in the different cultural zones of Africa so as to become truly pan-African in his outlook. His experience in each significant cultural area is reflected in specific novels giving the perceptive reader a comprehensive account of his outlook on Africa since the colonial era.

MAJOR WORKS AND THEMES

Ayi Kwei Armah's first major work, *The Beautyful Ones Are Not Yet Born*, was published in 1968. Set in Armah's hometown of Takoradi, the novel deals with postcolonial life in Ghana under the supposedly egalitarian government of Kwame Nkrumah. By focusing on three characters in differing circumstances, the novel presents a cross-sectional description of life in Takoradi, Ghana's gateway then to the world.

The main character, an insignificant clerk working in the nation's railway office and finding it hard to make ends meet, is revealed in his social anonymity by the nondefining name of "the man" that he bears. He is the representative of the ordinary person that the nationalist government of the Convention Peoples' Party (the CPP) under Kwame Nkrumah had claimed to be helping. "The man's" predicament as a poorly paid worker living in the slums is both depressing and desperate because nobody sees his plight as a product of the nation's economic malaise. He is despised by his wife and close relatives as a lazy person and loathed by the more affluent as an informer of the government. In his abject situation, he symbolizes the wretchedness of the ordinary Ghanaian in the post-colonial era.

The second major character in the novel is also portrayed as an insignificant and anonymous social being through the nondefining name of "the Teacher" that he bears. As his name suggests, he is *the* educator and the mentor of the society, the type that in the Far and Near East countries is revered as a guru. The point of the novel is that in the Ghanaian society this guru is marginalized and ignored. The society shuns the ethic of reflection that he seeks to introduce and prefers the "fineries" of the West.

The last major character, Koomson, is the symbol of the desire for materialism. It is part of the message of hopelessness in the novel that it is rather this representative of the negative influences on society who has a significant status and is even, rather cynically on Ayi Kwei Armah's part, the party man of the CPP, the party of the ordinary person. It is no wonder that when the coup d'état occurs toward the end of the novel and the old political and economic guards are swept away, the impression persists that the saviors of the society "are not yet born."

Ayi Kwei Armah's next major work, *Fragments*, was published in 1970. It is set in Accra and deals with the homecoming of Onipa Baako, the main character, from his studies in the United States. In terms of subject and treatment, this second published novel rather predates *The Beautyful Ones Are Not Yet Born*. Indeed, it is much more conceivable that Ayi Kwei Armah would start his major works with the homecoming of his hero and then follow him in his actions and reactions in his country in subsequent works. It would seem that the two works were handed to the publishers at the same time with *Fragments* as the first novel and *The Beautyful Ones* as the sequel, but that the publishers, naturally interested in a hot sell, chose to publish the sequel first.

As in *The Beautyful Ones*, *Fragments* focuses on certain significant characters in presenting a picture of a postcolonialist African society: the main character, Onipa Baako, his foil Brempong, his grandmother Naana, his mother Edin, and his girlfriend Juana, the psychiatrist. Onipa Baako, like "the man," "negates the negative" drive for Western materialism, although unlike "the man" he has a higher social status. Brempong and Edin are like Koomson in the sense that they symbolize the drive for materialism. Naana and the Teacher are alike in that they represent the saner but despised voice in society. Juana, the Puerto Rican psychiatrist who works in one of the state hospitals and who treats Onipa Baako later in the novel when he breaks down and then befriends him, is to be seen as the doctor in the country madhouse. The author uses Juana's perspective for the greater part of the novel because it is she who, by her training and situation as a concerned foreigner, poses the question: what has caused this malaise?

Ayi Kwei Armah's third novel, *Why Are We So Blest?*, was published in 1972. Set in the progressive decolonized country of Algeria, it, like the previous novels, focuses on the perspectives of certain characters: Modin Dofu, a Ghanaian who had abandoned his studies at Harvard on principle, his white girlfriend Aimee, and Solo, the eventual keeper of his diary, which is the substance of the novel.

In this novel, Armah gives himself a larger canvas in which he surveys the predicament of the entire decolonized continent of Africa. Solo, the representative of "freedom fighters," has been sidelined by his own comrades and now keeps a menial office job. In that sense, he is like "the man" in having been betrayed by his country's politicians. Unlike "the man," he is intelligent enough to understand the larger national and international forces at work against him and his continent. As if to take up the question posed by Juana in *Fragments*, he has found the answer but feels impotent to arrest the situation. At least, he feels impotent to warn Modin.

Modin, also intelligent enough to appreciate what is wrong, fails to understand that he is gradually compromising his principles to be of service to his people by his continued association with Aimee, who throughout the novel is presented as a symbol of the all-enticing West. The point is later made crystal clear in *Two Thousand Seasons* in the image of the "Springwater" flowing generously to the desert, which in turn gives nothing but destruction.

Aimee, in her frigidity, is like the barren desert. As Modin increasingly tries to arouse her and teach her the need for a warm relationship, he is forced to forgo his own inclinations and do things her way, and that becomes the message of the novel. Modin's life and death, as Solo explains in his footnotes to the diary, become the symbol of the entire Africa's progression from independence, "so woefully assimilated" (56) to the West.

The first three novels were first published by American companies. As Ayi Kwei Armah consistently dealt with the theme of Africa's identity and predicament in his novels, it was to be expected that he, like his fellow writers Wole Soyinka and Ngugi wa Thiong'o, would turn his attention also to the question of publication.

In East Africa in the 1970s, there was a publishing company, East African Publishing House, devoted to the dissemination of local texts for the populations. Ayi Kwei Armah went to the company for his next novel, *Two Thousand Seasons*, which was published in 1973, obviously to show that Africa is the center of his reading public.

The novel takes an extensive and epic canvas for its setting, "two thousand seasons" of the development of the entire black continent. The reason is to answer the question posed by *Fragments*: what has caused the malaise? As the full meaning of *Why Are We So Blest?* is explained in this novel, so also is the title of *Fragments* clarified: "Pieces cut off from their whole are nothing but dead fragments" (1). Armah's contention is that Africa's present malaise is the symptom of a thousand-year exploitation by foreigners and their African accomplices addicted to the fineries of the foreigners. To break the vicious cycle, he proposes comradeship: "There is no beauty but in relationships" (206).

Armah's next novel, *The Healers*, also first published by the East African Publishing House in 1978 and set in the Asante Empire late in the nineteenth century, attempts to show how a nation can be lost through greed and selfishness and won through comradeship. The healers are some of the traditional medicine practitioners. They take very little reward or none for their healing because greed and selfishness are anathema to their calling. In contrast are the power seekers who destroy rather than heal life. Such are most of the traditional leaders and chiefs.

As in his previous novels, Ayi Kwei Armah uses certain characters as representative viewpoints in this novel. The main character, Densu, loathes violence and greed and aspires to become a traditional medicine man. His foil, Ababio, is so ambitious that he destroys life in order to win power. Significantly, upon the coming of colonialist rule, Ababio hoists himself up as an ally of the colonialists in order to consolidate his power. As Ababio explains to Densu, "Those who take care to place themselves on the right side of big changes, when the big changes have taken place, become big men" (29). Reminiscent of Yambo Ouologuem's *Bound to Violence*, Ayi Kwei Armah seems to be saying, through Ababio, that such are Africa's present traditional leaders and politicians. No wonder, then, that in the postcolonial era Africa has become the place of the "wretched of the earth."

Ayi Kwei Armah has been working on his latest novel, *Osiris Rising*, which, judging solely from the title, promises to deal with the renascence of Africa as a result of the "healing" administered by the beneficent "healers" following "two thousand seasons" of her dark ages. Ayi Kwei Armah is also a literary critic with a number of outstanding articles to his credit. Most of his critical essays have been on essentially the same concerns as his novels: the identity and predicament of Africa. His main concern is for the establishment of a pan-African agency that will rope in all the diverse cultures and languages of the African continent. He calls, for instance, for the adoption of Kiswahili as the continental language of Africa. He expects that the adoption of a continental language will lead to the establishment of a continental publishing house to correct the present intolerable situation: "There is not a single African publishing house capable of printing works, distributing them throughout the continent, exporting the surplus and bringing home the profits, to plough them back into the further development of African literature" ("The Festival Syndrome," 727). There is ample evidence, therefore, in Ayi Kwei Armah's creative works and critical writings that his primary subject is the situation of Africa at the present time.

CRITICAL RECEPTION

Ayi Kwei Armah's first published novel, *The Beautyful Ones Are Not Yet Born*, was rapturously received in Ghana, the writer's native land. Outside Ghana, it was also received with considerable interest as an indication of the sophistication of the African novel. The editor, Eldred Jones, of *African Literature Today*, an authoritative critical journal of African literature, concluded an informative and sympathetic review thus: "Armah has taken the predicament of Africa in general, and Ghana in particular, and distilled its despair and its hopelessness in a powerful, harsh, deliberately *unbeautyful* novel" (57). *Fragments* confirmed Ayi Kwei Armah's reputation as a major African writer. He has often since been regarded as belonging to the next generation of African writers after Chinua Achebe. Indeed, his first two novels have been consistently on the reading lists of all departments of English in Ghana's universities and on the list of most departments of literature in Africa.

Although his reputation rests mainly on his first two novels, his later works have also been remarkably well received. Their style is much more oral, suggesting the presence of a traditional tale-teller. The critic Robert Fraser has sought to provide the following explanation for the more direct obtrusion of traditional techniques in those novels: "Armah has evidently become increasingly concerned with the democratic basis of his art. There has been a marked effort to reach out beyond the confines of the literati . . . to recapture some of the wider ancestral appeal of the oral artist" (*Novels of Ayi Kwei Armah*, x).

Ayi Kwei Armah's novels have a certain air of totality about them that would lead one to speculate that the writer imitates the French novel. However, Armah seems to warn such a possible speculator in his novels and essays that his style is all completely African. As presented in *The Healers*, his is the "tongue of the story-teller, descendant of the masters in the art of eloquence" (2).

BIBLIOGRAPHY

Works by Ayi Kwei Armah

Major Novels

The Beautyful Ones Are Not Yet Born. Boston: Houghton Mifflin, 1968; London: Heinemann Educational Books, 1969. Translated into Swahili as *Wema Hawajazaliwa*. Nairobi: Heinemann East Africa, 1976.

Fragments. Boston: Houghton Mifflin, 1970; London: Heinemann Educational Books, 1974; Nairobi: East African Publishing House, 1974.

Why Are We So Blest? New York: Doubleday, 1972; London: Heinemann Educational Books, 1974; Nairobi: East African Publishing House, 1974. The page reference in the text is to the Heinemann edition.

Two Thousand Seasons. Nairobi: East African Publishing House, 1973; London: Heinemann Educational Books, 1979. Page references are to the Heinemann edition.

The Healers. Nairobi: East African Publishing House, 1978; London: Heinemann Educational Books, 1979. Page references are to the Heinemann edition.

Major Articles

"African Socialism: Utopian or Scientific." *Présence Africaine* 64 (1967): 6–30.
"The Caliban Complex." *West Africa* March 18 and 25, 1985: 321–322; 570–571.
"The Festival Syndrome." *West Africa* April 15, 1985: 726–727.
"Dakar Hieroglyphics." *West Africa* May 19, 1986: 1043–1044.

Selected Studies of Ayi Kwei Armah

Achebe, Chinua. *Morning Yet on Creation Day*. London: Heinemann Educational Books, 1975; Garden City, N.Y.: Anchor Books, 1976.
Dseagu, Samuel. "The Nature of Oral Influence on the African Novel." Diss. University of Wisconsin–Madison, 1987.
Folarin, Margaret. "An Additional Comment on Ayi Kwei Armah's *The Beautyful Ones Are Not Yet Born*." *African Literature Today* 5 (1971): 116–128.
Fraser, Robert. "The American Background in *Why Are We So Blest?*" *African Literature Today* 9 (1978): 39–46.
———. *The Novels of Ayi Kwei Armah: A Study in Polemical Fiction*. London: Heinemann Educational Books, 1980.
Jones, Eldred Durosimi. "Review: *The Beautyful Ones Are Not Yet Born*." *African Literature Today* 3 (1969): 55–57.
McEwan, Neil. *Africa and the Novel*. London: Macmillan, 1983.
Ogungbesan, Kolawole. "Symbol and Meaning in *The Beautyful Ones Are Not Yet Born*." *African Literature Today* 7 (1975): 93–110.
Sackey, Edward. "The Relevance of Oral Traditions in the Novels of Ayi Kwei Armah." M. Phil. diss. University of Ghana, Legon, 1990.

SAMUEL A. DSEAGU

KOFI AWOONOR (1935–   )

BIOGRAPHY

Kofi Nyidevu Awoonor was born on March 13, 1935, in the small farming village of Wheta in the Volta region of Ghana. His maternal grandfather, Chief Nyidevu Besa, was a noted elder of the Asiyo division of the Ewe and a successful farmer. His father was a tailor by trade. Kofi Awoonor's primary-school education was at the Catholic Mission at Dzodze, which he attended from 1939 to 1943, and then at Bremen School at Keta, a school founded by Presbyterians on land given to them by Awoonor's great-grandfather in 1847. This early missionary education proved to be a significant factor in his work, which reflects, on many levels, the struggle to free himself from the values and attitudes acquired during his colonialist education. In his first volume of poetry, he was to make explicit reference to the necessity of abandoning the Christianity taught to him at the mission schools to embrace his traditional religion.

After attending the Achimota School in Accra, Kofi Awoonor received advanced degrees from the University of Ghana at Legon, the University of London, and the State University of New York, Stony Brook, where he earned the Ph.D. in comparative literature. From 1960 to 1965, Awoonor served as a faculty member at the University of Ghana at Legon, first in the Department of English and subsequently at the Institute for African Studies. While at the university, Awoonor was a participant in the International Socialist Solidarity of Kwame Nkrumah and helped to found the party study group at Legon. As part of the solidarity, he traveled to Russia in 1961, China in 1963, and Cuba in 1965. From 1965 to 1967, he served as director of the Ghana Film Institute and was closely associated with the Ghanaian literary magazine *Okyeame*, which published his poetry along with works by his compatriots Efua Sutherland, Ayi

Kwei Armah, and Ama Ata Aidoo. After the fall of the Nkrumah regime in February 1966, Awoonor left Ghana and on October 8, 1968, while at the University of London, changed his name from George Awoonor Williams to Kofi Awoonor. Awoonor spent eight years in exile, and more than half of those years were spent in the United States, in New York, California, and Texas. At the University of Texas, he held a visiting professorship, and at the State University of New York at Stony Brook, he chaired the Department of Comparative Literature. Upon his return to Ghana in 1975, Awoonor taught for a while at the Cape Coast campus of the university but was arrested in November of the same year and accused of collusion to subvert the Acheampong regime. The specific charge was harboring a fugitive from justice. He spent one year at the Ussher Fort Prison and, like South Africa's Dennis Brutus, Nigeria's Wole Soyinka, Kenya's Ngugi wa Thiong'o, and several other African intellectuals and artists, joined the ranks of "prison graduates." The year at Ussher Fort, however, yielded a collection of prison verse, *The House by the Sea* (1978). After a brief court appearance in October 1976, Kofi Awoonor was sentenced to another year in prison but was released mysteriously a few days later. During the 1980s, Kofi Awoonor rendered diplomatic service to Ghana, first as ambassador to Brazil and subsequently as permanent representative of Ghana to the United Nations, a position he held until 1994, when he returned to Ghana. He is currently residing in Ghana at Legon.

MAJOR WORKS AND THEMES

Kofi Awoonor's work, which includes poetry, fiction, and social and political history, is informed by his experience of colonialist cultural dominance, by his participation in the early success of independent Ghana, and by his experience of migration, exile, and return. In his poetry Awoonor re-presents and interrogates the African past as well as affirms new, developing African identities and sensibilities. In his fiction, however, he subjects to critique the African national bourgeoisie and its role in creating what he perceives to be a bankrupt postindependent Ghanaian society. In all his work, Awoonor renders consistently a forceful critique of and resistance to the colonizing and neocolonizing strategies of domination over Africa's economic and cultural production.

The publication of *Rediscovery and Other Poems* (1964) brought international attention to Awoonor's poetic talent and craft. The poems in this collection, referencing the rediscovery of cultural identity, speak specifically to the recovery of spiritual traditions and to the abandoning of Christianity, the "senseless cathedral of doom," to return to the energy, vitality, and power of the ancestral gods. The themes in this and in Awoonor's other early verse collections are also related to his conception of the role of the artist in society and to his close connection to Anlo-Ewe oral tradition.

As a young child, Awoonor attended funerary ceremonies and was exposed to the Ewe dirge, a traditional verse form of loss and lament. Later, as the more mature, self-conscious poet, he worked closely with the well-known dirge singer Akpulu. From his collaboration with Akpulu, Awoonor published *Guardians of the Sacred Word* (1974), a prolonged meditation on the role of the traditional poet, his skills, and his position in traditional society. From the dirge, Awoonor's poetry frequently incorporates themes of death, grief, and loss. At the same time, there are themes of regeneration, continuity, and survival, all of which are anchored, according to Awoonor, in the "faith, belief, and certainty that life is a cyclical process" ("Afterword," *Until the Morning After*, 216). Just as there are the grief and lament for the loss of traditional culture, seen as the wellspring of creative and spiritual power, there is hope for regeneration and continuity in the cultural work of the poet, the scholar, and ordinary people. The valorization of the traditional, first symbolized by the abandoning of his Christian name, George Awoonor Williams, speaks to the centrality of identity and the reclaiming of a knowledge of self. For Kofi Awoonor, cultural rediscovery is a gradual and ritualistic process. It is also that which marks him as a "traditionalist," that is, one who incorporates the materials and conventions from oral literature in his works. Unlike the first wave of "modern" African poets, primarily the Francophone poets of Negritude, whose verse demonstrated elaborate gestures of cultural affirmation, or the second-wave "Euromodernists" who debunked the attitudes of their predecessors, the traditionalists used verse forms to represent and explore the personal and political dimensions of their history and cultural legacy.

Sometimes labeled "nativist," traditionalist poets and writers promote the idea of an authentic ethnic identity that resides in traditional cultural forms and that, once "rediscovered," functions to heal the wounds inflicted by colonial subjugation and cultural displacement. The conscious reclamation of indigenous traditions and forms is also a means to reconnect with the masses and to challenge the political and social hegemony of the African national bourgeoisie. For Awoonor, this traditionalist aesthetic is manifested not only in the representation of oral forms, but in the clear, precise poetic diction and the use of verse as public utterance, as "message" to a communal audience.

Themes of disillusionment and decay and of loss and yearning inform Awoonor's fiction. In his first novel, *This Earth, My Brother* (1971), published the same year as his second verse collection, *Night of My Blood*, Awoonor gives metaphoric representation to the condition of modern Ghanaian society by means of thematic definitions of corruption and defilement. Experimental in form, impressionistic and expressionistic in technique, *This Earth, My Brother* is a complex rendering of the moral and spiritual degradation of the postcolonial African bourgeoisie. The text alternates between prose and poetic forms, using the first to describe the daily experiences and external reality of the protagonist and the other to represent his mythopoetic, spiritual consciousness. The movement between internal and external realities is paralleled by movements in time and space. Spatially the text moves back and forth between urban and village locales, between neighborhoods in the capital city and outlying districts in the eastern region of the country. Haunted by the memory of his dead female cousin, who is linked to images of a mythic water deity and who symbolizes the modern nation-state of Ghana (Innes, "Mothers or Sisters?" 132), the protagonist also moves back and forth in time, between recollections of a childhood past and the experiences of a vapid present. Amamu, a European-educated, "Been-to" lawyer, is so spiritually bankrupt and so alienated by the corrupt society he inhabits that he attempts to connect himself to the mythic, mammy water deity and suffers mental breakdown and death. Amamu's loss of identity and self is a metaphoric representation for the greater national malaise, disillusionment, and loss.

In *Comes the Voyager at Last* (1992), Awoonor moves from earlier themes of alienation and corruption to themes of betrayal, longing, and return within a transnational and transcultural context. The novel defines themes of forced migration and enslavement, displacement and confinement, reconciliation and return. Traversing geographical space and crossing national and cultural boundaries, the protagonist, Marcus Garvey MacAndrews, recoups an unsullied traditional past and is reconciled to an originary, indigenous homeland. From his birthplace in Virginia, he moves to New York, where he is betrayed and unjustly imprisoned. Disillusioned and bitter, he journeys to Africa and is able, through violence and murder, to move beyond the experience of racism and oppression to reconciliation.

As in *This Earth, My Brother*, Awoonor juxtaposes prose with poetic forms and moves back and forth in space and time. In this novel, however, the movement from rural and village locales to the city, from the diaspora back to the continent, imitates and parallels the various dimensions of identity. On one hand, identity, as racial or ethnic subjectivity produced through individual and collective experience, is constructed as a multiple and shifting phenomenon. On the other, identity is delineated as a unitary, "true" cultural self that, once rediscovered and reclaimed, restores what has been lost, stolen, and denied through economic, and cultural dominance. What distinguishes this novel from *This Earth, My Brother*, however, is that thematic definitions of loss and recuperation and of longing and return are situated within a transnational and transcultural context. In doing so, *Comes the Voyager at Last* makes possible a new kind of engagement and exchange between African people on the continent and those in the diaspora.

The Breast of the Earth: A Survey of the History, Culture, and Literatures of Africa South of the Sahara (1975), *Ghana: A Political History* (1991), and *Africa: The Marginalized Continent* (1994) are works in political and social history in which Kofi Awoonor addresses the effects of imperialism and colonialism on African politics, economy, and cultural production. In *Ghana: A Political History*, Awoonor first explains that he proceeds from the assumption that "no national effort to forge ahead can succeed without close reference to the national culture and history" (xii), and that the purpose of the book is to revise those external versions of history that have sought to "straight-jacket the

African predicament into well-wrought and neat ideological frames'' (x–xi). He then goes on to denounce the importation of Western democratic institutions to Africa, arguing that pre-European societies on the Gold Coast had viable political and social institutions that integrated all facets of life. Delineating the systematic destruction of these institutions under the British colonial order from 1844 to 1957, Awoonor recounts Ghanaian political history since independence, discloses the complicity of the African national bourgeoisie with the neocolonial strategies of Europe, and finally calls for an ''Alternative African Society,'' constructed on a new political, economic, and moral base (271).

In *Africa: The Marginalized Continent* (1994), the collection of essays and speeches made while Awoonor was Ghana's permanent representative to the United Nations, the focus is Africa's position in the post-Communist, post–Cold War era. Recognizing the far-ranging implications of the collapse of the Soviet Union for the developing nations of the South, Awoonor focuses on the issues of humanitarian relief and intervention, on the emergence of a unipolar world, and on global security and global apartheid. All of these, he contends, are crucial to the argument of whether democracy is a ''feasible proposition within any nation that is plagued by deprivation and grinding poverty'' (xiii). Asserting that ''Africa's crisis is the world's crisis,'' Awoonor sees this very crisis as a ''fundamental challenge to the moral basis of our common humanity'' (xv).

CRITICAL RECEPTION

The critical writing on Kofi Awoonor's work focuses primarily on his verse. He is regarded as preeminent among Anglophone African poets and is recognized for his skillful and imaginative use of language. At the same time, because his work links the ethical, the political, and the aesthetic, Robert Fraser in his study of West African poetry asserts that Awoonor is ''poet and propagandist,'' characterizing his poetry as verse in which ''personal self-expression and social criticism proceed hand-in-hand'' (161). Ken Goodwin in his study of ten African poets labels Awoonor a ''syncretist'' and delineates three stages in Awoonor's movement toward cultural synthesis. The first is the stage of rediscovery of tradition, with a heavy reliance on Ewe oral poetry; the second is the stage in which Awoonor juxtaposes, in a single poem, African and European traditions; the third is the stage of synthesis in which material from each culture reinforces rather than opposes the other (94–95). John Haynes devotes part of his study to Awoonor's poetry and its relationship to Ewe oral poems and songs, the dirge in particular. According to Haynes, while Kofi Awoonor, Okot p'Bitek, and Gabriel Okara situate traditional oral poetry as the basis for their art, these poets are also concerned with English as a translation language and with the question of ''Africanness'' in relation to it (40).

As one of the few studies to offer critical analyses of Awoonor's poetry and fiction, Richard Priebe's *Myth, Realism, and the West African Writer* deserves special mention. With a full chapter devoted to *This Earth, My Brother*, Priebe looks at the novel in terms of its structural and thematic similarities to the dirge. More important, he interprets the death of the protagonist, Amamu, as suicide and sacrifice, as a negation of the current social order, and as "symbolic of the recurrent transformations necessary to the health of any society" (70). In his analysis of Awoonor's poetry, Priebe offers a reading that links Awoonor, despite ideological and formal differences, to Wole Soyinka. The basis for the similarity, he argues, is liminality and the priestlike role of the personae in both Soyinka's and Awoonor's verse. Priebe likewise contends that there is a similar conception of the role of the poet as prophet, of the poet being the "priestlike" man who leaves his society only to return with the power to revitalize it (99). In much the same manner, Robert Fraser suggests that Awoonor claims the role and authority of the *heno*, the traditional custodian or guardian of the Ewe covenant with the ancestor. In reclaiming the tradition of the *heno* and asserting his prerogatives, Kofi Awoonor, Fraser maintains, becomes the medium by which "poetry becomes a means of continuity . . . and a channel of grace" (166).

BIBLIOGRAPHY

Works by Kofi Awoonor

Rediscovery and Other Poems. Ibadan, Nigeria: Mbari, 1964.
Night of My Blood. Garden City, N.Y.: Doubleday, 1971.
This Earth, My Brother. Garden City, N.Y.: Doubleday, 1971; London: Heinemann, 1972.
Ride Me, Memory. New York: Greenfield Center, 1973.
Guardians of the Sacred Word: Ewe Poetry. New York: Nok, 1974.
The Breast of the Earth: A Survey of the History, Culture, and Literatures of Africa South of the Sahara. Garden City, N.Y.: Anchor Doubleday, 1975.
The House by the Sea. New York: Greenfield Center, 1978.
Until the Morning After. Saline, Mich.: McNaughton and Gunn, 1987.
Ghana: A Political History from Pre-European to Modern Times. Accra: Woeli, 1990.
Comes the Voyager at Last. Trenton, N.J.: Africa World Press, 1992.
The Latin American and Caribbean Notebook. Trenton, N.J.: Africa World Press, 1992.
Africa: The Marginalized Continent. Accra: Woeli, 1994.

Selected Studies of Kofi Awoonor

Elimimian, Isaac. "Kofi Awoonor." *Theme and Style in African Poetry.* Lewiston, N.Y.: Edwin Mellen Press, 1991.
Fraser, Robert. *West African Poetry: A Critical History.* London: Cambridge University Press, 1986.
Goodwin, Ken. "Kofi Awoonor." *Understanding African Poetry: A Study of Ten Poets.* London: Heinemann, 1982.
Haynes, John. "Song and Copy: The Relation between Oral and Printed in Kofi Awoonor's

'Dirge.' '' *African Poetry and the English Language*. London: Macmillan, 1987.

Innes, C. L. ''Mothers or Sisters? Identity, Discourse, and Audience in the Writing of Ama Ata Aidoo and Mariama Bâ.'' *Motherlands: Black Women's Writing from Africa, the Caribbean, and South Asia*. Ed. Susheila Nasta. New Brunswick: Rutgers University Press, 1992, 129–151.

Kolawole, Mary. ''Kofi Awoonor as a Prophet of Conscience.'' *African Languages and Cultures* 5.2 (1992): 125–132.

Priebe, Richard. *Myth, Realism, and the West African Writer*. Trenton, N.J.: Africa World Press, 1988.

ALMA JEAN BILLINGSLEA-BROWN

MARIAMA BÂ (1929–1981)

BIOGRAPHY

Mariama Bâ was born in Senegal in 1929. She was orphaned at an early age and was raised by her maternal grandparents. The only way she knew her mother was through a photograph. Her father was one of the first ministers of state in the newly independent Senegal. The fact that she went to school did not dispense her from performing traditional tasks at home, especially since one did not know what the future might bring. As a young high-school student at the École Normale in Rufisque, she wrote her first published work. This piece was published in France and focused on colonial education in Senegal. After she completed her schooling, she worked as an elementary-school teacher and later as regional school inspector. She did not publish another major work until *So Long a Letter*, a book that won the Noma Award for Literature. This was followed by *Scarlet Song*, which was published posthumously. Her friends attribute the long hiatus in her literary production to marriage and motherhood. The fact that she was not writing did not mean that she was inert, as she was active in the women's movement in Senegal, promoting education and raising nine children.

As a writer, Bâ emerged from the oral tradition of the Senegalese griot women and wrote a "speakerly text." This tradition of orality in Senegal has been the major outlet for women's voices. The griot women—not controlled by society in ways other women are regarding speech—are given a license by society to say whatever they want without censorship. The tradition of the griot women is important to the Senegalese women, because it has always been one way of making themselves heard and listened to. So, for the Senegalese women, writing a speakerly text takes on added dimensions.

MAJOR WORKS AND THEMES

The problem of a female writer coming to voice has been a central theme in Mariama Bâ's fiction. This entry explicates Bâ's worldview as a writer. This worldview is located within the Wolof worldview. I will show that Bâ makes use of this worldview, and that an examination of issues of caste, friendship, fate, and women's relations is important to any developed reading of her texts. I will therefore locate Mariama Bâ's fiction in the oral tradition of the Senegalese griot women in particular, and Senegalese literature in general.

Mariama Bâ, I argue, writes in "Wolof" with the inflections of the spoken language. Bâ's expressions and structures do not change in the transition from speech to writing, as she gets Ramatoulaye to write herself not only into existence, but into a growth of self-consciousness. The autobiographical voice in the letter means coming out of muteness and speaking. This is important to the African who has been spoken for all her life. In gaining a voice, Ramatoulaye is a mature and articulate speaker; she addresses herself to her best friend Aissatou. Her voice is different from Celie's, yet both embark on a journey of discovery and soul searching at the beginning of their narratives and seem to have come to their own by the end of these narratives. Ramatoulaye tells Aissatou, "I felt that I had emerged" (*So Long a Letter*, 88). Ramatoulaye reflects on her past to understand the present.

Ramatoulaye is the narrator and writer of her letters, which makes her both narrator and protagonist. Therefore, in the tradition of the speakerly text, what we hear is Ramatoulaye's interpretation of what the other characters are saying in free and indirect discourse, although at times she uses quotation marks, showing that she is quoting a character's exact words. This is important to the African woman, because as she starts to tell her own story, she does not want to tell her sister's story for her and misrepresent it. So she creates some space, allowing her sisters to tell their own stories.

Ramatoulaye is educated and, therefore, assumed to be liberated automatically, but this is possible only up to a certain point, because Ramatoulaye lives in a society that relegates women to a certain position prescribed by society, a position that makes women important only as long as they are identified with men. Of course it has to be stressed here that this is a postcolonial position she has been assigned to by a conflicting tradition and Islam. There is also the Wolof view of fatalism that says that everyone's destiny is a fixed reality, impossible to avoid. As a result, Modou Fall sees his marrying a second wife as something destined by God. Ramatoulaye sees it as something she should accept, caught between the established order and a present given by Western education. Ramatoulaye is in a dilemma, a dilemma that her friend Aissatou did not seem to have when she chose divorce as an alternative. Mariama Bâ seems to be answering a call to speak out, but with more contradictions and opposition than the Western female writer has. Femi Ojo-Ade, whose position on feminism and women writers needs to be challenged, depicts the struggle of the female African writer as one that is located within tradition, colonialism, and modernization. Mariama Bâ as a writer is caught between tradition and the move toward modernity. This is inescapable. The contradiction in polygamy today is that the men have accepted the Western economic system and many of its social mores, but they refuse to give up the tradition of polygamy, a tradition that seems to have hardly any place in modern Africa.

The Wolof

The Wolof people, geographically, are located in the Senegambia region on the Atlantic coast of Africa. As the majority ethnic group in the region, Fatoumatta-Agnes Diarra asserts, "they have a tendency to believe themselves more fundamentally Senegalese than others." The Wolof have had sustained contacts with foreign cultures for centuries. These contacts have left an indelible mark on the lives of the people. As a result of these contacts and the fact that they mostly inhabit the urban area, the Wolof think highly of themselves in terms of being able to adapt and change foreign cultures. However, one foreign culture that has nearly overpowered Wolof society is the culture that came with Islam. Islam, therefore, becomes an important force that informs the Wolof worldview.

What is this worldview? The Wolof, as with other cultures in the world, have a way of looking at themselves and their relationship to the larger world. The Wolof have a sense of superiority over other ethnic groups and are ownership oriented, as their language illustrates. The French and other ethnic groups around them have described them as "arrogant," "haughty," and "think too highly of themselves." These comments are based on the posture the Wolof take regarding their unique culture.

As a society based on caste and family names, its biggest problem in modern times has been its inability to mediate between tradition and modernity. The caste system, as archaic as it seems, thrives today as much as it did in yesteryear. The reluctance of the upper caste to give up caste privilege is at the center of this perpetuation.

Caste, coupled with the discourse of fatalism coming through from both Islam and traditional practices, helps the perpetuation of the status quo. From Islam, only that which suits the society is highlighted and incorporated into their ways of life. Islam, it is evident, has no caste system, but from the Wolof worldview there can be no society without caste. Speaking of this stratification in the Wolof society, Abdoulaye Bara Diop explains that the caste system "continues to order groups, to determine their status, their functions and their comportment in reference to a social order—of old repute" (my translation, 28).

This kind of ordering and othering is based upon the society's view of inferiority and superiority. Though this caste system is not gender based, there is a problem regarding the way the different genders are viewed. Women, on the whole, are generally viewed as an important part of society and respected. Despite this respect, there are beliefs in the society that revolve around the evil and conniving nature of women, with sayings like "Djiguene sopal wai bul wolu ("You can love a woman but do not trust her"). I explain this kind of definition of woman as a male understanding of the disruption of patriarchy. Within this scheme of things is a concept and definition of the quintessential woman. This woman is the epitome of Wolof womanhood and exemplifies the concept of "gatt lamagne, gatt tank ("Short of tongue, short of feet")." This type of woman is the best *jabar* (wife) to have. The construction of women as cheats, liars, or saints feeds into a stereotyping of women in these categories. As oppressed people, women take these definitions and turn them around on other women. This interesting contradictory nature of relationships between women becomes a recurrent theme in Senegalese fiction, of course presented differently from different experiences.

Ousmane Sembène, probably more than any male writer in Senegalese fiction, contributes a balanced perspective in the discourse on women. He credits these positive portrayals to his experience, for what he saw growing up were powerful, resourceful women. The female writers in this tradition bring a whole new way of viewing women and their concerns. Therefore, constructions of the new knowledge of women arriving out of the particularity of female experiences finally joined the landscape of Senegalese literature, which was male dominated (at least in the written aspect of the literature). Perhaps no one is as poignant as Mariama Bâ in presenting the view of the women and the tensions inherent in such a presentation.

Claims of universality can be made about Mariama Bâ's work. Mariama Bâ herself, in her intellectual endeavors, has a sense of this universality, but at the same time she understands the particularity of the Senegalese (mainly Wolof) experience that she is writing about. She explains, "There is a cry everywhere, everywhere in the world, a woman's cry is being uttered. *The cry may be different*, but there is still a certain unity" (emphasis mine, Chamis, 1980). Without her particularly being situated in an Islamic Wolof society and having a Islamic/Wolof worldview, she could not have written these specific texts of hers in the context that she does.

Situating Bâ in this Wolof worldview requires defining her positionality and the different locations she inhabits. Even though Bâ locates herself as "an average Senegalese woman," the spot she inhabits is anything but average. She is a daughter born into high caste in a society where caste impacts on one's life. Caste determines one's status in life in the sense of expectations. Caste, like color, is not something to be worn or discarded depending on one's whim. Bâ's status as a *guer* (a non-casted person) distinguishes her and places her in a position that is different from that of other women who belong to the lower castes. By virtue of the circumstances of her birth, some kind of "superiority" is assumed. The fact that she is Western educated complicates matters further and puts her into a whole new category. Even though Western education does not keep one away from the daily duties of a woman, there is always the option of choices that are otherwise unavailable. Throughout *Une si longue lettre/So Long a Letter*, as Irene D'Almeida points out, the discourse of choice becomes central in the text.

Ramatoulaye and Aissatou always have the privilege of choice, as opposed to the non-Western-educated women in *Un chant écarlate/Scarlet Song* like Coumba, Ouleymatou, and Yaye Khady, who seem to have little or no choice in the kind of lives they live, or even Binetou, whose economic circumstances limit her choices. In reading Bâ, one then has to interrogate the interlocking systems of oppression of women in Dakar, Senegal. Caste, education, and class become important in this kind of discourse. The knowledge of how these three systems interact is automatically assumed by Bâ as she discusses these systems of oppression while not always naming them. Her positionings as female, Muslim, *guer*, Western educated, orphaned, mother, and a divorcée inform her experiences and the different tensions inherent in these multiple positionings.

How does Bâ's politics of location inform her intellectual project? Bâ's theoretical and practical concerns lie in the subjectivity of the Senegalese woman under multiple layers of oppression, under the guise of tradition—tradition here denoting something static. Senegalese society in general and the city of Dakar in particular are by no means inert. The city of Dakar, economically, structurally, and culturally, is continually changing, so to claim a static culture and tradition is problematic. Mariama Bâ herself believed that the mission of the writer in Senegalese society was to write against "the archaic practices, traditions and customs that are not a real part of our precious heritage" (Preface to *So Long a Letter*).

These are issues Bâ raises in trying to understand the logic behind the often contradictory worldview of her society. Bâ's canvas covers the different women in her society and their locations. As a female writer, Bâ is interested in a world where women will have choices and where monogamy is the order of the day. This world can only become a reality when women reexamine their relationships with each other and with their men. The *goros* (in-laws), the *xarits* (friends), and the *wugg* (wife), are all taken into account in this struggle.

In Bâ's fictional world, then, the most important and successful aspect of her literary presentation is, perhaps, her use of language (especially Wolof concepts). Bâ's texts, though written in French, show evidence that her use of language is situated in the tradition of the *tagg* of the griot women. This poetic act of extolling virtues takes the Wolof language to its highest forms. When one reads Mariama Bâ's texts, in essence, what one hears is this highly specialized poetics. The style in which both her letters and prose are written is informed by this style of *tagg*. At the same time, within the *tagg*, she uses the *xas* style, a style that shows contempt for the person receiving the *xas*. The Wolof language and Wolof concepts, therefore, become central in locating Mariama Bâ's work.

Tagg

In the beginning of both her texts, a *Scarlet Song* and *So Long a Letter*, Bâ starts by extolling the virtues of her characters. In *So Long a Letter*, Ramatoulaye starts her intimate letter/diary by extolling and invoking her lifelong friendship (*xaritya*) with Aissatou. This calling on Aissatou by Ramatoulaye, reaching into the past to show how important their friendship has been and continues to be, is important for this *tagg*. This *tagg* is not much different from the one Bâ dedicates to her Uncle in *Scarlet Song*. The dedication of the book to her uncle takes the form of a *tagg* poem. These two *taggs* set the tone for the two novels. Without this kind of grounding in the tradition of the griot, Mariama Bâ's texts would have felt and read differently.

The *tagg*, in the first instance, is used to call on and strengthen a *xaritya* that has gone through different changes and experiences. Even though the letter form is utilized in the *tagg*, it is because Aissatou is located across the Atlantic Ocean. The letter becomes the only link between Ramatoulaye and Aissatou as they inhabit two geographical spaces mediated by a body of water. This letter, it should be noted, is not written to anyone else but Aissatou. This is important, especially in looking at the way Ramatoulaye begins the letter with the *tagg*, because Aissatou is the "xariti ben bakan" (long-time friend).

Aissatou shares in Ramatoulaye's tears and joys. In the serious matter of announcing her husband's death, Ramatoulaye calls on Aissatou three times to call her attention to the seriousness of the matter she is about to discuss. She has to remind Aissatou of the fact that memories are "the salt of remembrance" (1), and the memories they share go back a long way.

Unlike the *tagg* poem for Aissatou with its intricacies, the *tagg* poem to her uncle, Ousmane Macoumba Diop, has a clear purpose. This man is evidently someone who has touched Mariama Bâ's life in ways she cannot even begin to describe. He is obviously an extremely religious man, as the poem shows with words like "prayers," "virtue," "piety," "solemn," and so on. It is no coincidence, then, that she presents us with a character like Djibril Gueye, who is the epitome of piety—the monogamist, the religious, the respecter of women, and the "level-headed" one. Djibril Gueye is the epitome of what men should aim to be like, according to Bâ. The praises that are sung about him in *Scarlet Song* show the respect and admiration his "creator" (Bâ) has for him. Through Ousmane, his son, the admiration for Djibril Gueye grows. But Oussou's admiration is reciprocated by his father's admiration. Djibril Gueye's admiration of his son is without equal. In his *tagg* of Oussou, he explains why Oussou deserves his praises.

This form of *tagg*, a praise of gratefulness, is a common one. It can take place among relatives, close friends, and neighbors in public and in private, but always ends in the form of a prayer. Bâ's presentation of this *tagg* is true to its original in Wolof. This is the kind of *tagg* many a child lives for to hear from his or her parents and loved ones. In this *tagg*, as in others, there is a listing of deeds that are highlighted. Ousmane's success would have been irrelevant if he had not sent his father to Mecca to perform the hajj. Children's worth is based on how much they honor their parents. This of course has its problems, which include parents' total control of their children's lives.

The *tagg* from the "griots, goldsmiths and *laobes* with their honeyed language" (7), the members of the lower castes, comes with a price tag. Lady Mother-in-Law, coming from a poor background, has to buy her *tagg*. Sharing her *tagg* in the public sphere makes Lady Mother-in-Law feel good about her achievements. When her name is broadcast over the radio, it makes her feel important and accepted into "high society." The fact that she has been awarded a space and position within the sorority of women "with heavy bracelets" makes her revel in a false sense of security. Bâ presents her situation to show that she was not aware of the temporality of her newfound wealth. In this context, the *tagg* becomes a *djei* because Lady Mother-in-Law would never have received this kind of attention if Binetou had not married Modo Fall.

In a different context in *Scarlet Song*, Yaye Khady also gets her share of public *tagg*—something she has always dreamt about and never thought possible—when Oussou marries a white woman, Mireille. With Ouleymatou in the family way with Oussou's child, Yaye Khady rejoices: finally, she is going to have her day in public. When the day comes, Yaye Khady won't be outdone.

Yaye Khady's narcissism, always under cover, comes out in full force as she participates in and does what is "required" of her in this naming ceremony. She feels redeemed in front of her age-mates after the disastrous naming ceremony of Gorgui during which she was shamed. "At last she had her day of glory among her peers" (134). The flattering to coax money out of the hands of the *guers* goes on with more and more *taggs*. Of course, at such a gathering the *tagg* is done mostly for financial gain, as the praises of "the open-handed ones" are sung. Bâ gives faithful representations of these *taggs* in translation. It is evident that she admires them for their literary finesse, but she also critiques the practice, especially in instances where it is not genuine, but done just for financial gain.

For Ousmane Gueye, the public *tagg* brings complications in his life. Ouleymatou uses Mabo the Dialli (griot) as part of the seduction process to "get" Ousmane. The Dialli made Ousmane feel good about his roots and determined that he was doing the right thing by being with Ouleymatou. The words the Dialli uses are carefully chosen and meant to touch Ousmane's heartstrings. Who will not be moved by high praises of one's ancestry? This is the human weakness the *tagg* exploits. Regardless of class and economic positioning, when one is reminded of one's glorious past, one's pride abounds.

In all its forms the *tagg*, therefore, operates as a way to show thanks and appreciation, to goad one to release money, to praise one's ancestry, and to ensure that things move smoothly at public functions, despite the fact that sometimes it has the opposite effect. Ramatoulaye complains about receiving the same calibre of praise as Binetou when in her calculations she should have received the most praises because she had been married to Modou for a longer period of time and has twelve children, while Binetou has only three. She sees this as hypocrisy on the part of her in-laws. "Our sisters-in-law give equal consideration to thirty years and five years of married life. With the same ease and the same words, they celebrate twelve maternities and three. I note with outrage this desire to level out, in which Modou's new mother-in-law rejoices" (4).

The *tagg*, as these examples have shown, is deeply rooted in the griot tradition of praise poetry, a form that can be both spontaneous and well thought-out and defined. Mariama Bâ's literary roots, I argue, are deeply rooted in the tradition of the griot.

Mirasse, Xas, and *Aha*

In *So Long a Letter*, Ramatoulaye's reflection on her life takes place during her *tenge*. This is the period when a woman is sequestered to mourn the death of her husband. It is a period of solitude, prayer, and reflection. The interesting thing, however, is that men do not have to go through this same process when they lose their wives. She uses the time of reflection that is afforded her to contemplate how the choices she has made in the past have impacted her life. Ramatoulaye decides to evaluate the man she had married with "the ear" of her friend Aissatou. She justifies sharing the most intimate details of her life with Aissatou by stating: "The *mirasse* commanded by the Koran requires that a dead person be stripped of his most intimate secrets; thus is exposed to others what was carefully concealed" (9). In keeping with the requirements of the *mirasse*, Ramatoulaye goes on to reveal the details of Modou's life she never thought of revealing.

The fact that Modou Fall dies of a heart attack is a shock to Ramatoulaye. "Modou is dead. How am I to tell you? One does not fix appointments with fate. Fate grasps whom it wants, when it wants" (2). This strong belief in fate, tied to her Islamic religion and the Wolof worldview, "lu yalla dogol, Diam mun si dara" (what god decides, man can do nothing about), is what pulls her through the difficult time.

Modou's death is a rapid death for someone who had accumulated so much *aha* (sin) in his life. It is widely believed in Wolof society that a major sin, such as the abandonment of one's wife and children, deserves a fate no less than an "ugly" death—Modou Fall deserved this kind of death. Thus, because God "never sleeps," Modou is "embarrassed" in death.

Modou Fall had lost his sense of shame and thought that money could right all his mistakes. It is discovered, according to Ramatoulaye, that he died "without a penny saved. Acknowledgement of debts? A pile of them: cloth and gold traders, home-delivery grocers and butchers, car-purchase installments" (9). At the time of his death, Modou had abandoned Ramatoulaye, his first wife, and their children for the younger Binetou, a friend of his oldest daughter. This type of abandonment (a form of betrayal known as *ur*) is frowned upon by the society, but Modou sees nothing wrong with his actions. He is going through a midlife crisis and needs a young woman to make him feel young again. Modou Fall's belief in having "fresh blood" with a young wife is what leads him to Binetou. In the prime of his life, when he is supposed to dedicate his whole life to Allah, it is more important for him to have a young woman than to have any orderly life he and Ramatoulaye may have had.

This position within which Modou is located is contradictory. Mariama Bâ makes it clear that the men in her fiction do not always follow the precepts of society (religious and traditional). On one hand, Modou knows and understands that tradition frowns upon abandonment; yet tradition sanctions more than one wife, and usually it is understood that the wife one takes in middle age is a young virgin. How does he reconcile these tensions in his life without committing sacrilege against tradition? Bâ offers some clarification regarding what Islam has to say about the taking of more than one wife: "A man must be like an evenly balanced scale. He must weight out in equal measures his compliments and his reproaches. He must give equally of himself. He must study his gestures and behavior and apportion everything fairly" (*Scarlet Song*, 7). With a prescription such as this one, no man is qualified to have more than one wife, because what kind of man will be able to be so fair minded as not to go against the teachings of Islam?

Modou Fall evidently does not have the presence of mind or the tenacity needed to have more than one wife, as "in loving someone else, he burned his path both morally and materially. He dared to commit such an act of disavowal" (*So Long a Letter*, 12). Modou Fall, Mbye Cham argues at this point, has a "selective adherence to tradition" (Cham, 1980, 90). This selectivity is based upon the idea of privilege, but never taking the responsibilities that come with one's privilege. This puts Modou Fall in a space where he cannot transform his possibilities from the positions he inhabits. Transforming tensions that result from his multiple positionings is something he is incapable of.

As a result of this inability to transform his situation, Ramatoulaye now has the right to call him out on his indecencies and blatant disregard for tradition where his first family is concerned. Thus the use of the *xas*. It should be pointed out here that the concepts *xas*, *mirasse*, and *aha* are used concurrently in the text. The occasion Ramatoulaye uses to lash out indirectly at Modou is when Tamsir, Modou's elder brother, proposes marriage to her. She decides that her voice, which was silenced during thirty years of marriage, will be heard. She names what she sees as Tamsir's lack of regard for her in a violent sarcastic *xas*.

Ramatoulaye's torrential tirade is a result of what she considers an affront to her sense of agency. She says that she commits this act of verbal violence to get back at Tamsir for announcing Modou's marriage to her years earlier. But it is more than a revenge. It is an act of courage for Ramatoulaye to speak up about her feelings. Tamsir bears the brunt of her anger that she has bottled up over the years. Tamsir becomes the whipping boy for Modou Fall, whom she did not have the chance to *xas* before his death. All the anger Ramatoulaye had kept under wraps, due to Modou's treatment of her and her children, surfaces in her somewhat misdirected anger at Tamsir.

What Mariama Bâ does in this *xas* episode is to call to the attention of her readers that silence does not always mean a lack of agency. When the occasion presents itself, women are as capable as men in defining their needs and wants. She is also levelling a critique of the use of women as property under the guise of custom. In this process of wife inheritance, women are exchanged and discarded as goods rather than as human beings with rights. A custom thought of to keep children within a family, wife inheritance is widely abused nowadays. Customs, Bâ seems to be saying, have their place in regulating society, but it is when people want to practice customs without all the responsibilities that come with them that they become problematic.

Tamsir wants to practice the custom of wife inheritance but cannot even afford to feed his own wives and numerous children. For a custom designed to financially and emotionally help a widowed woman, his request is unreasonable. His lack of resources and any kind of emotion for Ramatoulaye makes him unsuitable for the task at hand. He only sees Ramatoulaye as a ''milch cow'' to exploit. The exposure of Tamsir's motives in public (he is accompanied by the Imam and Mawdo), coupled with the disclosure of Modou's indiscretions to Aissatou, locates the *xas* within the concept of the *mirasse*, as these two terms work hand in hand to situate the *aha*.

Women and Caste

It is necessary to further explicate Bâ's fictional world by examining the caste system and women's relationship to it. What is caste and how does it operate in Bâ's fictional world? The caste system in the Senegambia area is as old as the histories of the people who inhabit the area. It needs to be suggested at this point that not all ethnic groups in the area have caste systems. The four major groups with the most sophisticated caste systems are the Peulh, the Toucouleur, the Wolof, and the Mandinka. What concerns us as we read Bâ are the Wolof and the Peulh systems, which are similar in a great many ways. The caste system in Senegambia is occupationally based and not always economic. I will try to briefly explain a complicated system.

The *guers* are the highest caste in the caste system. This caste comprises the descendants of nobles and farmers. In the past, supposedly, this group ruled the various kingdoms in the region before the advent of colonialism.

The *guewals* are the second-highest caste in this man-constructed hierarchy. This group is formed by the praise singers, the poets, the guardians of history and culture.

The *tegg* caste is made of highly skilled members who work with metals. They work with the elements of water and fire, a skill that requires mathematical abilities, scientific know-how, and creativity.

The *woodeh* caste, also highly skilled, works with leather and wood. Its members are mostly the artists of the society. Of course, this situation is being challenged as gifted artists from all castes practice their craft.

In Bâ's fiction the issue of caste is well woven into her texts. Her stance is one of resistance. She creates the possibility of a relationship between two women from two different castes. In Aissatou and Ramatoulaye, a *tegg* and a *guer* come together in a friendship based on equality and mutual respect.

Evidently, these two women have transcended the boundaries drawn by caste. Tante Nabou, Mawdo's mother and Aissatou's mother-in-law, cannot transcend the parameters set up by her society. To her it is each to his or her own. Mawdo's marriage to Aissatou is perceived by her as an affront to her noble birth. For people like Tante Nabou, the past cannot be separated from the present or the future. Her worldview (the kind Bâ critiques) rests on the belief in "ancient properties." Tante Nabou believes that as one who is descended from a long line of notable nobles, she is superior to the members of the lower castes. Her belief in perpetuating the traditional way of life is informed by her annals of history that teach her that there should be no intermarriage between the castes. Caught between tradition and modernity, she opts for the glorious days of the past in which people respected the old ways and lived faithfully by them. For someone of her standing, female solidarity has no meaning, because she cannot transcend caste to transform her possibilities.

Mariama Bâ, in her presentation of a woman like Tante Nabou, shows the problem involved in locating a female solidarity when caste, age, and "bloodlines" become more important than being female. Aissatou's crime, as Bâ presents it, is marrying the man she loves despite the fact that he belongs to a "superior" caste. Tante Nabou, Mawdo Bâ's mother and Aissatou's mother-in-law, totally disapproved of this kind of *rah* (mixing). She does not want grandchildren who will be located in a position where they will suffer from the violence of *xas* because of the "inferior" blood inherited from their mother. Therefore, from the day Mawdo Bâ married Aissatou, Tante Nabou lived exclusively to get Aissatou out of the household.

Thus Tante Nabou embarks on a journey of renewal of her roots that will purge her family of Aissatou. She travels to Diakhao, the place of Bour Sine, her revered ancestor. In Diakhao, she reexamines her location vis-à-vis her son and her daughter-in-law, Aissatou. She becomes more determined than ever, after her ritualistic search for selves, to get "rid" of Aissatou. She swears that Aissatou's existence "would never tarnish her noble descent" (28). Her offerings to her "*Tours* are a sign of her determination to live the "old way." Bâ comments on Tante Nabou's role as an upholder of the "canons of tradition" (*Cham*). Aunt Nabou "lived in the past, unaware of a changing world. She clung to old beliefs. Being strongly attached to her privileged origins, she firmly believed that blood carries its virtues, and, nodding her head, she would repeat that humble birth would always show in a person's bearing" (26). Tante Nabou's attitudes, it is important to note, do not exist in a vacuum; rather, they are the sum total of a way of positioning and naming people in her society. Her language reflects caste as conceptualized within the language of division and difference (in a negative way). To Tante Nabou, "those people" are not worthy of her company or family because they have a specific place and function in society. You call on them when you need their services; otherwise, each to his or her own when it comes to marriage.

The question raised by this kind of presentation is, does Bâ successfully critique women's relations based upon caste thoroughly, or does she contribute to the perpetuation in placing the lower-caste women in particular positions? Bâ, it can be argued, carefully negotiates the spaces inhabited by the different women in her fictional world. She does present women with tensions in their lives contingent on their locations, locations replete with tensions. These tensions are exacerbated further by generational gaps and caste pretensions, to the point where the women always seem to be in contention and opposition. These oppositions and tensions are not always negative, as Bâ seems to leave space for transformation, as in the relationship with Ramatoulaye and Farmata. Bâ sees transformations of culture and traditions as a solution to the problem of the alleviation of the situation of the woman in Senegalese society in particular and Africa in general.

At the same time, this does not absolve her from reinscribing caste in ways that can be read as acquiescence. For instance, even though Ramatoulaye tries not to be caught in the game of castes, she does turn to Farmata for help in sending a letter to Daouda Dieng. Farmata, she tells the reader, "was happy, having dreamed of this role right from our youth" (67). Farmata is supposedly happy to finally have the chance to act out the role of her subordination in society. The use of caste, though, seems to rest on Bâ's characters, who are rooted in their belief, in tradition. Yaye Khady, Tante Nabou, and Lady Mother-in-Law represent the last bastion of this tradition.

CRITICAL RECEPTION

When one looks at the state of the criticism on Mariama Bâ, there seem to be distinctions within the criticism. There is clearly an international interest in Bâ, probably more than in her other female compatriot writers. As a result, there is a distinctly Francophone body of criticism that places her in a Francophone literary tradition. The Europeans and the Americans identify her as a representative of African women, especially in the context of feminism. African-American critics, it should be added, claim her within the context of black women's writings. There is also a small but distinctly Senegambian form of criticism within this body of criticism. As opposed to "the other" areas of criticism, this area seems to offer an insider's view.

The pioneering contributions to the body of criticism on Bâ started from her home country of Senegal. Journalists and academics alike wrote mostly short pieces and interviews that dealt with her life and achievement. Among these people were Annette Mbaye D'Enerville, Aminata Ka Maïga, and Alioune Toure Dia, to name a few. One of the major critical pieces on Bâ that provided much insight into her work in the context of her society came from Mbye Cham. The article, titled "The Female Condition in Africa: A Literary Exploration by Mariama Bâ," brought into focus issues that moved away from the mostly biographical pieces of the time, contextualizing for readers Bâ's concerns. Aminata Maïge Ka and Sada Niang, in the same tradition, provide insight into the culture that Bâ wrote about. In their works on Bâ these two authors look at Wolof concepts and how Bâ worked them into her fiction. How is this different from the Western readings of Bâ?

There are diverse Western and Eastern readings of Bâ that show insights from cultural perspectives different from those of Bâ. These readings bring richness to her works but at the same time reiterate stereotypical themes of the supposed concerns of "African feminist writers." These works are too numerous to discuss here, but will make interesting reading.

Bâ's intellectual project leaves the baton to the young women to change the status quo. Her hopes are that through the younger generation, the archaic and negative attachment to tradition will make way for a different way of constructing knowledge within tradition, but in a positive manner. She firmly believed that this transformation can and will take place within Senegalese society.

BIBLIOGRAPHY

Works by Mariama Bâ

Un chant écarlate. Nouvelles Éditions Africaines, 1981. Translated into English by Dorothy Blair as *Scarlet Song*. Essex: Longman, 1986.
Une si longue lettre. Dakar: Nouvelles Éditions Africaines, 1980. Translated into English by Modupe Thomas as *So Long a Letter*. London: Heinemann, 1981.
"La fonction politique des littératures africaines écrites." *Écriture Française* 5.3 (1981): 3–7.

Studies of Mariama Bâ

Abubakr, Rashidah Ismaili. "The Emergence of Mariama Bâ." *Essays on African Writing, A Re-evaluation*. Oxford: Heinemann, 1993. 24–37.
Arnhold, Barbara. "The Long Road to Emancipation," (interview). *Afrika*, 1980.
Borgomano, Madeleine. *Voix et visages de femmes, dans les livres écrits par des femmes en Afrique francophone*. Abidjan, CEDA: Corlet, 1989.
Cham, Mbye. "Contemporary Society and the Female Imagination: A Study of the Novels of Mariama Bâ." *African Literature Today* 15 (1987): 89–101.
———. "The Female Condition in Africa: A Literary Exploration by Mariama Bâ." *Current Bibliography on African Affairs* 17.1 (1984–85): 29–52.
———. "Islam in Sénégalese Literature and Film." *Faces of Islam in African Literature*. Ed. Kenneth Harrow. London: James Currey, 1991. 163–186.

Champagne, John, " 'A Feminist Just Like Us?' Teaching Mariama Bâ's *So Long a Letter.*" *College English* 58.1 (1996): 22–42.

D'Almeida, Irene Assiba. "The Concept of Choice In Mariama Bâ's Fiction." *Ngambika: Studies of Women in African Literature.* Ed. Carole Boyce Davies and Anne Adams Graves. Trenton, N.J.: Africa World Press, 1986.

Diarra, Fatoumatta-Agnes, and Pierre Fougeyrollas. *Two Studies on Ethnic Group Relations in Africa: Senegal, the United Republic of Tanzania.* Paris: UNESCO, 1974.

Diop, Abdoulaye. *La société wolof: Tradition et changement: Les systèmes d'inégalité et de domination.* Dakar: Karthala, 1981.

Diop, Papa Samba. *Die frankophone Literatur des Senegal und ihre Beziehungen zu den afrikanischen Sprachen und Kulturen—am Beispiel des Wolof.* Translated by Janos Riesz. Munich: Edition Text and Kritik, 1994. 190–212.

Edson, Laurie. "Mariama Bâ and the Politics of the Family." *Studies in Twentieth Century Literature* 17.1 (1993): 13–25.

Fandio, Pierre. "Mariama Bâ et Angele Rawiri: Une Autre Verite de la Femme." *Dalhousie French Studies* 30 (1995): 171–178.

Fetzer, Glenn W. "Women's Search for Voice and the Problem of Knowing in the Novels of Mariama Bâ." *College Language Association Journal* 35.1 (1991): 31–41.

Flewellen, Elinor C. "Assertiveness vs. Submissiveness in Selected Works by African Women Writers." *Bâ Shiru: A Journal of African Languages and Literature* 12.2 (1985): 3–18.

Gavioli, Davida. "In Search of the Mother's Lost Voice: Mariama Bâ's *Une si longue lettre*, Francesca Sanvitale's *Madre e figlia*, and Amy Tan's *The Joy Luck Club.*" *Dissertation Abstracts International* 55.6 (1994): 1552A–1553A.

Grimes, Dorothy. "Mariama Bâ's *So Long a Letter* and Alice Walker's *In Search of Our Mothers' Gardens*: A Senegalese and an African American Perspective on 'Womanism.' " *Global Perspectives on Teaching Literature: Shared Visions and Distinctive Visions.* Urbana, IL: National Council of Teachers of English, 1993. 65–76.

Gueye, Medoune. "La Politique du roman feminin au Senegal." *Dissertation Abstracts International* 55.9 (1995): 2825A.

Herzberger-Fofana, Pierrette. "L'Islam dans les romans feminins senegalais." In *Frankophone Literaturen ausserhalb Europas.* Frankfurt: Peter Lang, 1987. 97–104.

Jaccard, Anny-Claire. "Les Visages de l'Islam chez Mariama Bâ et Aminata Sow Fall." *Nouvelles du Sud* 6 (1986): 171–182.

Jackson, Kathy Dunn. "The Epistolary Text: A Voice of Affirmation and Liberation in *So Long a Letter* and *The Color Purple.*" *The Griot* 12.2 (1993): 13–20.

Jagne, Siga Fatima. "African Women and the Category 'Woman': Through the Works of Mariama Bâ and Bessie Head." *Dissertation Abstracts International* 55.12 (1995): 3837A.

Ka Maïga, Aminata. "Ramatoulaye, Aissatou, Mireille et . . . Mariama Bâ." *Notre Librairie* 81 (1985): 129–134.

Kembe, Milolo. *L'image de la femme chez les romancières de l'Afrique noire francophone.* Fribourg: Éditions Universitaires Fribourg Suisse, 1986.

Kemp, Yakini. "Romantic Love and the Individual in Novels by Mariama Bâ, Buchi Emecheta, and Bessie Head." *Obsidian II: Black Literature in Review* 3.3 (1988): 1–16.

King, Adele. "The Personal and the Political in the Work of Mariama Bâ." *Studies in Twentieth Century Literature* 18.2 (1994): 177–188.

Larrier, Renee. "Correspondence et creation littéraire: Mariama Bâ's *Une Si Longue Lettre.*" *French Review: Journal of the American Association of Teachers of French* 64.5 (1991): 747–753.

McElaney-Johnson, Ann. "The Place of the Woman or the Woman Displaced in Mariama Bâ's *Une Si longue lettre.*" *College Language Association Journal* 37.1 (1993): 19–28.

Makward, Edris. "Marriage, Tradition, and Woman's Pursuit of Happiness in the Novels of Mariama Bâ." *Ngambika: Studies of Women and African Literature.* Ed. Carole Boyce Davies and Anne Adams Graves. Trenton, N.J.: Africa World Press, 1986. 271–282.

Mbaye d'Enerville, Annette. *Femmes africaines: Propos recueillis par Antte Mbaye d'Enerville sur les thèmes de femmes et société: Suivi de Une si longue lettre par Mariama Bâ: Avec cinq compositions de Gnagna Diène.* Romorantin: Éditions Martinsart, 1982.

Miller, Elinor S. "Two Faces of the Exotic: Mariama Bâ's Un Chant écarlate." *French Literature Series* 13 (1986): 144–147.

Miller, Mary-Katherine Fleming. "(Re)production of Self: Colonialism, Infanticide, and Autobiography in the Works of Mariama Bâ, Aminata Sow Fall, and Marguerite Duras." *Dissertation Abstracts International* 53.11 (1993): 3896A.

Mortimer, Mildred. "Enclosure/Disclosure in Mariama Ba's *Une Si Longue Lettre.*" *French Review: Journal of the American Association of Teachers of French* 64.1 (1990): 69–78.

Niang, Sada. "Modes de contextualisation dans *Une si longue lettre* et *L'appel des arènes.*" *Literary Griot* 4.1–2 (Spring/Fall 1992): 111–125.

Nwachukwu-Agbada, J. O. J. " 'One Wife Be for One Man': Mariama Bâ's Doctrine for Matrimony." *Modern Fiction Studies* 37.3 (Autumn 1991): 561–573.

Ojo-Ade, Femi. "Still a Victim: Mariama Bâ's *Une si longue lettre.*" *African Literature Today* 12 (1982): 71–87.

Plant, Deborah G. "Mythic Dimensions in the Novels of Mariama Bâ." *Research in African Literatures* 27.2 (summer 1996): 102–111.

Reyes, Angelita Dianne. "Crossing the Bridge: The Great Mother in Selected Novels of Toni Morrison, Paule Marshall, Simone Schwarz-Bart, and Mariama Bâ." *Dissertation Abstracts International* 46.6 (1985): 1619A.

Riesz, Janos. "Mariama Bâ's *Une Si Longue Lettre*: An Erziehungsroman." *Research in African Literatures* 22.1 (1991): 27–42.

Rueschmann, Eva. "Female Self-Definition and the African Community in Mariama Bâ's Epistolary Novel *So Long a Letter.*" In *International Women's Writing: New Landscapes of Identity.* Westport, CT: Greenwood, 1995. 3–18.

Sarvan, Charles Ponnuthurai. "Feminism and African Fiction: The Novels of Mariama Bâ." *Modern Fiction Studies* 34.3 (Autumn 1988): 453–464.

Staunton, Cheryl Antoinette. "Three Sénégalese Women Novelists: A Study of Temporal/Spatial Structures." George Washington University, 1986.

Staunton, Cheryl Wall. "Mariama Bâ: Pioneer Senegalese Woman Novelist." *College Language Association Journal* 37.3 (1994): 328–335.

Stringer, Susan. "Cultural Conflict in the Novels of Two African Writers, Mariama Bâ and Aminata Sow-Fall.'' *SAGE: A Scholarly Journal on Black Women* 5 supp. (1988): 36–41.

Treiber Jeanette. ''Feminism and Identity Politics: Mariama Bâ's *Un chant esarlate.''* *Research in African Literatures* 27.4 (Winter 1996): 109–123.

Walker, Keith L. ''Postscripts: Mariama Bâ, Epistolarity, Menopause, and Postcoloniality.'' *Postcolonial Subjects: Francophone Women Writers*. Minneapolis, MN: University of Minnesota Press, 1996. 246–264.

Wills, Dorothy Davis. ''Economic Violence in Postcolonial Senegal: Noisy Silence in Novels by Mariama Bâ and Aminata Sow Fall.'' In *Violence, Silence, and Anger: Women's Writing as Transgression*. Charlottesville, VA: University Press of Virginia, 1995. 158–171.

Yousaf, Nahem. ''The 'Public' versus the 'Private' in Mariama Bâ's Novels.'' *The Journal of Commonwealth Literature* 30.2 (1995): 85–98.

Zongo, Opportune Marie C. ''Body Politics: Representing the Body in *Le Vieux Negre et la medaille*, *The Beautyful Ones Are Not Yet Born*, and *Une Si Longue Lettre.''* *Dissertation Abstracts International* 53.7 (1993): 2366A–2367A.

SIGA FATIMA JAGNE

CALIXTHE BEYALA (1961–)

BIOGRAPHY

Born in 1961 in Douala, Calixthe Beyala is an Éton from Saa, situated about seventy-two kilometers from Yaounde, the capital city of Cameroon. In the early years of her life, Beyala lived with her Cameroonian mother and Central African stepfather in the Republic of Central Africa. She was separated from her mother at age five and was then raised by an elder sister, four years her senior, in one of the ghettos of Douala. Although her childhood was characterized by loneliness, with her elder sister as her only close companion, Beyala claims to have been raised in a women's world, one in which women like her aunt and her grandmother were extraordinarily powerful. These women, unlike many others, never chose prostitution as a means of survival. They were self-determined and hardworking and, according to Beyala, could divorce their husbands whenever they wanted. Beyala was therefore molded by these strong women and learned at an early age to have a firm grip on life.

The influence of her grandmother was particularly important. The young Beyala spent many an evening listening to her stories. Her grandmother once told her that in order not to provoke the wrath of evil spirits, tales could not be told during the day and that one had to wait for the first stars to appear in the sky. At sunset, Beyala would stand outside waiting for the first star to appear in the sky and would scream with joy and beckon her namesake to come and see the star. Then the storytelling would begin. The young girl enjoyed these worlds of energetic women and storytelling, and this made life bearable in the shantytowns of Douala. She was fascinated by the stars, and they became part of her world of fantasies and literary expression.

Her grandmother's stories and her fascination with the stars gave her a chance to dream dreams that most children in the ghetto do not and cannot. Most of these children are not given the care and the education that Beyala was fortunate enough to get. She attended primary school at the École Principale du Camp Mboppi in Douala and obtained her high-school education at the Lycée des Rapides à Bangui and the Lycée Polyvalent de Douala. She never really liked school, but had one teacher who would beat the daylights out of her if she stayed away from school. Beyala then took her schoolwork seriously and eventually won a scholarship. She left for Paris at the age of seventeen, where she wrote her *baccalauréat*. She then went to Spain, where she lived for six years with her husband and also studied management. She returned to France, where she earned a B.A. in letters. She held a variety of jobs and, among other things, was a florist and a model. She is now divorced, lives with her two children in Paris, and earns her living as a full-time novelist.

Beyala has always been saddened by the fact that children in her native country and continent who grow up as she did are left hungry and illiterate and are either used for manual labor or treated as a commodity. The plight of children has become one of the dominant themes in her writing and living. She has adopted dozens of orphans in Yaounde and Douala and dreams of the day when she will be able to take care of all the dispossessed children of the world. Beyala is also an advocate of women's rights. She states that the African woman has three types of struggles: her gender, her race, and her social integration. Children's and women's issues are therefore at the heart of her writing.

She has been hailed as the precursor of a new literary movement of writers born after independence. Their post-colonial experiences and writings distinguish them from their counterparts whose works span the colonial and post-colonial periods. Beyala particularly notes that being born after independence completely modifies and shapes her thinking in ways that are different from those of writers of the Negritude era. The oppressor is no longer white but the black brother who lives next door.

The recognition that she has been getting is important to Beyala the writer and African woman. She openly challenges the saying that goes that African women publish once and then vanish into oblivion. She is one of the rare African women writers who, from the beginning, has not had problems with publishing her novels and actually writes for a living. She maintains that her goal is to publish at least one novel every two years. Beyala writes in French, a language whose "elasticity" she finds comfortable to work with. She uses the French language as a tool that she can dominate, manipulate, and transform with her own culture and traditions. Rewriting languages, cultures, traditions, children's issues, and women's issues and putting the individual child or woman (instead of an elusive collective consciousness) at the center of her stories are part of the goals that Beyala has set for herself and her writing. (This biography has been gleaned from a few published interviews: Genevoix, Cévaër, Ormerod, Volet, Matateyou, and an unpublished interview given by Beyala to Eloïse Brière and Béatrice Rangira Gallimore.)

MAJOR WORKS AND THEMES

Calixthe Beyala has published five novels: *C'est le soleil qui m'a brûlée* (1987), *Tu t'appelleras Tanga* (1988), *Seul le diable le savait* (1990), *Le petit prince de Belleville* (1992), and *Maman a un amant* (1993). Three of these novels have been translated into English by Marjolin de Jager: *Le petit prince de Belleville* as *Loukoun* (1995), *C'est le soleil qui m'a brûlée* as *The Sun Hath Looked Upon Me* (1996), and *Tu t'appelleras Tanga* as *Your Name Shall Be Tanga* (1996). The first three novels are set in Africa and the last two in Paris. With a tone that is often harsh and sometimes ironic and humorous, Beyala paints a bleak picture of humankind and the plight of women and children in a male-dominated society. Her novels lay emphases on individuals instead of the ''masses,'' making universal points out of the consciousness and experiences of these individual characters.

Beyala told Mouellé Kombi II in an interview: "Le lien entre mes différents romans est constitué par les problèmes essentiels de la femme dans la société" (The connection between my different novels is constituted essentially by women's problems in society) (Mouellé Kombi II, 12; my translation). The main protagonists in her novels are teenagers or young women in their twenties. Ateba Léocadie is nineteen and Tanga is seventeen, while Mégrita is twenty-six. In the last two novels (which actually tell one story), the narrative voice is that of a naïve but pragmatic ten-year-old boy, Loukoum, who through his questions and observations puts into perspective the lives of his and other African immigrant families eking out a living in Parisian slums.

The effects of poverty, social degradation, and injustices occupy a significant space in Beyala's texts. Promiscuity, prostitution, and child abuse are dominant themes in the first three novels. They question and problematize the identities, be they constituted or constituting, and subjectivities of women and children in African post-colonial society. These three novels are an indictment of human depravity in African urban slums; of patriarchal society and the appropriation and misuse of power; and of a society that condones child abuse, child slavery, and prostitution, a society that is not only oppressive to women, but one in which women also act as oppressive agents toward other women. The brutal specter of revenge and death that permeates the setting in these novels, especially in *C'est le soleil qui m'a brûlée* and *Tu t'appelleras Tanga*, is balanced by a break for freedom in *Seul le diable le savait*. *C'est le soleil qui m'a brûlée* tells the story of one woman's struggles toward self-determination in an urban ghetto, QG, a male-dominated world where promiscuity and corruption reign supreme and where women's entrapment lies in marriage, multiple pregnancies, and prostitution. In *Tu t'appelleras Tanga*, this theme is further explored in darker, violent tones, in conjunction with the harsh realities of the exploitation of deprived children.

Abandoned as a child by her mother, who was a prostitute, Ateba, the heroine in *C'est le soleil qui m'a brûlée*, is raised by a domineering aunt who treats her niece and the array of lovers in her own life with contempt. Ada seeks to ascertain a position of authority, under the guise of family honor, by subjecting Ateba to the egg ritual. Ironically, Ateba is still a virgin, and it is this virginity that Ada publicly brandishes as if it were a trophy. It is by condoning and reinforcing such cruel practices on women's bodies that adults like Ada control and stifle the aspirations and womanhood of children like Ateba. The young woman rebels against what she considers to be a society that has no sense of direction or hope for a better future, and her introspective look at her society confronts this status quo. Her acts of defiance are seen in her questioning of women's sexuality and her strong eroticization of the woman's body. Humiliated and violated by the egg ritual, she seeks solace in her friendship with a young prostitute, Irène, and through this friendship observes the subjugation of women and their struggles to be free. When her friend dies from an abortion, she commits a murder that in the rashness of her adolescent mind is symbolic of the destruction of Man, the agent of Woman's subjugation: a violent act that both is self-liberatory and challenges the recurring statement in the novel that proclaims, "God created woman on her knees, at the feet of men."

This theme spills over into Tanga's story in *Tu t'appelleras Tanga*. Raised by a father who orders her not to look people in their faces, Tanga is an illustration of a woman who refuses "to be on her knees at the feet of men." Physically battered and psychologically damaged by rape and incest at the tender age of twelve by her father, forced to undergo a clitoridectomy and to go into the market of prostitution by her mother, Tanga, like Ateba, is determined not to let the tragedies that have become part of her daily life stifle her efforts toward self-actualization in a post-colonial climate of destitution and violence. Women are prostitutes and children a commodity. Tanga's story tells of the degradation that children in African slums are forced to live with; it is a direct indictment of a society that has lost its traditional family values. But in the bleakness and harshness of Beyala's stories is a persistent glimmer of light at the end of the tunnel. The women and the children that are at the center of her stories seek out other forms of self-liberation and self-determination. They are not condemned to rot in their slums or sell their bodies all their lives. What we see consistently is Beyala's ability to portray tragic conditions that Africans in the post-colonial era have created or have to live with, but she also leaves the post-colonial subject with a potential for change.

For instance, Ateba seeks out Irène's friendship, never judging her lifestyle, but using this friendship to understand what happened to her own mother and many other women like her. She also has an ability to fantasize, to dream about the stars, and to write letters to other women, acts that in themselves are liberatory, acts that most dispossessed children of the ghettos are incapable of. In the same way, Tanga's friendship with a group of disinherited, street-wise children brings her closer than most people to their daily lived realities and experiences and gives new meaning to her own existence, one that is different from the constant possession and objectification of her body. These children, and especially Mala (the son she adopts who later dies), become her support group. She spiritually survives her death through the woman Anna-Claude with whom she shares her story in prison. Women in Beyala's stories are an intrinsic component of a network of support for other women, even though individual women must eventually redefine their own lives.

Mégrita also benefits from such support and diverse friendships, and these help balance the inconsistencies that plague her life in *Seul le diable le savait*. Raised in a home by her mother and two fathers, the red-haired, mixed-race Mégrita lives a marginal life because she is different. Beyala uses Bertha Andela's "unusual" lifestyle and Mégri's "shady" origins to spin a yarn about Wuel, a society rife with superstition, tale mongering, and corruption. When a Stranger comes to town and gives them money, the people in the community neglect their work and seek to exorcise the demons within themselves by using the Pygmy's death as an opportunity to subject Mégri to a hallucinatory ritual performance and witch hunt. Mégri's road to self-discovery is paved by this ordeal and the friendships that she shares with her mother, Laetitia, and other women. They teach her to appreciate the complexities that are part of women's daily lives. She falls in love with the Stranger and has his baby, but never really marries him, for he is hunted down by the police and killed. Mutual respect and love between Mégri and the Stranger is a new development in Beyala's third novel. Whereas Ateba and Tanga shun and condemn motherhood, Mégrita gets pregnant out of love. Her love for the Stranger fuels and legitimizes her escape to freedom on her wedding day from the husband she had been forced to marry. She liberates herself from these oppressive conditions by fleeing, first, to the Stranger's village and then to Paris.

Paris becomes the setting of the next two novels, *Le petit prince de Belleville* and *Maman a un amant*. The focus shifts from the lives of post independence post-colonial subjects in Africa to the discrimination, adjustments, and integration that post-colonial subjects are confronted with when they move out of the former colonies to the countries and metropolitan spaces of the former colonizers. Particularly telling is the position of immigrant women, of women living in a polygamous family life, in a context where the laws and regulations offer them little or no protection.

The ten-year-old Loukoum, Abdou Traoré's son, tells the story of their Malian family living in a Parisian ghetto in an apartment that Traoré refers to as a "coffin." This metaphor succinctly highlights the stifling and devastating realities that poverty and clandestine living have on African immigrants, and the effects that the struggle for integration in their new "home" has on their lives as they simultaneously seek to maintain their Africanness. Abdou Traoré, the war veteran, Muslim, polygamist, and revered patriarch, is embittered by the treatment he has received at the hands of the French and the changes that he sees in his wives and children. He continues to fantasize about a fleetingly distant African past and traditions that he can no longer have or maintain under his control. Traoré remains locked up in his womanizing and in his inability to see women in nondomestic, nonsexual roles. M'ammaryam, his first wife, cannot have children. Soumana, his second wife, has three daughters. Loukoum's mother, his former mistress, is a prostitute and part-time singer. Under French law, M'ammaryam is the only and official wife. She is, therefore, the only wife and mother of Traoré's four children. Soumana, on the other hand, is "officially" not married and has no children, legal documents, or status. In other words, Soumana does not exist. Soumana becomes ill but in actuality dies out of frustration, anger, and despair both at a system that erases her very existence and at a husband who validates and buries his own bitterness under the skirts of countless other women. The process of integration into a different culture, therefore, radically redefines the African family institution and sexual politics, reshaping conceptions and inscriptions of masculinity and femininity.

Ironically, only in death is Soumana liberated. She "exists," becoming an agent for change, for her husband goes to prison on a charge of family-allowance fraud, and only then does M'ammaryam take charge of her own life. These circumstances force her to give new direction to her life by opening a jewelry business that she operates with the help of Loukoum. M'ammaryam and Loukoum's personal growths go hand in hand. Loukoum learns how to negotiate racist attitudes and ideologies, while M'am juggles her pursuit of literacy with her jewelry business. Learning to read and write becomes, for both of them, a valuable tool for resistance and self-determination. M'am's personal growth leads her to give up her white, French lover while negotiating a reentry into the lives of "her children." The choices she makes seek to complement her new lifestyle and the traditional African values that she strives to maintain. This correlation is also aptly illustrated by Beyala's integration of colloquial French-African expressions and specific street-wise language into the diction, expressions, and attitudes of the immigrants. M'am's ultimate goal is to enable these children of immigrants to grow up and have better lives than either Abdou, Soumana, or she herself had. The children therefore deserve a better deal. Following the publication of *Le petit prince de Belleville*, Beyala had this to say to Sylvia Genevoix:

Quand on est né dans un bidonville, on ne peut pas accrocher son passé à un porte-manteau et dormir en paix. Quand j'étais petite, on m'a aidée à manger, à aller à l'école. Je me suis dis tous les jours que j'ai eu beaucoup de chance, et c'est maintenant à mon tour de me battre pour que les enfants des bidonvilles aient un peu moins faim, pour qu'ils aient des chaussures à mettre à leurs pieds et qu'ils soient éduqués comme les autres. (18)

(When one is born in a ghetto, one cannot hang one's past on a coat-rack and sleep in peace. When I was young, I was given help with food, with going to school. I told myself every day that I had a lot of luck, and it is now my turn to fight so that all the children of the ghettos are a little less hungry, so that they can have shoes to wear on their feet and be educated like the others.)

CRITICAL RECEPTION

There is no doubt that Calixthe Beyala is being hailed as a writer in a class all her own with respect to other sub-Saharan Francophone women writers of the 1970s through the 1980s. Despite what Joseph Ndinda has lamented as "the conspiracy of silence" of readers and critics that has for too long cloaked the writings of Cameroonian women, if compared with their male counterparts (Ndinda, 12), Anny-Claire Jaccard has maintained that thanks especially to Calixthe Beyala and Werewere Liking, Cameroonian women's writing appears to be "the most original and the most innovative of all sub-Saharan francophone women's writing" (Jaccard, 161). Beyala has therefore positioned herself at the forefront of such innovative creativity. The themes that she forcefully addresses have made her a controversial author whose work will draw more (published) critical attention in the 1990s. Critical reception has been mixed. While most critics applaud her originality, both thematic and stylistic, others are uncomfortable with her subject matter and what they feel it says about Africa (Doumbi-Fakoly, 148), and some have openly condemned her work. For instance, Ndinda has pointed out that Cameroonians were, paradoxically, some of the worst critics when her first novel appeared and some even went so far as accusing her of plagiarism (Ndinda, 71), an accusation that unfortunately persists with the publication of more of Beyala's work.

Nevertheless, Jean-Marie Volet's views represent what many critics have said. Volet notes that Beyala is "developing into one of the most provocative writers of her generation" (309), and if her texts are taken as a whole, they "seem both distinctive and complementary insofar as they may well mirror the author's journey of discovery through the maze of her own life" (310). Volet also maintains that her novels "represent a set of texts daring in their narrative style, unmistakably feminist, strongly committed to the ideals of social justice, and open to the possibilities of a better future for humankind in general and African women in particular" (309). Feminist critics like Irène d'Almeida, for instance, have hailed not only the feminist stance of Beyala's novels but also the various ways in which she continually seeks to subvert patriarchal norms (48–51). Eloïse Brière also notes the reappropriation of women's bodies in Beyala's work that is distinctively feminine, is grounded in women's fantasies and desires, and definitely rejects and breaks away from the Negritude tradition of male authors and their portrayal and/or appropriation of the African woman's body as Mother Africa/exotic object/whore (*Roman camerounais*, 231–41). Not only do women's bodies undergo this radical "auto-appropriation" in Beyala's novels, but her narrative style is one that critics have pointed out brings together an interdependence of heterogeneous voices (Borgomano, 87–94; Ellington, 102–06). The voices of the main protagonists are always melded with other voices that serve as their doubles, their alter egos, sometimes replacing an elusive omniscient narrator and invariably serving as a mystical, spiritual guide and companion.

Some critics have raised the issue of homosexuality in Beyala's work, an issue that to some is at best controversial and is downright scandalous to others (Ndinda, 12; Atchebro, 29). Richard Bjornson maintains, "Beyala's lesbian approach to the reality of contemporary Cameroon is unusual within the context of the country's literate culture" (420). David Ndachi Tagne states, "Man is reduced to his penis, his obsessions, his corruption and his constant desire to see woman only as an instrument of pleasure." He goes on to say, "Ateba's homosexual yearnings . . . will raise an outcry from a number of African readers," and even claims that readers will be scandalized by the "pornographic" content of her first novel (97). But Rangira Gallimore disagrees with those critics who put a "pornographic" label on her work when they accuse Beyala of "commercialising African eroticism" (60). In her review of Beyala's work, Armelle Nacef also celebrates what she terms a feminine way of loving (55), and Arlette Chemain refers to her work as an audacious revolt by an African woman writer against violence against women (162–63). Finally, Thécla Midiohouan rightly contends that the fact that these issues are addressed "so bluntly by a woman, is a first in [sub-Saharan] literature of French expression. Calixthe Beyala's writing has startled by its audacity, its crudeness" (156).

BIBLIOGRAPHY

Works by Calixthe Beyala

C'est le soleil qui m'a brûlée. Paris: Éditions Stock, 1987.
Tu t'appelleras Tanga. Paris: Éditions Stock, 1988.
Seul le diable le savait. Paris: Le Pré aux Clercs, 1990.
Le petit prince de Belleville. Paris: Albin Michel, 1992.
Maman a un amant. Paris: Albin Michel, 1993.

Studies of Calixthe Beyala

Atchebro, Daniel. "Beyala: Trop 'brûlante' pour les mecs!" *Regards Africains* 8 (1988): 29.
Bjornson, Richard. *The African Quest for Freedom and Identity: Cameroonian Writing and the National Experience*. Bloomington: Indiana University Press, 1991. 416–20.
Borgomano, Madeleine. "Les femmes et l'écriture-parole." *Notre Librairie* 117 (April–June 1994): 87–94.
Brière, Eloïse. "Le retour des mères dévorantes." *Notre Librairie* 117 (April–June 1994): 66–71.
———. *Le roman camerounais et ses discours*. Ivry: Éditions Nouvelles du Sud, 1993.
Cévaër, Françoise. "Interview de Calixthe Beyala." *Revue de Littérature Comparée* 67.1 (January–March 1993): 161–64.
Chemain, Arlette. "L'écriture de Calixthe Beyala: Provocation ou révolte généreuse." *Notre Librairie* 99 (October–November 1989): 162–63.

d'Almeida, Irène A. "Femme? Féministe? Misovire? Les romancières africaines." *Notre Librairie* 117 (April–June 1994): 48– 51.

Diallo, Assiatou B. "Un nouveau roman de Calixthe Beyala." *Amina* 223 (November 1988): 85.

Doumbi-Fakoly. Review of *Tu t'appelleras Tanga*. *Présence Africaine* 148 (1988): 147– 48.

Ellington, Athleen. "L'interdépendance, un discours d'avenir Calixthe Beyala, Werewere Liking, et Simone Schwarz-Bart." *Notre Librairie* 117 (April–June 1994): 102– 06.

Gallimore, Beatrice R. "Le corps: De l'aliénation à la réappropriation: Chez les romancières d'Afrique noire francophone." *Notre Librairie* 117 (April–June 1994): 54– 60.

Genevoix, Sylvie. "Portrait: Calixthe Beyala." *Madame Figaro* July 24, 1993: 18.

Jaccard, Anny-Claire. "Des textes novateurs: La littérature féminine." *Notre Librairie* 99 (October–December 1989): 155–61.

Matateyou, Emmanuel. "Calixthe Beyala: Entre le terroir et l'exil." *French Review* 69.4 (March 1996): 605–15.

Midiohouan, Thécla M. "La parole des femmes." *Figures et fantasmes de la violence dans les littératures francophones de l'Afrique subsaharienne et des Antilles*. Ed. Franca Marcato Falzoni. Bologna: CLUEB, 1991. 149–62.

Mouellé Kombi II, Narcisse. "Calixthe Beyala et son petit prince de Belleville." *Amina* 268 (August 1992): 10–12.

Nacef, Armelle. "Sous le signe de l'amour au féminin." *Jeune Afrique* 1423 (April 13, 1988): 55.

Ndachi Tagne, David. Review of *C'est le soleil qui m'a brûlé*. *Notre Librairie* 100 (January–March 1990): 96–97.

Ndinda, Joseph. "Écriture et discours féminin au Cameroun: Trois générations de romancières." *Notre Librairie* 118 (July–September 1994): 6–12.

Nfah-Abbenyi, Juliana M. *Gender in African Women's Writing: Identity, Sexuality, and Difference*. Bloomington: Indiana University Press, 1997.

———. Review of *Le petit prince de Belleville* and *Maman a un amant*. *Notre Librairie* 118 (July–September 1994): 183.

———. "Woman's Sexuality and the Use of the Erotic in Calixthe Beyala." *1993 African Literature Association Selected Conference Papers*. Ed. Eileen Julien, Aliko Songolo, and Micheline Rice-Maximin. Forthcoming.

Ormerod, Beverley, and Jean-Marie Volet. *Romancières africaines d'expression française: Le sud du Sahara*. Paris: Éditions l'Harmattan, 1994.

Volet, Jean-Marie. "Calixthe Beyala, or The Literary Success of a Cameroonian Woman Living in Paris." *World Literature Today* 67.2 (Spring 1993): 309–14.

JULIANA MAKUCHI NFAH-ABBENYI

DENNIS VINCENT FREDERICK BRUTUS (JOHN BRUIN) (1924–   )

BIOGRAPHY

Dennis Brutus was born on November 28, 1924, in Salisbury, Southern Rhodesia, to South African parents. Francis Henry Brutus and Margaret Winifred Bloemetjie were teachers who, quite early in Brutus's life, moved to the coastal town of Port Elizabeth, where Brutus grew up in the district of Dowerville with his brother Wilfred and sisters Helena and Dolly. Brutus attended school there irregularly, and so his childhood was one of comparative solitude. Perhaps this was exacerbated by the breakup of his parents.

Too soon, the country's racial issues would dominate his mind. While Brutus suggests the strength of his literary readings on his development, school also had an important influence on him: it was a "mixed" school, so the color bar was not as evident as it was outside. Brutus realized that as a result of this influence he escaped state indoctrination.

While at high school, he began writing poetry and initiated and edited a student newspaper, the *Patersonian Spectator*. At age fifteen Brutus attended school regularly and won a City Council bursary to Fort Hare College, Cape; he was one of only two nonwhites to gain university entrance. At Fort Hare Brutus worked on the student newspaper *SANC* (*South African Native College*). Brutus's distinction in English won him a scholarship to do an M.A., but he could not take it up.

In 1948 Brutus became a high-school teacher of English and Afrikaans at St. Thomas Aquinas High School, Port Elizabeth. Though he worked there for a year, he refused to accept the school system's policies. At school he was in charge of sports and was a member of the editorial committee of *Education News*. Following his parents' lead (they were founding members), Brutus joined the Teachers' League of South Africa. He was active with the league in the 1940s and 1950s. After St. Thomas Aquinas Brutus worked at his old school, Paterson High, as senior English Master, and he returned to poetry after a love affair with a former student. Parents, education, and experience, therefore, as well as apartheid laws, were all influencing Brutus's direction.

In 1950 Brutus married May Jaggers, with whom he has eight children. From 1950 Brutus found himself, his family, and his students confronting increasingly more horrific laws. "Letters to the Editor" by Brutus appeared in a Port Elizabeth newspaper, as did his first published "mature" poem, thus giving him an outlet for his anger at the system; articles also appeared under a variety of *noms de plume* in the Port Elizabeth *Evening Post* and the *Herald*. Perhaps the most significant early piece (written in 1959) was "Sports Test for South Africa," as it defines the area of combat that Brutus would make his own: only in Atlanta's 1996 Olympics were South African athletes permitted to make a full return.

In 1955 Brutus helped establish the Co-ordinating Committee for International Relations in Sport to convince international sports bodies to associate only with interracial South African organizations. Brutus chose this method to assault the system, and with novelist Alan Paton as patron, Brutus, as secretary, founded the South African Sports Association (SASA) in October 1958. The organization's goal was to draw attention to South Africa's infringement of the Olympic Charter and to advocate nonracial sports. SASA was soon noticed, and Brutus fell under the scrutiny of the Special Branch. Undoubtedly, the attention of the latter was due to Brutus's lead in SASA's first victory: the ability to persuade the West Indies cricket team to cancel a trip to South Africa in October 1959.

The Sharpeville massacre of 1960 and the ensuing state of emergency may have contributed most fully to Brutus's active participation in the resistance. By 1960 the limited output of poetry became political too, through an intermingling of love for South Africa and for a young white woman with whom he was having an affair at the time. Forbidden to teach, write, and publish and fired from his teaching position in 1961, he was banned under the Suppression of Communism Act. Ironically, the same legal system that brought about the Republic of South Africa was denying the existence of an exemplary inhabitant. Brutus moved to Johannesburg to work as a secretary in a private school, Central High School, Johannesburg, for one year. From 1962 to 1963 he studied law at the University of the Witwatersrand. A further order that prevented the reproduction of writings by Brutus in any way was issued in July 1962. SASA became South African Non-Racial Open (later Olympic) Committee (SANROC) in 1962, and Brutus was placed under house arrest, pending trial, for his involvement in the organization. In 1963 South Africa was suspended from the 1964 Tokyo games.

The year 1963 saw some of Brutus's poems published in Ruth First's journal *Fighting Talk* and then his arrest. Brutus escaped in September while on bail. After leaving Swaziland legally, he was arrested at the Mozambique border by Portuguese secret police and handed over to the South African security police.

Brutus attempted to escape again, fearing that his arrest was not known to other activists and that his treatment at the hands of the police would reflect this fact. He was shot in the back. Hospitalization was followed by eighteen months of hard labor, including time on Robben Island.

Brutus was placed under house arrest in Port Elizabeth upon his release from prison and received a further ban on writing. This situation gave rise to *Letters to Martha*. The banning order and John Harris's execution severely weakened SANROC's activities in South Africa. On July 31, 1966, after a year under house arrest, Brutus arrived in London with his wife and children on an exit permit (that is, if he returned to South Africa, he would be subject to arrest). His decision to leave South Africa was based on renewing the fight against apartheid.

In London Brutus worked as a journalist and teacher, compiled a collection of Arthur Nortje's poems for Heinemann, and assembled *Letters to Martha* with Cosmo Pieterse, who selected the poems. A return to overt action occurred when Brutus was charged, and released, after he interrupted a tennis game at Wimbledon that featured the South African Cliff Drysdale. The previous week, Wilfred Brutus had been charged with disturbing the peace. As a result, when charged with the demonstration at Wimbledon, Dennis Brutus was also mistakenly charged with "violating his probation" because the police took him for his brother. The case was appealed and counterappealed until, funded by International Defence and Aid Fund (IDAF), Brutus took it to the House of Lords. In a decision entitled *Cousins vs. Brutus*, the Lords ruled in Brutus's favor and established a precedent for the right to demonstrate in public places.

Travels by the exile on a number of issues began: in January 1968, to Cuba for a cultural congress; in February 1970, to Texas for a colloquium on "The Black Experience"; and in March to testify before the United Nations Special Committee on Apartheid; he then visited Algiers for the Panafrican Arts Festival. He became a visiting professor at the University of Denver in September 1970. Brutus intended to return to the United Kingdom permanently; however, the year's stay at Denver revealed America to be a greater power base. On Brutus's return to London, four offers of employment in the United States arrived.

In 1970 South Africa was excluded from the Olympic Games, as was Rhodesia in 1972. In 1973 Brutus was a guest of the People's Republic of China (PRC). This visit was an added catalyst for Brutus's interest in minimalist poetry. From 1974 to 1975 Brutus was a visiting professor at the University of Texas at Austin. The African Literature Association (ALA) was founded at this time, with Brutus organizing the first conference and being elected the first president. In June 1974 Brutus was an African National Congress (ANC) delegate at the Sixth Pan-African Congress in Dar Es Salaam, Tanzania. He also broadcast to the people of South Africa on the ANC radio station in Lusaka. From 1975 to 1985 Brutus worked as a visiting professor in the Department of English at Northwestern University, and his well-publicized battle for asylum in the United States began. *Index on Censorship* notes that Brutus had to surrender his United Kingdom passport when Zimbabwe became independent. Brutus was ordered to leave the United States; he appealed, but the appeal was refused because "his waiver of excludability—had expired" (Ralph-Bowman, 13). The Reagan administration seemed determined to rid itself of Brutus's criticisms during the period of "constructive engagement" with South Africa. However, on September 6, 1983, Brutus was granted asylum in the United States.

In 1986 Brutus moved to the University of Pittsburgh, where he continues to teach and is the former director of the Department of Black Community, Education, Research, and Development. Activities continue in the form of prefaces and introductions to volumes on South Africa, in his perennial attendance and participation in the ALA, and in his chairing the important series of symposia on "Post Apartheid South Africa." One reason for this series of symposia is to address the limited quantity of forethought about the "reconstruction" of South African society after apartheid. The planning that had been undertaken was by a small group, an idea that displeases the egalitarian in Brutus.

Brutus's return to South Africa occurred in July 1991 for the South African Committee on Olympic Sport (SACOS) conference in Durban, where he received an award of merit for antiapartheid work. In an interview with Sondra Gair, Brutus talked briefly of the personal experience of return: "I would say that . . . for the majority of people, and particularly the non-whites, the blacks, life has become worse" (National Public Radio).

MAJOR WORKS AND THEMES

While in prison, Brutus learned that Mbari had published his first book, *Sirens Knuckles Boots*. Dennis Williams of Mbari, against Brutus's advice, chose to mix love poems and political poems in the volume rather than opting for a unidimensional volume. The volume won Brutus the 1962 Mbari Prize, but he refused the money because the prize was restricted to blacks only. The American writer Paul Theroux provided one of the first critiques of the collection; in "Voices out of the Skull," Theroux described Brutus's work as thematically centered on freedom. Theroux concluded that Brutus's poetry was remarkable for its political conviction. Many of these poems, as is the case with the majority of Brutus's works, are untitled because he thinks that they are self-explanatory. The volume has been well received critically. Clarity and sophistication in statement as well as the control and economy of form produce a dense volume of "metaphysical" poems.

Letters to Martha was published in 1968. These poems are based on Brutus's prison experiences and are written to his sister-in-law; Brutus's brother was in Robben Island prison at the time serving forty-five months for antiapartheid activities. This volume met with critical praise for individual poems, but many critics felt that the lack of chronological flow diminished the book, while exasperating the reader and weakening the political impact of the experiences described. Myrna Blumberg, for example, admired the "deft simplicity" of the first part, while C. J. Driver criticized the "unnecessarily polysyllabic, formless . . . generalised and generalising nature of several of the poems" (Driver, 109). It is most certainly an admirable work in the form and content of the individual letters. Individual experience contains an element of the communal experience, but the letter format, ingenious in its revolt against the banning order, is not accessible to a large readership. If not fully successful, the volume is the work of a writer nearing the end of his apprenticeship.

Poems from Algiers (nine poems) was published in 1970, as was *Thoughts Abroad*. The first volume is a mimeographed pamphlet of handwritten poems marked by an "oblique" and "indirect" approach to self-assessment. The poems are uneven in poetic quality; the first, "And I Am Driftwood," is the best in its measured flow and differentiation of the exile from those at/with home. The latter volume was published under the pseudonym of John Bruin (Bruin is Afrikaans for a nonwhite person) so that copies could be sent to South Africa, where Brutus's writing was still under a banning order. Brutus and the critic Bernth Lindfors established Troubadour Press to publish the work. *Thoughts Abroad*, which is an incomplete allusion to Browning's "Home Thoughts from Abroad," clearly reflects the state of exile. Brutus's penchant for punning also evokes a Sinatra-esque thought of "a broad," reflecting the parallel in Brutus's poetry between a woman and South Africa. Each poem carries a place name, a locale from which the experience or reflection was elicited. This form of labeling underscores the poet's prolonged exile, his travels to advance the cause of antiapartheid groups, and, not insignificantly, the poet's lack of a home. These poems are, then, produced in flight (literally); they evoke a sense of the place visited; they suggest, through absence, the homeland that was Brutus's rightful subject. Indeed, the sensuous nature of several of the descriptions is a reminder of the earlier verse, where woman is used as a metaphor for the persona's engagement with his land. In *Thoughts Abroad*, not surprisingly, the connection is never fully made with the new landscapes. Nadine Gordimer offered an early positive review of the volume. Copies were available in South Africa until the publication of *A Simple Lust*, which ultimately gave away Bruin's real identity. Brutus remembers the Troubadour Press as successful in that a reasonable number of volumes were sold to cover costs.

Cosmo Pieterse published some of Brutus's poetry in the influential *Seven South African Poets* (1971). *A Simple Lust* (1973) offered new and selected poems from *Sirens Knuckles Boots, Poems from Algiers*, and *Thoughts Abroad* as well as a reordered *Letters to Martha*. *A Simple Lust* is Brutus's most important collection because it provided a retrospective of his career to date. Revisions to earlier poems, as has been noted by G. D. Killam, reveal a more assured editorial sense, while the reordering of *Letters* answered and nullified the criticism of that earlier volume. Paul Kameen emphasizes the "more convincing, and often poignant" (298) nature of Brutus' meditative work in this volume, while cautioning poet and reader against those poems that offer numerous unrealizable possibilities because they tend toward the diffuse, abstract, and unfocused sentiment.

China Poems and *Strains* were published in 1975. *China Poems* represents only Brutus's drafts, as many of the poems written in China were given to the PRC as a gift when he left. These pieces lack the natural images found in traditional *chueh chu*. Most are devoid of personal emotion, offering instead uncritical political statements of a general nature. Brutus gave up writing for a time after the publication of this pamphlet, as he had done in the past when he felt that the writing was obvious and effortless. He also felt that there were too many problems he had to address at that time before he could write. His need was to find out where he was and to act. For Brutus the first principle is the fight against injustice. The art may suffer on occasion, but for good reason:

In order for me to make a total commitment to poetry, I would have to remake myself. This is not impossible, in the sense that I could wholly shut out, say, my political activity, my organising work, my sport, the kind of chores I do from day to day with this or that committee, and so on. I think it would not be impossible, but it would be immoral. This is what really stops me: that a total commitment to the craft of poetry, with the kind of integrity which that implies, would do damage to what I now regard as essential to integrity for me. Which means social concern. (Lindfors, "Somehow," 51)

Stubborn Hope preceded the announcement of Brutus's receipt of the 1979 Kenneth Kaunda Humanism Award by one year. Goodwin and Amuta represent the two principal positions critics have taken over this text. Goodwin sees the volume as "carelessly arranged," even repeating "one poem" (22); he argues that they "are crude poems obviously designed—for political rallies," (23), whereas his "earliest poems are bejewelled metaphysical artefacts in imposed forms" (27). Amuta, on the other hand, advances a positive review of the poems, placing a Marxist emphasis on Lindfors's earlier espousal (which ended with *Strains*) of Brutus's "Dialectical Development."

Brutus is merely exploring the general through the specific by stressing their dialectical relatedness. *Stubborn Hope* represents an advancement, politically, on Brutus' earlier verse. . . . In *Stubborn Hope* . . . it would appear that the experience of exile and the compelling need for urgent militant action against apartheid forces him to abandon his earlier approach in favour of more direct, declamatory and structurally uncomplicated verse. (179, 180)

Goodwin's analysis, which also parallels Lindfors's sense of Brutus's direction, is the more balanced. Ultimately, the choices and the changes in expression are aimed principally at a non–South African audience, one that is aware of the injustices of apartheid, but also one that has a developed critical sensibility. Perhaps, now that Brutus's banning order is lifted, the South African masses will be more receptive to the new aesthetic in his poetry. Brutus's *Stubborn*

Hope fits Amuta's specific prescriptions about art. Brutus, on the other hand, sees that "there is no uncommitted writing. . . . You have to decide which side you are on: there is always a side" (Brutus, "Literature and Commitment," 81). Brutus's commitment is a commitment to "recovering our humanity" (82), whether in early metaphysical work or more recent and overt political statement. In *Stubborn Hope* the writing is clear and direct; while the volume lacks literary experimentation, it compensates with a consistent and dogged concern for the exposure of injustice, a call for change. Some of the best pieces in this collection are the meditations on people who have shared in apartheid's suffering, for example, his children's loss of a father (4).

Salutes and Censures was published in Nigeria in 1982. It marks a return to an African publisher, as well as a broadening of material, but like *China Poems*, it is aesthetically weak. Much of Brutus's poetry in exile has been occasional poetry.

Later verse commemorates real martyrs, victims, and heroes as well as their battles, defeats, and causes. Brutus's writing is an aesthetic experience because of the insight and value it reveals at the core of political events, experiences, and the people involved. The resonance found in the poetry is due to the fact that Brutus writes to life. Thus the poems are catalysts that refresh commitment, not package it for storage. Above all else, these occasional poems provide intellectual, cultural, and social validation of important issues, items needed in a society dominated by mass media.

Both *A Simple Lust* and *Stubborn Hope* were unbanned in South Africa in 1988. The year 1989 also brought forth *Airs and Tributes*, a chapbook of seventeen judiciously selected poems. Concern with place and its experiential value remains a consistent thread with his earlier work. There is a return to the precision of *Sirens Knuckles Boots* and *Letters to Martha*, the opposition of reasons for hope and the necessity of continued resistance. These poems are kin to "Sequence for South Africa" first published in *South African Voices*, then reprinted in *Stubborn Hope: "Victory Edition"*: deliberated and worked-upon meditations that affirm the poet's maturity, the balance of the poetic with the political.

Still the Sirens suggests a cycle, a return to the first volume. The poems, again, are occasional in nature, representing a slim chapbook of Brutus's concerns and poetics throughout his career. Many pieces address comrades and family felled on the path to a victory that remains incomplete for Brutus. "Endurance" is the most significant and complex poem.

CRITICAL RECEPTION

Brutus's work, as McLuckie and Colbert's annotated bibliography confirms, has been widely reviewed and analyzed. Critical reception internationally confirms the impact and longevity of the first major volume, *A Simple Lust*. Too little critical work has been undertaken with respect to Brutus's numerous writings for the press. This work needs to be collected into an accessible volume because of its historical and human significance. Relatedly, a critical biography, placing the poems in the context of the activism, is much needed. Collections of Brutus's writings are available at the Michael J. Herskovits Library of Africana, Northwestern University; the Schomburg Center Collection, New York; the School of Oriental and African Studies, University of London; and the Centre for Southern African Studies, University of York, England.

BIBLIOGRAPHY

Selected Works by Dennis Vincent Frederick Brutus

Poetry

Airs and Tributes. Ed. Gil Otto. Introd. Samuel Allen. Camden, N.J.: Whirlwind Press, 1989.
China Poems. Austin: African and Afro-American Studies and Research Center, University of Texas at Austin, 1975.
"For the Prisoners of South Africa" (a broadsheet). n.p.: Slash and Burn Press, 1986.
Letters to Martha, and Other Poems from a South African Prison. London: Heinemann Educational Books, 1968.
Poems from Algiers. Austin: African and Afro-American Research Institute, University of Texas at Austin, 1970.
Salutes and Censures. Enugu, Nigeria: Fourth Dimension Publ. Co., 1982.
"Sequence for South Africa." *South African Voices.* Ed. Bernth Lindfors. Occasional Publication 11. Austin, TX: African and Afro-American Studies and Research Center, 1975. 31–34.
A Simple Lust: Collected Poems of South African Jail and Exile Including "Letters to Martha." London: Heinemann Educational Books; New York: Hill and Wang, 1973.
Sirens Knuckles Boots. Ibadan, Nigeria: Mbari Productions; Evanston, IL: Northwestern University Press, 1963.
Still the Sirens. Santa Fe: Pennywhistle Press, 1993.
(John Bruin) *Strains.* Ed. Wayne Kamin and Chip Dameron. Del Valle, TX.: Troubadour Press, 1975.
Stubborn Hope. Washington, DC: Three Continents Press, 1978; London: Heinemann, 1978. Reprint. London: Heinemann, 1991.
Stubborn Hope: "Victory Edition": New Poems and Selected Poems from China Poems and Strains. Augmented ed. Washington, DC: Three Continents Press, 1983.
(John Bruin) *Thoughts Abroad.* Del Valle, TX: Troubadour Press, 1970.

Nonfiction

Brutus and Robert Baker. "The Conference on International Sport, Politics, Racism, and Apartheid—An Overview." *Journal of Sport and Social Issues* 2.2 (Fall/Winter 1978): 4–6.
Denis [*sic*] Brutus. "Cultural Liberation and the African Revolution." *World Inequality: Origins and Perspectives of the World System.* Ed. Immanuel Wallerstein. Montreal: Black Rose Books, 1975. 152–156.

"Founding the A.L.A.: African Publishing Houses: A Proposal." *Antioch Review* 38 (Spring 1980): 233–236.

"From the Introduction to *Salutes and Censures*." *From South Africa*. Ed. David Bunn et al. Chicago: University of Chicago Press, 1988. 363–367.

"In Memoriam: Arthur Nortje, 1942–1970." *Research in African Literatures* 2 (1971): 26–27.

"International Declaration: U.N. Action—Summary." *Journal of Sport and Social Issues* 2.2 (Fall/Winter 1978): 1–3.

"Introduction to 'Two Unpublished Poems by Arthur Nortje.' " *Gar* 33 (February 1979): 25.

(Panelist). "Literature and Commitment in South Africa." *Contemporary Black South African Literature: A Symposium*. Ed. Bernth Lindfors. Washington, DC: Three Continents Press, 1975, revised and augmented in 1985.

"Poetry of Suffering: The Black Experience." *Ba Shiru* 4.2 (1973): 1–10.

"Protest against Apartheid." *Protest and Conflict in African Literature*. Ed. Cosmo Pieterse and Donald Munro. London: Heinemann Educational Books, 1969. 93–100.

D.A. "Sports Test for South Africa." *Africa South* 3.4 (July–September 1959): 35–39.

"The Sportsman's Choice." *Apartheid, a Collection of Writings on South African Racism by South Africans*. Ed. Alex La Guma. London: Lawrence and Wishart, 1972.

"[Statement for a Cultural Boycott]." *Index on Censorship* 4.1 (Spring 1975): 42.

"Testimony." *South African Prisons and the Red Cross Investigation* (white paper). London: Christian Action Publications for International Defence and Aid Fund, 1967.

"Two Poems by Nortje, with a Note by Dennis Brutus." *African Literature Today 10: Retrospect and Prospect*. London and Ibadan: Heinemann; New York: Africana, 1979. 231–232.

Witness. United Nations Unit on Apartheid, Department of Political and Security Council Affairs. Special Committee on Apartheid Hears Mr. Dennis Brutus, no. 7/70. New York, March 1970.

Panel discussant for various sessions. *The Writer in Modern Africa: African-Scandinavian Writers' Conference* (Stockholm, 1967). Ed. Per Wastberg. New York: African Publ. Corp., 1969.

Selected Studies of Dennis Vincent Frederick Brutus (Mainly Post–1975)

Abasiekong, Daniel. "Poetry Pure and Applied: Rabearivelo and Brutus." *Transition* 5.23 (1965): 45–48.

Abrahams, Cecil. "Aesthetics and Protest in South African Literature." *MANA* 5.2 (1980); *ACLCLSB* 6.1 (1982).

———. "The South African Writer in a Changing Society." *Matatu* 2.3–4 (1988): 32–43.

Alvarez-Pereyre, Jacques. "The First Generation of Committed Black Poets." *The Poetry of Commitment in South Africa*. Trans. Clive Wake. London: Heinemann Educational Books, 1984. 130–145.

Amuta, Chidi. "Private Experience as Public Protest: Dennis Brutus' *Stubborn Hope*." *The Theory of African Literature*. London and New Jersey: Zed Books, 1989. 178–185.

Asein, S. O. "Troubadours, Wanderers, and Other Exiles." *Comparative Approaches to Modern African Literature*. Ed. S. O. Asein. Ibadan: Dept. of English, 1983. 125–132.

Barnett, Ursula A. *A Vision of Order: A Study of Black South African Literature in English (1914–1980)*. London: Sinclair Browne; Amherst: University of Massachusetts Press, 1983. 89–100.

Benson, Peter. *"Black Orpheus," 'Transition,'' and Modern Cultural Awakening in Africa*. Berkeley, Los Angeles, and London: University of California Press, 1986. 27, 31, 42, 59, 123, 126, 282.

Blumberg, Myrna. "Of Degradation and Joy." *The Guardian Weekly* 100. 10 (March 6, 1969): 114.

Diuto. "The Life and Loves of a Mirthless Troubadour: The Poetry of Dennis Brutus." *Muse* 12 (1980): 50, 53.

Donne, John. "Remembering Dennis Brutus." *Medu Art Ensemble Newsletter* 2.2: 15–20.

Driver, C. J. "The View from Makana Island: Some Recent Prison Books from South Africa." *Journal of Southern African Studies* 2.1 (October 1975): 109–119.

Duerden, Dennis, and Cosmo Pieterse, eds. *African Writers Talking*. 2nd ed. London: Heinemann, 1975. 52–61.

Egudu, Romanus N. "African Literature and Social Problems." *Canadian Journal of African Studies* 9.3 (1975): 421–447.

———. "Pictures of Pain: The Poetry of Dennis Brutus." *Aspects of South African Literature*. Ed. Christopher Heywood. London: Heinemann Educational Books; New York: Africana Publ. Corp., 1976. 131–144.

Elimimian, Isaac I. "Form and Meaning in the Poetry of Dennis Brutus." *Literary Half-Yearly* 28.1 (July 1986): 70–78.

Ezenwa-Ohaeto. "Art in Pain: A Study of the Dangers and Prospects of Protest Poetry through Two Representative South African Poets." *Literary Half-Yearly* 25.1 (1984): 17–38.

Gair, Sondra. National Public Radio interview with Dennis Brutus. WBEZ/Chicago. July 26, 1991.

Gardner, Colin. "Brutus and Shakespeare." *Research in African Literatures* 15.3 (Fall 1984): 354–364.

Goodwin, Ken. "Dennis Brutus." *Understanding African Poetry: A Study of Ten Poets*. London: Heinemann Educational Books, 1982. 1–29.

Imfeld, Al. "Dennis Brutus—Apartheid und Atomkraft vernichten uns." *Vision und Waffe: Afrikanische Autoren, Themen, Traditionen*. Zurich: Unionsverlag, 1981. 295–304.

Jacobs, J. U. "In a Free State: The Exile in South African Poetry." *Momentum: On Recent South African Writing*. Ed. M. J. Daymond et al. Pietermaritzburg, South Africa: University of Natal Press, 1984. 243–259.

Kameen, Paul. *Bestsellers* 33.13 (October 1, 1973): 298.

Katz, Jane. *Artists in Exile*. New York: Stein and Day, 1983. 31–42.

Killam, G. D. "*A Simple Lust*: Selection, Structure and Style." *Cultural Perspectives on Dennis Brutus*. Ed. Craig W. McLuckie and Patrick J. Colbert. Colorado Springs: Three Continents Press, 1995. 86–98.

Lapchick, Richard. *The Politics of Race and International Sport: The Case of South Africa*. Westport, Conn.: Greenwood Press, 1975.

Legum, Colin, and Margaret Legum. *The Bitter Choice: Eight South Africans' Resistance to Tyranny.* Cleveland and New York: World Publ. Co., 1968. 151–162.

Lindfors, Bernth. "Dennis Brutus and His Critics" and "Dialectical Development in the Poetry of Dennis Brutus." *The Blind Men and the Elephant and Other Essays in Biographical Criticism.* Adelaide: Centre for Research in the New Literature in English, The Flinders University of South Australia, 1987. 14–25 and 26–36, respectively.

———. "Dennis Brutus' Mousey Tongue" (from the symposium on South African Literature and the inaugural meeting of the African Literature Association held at the University of Texas, Austin, March 19–22, 1975). *World Literature Written in English* 15: 7–16.

———. "John Bruin: South African Enigma in Del Valle, Texas." *Africa Today* 18.4 (1974): 72–77.

———. " 'Somehow Tenderness Survives': Dennis Brutus Talks about His Life and Poetry." *Benin Review* 1.1 (1974): 44–55.

McLuckie, Craig W., and Patrick J. Colbert, eds. *Critical Perspectives on Dennis Brutus.* Colorado Springs, CO: Three Continents Press, 1995.

Meester, Ria de. "An Introduction to Dennis Brutus' Prison Poems." *Restant* 8.2 (1980): 47–56.

Moyana, T. T. "The Problems of a Creative Writer in South Africa." *Aspects of South African Literature.* Ed. Christopher Heywood. London: Heinemann, 1976. 85–98.

Mphahlele, Ezekiel. "Contemporary African Literature." *Lincoln University African Center Quarterly Review* 1.2 (1969): 1–28.

Ndu, Pol. "Passion and Poetry in the Works of Dennis Brutus." *Black Academy Review* 2.1–2 (Spring–Summer 1971): 41–54.

Ngara, Emmanuel. *Ideology and Form in African Poetry.* London: James Currey, 1990. 57, 131–133, 143, 192–193, 199.

Nkondo, Gessler Moses. "Dennis Brutus and the Revolutionary Idea." *Ufahamu* 10.3 (1981): 78–91.

———. "Dennis Brutus: The Domestication of a Tradition."*World Literature Today* 55.1 (Winter 1981): 32–40.

Nkosi, Lewis. *Tasks and Masks.* London: Longman, 1981. 101, 114, 116–167.

Ogundele, Wole. "The Exile's Progress: Dennis Brutus' Poetry in the First Phase of His Exile." *Commonwealth Essays and Studies* 10.2 (Spring 1988): 88–97.

Ogunyemi, Chikwenye Okonjo. "The Song of the Caged Bird: Contemporary African Prison Poetry." *Ariel* 13.4 (October 1982): 65–84.

Ojaide, Tanure. "The Troubadour: The Poet's Persona in the Poetry of Dennis Brutus." *Ariel* 17.1 (January 1986): 55–69.

Onuekwusi, Jasper A. "Pain and Anguish of a South African Poet: Dennis Brutus and South African Reality." *Literary Criterion* 23.1–2 (1988): 59–68.

Ralph-Bowman, Mark. "Dennis Brutus: Shall I Be Deported from the USA?" *Index on Censorship* 12.3 (1983): 13–16.

Riemenschneider, Dieter. "Yet Somewhere Lingers the Stubborn Hope." *Salutes: Selected Essays.* Ed. Monika Idehen. Evanston, IL: Troubadour Press/Whirlwind Press, 1994. 121–128.

Salt, M. J. "On the Business of Literary Criticism: With Special Reference to Bahadur Tejani's Article: 'Can the Prisoner Make a Poet?' " *African Literature Today* 7 (London: Heinemann, 1975): 128–141.

Shava, Piniel Viriri. "From Sophiatown to Robben Island: Protest Writings in the 1950s and 1960s." *A People's Voice: Black South African Writing in the Twentieth Century*. London: Zed Books, 1989. 38–47.

Tejani, Bahadur. "Can the Prisoner Make a Poet? A Critical Discussion of *Letters to Martha* by Dennis Brutus." *African Literature Today* 6 (London: Heinemann, 1973): 130–144.

Theroux, Paul. "Voices out of the Skull." *Black Orpheus* 20 (August 1966): 41–58.

Ungar, Andre. "South Africa." *Resistance Against Tyranny*. Ed. Eugene Heimler. London: Routledge and Kegan Paul, 1966. 31–33.

CRAIG W. MCLUCKIE

DRISS CHRAÏBI (1926–)

BIOGRAPHY

Driss Chraïbi, a prolific writer, is considered to be the father of the modern Moroccan novel. Born in 1926 in El Jadida, Morocco, he attended Koranic school as a young boy. His father, a successful tea merchant, was orphaned by age thirteen with seven siblings and no skills or education. Although he maintained a Muslim household, the father perceived Western education as a means to a modern Morocco. When the family moved from El Jadida to Casablanca, he sent his sons, including Driss, to the French Lycée. A good student, Chraïbi was interested in writing and literature and holds fond memories of his teachers. As an adolescent, he became aware of social injustices that are consistently reflected in his work. As a young man, he studied chemical engineering in France and considered becoming a doctor. Continuing to reside in France with his first wife and their children, he devoted himself to writing in 1952 and published his first novel, *Le passé simple*, in 1954. In 1956 he began writing for French radio and television and has written for many journals and newspapers. He taught in Canada for a year after his second divorce but returned to live in France. However, his unabated love of Morocco is manifested in much of his writing. Although he is critical of the injustices within French society and perpetuated by France in North Africa, his humanism draws on French and Western culture as a source of enrichment rather than effacement. He is a writer who has been the center of much controversy and misunderstanding; his continuing writing career includes fifteen novels and two children's books. As with many Maghreb writers, his works draw heavily from his own life and probe the writer's role as healer and educator in modern society. Like other modern Maghreb writers, Chraïbi was influenced by the American writer William Faulkner.

Chraïbi's novels place themselves in both a universal and national context by their references to other literary works, to his other works, and to historical and contemporary political events.

MAJOR WORKS AND THEMES

Chraïbi's first novel, *Le passé simple*, caused a furor when it was published in 1954 and continues to elicit critical discourse. The novel, which begins realistically, tells of a young French-educated man's revolt against his tyrannical Moslem father. It depicts the clash of two cultures as well as two generations. Through the harsh perception of the adolescent protagonist, the novel is a revealing indictment of the strict and often hypocritical Islamic traditions that hold people prisoners from finding self-fulfillment. The young man, a bright student, riddled with patricidal fantasies, sympathizes with his submissive mother. While Driss accompanies his mother on a visit to her family, the father strikes the younger and sickly brother twice in the head for helping Driss take the necessary finances for his mother's trip. Consequently, the younger brother dies and Driss can no longer abide his father. He is equally disillusioned by his mother, who makes herself up in an effort to seduce the father in order to have another child. He begins his odyssey of revolt by emptying the father's storehouse and by revealing to the family the hypocritical behavior of the father, such as his illegitimate children and his cabinet of alcohol. The father banishes Driss from the home. At this point, the novel departs from its realistic style, and the narrative becomes self-conscious of its own evolvement into the form of a novel. The narrator begins to intrude on the plot narrative to comment on the re-creation of his life as a novel and to include observations on Moroccan society. When Driss is thrown into the streets, the range of the novel moves with its protagonist out of the domestic situation into the streets of Morocco. Driss turns to his friends for solace but is refused their hospitality; subsequently he realizes the powerful and far-reaching extent of his father's influence. After passing his exams with distinction, Driss returns home only to find that his mother has committed suicide in his absence. The father blames Driss for planting the seeds of revolt in his mother. Yet in a touching scene, the father begins to treat Driss as an adult in an effort at reconciliation. He confides to Driss, as a means of explanation, his life and rather unhappy but respectable marriage to the mother. The father shares his hopes for Driss's future and his disappointment in his other sons. The novel closes with Driss's departure for France, which he, like many other young Moroccans, conceives of as the land of liberty. The novel's final image is Driss's urine falling from the plane to France on the heads of those back home.

Chraïbi's second novel, *Les Boucs*, is a bitter portrayal of the Arab immigrants living in poverty in France. The title refers to the French racist terminology for the immigrants, and the novel's bitter realism and scenes of the Boucs' campsites are reminiscent of Gorky's *Lower Depths*. The novel's protagonist is Walid, an Algerian writer who has a son, Fabrice, by a French woman, Simone. Upon Walid's release from prison for assault, he returns to the squalor of poverty. His son is dying of meningitis, the disease whose menacing threat haunts Chraïbi's later novels and also claimed the author's youngest brother, Hamid, at the age of nine. As in *Le passé simple*, the tragedy of youth and hope is the indictment of society and the catalyst that destroys human relationships. Walid's profound despair moves him into a course of self-destruction. Mac O'Mac, an expert on Arab culture, is an acrid portrayal of the publishing industry, and some critics read his character as a reproach of the French writer François Mauriac. Mac considers publishing Walid's manuscript, but in the process, he callously dismisses Walid by purchasing an airplane ticket back to Algeria for Walid. Mac seduces Simone with small luxuries such as cordials, cigarettes, and, ironically, a story. Walid turns to his friend Rauss and wine for refuge. Rauss introduces Walid to the prostitute Isabelle, an orphaned survivor of the war and Nazi occupation. She has no pity for Walid and tells him to stop blaming others. She represents some hope for Walid, who is at home neither with the Boucs, who treat him like a Christian and do not understand his desire to write his story, nor the French pseudo-intellectuals. The novel, whose plot does not follow a linear time frame, closes with the image of a Young Arab who could be Walid whose family sells their last goat to finance his trip to France at the urging of a Priest, which suggests a cycle of displacement and the devastation of French hypocrisy.

Chraïbi's next three works move from the realism of *Les Boucs* to a more symbolic realm but preserve his concern with the political realities and spirituality of man. Each of these works explores the role of the individual caught in a historical whirlwind of modernization that erodes an innate spiritualism and in the crowd's engulfment of individuality. *L'âne* (1956) is set in Morocco during the colonization. The novel explores the despair caused by the dashed hopes and illusions of freedom in the modern world and suggests the possibilities of drawing on a heritage of spirituality as a source of strength. The novel depicts its characters during a rapidly changing Morocco. The main character, Moussa, is a rural barber who leaves his donkey behind and takes the train for the very first time. In leaving his previous occupation behind, he finds a prophetic mission in the midst of confusion and changes. The novel's ending, the lynching of the passive and mystical Moussa by a mob that later builds a mausoleum to its scapegoat, foreshadows the later political fable, *La foule*. In 1958 Chraïbi published *De tous les horizons*, a provocative collection of stories and parables that the author refers to as a novel, and that was republished in 1986 as *D'autres voix* in Morocco. *La foule* contains both political satire and comedy in its examination of the illusion of leadership and the role of political discourse in the creation of both a communal reality and the future. In the novel, Mathurin, a retiring history teacher, finds himself President, and his presidency is covered in the African press by the two twin journalists who have taken great care with their attire but cannot read or write.

Chraïbi returns to the milieu of *Le passé simple* and his protagonist "Driss" in *Succession ouverte*, published in 1962. The novel opens with Driss's visit to a doctor because he is experiencing an anxious restlessness and has become unpleasant with his loved ones. His health problems are a manifestation of his crisis over the value of civilization. The crisis of the "prodigal son" who has previously refused his father's financial support even though he has faced many difficulties in France is a filial premonition. While Driss is in the doctor's office, he receives word of his father's death. Upon his return to Morocco for his father's funeral, the novel introduces an endearing panorama of Moroccan society through his diverse brothers and aged but lively mother. His father's death marks the end of one era, and his brothers are left with the legacy of decolonization. Overtly his father leaves Driss out of his tape-recorded legacy, but he actually sends Driss on a quest as his final paternal gesture. Before returning to France, Driss begins to appreciate his father's foresight, and his death quest reaffirms their affinity rather than severance.

Un ami viendra vous voir moves out of Morocco and into the modern bourgeois of Paris as two men, a doctor and a talk-show host, examine a young woman's life. A young mother, a documenter for the Institute de Documentation, is haunted by an angst of emptiness. She appears on a national talk show in an effort to find a solution to her alienation, but the experience only increases her sense of isolation. When the cameras and the talk-show host leave, she murders her toddler son and is admitted to a mental hospital. Her assigned middle-aged doctor, who has problems with his own wife and leads a stagnated life that he relieves with food, realizes that her angst is her thirst for life. She, the patient, cures the doctor of his own malaise as they become lovers. The novel, which leaves the reader in the air as to the outcome of the affair, questions our mode of communication, value standards, and perceptions of others in the modern world.

La civilisation, ma mère! (1972) is the affectionate story of a cloistered Arab mother's liberation through education and contact with the Western world. Her education begins at home when her elder son, Nagib, brings a radio into the house, a magic box that speaks and comes to be known as Monsieur Kteu. Her two sons buy her Western clothes and begin to take her on outings, awakening her innate quest for knowledge, life, and justice. She becomes a vital member of the outside community when she enrolls in school for the first time and eventually utilizes her indomitable social skills to organize protests against World War II. The novel ends with the mother and Nagib's departure from Morocco to join Driss in France.

In *Mort au Canada*, Chraïbi returns to the Western world in a novel that recalls *Un ami viendra vous voir*. The novel recounts the failed and poignant love story of the protagonist, a composer and a doctor at a psychiatric clinic. In Canada, the composer meets a young girl of twelve who has lost her father first to divorce and then to death. His relationship with the young girl elicits his painful memories of his failed love affairs and his own neglected children. Despite his pain, the novel is a celebration of the generous human capacity to love and to rejuvenate itself. Like the love affair of *Un ami viendra vous voir*, the novel juxtaposes the psychological idea of health and the instinctive thirst for life.

Driss's epic Berber trilogy which includes *Une enquête au pays, La Mère du Printemps (L'Oum-er Bia)*, and *naissance à l'aube*, is a monumental tapestry of moods, writing style, and history. The three novels date from the Arab conquest of North Africa to the present. The first novel, *Une enquête au pays*, begins with the arrival of the delightfully humorous Inspector Ali and his superior, the Chief of Police, in the hot and isolated Berber mountains on a mysterious detective mission. Inspector Ali is caught between the ineffective tantrums and advice against any "insectuals" of his chief and the villagers, who have maintained their difficult but hospitable way of life. The comical clash between the modern city dwellers and the mountain Berbers borders on farce but takes an abrupt stylistic and thematic twist when the chief's mission is revealed. In the subsequent role reversal, Ali, who fantasizes about leaving his city life to return to the village life to take a rural wife, finds himself defending the bureaucracy before the village tribunal council in order to save his life. The novel ends with Ali's armed return to the village.

The second novel of the trilogy, *La Mère du Printemps*, is dedicated to the river Oum-er Bia, the mouth of the river that begins in Chraïbi's birthplace, El Jadida. Historical and mythical, the novel of the Berbers begins the journey into the past, to the Arab conquest of North Africa under the banner of Islam in the late 600s. The novel continues the clash between the village and the city and opens with an ironic depiction of the problem of population records that the tribal unit presents for the French bureaucrats. From the historical imposition of colonization, the novel's focus heralds back to the story of Azwan, the ancient tribal leader, and the consistent presence of the river Oum-er Bia. Azwaw, who converts to Islam to save the lives of his tribesmen, vows to keep their Berber identity that is intricately connected to the water and the land. He uses the minaret and call to prayers to warn the other tribes, and, fulfilling the prophecy, his punishment upon being discovered is to have his tongue cut out.

The final novel, *la naissance à l'aube*, which is dedicated to Morocco and its people, continues to discuss the Berbers and their intrinsic relationship to the water. In its completion of the story of Azwan and his modern descendants who are once again displaced by the French colonization, the reader is introduced to the historical Moor conqueror Tarik, who conquered Spain in the name of Islam. The trilogy, which, like many other modern Maghreb novels, does not follow a linear narrative, nevertheless underscores the importance of the past and human spiritual relationships to nature and to each other. The descendant of the mythic and spiritual Berber leader, Azwaw, is a modern-day porter at the train station and card shark at the cafes. The tenets of Islam have not been an effective sword against the spiritual erosion of modern life.

Chraïbi's two most recent novels recall the humor of *La civilisation, ma mère!*

L'inspecteur Ali (1991) introduces the author of the successful Inspector Ali series, and *Une place au soleil* (1993) reintroduces the character, Inspector Ali, in his first detective search. *L'inspecteur Ali*, a domestic comedy of Brahim Orourke and his family's adventures, mischievously brings to life the author at home, at the bank, and at the university. He is under financial pressure to write another novel but is having difficulty finding inspiration upon demand. Simultaneously, his family is preparing for the arrival of their third child and the visit of his wife's British parents. The cultural clash is a pretext for humor in this recent novel. Although *L'inspecteur Ali* depicts life in El Jadida as rather idyllic, the novel refers to the current political turmoil of the Gulf War and the Middle East. The author-protagonist, Orourke, is surprised by his elevated artist stature and decides to write *Le second passé simple*, an obvious reference to the real author's first text. Orourke himself hears the voice of his character Ali during the course of his day. The self-reference highlights the proximity between the author and the text. The references to past literary success and critical debate draw attention to the possible stagnation of literature and criticism that continually reiterates itself. Through his wit, Chraïbi examines serious questions about the adverse effects of literary consumerism. The birth of Orourke and his wife's baby is a humble reminder of the importance of life and creation in the midst of our modern pretentiousness.

Chraïbi's most recent novel, *Une place au soleil*, is the first adventure of Inspector Ali and can be read as the novel Orourke writes in *L'inspecteur Ali*. Inspector Ali is taken from his armed arrival in the Berber mountains that disturbs the community and set in the city, where he reestablishes such time-worn values as justice. His detective novel playfully exploits the character of the "street-smart" and moral detective who has a risqué way with women and is able to see directly to the heart of men. Single-handedly, he reestablishes justice in Morocco when he manages to derail the corrupt plots of the international wealthy and spare the innocent. Inspector Ali cleans house at home as well by ridding himself of his wife, who wants everything that she sees on TV. Although Inspector Ali is dressed in dungarees with a moderate income, he has an appreciation of traditional Oriental music and a worldly knowledge of literature that he often manages to misquote with no loss of significance. Chraïbi plays on the reader's expectations and good-naturedly fulfills them. Naturally, Inspector Ali falls in love with the beautiful and pure Sophia. Like so many of Chraïbi's characters, Inspector Ali gets another chance at life, and his story is a confirmation of human benevolence.

CRITICAL RECEPTION

The reception of the controversial *Le passé simple* was a critical maelstrom. Many of Chraïbi's compatriots saw him as a traitor to the Arab world and referred to the author as an "assassin of hope." For the French conservatives, the novel was a realistic document that depicted the savagery of everyday life in the Arab world that justified their continued presence in Morocco. At one point, the young writer was even moved to deny his early literary efforts. Other critics drew the parallel between the patriarchal authority and the French presence, and still others noted the love for the mother as a manifestation of love for the motherland. Chraïbi's first novel continues to generate critical discussion and interpretation. Although previous critics read the mother's suicide as indicative of her submission, for Moroccan critic Abderrahman Tenkoul, the mother's suicide is her fatal revolt motivated by her sense of dignity. Rather than a passive act, her suicide is an act of defiance. "Elle a voulu la manifester par un geste fatal, subversif. Ni l'éthique sociale, ni l'interdite religieux n'ont pu contraindre sa décision tragique de transformer sa faiblesse en défi absolu" (Tenkoul, 128).

The change of setting and criticism from Morocco to France in Chraïbi's second novel, *Les Boucs*, caused critics to speculate that it was the author's attempt to balance his criticism of the Arab world with a criticism of France. The influence of his treatment of patriarchal oppression, exile, and social injustices is easily evident in the later writings of younger Moroccan writers such as Tahar Ben Jelloun, Mohammed Khaïr-Eddine, and Abdelhak Serhane. The importance of *Le passé simple* and *Les Boucs* as initiating a new era of Maghreb literature cannot be overestimated. The *Souffles* generation, the second generation of modern Moroccan writers, readily proclaim their admiration for Chraïbi and acknowledge his influence on their own writing. Although he claims to be neither a colonist nor a decolonist, Chraïbi has been viewed by younger Maghreb writers as a predecessor in the fight against the cultural reduction to consumer folklore and the artistic void triggered by colonization.

Chraïbi's writing has been referred to as a literature of rupture and alienation. He has been influential in subject matter but also in his style and use of language. His polyphonic novels do not follow a linear temporal structure, which gives freedom to the width and depth of his verbal rendering of the modern world. Although he writes against the stagnation of civilization, his novels celebrate our perpetual ability to rejuvenate. Whether through the violence of his early novels, his symbolic mysticism, his epic scope, or his humor, Chraïbi constantly and humbly reminds us of our basic human dignity and of our obligations to ourselves, others, and our world.

Chraïbi's fight against social oppression and injustices, which has included support of women, has won him the respect and admiration of Arab feminists. He never presumes to speak for women, as some well-meaning writers do, but presents his women characters in light of his generous humanism in all his works, not only in the most obvious example, *La civilisation, ma mère!* His sympathetic treatment of women shows warmth and understanding, as exemplified by the doctor's question in *Un ami viendra vous voir*; the doctor asks the woman's husband if he knows his wife's thoughts, dreams, and desires. The woman's anguish is never minimized or portrayed solely as a middle-class malaise. Chraïbi's compassion toward women is never judgmental; in *Succession ouverte*, when Driss's mother confides to him that a prisoner learns to love her prison, Driss understands rather than promote a different lifestyle.

Unfortunately, the importance of *Le passé simple* and the enormous amount of criticism that it has generated have seemed to overshadow Chraïbi's later work. Yet in all of Chraïbi's novels, there is a great capacity for love and perpetual rebirth of man's spirituality as well as a disparagement of social injustices and individual stagnation. His range of style from epic to comedy is testimony to his versatility. Hopefully, younger critics will continue to appreciate his early works but also begin to focus on his more recent works.

BIBLIOGRAPHY

Works by Driss Chraïbi

Le passé simple. Paris: Éditions Denoël, 1954.
Les Boucs. Paris: Éditions Denoël, 1955.
De tous les horizons. Paris: Denoël, 1958.
L'âne. Paris: Éditions Denoël, 1956.
La foule. Paris: Éditions Denoël, 1961.
Succession ouverte. Paris: Éditions Denoël, 1962.
Un ami viendra vous voir. Paris: Éditions Denoël, 1966.
La civilisation, ma mère! Paris: Éditions Denoël, 1972.
Mort au Canada. Paris: Éditions Denoël, 1974.
Une enquête au pays. Paris: Éditions du Seuil, 1981.
La Mère du Printemps (L'Oum-er Bia). Paris: Éditions du Seuil, 1982.
D'autres voix. El Jadida: Éditions Soden, 1986.
Naissance à l'aube. Paris: Éditions du Seuil, 1986.
L'inspecteur Ali. Paris: Éditions Denoël, 1991.
Une place au soleil. Paris: Éditions Denoël, 1993.

Translations of Works by Driss Chraïbi

Heirs to the Past. London: Heinemann International, 1971.
The Butts. Trans. Hugh A. Harter. Washington, D.C.: Three Continents Press, 1983.
Mother Comes of Age. Trans. Hugh Harter. Washington, D.C.: Three Continents Press, 1984.
Flutes of Death. Trans. Robin Roosevelt. Washington, D.C.: Three Continents Press, 1985.
Mother Spring. Trans. Hugh Harter. Washington, D.C.: Three Continents Press, 1989.
Birth at Dawn. Trans. Ann Woollcombe. Washington, D.C.: Three Continents Press, 1990.
Inspector Ali. Trans. Lara McGlashan. Colorado Springs, Colo.: Three Continents Press, 1994.
Translation of *A Place in the Sun* is forthcoming by Three Continents Press.

Selected Studies of Driss Chraïbi

Accad, Evelyne. *Veil of Shame: The Role of Women in the Contemporary Fiction of North Africa and the Arab World.* Quebec: Editions Naaman, 1978.

Bet, Marie-Therese. "La Littérature maghrébine francophone." *Cahiers de l'Association Internationale des Études Françaises* 44 (May 1992): 67–80.

Kadra-Hadjadji, Houaria. *Contestation et révolte dans l'oeuvre de Driss Chraïbi.* Algers: E.N.A.L., 1986.

Khatibi, Abdelkebir. *Le roman maghrébin.* Rabat: Société Marocaine des Éditeurs Réunis, 1979.

Marx-Scouras, Danielle. "A Literature of Departure: The Cross-Cultural Writing of Driss Chraïbi." *Research in African Literatures* 23.2 (Summer 1992): 131–44.

Sellin, Eric, ed. *Revue CELFAN* 5.2 (February 1986): issue devoted to Driss Chraïbi.

Tenkoul, Abderrahman. *Littérature marocaine d'écriture française.* Casablanca: Afrique Orient, 1985.

LYNNE DUMONT ROGERS

J. P. CLARK-BEKEDEREMO (1935–   )

BIOGRAPHY

Johnson Pepper Clark-Bekederemo, known more commonly as J. P. Clark, was born in Kiagbodo, a bilingual town of Ijo and Urhobo speakers in the Delta State of Nigeria, on April 6, 1935, to Chief Clark Fuludu Bekederemo and his wife Poro. His great-grandfather, Ambakederemo, seems to have played an important role in his literary consciousness. One of the wealthiest men of his time, Chief Ambakederemo had no less than sixty-one wives. This polygamous setting of sibling tensions and rivalries was a real cultural school for Clark, almost all of whose plays involve some form of kinship antagonism. Equally important is his proficiency in the two languages of his native place, giving him access to two separate, if contiguous and related, cultures.

Clark attended primary schools in Okrika, Rivers State, and Otughievwen, Delta State, from 1941 to 1948 before going on to Government College, Ughelli, where he took his Cambridge School Certificate in 1954. After a year as a clerk in the office of the Chief Secretary to the Government of Nigeria, in Lagos, he was admitted to University College, Ibadan. It was at UCI that his literary talents began to flower. In 1957 he founded the *Horn*, a poetry journal where some of his earliest poems appeared. He was also editor of the UCI Students' Union journal, the *Beacon*. He took his B.A. (Honours) degree in English in 1960.

Clark-Bekederemo began his working career as information officer in the Western Regional Ministry of Information in 1960, but the following year he joined the staff of the *Daily Express* as editorial writer and head of features. It was at this time that he published his first two works, *Poems* and *Song of a Goat*, both by Mbari Publications, Ibadan. However, his journalistic career turned out to be brief, for in 1962 he left for Princeton University on a yearlong

Parvin Fellowship. On his return, he was appointed research fellow at the Institute of African Studies, University of Ibadan. While there, he researched and recorded *The Ozidi Saga*, which was to remain unpublished for a decade and a half. The year 1964 was a very fruitful one for Clark, for it witnessed the publication of *Three Plays* by Oxford University Press, which included *Song of a Goat* as well as two new plays, *The Masquerade* and *The Raft*. Also published in 1964 was *America, Their America* by Andre Deutsch. It was also the year of Clark's appointment as lecturer in the Department of English, University of Lagos, of his marriage to Ebun Odutola, and of the birth of their daughter Ebiere.

Clark-Bekederemo published in 1965 a new collection of poems, *A Reed in the Tide*, made up partly of poems from his first collection. It was followed by a new play, *Ozidi*, in 1966, the year he became coeditor, with Abiola Irele, of *Black Orpheus*, a journal of African literature and culture. These were to be his last major literary activities for about half a decade because of the Nigerian civil crisis and war between 1966 and 1970. His war activities have given rise to a certain amount of controversy. What is certain is that he supported the federal cause, that is, Nigerian unity, and was strongly enough opposed to the Biafran secession to speak against it publicly in and outside Nigeria, although he had several friends, like the writers Christopher Okigbo, Chinua Achebe, and Michael Echeruo, on the Biafran side. In the course of the war, in 1968, another daughter, Tamara, was born to Clark.

The end of the war saw the publication of *Casualties*, a collection of new poems occasioned by the war. In the same year, 1970, *The Example of Shakespeare*, five essays previously published in various journals, was issued by Longman. A third daughter was born the following year. In 1972 Clark was appointed professor of English at the University of Lagos. But thus began as well a long creative lull. *The Ozidi Saga* was published in 1977 from his research fourteen years earlier. A son, Ambakederemo, was born in 1978, and two years later Clark retired from the University of Lagos.

Since then, a new creative surge seems to have begun. In 1981 he published *A Decade of Tongues*, a selection of his earlier poems, *State of the Union*, new poems, followed in 1985. That same year he published *The Bikoroa Plays*, a new trilogy consisting of *The Boat*, *The Return Home*, and *Full Circle*. The PEC Repertory Theatre, which Clark established with his wife, Ebun, in Lagos, has also issued another play, *The Wives' Revolt*. Clark now spends his time between his work at the PEC Repertory Theatre in Lagos and his native home, Kiagbodo.

MAJOR WORKS AND THEMES

Clark-Bekederemo's first major publication, *Poems* (1961), contains some of his best-known and best-loved poems—"Ivbie," "Night Rain," "Agbor Dancer," and "Abiku." In spite of the occasional nature of the subjects of the poems, two related concerns predominate in this collection: the celebration of

African cultural experience and achievements, as exemplified among the Ijaw and Urhobo people of the Niger Delta, as well as lamentation and criticism of European colonialist exploitation, along with the psychological crisis produced in modern Africans by the European encounter. Significantly, Clark followed up the poetry that same year with what remains perhaps his most popular play, *Song of a Goat*, thus signalling his competence in the two genres in which he has done most of his writing.

The play and its companion piece, *The Masquerade*, two parts of an incomplete trilogy, both of which were published along with *The Raft* three years later, are family tragedies of incest, betrayal, murder, and suicide, conceived somewhat along classical Greek models, notably Aeschylus's Orestian cycle. In them, Clark demonstrates not only the universality of the tragic impulse and its ritual basis, but also, as proof perhaps of this premise, the amenableness of the African traditional social experience to the classical tragic form. In other words, tragedy is not the preserve of Europe, since African experience was the stuff of great tragedy in the hands of any capable artist. The last play, *The Raft*, is a satirical allegory of the divisive ethnicism of the Nigerian nation, with its four characters, Kengide, Olotu, Ogro, and Ibobo, representing the four regions, all heading in their strife-torn boat for disaster.

Clark followed up the plays the same year with *America, Their America*, his only general prose writing to date. The book is part travelogue (that is, a narrative of his experiences as Parvin Fellow in Princeton University and as New York sojourner) and part criticism of American social and political life: the crass materialism, its superpower imperialism, and the endemic racism. These themes tie closely with Clark's long-standing anticolonial, anti-Western resentments. However, the dualistic focus of the text inevitably manifested a certain stylistic tension between the bombast and sensationalism of journalism and the felicities of poetic prose.

Interestingly, the text incorporated a number of explicit poems that were republished the following year as part of *A Reed in the Tide*, Clark's second collection of poems and the first to be issued by an established international publisher, Longman, in the West African subregion. Of the thirty-three poems in this collection, more than half had appeared in *Poems* and others in *America, Their America*. What new materials Clark included, for example, the poems "The Leader," "Emergency Commission," and "His Excellency the Masquerader," were directly inspired by the worsening Nigerian political situation. There was little to indicate that any direct or indirect connection had been made between these events and the colonial heritage of which the very nation of Nigeria was an expression and that had been an important theme in his earlier writing.

Clark wrote one last major play, *Ozidi*, before the start of the Nigerian civil war. The theme of revenge, of retributive justice and its excesses, seems to have exercised endless fascination for Clark, for this was also the subject of his oral epic, *The Ozidi Saga*, published in 1977, as well as of the documentary film of a festival drama titled *Tides of the Delta*. But in the play, Clark subtly allegorizes the traditional play of the Ijo, elaborating a ritual of national cleansing after the excesses of corruption, strife, and bloodletting. This was Clark's last effort in the dramatic genre for twenty years.

Soon after the war, in 1970, he published one of the most lyrical and poignant laments to emerge from that terrible event. This is *Casualties*, made up of two parts, "Casualties" and "Incidental Songs for Several Persons." The tone of lamentation for the dead, for the country caught in the throes of a human and moral agony, is entirely dominant. However, several of the poems are rendered in the form of animal allegories, though Clark leaves no one in doubt as to his thrust through the extensive reference notes he provides. This allegorical form may have blunted the poignancy somewhat, but it equally lifts many of the poems from a maudlin slide. Even more important, it relocates them within the kind of traditional African idiom and the proverbial and riddling forms of expression Clark continuously cultivated, which seem to have made a little more tolerable for him the painful consciousness of expressing African experience in a foreign language. But *Casualties* remains Clark's last successful poetic work, since *State of the Union* (1985) has been unable to recapture the vitality of that idiom.

Much more successful has been his recent drama. In 1985 Clark published *The Bikoroa Plays*. In this full-fledged trilogy, consisting of *The Boat*, *The Return Home*, and *Full Circle*, Clark again returns to the theme of the family feud and curse: fratricide, vengeance, and its aftermath. Biowa's wilful murder of Bradide in a dispute over the use of a jointly owned boat (*The Boat*) corresponds to the accidental killing of Kari by Ojoboro—both of them Bradide's sons—in a scuffle a generation later (*Full Circle*). But what ironically unites both plays is *The Return Home*, which is conceived as a festival drama of ritual purification where the curse of the earlier fratricide was ostensibly undone, though it never really was, judging from the action of *Full Circle*. In all these plays, the essential tragic statement Clark-Bekederemo intends to make is far from domestic, or even ethnodirectional. His vision is fundamentally national and, by extension, racial and continental. The Nigerian condition and, from there, the African and black condition, that tragic cycle of repeated bloodletting and political and socioeconomic stagnation, are the real focus of these apparently merely domestic disasters. It is less a comment on the dramaturgic skills of Clark-Bekederemo than a failure of critical imagination that this has not been properly recognized.

CRITICAL RECEPTION

From the beginning, the criticism of Clark's drama has recognized the theatrical difficulties and challenges they pose to producers and directors. For example, a theatre critic complains of *Ozidi*: "The pulsating drama of *Ozidi* with its expansive scope of action and unbounded vision, is capable of exhausting the physical resources of the living stage'' (Umukoro, 137). Not only the themes but also Clark's dramatic technique, which necessitates the presence on stage of violence, whether of a ritual kind or otherwise, has often been held accountable for the problems of performing Clark's plays. They have thus been sometimes regarded as closet dramas (Wren, 76). Neither have the themes been sufficiently appreciated or understood. On the other hand, the evocative language of the plays, either explicitly poetic, as in *Song of a Goat*, or idiomatic, as in most of the others, has been widely admired. More recent criticism has focused on the rich traditional cultural background of his plays (Ifie).

Much better appreciated generally is Clark's poetry. His gift for visual metaphor has been often remarked and commended, especially in his early poetry (Udoeyop, 85). As the first modern West African poet of note, Clark's place in African literature was made secure primarily in this genre. However, the occasional nature of his subjects and themes has been pointed out, indicating a lack of any substantive ideological base or controlling ethic. Equally less appealing is the variety of the styles in his early poetry, with distinct echoes from Yeats, Hopkins, and Eliot. His later work has not achieved as much recognition and admiration. While the allegorical style of *Casualties* has elicited critical praise, his language has been adjudged somewhat stilted (Biakolo, 182). Neither has his latest poetry been at all favorably received. The experiment with prosaic language in *State of the Union* and the attention to non-Nigerian themes in *Mandela and Other Poems* have been adjudged not very successful. Thus in critical terms, Clark's earlier writing, with its thematic concentration on the colonial experience and its impact, seems to have done greater credit to his talents and reputation than his later work, which has focused more on the pains of Nigerian nationhood.

BIBLIOGRAPHY

Works by J. P. Clark-Bekederemo

Poems. Ibadan: Mbari, 1961.
Song of a Goat. Ibadan: Mbari, 1961.
America, Their America. London: André Deutsch, 1964; London: Heinemann, 1968.
Three Plays. London: Oxford University Press, 1964.
A Reed in the Tide. London: Longman, 1965.
Ozidi. London: Oxford University Press, 1966.
Casualties. London: Longman, 1970.
The Example of Shakespeare. London: Longman, 1970.
The Ozidi Saga. Ibadan: Ibadan University Press; Oxford University Press, 1977.
The Hero as Villain. Lagos: University of Lagos Press, 1978.
A Decade of Tongues. London: Longman, 1981.
The Bikoroa Plays. London: Oxford University Press, 1985.

State of the Union. London: Longman, 1985.
The Wives' Revolt (mimeograph). Lagos: PEC Repertory Theatre, 1985.
Mandela and Other Poems. London: Longman, 1988.

Selected Studies of J. P. Clark-Bekederemo

Akyea, Ofori E. "Traditionalism in African Literature: J. P. Clark." *Perspectives on African Literature.* Ed. Christopher Heywood. New York: Africana, 1971. 117–25.

Ashaolu, Albert O. "The Classical Temper in Modern African Drama." *Comparative Approaches to Modern African Literature.* Ed. Sam O. Asein. Ibadan: Department of English, 1983. 77–93.

Biakolo, Emevwo. "The Structure of Metaphor in Clark-Bekederemo's Poetry." *Review of English and Literary Studies* 3.2 (December 1986): 175–82.

Egudu, Romanus. *Four Modern West African Poets.* New York: Nok, 1977.

Ifie, Egbe. *A Cultural Background to the Plays of J. P. Clark-Bekederemo.* Ibadan: End-Time Publishing House, 1994.

Nwachukwu-Agbada, J. O. J. "Hands over Head: The Nature of Tragedy in Clark Bekederemo's *The Bikoroa Plays.*" *Review of English and Literary Studies* 3.2 (December 1986): 126–35.

Povey, John F. "Two Hands a Man Has': The Poetry of J. P. Clark." *African Literature Today* 1 (1968): 36–47.

Udoeyop, N. J. *Three Nigerian Poets.* Ibadan: Ibadan University Press, 1973.

Umukoro, Matthew M. "The Theatrical Challenges of *Ozidi.*" *Review of English and Literary Studies* 3.2 (December 1986): 136–47.

Wren, Robert. *J. P. Clark.* Boston: Twayne Publishers, 1984.

EMEVWO BIAKOLO

MIA COUTO (1957–   )

BIOGRAPHY

Mia Couto was born in Beira, Mozambique, in 1957, the son of Portuguese immigrants. His father was a journalist in search of more opportunities, and his mother was an orphan. Upon arrival, his father was shocked by the social inequalities and abuses in Mozambique, and although Mia Couto grew up in a more privileged situation in Mozambique, he was conscious that the world around him was not how it should be. In the schools he attended while growing up, there were very few blacks, and his teachers did what they could to keep the blacks in their place. He says that it was Europe inside his house, but Africa in the streets. Mia Couto, on the one hand, describes Beira as very volatile because of the barriers between the whites and the blacks. But he also speaks of the city in idyllic tones, talking about his childhood as a time in which he mixed freely with blacks, spoke the African language Sena, and attended storytelling sessions. In this environment of tension and opportunity, Couto grew up with both a regard for mankind and a love of literature.

Mia Couto went to Maputo, then called Lourenço Marques, to study medicine at the university. It was precisely at this same time that Frelimo, the socialist party in Mozambique, was growing in its struggle to overthrow the colonial government. Mia Couto was deeply involved in the struggle, and he says of that time in school that he was more a militant than he was a student; however, as a white, his participation in the resistance was very problematic. He was suspected of being an infiltrator by blacks, while the Portuguese saw him as a traitor. Although he originally came to Maputo to study medicine, he had, like his father, practiced some journalism on the side. Because the majority of the journalists were Portuguese, in 1974 Frelimo asked Couto to leave his studies for a year to help spread information and propagate their cause. He first worked at the newspaper *Tribuna*, then served as the director of the Agência de Informação Nacional (National Information Agency) for a few years before working as the director of the magazine *Tempo*, and eventually returned to newspaper work with *Notícias*. Twelve years after "temporarily" leaving his studies, Couto asked to step down and returned to the university to study biology. He says that he felt that his youth had slipped away from him; he wanted to rediscover his country and affirm the connections that he had felt during his childhood.

Mia Couto did not leave journalism entirely. He has continued to write and publish through the local periodicals. Many of his shorter writings were previously published in Maputo. He also continues to publish a weekly article "Queixatório" in the paper *Domingo*. Mia Couto has also recently formed his own business doing work in biology.

MAJOR WORKS AND THEMES

Mia Couto began as a poet, publishing his first poem at the age of fourteen. Numerous poems since then appeared in periodicals before the release of his collection *Raiz de Oravalho* in 1983. Various other poems have been published in anthologies listed in the Bibliography. Differing from his prose writing, the poetry is more introspective and self-reflexive and raises principally questions of identity. For example, in the poetry collected in *No reino de Caliban*, many of the poems contain images of dispersion and the consequent need for reconstruction. In "Segundo poema da alienação," he writes of his name, "estilhace-se em mil pedaços" (broken into thousands of pieces), which the poem then reconstructs "like a vein that finds its body again." The imagery is frequently informed by Marxist thought, reflecting Couto's involvement with Frelimo. His later writing reflects a more critical position on Marxist rhetoric, as can be seen in "O secreto namoro de Deloinda" and "O retro-camarada" of *Cronicando*. This more personal poetry, with its emphasis on metaphysical aesthetics, shows the influence of the poet José Craveirinha, considered the father of Mozambican literature. It also reflects the resistance taken up by the Associação de Escritores Moçambicanos (Association of Mozambican Writers) to the poetry of combat that dominated the period.

Mia Couto is currently better known for his prose writing. His shorter prose pieces are "estórias" and "crónicas." The "estórias," or short stories, are included in the collections *Vozes Anoitecidas* and *Cada homem é uma raça*. The "crónicas" are short journalistic pieces, usually published in periodicals, and are part of a well-established Lusophone tradition. Under "crónicas" fit *Cronicando*, the noun made into a gerund, and *Estórias Abensonhadas*. Rather than looking at Mia Couto's published work chronologically or in such generic categories, this discussion will instead trace a few themes found throughout his work.

Like many post-colonial writers, Mia Couto confronts the question of language. With respect to the colonial language legacy, authors like Ngugi wa Thiong'o in *Decolonising the Mind* advocate for authors the exclusive use of indigenous African languages. Mia Couto seems to respond to such calls in two ways. For Couto, as for many "assimilated" Mozambicans, Portuguese is his mother tongue. Further, Couto believes that the Portuguese language has been appropriated and reborn as an African language. Throughout his work, Couto himself participates in this transformation with an infusion of neologisms, hybrid words, and local terminology. He often also inverts the standard Portuguese syntax to reflect the spoken word, which raises the second part of the language question: the relationship of writing to the oral tradition.

Couto draws heavily on the stories from the oral tradition, both from his own experiences (see the interviews listed in the Bibliography) and from ethnographic sources (see the epigraph to "Lenda de Namarói" in *Estórias Abensonhadas*). In an attempt to minimize the influence of the European literary tradition, many Africanists trace the origin of African literature to the oral tradition, with writing being merely another material extension of the same. Couto occasionally reverses this relationship, with the transference being from the written to the oral. For example, in *Terra Sonâmbula*, the boy Muidinga spends most of the evenings reading to his "uncle" Tuahir from some notebooks they found. This is already a reversal of the traditional storytelling order of the old instructing the young. During one of their excursions, Tuahir wishes that they had the notebooks to read. Muidinga responds, "Deixei os cadernos lá no machimbombo. Mas eu já li outro caderno, mais à frente. Lhe posso contar o que diz, quase sei tudo de cabeça, palavra por palavra" (I left the notebooks back at the bus. But I already read ahead in another notebook. I can tell you what it says; I almost know it by heart, word for word). A similar reversal can also be seen in the story "A carta" of *Cronicando*.

In addition to questioning the relationship between writing and orality, many of Mia Couto's stories do not define the boundaries between the real and the unreal, the inside or outside of the text. As he says in the introduction to *Vozes Anoitecidas*, the stories came "a partir de qualquer coisa acontecida de verdade mas que me foi contada como se tivesse ocorrido na outra margem do mundo" (from something that really happened but that was told to me as if it had happened on the other side of the world). Recall that Couto was a journalist and that many of these stories were first published in newspapers. This play between the real and the fictional becomes even more interesting in light of the expectation that journalism relay the news, that is, facts. But Couto in interviews and in his stories critiques these conventions. For example, in *Estórias Abensonhadas*, the story "Pranto de coqueiro" opens with "It was an event that came out in the newspaper"; "No rio, além da curva" begins with "I quote the true news from the paper." What follows, then, is not what one would expect to read in a news article. In the story "Sangue da avó, manchando a alcatifa" (Grandma's blood is staining the carpet) in *Cronicando*, old grandmother Carolina moves to Maputo to live with her son's family. As she is watching television, a report on armed bandits comes on. The grandmother leaps from the couch and attacks the television, accuses her son of allowing bandits into his home, and then returns to her home in the interior. The grandmother is unable to separate what happens within the television from what she has experienced. As in the works of many Lusophone writers today, such as Pepetela and Ungulani Ba Ka Khosa, Couto questions the distinctions between the factual and the fictional.

For at least thirty years preceding the peace accord in 1994, Mozambique was at continual war, initially combating colonial rule and subsequently thrown into civil war. Within the devastated landscape that occupies much of Couto's stories, children play the role of both victims and the hope for the future. The story "O apocalipse privado do tio Geguê" of *Cada homem é uma raça* tells of an orphan turned bandit, something that anyone familiar with the news from Mozambique knows was not uncommon. The story opens with "História de um homem é sempre mal contada" (A man's history is always poorly told). Here the two main characters are an uncle and his young, unnamed orphan. They live near a swamp, on the edges of society. In order to survive, the uncle Geguê trains the young boy as a bandit and teaches him how to live from terror and violence.

In many respects, "O apocalipse privado do tio Geguê" is similar to *Terra Sonâmbula*. However, in the novel Couto turns the narrative into one of hope; the brutal reality is mixed with mythology portending rebirth. Again the main characters are an uncle, Tuahir, and an orphan. This time the orphan is given a name, Muidinga. They also live on the edges, in a burned-out bus. The narrative goes back and forth between the adventures of Tuahir and Muidinga and those of Kindzu. Kindzu is the first-person narrator of the notebooks already mentioned. The place where Muidinga and Tuahir live is not one of desolation only, but implies a kind of underworld. Tuahir is like a shade, seemingly without body; he is described as "magro, parece ter perdido toda a substância" (thin, he looks as though he had lost all substance). His role is that of a guide to Muidinga: "O velho teve que lhe ensinar todos os inícios" (The old man had to teach him all the beginnings). Their cyclical journeys to and from the bus turn into initiations. Although *Terra Sonâmbula* ends without completing the rite of passage, the pattern points toward Muidinga's pending integration into society, and the story ends portending mythical transformation. Aware of the contemporary realities, Couto's mythic optimism points toward the emergence of a new era in Mozambique. In many ways, this shift toward a more optimistic view can be traced chronologically in Couto's works. He indicates the change himself in the introduction to *Estórias Abensonhadas*, where he describes the pieces as "foram escritas depois da guerra" (written after the war).

It is not surprising that for a biologist, nature would be a recurring image. In many stories, nature plays more of a scenic role, with the landscape or water as a metaphor. At other times, as in *Cronicando*, three playful but equally polemic pieces discuss the mistreatment and destruction of animals. In "Animais, ani-menos" and "No zoo-ilógico," Couto does this through a series of wordplays with the names of animals, as the titles indicate. In "O monstro infantil," the victim is the elephant whose murder Couto calls "elefanticínio." In *Estórias Abensonhadas*, Couto also addresses nature and its exploitation. For example, in "O adeus da sombra," a young person travels into the interior in search of an herb necessary to cure an ailing friend. When he arrives at an old herbalist's home, she tells him that the people in the "cidade cortam tudo, nem as raízes nos deixam" (city cut everything, not even leaving the roots).

Differing from these few examples of the exploitation of the environment, in the majority of the writing here discussed, Couto does not usually address political issues directly. He draws a distinction between his two genres of writing, reserving his more polemical and didactic words for other venues. For example, he addresses the destabilized condition of Mozambique through an almost allegorical story in "A guerra dos palhaços" of *Estórias Abensonhadas*. Here two clowns come into town and begin to fight. At first the observers watch with curiosity, but eventually the entire town is drawn into the fight. By the end, the clowns stop fighting and walk away laughing, leaving the town behind in ruins. Couto's double engagement with writing as an aesthetic enterprise and writing as journalism, highly conscious of the harrowing conditions, is part of what makes his works so engaging. He has not divorced art from reality but works out of common and brutal experience a hopeful narrative.

It is this very role that Couto assumes, however, that places him in a problematic position familiar to many postcolonial writers. His work reflects a preoccupation with the marginalized, the orphans, the elderly, the abused women, the mulato, the *monhé* (Indian), and the displaced. In many ways, Couto tries to give voice to them, to represent them in his stories. His writing is not naïve, but seeks to promote possibilities and reconcile conflictive differences. But, as noted at the beginning, Couto is himself from a more privileged class, which has over time distanced him from the more common experience. Gayatri Chakravorty Spivak has described in her seminal essay "Can the Subaltern Speak?" how the "postcolonial intellectuals learn that their privilege is their loss" (*Marxism and the Interpretation of Culture*, ed, Cary Nelson and Lawrence Grossberg [Urbana: University of Illinois Press, 1988], 287). As mentioned earlier, Couto is conscious of this distance and attempts to bridge it. However, the suspicion that Couto encountered in the struggle for independence has continued to some degree, including among some fellow writers who attribute his publishing success to his privileged upbringing and newspaper work.

CRITICAL RECEPTION

The majority of critics to date highly praise Mia Couto as an important voice in Lusophone literature. In 1989 *Cronicando* was awarded the Prémio Anual de Jornalismo Areosa Pena by the Organization of Mozambican Journalists. The popularity of his writing has inspired some to adapt the stories, like "Sidney

Poitier na barbearia de Firipe Beruberu'' from *Cada homem é uma raça*, to the theater. Nevertheless, the majority of the scholarship on Couto has played the perpetual role of introduction that much of Lusophone African literature faces. In an analysis of the development of Mozambican literature, Patrick Chabal concludes his discussion of emerging writers with Mia Couto, describing him as the most original new prose writer. The reason cited is Couto's inventive use of language.

It is in this inventive vein that other scholars, like Mary L. Daniel, have begun to open the discussion on the influence of the Brazilian writer João Guimarães Rosa. During the enormously important Regionalist movement in Brazil during the mid-twentieth century, Guimarães Rosa emerged as a writer who was conscious of the social situation of the interior of Brazil, but even more concerned in his writing with a reconfiguration of language. As a consequence of the use of regionalist dialect and erudite linguistic inventiveness, Guimarães Rosa has been credited with the creation of a uniquely Brazilian literary language. The echoes are obvious, not in the least because of the ubiquitousness of neologisms in Mia Couto's prose. He has himself expressed in interviews the influence of Guimarães Rosa. Couto also appears to pay homage to him in his most recent collection, *Estórias Abensonhadas*. The first word of the title reminds one of Guimarães Rosa's *Primeiras Estórias*. They are both collections of very short pieces. The second half of Couto's title is a past-participle neologism combining ''abençoar'' (to bless) and ''sonhar'' (to dream).

The scholarship on Mia Couto will undoubtedly continue to increase as scholars begin to further examine, for example, the central role that the mythology of the oral tradition plays or the mistreatment of women. Couto is still a relatively young writer, and there is most likely much more to look forward to. In fact, Mia Couto's most recent work, *A Varanda do Frangipani*, was released just as this volume was being finalized to go into press.

BIBLIOGRAPHY

Works by Mia Couto

Cada homem é uma raça. Uma Terra Sem Amos 44. Lisboa: Caminho, 1990.
Cronicando. Maputo: Notícias, 1988. 2nd ed. Uma Terra Sem Amos 52. Lisboa: Caminho, 1991.
Estórias Abensonhadas. Uma Terra Sem Amos 69. Lisboa: Caminho, 1994.
''Identidade,'' ''A voz do pedreiro,'' ''Poema da minha alienação,'' ''Confidência,'' ''Incompleta reflexão,'' ''Segundo poema da alienação.'' *No reino de Caliban: Antologia panorámica da poesia africana de expressão portuguêsa*. Ed. Manuel Ferreira. Vol. 3. Lisboa: Seara Nova, 1985.
''Música sem poente,'' ''No teu corpo . . . ,'' ''Mil carícias não valem. . . .'' *África* 2.10 (October/December 1980): 543–45.
Raiz de Orvalho. Gostar de ler. Maputo: Cadernos Tempo, 1983.

"Sem ti," "Sobre algumas palavras de Alberto Lacerda." *As palavras amadurecem.*
    Beira: Diario de Moçambique, 1988. 109–10.
Terra Sonâmbula. Uma Terra Sem Amos 62. Lisboa: Caminho, 1992.
Vozes Anoitecidas. Karingana 1. Maputo: Associação de Escritores Moçambicanos, 1986.
    2nd ed. Uma Terra Sem Amos 34. Lisboa: Caminho, 1987.
A Varanda do Frangipani. Uma Terra Sem Amos 76. Lisboa: Caminho, 1996.

Translations

Every Man Is a Race. Trans. David Brookshaw. Oxford: Heinemann, 1994.
"Grandma's Blood Is Staining the Carpet." Trans. by Peter Bush. *Literary Review* 38.4
    (Summer 1995): 604–5.
A Sleepwalking Land (excerpt). Trans. by David Brookshaw. *Literary Review* 38.4 (Sum-
    mer 1995): 593–603.
Voices Made Night. Trans. David Brookshaw. African Writers Series. London: Heine-
    mann, 1990.

Selected Studies of Mia Couto

Chabal, Patrick, ed. *The Post-Colonial Literature of Lusophone Africa.* Evanston, IL:
    Northwestern University Press, 1996.
Couto, Mia. Interview. "Cada hombre es una raza." By Ignacio Cabria. *Quimera* (Oc-
    tober 1992): 71–74.
———. Interview. "Mia Couto: Escrevo por mãos de outros." By Nelson Saúte. *Jornal
    de Letras, Artes & Ideias* 11.475 (August 13, 1991): 10–11.
———. Interview. *Vozes Moçambicanas.* By Patrick Chabal. Lisboa: Vega, 1994. 274–
    291.
Daniel, Mary L. "Mia Couto: Guimarães Rosa's Newest Literary Heir in Africa." *Luso-
    Brazilian Review* 32.1 (1995): 1–16.
Louro, João. "O mito e a realidade." *Jornal de Letras, Artes & Ideias* 11.501 (February
    11, 1992): 6.
Medina, Cremilda de Araújo. "No rastro da expressão mestiça" and some excerpts.
    Sonha Mamana África. São Paulo: Edições Epopeia, 1987. 54–68.
Ornelas, José. "Mia Couto no Contexto da Literatura Pós-Colonial de Moçambique."
    Luso-Brazilian Review 33.2 (Winter 1996): 37–52.

JARED BANKS

TSITSI DANGAREMBGA (1959–   )

BIOGRAPHY

Tsitsi Dangarembga was born on February 14, 1959, in colonial Rhodesia. At the age of two, she moved with her parents to England, where she remained until 1965. Upon her return to Rhodesia, Dangarembga entered a mission school in Mutare and then completed her secondary education at an American convent school. By her own account, she felt isolated as a child and began writing to herself as a way of coping with her sense of alienation. At home and at school, she read mostly the English classics, although her academic interests shifted to the sciences. She read her first African novel (Ngugi wa Thiong'o's *A Grain of Wheat*) as a teenager, but it was not until she returned from Cambridge shortly before Zimbabwean independence in 1980 that she became avidly involved with African and African-American literature.

Dangarembga went to Cambridge in 1977 to study medicine. Her experience in England was difficult and alienating; she abandoned her studies three years later and returned to Zimbabwe. She worked for a short while at an advertising agency and ultimately returned to university (this time the University of Zimbabwe) to study psychology. The independence celebrations and the period immediately following it were a formative time for Dangarembga. She became increasingly aware of Shona oral traditions, read avidly in contemporary African literature, and was swept up by the writings of Afro-American women. At the university she became actively involved with the Drama Club. She wrote and staged three plays, *She No Longer Weeps* (published in 1987), *The Lost of the Soil*, and *The Third One*.

Dangarembga's reputation was established by the success and acclaim of her first novel, *Nervous Conditions*, which appeared in Great Britain in 1988 and in the United States in 1989. *Nervous Conditions* was awarded the Commonwealth Writers' Prize in 1989. More recently, Dangarembga has turned her attention to film. She wrote the story on which the film *Neria* (directed by Godwin Mawuru, 1992) was based. *Neria* showed at several African film festivals in the United States in 1992–93, including New York, Chicago, and Los Angeles.

MAJOR WORKS AND THEMES

Dangarembga's earliest published work, *She No Longer Weeps*, is a feminist play that examines contemporary Zimbabwean society. *She No Longer Weeps* chronicles the unsuccessful effort of a female university student to emerge from the restrictive familial roles of daughter, wife, and mother.

In a long soliloquy at the beginning of the play, Martha (visibly pregnant) explains how she has already broken up with the child's philandering father because of his physically and emotionally abusive behavior. Then, in a confrontation with her mother, Martha casts her refusal to marry Freddy in revolutionary terms: she can only change society by choosing a course for herself that maps a new path. If she acquiesces to society's expectations (a position made amply clear by her father's mixture of Christian and traditional morality), she will be destroying herself.

This strong sense of self serves Martha well: she is able to finish her education, raise her daughter, and pursue a lucrative career as a lawyer. Yet ultimately, the forces working against her are so aggressive that she is defeated. Her estranged lover, Freddy, returns with the sole intent to destroy her. He makes a claim for his daughter and declares that he wants "everything" from Martha. The successful, professional, single mother is cast by Freddy as the transgressive woman who must be put in her place. Recognizing that the courts are not likely to judge in her favor, Martha relinquishes her daughter, but returns in a desperate assertion of her own sense of justice and kills Freddy.

In her play, Dangarembga depicts a modern, urban society in which it is possible for Martha to attain both an education and a successful career despite her unplanned pregnancy. But Martha's personal accomplishments are not enough to ensure her independence. The play chronicles the betrayal of feminist aspirations in postindependence Zimbabwe, where traditional strictures on women's behavior continue to be aggressively pursued.

Dangarembga borrowed the title of her novel *Nervous Conditions* from Jean-Paul Sartre's introduction to Frantz Fanon's *Wretched of the Earth*. The "nervous condition" of the native is, according to Sartre, a function of mutually reinforcing attitudes between colonizer and colonized that condemn the colonized to what amounts to a psychological disorder. Dangarembga thus borrows from Sartre (and Fanon, of course) this politicized understanding of the native's psychology in order to investigate the possible solutions for a female subject.

Nervous Conditions is narrated by its heroine, Tambudzai. It is the story of a young girl's coming of age in colonial Rhodesia of the sixties and seventies.

Tambudzai states explicitly that she has a story to tell only because her brother died when she was a child: if it were not for the circumstantial elimination of her brother, she would not have had an education to speak of. Dangarembga gestures toward a rewriting of the male education novel that played such an important role in the development of African literature around the period of the independence struggles. The revisionary nature of Tambudzai's narrative has an analogue in the belated independence of Zimbabwe: both Tambudzai and Zimbabwe have the opportunity to rewrite stories that have already been written elsewhere in Africa.

By the time of her brother's death, Tambudzai has already proven her fierce determination to chart a different course. Pained by the realization that her mother's existence is confining and overburdened, resentful of her tyrannical brother and her second-rate status as a female child (women's needs are "not legitimate," she tells us), Tambudzai desperately pursues her opportunity to get an education. She grows her own harvest in order to raise the fees for her schooling. Her brother sabotages her efforts by stealing most of her crop. A sympathetic teacher intervenes and helps her sell the remainder of her crop. Thus she earns her fees for a few years to come.

Tambudzai channels her rebelliousness vicariously through her cousin Nyasha. Having spent five years in England, Nyasha is alarmingly Westernized. Most important, she lacks any sense of shame and behaves with scandalous immodesty. Tambudzai calls her relationship with her cousin "her first love affair." Although continuously shocked by Nyasha's brazenness, Tambudzai realizes that her cousin has opened her eyes to new possibilities of selfhood that were enabled only by the active negotiation of conflicting cultural codes.

Her personal circumstances place Tambudzai in the middle of two alternative worlds: her own immediate family, poor, rural, and essentially traditional, and, on the other hand, her cousin's Western-educated, affluent family. At first these two alternative worlds are presented in terms of class. Increasingly, however, Tambudzai places less emphasis on class and more emphasis on gender: Babamakuru, her uncle who was at first a "god" in her eyes because he was rich and educated, victimizes Nyasha because of her "femaleness" and reminds Tambudzai of her own victimization at the hands of her brother. Tambudzai increasingly questions the willingness of her family to accept the authority of her uncle because she now sees him as a victimizer of women.

If the class difference between the two sides of the family has been established as a result of opportunities presented through colonialism, then Babamakuru's dominance over his brother's family is an omen for the future of this society at large. Dangarembga does not make direct references to historical circumstances. Yet the repression of the political shapes the psychology of Dangarembga's characters in ways that make the reader confront the inevitable politicization of the self. Tambudzai rages against patriarchal domination and reveals how colonialism depends on a renewal of patriarchal principles. Babamakuru's authority becomes increasingly irrational. At his insistence, for example, Tambudzai's parents must have a Christian wedding; their traditional wedding of many years ago is deemed suddenly and urgently inadequate. This absurdly belated wedding throws Tambudzai into a total paralysis. She refuses to attend the wedding and at once rejects her uncle's authority and his formula for cultural survival. As a woman, Tambudzai must free herself from the dichotomy between tradition and modernity.

Godwin Mawuru's film *Neria* was based on a story by Dangarembga, where once more the focus is on a strong woman who confronts traditional practices and reveals their essentially misogynistic ethics. The heroine is widowed unexpectedly. Her husband's family, which still lives in the ancestral village, finds it paramount to send a male family member to the young widow, who is in the city. As custom requires, he must protect the widow, but this protection amounts to little more than plunder. Neria is stripped of her material possessions and loses custody of her children. With the help of a female friend she is able to seek legal action against her brother-in-law.

CRITICAL RECEPTION

As an African woman's coming-of-age novel, it is safe to say that *Nervous Conditions* has already attained the status of a classic. Several scholarly articles have appeared on *Nervous Conditions*, but it is clear that this is only the beginning of a continuing process of sustained critical appraisal of the novel.

Sue Thomas anchors her discussion of the hysteric in *Nervous Conditions* to Dangarembga's allusions to Sartre and Fanon. Dangarembga, Thomas argues, tries to amplify Fanon's analysis of the colonized's pathology by theorizing the problem of gender, which is inadequately treated by Fanon. In a strong reading of the novel that ties the critique of patriarchy to colonialism, Thomas also discusses at length Tambudzai's ambiguous relationship to her mother.

Sally McWilliams argues that Tambudzai must come to terms with the realization that the coherent self she is seeking is a myth. The female identity is not "natural" but "constructed," and therein lies its similarity to the colonized subject. Borrowing Homi Bhabha's concept of "mimicry," McWilliams demonstrates how Babamakuru initiates the subversion of his own authority. Tambudzai cannot bring herself to participate in the farcical mimicry of her parents' Christian wedding and loses her respect for her uncle.

Most of the discussions of the novel have followed the pattern set out by these examples. They have centered on the problems of womanhood and the intersection of feminist and colonialist debates. For a slightly different approach, one may turn to Etienne Galle, who has focused on Dangarembga's rendition of Shona words and phrases into English.

Neria is the highest-grossing film in Zimbabwean history. Despite its popularity in Zimbabwe, the film received a mixed reception in the United States, where the critics deemed it too ideological.

BIBLIOGRAPHY

Works by Tsitsi Dangarembga

She No Longer Weeps. Harare, Zimbabwe: College Press, 1987.
Nervous Conditions. London: Women's Press, 1988.
Neria (Film). Godwin Mawuru, director. Zimbabwe, 1992.

Studies of Tsitsi Dangarembga

Bardolph, Jacqueline. " 'The Tears of Childhood' of Tsitsi Dangarembga." *Commonwealth Essays and Studies* 13.1 (1990): 37–47.
Bosman, Brenda. "A Correspondence without Theory: Tsitsi Dangarembga's *Nervous Conditions*." *Current Writing* 2.1 (1990): 91–100.
Flockemann, Miki. " 'Not-Quite Insiders and Not-Quite Outsiders:' The 'Process of Womanhood' in *Beka Lamb*, *Nervous Conditions*, and *Daughters of the Twilight*." *Journal of Commonwealth Literature* 27.1 (1992): 37–47.
Fritz-Piggott, Jill. "Surviving Political Abuse." *Women's Review of Books* 6 (1989): 10–11.
Galle, Etienne. "Indigenous Embedments in Europhone African Literature." *Commonwealth Essays and Studies* 14.1 (1991): 16–20.
Marangoly George, Rosemary, and Helen Scott. "An Interview with Tsitsi Dangarembga." *Novel* 26.3 (1993): 309–319.
McWilliams, Sally. "Tsitsi Dangarembga's *Nervous Conditions*: At the Crossroads of Feminism and Post-colonialism." *World Literature Today* 31.1 (1991): 103–112.
Thomas, Sue. "Killing the Hysteric in the Colonized's House: Tsitsi Dangarembga's *Nervous Conditions*." *Journal of Commonwealth Literature* 27.1 (1992): 26–36.
Veit-Wild, Flora. "Women Write about the Things That Move Them: Interview with Tsitsi Dangarembga." *Matatu* 3.6 (1989): 101–108.
Vizzard, Michelle. " 'Of Mimicry and Woman:' Hysteria and Anticolonial Feminism in Tsitsi Dangarembga's *Nervous Conditions*." *SPAN* 36 (October 1993): 202–210.
Wilkinson, Jane, ed. *Talking with African Writers*. London: James Currey, 1990.

ELENI COUNDOURIOTIS

NAFISSATOU DIALLO (1941–1982)

BIOGRAPHY

Nafissatou Niang Diallo was born in a military camp near Tilène (Tileen in Wolof) Market in Dakar. Although her mother died when she was one and a half, Diallo's autobiography depicts a happy childhood in a large and loving family. Shortly after she started school, Diallo's family moved to a house in the elite Plateau section of Dakar—hence the title of her autobiography, *From Tilène to Plateau*. This move represented a rise in wealth and social status.

Diallo's education paralleled this move intellectually, for she learned Wolof and Toucouleur precepts and attended a Koranic school as well as a Western school. She attended the prestigious Van Vollenhoven High School and then received a degree in midwifery. At twenty-three she continued her education in France at the Toulouse Institute of Obstetrics and Pediatry. Diallo's portrayal of her educational experience clearly fits the model proposed by Senegal's first president, Léopold Sédar Senghor, who actively promoted efforts to blend Western, Senegalese, and Islamic traditions.

Although Diallo promotes what some might call a Senghorian educational model, she also describes some of the difficulties involved in uniting disparate cultural systems. Confusing relationships with men provoke the only emotional crises she shares with her readers. In her autobiography, she describes an early infatuation, inconclusive relationships, and an engagement that she decided to annul after falling in love with Mambaye Diallo, whom she married in 1961. In choosing to focus on marriage as a site of intergenerational conflict, Diallo echoes themes present in novels of the colonial period (particularly those of Abdoulaye Sadji); however, she strikes a very different tone by presenting herself as an independent, "modern" woman. The vexed notion of modernity haunts postcolonial theory, for it may represent the textual return of the colonizer and of positivist conceptions of culture. Diallo's autobiography raises this issue without offering a clear solution.

Like many other women writers, Diallo had difficulty finding time and "a room of her own" to write. She had six children (four girls and two boys) and a busy professional life as a midwife. In an interview, her husband explained that she wrote only after hours or on holidays. Perhaps Diallo had the assistance of a maid, as is common in many Dakar households; however, this would not free her from her many familial, professional, and social obligations. As a result, it took her ten years to complete and publish her autobiography. Diallo produced three novels after the publication of her autobiography, but her early and unexplained death cut off her career in its bloom.

Apart from Léopold Sédar Senghor's praise, Diallo received most of her honors posthumously. The Association Internationale des Parlementaires de Langue Française (The International Association of French Parliamentary Representatives) gave her the title of Knight of the Order. In addition, a school in Dakar was renamed Nafissatou Niang Diallo School in 1987.

MAJOR WORKS AND THEMES

Nafissatou Diallo's works all address issues of women's representation and roles in public life. Her novels criticize women's subordination as subtly as her autobiography does, leading many readers to assume that she supported the status quo; however, Diallo's indirect manner of criticism fits the speech practices typical of her first language, Wolof. Speech and action are inseparable, as many proponents of speech-act theory argue. Wolof speakers tend to be highly aware of this factor, as sociolinguistic studies indicate, so they use language in a highly conscious, sophisticated manner. This linguistic sophistication makes a high level of subtlety and indirection possible; an equally sophisticated code of etiquette makes it preferable. Highly conscious of her audience, Diallo presents her social criticism in subtle and diplomatic ways.

The private and the public spheres intersect in Diallo's autobiography. She places the narrative of her early years in the framework of the quest for national identity by presenting the story of an ordinary Senegalese woman as a historical document that traces the development of her generation and of her country. In a society in which silence is considered a characteristic of nobility, writing an autobiography is a delicate task. Diallo pulls it off by revealing that the personal is political.

Diallo's two historical romances allow her to envision alternative roles for women. In *Le fort maudit* (The accursed fort), she depicts the widespread misery caused by the depredations of the ruling classes in the nineteenth century. The protagonist, Thiané Sakher Fall, grows up in an idyllic village in Kajóor. Her happy life comes to an end when the ruler of a neighboring kingdom invades and kills or tortures all who are dear to her. Thiané avenges her family by killing the ruler and herself with the poisonous sap of a local plant.

Although the story is based on a historical event popularized in oral narratives, Diallo's retelling of the story has political significance in the postcolonial era. After decolonization, propagandists rehabilitated the nineteenth-century warlord of Kajóor, Lat Dior, casting him as a national hero in order to unify popular political sentiment. The correspondences between Diallo's predatory warlord, who comes from the neighboring kingdom of Baol, and the Kajóorian Lat Dior are unmistakable. Even though he ruled the kingdom of Kajóor, conflicts over succession led Lat Dior to retreat and then to attack from Baol. Many Senegalese readers are aware of the history of popular resistance to Lat Dior and earlier rulers that led most Wolof to convert and join Muslim leaders.

Past resistance has resonance today in light of the growing gap between elites and the rest of the population. Because a female character defeats the marauders and saves her village's honor, the novel implies that women play a more important role than society usually allots them. Thiané Sakher Fall's solution also echoes the story of the women who killed themselves at Nder to avoid dishonor. Suicidal solutions, however, cannot institute social change.

Although Diallo's later novel, *La Princesse de Tiali* (translated as *Fary, Princess of Tiali*), appears to be less pessimistic, the woman still sacrifices herself for the greater good of her community. In this novel, Diallo criticizes the caste system that continues to influence Senegalese society in light of Muslim values. Although her heroine and her community are Muslim, they cannot be buried because of their status as members of the bardic (griot or *géwël*) caste. Instead, their bodies are hoisted into the cleft of a baobab. One of the princes of the kingdom falls in love when he sees this heroine, and marries her. The girl must sacrifice her love for her fiancé to marry the prince—a dwarf—in order to use her new status as a princess to gain the right to proper burial for her caste. Again, Diallo uses historical romance to criticize contemporary social practice.

Awa, la petite marchande (Awa, the little market trader) is a juvenile novel that shows traits found in Diallo's other work, for it, too, is a romance that criticizes current social conditions. When Awa's father can no longer work because of illness, Awa has to leave school and sell fish at the market in order to support her family. When her father's health improves, he leaves for France with his daughter. Many impoverished Africans from former French colonies choose to emigrate to France for economic reasons; however, exile in a hostile environment poses many problems. Diallo's characters overcome them and return from their exile ready to use their Western education to build a better future in Senegal. In light of persistent neocolonial patterns of inequality, it is easy to criticize a narrative that portrays France as a source of wealth and economic stability; however, Diallo's tale also underscores the problems that Senegalese women face in France.

CRITICAL RECEPTION

Until recently, Diallo's work received little critical attention. This is surprising, for Stringer claims that "although other women from French-speaking Black Africa quickly followed her, Diallo can truly be called the first in the field of creative prose writing" (165). Stringer's overview of Diallo's work attempts to rectify the oversight. She insists on Diallo's importance, comparing her autobiography to Camara Laye's almost canonical work *L'enfant noir* (1953) in importance.

Stringer believes that critics have favored other women writers over Diallo because they take a more clearly feminist stance. Indeed, some critics believe that Diallo praises patriarchy in praising her own father. Volet writes that "son respect pour le père témoigne en faveur d'une vision du monde dominée par la figure du patriarche" (her respect for the father speaks in favor of a vision of the world dominated by the figure of the patriarch) (196). Stringer and other critics, however, have noted Diallo's distinctive and obliquely feminist perspective. D'Alméïda argues that Diallo's rebellious attitude allowed her to break the silence about women's lives. Charlotte Bruner, too, situates Diallo's work within a feminist context, stating that representations of childhood are "fundamental to the understanding of women's issues" (324).

The most recent published study, Susan Stringer's *The Senegalese Novel by Women: Through Their Own Eyes* (1996), strives to describe feminism in the plural. Stringer detects "conscious feminism in Diallo's work" (46); indeed, Diallo's depictions of strong decisive women who influenced events before, during, and after the colonial encounter "claim that western feminism has improved the situation of African women and [assert] her independence from western feminist trends" (47).

Most critics choose to focus on Diallo's autobiography. Carole Boyce Davies compares *De Tilène au Plateau* to several other autobiographies written by African women in an important article on the construction of self in autobiography. She sees Diallo's work as a document of the family and, by extension, as social history. Babacar Thioune agrees, describing the autobiography as a realist work with few literary pretensions and a Manichean narrative structure. D'Alméïda, on the other hand, perceives the influence of oral narrative in the text's structure. Most critics observe that Diallo's primary concern is to portray her society.

For this reason, few critics have dealt with the formal aspects of Diallo's work. Those who do concentrate on issues of narrative structure. D'Alméïda, for instance, perceives the influences of oral narratives on the structure of the text. My own work also emphasizes Diallo's attempts to bridge the gap between the colonial past and the neo-colonial present. Andre Patrick Sahel takes another approach in his review of *Le fort maudit*, suggesting that we can read the novel as the story of an individual or as a sociohistorical document. The first reading presents a plot structure typical of seventeenth-century French tragedies. The second interpretive strategy leads Sahel to argue that the novel represents a search for African identity in keeping with the aims of the Negritude movement. In contrast, Stringer (1996) focuses first on issues of genre. This brief discussion centers on the paradoxical similarities between autobiographical and fictional discourses. Stringer then moves back to the issues of narrative structure and then concurs with other critics that Diallo's works show a dualistic nature.

Diallo was a literary pioneer. Although more celebrated contemporaries have perhaps had a greater impact on Senegalese letters, she was the first Senegalese woman to publish a long narrative work. She was also the first to write an extended autobiography. Diallo thus facilitated other women's efforts to break their silence by writing.

BIBLIOGRAPHY

Works by Nafissatou Diallo

De Tilène au Plateau: Une enfance dakaroise. Dakar: Nouvelles Éditions Africaines, 1975.
Le fort maudit. Paris: Hatier, 1980.
Awa, la petite marchande. Paris: Les Nouvelles Éditions Africaines/EDICEF, 1981.
A Dakar Childhood. Trans. Dorothy Blair. London: Longman, 1982.
Fary, Princess of Tiali. Trans. Ann Woollcombe. Ed. Barbara Hetzner Scherer. Washington, D.C.: Three Continents Press, 1987.
La princesse de Tiali. Dakar: Les Nouvelles Éditions Africaines, 1987.

Studies of Nafissatou Diallo

Blair, Dorothy. *Senegalese Literature: A Critical History.* Boston: G. K. Hall, 1984.
Bruner, Charlotte. "First Novels of Girlhood." *College Language Association Journal* 31 (1988): 324–338.
D'Alméïda, Irène Assiba. *Francophone African Women Writers: Destroying the Emptiness of Silence.* Gainesville: University Press of Florida, 1994.
Davies, Carole Boyce. "Private Selves and Public Spaces: Autobiography and the African Woman Writer." *Neohelicon* 17.2 (1990): 183–210.
Hitchcott, Nicki. "African 'Herstory': The Feminist Reader and the African Autobiographical Voice." *Research in African Literatures* 28. 2 (1997): 16–33.
McNee, Lisa. *Selfish Gifts: Senegalese Women's Autobiographical Discourses.* Forthcoming.
Miller, Mary-Kay F. "My Mothers/My Selves: (Re)Reading a Tradition of West African Women's Autobiography." *Research in African Literatures* 28.2 (1997): 5–15.
Ormerod, Beverley, and Jean-Marie Volet. "Nafissatou Diallo." *Romancières africaines d'expression française: Le sud du Sahara.* Paris: L'Harmattan, 1994. 63–66.
Sahel, André-Patrick. "Une tragédie de la dissémination: *Le fort maudit*, de Nafissatou Diallo." *L'Afrique littéraire* 63–64 (1982): 83–85.
Stringer, Susan. "Nafissatou Diallo—A Pioneer in Black African Writing." *Continental, Latin-American, and Francophone Women Writers: Selected Papers from the Wichita State University Conference on Foreign Literature II, 1986–1987.* Ed.

Ginette Adamson and Eunice Myers. Lanham, MD: University Press of America, 1990. 165–171.

————. *The Senegalese Novel by Women: Through Their Own Eyes*. New York: Peter Lang, 1996.

Thioune, Babacar. *L'exploration de l'écriture féminine au Sénégal: La tentation autobiographique*. Thèse de doctorat de troisième cycle. Paris: Université de Paris–Sorbonne IV, 1987.

Volet, Jean-Marie. *La parole aux Africaines ou l'idée de pouvoir chez les romancières d'expression française de l'Afrique sub-saharienne*. Amsterdam: Rodopi, 1993.

Watson, Julia. ''Unruly Bodies: Autoethnography and Authorization in Nafissatou Diallo's *De Tilène au Plateau* (A Dakar Childhood).'' *Research in African Literatures* 28.2 (1997): 34–56.

LISA MCNEE

DAVID MANDESSI DIOP
(1927–1960)

BIOGRAPHY

David Mandessi Diop was born to a Senegalese father and a Cameroonian mother in Bordeaux, France. Among the many issues that shaped the character of the young Diop was his dual ethnic and national parentage. Diop lived an uprooted and transplanted life, for at an early age he moved between Cameroon and Senegal, where he had his primary education before attending the Lycée Marcelin Berthelot in Paris. He experienced a pronounced stay in France and only visited Africa occasionally during his childhood. His tendency to idealize Africa and to write scathingly of Europe was caused by his experience of exile.

David Diop's father died when he was under ten years of age, and he was raised by his mother, who introduced him to the work of the West Indian writer Aimé Césaire and the other Negritude writers. When Diop made his debut as a poet while still a schoolboy, he reflected the problems faced by other minority writers trying to negotiate their identity in a hostile world.

In France, Diop himself experienced firsthand the racism to which blacks were subjected, as he testifies in an early poem, "A White Said to Me." On account of ill health, Diop had to change from a medical career to the liberal arts. Though he obtained two *baccalauréats* and a *licence-ès-lettres*, his constant hospitalization contributed to his daily frustrations. In 1950 Diop married Virginie Kamara; in the poem "Rama Kam," he celebrates her as symbolizing the perfection and authenticity of the black life he sought. The marriage, however, resulted in a divorce after the birth of their third child.

Diop returned to Africa in the fifties to join the independence struggle. He published numerous poems and essays in the Paris-based influential journal of black studies *Présence Africaine*, vehemently opposing the injustices of colonialism. In 1956 his book of poems *Coups de pilon* was published. Active as a teacher in Dakar, Diop taught for a year at the Maurice Delafosse School. He lived in Guinea for two years and was the principal of a secondary school in Kindia, having gone to Guinea among the Africans who volunteered to salvage the manpower-strapped Sekou Touré regime following the withdrawal of French administrators opposed to the independence of that West African country.

David Diop died tragically on August 25, 1960, in a plane crash over the Atlantic along with his second wife. The manuscript of what should have been his second volume of poems also perished in that accident, thus leaving the slim poetry volume *Coups de pilon*, which has become available in English translation, Diop's definitive poetic legacy.

MAJOR WORKS AND THEMES

While critical thinking about David Diop's poetry has been consistent in locating it within the Negritude school of writing, the historical significance of the poet and the seminal nature of the poetic forms he adopted have yet to be accorded the emphasis they deserve. David Diop was essentially a freedom fighter of the pen, a cultural patriot, and an artist who lived ahead of his time. He was one of the few African poets emerging during the colonial period who chose to advocate a mother-tongue literature. Even in those early years, Diop showed a strong commitment to the use of African languages in literature, as when he argued in the 1956 essay "A Contribution to the Debate on National Poetry":

The African creator, deprived of the use of his language and cut off from his people, might turn out to be only the representative of a literary trend (and that not necessarily the least gratuitous) of the conquering nation. His words, having become a perfect illustration of the assimilationist policy through imagination and style, will doubtless rouse the warm applause of a certain group of critics. In fact, these praises will go mostly to colonialism which, when it can no longer keep its subjects in slavery, transforms them into docile intellectuals patterned after western literary fashions which besides, is another more subtle form of bastardization. (*Hammer Blows and Other Writings*, 59)

Diop exposed the notion of the adopted languages of the conquerors as a gift or privilege bequeathed to the colonized to be a sham, and he was among the earliest Africans who, although they recognized the necessity to release their creative energies through indigenous African languages, still found the use of the languages of the colonizers (in his own case, the French language) necessary to fight the freedom war. It is instructive to note that without the decisive role played by pioneers such as Diop, the work of other exiled writers, like Mazisi Kunene and Ngugi wa Thiong'o, who continue in our day to fight to ensure the legitimization of African-language literatures, might never have taken the current direction.

In *Coups de pilon* Diop's themes of love for Africa are incorporated with concerns for reinstating Africa's oral literary heritage, the fascination with the past, and criticism of the dehumanizing influences of Western civilization. The preoccupation with the techniques of African oral expression that marks the poetic style of David Diop is his attempt to achieve the decolonization of the African. He focuses upon the dilemma of his race since the colonial encounter and reveals the history of cruelty visited on his people by the West from the slave-trade era to the eventual colonial occupation. The silencing of African voices is one of the worst forms of the dehumanization of the natives, and so Diop sets out through a deliberately cultivated oral style to restore the authentic African voice. In the poems "Africa," "The Vultures," and "Listen Comrades," his employment of satire, allegory, ribald verse, fable, and exaggeration reminiscent of oral narrative makes poignant the attack on the atrocities of colonialism. Diop's style contrasts sharply, in its assertive, defiant tone, with that of his contemporaries like the Ghanaian Casely Hayford, Michael Dei-Anang, R. G. Armatoe, and others who tended to imitate the muted hymnal styles of minor nineteenth-century English poets; instead, Diop's style prefigured the mood of the Black Consciousness poets of South Africa such as Mafika Gwala and Don Mattera and the modern West African poet Kofi Awoonor in his angry response to the evils of colonialism.

The oral outlook may be evident through the use of parallel structures built on incremental repetition, as in the pieces "The True Road" and "The Hours," which draw a contrast between the African way of life that has been eroded by Western civilization—a lifestyle characterized by a strong and healthy sense of communal solidarity, gaiety, and warmth—and the supposedly mechanistic, alienating, duplicitous, and ravenous lifestyle of the West. A major attractive feature of the oral form for Diop in these poems is the entertainment quality that helps the poet rivet the audience's attention while instructing them.

The hardship suffered by women in Africa certainly predated colonialism; but women suffered a double colonization during the period of colonial occupation, since, in addition to their roles as housewives, mothers, and in-laws, many women worked alongside their male counterparts during forced labor. The achievement of David Diop is to write with the greatest incisiveness of the African women's contribution. As a poet committed to the oral forms of his social environment, Diop employed praise-names and often, like Senghor, conceived Africa in the image of a woman in order to reveal the poverty of her circumstances and her suffering, as well as her nurturing, caring, and life-giving potential. In the poems "Your Presence," "To a Black Dancer," "The Agony of Chains," and "Niger Tramp," Diop exploits the praise form to expose with penetrating clarity the indomitable female principle that enabled Africa to survive the cruel ordeal of colonialism. He depicts the women in both their strengths and their weaknesses. Diop's choice to glorify the indestructible will of Africans as the source of hope for the future counters the myth that Africans were passive victims of their historical circumstances, and through expressing the conviction that Africa owes her ability to survive the trauma of colonialism to the solidarity forged between women and men in times of great difficulties, Diop truly anticipates the gender studies currently in fashion. Through immortalizing the heroic image of the African woman, Diop joins the ranks of the first African writers who give due recognition to the important roles played by all the different segments of society in the liberation war. In this respect, he demonstrates that Africa's liberation struggle began not when the first shots were fired, but with endurance, self-sacrifice, and tireless labor for the collective good of the men and women folk, all of which had predated the armed struggle.

Another interesting feature of Diop's poetry in its historical context is that he did not limit his indictment to the white colonialists; in fact, he directs attack as much against the blacks who perpetrate their own subjugation as against the French originators of oppression. Diop urges a self-reassessment of the African as a precondition for the continent to overcome its problems; and in the poem "The Renegade," he conducts such a self-examination, reinforcing the oral quality of his work by employing the dirge form to expose with ruthless severity the harmful effects of inferiority complex and self-delusion. So long as the assimilated natives remain acculturated, Diop contends, for so long will the collective consciousness of the African continent remain in shackles. The denunciation of colonial mimicry is conducted via the forum of a conversational style, using a plethora of revolting images: One must be oneself and not what one is not, for apemanship is a debilitating self-enslavement.

David Diop was unquestionably one of the pioneers of mother-tongue literature in Africa, and it is regrettable that he did not live to put some of his convictions into practice, for much of what he wrote in the colonizer's language betrayed traces of anguish and a stretching for the echoes of his mother tongue. By infusing his poetry with the language of dirgers, incanters, and praise singers, David Diop wrote himself into the forefront among the African writers who helped lay a solid foundation for the decolonization of African literature that is currently under way. He remains the precursor writer for the realist writers of the present-day Africa, such as Meja Mwangi, Ayi Kwei Armah, Wole Soyinka, Ngugi wa Thiong'o, Ousmane Sembène, and a host of others.

CRITICAL RECEPTION

In his *African Literature in the Twentieth Century*, one of the earliest books on African literature, O. R. Dathorne correctly urges readers to view David Diop's poetry within the historical context in which the poet lived. David Diop, he observes, "lived during the time when negritude was in its infancy and he died at an early age" (235). Surprisingly, Dathorne himself betrays insensitivity to the context, literary goals, and strategies of Diop when he criticizes the poet for incessantly cataloging "the familiar grievances of a colonial" (236). The poet, he charges further, "offers no hope in his poems. They are morbid pieces"

(236). For Dathorne, Diop's poetry is quite simply the work of a promising poet who had not matured fully as a poet when he died.

In his *Tasks and Masks*, Lewis Nkosi upholds the view that the strength of Diop's poetry derives from being able to undermine the tendency toward posturing in Negritude writing while working within the tradition. Although he views Diop as one of "the three poets" who are "the founding fathers of African poetry of French expression," Nkosi believes that "a militant anti-colonial protest" marks out Diop (138). He notes "a deep fission" separating Diop and Senghor. From the beginning, Nkosi writes, Diop was "the most radical, the most aggressively direct and frankly internationalist in his concerns" (138). He claims a legitimacy for the battle Diop wages against the romanticized view of Africa and identifies "surrealist imagery and an austere blank verse" as being the hallmarks of Diop's poetry. But Nkosi uses scanty evidence to substantiate his assertion that "it was the actual condition of black people rather than the mythologies of blackness which interested David"; nor does he fully explain how Diop's poetry draws its "energy" from politics (139).

In *Modern African Poetry and the African Predicament*, Romanus Egudu examines Diop's use of "images of brutality, both physical and psychological, to depict the colonial monster" (17). The reader of Diop's poetry, he contends, confronts "powerful images [and] the combined effects of metonymy and personification [and] oxymoron" (18). The poet's concerns, Egudu discovers, are "the white man who imprisoned and muzzled the tramp and who stole all his wealth" and "the African renegade whom the white man has succeeded in changing into something detestable" (19–20). Egudu thus draws support from the arguments of Wilfred Cartey, who, in his *Whispers from a Continent*, notices Diop's deft use of "words and images denoting harshness, brutishness, destruction" (255).

BIBLIOGRAPHY

Works by David Mandessi Diop

Coups de pilon. Paris: Présence Africaine, 1956.
Hammer Blows and Other Writings. Bloomington: Indiana University Press, 1973.
Hammer Blows. AWS 174. London: Heinemann, 1975.

Selected Studies of David Mandessi Diop

Cartey, Wilfred. *Whispers from a Continent: The Literature of Contemporary Black Africa*. New York: Random House, 1969; London: Heinemann, 1971.
Dathorne, O. R. *The Black Mind: A History of African Literature*. 1st ed. Minneapolis: University of Minnesota Press, 1969. (A shorter version appears under the title *African Literature in the Twentieth Century*. London: Heinemann, 1975.)

Egudu, R. N. *Modern African Poetry and the African Predicament.* London: Macmillan, 1978.
Nkosi, Lewis. *Tasks and Masks: Themes and Styles of African Literature.* Harlow, Essex: Longman, 1981.

ODE S. OGEDE

ASSIA DJEBAR (1936–   )

BIOGRAPHY

Assia Djebar (Fatima Zohra Imalayen) is one of North Africa's best-known and most widely acclaimed writers. She was born in Cherchell, Algeria, and attended the primary school where her father taught French. After her studies at a French *lycée* and the University of Algiers, she became the first Algerian woman to be accepted at the École Normale Supérieure. A student of Louis Massignon, she eventually obtained an advanced degree in history. In 1958 she married Ahmed Ould-Rouïs, a member of the Resistance; they had a daughter and a son. They divorced, and she married poet Malek Alloula in 1980.

Assia Djebar has lived in Algeria, Morocco, Tunisia, and France. She has taught history, semiotics, theatre, and film at the University of Algiers and has lectured in many countries. Since the early 1980s she has held a research appointment at the Algerian Cultural Center in Paris. Her work includes novels, short stories, drama, poetry, and film, as well as essays, articles, reviews, film criticism, and translations. Her fictional works have been translated into several languages.

MAJOR WORKS AND THEMES

The corpus of Assia Djebar's work spans a period of forty years. Important issues raised in her early novels continue to be developed and explored in her recent works. Algerian women have faced a double colonization, colonial and patriarchal, and have had to fight to redefine their role in postcolonial Algerian society. Their struggle for social emancipation has been the deepest and most constant current in Djebar's writing.

In 1957 Djebar, then a twenty-year-old university student, published her first novel, *La soif* (Thirst). Fearing her father's disapproval, she adopted the pen name she has kept ever since. The author has described the heroine, Nadia, as "a typical westernized Algerian girl." Djebar's second novel, *Les impatients* (The impatient ones, 1958), also describes how a young woman of the Algerian bourgeoisie is trapped by Islamic and patriarchal traditions. Both novels emphasize the psychological dilemmas of young women struggling in a society in which women's position is inferior to men's, and where French and Muslim cultures clash.

In 1960 Djebar's works began to deal more specifically with the revolution. She wrote the play *Rouge l'aube* (Red is the dawn, performed in 1969), a series of scenes of men and women in the war. Her next two novels, *Les enfants du nouveau monde* (Children of the new world, 1962) and *Les alouettes naïves* (The naïve larks, 1967), were written in the realist style of the "engaged" novel. Both portray heroines with political roles in the revolution and who are involved in collective action. Djebar hoped that women's struggle in the revolution would mean liberation for all Algerians, male and female. These novels address basic themes that Djebar develops in subsequent works, including love and war, the past and the present, the role of the French language in forming the identity of colonial and postcolonial subjects, and the cultural legacies of centuries of invasion, settlement, and colonialism in Algeria.

Like her fellow North Africans who write in French, Djebar has had to come to terms with the nagging "language question." In the 1970s she began to feel that writing in French might not be the best way to express her Arab identity or to reach her Algerian sisters, most of whom do not know French and many of whom cannot read at all. After studying classical Arabic and attempting to write in it, she turned to cinema, producing two films. *La Nouba des femmes du Mont Chenoua* (The Nouba of the women of Mount Chenoua, 1979) combines oral testimony of Algerian peasant women with the story of a professional woman returning to her village. This combination is taken up again in Djebar's latest novel, *Vaste est la prison*. A second film, *La Zerda et les chants de l'oubli* (The Zerda and songs of forgetting, 1982), is a chronicle of life in the Maghreb from the early to the mid-twentieth century that mingles documentary footage, archival photographs, and ancestral songs and poems. Like Djebar's later novel, *L'Amour, la fantasia, La Zerda* parallels two eras: colonial Algeria of the 1930s and 1940s, corresponding to the narrator's childhood, and the period of the beginning of colonization, 1830–1850.

Djebar makes use of written documents from the colonial period and from Islamic history, oral testimony of peasants and revolutionary women, folk traditions, archeological finds, and events from her own life as well as those of her ancestors. She reclaims a history obscured by both colonial hegemony and patriarchal suppression. Through writing, she creates a personal identity and a collective identity of Algerian women that both acknowledges their past and looks toward their future. Her filmmaking resonates with the work of the Vietnamese Trinh Minh-ha; both attempt to reconstitute women's past, to fill in the blanks of history from the point of view of a postcolonial woman. Djebar's work with oral and musical traditions appears to have given her a deeper understanding of the politics of language in postcolonial Algeria (see Zimra, ''In Her Own Write''). The issue of language—and related themes of voice, body language, aphasia, sound, and silence—has been crucial in her subsequent work, beginning with *Les femmes d'Alger dans leur appartement* (Women of Algiers in their apartment, 1980), a highly acclaimed collection of six short stories written between 1959 and 1978. In a structure that, once again, juxtaposes colonial past and postcolonial present (''Yesterday'' and ''Today''), the author pans in on a closed world of women, such as the one Delacroix might have glimpsed in his painting. With a new sensibility and a new vocabulary both borrowed from film, she writes about the ''forbidden gazes'' and the ''muffled'' and ''severed'' sounds of the cloistered Algerian women who, more than a decade after ''independence,'' are still imprisoned in the harem like their foremothers of a century ago. An important question raised in this book is whether feminism and women's solidarity can actually change social relations in Algeria today. *L'amour, la fantasia (Fantasia: An Algerian Cavalcade*, 1985) is the first novel of a proposed quartet about Maghrebian women that will weave together history, autobiography, and fiction. Djebar creates a broad fresco of Algerian history during the period of French colonialism, from the capture of Algiers in 1830 to the War of Independence, 1954–62. This work is a testimony of resistance, of Algerians, and especially of women, whose stories have been erased in all the ''official'' histories. Djebar manipulates the French language, giving it the sounds and rhythms of Arabic, to reproduce the ''authentic speech'' of the women in her mother's urban community and the peasant women of the mountains nearby. This collective history merges with the history of the narrator, who grapples with her mixed Arabo-Berber-Andalusian and Franco-European heritage.

The issue of linguistic alienation, according to Djebar, is particularly difficult for the Algerian woman who writes in French. The author relates how, in her own life, the oral narrative in Arabic, the mother tongue, is joined by written French, the language her father taught. After much anguish about not writing in Arabic, which was so strongly promoted in her country after independence, she has learned to let these languages coexist in her. Although she recognizes French as the language of the colonizer, the ''adversary,'' she also appropriates it as a tool of empowerment. She calls it ''war booty'' and uses it to rebel against tradition, as a passage to the outside world, and as a secular language that can be used where Arabic might be difficult: to talk about subjects such as love, sex, the display of emotions, and religion.

Ombre sultane (A Sister to Scheherazade, 1987), the second novel of the quartet, takes up the theme of the harem found in *Les femmes d'Alger.* Djebar's harem is not the exoticized world of the orientalists, but a space of confinement opposed to the spaces of liberation outside it. This novel depicts two women,

Isma and Hajila, who were married to the same man. When Isma divorced him, she chose Hajila, who is cloistered and passive, to be his new wife. It is Isma who speaks for them both, describing her own liberated sexuality and the joy that Hajila experiences in leaving the house, unveiled, to go walking in the city. While Djebar makes allusions to Scheherazade and the sisterhood of women, the book ends on a foreboding note, describing Algeria, with the rise of fundamentalism, as "ce lieu de la terre où si lentement l'aurore a brillé pour nous que déjà, de toutes parts, le crépuscule vient nous cerner" (172) (this corner of the earth where the dawn has risen so slowly that dusk is already settling around us on all sides).

Djebar's passion for history is evident in her 1991 novel *Loin de Médine* (*Far from Madina*), a fictional chronicle about intelligent and powerful Arab women in the first two centuries of Islam. Djebar creates a host of female characters who speak out: Fatima, the Prophet's daughter, Aïcha, his youngest widow, Selma the Rebel, Kerama the Christian, and many others. Critics have pointed out similarities to *Sultanes oubliées* (The forgotten queens of Islam, 1990) by the Moroccan Fatima Mernissi. Both works argue that historically, women commanded respect and wielded political power. Both authors uncover models of female authority within the Islamic tradition itself. Djebar emphasizes women's revolt and opposition to various forms of male authority. Her heroines are "des Musulmanes de la plus rare espèce: soumises à Dieu, et farouchement rebelles au pouvoir" (299) (Muslim women of the rarest kind: submissive to God and rebelling fiercely against power), women like herself who are not afraid to speak out against injustices committed in the name of religion.

The author's most recent work is *Vaste est la prison* (Vast is the prison, 1995). In its richness of themes as well as in its graceful and poetic style, this novel, frankly autobiographical, is a culmination of Djebar's previous efforts. The narrator tells the story of her childhood, adolescence, and periods of her adult life, including her passion for a younger man and her divorce around age forty. She tells of filming at Mount Chenoua, where she "hunted for images." These stories are interspersed with the history and traditions of her female ancestors and relatives. She also writes of historical figures, from Jugurtha to Delacroix.

One of the many meanings of the "vast prison" is a symbol for contemporary Algeria, which denies its cultural diversity, cuts off all relations to the outside, and tries to suppress women's voices and hide their bodies. To widen this narrow conception of national culture, Djebar points out the existence of Berber language and culture in Algeria long before the arrival of the Arabs. She describes the ancient steeple at Dougga, engraved in two languages, one of which was an ancestor to today's Berber languages. She writes of Princess Tin Hinan from the fourth century A.D., foremother of the Tuaregs who helped pass on the "lybic" writing system. She recalls the centuries of contact between Europe and Africa. In a bold and touching passage at the end of the novel, she recounts the assassination of Yasmina, a young journalist, in June 1994 and reminds us of the fear and death that rage in her homeland today. Her latest novel is *Le Blanc de l'Algérie* (The Blank/white of Algeria, 1996).

CRITICAL RECEPTION

Djebar's writing has attracted critical attention from scholars internationally, with scores of books, theses, and articles dedicated to her work every year. Criticism of Djebar's work has tended to focus on postcolonialism, history, politics, feminism, and the questions of language and voice.

Certain critics compared her first novel, *La soif*, to Françoise Sagan's *Bonjour tristesse*, another first novel about a young woman's emancipation. Although praised in France, Djebar's first two novels were condemned by nationalist critics in Algeria for being too preoccupied with problems of individual women of the upper middle class and for ignoring the political realities of the day. Most critics approved of her next two novels for tackling the question of the revolution, while the Algerian Mostefa Lacheraf harshly criticized Djebar for writing in French in 1963, after independence, when writers were supposed to immediately switch to the national language, Arabic (''L'Avenir''). The Moroccan critic Abdelkébir Khatibi, who writes in French and celebrates the plurilingualism of the Maghreb, is more sympathetic to Djebar's work (*Le Roman Maghrébin*). Le Clézio's interview with Djebar focuses on the question of language, as do articles by Gragg, Mortimer, Murdoch, and Zimra. Zimra sees *Les femmes d'Alger dans leur appartement* as a turning point in Djebar's career as a Francophone writer. This work is also hailed by Hédi Abdel-Jaouad as a ''landmark'' in Djebar's writing and in Maghrebian literature in general, both for its style and its content.

A number of critics have written about the ways Djebar writes about history to restore women's past and to critique the present sociopolitical situation in Algeria. *L'Amour, la fantasia*, in particular, has been highly esteemed. It has been called a ''monumental novel'' and ''a masterpiece.'' Among those who have written about the historical and political significance of Djebar's works are Green, Marx-Scouras, Nolin, Page, Tahon, Turk, and Verthuy.

Djebar's strong feminist stance has earned her much praise. Her early novels were lauded for showing women struggling against patriarchy and repressive traditions. *La Nouba des femmes du Mont Chenoua* won the International Critics Prize at the 1979 Film Festival in Venice. After being shown on Algerian television, this film was criticized for being ''too feminist.'' Some critics have seen the endings of *Les Femmes d'Alger* and *Ombre sultane* as pessimistic about the future of Algerian women, who are portrayed as silenced and cloistered. The end of *Vaste est la prison*, by contrast, is a poignant cry against a regime that has become increasingly bloody. *Loin de Médine* tackles the current issue of Islamic fundamentalism. Accad wonders about the utility of a ''glorification and reinterpretation of tradition to show how today's Islam has been twisted'' (185).

Merini, Mortimer, and Zimra are some of the other critics who have written about questions of feminism and politics in Djebar's works.

It is interesting to note that because of her legitimate fear of being mistranslated, and undoubtedly for political reasons, none of the author's novels have been translated into Arabic in her native Algeria. By contrast, English translations of her works are eagerly read by a wide audience in Europe and North America. Djebar's works combine fascinating subject matter, a sophisticated style, and bold political and feminist messages. Assia Djebar has definitely made her mark as a postcolonial writer.

BIBLIOGRAPHY

Works by Assia Djebar

Books

Les alouettes naïves. Paris: Julliard, 1967.
L'Amour, la fantasia. Paris: J.-C. Lattès, 1985.
Le blanc de l'Algérie. Paris: Albin Michel, 1995.
Chronique d'un été algérien (essay by Djebar and photographs). Paris: Éditions Plume, 1993.
Les enfants du nouveau monde. Paris: Julliard, 1962.
Fantasia: An Algerian Cavalcade. Trans. Dorothy S. Blair. London: Quartet, 1989.
Les femmes d'Alger dans leur appartement. Paris: Éditions des Femmes, 1980.
Les impatients. Paris: Julliard, 1958.
Loin de Médine. Paris: Albin Michel, 1991.
Far from Madina. Trans. Dorothy S. Blair. London: Quartet, 1994.
Ombre sultane. Paris: J.-C. Lattès, 1987.
A Sister to Scheherazade. Trans. Dorothy S. Blair. London: Quartet, 1987.
Poèmes pour l'Algérie heureuse. Algiers: SNED, 1969.
Rouge l'aube. Algiers: SNED, 1969 (1960).
La soif. Paris: Julliard, 1957.
Vaste est la prison. Paris: Albin Michel, 1995.
Women of Algiers in Their Apartment. Trans. Marjolijn de Jager, afterword by Clarisse Zimra. Charlottesville: University Press of Virginia, 1992.
Women of Islam. (essay by Djebar and seventy photographs). London: Deutsch, 1961.

Other Works

La Nouba des femmes du Mont Chenoua (1979) (film).
La Zerda et les chants de l'oubli (1982) (film).
Djebar, Assia, and Assia Trabelsi, trans. (preface by Djebar). *Une voix de l'enfer.* By Nawal El Saadawi. Paris: Éditions des femmes, 1982.

Selected Studies of Assia Djebar

Abdel-Jaouad, Hédi. "L'Amour, la fantasia: Autobiography as Fiction." *Celfan Review* 7.1–2 (1987–88): 25–29.

————. Review of *Les femmes d'Alger dans leur appartement. World Literature Today* 55.2 (Spring 1981): 362.

Accad, Evelyne. Review of *Loin de Médine. World Literature Today* 66.1 (Winter 1992): 184–185.

Bouguarche, Ahmed. "Le Hammam: Sexualité, purification, et régénérescence dans l'oeuvre d'Assia Djebar." *L'Eau: Source d'une écriture dans les littératures féminines francophones.* Ed. Yolande Helm. New York: Peter Lang, 1995. 209–226.

Brahimi, Denise. "L'Amour, la fantasia: Une grammatologie maghrébine." *Littératures maghrébines: Colloque Jacqueline Arnaud.* Tome 2. Paris: L'Harmattan, 1990. 119–124.

————. "Orientalisme et conscience de soi." *Littérature maghrébine d'expression française, de l'écrit à l'image.* Ed. Guy Dugas, et al. Meknes: Faculté des lettres, Université Sidi Mohamed Ben Abdallah, 1987. 29–36.

Budig-Markin, Valerie. "La Voix, l'historiographie, l'autobiographie: Les dernières oeuvres d'Assia Djebar." *Francophonie Plurielle.* Ed. Ginette Adamson and Jean-Marc Gouanvic. Quebec: Hurtubise HMH, 1995. 21–28.

Chikhi, Beida. *Les romans d'Assia Djebar.* Alger: Office des publications universitaires, 1990.

Déjeux, Jean. *Assia Djebar, romancière algérienne, cinéaste arabe.* Sherbrooke, Quebec: Naaman, 1984.

Donadey, Anne. "Assia Djebar's Poetics of Subversion." *L'Esprit Créateur* 33.2 (Summer 1993): 107–117.

————. "Polyphonic and Palimpsestic Discourse in the Works of Assia Djebar and Leila Sebbar." Diss. Northwestern University, 1993.

Gadant, Monique. "La permission de dire 'je': reflexions sur les femmes et l'écriture, à propos d'un roman d'Assia Djebar." *Le nationalisme algérien et les femmes.* Paris: L'Harmattan, 1995. 269–285.

Geesey, Patricia. "Women's Words: Assia Djebar's *Loin de Médine.*" *The Marabout and the Muse: New Approaches to Islam in African Literature.* Ed. Kenneth W. Harrow. Portsmouth, NH; London: Heinemann, 1996. 40–50.

Ghaussy, Soheila. "A Stepmother Tongue: 'Feminine Writing' in Assia Djebar's *Fantasia: An Algerian Cavalcade.*" *World Literature Today* 68.3 (1994): 457–462.

Gracki, Katherine. "Assia Djebar et l'écriture de l'autobiographie au pluriel." *Women in French Studies* 2 (1994): 55–66.

Gragg, Michèle. "L'Amour, la fantasia: L'écriture, lieu de paradoxe." *Francographies* 2 (1993): 99–106.

Green, Mary Jean. "Dismantling the Colonizing Text: Anne Hébert's *Kamouraska* and Assia Djebar's *L'Amour, la fantasia.*" *French Review* 66.6 (May 1993): 959–966.

Hamm, Jean-Jacques. "Le regard de l'objet: sur l'oeuvre d'Assia Djebar." *Mises en scène d'écrivains.* Sainte-Foy, Québec: Les Éditions le Griffon d'argile, 1993. 37–48.

Khatibi, Abdelkébir. *Maghreb Pluriel.* Paris: Éditions Denoël, 1983.

————. *Le Roman Maghrébin.* Paris: Maspero, 1970.

Lacheraf, Mostefa. "L'Avenir de la culture algérienne." *Les Temps Modernes* 19 (October 1963): 721–45.

Lang, George. "Jihad, Ijtihad, and Other Dialogical Wars in *La Mère du Printemps, Le Harem Politique,* and *Loin de Médine.*" *The Marabout and the Muse: New Ap-*

proaches to Islam in African Literature. Ed. Kenneth W. Harrow. Portsmouth, NH; London: Heinemann, 1996. 1–22.

Le Clézio, Marguerite. "Écrire dans la langue adverse." *Contemporary French Civilization* 9.2 (1985): 230–43.

Marx-Scouras, Danielle. "Muffled Screams/Stifled Voices." *Yale French Studies* 82 (1993): 172–182.

Merini, Rafika. *Two Major Francophone Women Writers: Assia Djebar and Leila Sebbar.* New York: P. Lang, 1995.

Mortimer, Mildred. *Assia Djebar.* Philadelphia: CELFAN Monographs, 1988.

———. "Entretien avec Assia Djebar, écrivain algérien." *Research in African Literatures* 19.2 (1988): 196–205.

———. "The Evolution of Assia Djebar's Feminist Conscience." *Contemporary African Literature.* Ed. Hal Wylie, Eileen Julien, Russell J. Linneman, Sue Hutchins, and Marie-Denise Shelton. Washington, D.C.: Three Continents Press, 1983. 7–14.

———. "A Feminist Critique of the Algerian Novel of French Expression." *Design and Intent in African Literature.* Ed. David F. Dorsey, Phanuel A. Egejuru, and Stephen H. Arnold. Washington, D.C.: Three Continents Press, 1982. 31–38.

———. "La femme algérienne dans les romans d'Assia Djebar." *French Review* 49.5 (1976): 759–763.

———. "Language and Space in the Fiction of Assia Djebar and Leila Sebbar." *Research in African Literatures* 19.3 (1988): 301–311.

———. "Women's Voice." *Journeys through the French African Novel.* Portsmouth, NH: Heinemann, 1990.

Murdoch, Adlai. "Rewriting Writing: Identity, Exile, and Renewal in Assia Djebar's *L'Amour, la fantasia.*" *Yale French Studies* 83, *Post/Colonial Conditions.* Ed. Lionnet and Scharfman, 1993. 71–92.

Nolin, Corinne. "Intellectuels et pouvoir au Maghreb: Thématiques de l'exil et de la subversion." Diss. Northwestern University, 1994.

Page, Andrea. "Rape or Obscene Copulation? Ambivalence and Complicity in Djebar's *L'Amour, la fantasia.*" *Women in French Studies* 2 (1994): 42–54.

Roth, Arnold. "L'espace du harem dans *Ombre sultane.*" *Mises en scène d'écrivains.* Sainte-Foy, Québec: Les Éditions le Griffon d'argile, 1993. 49–60.

Tahon, Marie-Blanche. "Women Novelists and Women in the Struggle for Algeria's National Liberation." *Research in African Literatures* 23.2 (1992): 39–51.

Talahite, Claude. "*Femmes d'Alger dans leur appartement*: Problématique de la figure de l'observateur." Oran (Algeria): C.D.S.H., Université d'Oran, 1981.

Turk, Nada. "*L'Amour, la Fantasia* d'Assia Djebar: Chronique de guerre, voix des femmes." *Celfan Review* 7. 1–2 (1987–88): 21–24.

———. "Assia Djebar: Solitaire Solidaire: Une étude de la lutte des algériennes pour les libertés individuelles dans l'oeuvre romanesque d'Assia Djebar." Diss. University of Colorado, 1987.

———. "Assia Djebar, Voix au féminin." *Constructions* (1988–89): 89–98.

Verthuy, Maïr. "Histoire, mémoire, et création dans l'oeuvre d'Assia Djebar." *Mises en scène d'écrivains.* Sainte-Foy, Québec: Les Éditions le Griffon d'argile, 1993. 25–36.

Woodhull, Winifred. "Algeria Unveiled." *Genders* 10 (Spring 1991): 112–131.

———. "Feminism and Islamic Tradition." *Studies in Twentieth Century Literature* 17.1 (Winter 1993): 27–44.

————. *Transfigurations of the Maghreb: Feminism, Decolonization, and Literatures in French.* Minneapolis: University of Minnesota Press, 1993.

World Literature Today. "Special Issue on Assia Djebar." 70.4 (Autumn 1996).

Zimra, Clarisse. "Comment peut-on être musulmane? Assia Djebar repense Médine." *Notre Librairie* 118 (July–September 1994): 57–63.

————. "In Her Own Write: The Circular Structures of Linguistic Alienation in Assia Djebar's Early Novels." *Research in African Literatures* 11.2 (Summer 1980): 206–223.

————. "When the Past Answers Our Present: Assia Djebar Talks about *Loin de Médine.*" *Callaloo* 16.1 (1993): 116–131.

————. "Writing Woman: The Novels of Assia Djebar." *SubStance* 69 (1992): 68–84.

MARY B. VOGL

EMMANUEL BOUNDZEKI DONGALA (1941–   )

BIOGRAPHY

The early years of Emmanuel Boundzeki Dongala appear to have set the tone for his entire, eclectic life. Born in the Central African Republic to a Central African mother and Congolese father, he completed his secondary education in Brazzaville, Congo. In the mid-1960s Dongala set off to the United States to attend college, obtaining an M.S. in physics after seven years. During this period of study, Dongala also learned a lot about American music, especially jazz. Among his favorite musicians at the time were John Coltrane, Archie Shepp, and Ornette Coleman. What intrigued Dongala most about Coltrane's playing was the musician's interest in finding "the absolute," the mystic perfection of music. This beauty was in direct contrast to the political turmoil he experienced in the streets of New York during the civil rights movement. Years later in his short story, "A Love Supreme," Dongala wrote his own ode to this jazz legend.

His international itinerary continued when upon completion of his master's degree, Dongala went to Montpellier, France, to obtain his Ph.D. in physics. He then worked at the National Center of Scientific Research (CNRS) in France before returning to teach chemistry at the Université Marien Ngouabi in Brazzaville. He found the perfection of music resonating in the field of mathematics. For more than a decade, he divided his waking hours between his teaching and laboratory work and his literary writing.

In the late 1980s he began to devote much more time to artistic expression. He began by organizing and directing a theater troupe, Le Théâtre de l'Eclair, whose aim is to bring international theater to the Congolese. He believes that theater could have an enormous role to play in the Congo, since theater was one precolonial mode of communication. Dongala embraces traditional values but also values modern technology and innovation. He sees everything in its historical context and believes that we now need to be open to all kinds of influences. Toward this end, his troupe has performed works of Japanese playwright Yukio Mishima as well as those of French playwrights, like Jean-Paul Sartre. He has, however, noted that it is hard to work traditional Congolese values into a French-language script.

Dongala's multiculturalism has clearly influenced his literary and theatrical work. Music remains an important feature in Dongala's life and the style of his texts, though he never listens to music while writing. Furthermore, like many contemporary Congolese authors, Dongala has commented on his admiration for Latin American novelists like Gabriel García Marquez, Miguel Angel Asturias, and Alejo Carpentier. He frequently uses stream-of-consciousness writing and the circular motion of the oral tradition. At the same time, he differs from his literary compatriots by reaching into Asian literature for quotes from Lu Xin and the Bhagavad Gita. No matter the language or the theme, Dongala firmly believes that humor is crucial in literature since literature is to entertain as well as educate. As a result, his pessimistic view of contemporary African politics is tempered with sarcasm; the threat of censorship influences the way he approaches his political and social themes. He understands the power of the word to transform the world and writes to responsibly focus attention on political reform and the suffering of ordinary people.

MAJOR WORKS AND THEMES

Dongala has published two novels, *Un fusil dans la main, un poème dans la poche* and *Le feu des origines*, as well as a collection of short stories entitled *Jazz et vin de palme*. His first novel was translated into a number of European languages and received the Ladisla Dormandi prize as the best foreign book in 1974. Centering on the life of Mayela dia Mayela, a teenager at the time of independence of the fictitious country of Anzika, the novel describes the complexity and excitement of living at that period in Africa's history.

Written as a controlled stream-of-consciousness epic as Mayela awaits execution, *Un fusil* gives a psychological portrayal of a vain, privileged kid who grew up oblivious to the horrors of his own people. This naïveté melts in the hot savanna of Zimbabwe, where Mayela goes to fight for Africa's freedom from colonialism. Among his fellow rebels are a black South African whose family is murdered at Sharpeville and a black American whose romantic vision of the struggle intially clashes with Mayela's. Dongala incorporates these characters into his work to contextualize his views on both apartheid and the civil rights movement. Back in Anzika, Mayela finds himself having to choose about how best to help his own people. His rise to power is quite similar to the story of Patrice Lumumba, whose real-life martyrdom finds its way into the novel. The pessimistic view of the author, who concludes the novel with the death of a native son by his own countrymen, is reminiscent of Ambroise Bierce's "Occurrence at Owl Creek Bridge" and also places Dongala in the generation of disillusioned African writers.

Jazz et vin de palme brings together eight short stories, half about life in the United States and the other half about the Congo. The influence of music is clear in most of these stories; some stories develop slowly and then reach a crescendo, while others sway and bob to a beat all their own. The topics vary, but other than the title story, which deals with UFOs, the focus is the daily struggles of life—obtaining medicine for a sick child or the personal crises of public men. As in his first novel, Dongala focuses on the daily joys and tragedies of life. In this collection, Dongala names Congolese locations, a trait that distinguishes him from other Congolese authors who fear reprisals from censors.

For his most recent work, *Le feu des origines*, Dongala received both the Grand Prix de l'Afrique Noire and the Prix Charles Oulmont in 1988. In the novel, twentieth-century African history is reflected in the life of one centenarian, Mandala Mankunku. Born before the arrival of the French and growing up throughout the colonial period, including the French construction of the dreaded railroad, Mankunku becomes the African Everyman. In a scene reminiscent of Ferdinand Oyono's *Le vieux nègre et la médaille*, Mankunku's knowledge of trains is acknowledged and honored when he becomes the first native train engineer at independence. The influence of García Marquez is clear in Dongala's play with time, mixing actual events like Dien-Bien-Phu and famous Congo-Zairian musicians with fictitious places and people. Similarities with Ayi Kwei Armah of Ghana and Ngugi wa Thiong'o of Kenya are also apparent as Dongala reaches into the past to reclaim national pride in traditional culture and beliefs. In 1990 the National Congolese Theater adapted the novel for the stage and performed it to large crowds in Brazzaville.

CRITICAL RECEPTION

Considering the number of works (and their translations) created by Emmanuel Dongala to date, there is surprisingly little substantive literary criticism about his work. Koffi Anyinefa's *Littérature et politique en Afrique noire* is probably the most extensive discussion of Dongala's work to date. Anyinefa contends that Dongala has been misunderstood by European critics, specifically Chemain, who viewed Dongala's first book as an unsuccessful epic. Anyinefa, on the other hand, focuses attention on the political forces that drive Congolese writers and African writers in general. Benyacoub also sees Dongala as being in the generation of African "disenchantment" authors, but adds that Dongala's use of humor in the face of tragedy, both in stories about the Congo and the United States, raises his literary work high above the level of a political tract.

BIBLIOGRAPHY

Works by Emmanuel Boundzeki Dongala

Le feu des origines. Paris: Éditions Albin Michel, 1987.
Un fusil dans la main, un poème dans la poche. Paris: Éditions Albin Michel, 1973.
"Littérature et société: Ce que je crois." *Peuples Noirs, Peuples Africains* 9 (1979): 56–64.
Jazz et vin de palme. Paris: Hatier, 1982.

Studies of Emmanuel Boundzeki Dongala

Anyinefa, Koffi. *"Le feu des origines."* *Présence Africaine* 146 (1988): 262–265.
―――. "Intertextuality in Dongala's *Un fusil dans la main, un poème dans la poche.*" *Research in African Literatures* 24.1 (1993): 6–17.
―――. *Littérature et politique en Afrique noire: Socialisme et dictature comme thèmes du roman congolais d'expression française.* Bayreuth, Germany: African Studies Series, 1990.
Benyacoub, Latra. *"Jazz et vin de palme."* *Recherche, pédagogie, et culture* 62 (1983): 100–101.
Bestmann, Martin T. "Structure narrative et aventure révolutionnaire dans *Un fusil dans la main, un poème dans la poche.*" *Peuples Noirs, Peuples Africains* 30 (1982): 138–58; 31 (1983): 79–85.
Bousquet, Marie. "New York: L'Afrique et l'humour." *Jeune Afrique* August 4, 1982: 92.
Brezault, Alain, and Gerard Clavreuil, eds. "Emmanuel Boundzeki Dongala." *Conversations Congolaises.* Paris: L'Harmattan, 1989. 35–46.
Chemain, Arlette. "Une écriture plusieurs fois renouelée: Emmanuel Dongala." *Notre Librairie* 92–93 (1988): 134–135.
Chemain, Roger, and Arlette Chemain-DeGrange. "Un fusil dans la main, un poème dans la poche." *Panorama critique de la littérature congolaise contemporaine.* Paris: Éditions Présence Africaine, 1979. 93–101.
Daninos, Guy. *"Jazz et vin de palme."* *Présence Africaine* 125 (1983): 261–266.
Magnier, Bernard. "L'enfant aux yeux pers." *Africa International* 199 (1987): 57.
Midiohouan, Guy Ossito. *"Jazz et vin de palme."* *L'afrique Littéraire et Artistique* 65–66 (1982): 77–79.
Mpoyi-Buatu, Th. *"Jazz et vin de palme."* *Peuples Noirs, Peuples Africains* 29 (1982): 137–142.
Ravell-Pinto, Thelma. *"Un fusil dans la main, un poème dans la poche."* *Journal of Black Studies* 13.3 (1983): 369–371.

ANNE E. LESSICK-XIAO

BUCHI EMECHETA (1944–)

BIOGRAPHY

Buchi Emecheta (née Florence Onyebuchi Emecheta), Africa's most prolific female writer, with nineteen published books to date and numerous essays, was born in Lagos, Nigeria, in 1944, although her parents came from Umuezeokolo Odanta Village in Ibuza, Delta State, an Igbo-speaking area. After completing her primary education at Ladilak School and Reagan Memorial Baptist School, she won a scholarship to Methodist Girls' High School in Lagos. She passed her West African School Certificate Examinations with honors and subsequently married Nduka Sylvester Onwordi. Emecheta worked for the American embassy in Lagos for two years before she went abroad in 1962 to join her husband, who was studying for a degree in accountancy at London University. They had five children—three girls and two boys—but the marriage, which had difficulties exacerbated by the life of an African student struggling in London, ended in great bitterness.

Despite the emotional strains, social pressures, and financial problems of being a black woman and single parent in Great Britain, Buchi Emecheta earned an honors degree in sociology in 1974 and a master's degree in philosophy, both at London University. Her ability to write her first two novels while a student and single parent was "out of a necessity" (interview with Marie Umeh, *Ba Shiru*, 19). Emecheta's published books and essays have gained her both national and international recognition and rewards "after eight years of writing" (20). At London University she taught creative writing and also received a graduate fellowship. In 1980–81 she was a writer-in-residence at the University of Calabar in Calabar, Nigeria. However, she returned to London to be "reunited with [her] five children and to get on with [her] writing" (interview with Wendy

Davis, *Africa Now*, 75). Upon her return to London she lectured at the School of Oriental and African Studies. Additionally, she was a guest speaker at international conferences in Claremont, California, the University of Chicago, and Spelman College, to name only three. At present, Emecheta resides primarily in London with her four children. Her first daughter, Chiedu Onwordi, died in 1984 while a medical student at Edinburgh University. Nduka Sylvester Onwordi, from whom she was estranged, died in London in 1986. In addition to writing, teaching, and lecturing around the world, Emecheta operates her own London-based publishing company, Ogwugwu Afor, and smothers her two grandchildren with love and stories. She visits Nigeria regularly to be with her in-laws, nieces, and nephews.

Buchi Emecheta has garnered various literary prizes. *Second-Class Citizen* won the Daughter of Mark Twain Award in 1975. *The Slave Girl* earned her both the New Statesman/Jock Campbell Award in 1978 and the accolade in 1979 for the Best Third World Writer for 1976–79. In 1980 she received the Best Black Writer in Britain prize for her magnum opus, *The Joys of Motherhood*. Additionally, two of her novels, *Double Yoke* and *The Joys of Motherhood*, have been made into films. *The Joys of Motherhood* has also been translated into the French and German languages. Buchi Emecheta has been a member of PEN (Poets, Essayists, and Novelists), an Association of International Women Writers, since 1990. In 1992 Buchi Emecheta received from Fairleigh Dickinson University in New Jersey an honorary doctor of literature degree.

MAJOR WORKS AND THEMES

Buchi Emecheta has published twelve adult novels: *In the Ditch* (1972), *Second-Class Citizen* (1975), *The Bride Price* (1976), *The Slave Girl* (1977), *The Joys of Motherhood* (1979), *Double Yoke* (1982), *Naira Power* (1982), *Destination Biafra* (1982), *The Rape of Shavi* (1985), *A Kind of Marriage* (1987), *Gwendolen* (1989), also known as *The Family* (1990), and *Kehinde* (1994). She also has to her literary credit an autobiography, *Head above Water* (1986), and four children's books: *Titch the Cat* (1978), *The Moonlight Bride* (1983), *The Wrestling Match* (1983), and *Nowhere to Play* (1980). Two of her dramatic works, *A Kind of Marriage* (1975) and *Juju Landlord* (1976), were performed at the London Theater. According to Bernth Lindfors, Emecheta's essays, which appear in numerous magazines around the world, have "elevated her from a nonentity to a major minor writer" (33). Buchi Emecheta describes herself as a feminist with a small "f" (interview with Umeh, 23). The major theme in her books is the extirpation of retrogressive Igbo cultural norms that prevent women from participation in a wide range of activities said to be the preserve of men. Emecheta's literary achievement therefore marks a turning point in Nigerian literary history. For the first time, one observes a conscious effort by a female writer to speak out against the subjugation of Igbo women in the quest for social change.

In the Ditch is a semiautobiographical work wherein Adah Obi (Emecheta's alter ego) describes the plight of "welfare" women in the overindustrialized, bureaucratic society of London. Problems of adjusting to a new way of life befall the family, and Adah and her husband, Francis, who is unable to cope, separate. Besides Adah's grappling with her private life, the socioeconomic problems of the women in the "ditch" are highlighted in order to denounce the establishment's uncreative and life-denying roles for women. Indeed, one of Emecheta's most poignant stands is against a system that works to perpetuate broken homes and to foster the growth of dependent, unfulfilled women on the periphery of an affluent society. Emecheta's brand of feminism calls for the political consciousness of all women, coupled with questioning and challenging the marginalization of women in all social systems.

In another autobiographical work, *Second-Class Citizen*, Emecheta describes artistically how Igbo traditional culture exploits women through a system of assigned and devalued roles that emphasize sexual asymmetry. Reminiscing upon her childhood days, Adah Obi, Emecheta's fictional representative, recollects that after her father's death, all the family savings were put away for her brother's education. As a result, Adah studied hard to win a scholarship so that she could attend secondary school on her own. Adah later marries Francis, an accountant, works, and sends him to London. However, she realizes all too soon that only her financial contribution to the household stops Francis from walking out on her. *Second-Class Citizen* is thus a diatribe against Francis, a male chauvinist, the African man and his vaunted role as breadwinner, and the idea of manhood. Through her interaction with Francis Obi, Emecheta's main character in the book gives testimony to the fact that gender roles are learned behavior, not necessarily a biological fact.

What distinguishes Emecheta's individual talent from other contemporary Igbo writers is her consistent iconoclastic vision, her explicit articulation, and her depiction of the woes of Igbo women due to repressive patriarchal norms that condemn them to prescribed fates of subsistence and subjugation. *The Bride Price* emphasizes the individual's right to freedom of choice. Aku-nna, the protagonist in the book, operates in a society that places constraints on an individual's concept of life. The plot becomes complicated as Aku-nna falls in love with her schoolteacher, Chike Ofulue, an outcast slave (osu) and therefore an ineligible spouse for her, according to Igbo tradition. Aku-nna challenges the larger community's will to negate her spontaneous love for Chike, so together they elope and seek to exist as interdependent. Surprisingly enough, at the end of the novel, Aku-nna dies. The moral becomes clear. If Aku-nna had allowed custom to take its course, the ways of her clan might have ensured her a good marriage and a long life. This ending points to a conflict between Igbo and Western cultures within the writer herself.

In *The Slave Girl*, Emecheta further attacks the Igbo man's insensitivity to women by suggesting that a woman is a slave to her husband. Ojebeta, the main character, grows up outside her village as a slave. When she regains her liberty, it turns out to be short-lived, for Eze, a husband to her Aunt Uteh, conspires to force her into a marriage against her will. Consequently, she decides to elope to Lagos with her lover. However, her hopes of a happy married life prove illusory. In the first place, there is the question of her bride price to be settled, and, second, the relationship between Ojebeta and her new husband proves to be like that between a slave and her master. Indeed, for Buchi Emecheta, marriage in Igboland is a form of slavery (Ebeogu, "Igbo Tradition," 651).

As a literary artist preoccupied with promoting change, Emecheta, in her magnum opus, *The Joys of Motherhood*, breaks away from the prevalent portraiture in African writing in which motherhood is honorific. According to the protagonist, Nnu Ego, "the joy of being a mother is the joy of giving all to your children" (219). Emecheta goes on to unfold her metaphor of enslaved Igbo women, arguing that the society also programs women to be slaves of their male offspring as well as their husbands. In describing the "joys," Emecheta is at her best in the irony implied in the title. Children give joy, we all agree. From this premise, she builds an elaborate story to demolish the myth, while at the same time pretending to uphold the age-old idea. Nnu Ego gradually realizes that motherhood has not brought fulfillment.

In keeping with Emecheta's theme of female oppression, *Double Yoke* describes the tragic limitations of Nigerian women in pursuit of academic excellence and the anxiety of assimilation. By describing the sexual and cultural politics in Nigerian society, Emecheta again campaigns against female subjugation in Igbo society and champions the cause of female emancipation. Presenting her drama with strikingly new and provocative twists, Emecheta extends her argument that Nigerian men are similarly enslaved to retrogressive cultural norms. Apart from Ete Kamba's inability to throw off the precepts of traditional African society that give certain prerogatives to men and deny them to women, Nko, the main character in the novel, is also confused about the actual role the educated female should play in Nigerian society. Both African men and women are therefore in bondage. Living in two different cultures brings too much tension. Hence they must live with a "double yoke" for daring to walk where angels fear to tread.

The Rape of Shavi is first and foremost a satire. The novel also serves essentially to show how Ayoko's rape by Ronje, a Dane living temporarily in the village of Shavi following an airplane crash, is brilliantly handled by the women, as it is a problem beyond the men. In favor of women, interlocked images of solidarity and ingenuity in facing new problems emerge when the women punish Ronje for his crime by binding him in a large fish net and leaving him near the Ime Oja Hills for the desert vultures to devour. Emecheta's revisionist thrust insists that although the experiences of women are different from those of men, they are no less heroic.

In *Destination Biafra*, Emecheta once again turns her gaze to illuminating the need for social reform in regard to the position of women in Nigerian society. Significantly enough, Debbie Ogedemgbe, Emecheta's emancipated African woman, acts out the author's feminist philosophy. Through authorial comment we learn that Debbie wants "to do something more than child bearing and rearing and being a good, passive wife. She was going to help the Nigerian army, not as a cook or a nurse, but as a true officer" (45). As Emecheta dramatizes the virtues of Debbie during the war, her supportive camaraderie with the women with whom she travels, and her sense of mission, despite setbacks, to bring peace between eastern and western Nigeria, the word "female" loses its uncomplimentary status in African literature. In allegorical fashion, then, Debbie represents sacrifice and goodness. The allusion to the Nigerian Head of State and the Biafran leader in the depiction of their betrayal of countless Nigerians at the center of their power struggle during the Civil War reinforces the negative. The myth of male superiority is, of course, dismantled at the same time as the redemptive role Debbie acts out is exalted. It is by replacing heroes with heroines that both male and female writers can attest to the fact that women have similar talents to men and that they too suffer, economically and psychologically, from too rigid a constraint. Once given the chance, there is the probability that more African women can successfully hold leadership positions.

The adverse effects of money in Nigerian society are highlighted in *Naira Power*. According to Emecheta, it is because of *naira mania* that crimes are committed, ranging from the neglect of duty to stealing, kidnapping, prostitution, and murder. Romanu, one of the chief characters in the novel, is identified as a corrupt opportunist. Throughout the novel, the author goes on to demystify the general aura of grandeur surrounding young millionaires by describing the dazzling and handsome Romanu as a ritual murderer and drug peddler. Shocking details are given in the story portraying Romanu as the "taxi driver caught along the border with five kilos of marijuana in the boot of his taxi along with five human heads" (90). By treating one of the burning issues in Nigerian society, corruption, Emecheta affirms her identification with the aspiration of patriotism and stabilization of an African state.

A Kind of Marriage was first written in 1975 as a play for the Crown Court Series of the BBC. In 1986 it was published in novel form by Macmillan. In the book, one finds a portraiture of a professional woman, the modern African wife, coming to grips with her world and dealing with masculine infidelity, an almost exclusive male right in patriarchal societies. When Maria "Ubakamma," the protagonist, discovers that her husband deceives her and surreptitiously marries a second wife because of her inability to have more than one child, she is steadfast in her decision to maintain financial independence and educate their only son, Osita. On the other hand, Charles's attempt to live up to his family name, Ubakamma, meaning "it is better for us to be many" (63), proves to be his Achilles' heel. First, Obioma, Charles's second wife, walks out on him, abandoning their two children, Afam and Chioma. Second, Afam is responsible for his senior brother's premature death and subsequently his own. Estranged from his beloved wife Maria ever since his secret marriage to Obioma was exposed, Charles dies of heartbreak and despair shortly after burying his two sons. Maria's dedication to her nursing career becomes therapeutic. She survives the tragedy to witness the birth of Osita's pregnant widow's twin boys. With the characterization of Maria, Emecheta's idea of Igbo women enslaved to fathers, husbands, and sons becomes a question of déjà vu.

The potential evil of polygamous relationships illustrated in the novel is intended to educate and to reform Igbo society, given its patriarchal bias toward men and its premium on sons. Happiness in marriage should not necessarily depend on a house full of offspring. Couples should strive toward understanding each other and take procreation as secondary. In an interview Emecheta said, "Good men are the salt of the earth" (interview with Umeh, 23). And who was it that said, "Behind every successful man is a woman"?

Buchi Emecheta's autobiographical work, *Head above Water*, is a record of her triumph over the suppression of her spirit, her search for happiness and security outside the limited roles Igbo patriarchy has defined for its daughters. She says in her autobiography, "I love telling stories and now I could tell my stories from my new home and unlike my big mother Nwakwaluzo, I was even being paid for them" (243). Emecheta has come a long way, and it is wonderful that she has been able to recognize a certain aspect of women's subjugation and accordingly has sought to save herself. As Carole Boyce Davies puts it: "The struggle for equal rights between the sexes is going to prove even more difficult than that of decolonization because in essence it is a struggle between a husband and wife, brother and sister, father and mother" (Davies and Graves, *Ngambika*, 8).

The major theme in *Gwendolen*, also known as *The Family*, is the seduction of a daughter by fathers (biological and surrogate). Again in opposition to the conservative attitude of African people, Emecheta fails to sweep the dust under the carpet. Author Emecheta not only condemns the sexual abuse of children, but she also contends that it is not uncommon in the African-Caribbean world, but rather is quite pervasive. Gwendolen, the protagonist, is raped by Uncle Johnny at the age of nine in Kingston, Jamaica. A few years later in London, England, she is forced into a sexual relationship with her father while her mother is away for more than a year. Although Gwendolen leaves home and subsequently goes mad, she regains psychological balance through the help of "other mothers." When her child from the incestuous relationship with her father is born, she finds happiness and accepts her daughter "Iyamide" as the mother she never had.

With the publication of *Kehinde* in 1994, Emecheta again focused on wayward husbands. Kehinde Okolo has been married to Albert Okolo for over eighteen years. Bored in London, Albert is so determined to return to Nigeria "to be someone . . . to show off his own life style, his material success" (6) that he insists on his pregnant wife aborting her fetus so that he can go home in style. After the abortion, Kehinde makes the mistake of remaining in London to sell their house, while Albert, followed by their two children, Joshua and Bimpe, moves to Nigeria. Once home, it does not take long before Albert marries Rike, a university professor, and gives her two children. Although Kehinde is unable to sell their house, she takes the advice of Taiwo, her dead twin, who appears in a dream and warns her to go home and give Albert "the attention he needs to survive" in Nigeria (46). In Nigeria, Kehinde—jobless and lonely—finds her polygamous household unbearable. When her London-based friend, Moriammo, sends her a plane ticket to return to England, Kehinde accepts the offer. Back in London, Kehinde earns a first degree, secures a good-paying job, and begins an affair with a younger man. With the characterization of Kehinde, Emecheta comes to terms with the roles the twenty-first-century woman often plays to her benefit.

Emecheta's iconoclastic yet revisionist imperatives are laudable because her agitations aim at improving the quality of life between man and woman, individuals and community, for the total growth and complete fulfillment of the African woman as well as man. Her vision of a society where men and women act out roles in communion with their talents and personalities, where men and women "clasp hands truly" (Simone de Beauvoir *The Second Sex*, Trans. H. M. Parshley [New York: Vintage, 1974], 292) is what her explicit, ideological position is all about. For the other side of liberation is the efficient, creative, and total utilization of latent forces in both men and women for the benefit of the human race. Furthermore, the core of Emecheta's revolutionary imperative is her recognition of the need for "balance," "equalization," and "alliance" in male-female relationships within the Igbo sociocultural framework. The issue at stake—the "nurturance" of the gifted female—is not limited to femalism, but concerns the fostering of man's humanity to woman. In conclusion, Emecheta's novels are rooted in autobiographical realism and cultural facts. Reflected in her *oeuvre* and true to life are Igbo society's attitudes about the necessity of motherhood and the double standards for men and women. Men make the rules and women see that they are carried out. Nnu Ego in *Joys* found status in motherhood because of its availability and the importance her society attached to it.

Therefore, the depiction of African women as marginalized mirrors Emecheta's personal worldview and places her writing in the propagandist vein as the message is significantly reiterated. This often bores the reader, as in the case of Orisha Debbie in *Destination Biafra*, who repeatedly overstates her case for female transcendence even to the unconvincing extent of rejecting the man she loves. Emecheta's vision is also marred by a slanted, one-dimensional, almost vindictive characterization of the male in all her novels. Take these incredible personalities, for example: Francis in *In the Ditch* is animalistic, Pa Palagada in *The Slave Girl* is an opportunist, Nnaife in *Joys* never grows, Abosi and Monoh in *Destination Biafra* exert cruelties, and Charles in *A Kind of Marriage* and Albert in *Kehinde* are morally weak. Such bias against men in the face of multidimensional, strong, honest, and industrious women subtracts from the complexity of her artistic development. On the other hand, from a stylistic point of view, the language and plots in her earlier works are largely innovative and episodic. However, she has perfected the art of irony over the years, as limned in her later, technically mature creations.

CRITICAL RECEPTION

Buchi Emecheta is black Africa's most prolific female writer. Next to the late South African writer Bessie Head, Emecheta's voice of protest against the patriarchal myopic vision of Igbo women's roles and her unwavering attempt to improve the quality of African women's lives have generated much literary criticism. Emecheta's unique contribution to the Nigerian literary canon surrounds her realistic portraits of African women, which have helped to correct centuries of misconceptions regarding the status of African women in African society. On yet another level, her art advocates reformation of Igbo social systems and the anachronistic ideas emanating from them.

In *Womanist and Feminist Aesthetics: A Comparative Study*, Tuzyline Jita Allan posits womanism's multifaceted response to patriarchy as a corrective to feminism's selective preoccupation with sexual oppression. "There is no doubt," she writes, "that womanism offers a useful assessment of white women's insensitivity to racial and cultural difference on the one hand and black women's heightened awareness of these differentials on the other" (16). However, she cautions that the racially essentialist grounds on which womanism rests threaten its capacity as a viable critical tool. Reading Virginia Woolf's *Mrs. Dalloway*, Margaret Drabble's *The Middle Ground*, and Buchi Emecheta's *The Joys of Motherhood* against Alice Walker's *The Color Purple* ("the paradigmatic womanist text," 107), she discusses both the merits and drawbacks of the womanist position. Buchi Emecheta's narrative "strategy of resistance and accommodation," for example, is said to be feminist rather than womanist, thereby complicating Walker's race-based womanist argument.

Nancy Topping Bazin, in an article entitled "Venturing into Feminist Consciousness: Two Protagonists from the Fiction of Buchi Emecheta and Bessie Head," argues that Emecheta's heroine Nnu Ego in *The Joys of Motherhood* ventures into feminist consciousness, the awakening of self to the inequities in Igbo cultures, such as son preference, polygamy, rigid sex roles, and a glorification of motherhood, which all render women powerless. Bazin credits Emecheta with speaking "for millions of Black African women as to what it is like to be a female in a patriarchal African culture" (36).

In his book *Women Writers in Black Africa*, Lloyd W. Brown describes Emecheta as the African female writer with "the most sustained and vigorous voice of direct feminist protest" (34). It is Emecheta's vision for change that aligns her "more closely to the militant temper and rhetoric of contemporary feminism in Europe and the United States than any other female writer in Black Africa" (35). Emecheta's innovative and germane spectrum on the position of women in Igbo society is committed to the women in developing countries like Nigeria. This perspective, according to Brown, "heralds a promising future" for the author (36).

Barbara Christian, in her book *Black Feminist Criticism*, commends Buchi Emecheta for her realistic portraiture of motherhood in the novel *The Joys of Motherhood*. According to Christian, Emecheta's tendentious art challenges the prevailing views of motherhood held by Igbo society, in contrast to the literary tradition that preceded her. Emecheta's contribution to the Nigerian literary canon lies in her advocating societal change, for "freedom cannot exist unless women, mothers or not, are free to pursue it" (248).

Rhonda Cobham-Sander, in an article entitled "Class vs. Sex: The Problem of Values in the Modern Nigerian Novel," identifies some of the tensions plaguing ambitious young men and women in pursuit of academic degrees in Nigerian universities as recorded in the novel *Double Yoke* by Buchi Emecheta. According to Cobham-Sander, the main protagonist's burdens surround the shaking off of traditional African values that on one hand encourage dominance in the male and on the other subjugate the female into passive roles, along the lines of patriarchal sexual bias. Cobham-Sander concludes that "not until Nigerian women writers begin to question the function of education . . . will the values that inform their demand for a better deal for women be able to incorporate a critique of their own roles as female members of the privileged elite" (27).

In "Technique and Language in Buchi Emecheta's *The Bride Price, The Slave Girl*, and *The Joys of Motherhood*," Ernest N. Emenyonu examines Buchi Emecheta's imagery, figurative language, omniscient commentary, and irony in these early novels. He goes on to describe her writing in *The Bride Price* and *The Slave Girl* as basically ironical in nature, however marred they are by the author's ambivalence as to the fate of the African woman as well as by a profuse use of trite and flat figurative expressions such as "a child is as fat as a plump yam" and "Okoli croaked like a frog with a bad cold" (133). In *The Joys of Motherhood*, however, he contends that the author's style is much more secure, confident, and successful as she handles her themes and language in the tradition of African narrative art with precision, subtlety, and a sense of invaluable mission. The article ends with Emenyonu praising Emecheta as "one of the best storytellers in modern Africa" (141).

Katherine Frank in an article entitled "Women Without Men: The Feminist Novel in Africa" presents the view that the feminist novel in Africa is more radical, even more militant than its Western counterpart. She goes on to report that Africa's female writers' solution to sexism is repudiation of patriarchy and acceptance of a world without men (15). Although Frank's separatist view is supported with textual examples from Emecheta's novels *Double Yoke* and *Destination Biafra*, it is limited by the sociocultural fact that the masses of African women (both educated and uneducated) have chosen to be "women under husbands" even within polygamous households in contemporary African society.

Eustace Palmer in an article entitled "The Feminine Point of View: Buchi Eme-

cheta's *The Joys of Motherhood*'' exalts *Joys* as the first work in African literature to present the female point of view in registering its disgust at male
chauvinism and patriarchy's satisfaction with an unfair and oppressive system
toward women (39). Nnu Ego's famous words "God, when will you create a
woman who will be fulfilled in herself, a full human being, not anybody's
appendage?" contradict the "phallocratic" images of happy, cheerful women.
Palmer concludes that another first is Emecheta's creation of Adaku, Nnu Ego's
cowife, the "forerunner of women's liberation in Africa" (49).

Florence Stratton, in a brilliant and illuminating study, "The Shallow Grave:
Archetypes of Female Experience in African Fiction," contends that in the novels, *The Bride Price, The Slave Girl*, and *The Joys of Motherhood*, Emecheta's
women become paradigms of a shallow grave, the living dead (147). Stratton
goes on to prove by indirect analogy how patriarchy, regardless of the cultural
milieu, negatively affects the female psyche. The significance of this study is
that for the first time in African literary criticism, a comparison is made conveying the subtle similarities between the Western woman's sense of imprisonment and abnegation and the African woman's feeling of enslavement and
second-class status due to patriarchy's restrictions. Stratton's hypothesis that
there is "a female literary tradition that transcends all cultural boundaries" (144)
paves the way for more novel and exciting theories in African literature dealing
with gender.

The importance of Rolf Solberg's article "The Women of Black Africa, Buchi
Emecheta: The Woman's Voice in the New Nigerian Novel" is that it points
out that Emecheta's "dilemma is part and parcel of . . . her love and respect for
the African heritage vying with the pains of having to define her attitudes towards the problems of the post-colonial reality" (260). Emecheta's ambivalent
feelings toward Westernization are evident in her novel *The Bride Price*, in
which she has Aku-nna break away from the elders who represent tradition to
become a "full human being, not anybody's appendage." Solberg concludes
that Aku-nna's death during childbirth at the end of the novel is symbolic of
tradition's triumph.

In Oladele Taiwo's book *Female Novelists of Modern Africa*, Buchi Emecheta
admits that she supports the feminist movement because of her belief in the
individuality of everybody, man and woman. She goes on to assert that "a
citizen must be able to act in freedom and dignity. No sex should attempt to
dominate the other" (102). Emecheta's discourse can indeed be regarded as
revolutionary, with an undeniable emphasis on the need for change. As Taiwo
prophesies, "The elders may dominate the present, but the future certainly belongs to people like Chike and Aku-nna and their friends, Adegor, Rose and
Chima" (108).

Cynthia Ward, in "What They Told Buchi Emecheta: Oral Subjectivity and
the Joys of 'Otherhood,' " examines the oral ambiguity and ironic tensions in
Emecheta's novel *The Joys of Motherhood*. Ward shows how this author's "subtle interweaving of often contradictory perspectives suggests a flexibility of so-

cial and cultural roles, rankings and relationships that preclude any authoritative perspective or voice from telling us how to view the village or, indeed, read the novel'' (92–93). Ward goes on to say that the conflicting reports of the author herself account for the varied interpretations of her critics: Bazin, Frank, Ogunyemi, Solberg, and Umeh, to name only a few. Ward concludes that although Emecheta's recollections of Ibuza social customs and acceptable modes of behavior are contradictory, the bottom line is that they reflect the complexity of Ibuza life itself, and just as all of the author's renditions of Igbo life and culture are valid, so too are the varied exegeses of her critics.

Florence Stratton's book *Contemporary African Literature and the Politics of Gender* is one of the first books to examine gender politics in African literature and to include rather than exclude contemporary women writers' contribution to the canon. In placing Buchi Emecheta, as well as Flora Nwapa, Grace Ogot, and Mariama Bâ, next to great African male writers, such as Chinua Achebe and Ngũgĩ wa Thiong'o, Stratton challenges male hegemony in African literature. For example, in the chapter '' 'Their New Sister': Buchi Emecheta and the Contemporary African Literary Tradition,'' Stratton demonstrates the ways Emecheta (re)creates spheres of female influence to redeem the African woman's personality and inner reality that have been hidden under rapid generalizations, myths, and patent untruths. In a womanist thrust, Stratton also points to the ways in which Emecheta's fiction redirects men's tunnel vision and has transformed sexist concepts of masculinist authors who now attempt to write with sensitivity on gender issues.

Chikwenye Okonjo Ogunyemi in *Africa Wo/Man Palava: The Nigerian Novel by Women* examines the major female novelists of Nigeria and their womanist discourses, which she names ''wo/man palava.'' In her chapter entitled ''Buchi Emecheta: The Been-to (Bintu) Novel,'' Ogunyemi commends Emecheta for internationalizing sexual politics in an African society with encyclopedic range ''to restore order in the family and the rank and file to avert the enslavement and fall of the nation'' (225). Rich in postmodern theories of discourse, Ogunyemi's insider views are scintillating.

Marie Umeh's chapter ''Procreation, Not Recreation: Decoding Mama in Buchi Emecheta's *The Joys of Motherhood*,'' in *Emerging Perspectives on Buchi Emecheta*, focuses on female sexuality in Emecheta's magnum opus. According to Umeh, Emecheta in *The Joys of Motherhood* exposes patriarchal effacement of female sexual desire and expressivity by programming its female kith and kin to carry a ''moral albatross'' around their necks (191). It is my contention that Emecheta is redefining African women's sexuality and showing possibilities for happiness within the African world by exploring the roles of love, sexuality, and male companionship in African women's lives.

BIBLIOGRAPHY

Works by Buchi Emecheta

Adult Books

In the Ditch. London: Barrie and Jenkins, 1972.
The Bride Price. London: Allison and Busby 1975 (c1974); New York: George Braziller, 1976.
Second-Class Citizen. New York: George Braziller, 1975.
The Slave Girl. New York: George Braziller, 1977.
The Joys of Motherhood. New York: George Braziller, 1979.
Our Own Freedom. London: Sheba Feminist Publishers, 1981.
Destination Biafra. London: Allison and Busby, 1982.
Double Yoke. London: Ogwugwu Afor, 1982.
Naira Power. London: Macmillan, 1982.
The Rape of Shavi. New York: George Braziller, 1985.
Head above Water. London: Fontara, 1986.
A Kind of Marriage. London: Macmillan, 1986.
The Family. London: William Collins Sons and Co., 1989.
Kehinde. London: Heinemann, 1994.

Dramatic Works

Juju Landlord. British Broadcasting Company, 1976.
A Kind of Marriage. British Broadcasting Company, 1986.

Children's Books

Titch the Cat. London: Allison and Busby, 1978.
Nowhere to Play. London: Allison and Busby, 1980.
The Moonlight Bride. New York: George Braziller, 1983.
The Wrestling Match. New York: George Braziller, 1983.

Articles

"Should Husbands Control a Wife's Salary?" *African Weekly Review* 1.3 (1967): 8.
"Marriage: Does It Pay." *African Weekly Review* 1.20 October 1967: 12.
"Mixed Marriage." *African Weekly Review* 1.17 (1968): 13.
"Out of the Ditch and into Print." *West Africa* (London) April 3, 1978: 669–72.
"An African View of Church of England." *West Africa* (London) April 24, 1978: 805–6
"The Human Race Decides to March through London." *West Africa* (London) June 19, 1978: 1177–80.
"Buchi Emecheta on the Neglect of the Art of the Story Teller." *West Africa* (London) August 28, 1978: 1691–92.
"A Time Bomb." *West Africa* (London) October 30, 1978: 2139–40.
"Give Us This Day Our Daily Bread." *West Africa* (London) December 4, 1978: 2410–11.
"Christmas Is for All." *West Africa* (London) December 25, 1978: 2590–91.
"Buchi Emecheta Goes Jogging." *West Africa* (London) March 12, 1979: 444–45.

"Another Fear of Flying." *West Africa* (London) June 25, 1979: 1119–38.

"Darry and a Bouquet of Flowers." *West Africa* (London) July 9, 1979: 1215–16.

"Language Difficulties." *West Africa* (London) July 16, 1979: 1267–68.

"A Question of Dollars." *West Africa* (London) July 30, 1979: 1367–1438.

"US Longing for Roasted Yams." *West Africa* (London) August 27, 1979: 1560–62.

"US Police Convince Me I Am Lost." *West Africa* (London) September 24, 1979: 1761–62.

"Calabar Contrasts and Complaints." *West Africa* (London) January 12, 1981: 21–22.

"Lagos Provides a Warm Welcome." *West Africa* (London) January 19, 1981: 110–13.

"That First Novel." *Kunapipi* 3.2 (1981): 115–23.

"It's Me Who's Changed." *Connexions* 4 (1982): 4–5.

"A Nigerian Writer Living in London." *Kunapipi* 4.1 (1982): 115–19.

"African Women Step Out." *New Africa* 1 (November 1985): 7–8.

"Education: United States." *Women: A World Report*. New York: Oxford University Press, 1985. 205–18.

"Nwayi Oma, Biko Nodu Nma" (Beautiful woman, please farewell). *West Africa* (October 24–30, 1994): 1831.

Studies of Buchi Emecheta

Acholonu, Catherine. "Buchi Emecheta." *Guardian Literary Series* (Lagos, Nigeria) January 25, 1986: 13.

Allan, Tuzyline J. *Womanist and Feminist Aesthetics: A Comparative Study*. Athens: Ohio University Press, 1995.

Amuta, Chidi. "The Nigerian Civil War and the Evolution of Nigerian Literature." *Canadian Journal of African Studies* 17.1 (1983): 90–103.

Barthelemy, Anthony. "Western Time, African Lives: Time in the Novels of Buchi Emecheta." *Callaloo* 12.3 (1989): 559–74.

Bazin, Nancy T. "Venturing into Feminist Consciousness: Two Protagonists from the Fiction of Buchi Emecheta and Bessie Head." *Sage: A Scholarly Journal on Black Women* 2.1 (Spring 1985): 32–36.

Beik, Janet. "Women's Voice in African Fiction: Buchi Emecheta." Paper presented in a seminar at the University of Wisconsin–Madison, December 1979.

Benstock, Shari, ed. *Feminist Issues in Literary Scholarship*. Bloomington: Indiana University Press, 1987.

Berrian, Brenda. *Bibliography of African Women Writers and Journalists*. Washington, D.C.: Three Continents Press, 1985.

Brown, Lloyd W. *Women Writers in Black Africa*. Westport, CT: Greenwood Press, 1981.

Brunner, Charlotte. "The Other Audience: Children and the Example of Buchi Emecheta." *African Studies Review* 29.3 (September 1986): 129–40.

———. *Unwinding Threads: Writing by Women in Africa*. London: Heinemann, 1983.

"Buchi Emecheta." *African Women* 2 (January 1976): 48–49.

Chinweizu. "Times of Troubles." *Times Literary Supplement* February 26, 1982: 228.

Christian, Barbara. *Black Feminist Criticism*. New York: Pergamon Press, 1985.

Chukukere, Gloria. *Gender Voices and Choices: Redefining Women in Contemporary African Fiction*. Enugu: Fourth Dimension, 1995.

Chukwuma, Helen. *Feminism in African Literature: Essays in Criticism*. Abuja, Nigeria: New Generation Books, 1994.

————. "Nigerian Female Authors: 1970 to the Present." *Matatu* 1.2 (1987): 23–42.

Cobham-Sander, Rhonda. "Class vs. Sex: The Problems of Values in the Modern Nigerian Novel." *The Black Scholar* 17.4 (July/August 1986): 17–27.

Crichton, Sarah. "Buchi Emecheta." *Publishers Weekly* 215 (June 11, 1979): 10–11.

Davies, Carole Boyce. "Motherhood in the World of Male and Female Igbo Writers: Achebe, Emecheta, Nwapa, and Nzekwu." *Ngambika: Studies of Women in African Literature*. Ed. Carole Boyce Davies and Anne Adams Graves. Trenton, NJ: Africa World Press, 1986. 241–56.

————. "Private Selves and Public Spaces: Autobiography and the African Woman Writer." *College Language Association* 34.3 (1991): 267–89. Reprinted in *Crisscrossing Boundaries in African Literature, 1986*. Ed. Kenneth Harrow, Jonathan Ngate, and Clarisse Zimra. Washington, DC: Three Continents Press and the ALA, 1991. 109–27.

Davies, Carole Boyce, and Anne Adams Graves, eds. *Ngambika: Studies of Women in African Literature*. Trenton, NJ: Africa World Press, 1986.

Davis, Wendy. "Destination Biafra: Mission Not Quite Accomplished." *Africa Now* March 1982: 74–75.

Ebeogu, Afamefuna N. "Enter the Iconoclast: Buchi Emecheta and the Igbo Culture." *Commonwealth Essays and Studies* 7.2 (1985): 83–94.

————. "The Igbo Tradition in Nigerian Literature of English Expression." Diss. University of Ibadan, Nigeria, 1980.

Emenyonu, Ernest N. "Technique and Language in Buchi Emecheta's *The Bride Price, The Slave Girl*, and *The Joys of Motherhood*." *Journal of Commonwealth Literature* 23.1 (1988): 130–41.

Ezenwa-Ohaeto. "Replacing Myth with Myth: The Feminist Streak in Buchi Emecheta." Paper presented at the 1988 University of Calabar Conference, Calabar, Nigeria.

Fishburn, Katherine. *Reading Buchi Emecheta: Cross-Cultural Conversations*. Westport, CT: Greenwood Press, 1995.

Frank, Katherine. "Women Without Men: the Feminist Novel in Africa." *African Literature Today* 15 (1987): 14–34.

Ikonne, Chidi. "Biography into Fiction." *Guardian* (Lagos, Nigeria) January 9, 1985: 9.

Katrak, Ketu H. "Womanhood/Motherhood: Variations on a Theme in Selected Novels of Buchi Emecheta." *The Journal of Commonwealth Literature* 22.1 (1987): 159–70.

Kemp, Yakini. "Romantic Love and the Individual in Novels by Mariama Bâ, Buchi Emecheta and Bessie Head." *Obsidian II* 3.3 (1988): 1–16.

Lauer, Margaret R. "Buchi Emecheta's: *The Bride Price*." *World Literature Written in English* 16 (November 1977): 308–10.

Lelyveld, Joseph. "Out of Africa." *New York Times Book Review* November 11, 1979: 15, 39.

Lindfors, Bernth. "The Famous Authors' Reputation Test." *Kriteria: A Nigerian Journal of Literary Research* 1.1 (1988): 25–33.

Nichols, Lee. *Conversations with African Writers: Interviews with Twenty-six African Authors*. Washington, DC: Voice of America, 1981.

Nnaemeka, Obioma. "Feminist Protest in Buchi Emecheta's Novels." *International Third World Studies Journal and Review* 1.1 (1989): 1–10.

————. "From Orality to Writing: African Women Writers and the (Re) Inscription of Womanhood." *Research in African Literatures* 25.4 (Winter 1994): 137–57.

Nnolim, Charles E. "Trends in the Nigerian Novel." *Matatu* 1.2 (1987): 7–22.

Nwankwo, Chimalum. "Emecheta's Social Vision: Fantasy or Reality?" *Ufahamu* 17.1 (1988): 35–44.

Ogunyemi, Chikwenye O. *Africa Wo/Man Palava: The Nigerian Novel by Women*. Chicago: University of Chicago Press, 1996.

————. "Buchi Emecheta: The Shaping of a Self." *Komparatistische* Hefte 8 (1983): 65–77.

————. "The Nigerian Female Novelist and the Feminist Encounter." Paper presented at the Conference on The Black Women Writer and the Diaspora at Michigan State University, October 27–30, 1985.

————. "Womanism: The Dynamics of the Contemporary Black Female Novel in English." *Signs* 11.1 (1985): 63–80.

Oko, Emelia. "The Female Estate: A Study of Buchi Emecheta's Novels." Paper presented at the Literary Society of Nigeria Conference, University of Benin, February 1984.

Palmer, Eustace. "The Feminine Point of View: Buchi Emecheta's *The Joys of Motherhood.*" *African Literature Today* 13 (London: Heinemann, 1983): 38–55.

Perry, Alistar. "Buchi Emecheta: The Feminist Book Fair." *West Africa* June 18, 1984: 1263.

Petersen, Kirsten. "Unpopular Opinions: Some African Women Writers." *A Double Colonization: Colonial and Post-Colonial Women's Writing*. Ed. Kirsten Holst Peterson and Anna Rutherford. Mundelstrup, Denmark: Dangaroo, 1986. 107–20.

Ravell-Pinto, Thelma. "Buchi Emecheta at Spelman College." *Sage: A Scholarly Journal on Black Women* 2.1 (1985): 50–51.

Schipper, Mineke. "Mother Africa on a Pedestal: The Male Heritage in African Literature and Criticism." *Women in African Literature Today* 15 (1987): 35–54.

————. ed. "Women and Literature in Africa." *Unheard Words: Women and Literature in Africa, the Arab World, Asia, the Caribbean, and Latin American*. London: Allison and Busby, 1985. 22–58.

Skinner, Margaret. "The Theme of Barrenness in African Women's Literature: Buchi Emecheta and Flora Nwapa." Paper presented for the Women's Studies Colloquium, University of Wisconsin–Madison, February 1980.

Solberg, Rolf. "The Woman of Black Africa, Buchi Emecheta: The Woman's Voice in the New Nigerian Novel." *English Studies* 64.3 (June 1983): 247–62.

Stratton, Florence. *Contemporary African Literature and the Politics of Gender*. London and New York: Routledge, 1994.

————. "The Shallow Grave: Archetypes of Female Experience in African Fiction." *Research in African Literatures* 19.1 (Summer 1988): 143–69.

Strummer, Peter. "Buchi Emecheta und die Erfahrung der Schwarzen Frau." *Drama in Commonwealth*. Ed. Gerhard Stilz Gunter. Tübingen: Narr, 1983. 91–102.

Taiwo, Oladele. "Culture, Tradition, and Change in Buchi Emecheta's Novels." *Medium and Message* 1 (1981): 122–42.

————. *Female Novelists of Modern Africa*. London: Macmillan, 1984.

Tapping, Craig. "Irish Feminism and African Tradition: A Reading of Buchi Emecheta's Novels." *Medium and Message* (University of Calabar, Nigeria: Department of English) (1981): 178–96.

Umeh, Marie. "African Women in Transition in the Novels of Buchi Emecheta." *Présence Africaine* 116 (1980): 190–201.

———. "Children's Literature in Nigeria: Revolutionary Omissions." *Preserving the Landscape of Imagination: Children's Literature in Africa*. Ed. Raoul Granqvist and Jürgen Martini. In *Matatu*, 17–18. Atlanta: Editions Rodopi, 1997. 191–206.

———. *Emerging Perspectives on Buchi Emecheta*. Trenton, NJ: Africa World Press, 1996.

———, and Davidson Umeh. "Interview with Buchi Emecheta." *Ba Shiru* 12.2 (1985): 19–25.

———. "*The Joys of Motherhood*: Myth or Reality." *Colby Library Quarterly* 18.1 (1982): 39–46.

———. "The Poetics of Thwarted Sensitivity." *Critical Theory and African Literature*. Ed. Ernest Emenyonu. Ibadan: Heinemann, 1987. 194–206.

———. "Reintegration with the Lost Self: A Study of Buchi Emecheta's *Double Yoke*." *Ngambika: Studies of Women in African Literature*. Ed. Carole Boyce Davies and Anne Adams Graves. Trenton, NJ: Africa World Press, 1986.

Uwazurike, Chudi. "The Abuse of Igbo Culture." *National Concord* (Nigeria) February 4, 1981: 5.

Walker, Alice. "A Writer Because of, Not in Spite of Her Children." *In Search of Our Mothers' Gardens*. New York: Harcourt Brace Jovanovich, 1983. 66–70.

Ward, Cynthia. "What They Told Buchi Emecheta: Oral Subjectivity and the Joys of 'Otherhood.' " *PMLA* 105.1 (January 1990): 83–97.

Wilson, Judith. "Buchi Emecheta: Africa from a Woman's Voice." *Essence* February 1980: 9–11.

Zell, Hans M. *A New Reader's Guide to African Literature*. New York: Africana Publishing Company, 1983.

MARIE UMEH

FEMI EUBA (1941–)

BIOGRAPHY

Femi Euba, professor of theater and English at Louisiana State University, is a playwright, actor, director, short-story writer, and literary critic. Born April 2, 1941 in Lagos, Nigeria, he is the son of Alphaeus Sobiyi Euba (a confectioner) and Winifred Remilekun (Dawodu) Euba (a teacher). He is married to Addie Jane Dawson (a printmaker).

Femi Euba has been in the theater world since 1959. He was, with Wole Soyinka, a founding member of the 1960 Masks, a group that helped usher in a renaissance of the theater in independent Nigeria. Before then, his early creative efforts included poetry and short stories for Radio Nigeria. He studied acting and speech and drama at the Rose Bruford College of Speech and Drama in Kent, England, between 1962 and 1965. After his studies, Euba worked his way into professional acting in England, under the direction of Athol Fugard. Although opportunities were limited for black actors, Euba featured in such plays as *Macbeth* with the renowned actor Alec Guinness at London's Royal Court, where he was also a member of a writers' workshop created by one of England's innovative directors, William Gaskill. He has performed in many theater houses in England and the United States. He received an M.F.A. from the Yale School of Drama in 1973, an M.A. in Afro-American studies at the Yale Graduate School in 1982, and a Ph.D. in literature at the University of Ife (now Obafemi Awolowo University) in 1988. Teaching courses in playwriting, acting, and directing, Femi Euba was, for many years, a senior lecturer at the University of Ife Dramatic Arts Department. He has been residing in the United States since 1986, first in Williamsburg, Virginia, where he taught acting at the College of William and Mary, and then in Baton Rouge, Louisiana, where he still teaches playwriting and directing at Louisiana State University and also directs plays for LSU Theater.

In the three decades from 1960 to 1990, Femi Euba acted such prominent roles as Olunde in Soyinka's Nobel Prize–winning play *Death and the King's Horseman*, Colonel Moses and Lakunle in Soyinka's *Opera Woyonsi* and *The Lion and The Jewel*, respectively, Pamphillion in Derek Walcott's *Dream on Monkey Mountain*, and Von Lieres in Blau and Fenton's *The Biko Inquest*. He has directed such plays as Athol Fugard's *Sizwe Bansi Is Dead*, which won directing awards at the Kennedy Center/American College Theater Festival in 1993. He also directed Lorraine Hansberry's *A Raisin in the Sun*, Akin Ishola's *Madame Tinubu*, and many other African and European plays. In his capacity as a professional actor and talented director, Femi Euba has been significant to the vision of other artists such as Wole Soyinka and Athol Fugard, two of Africa's most notable playwrights. However, his own vision and dedicated love for the theater have been blanketed over in the often hidden role of director.

He has also written numerous plays, which have been produced on the BBC Radio in London, on Radio Nigeria, and at theaters in Nigeria and the United States. Current both in film and on stage, Femi Euba is concerned not just with the aesthetic engagement of writing and performance, not just with the teaching of creative writing and the production of scholarly papers, but primarily with the theoretical and performative ritual role of black dramatists in Africa and the diaspora. In a global setting of transnational economic collusions and epidemic violence, Euba takes seriously the role of the black dramatist as bearer of tradition and conscience of society. His political commitment is evident in the major genre in which he himself writes—satire. In such plays as *The Wig and the Honeybee, Tortoise*, and *Riddles on Greed: Three One-Acts*, written over the span of three decades, Euba satirizes the institutions of greed and corruption eating away at the moral fibre of his country, Nigeria. His clarion call of what-you-sow-you-shall-reap, a theme that runs through most of his plays, is aimed at willing Nigerians to self-reflexivity and change. Euba's 1989 publication of *Archetypes, Imprecators, and Victims of Fate*, a critical study of satire in black drama, is his attempt to locate the complex cartographies of black struggle in the Americas and in Africa. This landmark publication on black drama bears fruit in his most powerful play to date, *The Gulf*, which won the Association of Nigerian Authors Literary Award. In *The Gulf*, more so than in the one-act plays, Euba offers a recipe with a clear social vision for the postmodern realities of our time.

MAJOR WORKS AND THEMES

In Femi Euba's search for a definition of black diasporic theater and his attempts to articulate the contradictory, sometimes uncontainable, notion of the "essence" of blackness, it is not surprising that he should turn to his immediate experience of consciousness and identity within his cultural space—the cultural world of the Yorubas and its everyday engagement with the gods. In his critical study on black drama, *Archetypes, Imprecators, and Victims of Fate*, Euba attempts to sketch a unifying concept of identity through a physical and metaphysical journey of fate as controlled and directed by Esu-Elegbara, the god of fate, the messenger god who distributes both good and evil to the human race. By presenting the Yoruba trickster god in all its contradictions—the forces of good and evil are coexistent and complementary in Esu—Euba introduces the "principle of indeterminacy" (2) that manifests itself not only in the trickster god's unknowable ways but also in his evident trick of fate on the human race. The black race scattered across the Americas, for example, is tied to its African roots through the "essence of fate" (4) they share—the slave trade and the continued effects of the colonial encounter. Euba locates, in the black race's attempts to alter this fated encounter, both the ritual significance of "Esu" as a concept of theatrical expression and Esu's import as a master satirist. Satire in black drama, Euba argues, expresses, in historically specific terms, "the black condition of survival" (9). Thus, in embracing both ritual and satire as conditioning black theater, Euba captures the contemporaneous indeterminacies of black existence in chapter 4, which he significantly titles "Drama of Epidemic." As an archetype of black drama, Esu-Elegbara functions, through "destructive and restorative processes" (125), as a critique of the epidemic, the social malaise, present in black societies and cultures.

Euba's ritualized celebration of black struggle and survival in the face of the vicissitudes of life, of fate, is further adumbrated in his literary award-winning play *The Gulf*. The play opens with Inside-Out, a journalist, doing an on-the-scene investigation of a road accident for his socialist newspaper in Lagos. The accident has just taken place on a poorly constructed bridge over a gulf that has already devoured, even by Nigerian standards, an epidemic proportion of human lives through road accidents. Because of the gulf's notoriety, many believe that Ogun, the god of iron and technology, is merely requiring necessary devotion, through blood sacrifice, by causing accidents. The gulf is also the pathway to a former slaveholding fort. Thus Euba sets the stage for a realistic encounter between diasporic Africans and their homeland in all its present-day decadence. Gold Jackson, an African-American tourist, has come to Lagos to visit historical sites, like the fort, that will reveal her roots and history to her. This historical rememory, however, is constantly interrupted by the blatant institutional corruption of modern-day Lagos. For instance, Yangi's reckless driving of a passenger bus results in the death of all his passengers; however, when Yangi bribes the police, the police forego prosecution for manslaughter by helping him remove "the evidence." As expected, the community believes that Ogun has struck again and that the god has miraculously "disappeared" the evidence. Euba's metaphysical take, that Esu the god of fate actually wills the outcome of other gods' actions, as explored in *Archetypes*, is played out in *The Gulf* as the everyday drama of life in Lagos. Yangi, the bus driver, is named after Esu and becomes, if not Esu himself, then the representative of Esu. Yangi's father,

Babalorisa, is the symbol of tradition in the play, but like Yangi and the police, Babalorisa manipulates tradition to work for him in the face of the threat of modernity; for the narrative of survival to continue, tradition must be balanced with the postcolonial condition. Thus through ritual drama, Baba exposes both the Commissioner-for-Roads' total rejection of his culture for Western ways and Gold Jackson's obsessed search for "the real thing," for a pure unadulterated African tradition.

In satirizing the fate of Africa and its descendants through the drama of epidemic, Femi Euba, in postmodern relief, challenges us with the elusive, dynamic concept of "Esu," that "compromise between good and evil" (*Gulf*, 67), between tradition and modernity. Doubt and confusion, the result of progress and civilization, must be responded to with the concept of "Esu"—action, imaginativeness, irony, and wit. For, as Femi Euba provocatively states in *Archetypes*, "Esu is no other than our fate—by synecdoche, ourselves" (4).

CRITICAL RECEPTION

Femi Euba's *Archetypes, Imprecators, and Victims of Fate* has received much praise in Eugene Kraft's review of the work for the depth of ideas it explores, its textual density, and its scholarly magnitude. Kraft attempts to capture the complexity of the archetypal satirist Esu and his influence in human affairs when he paraphrases Euba thus: "Fate controls the human, yet the human's will is fate. The arrogance and greed manifested by the will produce retribution in the form of fate." Euba seems to suggest, in his painstaking explanation of the relationship between gods and humans, the reality of the effects of outside, "environmental" forces on human social perception and actions. But these effects, Euba insists, have been created by society itself and are therefore subject to change. Kraft further captures Euba's wry humor in "The African Model" section of chapter 4 where Euba highlights the glorious visibility of corruption in all walks of life in African nation-states today and the imminent consequences of such moral disintegration. Esu (evil) is the one who misguides, but Esu (good) is the one who also retributes the misguided one (31). Kraft also notes the further complexity of the Esu concept in its rather dramatic manifestations in the New World—the Americas. Slaves, empowered or embodied by Esu (the spirit of revolution), often used the "devil" in them to challenge the "devil" in the master. Kraft concludes that the work is "valuable primarily for its suggestiveness" and that it is "a most tempting invitation" for subsequent scholarship.

D. F. Dorsey, in a review of *Archetypes*, identifies Euba's discussion of Esu "not as metaphor or belief, but an existing divinity, manifest in art, but also in the historical experiences (such as slavery) and contemporary political and social realities (such as Nigerian traffic and 'dash')." Dorsey also points out that Euba's work offers "new trends in black literary theory."

In her review, Omofolabo Ajayi confirms Euba's theoretical trend when she asserts, "What *Archetypes* attempts to do for black theater is what the Greek classical theater has done for Western dramatic theory'' (150). Ajayi praises Euba's ''monumental archeological work'' (149) not only for its impact on African dramatic traditions, but for its very existence in the African diaspora, its impact on Western dramatic forms. Ajayi also notes that *Archetypes* not only straddles African and Western scholarship with its classical and postmodern sensibilities but also provides an interdisciplinary focus that makes the work a necessary sourcebook in studies such as religion and anthropology. As antidote for survival, as deconstructive tool, and as ''drama of epidemic,'' Euba's study of satire, Ajayi points out, is offered as a ''theory of crisis management'' against the ''accidents'' of colonial history (148).

Euba's philosophical position in *Archetypes* is reiterated in his play *The Gulf.* J. B. Alston, in *Yoruba Drama in English*, observes that even though Euba is working with the old theme ''western mechanization and its effect on African culture,'' Euba's emphasis is unique because it deals significantly with the ''cultural conditioning'' of both Africans and African Americans. In the face of cultural uncertainty, Alston notes, confusion is the all-present element. The characters are all confused, and even those, like Babalorisa and the Commissioner, who are somewhat assertive in their convictions ''are betrayed by their actions.'' In a world where both tradition and modernity fail, Euba's only solution, Alston confirms, is the ''trial and error of concerted compromise.''

On the technical aspect of the play, Alston comments on the ''clean crispness'' that makes the play ''a pleasure to read and analyze.'' Although Alston sees the ending of the play as almost extraneous to the rest, it has not in any way diminished his own investment in the play as a director of a very successful production at North Carolina Central University. Newspaper reviews of the production at NCCU refer to the plot's riveting structure and Euba's intellectual efforts at bridging the gulf between Africa and the black diaspora.

BIBLIOGRAPHY

Works by Femi Euba

Plays and Scholarship

''Abiku.'' *Five African Plays*. Ed. Cosmo Pieterse. London: Heinemann, 1972. 1–29.
Archetypes, Imprecators, and Victims of Fate: Origins and Developments of Satire in Black Drama. Westport, CT: Greenwood Press, 1989.
''Crocodiles.'' *Quarterly Journal of Ideology* 18. 1–2 (June 1995). *The Eye of Gabriel*, a full-length play (unpublished). Staged reading at the Schomburg Research Library in New York, March 1995.
''The Game.'' *Ten One-Act Plays*. Ed. Cosmo Pieterse. London: Heinemann, 1968; reprinted 1972. 85–107.
The Gulf. Lagos: Longman Nigeria, 1991. U.S. premiere production at North Carolina Central University, March 1993.

"Riddles of the Palm" and "Crocodiles." Bound copy. New York Public Library at Kennedy Center.
Riddles on Greed: Three One-Acts. 1991 (unpublished).

Articles

"Aldridge's Revolutionary Realism: An Evaluation of Ira Aldridge's Adaptation of An-icet-Bourgeois." *The Black Doctor*, in a new series of publications of W. E. B. Du Bois Institute. Ed. Henry L. Gates, Jr. New York: Oxford University Press, forthcoming.
"The Nigerian Theatre and the Playwright." *Drama and Theatre in Nigeria: A Critical Source Book.* Ed. Yemi Ogunbiyi. Lagos: Nigeria Magazine, 1981. 381–398.
"Report from London: The African Actor." *African Arts/Arts d'Afrique* Summer 1969: 62–64.
"Soyinka's Satiric Development and Maturity." *Black American Literature Forum.* 22.3 (Fall 1988): 615–627.

Radio Plays

Chameleon. British Broadcasting Corporation (BBC) Radio Monograph, 1968.
The Devil. BBC Radio Monograph, 1970.
Down by the Lagoon. BBC Radio Monograph, 1965.
The Game. BBC Radio Monograph, 1966.
The Telegram. BBC Radio Monograph, 1965.
Tortoise. BBC Radio Monograph, 1967.
The Wig and the Honeybee. BBC Radio Monograph, 1976.
The Yam Debt. BBC Radio Monograph, 1964.

Studies of Femi Euba

Reviews *of* Archetypes, Imprecators, and Victims of Fate

Ajayi, Omofolabo. "The Faces of Nigerian Theater . . ." *Research in African Literatures* 24.3 (Fall 1993): 141–150.
Dorsey, D. F. *Choice* 28 (September 1990): 123.
Kraft, Eugene. *Afro-Hispanic Review* January 1991: 30–31.

Reviews *of* The Gulf

Alston, J. B. *Yoruba Drama in English: Interpretation and Production.* Lewiston, NY: E. Mellen Press, 1989.
Fioupou, Christiane. *La route: Realité et representation dans l'oeuvre de Wole Soyinka.* Amsterdam and Atlanta, GA: Editions Rodopi, 1994. 69–70, 108, 113, 145n, 340, 371.
McDowell, Robert W. *Spectator* March 4, 1993: 20.
McLain, Kay. "NCCU Cast Shines in Nigerian Playwright's New View of Old Story." *Herald Sun* (Durham, NC) February 26, 1993: B14.

Bibliographic Entries

Black Writers: A Selection of Sketches from Contemporary Authors. 2nd ed. Ed. Sharon
    Malinowski. Detroit: Gale Research, 1994.
Marquis Who's Who in Entertainment. 2nd ed. Wilmette, IL: Marquis Who's Who,
    1992–1993.

IYUNOLU FOLAYAN OSAGIE

AMINATA SOW FALL (1941–   )

BIOGRAPHY

Born in Saint-Louis, Senegal, in 1941, Aminata Sow Fall writes in French although her mother tongue is Wolof. After high school she went to study in Paris; she stayed there between 1962 and 1969. When she returned to Senegal, she worked for a number of years as a teacher and was actively involved in educational reform and the development and implementation of pedagogic programs. Having held the position of Directrice des Lettres et de la Propriété Intellectuelle, she resigned in 1988 to devote her time to writing; in September of that year she founded the Centre Africain d'Animation et d'Échanges Culturels (CAEC). This center is a nonprofit organization that seeks to foster intellectual, literary, and cultural debate. It also serves as the headquarters for the National Union of Senegalese Writers, the International Association of Anthropologists, and the Association of Senegalese Translators and Interpreters. The center also has a desktop-publishing facility designed to encourage young writers to exchange their manuscripts, notably those written in African languages.

With the publication of *Le revenant* in 1976, Aminata Sow Fall became the first sub-Saharan Francophone African female writer to publish a work of literature that was not of autobiographical inspiration. She published *La grève des Bàttu ou les déchets humains* in 1979 (awarded the Grand Prix Littéraire d'Afrique Noire in 1980) and *L'appel des arènes* in 1982 (awarded the Alioune Diop International Prize for African Literature in 1982); this secured her place in African literature, but also set a precedent for future women writers.

MAJOR WORKS AND THEMES

The image of women as the incarnation of motherly and mythic values has been progressively eroded and has given way to thinking about issues relating to polygamy, arranged marriages, sexual mutilation, and education. Aminata Sow Fall's novels examine the social environment in which African women have to attempt to construct identity, but nevertheless without suggesting any radical or militant stance. She does, however, examine the various social mechanisms that are at work in contemporary African society and exposes the manner in which power is acquired, maintained, and manipulated.

When Aminata Sow Fall returned to Senegal in 1969, the society she had once known had undergone radical transformation. This transition from colonial to post-colonial rule provides the background to her first novel, *Le revenant* (1976), in which she explores the emergence of capitalism and the accompanying erasure of those cultural elements that had always provided the foundations to Senegalese society. Fall denounces the negative effects of outside influences on her culture, influences that ignore the intrinsic values of the region. We now find ourselves in a new world that has no direction and that is devoid of a cultural framework.

In *La grève des Bàttu ou les déchets humains* (1979), Mour Ndiaye (the Director of Public Health) dreams of being nominated the Vice-President of the imaginary country in which the story takes place. To ingratiate himself with the President, he rids the city of all its marginal figures (predominantly the beggars). In a somewhat paradoxical turn of events, the beggars, who are aware of Ndiaye's need to purge himself through charitable donations, decide to go on strike as retribution for his opportunistic treatment of them. Without their prayers, the position he seeks will continue to elude him. With this second novel, Aminata Sow Fall thus confronts a further aspect of contemporary social reality.

In *L'appel des arènes* (1982), the narrative follows the attempt by Nalla's parents to ensure that he receives a fundamentally Western education, and how this has placed them at odds with traditional values. These traditional values are exemplified by the wrestling matches that take place in the arena and the "Bàkks," the traditional poems chanted by the wrestlers. This work thus stands as an indictment of a system that has failed to take from tradition those elements that can help the individual find a place in modernity.

Aminata Sow Fall's fourth novel, *L'ex-père de la nation* (1987), continues along the lines of her previous work in that it focuses on contemporary post-colonial society, but it does differentiate itself to the extent that it deals specifically with the question of political power. The work presents itself as the "Memoirs" of Madiama and plots the rise to and fall from power of a "former President" and the accompanying disillusion and dilemmas that he faces. With the recent publication of her fifth novel, *Le jujubier du patriarche* (1993), arguably her most aesthetically ambitious, Aminata Sow Fall has taken a certain distance from the traditional linearity of her previous work. Whereas her first four novels concentrated on social issues and the crisis of values, money, power, social parasites, the collapse of society, and so on, this latest novel goes beyond the immediate problems facing post-colonial African society and looks toward the future.

Fall manifests a concerted effort to express herself in new ways, and her work betrays a deep concern for the aesthetic aspects of literary production. The position of the writer and the relationship between artistic and political considerations are central to her writings; her narrative structures have become more diverse with the integration of oral literature, elements of magic realism, and a plurality of narrative voices. A reconciliation with the past and traditional culture is now seen as the path to the future, for as Aminata Sow Fall has declared, "The future lies in a synthesis between a concern for social progress along with a profound respect for African values" (in an interview I conducted on May 19, 1993, at the University of Connecticut, where Aminata Sow Fall was a visiting professor for the spring semester).

CRITICAL RECEPTION

Literary works by sub-Saharan Francophone women writers have remained relatively unexplored and have not benefited from the same critical attention as, for example, their European or American counterparts. One of the most important attempts to fill this gap has been Christopher L. Miller's *Theories of Africans: Francophone Literature and Anthropology in Africa* (1990). The final chapter in this work, entitled "Senegalese Women Writers," examines the significance of the pre-1976 absence of women writers; although he focuses on another Senegalese female writer, Mariama Bâ, his discussion of "how women began the reappraisal of gender within the African novel while simultaneously confronting [their] own marginal status as a writer" (247) provides the most pertinent background to any reading of Aminata Sow Fall, but of course to other sub-Saharan Francophone African women writers also.

Arlette Chemain's *Emancipation féminine et roman Africain* (1980) provides a useful insight into gender issues, although much, of course, has happened since it was published. Dorothy Blair, who translated *La grève des Bàttu*, has also written on women authors; however, it is in literary journals that African women writers have received the attention and articulate critiques their works deserve.

BIBLIOGRAPHY

Works by Aminata Sow Fall

Le revenant. Dakar: Les Nouvelles Éditions Africaines, 1976.
La grève des Bàttu ou les déchets humains. Dakar: Les Nouvelles Éditions Africaines, 1979.
The Beggar's Strike. Translated by Dorothy S. Blair. London: Longman, 1981.
L'appel des arènes. Dakar: Les Nouvelles Éditions Africaines, 1982.
L'ex-père de la nation. Paris: L'Harmattan, 1987.
Le jujubier du patriarche. Dakar: C.A.E.C. Éditions Khoudia, 1993.

Selected Studies of Aminata Sow Fall

Abanime, Emeka. "*La Grève des Bàttu.*" *World Literature Today* 54.2 (Spring 1980): 327.

Blair, Dorothy. *Senegalese Literature: A Critical History.* Boston: Twayne Publishers, 1984.

Boni-Sirera, Jacqueline. "Littérature et société: Étude critique de *La Grève des Bàttu* d'Aminata Sow Fall." *Revue de Littérature et d'Esthétique Négro-Africaine* 5 (1984): 59–89.

Cazenave, Odile. "Gender, Age, and Reeducation: A changing Emphasis in Recent African Novels in French, as Exemplified in *L'Appel des arènes* by Aminata Sow Fall." *Africa Today* 38.3 (1991): 54–62.

Chemain, Arlette. *Emancipation féminine et roman africain.* Dakar: Les Nouvelles Éditions Africaines, 1980.

Crosta, Suzanne. "Les structures spatiales dans *L'Appel des arènes* d'Aminata Sow Fall." *Revue Francophone de Louisiane* 3.1 (Spring 1988): 58–65.

Gadjigo, Samba. "Social Vision in Aminata Sow Fall's Literary Work." *World Literature Today* 63.3 (Summer 1989): 411–15.

Guyonneau, Christine. "Francophone Women Writers from Sub-Saharan Africa: A Preliminary Bibliography." *Callaloo* 24 (1985): 473.

Hammond, Thomas N. "*L'Appel des arènes.*" *French Review* 57.6 (May 1984): 907–08.

———. "*La Grève des Bàttu.*" *French Review* 54.2 (December 1980): 363.

———. "*Le Revenant.*" *French Review* 54.4 (March 1981): 618–19.

Jaccard, Anny-Claire. "Les visages de l'Islam chez Mariama Bâ et Aminata Sow Fall." *Nouvelles du Sud* 6 (1986–87): 171–82.

Michelman, Fredric. "*L'Appel des arènes.*" *World Literature Today* 58.1 (Winter 1984): 153.

Miller, Christopher L. *Theories of Africans: Francophone Literature and Anthropology in Africa.* Chicago: University of Chicago Press, 1990. 246–93.

Miller, Elinor S. "Contemporary Satire in Senegal: Aminata Sow Fall's *La Grève des Bàttu.*" *French Literature Series* 14 (1987): 143–51.

Milolo, Kembe. *L'image de la femme chez les romancières de l'Afrique noire francophone.* Saint-Paul Fribourg: Editions Universitaires Suisse, 1986.

Minh-Ha, Trinh T. "Aminata Sow Fall et l'espace du don." *French Review* 55.6 (May 1982): 780–89.

Pfaff, Françoise. "Aminata Sow Fall: L'écriture au féminin." *Notre Librairie* 81 (1985): 135–38.

———. "Enchantment and Magic in Two Novels by Aminata Sow Fall." *College Language Association Journal* 31.3 (March 1988): 339–59.

Volet, Jean-Marie. "Romancières francophones d'Afrique noire: Vingt ans d'activité littéraire à découvrir." *French Review* 65.5 (April 1992): 765–73.

DOMINIC THOMAS

NURUDDIN FARAH (1945–   )

BIOGRAPHY

In the last decades of the nineteenth century the Somali Peninsula, located on the Horn of Africa, fell subject to the colonial ambitions of a series of states: Egypt, Ethiopia, France, Italy, and Britain. By the early part of the twentieth century the colonizers had divided the Somali Peninsula (the native land of ethnic Somalis who belong to one of six major clan-families) into five Somalilands: the British-controlled north central, the French southeast (contemporary Djibouti), the Italian south, the Ethiopian west (the Ogaden), and the "frontier district" in the southwest, not directly controlled by any state and later part of Kenya. The Somalilands were configured and reconfigured in the machinations of World War II: Italy conquered British Somaliland early in the war, but in 1941 British troops regained the north central part and subsequently captured the Italian south as well as the Ogaden. Nuruddin Farah was born in Baidoa in 1945, a city in Italian Somaliland at the time under British control. In 1948 the British restored the Ogaden to Ethiopian rule; in 1949 the recently formed United Nations returned the south to Italy.

Farah's father worked as a translator for the British, and he was transferred to the Ogaden to work for the British governor soon after Nuruddin's birth. When the Ogaden was transferred back to Ethiopian control in 1948, his father elected to remain. As a result, Nuruddin spent much of his childhood in the Ethiopian colony. Farah did not return to the southern region until his family fled from border conflicts in the Ogaden in 1963, three years after Somalia was granted independence by the British and Italians.

Farah received his primary education at schools in Kallafo, Ogaden, which, by colonial force, were hotbeds of cultural and linguistic diversity: he spoke

English, Arabic, and Amharic, the official Ethiopian language. He achieved great success in his studies and went on to pursue a degree in literature and philosophy at the Punjab University of Chandigarh, where he wrote and submitted the manuscript of his first novel, *From a Crooked Rib*. Following his education in India, he also attended the Universities of Essex and London. He has held teaching positions at universities in the United States, Germany, Italy, Nigeria, Sudan, Gambia, and India and has visited the former Soviet Union. Clearly a world citizen, Farah nonetheless identifies Africa, and particularly Somalia (despite the grievous difficulties that have haunted the country and the author since independence), as his home. Indeed, an abiding concern for post-colonial Africa forms the heart of Farah's artistic production.

Though Farah is fluent in Somali, Arabic, Amharic, Italian, and Punjabi, the majority of his essays, novels, short stories, plays, and film scripts are written in his fourth language, English. He has written a few essays and one novel in Italian, and another novel in Somali. The Somali novel, one of the first written using the newly developed script of the Somali language, was serialized in the local papers in 1973, but was discontinued when the government found his work politically objectionable. Siyad Barre's Somalian regime subsequently reviewed and banned all of his works in Somalia and ordered that the author be killed.

Farah escaped from Somalia in 1974 and has returned to his homeland and his native culture only through his novels. This condition of exile has significantly shaped the political and ethical dimensions of his artistic creation. This forced exile, in combination with the familial exile and migrancy of his youth and the migrancy of his academic and artistic careers, has influenced the character and complexity of his works and has contributed to the remarkably wide-ranging political insight and ethical urgency of his critiques of post-colonial reality.

MAJOR WORKS AND THEMES

Farah's works are marked by a series of thematic concerns that strongly characterize the postcolonial nature of his writings, and that underlie his unyielding criticism of neocolonial practices in contemporary Somali politics. Two concerns form the thematic foundation of his novels: the ethics of human freedom and the oppression of women in postcolonial Somaliland. Like other postcolonial writers, Farah perceives and critiques the horrors of oppression and celebrates the liberatory goals of African nationalism. However, while studying the historical dialectics of colonial and neocolonial political schemas, Farah passionately critiques the unenlightened realities of postcolonial Somali history. In the process his works indict the politicians and intellectuals who—through either action or inaction—support authoritarian regimes in postcolonial Somalia. Farah bemoans the transformation of nationalist ideas in the hands of neocolonial dictators whose self-aggrandizing ends progressively betray all aspects of human freedom. Farah critiques the ways in which the liberatory goals of Somali nationalism seem, ironically, to exclude questions of women's liberation, decrying the hypocrisy and vacuity of a political freedom that allows the ongoing oppression of women. Farah argues, through his novels, that a country can be free only when its female citizens are emancipated.

In order to postulate the ethical primacy of human freedom and women's liberty in postcolonial realities, Farah develops the question of freedom by investigating certain other related sociopolitical issues that regulate the nature of freedom in Somali culture. For example, in his novel *From a Crooked Rib*, Farah reveals the ways in which women are caught in positions of subservience as mere objects of male desire. Women are not able to escape from their subordinate positions: their efforts to evade the authoritarian role of the traditional patriarch are thwarted by the kinship practices of the nomadic clan-families, which deny women individual rights. Women are the property of the patriarch, who has the exclusive right to arrange their marriages and to settle their bride price. The situation of women is exacerbated by the constraints of the traditional Islamic law, which affords women limited status and few legal protections. The public and private sites of negotiation available for women, which might enable them to subvert the male social hierarchy, are confined within traditional family structures that end up suborning women's realities. The novel demonstrates the metaphorical relationship between political and domestic power: the authoritarian rule of dictatorship begins at home when the community of men controls women's bodies by enforcing social practices such as polygamy, female circumcision, and infibulation. The novel problematizes the question of Somalia's political independence by critiquing the vacuity of the country's nationalist agenda in the light of the continuing enslavement of women.

Farah further investigates issues of patriarchy and authoritarianism in postcolonial reality by examining Somalia's complex relationships with foreign powers, especially the Soviet Union, the United States, and Great Britain. In *A Naked Needle* Farah studies the crisis of Somali national identity in terms of Somalia's complicated international alliances. His novel traces this crisis allegorically, exploring the personal realities of Somali men and women who are in relationships with Westerners. By tracing the complications of these personal relationships, Farah narrates the tangled postcolonial politics of a socialist, Islamic, militaristic Somalia. The novel highlights how women participated in the struggle against colonial rule, but suggests that since the achievement of political independence women's lives are even more dominated by male authority and chauvinistic practices than they were in colonial times.

Farah devotes his next work, a trilogy titled *Variations on the Theme of an African Dictatorship*, to a multifaceted investigation of General Barre's dictatorship. In *Sweet and Sour Milk* he criticizes the repressive tactics of Barre's government while studying the evolution of postcolonial Somalia from a tribal oligarchy to an Islamic-based totalitarian dictatorship. The novel investigates the complexity of violence and political repression in postcolonial Third World dictatorships and how the sources of repression emanate from both local and foreign influences. In the novel Farah acknowledges that the First World superpowers have sustained the general's rule, but he also insists that Somali institutions cannot be absolved from censure. Farah perceives the general's power as authenticated and buttressed by the authoritarianism of Somali institutions, such as the family, clan, and tribe.

Political autocracy can be effectively implemented and maintained only when other institutions of a society participate in the authoritarian order. In *Sardines* Farah explores the complicated ways the Somali family structure authorizes the state to control both the public and private lives of women by manipulating the political and religious ideologies of Islam and Marxism. He also examines the role of Somali women in resisting the enslaving practices of the regime. Farah combines women's issues with state politics and explores the possibility of a feminist resistance to female circumcision and infibulation. As is so often true in his writing, the possibility of women resisting oppression is a powerful metaphor for the possibility of the emergence of a truly liberated Somalia.

The last work of the trilogy, *Close Sesame*, suggests the possibility of overthrowing the dictator by a renewed and redefined nationalism. The novel draws parallels between the violent colonial practices of the Italian authorities and the neocolonialist practices of the present militaristic regime. Farah suggests that the Barre regime has committed worse crimes against the people of Somalia than those committed by the colonizers during the colonial period.

Maps is the first novel of a second trilogy that will include *Gifts* and *Letters*. In *Maps* Farah explores the pain of cultural uncertainty in postcolonial reality. The precariousness of cultural identity is extended to include issues of race, gender, class, and sexuality. Farah subverts identities and nationalities by destabilizing the categories of gender and by displacing these uncertainties on the geographical boundaries of the nation, Somaliland. Farah is in the process of writing the last two novels. The central theme of this trilogy seems to suggest that as family structures are collapsing, society is orphaned; however, there is the possibility of a liberation from authoritarian structures through individualism and literacy.

CRITICAL RECEPTION

Derek Wright, in *The Novels of Nuruddin Farah*, emphasizes the postcolonial aspects of Farah's novels. He draws attention to the multicultural aspects of the work by concentrating on issues of nationality, gender, colonialism, and recent political and social developments in Somalia. Wright also provides close textual analysis that helps in deciphering the complex cultural contexts of Farah's works.

The feminist aspects of Farah's works are examined by Florence Stratton in "The Novels of Nuruddin Farah" and by Kirsten Holst Petersen in "The Personal and the Political: The Case of Nuruddin Farah." Stratton shows the interconnections between the powers of the state and religion to control women's lives. She illustrates how Farah uses the complexities of the traditional family as an image of state control. Stratton concludes her article by focusing on the subversive alternatives provided by Farah and his emphasis on education. Petersen draws attention to the ways in which Farah is different from other African writers in how he deals with questions of the personal and the political. She claims that he is probably the first feminist writer of Africa as "he describes and analyzes women as victims of male subjugation" (98). She does, however, fault Farah for not providing definite resolutions to the various problems raised in his work.

Both Francesca Kazan in "Recalling the Other Third World: Nuruddin Farah's *Maps*" and Rhonda Cobham in "Misgendering the Nation: African Nationalist Fictions and Nuruddin Farah's *Maps*" concentrate on the postcolonial and postmodern aspects of the novel *Maps*. Kazan analyzes the instability of human identity in terms of social and cultural altercations that affect a specific historical moment of postcolonial reality. She maintains that Farah's *Maps* challenges the Western necessity to secure a homogenous version of Africa. Kazan, however, explores the various "fissures"—national, personal, and linguistic—that are tearing apart postcolonial Somalia. She maintains that the novel raises the anguish of blurring identities and agencies. She analyzes the unstable categories of gender, nationality, and sexuality as being part of the colonial and imperial legacy inherited by Somalia.

BIBLIOGRAPHY

Works by Nuruddin Farah

From a Crooked Rib. London: Heinemann, 1970.
A Naked Needle. London: Heinemann, 1976.
Variations on the Theme of an African Dictatorship:
    Sweet and Sour Milk. London: Heinemann, 1980.
    Sardines. London: Heinemann, 1981.
    Close Sesame. London: Allison and Busby, 1983.
Maps. London: Picador, 1986.
"Why I Write." *Third World Quarterly* 10.4 (1988): 1591–99.
"Nuruddin Farah." *Interviews with Writers of the Post-colonial World*. Conducted and
    edited by Feroza Jussawalla and Reed Way Dasenbrock. Jackson: University Press
    of Mississippi, 1992. 42–62.
"Bastards of Empire." *Transition* 5.1 (65) (Spring 1995): 26–35.

Studies of Nuruddin Farah

Cobham, Rhonda. "Misgendering the Nation: African Nationalist Fictions and Nuruddin
    Farah's *Maps*." *Nationalisms and Sexualities*. Ed. Andrew Parker, Mary Russo,
    Doris Summer, and Patricia Yaeger. New York: Routledge, 1992.

Kazan, Francesca. "Recalling the Other Third World: Nuruddin Farah's *Maps*." *Novel* 26.3 (1993): 253–67.

Petersen, Kirsten Holst. "The Personal and the Political: The Case of Nuruddin Farah." *Ariel* 12.3 (1981): 93–101.

Stratton, Florence. "The Novels of Nuruddin Farah." *World Literature Written in English* 25.1 (1985): 16–30.

Wright, Derek. *The Novels of Nuruddin Farah.* Bayreuth, Germany: Bayreuth University, 1994.

HEMA CHARI

ATHOL FUGARD (1932–)

BIOGRAPHY

Harold Athol Lannigan Fugard was born on June 11, 1932, in the dusty Karroo town of Middelburg in the Cape Province, South Africa, the son of a general dealer. Later the family moved to Port Elizabeth, eking out a living keeping a boardinghouse and later acquiring the St. George's Park Tea Room. After his matriculation year, Fugard secured a scholarship to the University of Cape Town, enrolling for a B.A. in philosophy. It was here that he was equipped with the knowledge to understand Kierkegaard, Heidegger, Sartre, and Camus. He did not complete his degree, however, as he decided to hitchhike through Africa, with the poet Perseus Adams as his companion. They were arrested in Cairo for illegal entry into the country and deported to the Sudan, where they were promptly jailed for the same offense. Upon their release, the two men parted ways. In Port Sudan, Fugard was offered a job on a steamer, the S.S. *Graigaur*. His experiences on the ship, especially those relating to his fellow crew members, had a lasting impact upon him; in fact, it was on this ship that Fugard crossed the divide between the racially bound South African he was then and the cosmopolitan humanist he was to become. This would help him relinquish the shackles of convention and allow him to enter those seedy bars and illegal taprooms in his native land where he would meet people who would be re-created as characters in his plays. Eventually, with financial assistance from his mother, he returned to South Africa, where he wrote freelance articles for the Port Elizabeth newspaper, the *Evening Post*. In 1954 Fugard wrote a play, *Klaas and the Devil*, which he followed with *The Cell* (foreshadowing his later *The Island*). On September 22, 1956, he married Sheila Meiring, an actress and former fellow student whom he had admired but who, he felt, had not taken any notice of him.

In 1958 Fugard began working as a clerk in the Fordsburg, Johannesburg, Native Commissioner's Court. This experience crystallized his sympathetic attitude to the oppressed majority in South Africa and his outrage at the indignities endured by them. Fugard once commented: "My time in the Fordsburg court in Johannesburg was traumatic for me as a white South African. . . . I saw more suffering than I could cope with. I began to understand how my country functioned" (Introduction, *Three Port Elizabeth Plays*, viii). As he came into contact with more and more of the unfortunates, Fugard befriended, and was befriended by, an increasing number of black people from the townships. The distance he felt between himself and them was diminishing, and he could identify with the country as a whole and not only with its Eurocentric concerns.

On August 30, 1958, Fugard's *No-Good Friday* premiered at the Bantu Men's Social Centre in Johannesburg. Fortuitously, too, Fugard became stage manager for the National Theatre organization, founded in 1947 with the noble ideal of removing racialism and with the hope of achieving social reform. In 1959 *Nongogo* was staged, a glimmer of light in a particularly bleak period that continued when the Fugards went to London and Athol, to survive, was forced into doing housecleaning while Sheila had to do secretarial duties. By the beginning of 1961 the Fugards were back in South Africa living in Port Elizabeth with Fugard's mother.

In 1967 Fugard's passport was withdrawn and only returned in 1971 after considerable pressure was placed on the government. But the playwright was undaunted in the intervening period. In 1968 *People Are Living There* (in its draft form titled *The Silkworms* in 1962) was staged at the Citizens' Theatre in Glasgow. Extracts from another successful Fugard creation, *Boesman and Lena*, were published in 1968. *Sizwe Bansi Is Dead* (originally *Sizwe Banzi Is Dead*) opened on October 8, 1972, and the play, bizarrely, had to be staged furtively and in primitive circumstances. Fugard has since written many plays, and a novel, *Tsotsi*, was published in 1980, though it is speculated that it was probably written in the period 1952–60. Fugard and his wife still live in Port Elizabeth, the city where he has found his initial and continuing inspiration.

MAJOR WORKS AND THEMES

Fugard's novel *Tsotsi* was something of an enigma when it was first published. Most critics were (and still are) unsure of its actual date of composition. David Hogge writes that the first draft of the novel has been lost but that its systemization depended on notebooks kept during 1952–54. "This systemization took place in London in 1960–61," writes Hogge (unpublished Fugard novel, 60). Barrie Hough disputes the importance of the notebooks, considers 1960 to be the date of the novel's genesis, and suggests that the novel was written, mostly, while Fugard was on his sojourn in London (28).

The novel concerns a gangster, Tsotsi or David, and his followers. Within the first ten pages, the gang has killed a man—Gumboot Dhlamini—by shoving a spoke into his heart while he was caught up in a crowd on a commuter train. They were after his wages. The point is made that Gumboot had made some fatal mistakes in planning his journey and Tsotsi was not one to allow mistakes to pass unpunished. The novel culminates—like Graham Greene's *Brighton Rock*—in the death of the protagonist, the difference being that Tsotsi's death, unlike Pinky's, has a sense of poignancy about it, as he is trying to save a baby's life.

Fugard's *Tsotsi* is a complex novel, recalling other classical writers. Barrie Hough, for example, reflects that *Tsotsi* "has a complex narrative structure reminiscent of that in works by William Faulkner" (ii). The work contains those themes most often associated with the postcolonial novel, as Vandenbroucke writes: "These themes include the acceptance of responsibility for one's life, the recovery of past memories that lead to the affirmation of the present, and the heightening of individual consciousness" (49). Hough finds that "[d]iscovering the meaning of life through pain is a salient theme" (32–33) in the novel, as well as the theme of ontological insecurity that leads to so much of the work's exposition. The city of Johannesburg, the city of Eurocentric culture, the city of the white man, lurks in the background, while the action takes place in a township reserved for the black community. Fugard suggests that it is this unnatural separation that contributes to the violence and appalling suffering occurring in the township. The conclusion of the novel indicates latent hope. Yet it is hope bounded by the knowledge that the death of Tsotsi, imbued as it is with a feeling of poignancy, nevertheless signifies the existence and the future birth of legions like him, as the system within which they exist will remain immutable.

The Blood Knot (first published in 1963) "is not about apartheid, but about its victims," writes David Hogge (unpublished Fugard novel, 74). Its themes are those concerning "confinement, poverty, and deprivation" (74) and family relationships. These themes are interwoven with the exploration of time and its effect on relationships. Time is most often associated with mutability, with change, and with decay. In *The Blood Knot* time also assumes significance in the way individuals are tied to it.

Russell Vandenbroucke points out that both the alarm clock and the calendar play significant roles and that as soon as the clock ceases to function, the protagonists can assume control of their destinies instead of being controlled by them (60–61). The last words of the play, too, recall time past, present, and future: "MORRIS. No. You see, we're tied together, Zach. It's what they call the blood knot . . . the bond between brothers" (Fugard, *Three Port Elizabeth Plays*, 97). Their past lies in their conception and birth, their present in the realization of the fact that they are related as brothers, and their future in living with this knowledge.

Fugard manages to imbue the play with its drama and tension by having one of the brothers (Zach) dark skinned and the other (Morris) light skinned. Morris has tried to pass as a white man and has succeeded, making the play "uniquely South African" (Hough, ii). In the South Africa of the age, this was a situation fraught with the danger such impersonation could bring, as the strict enforcement of apartheid laws could lead to imprisonment and relegation to the hazards and deprivations of life in the black ghettoes. With almost every public amenity segregated and with personal relationships dictated by the edicts of the apartheid state, race classification plays an important role in the play. But Morris's decision alienates him from his brother, and he attempts to ingratiate himself once again with him.

Boesman and Lena (1973) and *Hello and Goodbye* (1966) explore "the effect of time and alienation on man, but do so in more depth. These two works also display a new kind of minimalism as far as both language and theatrical techniques are concerned" (Hough, ii). It is the extent to which Fugard explores his themes in these plays that set them apart. In *People Are Living There* (1969) and *The Occupation* (1970), Hough (ii) observes that "man's alienation and the effect of time on people" are also considered, but are treated in a different way.

In *"Master Harold" . . . and the Boys* (1985), Fugard uses the drama as an autobiographical vehicle to expiate some unresolved guilt he still nurtures. Although the incident leading to Fugard's feelings of guilt occurred when he was a young boy, it was only in 1981 that he was able to start writing about it. The incident referred to concerned Fugard's attempt as a young boy (then known as "Hally") to coerce an older black man into calling him "Master." The older man's refusal and his deft handling of the situation led to Hally spitting in his face, an action Fugard has regretted since.

CRITICAL RECEPTION

Although the dynamics of the situation in South Africa are changing, and although many more artists, authors, and playwrights are gaining recognition for their excellence, Fugard remains undeniably the best-known dramatist abroad—and, indeed, within South Africa—more renowned than any of his peers in the genre. The reason for this is not quite clear. Perhaps it is because he struck a chord in his early years with international audiences and producers; perhaps it is his minutely portrayed regional characters that enthrall audiences worldwide. Nevertheless, the critical reception afforded his works must surely draw on his familiarity and early achievement.

Two plays—*The Blood Knot* and *Boesman and Lena*—deal as do all of Fugard's works, in one way or another, with the apartheid problem. Yet it would be too simplistic to regard this blight on the African continent as the sole theme in these works. Fugard tends to focus on the minutiae in relationships, trying to express the motives in the characters, the forces that drive and control them, and the internal and external powers affecting and effecting attitudes.

The Blood Knot (completed and produced in 1961) ran for 140 performances in 1962. The play won critical acclaim in London and New York, culminating in its being selected as 1964's best play by the *New York Times*, a selection vindicated when the play opened at the Theatre Royal in Brighton, England.

Boesman and Lena (grouped with *The Blood Knot* and *Hello and Goodbye* in the work published in 1974, but written in the period 1967–69) shares certain characteristics with *The Blood Knot*. Barrie Hough writes that these elements are

the characters' search for their true identity; scenes in which characters hark back to the past in order to solve existential dilemmas of their present experience; language which, although primarily English, is spiced with Afrikaans' words and phrases and sometimes English is spoken in Afrikaans' word order; and local settings with very specific points of reference. (42)

Although the conflict between the sexes—patriarchy as opposed to gender liberation—is central to the play, more than anything else, *Boesman and Lena* is an existential allegory of man's ceaseless journey and search for the ultimate peace, while beset by inexorable insecurity in a world of chaos.

From the bleakness of the South African social landscape, Fugard is able to conjure hope, especially as it relates to individuals within a damaged society. Fugard intimates that self-affirmation cannot be found in society as a whole but in relationships between individuals and within individuals themselves. There is a feeling about Fugard's work that impels the critic toward a reconsideration of a man's universally tenuous position. Although the works are localized within South Africa, the universal nature of his characters—their ability to deal with cosmic forces beyond their control by grappling with their own situations—sets his writing apart from that of the sociopolitical pamphleteer.

BIBLIOGRAPHY

Works by Athol Fugard

Plays

"Master Harold" . . . *and the Boys*. Oxford: Oxford University Press, 1985.
Statements: Three Plays. London: Oxford University Press, 1974. Includes "The Island," "Sizwe Banzi Is Dead," and "Statements After an Arrest under the Immorality Act."
Three Port Elizabeth Plays. London: Oxford University Press, 1974. Includes "The Blood Knot," "Hello and Goodbye," "Boesman and Lena," subsequently published as *Boesman and Lena and other Plays* with the addition of "People Are Living There," London: Oxford University Press, 1980.

Novel

Tsotsi. Johannesburg: Ad. Donker, 1980.

Studies of Athol Fugard

Hogge, David. ''From Novice to Master Craftsman: A Study of Athol Fugard's Plays.''
    Thesis Rhodes University, 1977.
————. ''Unpublished Fugard Novel.'' *Contrast* 12.1 (1978): 60–78.
Hough, B[arrie]. ''Athol Fugard's Writing (1958–1969): His Early Development.'' Diss.
    Randse Afrikaanse Universiteit, 1979.
Read, John. *Athol Fugard: A Bibliography*. Grahamstown, South Africa: National English
    Literary Museum, 1991.
Vandenbroucke, Russell. *Truths the Hand Can Touch*. Johannesburg: Ad. Donker, 1986.

JO E. NEL

NADINE GORDIMER (1923–   )

BIOGRAPHY

Winner of the 1991 Nobel Prize for Literature, Nadine Gordimer was born of Jewish parents in Springs, a gold-mining town east of Johannesburg, South Africa. Both of her parents were immigrants. In his teens, her father had fled the czarist anti-Semitism of Lithuania, and in Springs he learned watchmaking and became a jeweler. Her mother was born in England.

Gordimer's childhood was highly unusual. She has portrayed her father as a recalcitrant racist in spite of his own experiences with anti-Semitism and poverty and her mother as a woman who sought to do good for blacks in a nearby township. Gordimer, however, fell under the control and influence of her mother, who could find neither adequate outlet for her talents nor reprieve from her own emotionally barren marriage. When Gordimer was diagnosed, at age eleven, with a nonexistent heart ailment, her mother, for her own emotional purposes, as Gordimer later discerned, withdrew her from school until she was sixteen. Privately tutored at home, confined to the world of her parents, and isolated from the influence of peers, Gordimer became deeply involved with reading and writing.

Gordimer's private education at home meant that she could not meet university admissions requirements. Therefore, she audited classes at the University of the Witwatersrand. Nevertheless, despite her limited formal education, Gordimer has been publishing stories since she was fifteen, when her first adult story appeared in the *Forum*, a liberal South African magazine, but she met with serious, international acclaim in 1949 when she had a story published in the *New Yorker* and when her first collection of stories, *Face to Face: Short Stories*, appeared in print.

Two of the dominating influences on Gordimer's life and writing have been apartheid and her affiliation with the multiracialism of Sophiatown of the 1950s. At that time, she was involved with *Drum* magazine and several black artists, writers, and critics. During the fifties and sixties, she also witnessed great national tumult, most notably the Sharpeville massacre, the 1960 treason trial, the state of emergency, the incarceration of Nelson Mandela, and the Rovonia trial of 1963. By the middle of the sixties, repressive government measures had silenced her black fellow writers who left South Africa. Gordimer, however, was able to stand fast and published her study of black South African writing, *The Black Interpreters*, in support of her colleagues.

By the 1970s, with the ascendancy of Black Consciousness, white South African writers also experienced silencing as they were increasingly marginalized by black writers and activists. This period witnessed the dissolution of the multiracial writers' association of which Gordimer was a member, and black writers formed an independent group that disavowed the need for white spokespersons. The recognition of increasing black intellectual autonomy appears to have led Gordimer to recognize the necessity for whites to play a significant role in the future of South Africa on black terms. Her public statements about the relationship between blacks and whites, from her condemnation of apartheid to her acknowledging the obligation of whites to reconsider the terms on which they should remain in South Africa, have annoyed many South Africans, who have viewed her as a traitor. At the same time, her refusal to adhere to the blind orthodoxy of revolution has alienated her from many black writers and critics. Nonetheless, Gordimer persists in her documentation of the South African experience in particular and the African experience in general, and she continues to work in South Africa, where, she maintains, she must stay and write.

MAJOR WORKS AND THEMES

Gordimer is one of the world's most prolific living major writers. Her great literary output spans nearly fifty years. While she is obviously an African writer, her fiction and essays capture the perception, voice, and experience of the white African settler who, for good or for ill, is spiritually and psychologically enmeshed with the indigenous black African whom he has sought to displace and exploit. Given, however, her political persuasion and the tough moral and political questions she raises in her work, Gordimer is actually a minority within a minority, for she is a white, South African woman who has openly opposed the prevailing ethos of the politically and economically powerful white South African minority. In her confrontation of the status quo, she is accompanied by such writers as Alan Paton, Athol Fugard, J. M. Coetzee, and Andre Brink.

Through her fiction, from *Face to Face: Short Stories* (1949) and *The Lying Days* (1953) to *None to Accompany Me* (1994), the reader, mindful that truth is a power-based social and political construct, perceives the historical evolution of South Africa from the construction of apartheid through the first democratic elections and the political transition of 1993. In the chronology of her work, therefore, as it mirrors historical and political change in South Africa, the reader experiences Gordimer's moral outrage at apartheid as well as her confrontation of the problems inherent in blind adherence to orthodox opposition.

While Gordimer has brilliantly mastered the short story, her novels, given the greater scope of the novel form, stand out for their exploration of life in South Africa in particular and in newly emerging African nations in general. Gordimer's early works form the genesis of the South African tale that she tells repeatedly throughout her career. Her first three novels and her early short stories document the inception and early years of apartheid, which she describes as "the ugliest creature known to man . . . baptised in the Dutch Reformed church" (*Essential Gesture*, 262). The works explore the insidious effects of an ideology grounded exclusively in skin color and demonstrate its impact on all South Africans. In addition, the works examine and challenge aspects of colonialism that characterized South Africa at that time. As we read the confluences of apartheid and colonialism in Gordimer's early texts, we experience the traditional relationship between Prospero and Caliban in the acceptance within the world of the text of the European center and the native African margin. Repeatedly in these early texts the reader is confronted by the concept of the Native Other. In short, in the South African world prior to the 1960s, the civilized life is a modified replica of European customs and manners with a strong allegiance to the physical and psychological links to Europe. In Gordimer's first three novels, for example, the idea of returning to England finds open expression.

One of the looming issues in Gordimer's early fiction is the relationship between the colonial settler and his overseas home. This concern has frequently been explored in the work of colonial writers. In *The Lying Days*, for example, Helen Shaw, born in South Africa, is caught between a mere intellectual or vicarious experience with Europe and the realities of apartheid in addition to shifting social norms in white South African society. The colonial dilemma raised in Gordimer's early texts is compounded by an even greater moral variable, namely, the race question, which is so systematically and deliberately woven into all aspects of South African life and culture that liberal humanism and fundamental human goodwill fail in its wake. In *The Lying Days*, Helen's well-intended overtures toward Mary Seswayo ultimately cannot withstand the weight of apartheid. The initial courage and curiosity that permit Helen early in the novel to venture outside the mine compound and into university life are insufficient to equip her to challenge meaningfully the social expectations of her world. Thus, even in her witnessing the shooting of a black protester, she is not sufficiently empowered to take action.

Gordimer further explores the moral failure of colonialism and the tenuous relationship between the colonial settler and his overseas home in *A World of Strangers*, sometimes termed her Sophiatown novel, and *Occasion for Loving*. In *A World of Strangers*, the protagonist, Toby Hood, arrives from England and exercises the option of leading an unconventional life in Sophiatown as opposed to the traditional white existence in Johannesburg. As an outsider, however, Toby is able to exist in both worlds, as symbolized by his relationships with his "native" friend Steven Sithole and his white lover Cecil, who, because of apartheid, never encounter each other. Similarly, Toby is free to cross the racial divide between High House, the Alexanders' mansion, and the House of Fame in Sophiatown. Nevertheless, the goodwill that Toby embraces, informed in the novel by the allusions to the novels of E. M. Forster and their ethos of individual goodness, fails. He is unable to influence Cecil out of her acceptance of racial superiority and loses her to a conventional marriage in the comfortable world of apartheid, and he loses Steven to death in a police raid. While Steven's death jolts Toby into acknowledging the racist horrors of South Africa, it is insufficient to galvanize him into moral action. Thus the novel ends with his exercising the option available to all colonials—the return to the mother country.

Perhaps the worst example of the spiritual and psychological destruction that occurs as a result of the moral failure of colonialism is evident in *Occasion for Loving*. In this text, Gordimer raises the issue of miscegenation, which was outlawed in South Africa by the Immorality Act (1950). In the novel, Gordimer does not make interracial love a fairy-tale solution to the race question. Instead she portrays the white colonial option of sexual adventurism and ignoring the moral high ground. In the novel, Anne Davis, an English visitor to South Africa, has an adulterous affair with an African artist, Gideon Shibalo. When the intrusion of dehumanizing laws into her private existence proves overwhelming to her as a white woman, she callously abandons Gideon and leaves South Africa with Boaz, her husband. Gideon, embittered, turns to alcoholism, and her friend, Jessie Stilwell, from whose perspective we see these events, retreats into avoidance, too weak willed to adopt a clear moral position.

While Gordimer's early works are informed by the colonial experience and the entrenchment of apartheid, they also reflect the push for multiracialism, the developing black arts movement, and gradually escalating resistance to apartheid. Building on these themes, the works of her middle years portray more aggressive resistance to apartheid and the turbulent growth of developing African nations. In this group of works are *The Late Bourgeois World* (1966); *A Guest of Honor* (1970); *Livingstone's Companions* (1971), a short-story collection that portrays variables of existence in post-colonial Africa; *The Black Interpreters: Notes on African Writing* (1973), a critical work; *The Conservationist* (1974); and *Burger's Daughter* (1979). The term that most appropriately describes the subject matter of her fiction in this period is "Africa emergent," the title of one of the stories from *Livingstone's Companions*. The works in this group portray an Africa coming of age and experiencing the accompanying turbulence. Moreover, in this group of texts, the reader is aware of an increasing repositioning of the Native Other from margin to center and the trauma to the white soul and psyche as a result of the shift.

The concerns found in Gordimer's middle works clearly speak to the issue raised in her essay "Where Do Whites Fit In?" (1959), in which she discusses the place of whites in a changing Africa. Such a question has no pat answers, particularly for white settlers whose sense of belonging is more rooted in Africa than in Europe. Nevertheless, in the essay, she submits that the white man who wishes to remain in Africa will have to "forget the old impulses to leadership and the temptation to give advice backed by the experience and culture of western civilization" (*Essential Gesture*, 35). More significantly, she concludes, "If one will always have to feel white first and African second, it would be better not to stay on in Africa" (*Essential Gesture*, 37). In the novella *The Late Bourgeois World*, the question of the place of whites in a changing South Africa that is experiencing resistance to apartheid is evident in the story of Max and Liz Van Den Sandt. Gordimer has taken the title of the novella from Ernst Fischer's *The Necessity of Art* (1963), which also provides an intertext to the work. Fischer's work argues that society must reclaim its sense of community by exploring the collective, transformative function of art. So it is also that with the novella Gordimer achieves a melding of the political and aesthetic functions of art. That she does so self-consciously is evident in one character's referring to the prevailing ethos of the fictive world as "the late bourgeois world."

In weaving her tale, Gordimer probes the white liberal bourgeois dilemma posed in the novel's two epigraphs: Franz Kafka's "There are possibilities for me; but under what stone do they lie?" and Maxim Gorky's "The madness of the brave is the wisdom of life." As these epigraphs address the role of Max in the world of the text, the reader understands the failure of weak-willed narcissistic liberalism that contributes nothing to the destabilization of apartheid and results in Max's suicide. On the other hand, the epigraphs point to the options faced by Liz, his surviving ex-wife. She can remain insulated in her whiteness, or she can support the liberation cause.

The dilemma posed in *The Late Bourgeois World* and the question of where whites fit in are further examined in *A Guest of Honour* through the character of Evelyn Bray, a retired English colonel. This novel is set outside South Africa in a fictive central African country that in its newly independent state is experiencing the evils of neocolonialism. Having facilitated the anticolonial work of the People's Independence Party led by Adamson Mweta and Edward Shinza, Bray has been invited back to Africa for the country's independence. Although he is Mweta's guest, he becomes increasingly involved in the destructive factionalism within the emerging nation when he learns of Shinza's allegiance to the rural population and the exploited workers of the mining and fishing industries. Eventually, as he is leaving the country to procure arms for Shinza, he is mistakenly ambushed and killed by Shinza supporters. Like Max and Liz Van Den Sandt, Bray has an authentic recognition of the moral imperatives guiding his presence in Africa. Bray chooses to act on these imperatives with integrity. Nevertheless, Gordimer warns her readers that liberal idealism, although well intended, is fraught with peril and personal sacrifice. Bray's existence, like that of moral whites in Africa, reflects the two concepts of honor and bravery that are the epigraphs of the novel: Turgenev's "An honourable man will end by not knowing where to live'' and Ernesto Che Guevara's "Many will call me an adventurer—and that I am, only one of a different sort—one of those who risks his skin to prove his platitudes.''

In sharp contrast to Evelyn Bray is Mehring, the pig-iron tycoon of *The Conservationist*. Mehring epitomizes the white person who negotiates his African environment as a white man first and an African second. In this sense, he is reminiscent of the narcissistic Max Van Den Sandt, the obvious difference between the two being that Mehring, rooted in the worst capitalist way to the land and its resources, embraces none of Max's liberal idealism, however misguided it might have been. Thus Mehring has no investment in a moral South Africa. Worse yet, he presents a new white South African who in his rugged individualism has no sense of community. As opposed to the neighboring Boer farmers, Mehring is a recreational farmer. A divorced man, he is emotionally and ideologically alienated from his son, and he feels no investment in his mistress. Moreover, he also embraces misogyny and racism, which temporarily secure his gender, race, and class privileges but also guarantee his isolation, psychological collapse, and ultimate flight from the land into an uncertain future. In his psychological deterioration and flight, Mehring anticipates Maureen Smales of *July's People*. Panic ensues because neither character can envision or cope with his own shift from center to margin. Each abandons the land and its future to those no doubt better equipped to be its "conservationists.''

The central motif for Mehring's dilemma (and by extension that of all of white South Africa) and its solution is the body of the murdered African that appears on the farm and remains a disruptive presence to the Africans there. Initially the police give the body a hasty, improper burial, but by the end it is unearthed by a major storm that blows in from the Mozambique Channel. In its powerful, destructive, but cleansing symbolism, the storm's washing up the body represents the repressed white South African fear of the uncontrollable rising up of Native Africans. Gordimer underscores the vision of this inevitability, as critics have observed, through her juxtaposition of Mehring's narcissism and equally disordered mental state and quotations from Zulu belief that she has taken from Henry Callaway's *The Religious System of the Amazulu*. Similarly, the novel's epigraph, Richard Shelton's "The Tatooed Desert,'' points to the inversions created by the white presence in South Africa. It is significant that in his madness Mehring abandons the farm to no one but its native occupants. Ultimately it falls to the indigenous Africans on the farm, with Mehring's financial help, to give the unknown man a proper ritualistic burial to guarantee his possession of the earth and his place in their community.

Gordimer continues her exploration of the changing role of white South Africans through her use of the bildungsroman format in *Burger's Daughter*. In this highly complex text, she portrays the coming of age of Rosa Burger, daughter of an imprisoned Marxist activist, Lionel Burger. For her portrait of Lionel Burger, Gordimer drew on the actual figure of Bram Fischer, an Afrikaner lawyer who had abandoned his racist origins, involved himself in the antiapartheid movement, and ultimately died in prison. In 1961 she had published the essay "Why Did Bram Fischer Choose to Go to Jail?" in which she discussed his life and contribution. Like Bram Fischer and the liberals of his generation, however, Lionel Burger represents a paternalism that has become problematic.

The novel is ambitious in its scope, its action ranging from the fifties through the repressive sixties to the Black Consciousness movement of the mid-seventies, with the Soweto children's uprising occurring toward the end. When the novel opens, Rosa is a schoolgirl governed by the expectations and value system of her liberal parents. Her existence is shaped by the demands of the antiapartheid movement at the expense of her personal development and needs. At this stage she has no identity other than that of Lionel Burger's daughter in much the same way that the antiapartheid movement bore the stamp of paternalistic white men.

In order for her to come of age, therefore, and to develop autonomy even as a white South African, it is necessary for her to separate from her South African formative influences and to become distinct from her father's Marxist legacy. Thus in the second phase of the novel, Rosa goes to Europe, where she develops not only an individual identity but also a sense of what it means to be a liberal white South African. This realization comes during a particularly traumatic exchange in London between Rosa and Zwelinzima, her adopted "brother" from childhood who is an activist in exile. This exchange also represents a turning point in Gordimer's fiction, for in this scene Zwelinzima as Caliban has found his voice and in challenging Rosa and her legacy of paternalism has called both Prospero and Miranda into question. At this point, Rosa can examine herself. In the third phase of the narrative, she returns to South Africa to determine her own sense of political commitment, which eventually leads her, like her father, to prison. While Rosa continues in her family's heritage of political activism, her own maturity and the rising tide of black awareness force her, and by implication all liberal whites, to reassess the white role in the antiapartheid struggle.

Gordimer's insistence that white South Africans see themselves as Africans first and as whites second continues in her later works, which we can date from 1981 with the publication of *July's People*. In her collection of short stories *Jump and Other Stories* (1991), she includes "Once upon a Time," a fable that epitomizes the ultimate destructive consequence of white South African resistance to change in that country. In the tale, a Johannesburg couple, fearful of the winds of change and the ensuing lawlessness in South Africa, enclose their home in barricades designed to harm intruders, only to experience the horror of having their own child killed by the very implements designed to protect them. In this cautionary tale, the moral of which undergirds her writing during this period, Gordimer emphasizes that white South Africans, in their refusal to adapt, become the agents of their own destruction and kill off their own future.

The psychic toll that resisting change exacts from white South Africans and the uncertain future resulting from that resistance are the themes of *July's People*. The novel speaks to the black South African spirit of resistance of the seventies that was largely inspired by the overthrow of the Portuguese in Angola and Mozambique. Set in a fictive South African future in which Johannesburg is in the midst of a guerrilla takeover, *July's People* explores the psychological dynamics of what Gordimer calls ''life in the interregnum,'' that excruciatingly difficult period of waiting for inevitable change. The epigraphs of the novel, taken from Antonio Gramsci's *Prison Notebooks*, address the historical moment: ''The old is dying and the new cannot be born; in this interregnum there arises a great diversity of morbid symptoms.'' The novel, therefore, presents a bleak future as a way of exploring the anxious present of the eighties.

The most apocalyptic of her texts, *July's People* is the story of Bam and Maureen Smales and their servant of fifteen years, Mwawate, whom they have known only as July and whom, for all their apolitical, trendy liberalism and antiapartheid sentiment, they have relegated to the ranks of Native Other. July has divided his existence between the Smales household and a remote Bantustan where his family lives and that he has been able to visit only every two years. When violence erupts in Johannesburg, Bam, Maureen, their children, and July make the three-day trip in the family's truck to Bantustan, where they find refuge in July's hut.

Their flight from Johannesburg initiates them into the black South African experience of forced relocation, deprivation of freedom of movement, and ultimate loss of power over themselves. Because of their insistence on remaining whites first and Africans second, Bam and Maureen cannot cope with their reduced circumstances and loss of authority and privileged middle-class status. Their marriage falls apart. Bam devolves into total shame, and Maureen, at the end of the novel, abandons her family and rushes toward an unmarked helicopter and uncertainty. That only the Smales children remain functional indicates that the hope for white South Africa lies in a new and adaptable generation.

Gordimer's focus on the massive error inherent in white South African resistance to change continues in *A Sport of Nature*, a picaresque narrative in which the protagonist, Hillela, appears as an aberrant, amoral, self-serving creation in the context of conventional South African expectations. Gordimer's use of the *Oxford English Dictionary* definition of a ''sport of nature'' as the epigraph of the text underscores Hillela's picaresque characterization manifested in the success she finds in her increasingly Afrocentric identity, which, in turn, supports Gordimer's insistence that ''whites of former South Africa . . . redefine themselves in a new collective life within a new structure'' (*Essential Gesture*, 264).

Of Gordimer's novels, *A Sport of Nature* most demands subversive reading, for in her narrative strategy, Gordimer includes a biased and, therefore, unreliable narrator who subtly disapproves of Hillela's departure from the ''parent stock'' while failing to pass judgment on the obvious moral failings of the larger South African world and on the specific ''parent stock'' from which Hillela has departed. The events of the narrative are simple. Abandoned by her adulterous mother, Hillela has been sent from Rhodesia to her aunts in Johannesburg because of her friendship with a "coloured" boy. She is later expelled from her adoptive home to a vagabond existence after she has been caught in a sexual relationship with her cousin, Sasha. She later marries an ANC leader who is murdered, and after his death she travels abroad as a refugee and a single mother of an interracial child whom she names after Winnie Mandela. She finally marries an exiled African leader who successfully regains power and becomes the director of the Organization of African Unity and with whom she eventually returns to Cape Town for the inauguration of South Africa's first majority government.

Throughout the narrative, the reader is aware of Hillela's position on the margin of South African society, from which she, like the traditional picaro, innocently presents and judges life. Thus her perspective lies in counterpoint to that of the narrator; and as she moves through space and society, her very existence calls into question established institutions, norms, and attitudes, not the least of which are apartheid and liberalism. Hillela, then, becomes the symbol of a South African spirit that flouts conventional expectations and embraces its African essence in order to celebrate both personal freedom and a healthy future.

From an overt concern with the place of whites in a changing South Africa, Gordimer shifts her focus in *My Son's Story* to the experience of colored South Africans and their role in the antiapartheid movement. Like *Burger's Daughter*, *My Son's Story* is a novel of development. In *My Son's Story*, she demonstrates the perils and dangers of entwined personal and political deceit both facilitated and made necessary by the overarching immoral construct of apartheid. In the narrative, Gordimer also makes use of metafiction, which is apparent in both the title of the text and in the epigraph, taken from Shakespeare's sonnet 13: "You had a father, let your son say so." This tale, then, is a son's telling of both his own and his father's stories. The challenge, therefore, falls to the reader to trust the son to be a reliable narrator of both stories.

In the novel, Will recounts how his adulterous father, Sonny, betrays both his family and the resistance movement when he has an extramarital affair with Hannah Plowman, a white activist. Will's accidental discovery of the affair draws him both into his father's deceit and into the limited but safe harbor of storytelling. Because, however, Will is also loyal to Aila, his mother and Sonny's wife, he also gradually assumes the central male position in the family as they become increasingly involved in the resistance movement independently of Sonny. Worse yet, Sonny has lost touch with the family so greatly that the state is able to destroy the unit before he realizes that they are at risk. In addition, he loses Hannah when she accepts a United Nations position outside of South Africa.

That Sonny should find himself alone and marginalized is significant. His ultimate condition speaks to the peripheral state of the colored community. The reader is aware of Sonny's early orientation toward colonialism, his initial detachment from the antiapartheid movement, and his falling into the resistance by default. Similarly, the deceit inherent in his liaison with Hannah and his increasing loyalty to her at the expense of his family and the resistance implies a loss of perspective and indifference to the moral improvement of South Africa. Like Gordimer's other fiction, then, *My Son's Story* also emerges as a cautionary tale that stresses the need for personal and political commitment to the idea of a healthy and unified state.

In her most recent novel, *None to Accompany Me*, a postapartheid text, Gordimer returns to the question of where whites fit in. She couples this question with her portrayal of the complicated existence of a new politically empowered black South African, the returning exile. Set just before South Africa's first nonracial election and the beginning of majority rule, the novel portrays a new South Africa, one in which individuals who have lived through the old order are forced to carve out a new place and to develop a new world for themselves. In so doing they also must redefine the meaning of family, community, and society at large.

Vera Starks, the protagonist of the novel, is a lawyer who represents black South Africans in their struggle to reclaim their land. In her commitment to her vocation, she is reminiscent of Anna Louw, a similar character in *A World of Strangers*. History, however, has overtaken the prototype. Instead of becoming an enemy of the state as Anna does, Vera represents the white liberal who decides to remain in South Africa through national changes on African terms. Such a transition, the text emphasizes, assumes the form of a lonely, highly individual journey. In keeping with her style, Gordimer's epigraphs underscore the larger theme of the novel and the relevant symbolism of events in Vera's life and in the complicated lives of her family members as well as those of returning exiles. The quotations from Proust, "We must never be afraid to go too far, for truth lies beyond," and from Basho, "None to accompany me on this path: / Nightfall in Autumn," stress the need for individuals in and beyond the fictive world to slough off the old life and to confront with courage and hope an inevitable, albeit uncertain, future.

With the publication of *None to Accompany Me*, Gordimer has brought her readers into contemporary South Africa. The direction her subsequent work will take remains to be seen. In one of her most recent essays, "That Other World That Was the World" (*Writing and Being*, 114–134), she addresses the death of that particular "double colonization" in South Africa that took place in April 1994, when all South Africans went to the polls. In this essay, she acknowledges the challenging task of transition now facing her country. For now, whether or not the throes of transition will be the focus of her work is a matter of speculation. Nevertheless, a survey of her total output to date reveals that she has consistently been a fine literary artist and astute social and political observer whose works not only portray the specific South African story but also address difficult issues in the larger human condition. In blurring the distinction between the center and the margin and in choosing relentlessly to call into question

definitions of and relationships between "self" and "other," she has successfully challenged and destabilized generations of assumptions that have privileged
the notion of Eurocentric superiority. Her stand has been an unpopular one;
nevertheless, it has garnered her wide readership and international acclaim.

CRITICAL RECEPTION

Gordimer's winning the Nobel Prize for Literature attests to the place of her
work in the canon of great literature. Prior to her winning the Nobel Prize,
however, her work had been widely read and accepted with spectacular success,
particularly among international readers. On the other hand, because of the controversial nature of her subject matter, her work has often met with hostile
critical reception within South Africa and has, upon occasion, been censored.
The widely read and taught *Burger's Daughter*, for example, was published in
England in 1979. On July 11, 1979, the novel was banned in South Africa by
a spurious censorship committee. Shortly thereafter, a state security expert indicated that the novel posed no national threat, and in April 1980 Gordimer was
awarded the CNA Prize for *Burger's Daughter*.

In addition to the Nobel Prize and the Central News Agency (CNA) Literary
Award, Gordimer has also received such prestigious awards as the James Tait
Black Memorial Prize, the Booker prize, and the Grand Aigle d'Or. All of her
novels are in print, available in paperback, and accessible in English and in
translation to a wide reading public. Her frequent contributions to such
publications as the *New Yorker* and *New York Review of Books* continue to
secure her prominence in the minds of a sophisticated reading public. Moreover,
Gordimer's work is the focus of increasing academic attention. Leading studies
have been written by such literary scholars as Stephen Clingman, John Cooke,
Judie Newman, and Kathrin Wagner. Gordimer's works continue to be the subjects of several doctoral dissertations and scholarly articles. In short, Gordimer's
literary reputation is indisputable and permanent.

BIBLIOGRAPHY

Works by Nadine Gordimer

Novels

The Lying Days. New York: Simon and Schuster, 1953.
A World of Strangers. New York: Simon and Schuster, 1958.
Occasion for Loving. New York: Viking, 1963.
The Late Bourgeois World. New York: Viking, 1966.
A Guest of Honour. New York: Viking, 1970.
The Conservationist. New York: Viking, 1974.
Burger's Daughter. New York: Viking, 1979.
July's People. New York: Viking, 1981.

A Sport of Nature. New York: Alfred A. Knopf, 1987.
My Son's Story. New York: Farrar Straus Giroux, 1990.
None to Accompany Me. New York: Farrar Straus Giroux, 1994.

Story Collections

Face to Face: Short Stories. Johannesburg: Silver Leaf, 1949.
The Soft Voice of the Serpent and Other Stories. New York: Simon and Schuster, 1952.
Six Feet of the Country. New York: Simon and Schuster, 1956.
Friday's Footprints and Other Stories. New York: Viking, 1960.
Not for Publication and Other Stories. New York: Viking, 1965.
Penguin Modern Stories 4 (with others). London: Penguin, 1970.
Livingstone's Companions. New York: Viking, 1971.
No Place Like. London: J. Cape, 1975.
Selected Stories. New York: Viking, 1976.
Some Monday for Sure. London: Heinemann, 1976.
A Soldier's Embrace. New York: Viking, 1976.
Town and Country Lovers. Los Angeles: Sylvester and Orphanos, 1980.
Something Out There: Stories by Nadine Gordimer. New York: Viking, 1984.
Crimes of Conscience. London: Heinemann, 1991.
Jump and Other Stories. New York: Farrar Straus Giroux, 1991.
Why Haven't You Written? Selected Stories, 1950–1972. London: Penguin, 1992.

Nonfiction

The Black Interpreters: Notes on African Writing. Johannesburg: SproCas/Ravan, 1973.
On the Mines (with David Goldblatt). Cape Town: Struik, 1973.
Lifetimes under Apartheid (with David Goldblatt). New York: Knopf, 1986.
The Essential Gesture: Writing, Politics, and Places. Ed. Stephen Clingman. New York: Alfred A. Knopf, 1988.
Writing and Being. Cambridge, Mass.; London: Harvard University Press, 1995.

Interviews with Nadine Gordimer

Conversations with Nadine Gordimer. Ed. Nancy Topping Bazin and Marilyn Dallman Seymour. Jackson and London: University Press of Mississippi, 1990.

Selected Studies of Nadine Gordimer

Books

Clingman, Stephen. *The Novels of Nadine Gordimer: History from the Inside*. London and Boston: Allen and Unwin, 1986.
Cooke, John. *The Novels of Nadine Gordimer: Private Lives/Public Landscapes*. Baton Rouge: Louisiana State University Press, 1985.
Driver, Dorothy, et al. *Nadine Gordimer: A Bibliography of Primary and Secondary Sources, 1937–1992*. London and New Providence: H. Zell, 1994.
Ettin, Andrew V. *Betrayals of the Body Politic: The Literary Commitments of Nadine Gordimer*. Charlottesville: University Press of Virginia, 1993.

Fletcher, Pauline, ed. *Black/White Writing: Essays on South African Literature*. Lewis-
	burg: Bucknell University Press; London: Associated University Presses, 1993.
Haugh, Robert F. *Nadine Gordimer*. New York: Twayne Publishers, 1974.
Heywood, Christopher. *Nadine Gordimer*. Windsor: Profile, 1983.
King, Bruce, ed. *The Later Fiction of Nadine Gordimer*. New York: St. Martin's Press,
	1993.
Nell, Racilia Jilian. *Nadine Gordimer: Novelist and Short Story Writer: A Bibliography
	of Her Works and Selected Literary Criticism*. Johannesburg: University of the
	Witwatersrand Department of Bibliography, Librarianship, and Typography,
	1964.
Newman, Judie. *Nadine Gordimer*. London and New York: Routledge, 1988.
Smith, Rowland, ed. *Critical Essays on Nadine Gordimer*. Boston: G.K. Hall, 1990.
Wade, Michael. *Nadine Gordimer*. London: Evans Bros., 1978.
Wagner, Kathrin. *Rereading Nadine Gordimer*. Bloomington: Indiana University Press,
	1994.

Articles

Barnouw, D. "Nadine Gordimer: Dark Times, Interior Worlds, and the Obscurities of
	Difference." *Contemporary Literature* 35 (Summer 1994): 252–280.
Bazin, Nancy Topping. "Sex, Politics, and Silent Black Women: Nadine Gordimer's
	Occasion for Loving, A Sport of Nature, and *My Son's Story*." *Bucknell Review*
	37.1 (1993): 30–45.
Beresford, David. "Caught in the Chains of Idealism." *Guardian* (June 18, 1992): 25.
Boyers, Robert. "The Art of Nadine Gordimer." *Salamagundi* 93 (1992): 188–202.
Cooper, Brenda. "New Criteria for 'Abnormal Mutation'? An Evaluation of Gordimer's
	A Sport of Nature." *Rendering Things Visible: Essays on South African Literary
	Culture*. Ed. Martin Trump. Athens: Ohio University Press, 1990. 68–96.
Glenn, I. "Nadine Gordimer, J. M. Coetzee, and the Politics of Interpretation." *South
	Atlantic Quarterly* 93.1 (Winter 1994): 11–32.
Halil, K. "Travelling the 'World Round as Your Navel': Subjectivity in Nadine Gordi-
	mer's *Burger's Daughter*." *Ariel* 25.2 (April 1994): 31–45.
Huggan, G. "Echoes from Elsewhere: Gordimer's Short Fiction as Social Critique."
	Research in African Literatures 25.1 (Spring 1994): 61–73.
Kinkead-Weakes, Mark. "Sharp Knowing in Apartheid? The Shorter Fiction of Nadine
	Gordimer and Doris Lessing." *Essays on African Writing*. Ed. Abdulrazak Gur-
	nah. London: Heinemann, 1993.
Knipp, Thomas. "Going All the Way: Eros and Polis in the Novels of Nadine Gordi-
	mer." *Research in African Literatures* 24.1 (Spring 1993): 37–50.
Lazar, K. "*Jump and Other Stories*: Gordimer's Leap into the 1990's: Gender and Pol-
	itics in Her Latest Short Fiction." *Journal of Southern African Studies* 18.4
	(1992): 783–802.
Neill, Michael. "Translating the Present: Language, Knowledge, and Identity in Nadine
	Gordimer's *July's People*." *Journal of Commonwealth Literature* 25.1 (1990):
	71–97.
Rich, Paul. "Tradition and Revolt in South African Fiction: The Novels of Andre Brink,
	Nadine Gordimer, and J. M. Coetzee." *Journal of Southern African Studies* 9
	(October 1982): 54–73.

Temple-Thurston, Barbara. "Madam and Boy: A Relationship of Shame in Gordimer's *July's People.*" *World Literature Written in English* 28.1 (1988): 51–58.

———. "Nadine Gordimer: The Artist as a Sport of Nature." *Studies in Twentieth Century Literature* 15.1 (1991): 175–184.

Visser, Nicholas. "Beyond the Interregnum: A Note on the Ending of *July's People.*" *Rendering Things Visible: Essays on South African Literary Culture.* Ed. Martin Trump. Athens: Ohio University Press, 1990. 61–67.

———. "The Politics of Future Projection in South African Fiction." *Bucknell Review* 37.1 (1993): 62–82.

White, Jonathan. "Politics and the Individual in the Modernist Historical Novel: Gordimer and Rushdie." *Recasting the World: Writing after Colonialism.* Ed. Jonathan White. Baltimore: Johns Hopkins University Press, 1993. 208–240.

Wienhouse, L. "The Paternal Gift of Narration: Nadine Gordimer's *My Son's Story.*" *Journal of Commonwealth Literature* 28.2 (1993): 66–76.

CAROL P. MARSH-LOCKETT

MAFIKA GWALA (1946–   )

BIOGRAPHY

Born in Verulam, near Durban (Natal), in 1946, in a region where the majority of the population consisted of Zulus and Indians, Mafika Gwala grew up in a mixed environment. Gwala was eight years old when the nationalists began separating the ethnic groups. His adolescence was during the period of the institutionalization of apartheid, which led to a radicalization of the younger generation of blacks; and Gwala, like many others, gave up his academic career for the sake of the political struggle against the power structure of the apartheid regime. After matriculating, he enrolled at the University of Zululand. At this time the South African Student Organization (SASO) was founded. Gwala gave up his university studies in order to devote himself to the Black Consciousness movement. He earned his living by various jobs such as legal clerk, secondary-school teacher, factory worker, personal assistant, and publications researcher. Gwala started writing poetry between 1966 and 1967, but his career as a writer began with short stories. There were problems with publication. One of his short stories and his first poems were published in the *Classic*. While his poems have been published in several anthologies, his short stories have remained mostly unpublished. In the interview with Thengamehlo Ngwenya ''Mafika Gwala: Towards a National Culture,'' Gwala discusses his fascination for jazz and his love for Miriam Makeba's song with the same title as the reason why he entitled his first collection *Jol'inkomo*. From 1970 through 1972 he was in the countryside of Transkei. In this collection there is sometimes an attempt to handle the rural context, and its title was a declaration of solidarity with the rural masses. His best contribution to Black Consciousness and SASO came out during this time. He sees his role as one of awakening consciousness and dismantling the deception of the negative reality.

Since this publication Gwala has contributed poems and essays to the magazine *Staffinder*, which has become well known as a medium of political discourse on literature. He contributed to the student organization's newsletter and edited the 1973 edition of *Black Review*, published by the Black Community Programme, an organization that was later banned. By making information about events accessible, *Black Review* made debate possible in the community. The collection of data signified deep involvement on the part of the editor. Gwala himself was detained in 1977 and released nine months later without being charged. In 1974 he took part in the Black Renaissance Convention, which was an important step toward bringing together the different political streams in this community divided on strategies. Here he gave a speech that brought him into focus as an important representative of the Black Consciousness movement. In 1982, when Gwala's second volume of poetry, *No More Lullabies*, came out, his reputation as a committed writer had already been established.

In the eighties Gwala went to Manchester in England to further his studies. Here he read his poems at the world conference of the Association of Commonwealth Language and Literature and contributed to the cultural programs of the African National Congress. In 1992 he edited and translated the anthology of Zulu praise poems, *Musho*, in cooperation with Elizabeth Gunner, a teacher at the School of Oriental and African Studies in London.

MAJOR WORKS AND THEMES

Gwala is a visionary poet. His poetry is conspicuous for its tone of optimism. In "Getting off the Ride" from the *Jol'inkomo* collection he calls himself "the Africa Kwela instrumentalist whose notes profess change." He is convinced that there is truth and hope too, even though it is difficult to cherish it in the face of adversity. For him, to be black means to struggle. He knows that history is written by the suffering of the people, but also that it contains positive changes, only they demand sacrifice. Gwala wants to see change in the spirits of the people, who must give up their deceiving comforts and stand up in order to change their situation for themselves. His poems, therefore, are full of exhortation, not to yield, but to fight for truth. Past glory leads them to value themselves in a positive way. He conjures up a proud ancestry that has been distorted and counts the virtues in order to make his people aware of their potential capacity to be a free people through a positive value system.

Gwala's criticism is directed against those who call themselves nationalists, when in reality they are exploiting their own people. In "Black Status Seekers," from the same collection, there is an outburst of anger against those who avoid ghetto truths while pretending to represent the cause of its dwellers. Gwala is sarcastic about the higher-class blacks who, in their superficial way of thinking, exhibit their consciousness by wearing dashikis, but at the same time do not hold back from sacrificing their brothers for their own profit. Gwala is equally ironical about the concept of progress which produces what he calls "plastic syphilization" ("Vo Nguyen Giap" in *No More Lullabies*). He is adept at coining new phrases to express this contempt, as when he writes "I eye-mock this plastic arrogance" ("Getting off the Ride").

Gwala's literary theory as well as his evaluation of Black Consciousness has become explicit in his essays like "Towards a National Culture." Here he stresses the responsibility of an artist that should be aroused by his identifying with black reality. For Gwala, black art cannot be a form of escapist art; authentic theatre represents the truth even if it is ugly. In "Tracing the Steps" he elaborates further on this theme and maintains that if writers are to write about African greatness, it has to be linked with the present. Black writers cannot write outside their experience if it is their intention to change it. As a matter of necessity they have to assume a role in the social conflict that should constitute their function as cultural workers. For Gwala, Black Consciousness is not an end in itself. It can be fruitful if it strives for a nonracial society in South Africa. By pointing out the importance of exploring indigenous values in his criticism "Black Writing Today," Gwala warns against assuming parochial attitudes. He is skeptical about the intellectuals who, assimilating foreign culture, tend to alienate themselves from their own people. In his previously mentioned speech at the Black Renaissance Convention, "Towards the Practical Manifestations of Black Consciousness," he exhorts them to accept that they are a part of the collective will. Liberation can come only by making Black Consciousness a "Back to the People Movement."

In his article on Steve Bantu Biko, Gwala's stance on Black Consciousness becomes very clear. He defines it as a path to National Consciousness. In spite of their shared bourgeois overtones, Black Consciousness showed a different approach than Negritude. While a regard for the past is essential to bring about a change, it cannot be without a critical awareness and also a vision of the future. To be a cultural weapon, writing must become an act of solidarity with the "wretched of the earth." Gwala finds that literature of most black writers will continue to reflect the language of the people, although most critics prefer the language of the elite.

In the already mentioned interview, "Mafika Gwala: Towards a National Culture," he again urges black writers to favor the popular language as opposed to the purist language by including expressions of the ghetto dwellers and rural blacks in literature. He describes the trend of writing in indigenous language by worker poets and the reintroduction of oral forms as an expression of black awareness. In his book review of Mbuli's oral poetry, he characterizes this kind of poetry as mass based.

CRITICAL RECEPTION

Povey considers Gwala's verse as the most original and yet the most typical of the "Soweto poets," as he calls the group, but not without some reservations. He discerns two triple elements in the pattern of Gwala's work: three stylistic and three thematic. Gwala's way of writing shows a crudely worded, traditional oral style and urban colloquialism. Thematically his writing attempts to conjure up the past, represents his immediate environment, and criticizes those who strive for white values. Povey is aware that in his analysis he is "trapped into applying too formal a paradigm" (92). He points out that "within this double trio of patterns, Gwala's work combines in opposing tension, tender concern and angry passion. Balanced, they achieve a kind of lyric harmony, linking the present political despair to the humane optimism which is surely the basis of all poetry" (86). Ngwenya argues, "The range and complexity of Gwala's work defies neat categorisation" ("Poetry," 44) and suggests that his poetry is to be considered not only as a literary, but also as a social phenomenon "which has to be evaluated according to the sociopolitical exigencies of our time and place" (50).

Mpe's article is what he himself calls a reply to the interview "Mafika Gwala: Towards a National Culture." He disagrees with Gwala on the issue of language and contends that Gwala's exhortation to Africanize English cannot be fulfilled because "such an imposition of responsibility upon a writer will curb his or her artistic capabilities. Furthermore, with many people unable to read or understand English it is very naive to see the possibility of its being 'the language of the people' at the moment" (30).

Alvarez-Pereyre deals with the question of language in Gwala's writing from a different aspect. He finds that of all his contemporaries, Gwala and also Arthur Nortje handle "the English language with the greatest freedom. Contrary to the fears of some purists, it is less a case, in fact, of his exploiting it than of his serving it, since he contributes so much to its renewal" (240).

BIBLIOGRAPHY

Works by Mafika Gwala

"Towards a National Culture." *South African Outlook* (Cape) 103.1227 (1973): 131–133.
"Towards the Practical Manifestations of Black Consciousness." *Black Renaissance: Papers from the Black Renaissance Convention*. Ed. T. Thoahlane. Johannesburg: Ravan, 1975. 24–33.
Jol'inkomo. Johannesburg: Ad. Donker, 1977.
"Steve Bantu Biko." *Reconstruction*. Ed. M. Mutloatse. Johannesburg: Ravan, 1981. 229–237.
"The Oral Poetry of Mzwakhe Mbuli and the COSATU Workers" Book Review. *Staffrider* 7.1 (1988): 83–91.

"Black Writing Today." *Soweto Poetry*. Ed. M. Chapman. Johannesburg: McGraw-Hill, 1982. 169–175.

No More Lullabies. Johannesburg: Ravan Press, 1982.

"Tracing the Steps." *Matatu: Zeitschrift für afrikanische Kultur und Gesellschaft* 2 3–4 (1988): 76–95.

Selected Studies of Mafika Gwala

Alvarez-Pereyre, Jacques. *The Poetry of Commitment in South Africa*. London: Heinemann, 1984.

Barnett, Ursula A. *A Vision of Order: A Study of Black South African Literature in English (1914–1980)*. Cape Town: Maskew Miller, 1985.

Mpe, Phaswane. " 'Literary Language' and the 'Language of the People' in Contemporary South African English Poetry." *Staffinder* 10.2 (1992): 27–30.

Ngwenya, Thengamehlo, "Mafika Gwala: Towards a National Culture" (interview). *Staffinder* 8.1 (1989): 69–74.

―――. "The Poetry of Mafika Gwala." *Staffinder* 10.2 (1992): 43–51.

Povey, John. "The Poetry of Mafika Gwala." *Commonwealth Essays and Studies* 8.2 (1986): 84–93.

JOGAMAYA BAYER

BESSIE HEAD (1937–1986)

BIOGRAPHY

Bessie Head was born on July 6, 1937, in the Fort Napier Mental Institution in South Africa. Her mother was white and her father black, and at the time of her birth, extramarital sexual relations between blacks and whites had been punishable in South Africa for a decade. Her mother was incarcerated by her family, according to biographer Gillian Stead Eilersen (1), in her seventh month of pregnancy. Nothing is known of the father, though Bessie liked to say that he had worked in the family's stables and taken care of their racehorses, but they did not have horses. The family was upper-class in South African white society and dealt with the problem of their daughter violating their racial and class taboos by putting her and her child far away. But Bessie Amelia, née Birch Emery, named her daughter Bessie Amelia Emery and left her a little money. Bessie Emery, senior, died in 1943 in the mental hospital. Her surname came from her Australian–South African husband, with whom, before the marriage ended, she had had a son, Ronald.

Bessie Emery, the daughter, was fostered from birth by a mixed-race woman, in South African apartheid terminology "coloured," and her husband, Nellie and George Heathcote. The child accepted Nellie as her mother, knowing nothing of her real mother until she went off to boarding school. Head notes that this woman was paid a pittance for taking care of the baby but clearly loved and protected her. When she was thirteen, Head was sent to a severe mission orphanage for "coloured" girls. Here she was abruptly told about her real mother and father, described respectively as "insane" and "a native," indicating that she might be at risk of also becoming insane. This began lifelong hatred of missionaries and Christianity as organized religion. But eventually she was able to obtain a little information about her mother from the mission's files and learned that she had cared about her daughter, had desired that she have an education, and had left money to be used for this purpose. For Head, the paradoxes of racial identity were thus, understandably, particularly acute. White rule in South Africa and her mother's family accepting this meant that she was cast out as mixed race and abandoned. The young woman needed to belong somewhere and at times during her later life very strongly desired that African culture or black identity become her source of emotional security. But she was cut off in her formative years entirely from a sense of belonging to a specific ethnic African identity. Additionally, South Africa's legal controls of human relations were barbaric during her whole experience there and taught her that her very existence was an affront to racist laws: that the opportunity for a vulnerable child to benefit from and learn family bonds, affection, loyalty, support, community, and inheritance were easily destroyed by the system of apartheid.

There were two important positive aspects to the last phase of her schooling: her first publication, a short piece of moralistic fiction for a 1951 children's anthology, and the meeting with Margaret Cadmore, an influential friend and an English missionary appointed lady warden at St. Monica's in 1954, two years before Bessie Emery left school. Bessie Emery completed her Natal Teachers' Senior Certificate in 1957 and after teaching for a while at Clairwood Coloured School became, at the age of twenty-one, a journalist in Cape Town and then Johannesburg, writing for the *Golden City Post*, a weekly tabloid with a black readership. She lived for some time in District Six, the integrated Cape Town neighborhood bulldozed out of existence by the South African government because President Botha wanted an all-white space there instead. In Johannesburg, she also worked for the important literary and political magazine *Drum* and met important writers, such as Dennis Brutus, the journalist, poet, and activist, and Lewis Nkosi, the journalist and novelist, and became interested in Hinduism and pan-Africanism.

After a breakdown in 1960 that involved a suicide attempt, she returned to Cape Town still unable to work, but eventually founded her own political broadsheet, the *Citizen*. In 1961, the year apartheid South Africa cut itself off from the Commonwealth by becoming a republic, she married Harold Head, who was a freelance journalist. Both Harold and Bessie began to contribute to the *New African*, which often ran into trouble with the Security Police, and then to *Transition*. During this highly politicized period, Bessie Head experimented with fiction and poetry and had a son, Howard, born in 1962.

By the mid-1960s, when Bessie was in her middle thirties, she had separated from Harold. Her husband escaped from police harassment in 1964 and finally settled in Canada. Earlier the same year, Bessie had left South Africa with a one-way exit visa, making her an exile, and went to the then British Protectorate of Bechuanaland (now called Botswana). She would not acquire citizenship in Botswana until 1979. Harold's arrival in Serowe after his dramatic border crossing later became, as Eilersen's research shows, the basis for a similar experience for her character Makhaya Maseko in her first published novel, *When Rain Clouds Gather* (1968).

As a newly arrived refugee, she was at first a primary-school teacher in Serowe and continued after 1965 to contribute to the *New Africa*. In 1966, the year Botswana became independent, she left Serowe to work on an experimental farm. Simon and Schuster also commissioned her first novel, *When Rain Clouds Gather*, completed in 1967. In August 1966 she published "The Woman from America" in the *New Statesman*, and British agents and publishers paid her some attention, though still had trouble placing her manuscripts of stories and an early novel.

When Rain Clouds Gather was published a year before Bessie suffered a serious nervous breakdown and was hospitalized in 1969. But she was seriously involved in the Boiteko self-help rural development project that began in 1969–70. She remained ill on and off until early 1971 but wrote her second novel, *Maru*, published in 1971, and built a house out of the royalties from her first book. Her masterpiece, *A Question of Power*, appeared in 1973, the same year her imaginative study of her adopted home, *Serowe: Village of the Rain Wind* was commissioned, though this was not published until 1981. In 1977 her story collection *The Collector of Treasures* appeared, and in 1984 *A Bewitched Crossroad*. In 1979 she became a citizen of Botswana. In 1986 Head died prematurely of hepatitis at the age of forty-nine. Since her death, three collections of her writing have appeared: *Tales of Tenderness and Power* (stories) edited by Eilersen (1989), *A Woman Alone* (autobiographical pieces) edited by Craig MacKenzie (1990), and *A Gesture of Belonging* (letters, 1965–79), edited by Randolph Vigne (1991). Also, in 1993 her very early novella *The Cardinals* was published with her short fiction.

MAJOR WORKS AND THEMES

Head's life contributed importantly to her fictional concerns. Recent theoretical developments in the field of women's autobiography argue that whereas textual constructs of the self are always fictional and the individual's narrative of a life is in effect a creative work, it is still very important to acknowledge that women's versions of their own experience have been vital in constructing necessary subjectivities to challenge hegemonies of gender, race, and class. Head's narrative of her life in the form of her texts is inward-looking, which marks her writing out as unusual among African women writers' texts in the sense of being centrally concerned with the ways in which one individual woman constructs enough of a sense of coherent self to stay sane. There is little in Head's writing of a sense of community or connection to African tradition, and sometimes there is evidence of a disturbingly strong attachment to the very "mission" idealism that so outraged her. But her experience, as migrant and official refugee, as an effective orphan of mixed race in an apartheid society, and as divorced mother, certainly separates her from that of writers living in their natal societies and in relatively secure family units connected to a strong community. She always knew herself to be an outsider, even after many years in Botswana.

Indeed, her work might be said to have certain identities in common with other women's texts about serious displacement and the threat of fragmentation, such as those of Jean Rhys, Anita Desai, Buchi Emecheta, and Michelle Cliff, rather than with texts that narrate an unconflicted ethnic, cultural, or racial identification with Africa. Head is unquestionably an African writer: she was born in South Africa and wrote about Botswana. Her entire life was lived in Africa. But her sense of what this means is idiosyncratic, understandably, given her personal history.

Head's published texts, which now consist of novels, stories, nonfiction, and letters, register the contribution of a highly original woman to the literature and politics of Southern Africa. One of the most interesting issues in the study of Head's work is the question of her use of genre. Susan Gardner in her introduction to *Bessie Head: A Bibliography* mentions the challenge that Head's texts pose for the bibliographer and how it was necessary to add some categories to the usual list such as "cultural comment," "semifictional prose" (which would now most likely be called "creative nonfiction"), and "semifictionalised history" (7).

Much of Head's writing was an effort to portray the people with whom she lived from 1964 onwards, namely, the people of Botswana. Like any migrant, she found the move to a new society challenging and the people different. She remarked, for example, in 1979 that whereas in South Africa people were oppressed and did not know what it was for their ambitions to be aroused, she found the people in Botswana initially much harsher. She explained that she had never before encountered human ambition and greed in black people. Botswana, and particularly Serowe, where Head finally settled, therefore became for her a kind of moral microcosm of the world in which all human traits were in play within an almost entirely African community. South Africa, which haunts these texts without being present directly in them, is by contrast the prison in which human personalities are distorted away from their free expression. In a letter to Randolph Vigne (1966), Head said that she felt she could never write about people in South Africa because they were "all torn up" and had no "definite kind of wholeness" (*Gesture*, 27). The African world, to people in Botswana, was naturally the center of their perceptions of the world: it was never, to them, as Head said in *Serowe: Village of the Rain Wind* (1981), a "dark continent."

It should also be said that the hardships that Head suffered, such as her ill health, sense of displacement, poverty, and isolation, seemed to her to deepen her perceptions of human culture and nature and therefore to shape the writing in important ways. She said (to Randolph Vigne, 1968) that the "best and most enduring love is that of rejection" (*Gesture*, 58), a remark that could not be made except by one who has been forced to accept rejection and work through it. Her racial identity meant that she felt not only shut out of white society but also that some people rejected her for not being black enough. She decided to opt for "mankind as a whole" after her black nationalist phase was ended by such criticism. She also valued what she could learn from her mother's tragic situation, which she read as that of an impulsive and very lonely woman reaching out for love and happiness. Head's interpretation of cultural constructs of race is perhaps clearest in *Maru* (1971). It should be remembered, however, that she writes about African experience. Her African worldview in a very strong and original way manages to include both the details of a particular community and the ways in which this is a microcosm of all human possibilities.

When Rain Clouds Gather (1968) opens with the escape of Makhaya Maseko, formerly a political prisoner, from South Africa and his illegal entry into Botswana. He eventually works with a British expatriate, Gilbert Balfour, an agriculturalist who is trying to develop the skills of the 400 people who live in Golema Mmidi. These villagers have fled there to "escape the tragedies of life" (22). Their village's name signifies that they grow crops for a living. Dinorego, an elder who is responsible for bringing Makhaya to the village from the border, his daughter, and a few others become Makhaya's allies along with Gilbert, but the local chief is hostile to his presence.

Eventually Makhaya becomes involved with Paulina Sebeso, also a recent arrival in the village. She is a widow with two children whose husband committed suicide because of the affront to his honor after being suspected of stealing money from his employers. Gilbert also marries Dinorego's daughter, Maria. These relationships are both culturally complex, as Paulina is from northern Botswana, for example, and Gilbert and Maria are of different races as well as national cultures. Head therefore can explore the implications of home and exile through these relationships. Eventually Paulina's son is killed and she is accused by the chief, Matenge, of being involved in his death. The village resists their chief over this issue, and Makhaya becomes a part of the community, marrying Paulina. Matenge has a brother, Sekoto, who is Paramount Chief and a friend, Joas Tsepe, who is a disgruntled nationalist. Through characters like Tsepe, Matenge, and Sekoto, Bessie Head discusses the political environment as Botswana moves from colonialism to self-government, including pan-African nationalism, the role of the chiefs, and the insecurity of leaders. This novel initiates some of the major concerns of Head's later fictional texts: class, racial, and gender tensions within African society; unusual alliances against abuses of power; identity and displacement; and the importance of inner conviction and spiritual clarity in developing the strength to fight corruption and to follow personal desires.

Maru appeared in 1971. In this text, Head explored race as a cultural narrative, using a fictional form strongly influenced by folktale and moral fable. The outsider figure is Margaret Cadmore, named for her adoptive mother, who is British and a missionary but also a sensitive artist. As in Bessie Head's own life, mother and daughter have the same name but are of different races and are eventually separated when the older Margaret returns to Britain. Head said that she took the name Margaret Cadmore from her mission teacher, whom she loved "for her personality" (*Tales*, 8).

Margaret Cadmore, the daughter, is a Masarwa, a member of the Bushman people despised by both white and black. Her mother dies when she is a baby, and Margaret Cadmore the elder decides to conduct a kind of experiment, raising the young woman to know that she must belong to her own people while putting into practice her belief that environment is everything, heredity nothing. The younger Margaret, left to make her way alone after her teacher training, comes to Dilepe to teach. Her involvement with Dikeledi, who befriends her like a good sister, her brother Maru, whom Margaret finally marries, and Moleka, who has the potential to damage Margaret's sense of self and autonomy, provides Head with a way into discussion of the nature of love, constructs of race, and the relation between mind, feeling, body, and spirit. The style of this novel, which has provoked very different kinds of critical responses, is rather poetic, compressed, and full of philosophical and moral statements, such as "How universal was the language of oppression!" (109). *Maru* makes it clear that any human society can fall into the practice of racism against any other human group, and so explores the essential nature of the process that culminates in excluding or mistreating persons according to their race. The text is more economical than *When Rain Clouds Gather*, and it is even clearer that the plot and characters serve the moral purpose of the storyteller in the way of didactic oral tales.

A Question of Power (1973) is without doubt Head's most powerful and achieved text. Like her previous two novels, it sets out to explore the intersections of narratives of gender, race, and class in Botswanan culture as they impact on an individual who joins a community as an outsider. In this case, some of the details of Elizabeth's life are very close to Head's own: she was born in a mental hospital to a white mother from a racehorse-owning family and fostered as a young child by a woman of mixed race whom she thinks of as her mother. She eventually marries, has a son, breaks the marriage with her husband, and leaves South Africa for Botswana. Even the village she joins, called Motabeng in the novel, is named "Village of the Rain-Wind" by Elizabeth. This naming would return in the title *Serowe: Village of the Rain Wind*.

Elizabeth has a serious breakdown, which of course also happened to Bessie Head: one of the strengths of this text is its insider knowledge of mental and emotional fracturing and of the healing process that follows. *A Question of Power* charts Elizabeth's struggle to emerge from psychic fragmentation to some sense of wholeness, which involves her working through the tension between her inner sense of identity and the narratives of gender, race, and class that her cultural situation visits upon her. A major element in the novel is her relation with two male figures, Dan (who is destructively and aggressively sexual and controlling) and Sello (who is Elizabeth's "twin soul" and highly spiritual), who are both extensions of Elizabeth's mental world and also actual individuals, separate and apart from her. Elizabeth knows them mainly through her idea of them. This is a successful attempt to dramatize what is meant by our construction of reality: we believe and know what we narrate to ourselves about experience. Our understanding of other people is dependent on our including them in our own individual cultural narrative, just as our sense of self is dependent on our making sense of the ways in which culture and society construct us as well as our response to that construction.

The major contradiction of using an essentially logical, narrative literary form to convey madness has obviously been explored by many writers in different ways, but Head's attempt conveys an immediacy that is startling precisely because it is a faithful, if stylized and shaped, rendition of her own knowledge of mental breakdown. Also, this fracturing of identity occurs at the intersection of racial, class, and gender tensions in Elizabeth.

In 1977 Head published a collection of "Botswana Village Tales," *The Collector of Treasures*. She had been publishing short pieces of journalism or fiction since 1962, and one of these stories, "Looking for a Rain God," was first published in 1966 in *New African*. Most of this volume, however, was written during the 1970s, by which time Head's style and mature concerns were apparent. By 1974 she had also had a decade of residence in Botswana and had already established the interest that sustained her for the rest of her writing life, that is, the interpretation in fiction and fictionalized history of her adopted home. The stories are, like *Maru*, written as mythic tales of human encounters in an African village, where a sense of evil and good is very strongly developed.

"Witchcraft," for example, recounts the story of a hardworking, sensible woman who takes ill mysteriously just after she and her sister have come to some financial security in finding reasonable jobs. She resists giving her hardearned money to the village traditional healer because she knows from having watched him over the years that he has no talent to cure anyone of anything serious. She does consult him, though, just as she goes to the local hospital. In the end, she triumphs over her suffering on her own, after resting for a number of days in her house, and tells those who ask that she had to recover because she has to support those who depend on her. The story teases the reader with possible causes of the illness: in the end it seems likely that it is malnutrition and exhaustion, the diseases of the poor, and that better food and rest have a part to play in the woman's recovery. Similarly, "Jacob: The Story of a Faithhealing Priest" portrays a man of simple and intense goodness and great faith, but expresses deep skepticism about his vision of God because God provides no practical help for the innocent and the poor. The powerful and wealthy rival to Jacob, Lebojang, is arrested at the end of the story for ritually killing a child as part of his magic to encourage riches and power to come to his clients. As in *A Question of Power*, then, organized religion, like politics, is a system prone to worldly corruption. The human spirit, however, can develop beyond this to demonstrate profound love for others.

Head's last two works published in her lifetime were both fictionalized historical or sociological portraits of Botswana: *Serowe: Village of the Rain Wind* (1981) and *A Bewitched Crossroad* (1984). These two texts show Head moving into a phase of writing in which she attempted to bring together historical research about important events or people, such as Khama the Great, her established concerns with race, identity, and human community, the necessity for individuals or communities to heal or strengthen themselves, and the forms of orature that most suited her purpose, such as the testimony of older villagers. Head was self-declaredly didactic and autobiographical in her writing. But in these two texts, she sought particularly to demonstrate her understanding of a particular corner of Africa, human society in microcosm.

Four posthumously published texts have given us stories, *Tales of Tenderness and Power* (1989); autobiographical sketches, *A Woman Alone* (1990); letters, *A Gesture of Belonging* (1991); and a novella, *The Cardinals* (1993). The material in the first two of these works somewhat overlaps. But each of these texts adds something important to our understanding of Bessie Head. The letters, written between 1965 and 1979 to Randolph Vigne, give the impression of a brilliant, mercurial, troubled woman who wrestled bravely with her demons and who, more than anything, longed to get her writing done, see it published, and receive the dignity of decent pay for it. In *A Woman Alone*, Head's most autobiographical public voice speaks, albeit still fictionalized. She makes direct reference to what shaped some of her major texts, for example, her concern with various manifestations of evil, particularly racism. *Tales of Tenderness* contains autobiography, mythic tales, fictionalized history, and stories. "The Woman from America," which was first published in the *New Statesman* (1966), is one of the most characteristic pieces in relation to Head's novels. It is about an unusual African-American woman who marries a Botswaman man and comes to live in Serowe, and about Serowe's reaction to such an unconventional life. The woman has a capacity to join together elements of many different cultures, both in her ancestry (African, German, Cherokee) and in her making a success of migrating to Africa. Head comments that many people in Southern Africa are used to authoritarianism and tend to be cautious, even timid, and to fear something new. The admiration for someone brave enough to defy convention is very strong in this piece and informs the comments on Southern African and American culture.

Head commented on her major themes and indicated that her concern in *Maru* was to write a piece on racial hatred expressing her view that lack of communication is at the root of it; and in *A Question of Power*, to make a "private and philosophical journey to the roots of evil" (Abrahams, *Tragic Life*, 15). She saw her work as including all major Southern African concerns: enforced migration and displacement, race, evil, and the history of settlement of Southern African peoples. She spoke of being able to absorb "the peaceful world of black people simply dreaming in their own skins" (17).

CRITICAL RECEPTION

Though Bessie Head's papers are available for scholars in the Khama III Memorial Museum in Serowe and in the Mugar Memorial Library in Boston University, there have been comparatively few biocritical studies of length and substance. But a short volume of letters from Bessie Head to Randolph Vigne (1991) is very helpful, as is his comment that she was a superb correspondent. He mentions the large quantity of Head's letters (several thousand) in the Bessie Head archive in Serowe, which one day should be published in a definitive edition.

Gillian Stead Eilersen's most readable biography is very important and supersedes, in its detail and inclusiveness, previous work done by Craig Mackenzie (*A Woman Alone*, 1990), who warns that Head is a difficult subject because she was an "unreliable witness" of her own life, and Virginia Osoma Ola's *The Life and Work of Bessie Head* (1994). There is an article on Head in the *Dictionary of Literary Biography* (Little, 1992). Mackenzie and Clayton (1989) have edited interviews with Head.

There are some fascinating contradictions in Head's writing that have sometimes provoked critical comment: a tendency to use Western or Eurocentric imagery (for example, "a black rage"), and yet to be provocatively insightful about race and racism; a capacity to draw strong women characters who nevertheless often allow themselves to be damaged by men; and an awareness of class and economic issues along with a cynicism about politics and an emphasis on moral rather than economic or political solutions to human misery. It is the contradictions, however, that are essential to understanding her texts.

Some critics have paid detailed attention to the difficult questions that these contradictions can raise. Psychoanalytic studies are fairly common (Campbell, 1994; Rose, 1994; Olaogun, 1994; Hogan, 1994). Roger Berger (1990) writes on *A Question of Power* that people who are sources of fear for Elizabeth are black. Berger suggests therefore that it is useful to consider some aspects of Frantz Fanon's analysis of racial psychopathologies in *Black Skins, White Masks* (1967). In Berger's reading, Dan and Sello manifest European racist notions of Africans (oversexed, irrational), and Elizabeth's relation to the land is the only possible avenue for her curing herself of her neuroses.

Another obvious theme in Head's texts is land and nationality (Sample, 1990, 1991; Menager-Everson, 1992; Lionnet, 1993). Lloyd Brown in his early study of African women writers (1981) points out that Head's fiction reflects "the exile's prevailing sense of homelessness" (158). He also claims that Head was the only nonwhite South African woman at the time writing about the relation between "sexual roles" (gender) and racial identity. Susan Gardner, however, quotes Head's distaste for political movements (129) and that she certainly resisted being labeled feminist. Nevertheless, feminist studies of Head are also common (Bazin, 1990; Achufusi, 1991, 1992; Chetin, 1992). Feminist studies of Head often use postcolonial theory. Head is, at best, however, an ambivalent feminist, constructing narratives of female struggles for autonomy and selfhood and against male power, but sometimes resolving them by the arrival of a protective man, such as Maru. Also, her attitudes to race and class as reflected in her texts are complicated and often contradictory.

Cecil Abrahams edited a collection of critical essays, *The Tragic Life: Bessie Head and Literature in Southern Africa* (1990), that brought together some of the characteristic elements developed in 1980s critical responses to Head: biographical interest in her "tragic life" and in her autobiographical texts; studies of politics and madness, feminism, and good and evil; and analysis of structural elements such as narrative techniques and tones. This work collectively establishes psychological, political, and moral themes as major in Head's texts. There are also several essays on Head in Gurnah's volume (1993).

The bibliographical work by Susan Gardner and Patricia Scott (1986) is very useful and lists critical responses to Head's texts by year of appearance, beginning with N. J. Marquard's 1963 response to her piece "The Gentle People" published in *New African* in 1962. It was, of course, after the publication of *A Question of Power* (1973) that extensive critical interest began to develop, though *Maru* provoked very diverse responses.

Head's place as an important African writer is assured by now, but it still remains for her special identity and that of her texts to be explored fully, permitting all facets to emerge and to relate to one another in critical reading. This, at the moment, happens only rarely. She is, for example, certainly both a South African and a Botswanan writer, and at the same time, neither of these national categories exactly fits her. Her texts have remarkable insights into prejudice and reflect and continue prejudice at the same time. Critics tend to construct writers and texts according to their own prevailing cultural narratives: perhaps at some time soon, as we continue to work on realizing intellectually how inadequate the usual categories of race, nation, gender, and class so often prove to be and how innate contradiction is to human experience, we will see her more clearly as a cultural and literary pioneer.

BIBLIOGRAPHY

Works by Bessie Head

Novels and Stories

When Rain Clouds Gather. New York: Simon and Schuster, 1968.
Maru. London: Gollancz; Heinemann, 1971.
A Question of Power. London: Davis-Poynter, 1973.
The Collector of Treasures, and Other Botswana Village Tales. Oxford: Heinemann, 1977.
Serowe: Village of the Rain Wind. Oxford: Heinemann, 1981.
A Bewitched Crossroad: An African Saga. Craighall, South Africa: Donker, 1984.

Tales of Tenderness and Power. Ed. Gillian Stead Eilersen. Johannesburg, South Africa: Donker, 1989; Oxford: Heinemann, 1990.
The Cardinals: With Meditations and Short Stories. Ed. M. J. Daymond. Cape Town: David Philip, 1993.

Letters and Autobiography

A Woman Alone. Ed. Craig MacKenzie. Oxford: Heinemann, 1990.
A Gesture of Belonging: Letters from Bessie Head, 1965–1979. Ed. Randolph Vigne. London and Portsmouth, N.H.: SA Writers and Heinemann, 1991.

Selected Studies of Bessie Head

Books, Articles, and Dissertations

Abrahams, Cecil, ed. *The Tragic Life: Bessie Head and Literature in Southern Africa*. Trenton, N.J.: Africa World Press, 1990.
————. "The Tyranny of Place: The Context of Bessie Head's Fiction." *World Literature Written in English* 17 (November 1978): 22–29.
Achufusi, Ifeyinwa Grace. "Conceptions of Ideal Womanhood: The Examples of Bessie Head and Grace Ogot." *Neohelicon* 19.2 (1992): 87–101.
————. "Female African Writers and Social Criticism: A Study of the Works of Bessie Head and Grace Ogot." *Dissertation Abstracts* 52.5 (November 1991): 1745A–46A, DAI no. 91246652, University of Wisconsin, Madison.
Balseiro, Isabel. "Nation, Race, and Gender in the Writings of Bessie Head and Rosario Ferre." *Dissertation Abstracts* 53.8 (February 1993): 2802A, DAI no. 9237923, New York University.
Bardolph, J., ed. *Short Fiction in the New Literatures in English*. Nice: Faculté des Lettres et Sciences Humaines, 1989.
Bazin, Nancy Topping. "Madness, Mysticism, and Fantasy: Shifting Perspectives in the Novels of Doris Lessing, Bessie Head, and Nadine Gordimer." *Extrapolation* 33.1 (Spring 1992): 73–87.
————. "Venturing into Feminist Consciousness: Bessie Head and Buchi Emecheta." *The Tragic Life: Bessie Head and Literature in Southern Africa*. Ed. Cecil Abrahams. Trenton, N.J.: Africa World Press, 1990. 45–58.
Beard, Linda Susan. "Bessie Head's *A Question of Power*: The Journey through Disintegration to Wholeness." *Colby Library Quarterly* 15 (1979): 267–74.
————. "Bessie Head's Syncretic Fictions: The Reconceptualization of Power and the Recovery of the Ordinary." *Modern Fiction Studies* 37.3 (Autumn 1991): 575–89.
Berger, Roger. "The Politics of Madness in Bessie Head's *A Question of Power*." *The Tragic Life*. Ed. Cecil Abrahams. Trenton, N.J.: Africa World Press, 1990.
Brown, Lloyd W. "Creating New Worlds in Southern Africa: Bessie Head and the Question of Power." *Umoja* 3.1 (Spring 1979): 43–53.
————. *Women Writers in Black Africa*. Westport, Conn.: Greenwood Press, 1981.
Bruner, Charlotte. "Bessie Head: Restless in a Distant Land." *When the Drumbeat Changes*. Ed. Caroline Parker and Stephen Arnold. Washington, D.C.: African Literature Association and Three Continents Press, 1981. 261–77.

———. "Child Africa as Depicted by Bessie Head and Ama Ata Aidoo." *Studies in the Humanities* 7.2 (1979): 5–12.

Campbell, Elaine. "Bessie Head: Model for Agricultural Reform." *Journal of African Studies* 12.2 (1985): 82–85.

———. "The Theme of Madness in Four African and Caribbean Novels by Women." *Commonwealth Novel in English* 6.1–2 (Spring–Fall 1993): 133–41.

Chase, Joanne. "Bessie Head's *A Question of Power*: Romance or Rhetoric?" *ACLALS Bulletin* 6 (November 1982): 67–75.

Chetin, Sara. "Myth, Exile, and the Female Condition: Bessie Head's *The Collector of Treasures*." *Journal of Commonwealth Literature* 24.1 (1989): 114–37.

———. "Rereading and Rewriting African Women: Ama Ata Aidoo and Bessie Head." *Dissertation Abstracts* 53:3 (1992): 808A, DAI no. BRDX96438, Kent University.

Davison, Carol Margaret. "A Method in the Madness: Bessie Head's *A Question of Power*." *The Tragic Life*. Ed. Cecil Abrahams. Trenton, N.J.: Africa World Press, 1990. 19–30.

Dovey, Teresa. "A Question of Power: Susan Gardner's Biography versus Bessie Head's Autobiography." *English in Africa* 16 (May 1989): 29–38.

Eilerson, Gillian Stead. "Social and Political Commitment in Bessie Head's *A Bewitched Crossroad*." *Critique: Studies in Contemporary Fiction* 33.1 (Fall 1991): 43–52.

Elder, Arlene. "Bessie Head: New Considerations, Continuing Questions." *Callaloo* 16.1 (1993): 277–84.

Evasdaughter, Elizabeth N. "Bessie Head's *A Question of Power* Read as a Mariner's Guide to Paranoia." *Research in African Literatures* 20 (Spring 1989): 72–83.

Flewellen, Elinor C. "Assertiveness v. Submissiveness in Selected Works by African Women Writers." *Ba Shiru* 12.2 (1985): 3–8.

Fontenot, Deborah Yvonne B. "A Vision of Anarchy: Correlate Structures of Exile and Madness in Selected Works of Doris Lessing and Her South African Contemporaries." *Dissertation Abstracts* 50.2 (August 1989): 449A.

Gardner, Susan. "Don't Ask for the True Story." *Hecate* 12.1–2 (1986): 110–29.

———. "Production under Drought Conditions: Some Observations Concerning the Work of Bessie Head." *Women and Writing in South Africa: A Critical Anthology*. Ed. Cherry Clayton. Marshalltown, South Africa: Heinemann, 1989. 225–35.

Guerts, Kathryn. "Personal Politics in the Novels of Bessie Head." *Présence Africaine* 140 (1986): 47–74.

Gurnah, Abdulrazak, ed. *Essays on African Writing, I: A Re-Evaluation*. Oxford: Heinemann, 1993.

Harrow, Kenneth W. "Bessie Head's *A Collector of Treasures*: Change on the Margins." *Callaloo* 16.1 (Winter 1993): 169–79.

Hogan, Patrick Colin. "Bessie Head's *A Question of Power*: A Lacanian Psychosis." *Mosaic* 27.2 (June 1994): 95–122.

Ibrahim, Huma. "Bessie Head: A Third World Woman Writer in Exile." *Dissertation Abstracts* 49:9 (March 1989): DAI no.

Johnson, Joyce. "Metaphor, Myth, and Meaning in Bessie Head's *A Question of Power*." *World Literature Written in English* 25.2 (February 1985): 198–211.

———. "Proper Names and Thematic Concerns in Bessie Head's Novels." *World Literature Written in English* 30.1 (1990): 132–40.

————. "Structures of Meaning in the Novels of Bessie Head." *Kunapipi* 8.1 (1986): 56–69.

Katrak, Ketu H. "From Pauline to Dikeledi: The Philosophical and Political Vision of Bessie Head's Protagonists." *Ba Shiru* 12.2 (1985): 26–35.

Kemp, Yakini. "Romantic Love, and the Individual in Novels by Mariama Bâ, Buchi Emecheta, and Bessie Head." *Obsidian II* 3.3 (Winter 1988): 1–16.

Kincaid-Weekes, Mark. "Replacing the Exiled Imagination: D. H. Lawrence and Bessie Head." *Swansea Review* (1994): 43–62.

Larson, Charles. *The Novel in the Third World.* Washington, D.C.: Inscape, 1976.

Lionnet, Françoise. "Geographies of Pain: Captive Bodies and Violent Acts in the Fictions of Myriam Warner-Vieyra, Gayle Jones, and Bessie Head." *Callaloo* 16.1 (Winter 1993): 132–52.

Lorenz, Paul H. "Colonization and the Feminine in Bessie Head's *A Question of Power.*" *Fiction Studies* 37.3 (Autumn 1991): 591–605.

Macenzie, Craig. *Bessie Head: An Introduction.* Grahamstown, South Africa: National English Literature Museum, 1989.

————. "Bessie Head's *The Collector of Treasures*: Modern Story-Telling in a Traditional Botswanan Village." *World Literature Written in English* 29.2 (1989): 139–48.

————. "Short Fiction in the Making: The Case of Bessie Head." *English in Africa* 16 (1989): 17–28.

Marquard, Jane. "Exile and Community in Southern Africa: The Novels of Bessie Head." *London Magazine* 18.9–10 (1978–79): 48–61.

Matsikidze, Isabella Pupurai. "Connecting the Spheres: The Home Front and the Public Domain in Bessie Head's Fiction." *Dissertation Abstracts* 52:11 (May 1992): 3925A–26A, DAI no. 9207434, University of Massachusetts.

————. "The Postnationalistic Phase: A Poetics of Bessie Head's Fiction." *Bucknell Review* 37.1 (1993): 123–33.

————. "Toward a Redemptive Political Philosophy: Bessie Head's *Maru.*" *World Literature Written in English* 30.2 (1990): 105–9.

Menager-Everson, V. S. "*Maru* by Bessie Head: The Dilepe Quartet from Drought to Beer." *Commonwealth Essays and Studies* 14.2 (Spring 1992): 44–48.

Mitchison, Naomi. "Bessie Head." *Contemporary Novelists.* Ed. James Vinson. New York: St. Martin's Press, 1972. 580–82.

Mphahlele, Ezekiel. *The African Image.* 2nd ed. London: Faber, 1974. 274–80.

Newmarch, David. "Bewitched Crossroads: The Problematic of Bessie Head's Contribution to a Literature of Botswana." *Swansea Review* (1994): 439–49.

Nkosi, Lewis. *Tasks and Masks: Styles and Themes in African Literature.* London: Longman, 1981. 100–102.

Ogunbesan, Kolawole. "The Cape Gooseberry Also Grows in Botswana: Alienation and Commitment in the Writings of Bessie Head." *Présence Africaine* 109 (1979): 92–106.

Ojo-Ade, Femi. "Bessie Head's Alienated Heroine: Victim or Villain?" *Ba Shiru* 8.2 (1977): 13–21.

Ola, Virginia Osoma. "Power and the Question of Good and Evil in Bessie Head's Novels." *The Tragic Life.* Ed. Cecil Abrahams. Trenton, N.J.: Africa World Press, 1990. 59–72.

————. "Women's Role in Bessie Head's Ideal World." *Ariel* 17.4 (1986): 39–47.

Olaogun, Modupe O. "Irony and Schizophrenia in Bessie Head's *Maru.*" *Research in African Literatures* 25.4 (Winter 1994): 69–87.

Osagie, Iyunolu Folayan. "Technologies of Myth and the Inscription of Subjectivity: Reading Bessie Head's *A Question of Power* and Toni Morrison's *Beloved.*" *Dissertation Abstracts* 53.8 (February 1993): 2805A, DAI no. 9300831, Cornell University, 1992.

Pearse, Adetokunbo. "Apartheid and Madness: Bessie Head's *A Question of Power.*" *Kunapipi* 5.2 (1984): 81–93.

Peek, Andrew. "Bessie Head and the African Novel." *Span* 21 (October 1988): 121–36.

———. "Bessie Head in Australia." *New Literature Review* 14 (1985): 5–13.

Phillips, Maggi. "Engaging Dreams: Alternative Perspectives on Flora Nwapa, Buchi Emecheta, Ama Ata Aidoo, Bessie Head, and Tsitsi Dangaremgba's Writing." *Research in African Literatures* 25.4 (Winter 1994): 89–103.

Ramelb, Carol, ed. *Biography: East and West.* Honolulu: University of Hawaii Press, 1989.

Ravenscroft, Arthur. "The Novels of Bessie Head." *Aspects of South African Literature.* Ed. Christopher Heywood. London: Heinemann, 1976. 174–86.

Rose, Jacqueline. "On the 'Universality' of Madness: Bessie Head's *A Question of Power.*" *Critical Enquiry* 20.3 (Spring 1994): 401–18.

Sam, Agnes. "Bessie Head: A Tribute." *Kunapipi* 8.1 (1986): 53–56.

Sample, Maxine. "Landscape and Spatial Metaphor in Bessie Head's *The Collector of Treasures.*" *Studies in Short Fiction* 28.3 (Summer 1991): 311–19.

Sarvan, Charles Ponnuthurai. "Bessie Head: *A Question of Power* and Identity." *Women in African Literature Today* 15. Ed. Eldred Jones. London: James Currey, 1987. 82–88.

Severac, Alain. "Beyond Identity: Bessie Head's Spiritual Quest in Maru." *Commonwealth Essays and Studies* 14.1 (Autumn 1991): 58–66.

Taiwo, Oladele. *Female Novelists in Modern Africa.* London: Macmillan, 1984.

Thomas, Nigel. "Narrative Strategies in Bessie Head's Stories." *The Tragic Life.* Ed. Cecil Abrahams. Trenton, N.J.: Africa World Press, 1990. 93–104.

Thorpe, Michael. "Treasures of the Heart: The Short Stories of Bessie Head." *World Literature Today* 57.3 (Summer 1983): 414–16.

Tucker, Margaret E. "A 'Nice-time Girl' Strikes Back: An Essay on Bessie Head's *A Question of Power.*" *Research in African Literatures* 19.2 (Summer 1988): 170–81.

Uledi-Kamanga, Brighton. "Alienation and Affirmation: The Humanistic Vision of Bessie Head." *Journal of Humanities* 1 (April 1987): 21–35.

Vanamali, Rukmini. "Bessie Head's *A Question of Power*: The Mythic Dimension." *Literary Criterion* 23.1–2 (1988): 154–71.

Visel, Robin. " 'We Bear the World and We Make It.': Bessie Head and Olive Schreiner." *Research in African Literatures* 21.3 (Fall 1990): 115–24.

Interviews

Beard, Linda Susan. "Bessie Head in Gaborone, Botswana: An Interview." *Sage* 3.2 (Fall 1986): 44–47.

Fradkin, Betty McGinnis. "Conversations with Bessie." *World Literature Written in English* 17.2 (November 1978): 427–34.

"Interview." *MS* September 1975: 72–73, 75.

Mackenzie, Craig, and Cherry Clayton, eds. *Between the Lines: Interviews with Bessie Head, Sheila Roberts, Ellen Kuzwayo, Miriam Tali.* Grahamstown: National English Literature Museum, 1989.

Nichols, Lee. "Bessie Head, South Africa." *Conversations with African Writers.* Washington, D.C.: Voice of America, 1981. 49–57.

Critical Biographies

Eilersen, Gillian Stead. *Bessie Head: Thunder behind her Ears.* Claremont, South Africa: David Philip, 1995; London: James Currey, 1995.

Ola, Virginia Osoma. *The Life and Work of Bessie Head.* Lewiston, N.Y.: Edwin Mellon Press, 1994.

Bibliographies

Berrian, Brenda. *Bibliography of African Women Writers and Journalists.* Washington, D.C.: Three Continents Press, 1985.

Gardner, Susan, and Patricia E. Scott. *Bessie Head: A Bibliography.* Grahamstown, South Africa: National English Literary Museum, 1986.

Little, Greta. "Bessie Head." *Dictionary of Literary Biography.* 117 Ed. Bernth Lindfors and Reinhard Sander. Detroit: Gale Research, 1992. 186–93.

*ELAINE SAVORY**

*Elaine Savory used to write as Elaine Savory Fido.

VINCENT CHUKWUEMEKA IKE (1931–   )

BIOGRAPHY

Vincent Chukwuemeka Ike was born in Ndikelionwu in Orumba area of Anambra State of Nigeria. He attended the Government College, Umuahia, from 1945 to 1950, where he obtained his Cambridge School Certificate. He earned his B.A. from the University College, Ibadan, in 1955 and his M.A. from Stanford University in 1966. He has been a fellow of the Nigerian Institute of Management (1987); a member of the Committee on Examinations in West Africa, University of London (1971–75); a member of the founding committee of *Okike: An African Journal of New Writing* (1970–71); Editorial Committee member, *The African Writer: Journal of the African Authors Association* (1961–62); refugee officer in charge of Umuahia Province, Biafra (1968–69); convener, Nigerian Book Development Forum (since 1990); and commissioner, Headquarters Scout in charge of Nsukka Province (1970–71.

His full-time service includes his tenure as a teacher in Amichi Central School, Amichi, from 1950 to 1951 and Girls' Secondary School, Nkwere, Orlu, from 1955 to 1956; administrative assistant/assistant registrar (in charge of students), University College, Ibadan, from 1957 to 1960; deputy registrar of the University of Nigeria, Nsukka, from 1963 to 1971; chairman of the Planning and Management Committee of the University of Nigeria, 1970; and registrar and chief executive of the Multinational West African Examination Council with headquarters in Accra, Ghana, from 1971 to 1979. In 1979 he retired from public service. However, he became a visiting professor of English at the University of Jos, Jos, from 1983 to 1985, and the pro-chancellor and chairman of Council, University of Benin, Benin City, a post he held until 1991.

On a part-time basis, he has served as chairman, Culture Sector, Nigerian

National Commission for UNESCO, since 1986; director, University Press, Ibadan, since 1978; and member, Governing Board, Nigerian Copyright Council (and chairman of its Technical Committee) since 1989. He was the director of a national newspaper, the *Daily Times*, from 1971 to 1987; consultant to the Botswana, Lesotho, and Swaziland Schools Examination Council in 1974; the organizing secretary of the Students' Christian Movement of Nigeria, Eastern Region, in 1956; and the editorial adviser of the *Nigerian Christian* from 1966 to 1971. He is married to a Yoruba, Adebimkpe O. Ike (née Abimbolu), who is the university librarian and dean of students, Abubakar Tafawa Balewa University, Bauchi. They have a son, Osita.

MAJOR WORKS AND THEMES

Ike's diverse experiences as primary- and secondary-school teacher, university registrar and professor, official in war-ravaged Biafra, participant in various committees, and holder of other offices, as well as his interest in breaking the boundaries of ethnicity, are easily discernible as influences in his novels. *Toads for Supper* (1965) deals with the "activities of a fictional individual" at a particular moment in history (Jonathan Peters, *A Dance of Masks* [Washington, D.C.: Three Continents Press, 1978], 94). The moment is the early colonial period when Africans were trying to grapple with the intrusion of Western culture, and the individual is an undergraduate of the University of Southern Nigeria, Amadi Chukwuka, who is being sponsored by his town's league. His connection with his village association is important because it lubricates his continued attachment to his roots as he strives to live above his ethnic background and be a modern man. The most pressing conflict arises out of his desire to marry a girl of his choice. The situation is complicated by the presence of Nwakaego, a girl from his village, already chosen for him, as well as the strong objection of his father, Mazi Chukwuka, to Amadi's marriage with a non-Ezinko girl. Compounding the difficult situation is the fact that Amadi's choice belongs to another ethnic origin, Yoruba. He, however, persists with his desire to marry his choice, Aduke. In a moving story doused with humor and pathos, Ike dramatizes the conflict between the hero's attachment to his roots and his attitudes as a modern man, striving to find a balance between the two cultures to which he has become inextricably bound in the new dispensation.

In the new order of postindependence, portrayed in *The Naked Gods* (1970), Ike shows awareness of the complexities of neocolonial politics by focusing on what Izebvaye would regard as Africa's "relation to the modern European world" (D. S. Izebvaye, "Shifting Bases: The Present Practice of African Criticism," *Research in African Literatures* 21.1 [1990]: 127). Using a small university community as the center of vision, he dramatizes through allegory the neocolonial intrigues involved in the choice of African leaders. The action revolves around the politics of choosing a new vice chancellor for Songhai University. The contenders are Dr. Okoro and Professor Ikin, each fortified by his own ideas of why he merits the intellectual throne. Like Chief Nanga in Chinua Achebe's *A Man of the People*, they exhibit the bigotry of those African politicians who would go to any length to achieve power or retain it. Dr. Okoro, who has rejected the use of charms and amulets all his life, has to subject his will to the direction of a medicine man who gives him sacrificial objects to deposit on his opponent's door. Professor Ikin's wife sells her virtues in order to influence events. The battleground extends outside the homes of the aspirants to implicate the international community. Through the exposition of intracampus intrigues involving the British, who support Professor Ikin, and the American group supporting Dr. Okoro, the author dramatizes foreign involvement in African politics. The groups seek to retain their interests permanently in Songhai University through the new vice chancellor, symbolizing those African leaders who are puppets of foreign powers. In simple language that leans on copious metaphors and exaggeration, the corruption, insecurity, arrogance, pettiness, and insensitivity of the ruling class and its supporters are exposed as they indulge in intrigues that drain their energy while neglecting the vital affairs of the university.

The Potter's Wheel (1973) centers on child abuse and education as a means of examining how the "mental universe of the colonised" (Ngugi wa Thiong'o, *Decolonising the Mind*, 17) was invaded by new attitudes of the colonizer. To enable their only son to get formal education in the nearby colonial school, Maza Laza and his wife send him to live with the schoolteacher, Zaccheus Kanu, and his wife, Madam, both of whom overwork and underfeed the boy and other domestics, in addition to subjecting them to extreme punishments for minor offenses. Through the boy's experience in school, the writer criticizes the inability of Africans to improve on the system of education inherited from the colonialists. The attempt of the African officer to exhibit the same arrogance as the colonial education officer appears comical, especially when he attempts to parody the European accent, thereby showing how the African psyche has been dented by colonialism. Through the use of direct references and animal images that denigrate the offenders, Ike achieves his aim of satirizing attitudes and practices that constitute obstacles to children's development.

Sunset at Dawn (1976) deals with the events of the Nigeria-Biafra war. The unacceptability of interethnic marriage between an Igbo man and a Hausa woman is presented as a front for examining the contradictions of the war. Contrary to popular expectation that it is a collective struggle and suffering, the reader is made to appreciate the class structure of the war experience. While the poor are starving, suffering, and dying in the war front and refugee camps, members of the military ruling class still have the time and resources to build houses and provide their families with luxuries such as electric generators, refrigerators, and deep freezers. In time of extreme emergency, they are evacuated to safety with their property, while the masses in the refugee camps are left to their fate. A character, Uduji, queries the situation: "Why should they be allowed to carry Doctor's belongings? . . . Don't we all here have property which we value?'' (199). The insecurity of the situation leads to the emergence of prayer houses that rehabilitate the poor and offer them the expectation of paradisal bliss that is denied them. The disillusionment of the war is well exemplified by the character of Dr. Bassey, who, after a series of misfortunes, becomes frustrated and an easy victim of the houses, which turn him into a religious fanatic. The title of the novel is thus symbolic of the events that show how the new republic is plagued by the disease (sunset) of injustice and exploitation even in its infancy (dawn).

Expo '77 (1980) examines the leakage of examination-question papers, which has become one of the most pressing problems at all levels of education in Nigeria. There is widespread leakage of the Certificate of Secondary Education (CSE) Examination. The chairman of the National Examinations Board invites a detective to investigate the matter. The determination of Dr. Buka, the Acting Registrar of the Board, to ''smoke out the defaulting officers'' (91) is met with stiff opposition not only from his subordinates but also from the students themselves, who contrive a plot to implicate him in the misdemeanor. They question the right of the Acting Registrar to thwart their plans by alleging that he himself sends the question papers to his alma mater for the benefit of the candidates. They support their right to indulge in examination malpractice when the whole society is wallowing in corruption—a person neither learns how to drive before obtaining a driving licence nor fulfills the requirements for a contractor's licence in order to ''land a multi-million contract'' (93). The social canvas of corruption is further widened by the herbalist who posits that students should not be castigated for misconduct in a society that is corrupt: ''Soja dey chop. Bishop dey chop. Trader dey chop. Clerk for office dey chop. Why student no go chop, If 'im hand fit reach am?'' (183). Thus the Expo is seen in the wider context of a disintegrating society, a fact that is confirmed by Mora's discovery that examination leakage is not a simple matter but a complex system of corruption that involves various segments of the establishment—the staff of the examination office, invigilators and examiners, authorities of the schools, and the students. The novel ends on a positive note as the Acting Registrar maps out strategies for combating the disease, drawing inspiration from the experience of some other establishments in the country.

The Bottled Leopard (1985) focuses on child development as a means of examining how the ''mental universe of the colonized'' is invaded by the culture and religion of the colonizer. Through the events revolving around the hero, Amobi Ugochukwu, a first-year student at a popular college, the conflict between Western and African cultures is explored. He is shocked by the injustice and pretensions of the intellectual community. The initiation ceremony organized by the Form Two boys turns out to be a nightmare of vandalism aimed at punishing the new entrants, called ''fags'' (7–12). The school authority officials, most of whom are British, scoff at African culture and strive to Westernize the students. The conflict of cultures also manifests itself in the rural community outside the college where the Christian mission tries to suppress African customs and practices. This compels the people to cope with the situation by pretending to be Westernized. Amobi's father, Mazi Eze, for example, can stay away from a ritual ceremony he sponsors so that the Christian authority will not expel him from the church. Amobi's spiritual oneness with a leopard is a serious problem for the young student, who is eager to discard his heritage and accept all the Western scientific attitudes the school has to offer. Not finding a solution to his problem through the school, he resorts to the remedy provided by the traditional healer, Dibia Ofia, who performs a ritual that seals the pot containing the spirit of Amobi's leopard. Through one of his transformation experiences witnessed by his friend and classmate, Chuk, news of his leopard linkage spreads in the school. It takes the intervention of the British Principal to lay the rumor to rest. Henceforth Amobi resolves to take the advice of the African teacher, "Computer," and "chew his stick diligently in the privacy of his room" (168), meaning that he would suppress his knowledge of the supernatural phenomenon while he pretends, as the school authority dictates, to dismiss it as African superstition. The novel is similar to Flora Nwapa's *Idu* and *Efuru*, in which "built-in folk superstitions" are used to weave the plot and situate characters (Chidi Ikonne, "The Folk Roots of Flora Nwapa's Early Novels," *African Literature Today* 18 [1992]: 96). Ike's handling of the plot shows the depth of colonial influence in the villages and schools and contradicts Egejuru's idea that "there is no way in which an African child who for the most part grows up in the village and does not leave Africa until after Higher school can lose his culture" (Phanuel Egejuru, "Who Is the Audience of Modern African Literature?" *Obsidian: Black Literature in Review* 5.1–2 [1979]:53).

Our Children Are Coming (1990) provides a deep insight into a major problem of the contemporary African society: the conflict between the old and the new generation. Removed from the relatively defined mores of the traditional society, the individuals fumble in an attempt to reconcile with new structures of the modern society. Parents worry and blame their children for not living up to their expectations. It is this situation that compelled the government to set up a Presidential Commission of Juveniles below Twenty-one to investigate the problems of young people. The submissions of the parents who appear before the commission reveal that most of them are as guilty as the children they castigate. The members of the commission are no better. The chairman, for example, is responsible for the sexual exploitation and destabilization of a female student, Apollonia, whose father has come to testify about her waywardness. As a reaction to their exclusion from the government's commission, the young people themselves, under the auspices of the Students' Union, set up another commissioner. Through the submissions by the young people who appear before the students' commissioner, the reader appreciates the problem from their point of view: many parents neither give their children the expected leadership by showing them good examples nor give them the expected parental support in times of distress. The students try to expose the corruption of members of the Presidential Commission who have gone off to Europe on a supposedly working tour, which in fact is a means of squandering the nation's money. At the crisis point, the government disbands the two commissions and sets up another one, the National Moral Reorientation Commission, to study the impact of the decline of traditional African life and find possible ways of incorporating its mores in the contemporary society. All segments of the society, including women and students, who are usually marginalized, are represented in the new commission. The author thus demonstrates the need for all, irrespective of gender, age, class, and ethnic origin, to join hands in revamping the precarious situation of neocolonial Africa. The novel ends with an indication of new awareness and respect for young people who have demonstrated their ability to pilot affairs and fight for their rights. One therefore agrees that the novel should be read by "every parent, teacher and child" (back cover) because of its comprehensive analysis of the problem.

CRITICAL RECEPTION

Ike's novels are widely hawked by book vendors and read by students, yet the critical attention to them is relatively below expectation, considering their quality. Ibegbulem's study of *Toads for Supper, Sunset at Dawn, The Naked Gods*, and *The Potter's Wheel* concentrates on the influence of traditional beliefs and practices in them. She examines their manifestation in the modern setting of the novels and sees a mixture of tradition and modernity in contemporary ethics that she posits as an important concern of the author. Njoku looks at the thematic preoccupation of three novels: *Toads for Supper, The Naked Gods*, and *The Potter's Wheel*. She focuses on the corruption depicted in the novels and commends Ike's dialectics of irony, wit, and humor, which enhance appreciation of his satiric tone. The novelist's depiction of and sensitivity to women's relegation in the society is also appraised, and she sees a concern for women's issues that impinges on the author's progressive stance in the novels.

BIBLIOGRAPHY

Works by Vincent Chukwuemeka Ike

Toads for Supper. London: Harvill, 1965.
The Naked Gods. London: Harvill, 1970.
The Potter's Wheel. London: Harvill, 1973.
Sunset at Dawn: A Novel about Biafra. London: Harvill, 1973.
University Development in Africa: The Nigerian Experience. Ibadan: Oxford University Press, 1976.
The Chicken Chasers. London: Fontana, 1980.
Expo '77. London: Fontana, 1980.
Emmanuel Obiechina, Chukwuemeka Ike, and John Umeh. *The University of Nigeria, 1966–1985: An Experiment in Higher Education*. Nsukka: University Press, 1986.

The Bottled Leopard. Ibadan: Spectrum, 1990.
Our Children Are Coming. Ibadan: Spectrum, 1990.

Studies of Vincent Chukwuemeka Ike

Ibegbulem, Jacqueline Adaku. "Ethics in Some Novels of Chukwuemeka Ike." B.A. thesis University of Nigeria, Nsukka, 1985.
Njoku, Theresa Ukaejunti. "Social Criticism in the Novels of Chukwuemeka Ike." B.A. thesis University of Nigeria, Nsukka, 1977.

CHINYERE GRACE OKAFOR

FRANCIS IMBUGA (1947–   )

BIOGRAPHY

Francis Davis Imbuga is among the most productive and respected of Kenya's contemporary writers and scholars. He is a leading member of a "second generation" of postcolonial writers, coming shortly after and having been influenced by such first-generation figures as Ngugi wa Thiong'o, Grace Ogot, and Leonard Kibera. Although he is most widely recognized for his active involvement in Kenyan drama during the decades since independence, Imbuga's prodigious creative energies have also encompassed other genres such as poetry, narrative, and television, in addition to his work as a teacher, scholar, and administrator at Kenyatta University. Despite the variety and volume of his output, there is in all of Imbuga's work a notable recurrence of social criticism, a concern with issues of cultural identity, and above all a powerful sense of sympathetic humor in dealing with the vagaries and ironies of life in a postcolonial African setting.

Imbuga was born on February 2, 1947, in the Maragoli District of Kenya's Western Province. His rural upbringing as well as the strong oral tradition in which he was raised have informed both the themes and the style of his works; he credits his grandparents with significantly influencing his dramatic voice (Ruganda, *Telling the Truth*, x). Imbuga's childhood corresponded with an era of uncertainty and change in what was then Britain's Kenya Colony. Following World War II, there was a dramatic increase in European settlement in the colony, and a concurrent increase in resistance to colonial rule. The 1950s saw an intensification in this resistance, including the armed struggle that came to be known as Mau Mau, leading eventually to independence in 1963. Imbuga's father had served in the King's African Rifles during World War II and following the war worked as a security guard in Nairobi, meaning that he was away from his family for much of the year. Imbuga's mother died in 1964.

It was at school that Imbuga's dramatic talents first developed in a formalized way. Although he came from a relatively poor family, Imbuga's academic achievements earned him a place at the elite Alliance High School in Nairobi, where he pursued his secondary education from 1964 to 1969. At Alliance, Imbuga began to discover and explore his interest in drama; he wrote, directed, and acted in *Omolo*, a play that was entered in the Kenya National Schools' Drama Festival and for which he won the Best Actor's Award.

Imbuga attended the University of Nairobi in the early 1970s, during an era in which the campus was a center of lively debate about the role of the arts, education, and literary and cultural production in postcolonial Africa. Ngugi wa Thiong'o, Taban lo Liyong, and Owuor Anyumba had led a move to revamp the university's literature curriculum, changing it to reflect an African focus. Other first-generation East African writers like Leonard Kibera, Okot p'Bitek, and Jared Angira were also active members of the university community. While at university, Imbuga demonstrated the prolific literary production that has become his hallmark. In addition to his regular studies, he continued his acting career, published three plays and wrote others, and wrote, directed, and acted in over fifty dramatic productions for the Voice of Kenya television's African Theatre Series. Another important influence on him at this time was Joe de Graft, a dramatist and senior lecturer at the University of Nairobi whose widely acclaimed play *Muntu* was written with Imbuga in mind as a lead character.

Since graduating from university, Imbuga has continued to balance an academic vocation with a highly productive writing career. He studied at University College, Cardiff, Wales, from 1974 to 1975, was involved in theatre workshops and productions in Nigeria and Ghana in the mid-1970s, and participated in UNESCO-sponsored workshops in Zaire (1979), Paris (1980), and Sofia (1982). He completed a Ph.D. at the University of Iowa and also participated in the university's acclaimed International Writing Program from 1988 to 1991, where he wrote *The Burning of Rags* (1989) as well as the first draft of his novel *Shrine of Tears* (1993). During the 1994–95 school year he was Fulbright Scholar-in-Residence at Tennessee State University.

Despite his frequent international studies and experiences, the focus of Imbuga's professional and creative work has always been on Kenya. *Betrayal in the City* (1976), Imbuga's most popular play to date, was selected as one of Kenya's official entries (along with Ngugi wa Thiong'o and Micere Mugo's *The Trial of Dedan Kimathi*) to the Second World Black and African Festival of Arts and Culture (FESTAC) in Lagos, Nigeria, in 1977; it was later read by a generation of secondary students as a set text in the Kenyan schools. In another measure of his high national reputation, Imbuga won the Kenya National Academy of Sciences Distinguished Award in Arts in 1987. Imbuga served as senior lecturer and chair of the Department of Literature at Kenyatta University until

1988, after which he pursued his doctoral degree at Iowa. Since returning to Kenyatta University, he has served as dean of the Faculty of Arts and continues to be active in his writing.

MAJOR WORKS AND THEMES

East African fiction, like African writing in general, has generally been characterized by a high level of political engagement and a commitment to positive social change. In this arena where poetics and politics are so closely intertwined, and where writers are often jailed, exiled, and even killed for their political messages, Imbuga's writing runs a careful line between pointed criticism and diplomatic tact.

Perhaps the overriding trait in all of Imbuga's work is the concept of indirect criticism. If Imbuga's works are not as overtly ideological or obvious in their criticisms as (for example) those of his compatriot Ngugi wa Thiong'o, they nonetheless contain hard-hitting commentary about postcolonial East African politics and society. The title of a study of Imbuga's works by John Ruganda, himself a Ugandan playwright, is telling: Imbuga, claims Ruganda, "tells the truth laughingly" through his indirect criticism. Imbuga's texts allow the targets of his criticism to save face and provide them room to reform themselves by avoiding direct confrontation. Imbuga participates in the trickster tradition, telling truth to power but in a manner that depends on the "survivalist principle . . . that good art must protect itself from vilification, and its creator from incarceration" (Ruganda, *Telling the Truth Laughingly*, xxi).

Certainly his criticism is hard-hitting at times. Imbuga's weekly column in the *Sunday Nation* and his cartoon strip, *Nyam-Nyam*, were withdrawn when editors and politicians became uncomfortable with their overtly critical messages. His play *The Successor* (1979) was written during the time leading up to the death of Kenya's first president, Jomo Kenyatta, when it was considered treasonous to even think about the death of the president, let alone express those thoughts in writing. The overtly political *Man of Kafira* was originally produced in 1979 as *Day of Truth* and performed for the new Kenyan president, Daniel arap Moi.

Like many of his literary colleagues, Imbuga's primary concern is the direction of African society in the postcolonial era. Important among his concerns are the megalomaniacal tendencies of political rulers: *Man of Kafira* (1984) investigates the psychology of deposed heads of state in places like Kafira (an anagram of Afrika) and Abiara (Arabia). A more recent concern for Imbuga has been the status of women in postcolonial African society. *Aminata* (1988), originally commissioned for the United Nations Decade for Women Conference in Nairobi in 1985, investigates the intersection of feminist issues with East African traditions. *The Burning of Rags* (1989) is essentially a rewrite of *The Married Bachelor* (1973), but vitalized with a new interest in the women of the story.

In the 1990s Imbuga began to experiment with new forms and an increased concern with cultural identity. His novel *Shrine of Tears* (1993), set in the loosely fictional nation of Kilima, focuses on the role of the national theatre in the dissemination of cultural values. The conflict surrounds who in fact controls the proceedings at the theatre, who has access to productions as either participants or spectators, and the extent to which the Shrine is or is not in fact a "national" institution. In the process, the text also examines the contradictory roles of politicians, of the police forces, of the universities, of expatriate "experts," and of traditional cultural forms.

Imbuga's firsthand experience with international representations of East Africa in film, particularly in *Gorillas in the Mist*, and his discomfort with the cultural dynamics that they represent feature prominently in his novel. Throughout *Shrine of Tears*, the concern is with "decolonizing the spirit," as the mentor character of Headmaster puts it, which is a reference to and a step beyond the "decolonizing the mind" that Ngugi has written about. In his novel, Imbuga is also experimenting with form, creating a text that participates in its own interpretation. There are various narrative voices, and we eventually discover that one of the characters and narrators, Headmaster, is also writing a novel whose title is, interestingly enough, *Shrine of Tears*.

CRITICAL RECEPTION

Francis Imbuga's literary reputation is unquestioned in East Africa, and he is steadily gaining recognition internationally. Most of what has been written about Imbuga's work consists of reviews or commentary in Kenyan newspapers such as the *Daily Nation* or the *Standard*, or in Kenyan magazines such as the *Weekly Review*.

John Ruganda, the Ugandan playwright, has produced the first full-length study of Imbuga's work, in which he discusses Imbuga as a master of "transparent concealment," writing socially critical drama in a political arena that is essentially antagonistic toward theatre. Drama is the most popular and dynamic literary form in contemporary Kenya, and potentially the most explosive. During the 1980s and since, government control of dramatic productions has been tight. Performances have been denied permits and playwrights have been detained: Ngugi wa Thiong'o—the country's most internationally renowned writer—was ostensibly imprisoned (and later exiled) for his work with popular theatre on *Ngaahika Ndeenda* (*I Will Marry When I Want*), and Alamin Mazrui was detained for his play *Kilio cha Haki* (*Cry for Justice*).

Imbuga, therefore, in working with political themes in dramatic form, is participating in a potentially volatile arena. What has characterized both his plays and his other writings, however, is an ability to criticize postcolonial Kenyan society in a powerful but humorous form. Given his productivity to date, there can be no doubt that much more can be expected from the pen of Francis Davis Imbuga.

BIBLIOGRAPHY

Works by Francis Imbuga

Published Plays

The Fourth Trial (two plays). Nairobi: East African Literature Bureau, 1972.
Kisses of Fate. Nairobi: East African Literature Bureau, 1972.
The Married Bachelor. Nairobi: East African Publishing House, 1973.
Betrayal in the City. Nairobi: East African Publishing House, 1976.
Game of Silence. Nairobi: Heinemann Educational Books, 1977.
The Successor. Nairobi: Heinemann Educational Books, 1979.
Man of Kafira. Nairobi: Heinemann Educational Books, 1984.
Aminata. Nairobi: Heinemann Kenya, 1988.
The Burning of Rags. Nairobi: Heinemann Kenya, 1989.
Usaliti Mjini (Swahili translation of *Betrayal in the City*). Nairobi: East African Educational Publishers, 1994.

Published Fiction

Imbaalo Ya Vaana Va Magomere (The initiation of the children of Magomere). Nairobi: Heinemann Kenya, 1986.
"Facelift for Regina" and "To the Shameless One." *An Anthology of Poetry for Schools*. Ed. Andrew K. Amateshe. London: Longman, 1988.
"The Forgotten Clay," "The Ugly Beauty," and "Celebration of the Unknown." *Boundless Voices: Poems from Kenya*. Ed. Arthur Luvai. Nairobi: Heinemann Kenya, 1988. 39–41.
Shrine of Tears. Nairobi: Longman Kenya, 1993.
Magomere's Children (translation of *Imbaalo Ya Vaana Va Magomere*). Nairobi: East African Educational Publishers, 1995.

Literary Criticism

Notes on Joe de Graft's "Muntu." Nairobi: Bookwise, 1981.
Notes on Austin Bukenya's "The Bride." Nairobi: Heinemann Educational Publishers, 1987.
"Thematic Trends and Circumstances in John Ruganda's Drama." Diss. University of Iowa, 1992.
"East African Literature in the 1980s." *Matatu* 10 (1993): 121–35.
"John Ruganda." *Twentieth-Century Caribbean and African Writers* (*Dictionary of Literary Biographies*, Vol. 157, Third Series). Detroit: Gale Research, 1996, 323–30.

Film Appearances

Raising the Daisy (1975).
The Willoby Conspiracy (1976).
Kolo Mask (1986).
Gorillas in the Mist (1987).
Miracles of the Forest (1989).

Selected Studies of Francis Imbuga

Arden, Richard, and Austin Bukenya. *Francis D. Imbuga: Betrayal in the City*. Longman Guides to Literature. Nairobi: Longman, 1978.

Gachugu, Makini. *The Plays of Francis Imbuga*. M.A. thesis University of Nairobi, 1985.

Harb, Ahmad. "The Aesthetics of Francis Imbuga: A Contemporary Kenyan Playwright." *Literary Review* 34.4 (Summer 1991): 571–82.

Muli, James. "Francis Imbuga." *Twentieth Century Caribbean and African Writers* (*Dictionary of Literary Biographies*, vol. 157, Third Series.) Detroit: Gale Research, 1996. 323–30.

Obyerodhyambo, Oby. "Of Betrayal in *Betrayal in the City*." *Literary Review* 34.4 (Summer 1991): 583–88.

Ruganda, John. "Alienation and Leadership in the Plays of Francis Imbuga." Diss. University of New Brunswick, 1990.

———. *Telling the Truth Laughingly: The Politics of Francis Imbuga's Drama*. Nairobi: East African Educational Publishers, 1992.

J. ROGER KURTZ

FESTUS IKHUORIA OJEAGA IYAYI (1947–)

BIOGRAPHY

Winner of the Commonwealth Prize for Literature, novelist, short-story writer, and political activist, Festus Iyayi was born on September 29, 1947, at Eguare-Ugbegun in Edo State of Nigeria. From a privileged background, young Festus attended C.M.S. Primary School from 1955 to 1960. He proceeded to Annunciation Catholic College in 1962, where he obtained his West African School Certificate (WASC) in 1966. His spectacular result influenced his easy admission into the then-exclusive Government College, Ughelli, for his Higher School Certificate (1967–68). He distinguished himself in the school by winning the Kennedy Essay Competition for the zone in 1968. He earned a master's degree in 1974 in industrial economy at the Kiev Institute of Economics, Kiev, in the USSR. His Ph.D. degree in management and administration was obtained from the University of Bradford, England, in 1980. He specialized in organizational analysis and behavior.

His full-time working employment includes his experience as a teacher in Immaculate Conception College, Benin City, in 1969; economic correspondent, business editor, and editorial staff writer of Bendel Newspapers, Benin, from 1974 to 1975; industrial training officer in engineering, University of Benin, Benin City (1975–77); lecturer, Department of Business Administration, University of Benin (1980–87); and from November 1987, the executive director of Centre Piece, a consultancy outfit in Benin City.

As a young, intelligent, and enthusiastic lecturer, critical of structures and forces inimical to human progress, he was popularly elected the chairperson of the Academic Staff Union of Universities (ASUU), University of Benin Branch, in 1984, a post he held until 1986, when he became the national president of the same union. He was detested by the military regime then in power for his radical views and stance, and this did not endear him to the university authorities, who ejected him from the university in 1987. He experienced a period of severe economic hardship with his young family but began to have some respite after he was propelled to the limelight in 1988 when he won two international and one national prizes for literature: the Commonwealth African Regional Prize, the Commonwealth Prize, and the Association of Nigerian Authors' (ANA) Prize for Literature. In his period of harassments, detentions, and humiliations, Iyayi received the sympathy and support of his colleagues, climaxed by the meritous award from the University of Nigeria branch of the ASUU for his "protection of welfare of academics and the common man" (Certificate of Merit, 1988).

He is married to Grace Aimenya Iyayi (née Akhuetie), a health administrator and manager in the University of Benin Teaching Hospital, whom Iyayi regards as a courageous and supportive friend, wife, and mother of his four children. They live in Benin City.

MAJOR WORKS AND THEMES

Iyayi's first novel, *Violence*, is set in Benin City, which is representative of other neocolonial African cities. With its juxtaposition of traditional African and modern, Westernized cultures, Benin becomes an appropriate setting for exposing the injustices and suffering of the masses, who appear to be trapped in an endless cycle of distress and pain, or what Iyayi regards as violence, which is the exploitation, brutalization, and dehumanization of the masses by the system (Okafor, interview, 1994). The novel is a description of the nature and kinds of violence, as well as reactions to it. One appreciates the pictures of suffering through the events involving the characters.

The hero, Idemudia, is portrayed as a good citizen, husband, and father, as well as a strong, enthusiastic, and conscientious workman. His poverty is presented as a serious disadvantage, a crime that impinges on his noble qualities, for it is depravity that propels him to change and abrogate his responsibilities. He becomes ashamed in the presence of his wife because he cannot fend for her and his son, whom he therefore sends to the village. He steals and becomes self-conscious, ashamed, and alienated from his family and the economic and political system that gives him no chance to be a responsible citizen. His predicament strikes a concordant note with the dilemma of Obi in Chinua Achebe's *No Longer at Ease*, whose ideals could not be practicalized, as he is plagued by contradictions of the neocolonial society (Okeke-Ezigbo). Just as Obi succumbs to corruption, Idemudia breaks custom and taboo by selling his own blood, a humiliating act for which he hates himself. Through her own character development akin to that of her husband, Adisa is forced by circumstances to change and to sell her most revered sacred possession in order to save her husband. She rationalizes her action in order to alleviate the emotional anguish she suffers as a result of her action: "We need the money. . . . Nobody will ever find out" (176). But even this hateful subjection of her body to defilement by the rich and callous Obofun does not solve their problem.

Violence in the novel manifests itself psychologically, for it gradually invades and erodes the emotions and mental capacity of the victims. They internalize and externalize their pain by hating self, family, and the structure that impedes their attempts to overcome problems. There are also instances of physical violence seen from the action of the oppressors who exploit the poor. Queen slaps and spits at her workers when they ask for more money, and the politicians use thugs to bully and intimidate the electorate. The old man's wife is raped and killed in his presence by political thugs because he cannot afford the registration fee for joining the party (154). Brutalized by various structures of the system, some of the frustrated people also mete out violence on others, and according to the Defence Council in the play-within-text, "they are only in a certain measure, answering violence with violence" (185), a phenomenon that can be galvanized into Frantz Fanon's liberative violence, a kind of counterforce by the oppressed to their oppressors.

The writer not only portrays the predicament of the poor people but also identifies the cause in the class structure of the postcolonial system, in which modern ideas and structures are superimposed on an organization that has not fully emerged from its traditional roots. With its own problems, the traditional still provides the much-needed anchor that the modern cities fail to provide. This is why the characters revert to the village base for encouragement and support. On the whole, through a mixture of omniscient and first-person point of view, the novelist provides an in-depth fictional analysis of the nature and forces that are inimical to progress in the neocolonial setup. His intention is to sensitize the masses to new awareness of their predicament and the structures that torment them. Like Achebe, he opts for very simple diction that expresses his ideas easily without any attempt at sophistication that might divert attention from his purpose ("Nigerian Writers," 1983).

In *The Contract*, Iyayi portrays the oppressive machinery of the neocolonial system and the contradictions inherent in its organization. He goes further to depict the various options individuals have chosen, trying to survive in a world that is unjust. The action centers on a modern man, Ogie Obala, who has just returned from studies abroad. He is patriotic and enthusiastic about changing the corrupt system. After initial hesitation, he accepts a job as the Principal Secretary of Oghe City Council and rationalizes his action by naïvely believing that he would change the system by joining it as an employee. Iyayi shows this to be an unrealistic approach to purging a corrupt machinery, for "one cannot change a system by joining it" (Okafor, interview, 1994). After his initial attempt at introducing changes such as organizing the documentation system, he faces stiff opposition from powerful men, including his father, who expect him to manipulate contracts in order to enable him to have a high percentage of the bribes (Olaniyan, 303). In the end he himself succumbs to the pressure and accepts a bribe from Chief Ekata, with whom he colludes in defrauding his father. He rationalizes his action by arguing that if he makes enough money, he would invest it in a business in the city and thus provide labor for the people, unlike his father and other members of his class who bank their "stolen money" in foreign banks where it is used to develop foreign economies (Fatunde, "Two African Writers," 53). Thus Ogie becomes corrupt, but unlike his father he remains patriotic, what he calls "corruption with human face" (12). However, he exhibits the selfish tendencies of the exploiter. He uses women for his own selfish aims and rejects them in moments of trial. He frustrates the efforts of his girlfriend, Rose Idebale, to improve herself educationally and uses her pregnancy as a means of thwarting her plans. He also derives sexual pleasure from Eunice, his father's secretary, but abrogates his responsibility when she gets pregnant. Rose's choice is presented as an alternative to her boyfriend's role. She detests the system and elects to remain outside the system of corruption. This is why she says that Ogie's action of joining the corrupt machinery is "unrealistic" (28), because she believes that one cannot "single-handedly fight a vast organisation" (28). Unlike Ogie, who easily yields to pressure, Rose has the willpower to sustain her principles. In spite of the abject poverty of her family, like Warringa of Ngugi's *Devil on the Cross*, she refuses to give her body as a bribe for economic upliftment. She opts for education as the vehicle of further emancipation and systematically plans toward a realization of her goal. While she fails to carry her boyfriend along in her antiestablishment campaign, she succeeds in winning over her friend, Eunice, and getting her to reject corruption. Eunice resigns from the job that requires her to subject herself to sexual abuse by customers in order to boost her employer's business.

Like Rose, Oniha Obala, Ogie's brother, opposes the system. He is dynamic and intelligent and tries to assert his uniqueness in the Obala family by galvanizing other students of Omani University to fight the corrupt system typified by his father, Chief Obala, whose stance as a petty bourgeois plunges the country into economic dependency. Like his counterpart, El Hadji abdou Kader Beye, in Ousmane Sembène's *Xala*, who is a symbol of African economic dependency, Chief Obala promotes the economic backwardness of his nation. While El Hadji allows himself to be used by foreign capitalists, Chief Obala embezzles the people's money for onward shipment to foreign banks. When he discovers his son Ogie's duplicity in the business deal, he kills him. Thus the high chief of corruption, Chief Obala, loses the money and his son, Ogie, in the bargain. This is a device that the novelist uses to show that the capitalist system contains the seeds of its own destruction. Iyayi deliberately prevents the symbol of neocolonial oppression from "having the last laugh" (Ajibade, 16). Instead, it is the action of the students that is invested with optimism, seen in their smashing of the council office door, a symbolic action denoting the cracking of the corrupt machinery. Rose's unborn baby is also a sign of hope because just as Ogie is better than his father, it is expected that "his child will be an improvement on Ogie himself" (Okafor, interview, 1994). Moreover, the child symbolizes a future that combines Rose's purity and Ogie's patriotism, albeit smeared with a streak of corruption.

Heroes centers on the exploitation of the ordinary soldier and civilian in the Nigeria-Biafra war. The linking character, Osime Iyere, who is a political correspondent of the *Daily News* newspaper, makes it possible for the reader to appreciate the scenes of the war both in the front and in the rear. Through the omniscient viewpoint, a narrator overviews the action as the reader appreciates an epistemological analysis of the events through the correspondent's consciousness explored in the first-person viewpoint. Iyere starts by regarding the secessionist Biafran troops as enemies while having implicit faith in the federal troops. He cannot agree with his friend Ade's opinion that both the federal and Biafran soldiers represent one side—the elephants—that "trample on the grass most crudely, most viciously" (15). However, his manhandling by the federal soldiers at the stadium jolts his consciousness to new awareness that does not quite prepare him for witnessing the brutal shooting of nine Ibo civilians, including his landlord, Mr. Ohiali, by federal soldiers. Taking Mr. Ohiali's family home to Oganza with the corpse enables him have further insight into the mechanism of the war. The military maneuvering in the area cuts him off from his girlfriend, Ndudi, and he gets stuck in an army camp in Asaba. His interaction with the ordinary soldiers, such as Sergeants Audu and Kush Kush, as well as civilians, such as the Umunnas, enables him to appreciate the class structure of the war: the Biafran and Nigerian upper classes contrived the war as a result of their conflict and implicated the lower class to fight the war for them while their own children are protected from the war. Iyere shares his conviction with soldiers, most of whom already notice the exploitation of the lower ranks, the real heroes, who take the risks, do the actual fighting, and lose their lives while the upper ranks get the credit for the achievements of the men under them, attend lavish parties when their men barely have enough to eat, and stay out of danger most of the time. Thus, as in Ngugi's *Devil on the Cross*, the world is classified into two: the eaters and the eaten.

Iyere is finally reunited with his girlfriend, Ndudi, just after she is brutalized and raped first by Biafran and then by Nigerian soldiers, all of whom the hero sees as victims of the machinations of the military and political ruling class. By the end of the novel, one is not sure of the direction of the war, but one is convinced of the need for a third army comprising the masses of both civilians and soldiers of the warring sides, who would liberate themselves from the upper class. Thus through a systematic probing of events and analysis of the protagonist, Iyere, Iyayi gradually unmasks the capitalist structure and prevailing conception of the war as a tribal conflict while suggesting new views and radical alternatives.

CRITICAL RECEPTION

Okojie (1983) examines Iyayi's portrayal of class inequalities, exploitation, and corruption and its repercussions in *Violence* and *The Contract*. She lauds the author for his courage in dissecting the neocolonial setup in spite of the risks of harassment by the hierarchy. Fatunde ("Two African Writers," 1985) focuses on the similarity of Iyayi's stance as a novelist to that of Ngugi wa Thiong'o since both expose the nature of corruption, emphasizing its link with the system of exploitation. In another essay (1986), he compares Iyayi's portrayal of the masses with Ouologuem's and posits that while the workers of Ouologuem's *Bound to Violence* do not show the potential for liberation through struggle, Iyayi's workers always "face the future with determination" (117). Osifo finds the characterization of *The Contract* effective in showing the impact of the neocolonial system on individuals, relationships, and ideals as well as the conflict between opposing views: conservatism and idealism, reactionary and progressive. Tejumola Olaniyan focuses on Iyayi's new kind of literature and discourse that is based on socialist realism. Comparing his handling with Saro-Wiwa's treatment of the same subject of war, Chiji Akoma places him far above Saro-Wiwa, especially because of the insight of his protagonist, but faults him for not checking the protagonist's leftist rhetoric. Akachi Ezeigbo appraises Iyayi's stance as a social realist who marries ideology with form and commends his choice of a journalist as a protagonist who carries out his pedagogical intention in the novel.

BIBLIOGRAPHY

Works by Festus Ikhuoria Ojeaga Iyayi

Violence. London: Longman, 1979.
The Contract. London: Longman, 1982.
"Nigerian Writers and the Conscience of the Nation." Paper delivered at the English and Literature Students' Association lecture, May 5, 1983.
"Lateral Power in British and Nigerian Organisations." *Aman* 3.1 (1984): n.p.
Heroes. London: Longman, 1986.
"The Primitive Accumulation of Capital in a Neo-Colony: The Nigerian Case Example." *Review of African Political Economy* 35 (1986): n.p.
"Managing Goal Contradictions in Public Bureaucracies." *Journal of Social Sciences* (1987): n.p.
"Iyayi: In the Cell, Each Face Looks like a Character from Michael Jackson's Thriller." *Guardian* December 11, 1988: 10–11.
Awaiting Court Martial: A Collection of Short Stories. Lagos: Malthouse, 1993.
B. A. Agbonifo, Ehiametalor, Inegbenebor, and Iyayi. *The Business Enterprise in Nigeria.* Lagos: Longman, 1993.
The Rainbow Has Only One Colour: A Collection of Short Stories. Forthcoming.

Studies of Festus Ikhuoria Ojeaga Iyayi

Ajibade, Kunle. "Iyayi: The World as It Looms around a Winner." *Guardian* December 12, 1988: 16.

Akoma, Chiji. "Artistic Truth or Narrative Fallacy: Iyayi, Saro-Wiwa on Civil War"
    (1). *Guardian* May 15, 1993: 19.
————. "Artistic Truth or Narrative Fallacy: Iyayi, Saro-Wiwa on Civil War (2). *Guard-
    ian* May 22, 1993: 22.
Fatunde, Tunde. "Images of Working People in Two African Novels: Ouologuem and
    Iyayi." *Marxism and African Literature.* Ed. Georg M. Gugelberger. Trenton,
    N.J.: Africa World Press, 1986. 110–17.
————. "Two African Writers on Corruption: Ngugi and Iyayi." *New Beacon Review*
    1 (1985): 53.
Okafor, Chinyere Grace. Interview with Festus Iyayi, Benin City, March 15, 1994.
Okeke-Ezigbo, Felix. "The Impossibility of Becoming a Gentleman in Nigeria: A Ne-
    glected Theme of Chinua Achebe's *No Longer at Ease.*" *Journal of African
    Studies* 12.2 (1985).
Okojie, Augustina Esohe. "The Concept of Violence in Festus Iyayi's Novels: *The Con-
    tract* and *Violence.*" Diss. University of Benin, Benin City, 1983.
Olaniyan, Tejumola. "Festus Iyayi." *Perspectives on Nigerian Literature, 1700 to the
    Present.* Vol. 2. Ed. Yemi Ogunbiyi. Lagos: Guardian, 1988. 303.
Osifo, Emmanuel Osagie. "Characterisation and the Conflict between Conservatism and
    Idealism in Festus Iyayi's *The Contract.*" Diss. University of Benin, Benin City,
    1989.

CHINYERE GRACE OKAFOR

TAHAR BEN JELLOUN (1944–   )

BIOGRAPHY

Tahar Ben Jelloun was born in Fès, Morocco, in 1944, twelve years before the country became independent from the French. He attended the lycée français of Tangier from 1954 to 1962. It is important to note these dates because of their significance for the Maghreb, for the Maghrebian people, and particularly here, for what they might have meant to most ten-to-eighteen-year-olds at that time and in that part of the world, specifically to Tahar Ben Jelloun. He later insisted that writing is always intimately connected to the political situation, in this case decolonization movements and struggles, and later on to mistreatment of the North African immigrant in France, as we shall see. Indeed, just a month or two after he had started attending the lycée français of Tanger, on November 1, 1954, neighboring Algeria, determined and uncompromising, launched a long fight for independence against the 132 years of French presence and colonialism. In fact, the endurance and effective strategies of the Algerian people lasted the whole time Tahar Ben Jelloun was attending the lycée français of Tanger, until independence on July 1, 1962. In the meantime, 1956 marked the end of the French Protectorate at home (since 1912) and in neighboring Tunisia (since 1881). Thus by the time Tahar Ben Jelloun was eighteen and graduating from high school, Algeria, Morocco, and Tunisia were newly independent countries.

Upon graduation from the lycée français of Tanger, Tahar Ben Jelloun went on to study philosophy at the University of Rabat. In 1968 he taught philosophy in Tétouan and then in Casablanca. Afterwards, he studied in Paris, where he completed a *thèse de 3e cycle* in social psychiatry and worked as a psychoso-ciologist.

As he likes to put it, he lives "*entre* la France et le Maroc" (between France and Morocco) and considers himself to be from both sides of the Mediterranean ("je suis des deux rives"), although his primary residence has been in Paris since 1971, that is, his "physical" residence, considering the multiplicity of geographic spaces that have become the terrain of his writing, and indeed his work on, in, and out of the "in between" of border zones.

Tahar Ben Jelloun is a highly respected and prolific poet, novelist, essayist, journalist, and playwright. His writings emanate from very real and concrete situations and position him clearly as a postcolonial author on both sides of the Mediterranean, in the Maghreb and in France—understandably so, perhaps, if we consider the political and intellectual climate that continues to influence his writings, and that he in turn influences, giving voice to his concerns and hopes (for the Maghreb, North Africans, immigrants, and Palestinians, in particular), and the creative energy that becomes the realm of resistance to hegemonic discourses and practices and operates primarily through the explosion of boundaries, multiple in all its dimensions and polyphonic, in a gesture perhaps better characterized today by the "always-already not-yet-being" of the Cuban critic Gustavo Pérez Firmat ("el no-ser-siempre-todavia"). Several key moments of Tahar Ben Jelloun's life (historical and personal) and influences (political and intellectual) contribute to his development and pursuits as a writer.

In the Maghreb, as a young boy, he was surrounded by decolonization movements and struggles, as stated earlier. As a young man in newly independent Morocco, he was quick to join the team of the revolutionary review *Souffles*, which was founded in 1966 in Morocco by Abdellatif Laâbi and gathered intellectuals who would quickly become high-profile innovators and key leaders in postcolonial Francophone literature (Mohammed Khaïr-Eddine, Abdelkebir Khatibi, Mostafa Nissaboury, Abaham Serfati), and, as in the case of Abdelkebir Khatibi, for instance, influence profoundly contemporary French "postmodern" philosophical thought and African and continental "postcolonial" theory.

In France, and as a man who lives "between" Morocco and France, Tahar Ben Jelloun relentlessly speaks against injustice, racism, indifference, economic oppression, hypocrisy, torture, and silencing while, since his involvement and "engagement" with *Souffles*, he continues to explore and explode the boundaries of writing ("faire un travail de l'écriture sur l'écriture même") through a mixing of genres and intense questioning ("une remise en question de l'écriture"), in an attempt to create a space for what Khatibi has called the unthinkable ("l'impensable"), whereby difference does not have to suffocate, but can exist in all its multiplicity, complexities, and contradictions, in ways that do not have to be exclusive. In other words, Tahar Ben Jelloun works in the realm of a revolutionary space.

MAJOR WORKS AND THEMES

Tahar Ben Jelloun was in a remarkably vibrant intellectual climate early on. As is often the case with all major changes, the *Souffles* team was well ahead of its time. Its main goal was to participate in the elaboration of national culture through a literature of decolonization in Frantz Fanon's sense of a "decolonisation radicale" that concerned itself with a total cleansing (*nettoyage*) of colonialism and of the colonial mind-set through a sharp criticism and refusal of all that is reminiscent of it, both internally and externally.

Influenced by the empowering message of Fanon that it is time to "faire peau neuve," which includes also the need for an in-depth reflection and new approach to the making of national culture, Ben Jelloun and others see, like Fanon, the role of the intellectual and of the writer as one of ultimate responsibility, keeping in mind that the poet is neither a "guide" nor a "prophet," in *La mémoire future*—"faire peau neuve" in the political, cultural, psychological, emotional and literary sense. They each necessitate an "engagement" (in the concrete and existentialist Sartrian sense) that aims for the elaboration of a (new) national culture. This "engagement" calls for a complete revision of the existing structures, practices, beliefs, convictions, and texts for the creation of the new and revolutionary national culture. It is an ongoing task that must not bring any satisfaction unless it is constantly on the move. Obviously, then, stagnation and paralysis are its worst enemies, and memory becomes an important vehicle and theme.

This revision of existing models, beliefs, and texts must be at times categoric and uncompromising. Particularly in the domain of the social sciences and the humanities, since the colonial mind-set and apparatus have used these fields of study to promote and justify racist ideology and inhumane practices (certainly not a minor factor today with a European community overly concerned with border zones and papers—carte d'ebergement, carte de séjour, permis de travail, passeport, and so on). Fanon, in his too-often unnoticed and yet crucial chapter of *The Wretched of the Earth* entitled "Colonial Wars and Mental Disorders" (215–28), takes upon himself to dismantle the racist theories that so-called experts elaborated at the service, as the result, and as the victims of the colonial machinery, and that insisted that the North African, and in particular the Algerian man, kills "frequently" and "savagely," that he has a need to see blood, which is proven by the fact that he "kills for no reason . . . a gesture, an allusion" (217–18). In fact, the North African was said to be a "born criminal" who "likes extremes" and whose violence is "hereditary" (219), and he must, therefore, never be trusted. Interestingly enough, Tahar Ben Jelloun not only addresses these points in his own way, which is facilitated by his own study of psychology and expertise in the field of social psychiatry (not unlike Fanon), but "calls things by their real name" when necessary.

To revise, question, and dismantle also means to "call things by their real name." In a Fanon gesture Tahar Ben Jelloun does not hesitate to do so ("appeler les choses par leur juste nom"). For Tahar Ben Jelloun, "calling things by their real name" takes the form of a passionate testimony ("témoigner sur une époque, avec ses contradictions, ses bavures et ses silences") and criticism of all forms of abuse, specifically those inherent in colonialism and neocolonialism; cultural and linguistic impositions; racial and ethnic intolerance; class, gender, and sexual oppression; religious fundamentalism; and even an intense questioning of what constitutes sanity and insanity.

In so doing, he also accuses the average Frenchman of having been "preparing his guns for centuries" with the encouragement of his neighbors, who "bring him the bullets" and "encourage him," with the support of the local and national press, and, of course, with the help of extreme right-wing rhetoric and politicians (*Hospitalité française*, 1984, 42). Why? Because, as the author points out passionately, it has been the case for a long time in France that "the color of one's skin," "the way of speaking" ("le son de la langue"), "the smell of cooking," and even "the noise of a party" can trigger racial hatred (107).

Besides the need to "rethink thoughts" ("repenser la pensée") and "call things by their real name," Tahar Ben Jelloun is also interested in what Khatibi has best articulated, perhaps, as the need to go into the depth of memory and imagination, even "to think the unthinkable" ("de penser l'impensée") (see Abdelkebir Khatibi's *Maghreb Pluriel*, in particular). If memory and imagination are important themes in *Cicatrices du soleil*, *Harrouda*, and *A l'insu du souvenir*, they are further explored in *La prière de l'absent*. Perhaps influenced by Kateb Yacine, *La prière de l'absent* takes Tahar Ben Jelloun's readers to the deep South and the Ancestor in a sort of mystical pilgrimage of initiation that is purifying, as Jean Déjeux points out. He also reports that Tahar Ben Jelloun talks about *La prière de l'absent* as an autobiographical piece: "Ben Jelloun en parle comme d'une oeuvre 'autobiographique' " (*Dictionnaire des auteurs maghrébins de langue française*, 225). A provocative book, *L'enfant de sable* reaches the domain of the "unthinkable" in the sense that the father is determined to have a son "even if it is a girl."

Influenced by all those who promote a "pensée de la différence," or "pensée plurielle" as Abdelkebir Khatibi puts it, such as Heidegger, Nietzsche, and others (whom Ben Jelloun and most of the others studied), the *Souffles* group attacked vehemently all forms of "totalitarisme," denouncing how all forms of "totalitarisme" operate through exclusion, in extreme cases through imprisonment, torture, and killing, and in most cases through reductionism and silencing. Specifically, Tahar Ben Jelloun and Abdelkebir Khatibi work in the realm of difference, a difference that cannot be reduced, seduced, nor contained, and certainly not rendered invisible. "Une différence intraitable," for Abdelkebir Khatibi, yet one that must be named: "J'écris pour dire la différence" says Tahar Ben Jelloun. Here, all oppressed characters find a voice in his work, even when they cannot speak for themselves: "Trempe ta plume dans l'encre de mon âme et écris" is the beginning statement in *L'écrivain public*.

In fact, it is fair to say that "la revendication de la parole" or "la prise de la parole" is the central theme of the group's concerns. Indeed, Tahar Ben Jelloun meticulously and skillfully creates spaces in which those who tend to be excluded and silenced speak for themselves, even if that means that in order to do so they must (pretend to?) be insane and are certainly considered as such by those whom they criticize, precisely because they are so clear minded in their observations, criticisms, and actions, as is the case with *Moha le fou, Moha le sage*. For Tahar Ben Jelloun, silence is a shroud which buries people alive (*Hommes sous linceul de silence*). To speak, then, is to affirm one's existence. It is a liberating act. Tahar Ben Jelloun writes in *Harrouda* that "to speak, in a society where silence is the law, is a true political manifesto" ("la prise de la parole—dans une société où le silence est une loi—est un véritable manifeste politique"). "A book is not much," he continues, "and yet my ambition is to open the windows in the house of silence, indifference or fear" ("ouvrir les fenêtres dans la demeure du silence ou de la peur," *Hospitalité française*).

Language is often explosive in an abundance of polyphonic voices perhaps precisely because of the proximity between silence and death. *La réclusion solitaire* offers a good example of various unusual characters whom Tahar Ben Jelloun calls "les voix" (the voices). These voices (a homeless bird, a student/author, Moha, the image, the immigrant, and the Palestinian people) interact with the other characters and with each other in a fashion that calls into question the linear approach to time in favor of movements in spiral. They offer a way perhaps to "re-create" French language and thought, to dismantle the French language from inside, and, in some cases, to participate in "linguistic terrorism" ("le terrorisme linguistique"), as Khatibi had suggested in 1968.

Under the influence also of Marx, Mao, Fanon, and Césaire, class oppression, economic exploitation, and imperialism became one of the intense focuses of the group. These themes are constant in the writings of Tahar Ben Jelloun and were already predominant at the time in the works of the renowned Algerian authors Mohammed Dib and Mouloud Feraoun. Although *Moha le fou, Moha le sage* certainly addresses the theme of class oppression in the Maghreb, for Tahar Ben Jelloun, the theme of economic exploitation is found most acutely when he writes and talks about North African immigrants in France. The state of isolation to which they are condemned is another of Tahar Ben Jelloun's recurrent themes. "He had taken with him a handful of earth from his home, he would smell it, put it all over his face to get rid of his solitude" (my translation), writes the author in *Les amandiers sont morts de leurs blessures*; he depicts that solitude, a complete state of isolation, misery, and impotence, most poignantly in *La réclusion solitaire* and in *La plus haute des solitudes*.

Not surprisingly, internally, the founders, members, and contributors of the revolutionary review were considered to be dangerous by the rulers and a Moroccan bourgeoisie comfortable with the status quo, for it was understood that their objective was to prepare the next Moroccan revolution, which, of course, threatened the existing political structures as well as the social and cultural organizations of Moroccan society, particularly when in 1970 the group published its "Manifeste pour une culture du peuple" (Manifesto for the culture of the people). Thus when *Souffles* was banned by the government and its founders imprisoned (Abdellatif Laâbi spent eight years in prison and was released only in 1980), Tahar Ben Jelloun and other members of *Souffles* helped found *Intégral*, which focused on literature and the plastic arts, and even those who were imprisoned continued to write letters, essays, and poems (see, for example, Abdellatif Laâbi's *Sous le bâillon, le poème* [1981], *Le chemin des ordalies* [1982], and *Chroniques de la citadelle d'exil* [1983]).

In an electric style and a passionate outcry against racism, Tahar Ben Jelloun excels specifically in *Hospitalité française*. As emphasized earlier, throughout his writings Ben Jelloun is concerned with the disenfranchised. In the case of those who, due to various circumstances, are made to be silent and silenced, his sense of urgency not merely to speak for them but to create a space in which they can speak is tremendous, although at times he is so outraged that he literally becomes those voices. This was clearly the case after a young nine-year-old boy, Taoufik Ouanès, was assassinated in France "à la cité des 4000 à la Courneuve," on July 9, 1983, in the turbulent period of time that was referred to as "the bloody summer of 1982 and the bloody year of 1983" by members of the North African community in France, and that prompted Tahar Ben Jelloun to write *Hospitalité française*. He talks about having "felt" this book like an "urgency" ("Ce livre, je l'ai senti comme une urgence"); he explains how it felt like a "burning in his stomach" ("une espèce de brûlure dans le ventre") (16). As an Arab who, as he likes to insist, lives "between France and Morocco," he felt the deep scarring caused by the vicious and dreadful form of racism in France, which, as he explains, "is not merely a desperate hatred" ("n'est pas qu'une animosité désespérante"), but also "a state of fact that kills" ("un état de fait qui tue") (16). Equally critical of what goes on in the Maghreb and, in this case, precisely of what does not go on, Tahar Ben Jelloun is further outraged by the indifference vis-à-vis those deaths (on both sides of the Mediterranean) and, in particular, by the absolute silence of North African governments, because the fact remains that "cette mort échoue ici et là-bas dans une espèce d'indifférence due à la fatalité [the Mektoub] ou à l'inconscience" (16).

Not surprisingly, Tahar Ben Jelloun is often regarded as an expert on immigration and is frequently called upon by the French press, *Le Monde, L'express, Le Nouvel Observateur*, and television's *Antenne 2*, and by the prestigious magazine *Jeune Afrique*. As well, he is generally considered to be a spokesperson for North African immigrants in France, both by the French and by North Africans, although the younger generation—*la génération beure*—more frequently opts to speak for itself or to elect its representatives.

CRITICAL RECEPTION

There is a great amount of research and an abundant body of literature and critical texts on Tahar Ben Jelloun, due perhaps to the following reasons: first, the author is a prolific writer in all genres who is best known for his novels, but also for his poems, essays, and articles. A look at the bibliography reveals that Tahar Ben Jelloun has been publishing for over twenty-five years, just about every single year. Second, he excels in all genres, does not hesitate to venture beyond their respective limits, and offers an innovative and at times provocative exploration of the very "acte de l'écriture," moving comfortably from the realism and criticism of concrete sociopolitical situations and astute analysis to an in-depth examination going back into memory (and time) that leads to an original poetic discourse, to pushing the limits of imagination, whereby what is real and what is not cannot be disassociated and are destabilizing at times, to the inscription of polyphonic voices. Third, his "engagement" as a writer contributes to his popularity, particularly when he concerns himself with universal themes and the disenfranchised, although he is always careful to be very specific. Deeply rooted in the Maghreb, in France, and in between, Tahar Ben Jelloun's voice is forceful and passionate; it demands to be listened to, because as a major and profoundly postcolonial author he has much to offer. This has been recognized by the international community, as proven by the numerous publications on him (as well as radio and television programs), particularly in France, the Maghreb, Italy, Germany, the United States, and Canada. Tahar Ben Jelloun has received several awards, the most important of which are Le Prix de l'Amitié franco-arabe in 1976, Le Prix des bibliothécaires de France et de Radio-Monte-Carlo in 1979, and the highly prestigious Prix Goncourt in 1987. It is pleasing indeed to see that Tahar Ben Jelloun's writings are translated more and more frequently, as indicated in the bibliography.

It is impossible to do justice here to the immense body of work Tahar Ben Jelloun has inspired so far. For details on critical reception the reader should refer to the section on Selected Studies of Tahar Ben Jelloun in the bibliography. Given the amount of what has been written on Tahar Ben Jelloun, the focus is primarily on the critical reception of the past fifteen years. Thus it is my intent here to focus only on one or two points that purposefully emphasize connections, in the hope to fill what I think is a void, although very recent studies on Tahar Ben Jelloun are quite promising, a void that, in my opinion, we do not have the luxury nor the time to continue to ignore if we are to survive the very turbulent and racist times of today. In North Africa, and in particular in a tormented Algeria, an Algeria where the very act of writing or thinking out loud is threatened by death, people do die for and because of their ideas. This concerns not just Tahar Ben Jelloun and North African intellectuals, but should concern us all. In Western Europe, the responsibility of France, England, Germany, and Italy for the unacceptable crimes against certain targeted immigrant populations, more specifically North Africans in France, and in particular Algerians (including, ironically enough, so-called French citizens like the Beurs who have become the primary targets of French racism and die young), Pakistanis and Indians in England, Turks in Germany, and Moroccans in Italy, to name a few, also concerns Tahar Ben Jelloun. The United States of America with its rampant racism, as the black community and its institutions (most recently the burning of black churches in the South) continue to be the main target of U.S. racism, as black people (men in particular) still die in disproportionate numbers compared to the rest of the population, as black children disappear, as attempts to discredit the American Muslim community increase in number, and also as the Arab-American community is targeted, perhaps in a more subtle, but nonetheless unacceptable, form in the very heart of its civil liberties (following, of course, the anti-Arab and anti-Muslim campaign of international politics and racist ideology), raises concerns that Tahar Ben Jelloun addresses, even if, in some regard, indirectly. Finally, for every Arab, of course, inside or outside the Arab world, the Palestinian people and what Edward Said calls *The Question of Palestine* are at the forefront of one's reality, concerns, and hopes. Tahar Ben Jelloun is also clear on that point. Most important, despite for all the disasters mentioned earlier and others, Tahar Ben Jelloun is a vehement believer in dialogue.

Perhaps because Tahar Ben Jelloun is considered to be a spokesperson for North Africans in France, and without doubt an "expert" on immigration, Nacer Kettane, founder of Radio Beure (1983), followed in his footsteps with his equally forceful and certainly empowering "Beure version" of *Hospitalité française* in *Droit de réponse à l'hospitalité française*, published two years later, in 1986. Both works need to be placed in the context of what is referred to by the North African immigrant and Beure community in France as the bloody summer of 1982 and the bloody year of 1983, during which North African males became (and continue to be) the target of racist violence, crimes, and murders. In fact, Tahar Ben Jelloun reports in *Hospitalité française* that between May 1982 and October 1983 alone, there were more than forty-five victims, mostly males and averaging twenty-three years of age, of racist assaults and crimes that resulted in the death of most at the hands of French citizens and police, in more than suspicious circumstances (a situation not unfamiliar to what most Beurs consider to be their counterparts, "USA style," as more and more of their "Black Brothers" in the same age range were also, and continue to be, victims of the same racist crimes, in such similar circumstances that James Baldwin and others' theory of an international conspiracy against people of color is not far-fetched at all; see *The Fire Next Time* and *Conversations with James Baldwin*) a situation that the Beure community in France is acutely aware of. Unfortunately, the reverse is usually not true, perhaps for very understandable reasons, linked most likely to local, national, and international politics and manipulation, and probably also to the theory of conspiracy.

However, it is quite alarming when critics, intellectuals, and scholars miss the point by failing to establish those vital connections that, without minimizing individual circumstances and their significance, transcend linguistic, geographic, and national boundaries and question political agendas based on notions of space and spaces that are clearly and simply limiting if not archaic and—why not admit it?—"dépassés." In fact, it would be wise to say that what prompted James Baldwin to give the warning in 1963 that unless the United States realizes, acknowledges, and accepts that it is a "mixed" (multiracial) nation, "next time, the fire," is not so different than what prompted the North African community in France, and in particular the Beurs, to state in no uncertain terms, "The

France of tomorrow *is* walking by,'' during the march (referred to as ''La marche des Beurs'') in October 1983 to protest the deaths and assaults of a racist France unwilling to realize, to acknowledge, and to accept that it is a ''mixed'' nation (''une nation métissée''), multiracial, multiethnic, multireligious, and multidimensional. In other words, ''French people wake up! This *is* the France of tomorrow''; otherwise, ''next time, the fire.'' While Los Angeles was burning twenty years after James Baldwin's warning, the south of France was also burning at the same time, and on both sides, children continue to mysteriously ''disappear.'' Consequently, it is also in the context of the march that Ben Jelloun's *Hospitalité française* and Kettane's *Droit de réponse à la hospitalité française* must be read, without overlooking other international concrete situations.

James Baldwin remarked not so long ago, when he was asked to investigate (with others) the ''mysterious'' disappearances of several black children in the Atlanta area that American life was poisoned by the death of a Black child, and this death was a poison because it was not acknowledged as such by the United States. Transposed into the context of Tahar Ben Jelloun's France of *Hospitalité française*, in 1984, James Baldwin's remark remains, not surprisingly, pertinent: ''Life in France is poisoned by the death of a child of immigration, and this death is a poison because it is not acknowledged as such by France,'' as mentioned earlier and criticized by Tahar Ben Jelloun, nor by the Maghreb. In memory, still pianissimo style, as stated by the only slogan of the march, ''The France of tomorrow *is* walking by,'' and some will be reminded of Tahar Ben Jelloun's *La mémoire future* (not a gratuitous play on words and time), because today's Maghreb, Palestine, France, and United States are unable to answer the very relevant question of Algerian poet Mohammed Mebkhout: ''Where can I find the word / Where can I find the voice / Where can I find the courage / Where can I find the space / To say 'I love you'?''

BIBLIOGRAPHY

Works by Tahar Ben Jelloun

Cicatrices du soleil (poems). Paris: Éditions Maspero, 1972.
Harrouda (novel). Paris: Éditions Denoël, collection ''Les lettres nouvelles,'' 1973; collection.
''Relire,'' 1977; collection ''Médianes,'' 1982.
La réclusion solitaire (novel). Paris: Éditions Denoël, collection ''Les lettres nouvelles,'' 1973; Seuil, collection ''Points roman,'' 1981. Translated as *The Solitaire* by Gareth Stanton and Nick Hundley. London: Quartet, 1988.
Le discours du chameau (poem). Paris: Éditions Maspero, 1974.
Grains de peau, Asilah . . . mémoire d'enfance, (photography by Mohammed Benaïssa, poetry by Tahar Ben Jelloun). Casablanca: Éditions Shoof, 1974.
Les amandiers sont morts de leurs blessures suivi de Cicatrices du soleil, and Le discours du chameau (poems and short stories). Paris: Éditions Maspero, collection

"Voix," 1976; PCM, 1979; Seuil, collection "Points roman," 1985. Prix de l'Amitié franco-arabe, 1976.

La mémoire future, anthologie de la nouvelle poésie du Maroc (anthology of the new Moroccan poetry, with a selection of poems by authors who write in Arabic and in French; introduction by Tahar Ben Jelloun). Paris: Éditions Maspero, 1976.

La plus haute des solitudes (essay in psychiatry based on the author's doctoral thesis in social psychiatry). Paris: Éditions du Seuil, collection "Combats," 1977; collection "Points actuel," 1979.

Moha le fou, Moha le sage (novel). Paris: Éditions du Seuil, 1978; collection "Points roman," 1980. Prix des bibliothécaires de France et de Radio-Monte-Carlo, 1979.

A l'insu du souvenir (poems). Paris: Éditions Maspero, collection "Voix," 1980.

La prière de l'absent (novel). Paris: Éditions du Seuil, 1981; collection "Points roman," 1982.

Haut Atlas: L'exil de pierres (photography by Philippe Lafond, text by Tahar Ben Jelloun). Paris: Éditions Chêne-Hachette, 1982.

L'écrivain public (essay). Paris: Éditions du Seuil, 1983.

La fiancée de l'eau suivi de Entretiens avec M. Saïd Hammadi, ouvrier algérien (play and interview). Paris: Actes Sud, 1984.

Hospitalité française, racisme, et immigration maghrébine. Paris: Éditions du Seuil, collection. "L'histoire immédiate," 1984.

L'enfant de sable (novel). Paris: Éditions du Seuil, 1985. Translated as *The Sandchild*. Alger: Laphomic, 1988.

La nuit sacrée (novel). Paris: Éditions du Seuil, 1987. Prix Goncourt, 1987. Translated as *The Sacred Night* by Alan Sheridan. London: Quartet, 1989.

Jour de silence à Tanger (essay). Paris: Éditions du Seuil, 1990. Translated as *Silent Day in Tangier*. London: Quartet, 1991.

La remontée des cendres suivi de Non identifiés. Paris: Éditions du Seuil, 1991.

Strategies d'ecriture. Paris: Éditions du Seuil, 1993.

L'ange aveugle (collection of short stories). Paris: Éditions du Seuil, 1992. Translated as *State of Absence*. London: Quartet, 1994.

Les yeux baissés (novel). Paris: Éditions du Seuil, 1992. Translated as *With Downcast Eyes*. Boston: Little, Brown and Company, 1993.

L'homme rompu (novel). Paris: Éditions du Seuil, 1994. Translated as *Corruption*. New York: New Press, 1995.

La soudure fraternelle. Paris: Éditions, Arléa, 1994. Librairie Arthème Fayard, 1996.

"Hommes sous linceul de silence." Section II of *Poésie Complète, 1966–1995*, 25–47.

Le Premier amour est toujours le dernier. Paris: Éditions du Seuil, 1995.

Poésie Complète, 1966–1995. Paris: Éditions du Seuil, 1995.

Les raisins de la galère (novel). Paris: 1996. Translated as *Nadia*. Milano: Bompiani, 1996.

The author has made several contributions to the review *Souffles* (especially between 1968 and 1970), has published numerous articles in the French press, and writes regularly for *Le Monde*. Also, he has translated from the Arabic Mohammed Choukri's important autobiographical text *Le Pain nu* (Maspero, 1980). "Écrire dans toutes les langues françaises" is his most recent article, in *La Quinzaine Littéraire* March 1996: 16–31.

Selected Studies of Tahar Ben Jelloun

Ben Abda, Salwa. *Bilinguisme et poétique chez Tahar Ben Jelloun*. Paris: Sorbonne, 1990.

Bet, Marie-Thérèse. "La littérature maghrébine francophone." *Cahiers de l'Association Internationale des Études Françaises* 44 (May 1992): 67–80.

Bourkis, Ridha. "La connotation du corps dans l'oeuvre de Tahar Ben Jelloun." *IBLA: Revue de l'Institut des Belles Lettres Arabes* 55.2 (170) (1992): 275–82.

Bousta Saigh, Rachida. *Lecture des récits de Tahar Ben Jelloun: Écriture, mémoire, et imaginaire.* . . . Casablanca: Afrique Orient, 1992.

Cazenave, Odile. "Gender, Age, and Narrative Transformations in *L'Enfant de sable* by Tahar Ben Jelloun." *French Review: Journal of the American Association of Teachers of French* 64.3 (February 1991): 437–50.

Chalier, Chantal. "*La Nuit sacrée*: Un roman musulman qui ose s'exprimer contre l'hypocrisie et le fanatisme religieux." *Australian Journal of French Studies* 28.1 (January–April 1991): 80–91.

Corcuera Ibanez, Mario. "Ben Jelloun, un escritor del Mediterraneo." *Suplemento Literario La Nacion* (Buenos Aires) September 12, 1993: 1–2.

Déjeux, Jean. *Dictionnaire des auteurs maghrébins de langue française*. Paris: Éditions Khartala, 1984.

———. *Littérature maghrébine de langue française*. 3rd ed. Quebec: Editions Naaman de Sherbrooke, 1980.

———. "Tahar Ben Jelloun, romancier, poète, et essayiste marocain." *Lettres et Cultures de Langue Française* 12 (1987): 1–5.

Diglio, Carolina. "La memoria dalle ceneri: *La remontée des cendres* di Tahar Ben Jelloun." *Annali Istituto Universitario Orientale, Napoli, Sezione Romanza* 35.1 (January 1993): 83–99.

Elbaz, Robert. *Tahar Ben Jelloun ou L'inassouvissement du désir narratif*. Paris: L'Harmattan, c. 1996. Collection Critiques Littéraires dirigée par Gérard Da Silva.

Erickson, John D. "Veiled Woman and Veiled Narrative in Tahar Ben Jelloun's *The Sandchild*." *Boundary 2* Spring 1993: 46–64.

———. "Writing Double: Politics and the African Narrative of French Expression." *Studies in Twentieth Century French Literature* 15.1 (Winter 1991): 101–22.

Fayad, Marie. "Borges in Tahar Ben Jelloun's *L'enfant de sable*: Beyond Intertextuality." *French Review* 67.2 (December 1993): 291–99.

Gaillard, Philippe. "Tahar le fou Tahar le sage." *Jeune Afrique* 1404 (December 2, 1987): 44–46.

Geesey, Patricia, and Mustapha Marrouchi. "Breaking up/down/out of the Boundaries: Tahar Ben Jelloun." *Research in African Literatures* 21 (Winter 1990): 71–83.

Gnisci, Armando. *Il rovescio del gioco*. Rome: Sovera, series "Studi di Litteratura Comparata," 1993.

Tahar Ben Jelloun, *La poussière d'or et La face masquée*. Paris: L'Harmattan, c. 1995. Collection Critiques Littéraires durigée. Gérard Da Silva.

Joubert, Jean-Louis. "Trio majeur: Tahar Ben Jelloun, Jours de silence à Tanger, Ahmadou Kourouma Monne, Outrages et Défis, Henri Lopes, Le Chercheur d'Afrique." *Diagonales* 15 (July 1990): 17–18.

Khatibi, Abdelkebir. *Maghreb pluriel*. Paris: Éditions Denoël, 1983.

Landwehr, Silvie. "Comment le sort de l'immigré en France est-il représenté dans le nouveau roman marocain?" *Französisch Heute* 17.1 (March 1986): 159–64.

Litherland, Caren, and Thomas C. Spear. "Politics and Literature: An Interview with Tahar Ben Jelloun." *Yale French Studies* 83 (1993): 30–43.

Lowe, Lisa. "Literary Nomadics in Francophone Allegories of Postcolonialism: Pham Van Ky and Tahar Ben Jelloun." *Yale French Studies* 82 (1993): 43–61.

Maazaoui, Abbes. "*L'enfant de sable* et *La nuit sacrée* ou Le corps tragique." *French Review* 69 (October 1995): 68–77.

Madelain, Jacques. *L'errance et l'itinéraire: Lecture du roman maghrébin de langue française*. Paris: Éditions Sinbad, 1989.

Memmi, Albert. *Écrivains francophones du Maghreb*. Paris: Éditions Seghers, 1985.

Mouzouni, Lahcen. *Le roman marocain de langue française*. Paris: Éditions Publisud, 1987.

Nicolini, Elisabeth. "Le Goncourt à Tahar Ben Jelloun." *Jeune Afrique* 1403 (November 25, 1987): 22.

Nicolini, Elisabeth, and Renaud de Rochebrune. "Comment travaillent les écrivains: Tahar Ben Jelloun." *Jeune Afrique* 1177 (July 27, 1983): 54–55.

Nisbet, Anne-Marie. *Le personnage féminin dans le roman maghrébin de langue française des indépendances à 1980: Représentations et fonctions*. Quebec, Canada: Éditions Naaman de Sherbrooke, 1982.

Pallister, Janis L. "Tahar Ben Jelloun and the Poetry of Refusal." *Revue Celfan/Celfan Review* 2.3 (May 1983): 34–36.

Silva, Edson Rosa da. "O Menino de Areia: Un Romance Arabe Escrito en Frances (ou os Laberintos da Escritura)." *Revista Letras* 38 (1989): 157–66.

———. "Tahar Ben Jelloun: Identité arabe/expression française." *Présence Francophone: Revue Internationale de Langue et de Littérature* 34 (1989): 63–72.

Taleb-Khyar, Mohammed B. "Tahar Ben Jelloun and *The Water's Bride*: Introductory Notes." *Callaloo: An Afro-American and African Journal of Arts and Letters* 13.3 (Summer 1990): 396–425.

Toësca, Georgette. *Itinéraires et lieux communs*. Paris: Agence de coupération culturelle et Technique, Éditions Silex, 1983.

Verheyen, Günther. "Tahar Ben Jellouns Aufbruch in die Weltliteratur: Einige Gedanken zu *L'enfant de sable* und *La nuit sacrée*." *Französisch Heute* 24.3 (September 1993): 267–80.

Zahiri, Mohammed. "*A l'insu du souvenir* de Tahar Ben Jelloun: Étude et analyse de l'isotopie de la 'Mort.' " *Présence Francophone: Revue Internationale de Langue et de Littérature* 23 (Autumn 1981): 21–42.

Zappala, Margueritte Rivoire. "Les Erotismes dans *La Nuit sacrée* de Tahar Ben Jelloun." *Francofonia: Studi e Ricerche sulle Letterature di Lingua Francese* 9.16 (Spring 1989): 99–113.

SORAYA MÉKERTA

MOHAMMED KHAÏR-EDDINE
(1941–1995)

BIOGRAPHY

Born in Tafraout, Morocco, in 1941 into a bourgeois family, Mohammed Khaïr-Eddine received a French education in Casablanca. As a student, he began to read an array of poetry that included St. John Perse, the French surrealist poets, and Arab poets. For a short time, he was a civil servant for the government before going into temporary exile in France. Khaïr-Eddine belongs to the second generation of Maghreb writers after Moroccan independence. In 1964 he began the poetic manifesto *Poèsie Tout* in Casablanca and later became one of the founders of *Souffles* in 1966. *Souffles*, a seminal journal, was a reaction to the disenchantment of Morocco's decolonization. The euphoria of Morocco's independence from France in 1956 soon gave way in the 1960s to the riots and strikes of students and unemployed workers. *Souffles* urged Moroccan artists and writers to collectively become active in the formation of a new national identity and to participate in a cultural revival that would fill the void left by colonization. Khaïr-Eddine's work, subversive in both form and content, has been referred to as "guerrilla linguistics" (Gontard, 109). He constantly scrutinizes, rejects, and transgresses traditional values and boundaries in his efforts to revitalize literature.

Khaïr-Eddine left Morocco for France, where he lived from 1965 to 1979 and later from 1989 to 1993. His first novel, *Agadir*, won the Prix des Enfants Terribles, and in 1966 he was awarded the Prix de la Nouvelle Maghrébine (*Revue Preuve Juin*). Although Khaïr-Eddine is a very private person, critics have noted the striking proximity between his literary works and his life. His love for his Berber grandfather and southern Morocco permeates all his work. Khaïr-Eddine rejects the assimilation offered by Europe and refuses to find refuge in the comfort of ethnic nativism. As a mature writer, Khaïr-Eddine is steadfast in his political commitments, which continue to inform his writing. His polyphonic novels are complex allegories that draw on the oral traditions of southern Morocco and on Sufi mysticism, as well as the Western literary canons. In their oneiric narratives that wrestle with their past, his narrators address themselves as well as their deities, historical figures, families, and, finally, the reader. His poetry uses scientific and geological terminology to weave intricate metaphors that carry the reader from one dimension to another with meteoric speed. Despite his harsh perception of the modern world, his poetry and novels are an affectionate gesture to the reader that glimmers with humor and beauty.

MAJOR WORKS AND THEMES

Like Khaïr-Eddine, the narrator of his first novel, *Agadir*, is a bureaucrat sent to Agadir after the 1960 earthquake that destroyed the Moroccan port town. The novel, which begins as the narrator's journal, is a medley of dreams, memories, and play vignettes of historical figures who converse with both the narrator and other characters. It is a kaleidoscope of parody, political satire, black humor, and youthful tenderness. The narrator, who becomes increasingly alienated, eventually decides to flee his homeland for France to pursue his career as a poet. Khaïr-Eddine's narrators continually look to fellow writers as fraternal figures. His works abound with literary allusions, such as ones to *Gulliver's Travels* and to his Maghreb peers. An ambitious early novel, *Agadir* begins to explore many of the themes raised in his later novels. The novel contains the creation story of the birth of negative man, the offspring of two hostile species, a wolf who substitutes for earth's language and a rattlesnake. The complex metaphor of necrophagous animals, African birds, and reptiles simultaneously expressing both destruction and creation typifies his work.

Although Khaïr-Eddine rejects the traditional God of Islam, he continues to struggle and play with the sacred role of writing and the word that is rooted in the Koran. His second novel, *Corps négatif suivi de Histoire d'un Bon Dieu*, also has a narrator-writer facing the problems of writing and the past. In a diffusion of the traditional boundaries among characters, humans, and deities, the reader, together with the narrator of *Histoire d'un Bon Dieu*, reads the story of a dubious God.

Le déterreur begins with the arrest and death sentence for necrophagia of a young poet who is living in exile in Paris. Through his confession, a condemnation of both French and Moroccan society, the narrator exerts his control over his identity by inverting the situation, making himself the victim and society the criminal. Similar in style and tone to Khaïr-Eddine's other novels, the narrator wins the reader's affections through his irony and his defense, based on moral and ecological grounds, which includes his dreams, conversations with God, and poetry. The young poet who left Morocco full of hope and finds only racism in

France bravely transcends the bleakness of urban life to bid a fraternal farewell to the reader.

Une odeur de mantèque introduces another endearing but roguish narrator who shares his youthful reminiscences and crimes with the reader. He is an older man who has stolen a magic mirror. His crime backfires because the mirror witnesses the crime it inspired, and subsequently the old man is bound by a superior being who leads him into Hell and Paradise. The reader accompanies him backwards through Moroccan history and to the southern countryside of his youth. The narrator's irony and honesty paint an unsentimental picture of modern Morocco and deconstruct any romantic notion of pre-colonial Morocco. The author's focus on memory and exiles continues in *Une vie, un rêve, un peuple toujours errants*. The novel, which also contains childhood memories and historical dramas, begins with a futuristic nightmare set among the ruins of the modern world.

Although concerned with similar themes, Khaïr-Eddine's most recent novel, *Legende et vie d'Agoun'chich*, is a slight departure of style from the poet narrator. Continuing to draw on the oral tradition, the modern novel recounts the adventures of legendary bandit Agoun'chich and his companion, a rapist. The hero witnesses the devastating changes of Moroccan society brought about by the French colonization. Khaïr-Eddine's most recent collection of poetry, *Mémorial*, maintains his subversive stance, but its concerns are more global. The complex images and the cosmic vastness of references of *Mémorial* are testimony to the endurance of Khaïr-Eddine's poetic vision.

CRITICAL RECEPTION

The hostile universe of Khaïr-Eddine is never without hope and human warmth. Like those of other African and Maghreb writers, his references to the native landscape and the sun are political, mythical, and symbolic. In his love/hate relationship with his homeland, his poetry describes not only the destructive monster born of his landscape but also the beauty. As Jacqueline Arnaud points out, the South for Khaïr-Eddine is the land of resistance, the myth of lost paradise, and the perpetual ideal to be reinvented (9). Although he occasionally mocks the bravado of his Berber heritage, his poetry is a lyric tribute to the essence of southern Morocco that consistently fortifies the tortured poet. Hédi Abdel-Jaouad notes that "geographic, temporal, mythical or imaginary" wandering is a major theme of Khaïr-Eddine's work and that his "linguistic guerilla" hinders any plot or character development (147). His wandering is imaginative, temporal as well as intellectual. Jean Déjeux summarizes the intention of Khaïr-Eddine's work as a "contestation" (409) of everything that never settles into an ideology. The Oedipal motif is manifested throughout his fiction in his rejection of his origins and patriarchal society. Yet his refusal never extends to the reader. Moroccan critic Abderrahman Tenkoul observes that the project of social transformation is inseparable from the fiction of Khaïr-Eddine.

Tenkoul perceives Khaïr-Eddine's use of the oral tradition as both a strategy of critical interrogation and a gesture to the reader (151). Although Khaïr-Eddine is acknowledged to be one of the more talented writers of the *Souffles* generation and his work maintains his radical stance, he has generated less criticism outside of Morocco than the celebrated Tahar Ben Jelloun. Much critical work on Khaïr-Eddine's elusive and rich writing remains to be done.

BIBLIOGRAPHY

Works by Mohammed Khaïr-Eddine

Nausée noire. London: Éditions Siècle à mains, 1964.
Agadir. Paris: Éditions du Seuil, 1967.
Corps négatif suivi de Histoire d'un Bon Dieu. Paris: Éditions du Seuil, 1968.
Soleil arachnide. Paris: Éditions du Seuil, 1969.
Moi l'aigre. Paris: Éditions du Seuil, 1970.
Le déterreur. Paris: Éditions du Seuil, 1973.
Ce Maroc! Paris: Éditions du Seuil, 1975.
Une odeur de mantèque. Paris: Éditions du Seuil, 1976.
Une vie, un rêve, un peuple, toujours errants. Paris: Éditions du Seuil, 1978.
Résurrection des fleurs sauvages. Rabat: Éditions Stourky, 1981.
Légende et vie d'Agoun'chich. Paris: Éditions du Seuil, 1984.
Mémorial. Paris: Aux Éditions du Cherche Midi, 1991.

Selected Studies of Mohammed Khaïr-Eddine

Abdel-Jaouad, Hédi. "Mohammed Khaïr-Eddine: The Poet as Iconoclast." *Research in African Literatures* 23.2 (1992): 145–50.
Arnaud, Jacqueline. "Khaïr-Eddine le sudiste." *Présence Francophone* 21 (Fall 1980): 7–19.
Déjeux, Jean. *Littérature maghrébin de langue française*. Quebec: Naaman, 1978.
Gontard, Marc. "La littérature marocaine de langue française." *Europe* 57 (June–July 1979): 102–23.
Tenkoul, Abderrahman. *Littérature marocaine d'ecriture française: Essais d'analyse sémiotique*. Casablanca: Afrique Orient, 1985.

LYNNE DUMONT ROGERS

UNGULANI BA KA KHOSA (1957–   )

BIOGRAPHY

On the back cover of his collection of stories *Orgia dos loucos*, Ungulani Ba Ka Khosa introduces himself as follows: "I was born on August 1, 1957, at 0.45 A.M. in Inhaminga, Sofala [Mozambique]. The rest is irrelevant, because according to Barthes 'There is only biography when life is unproductive. As long as I produce, as long as I write, it is the text itself that appropriates (happily) my narrative time.' " A biographical sketch, therefore, seems ironic. Nevertheless, a few words on Khosa's background will here serve as a brief introduction to the reader of this vibrant Mozambican author before proceeding to his texts.

Khosa was born to a Sena mother and a Shanga father. His parents were "assimilated," and Khosa says that his mother tongue is Portuguese. His registered name is Francisco Esau Cossa. Both of his parents were nurses working in the interior of Mozambique. When Khosa was still very young, his father decided to go south, and so Khosa stayed with his mother. At the end of elementary school he joined his father in the south of France, began to learn Tsonga, and was given the name Ungulani Ba Ka Khosa. With the assistance of a scholarship, Khosa traveled to Maputo, where he took an intensive course designed for public teachers. In 1978 he began to teach in Nyassa, the northernmost state in Mozambique. It was apparently a lonely period, and Khosa says that it was here that he began to want to write. In 1980 he returned to Maputo, where he took education courses in history and geography in order to teach high school. He also began to write and published his first story in 1982, the same year in which the Associação de Escritores Moçambicanos (Association of Mozambican Writers) was founded.

A group within the association that has been described as "maluca, sonha-

dora, esquizofrênica'' (crazies, dreamers, schizophrenics) started a literary review called *Charrua*, which means "plow." They advocate the reworking of
Portuguese and question the current literary conventions. They are opposed to
any kind of prescriptive rule for writing. Khosa, one of the leaders of the group,
wishes to break through the bourgeois domination of literature that he says
preceded and has continued since independence. Similar to the writing of others
in this group, Khosa's style is often caustic and certainly impassioned, for the
Charrua writers are engaged in a process of redefining Mozambican literature.
Although they often draw on the oral tradition and style, Khosa himself usually
makes no typographical distinctions to indicate speech or thought in the text.
The reason that Ungulani Ba Ka Khosa gives for writing *Ualalapi* is itself
interesting: He says that he saw one of his stories being used as toilet paper and
decided to avenge himself. Though perhaps this anecdote is metaphorical, Khosa
says in an interview that the reason he started writing was to put down on paper
the absurd reality that he encountered.

MAJOR WORKS AND THEMES

Set during the nineteenth-century scramble for Africa, *Ualalapi* engages in a re-
contextualization of past representations. After the General Act of Berlin in 1885
there commenced what has been called the Scramble for Africa in which the major
colonial powers fought to finalize Africa's partition. Although the Portuguese by
this time had control of the coastal areas of Mozambique, they began in 1895 a series of campaigns to conquer the interior of Mozambique. At this time Ngungunhane (also spelled Gungunhana), who was the ruler of Gaza from 1884 to 1895,
was the most feared African force in Mozambique. There were serious questions
about whether the Portuguese would have the military strength necessary to defeat
him, and if the Portuguese did not do so in time, that the English would take the
land instead. The novel is interwoven with Portuguese historical documents from
the period, such as those by Ayres D'Ornellas, Mouzinho de Albuquerque, Dr.
Liengme, and António Ennes, who exotically vilify Africa for their own aggrandizement. For example, on the opening page of epigraphs Khosa juxtaposes General Ayres D'Ornellas's glorification of Ngungunhane as one with "um certo ar de
grandeza e superioridade" (a certain air of greatness and superiority) with the description of him by the Swiss missionary, Dr. Liengme, as "um ébrio inveterado"
(an inveterate drunk) with an "expressão bestial" (bestial expression). In Canto 5
of Camões' *Os Lusíadas*, the Cape of Good Hope is personified as Adamastor,
which has been interpreted both as the personification of all that is ugly and evil
and as an embodied representation of Africa. Adamastor dares to confront the Portuguese as they round the African continent and is subsequently silenced. Thus,
forming a continuity in Portuguese colonial discourse, Ngungunhane becomes a
kind of nineteenth-century Adamastor who also must be conquered and tamed by
the Portuguese.

    The novel follows Ngungunhane's rise to power and subsequent capture by the Portuguese. However, the narrative does not proceed in a linear fashion, but is more like a series of separate accounts, all of which circle around Ngungunhane. It is interesting to note that the first edition was published as "contos" (short stories). Each chapter of the book is first introduced with "Fragmentos" (Fragments) of a historical document and then an epigraph, usually biblical. The first chapter centers on one of Ngungunhane's warriors, Ualalapi, who goes insane after killing Ngungunhane's brother in a consolidation of power. Another chapter centers on Ngungunhane's aunt, Damboia, who dies from an interminable menstruation. The final chapter, entitled "O Último discurso de Ngungunhane" (Ngungunhane's final speech or discourse), recounts his final words before sailing away into exile. The apocalyptic speech is presented here as retold by an old man who had been there. Ngungunhane's final prophetic pronouncements resonate with Adamastor's threats. Ironically, the curses that both Adamastor and Ngungunhane pronounce on the Portuguese appear to actually have fallen upon Mozambique during and immediately following colonialism, a situation of which Khosa is poignantly aware.

Khosa recognizes the violence inherent in any representation. He appears to be working in two directions: (1) against the colonial demonization of Ngungunhane and (2) against the reappropriation of Ngungunhane by Frelimo as the "Herói da resistência à ocupação colonial" (Hero of resistance against colonial occupation). Yet, having been influenced by French literary theory, Khosa is aware of the violence of his own text. He makes it impossible to distinguish between the historical and the fictional. Although the title of his book is literally the historical name of the warrior who assassinated Ngungunhane's brother, I assert that Khosa also chose the title for another reason. The very title of the book may be broken down as a false etymology to imply "howling pen" ("ulular," to howl, "lápis," pencil). The very (re) writing of history inherent in the construction of a national identity thus howls within the text.

If the violence of *Ualalapi* is one of historical representation, then that of Khosa's collection of short stories is one of the contemporary brutality of life. In *Orgia dos loucos*, Khosa moves back and forth between the city and the country, and the stories present snapshots of common life. A quote by Jorge Viegas that Khosa includes as an epigraph to the collection asserts that insanity is the only form of liberty permitted, ("A unica forma de liberdade permitido"). In "Fragmentos de um diário," a mother has given up hope; Dolores writes lucidly in her diary of her visits to her mother in a psychiatric hospital and of her decision to kill herself and her son. The insanity was not within Dolores, but all around her. The presence of insanity also resonates with *Ualalapi*, in which, besides Ualalapi himself, Ngungunhane's son also goes mad during his return from Portugal.

Khosa works often with inversions. The colonizers frequently portrayed the Africans as bloody savages; "A praga" is a kind of macabre response to that representation. At the end of the story the son "comia as crostas das feridas mal saradas que cobriam o corpo" (was eating the scabs of the hardly healed sores that covered his body). The father shouts at him to stop. Khosa writes, "Por entre os lábios havia bocados de sangue e pequenas crostas" (between his lips there was lots of blood and small scabs), and the son answers his father, "Estou com fome, pai" (I'm hungry, dad). In "Morte inesperada," a father decides to go to school despite an earlier pledge that he had sworn not to. As he is waiting for the elevator, he sticks his head through a small window to see if it is coming. Unable to draw his head back, he is trapped and dies. The description is grueling. As the alarm rings, his children are crying and tugging at his pant legs. The man's attempt to progress socially and financially is thus ended by the rather symbolic elevator.

Although Khosa's stories are haunting and caustic, they are not all pessimistic. Khosa concludes the collection with a short fable, "Fábula do futuro" (Fable of the future). In it he compares the flow of a river to "a democracia na natureza" (democracy in nature). However, as with many of the members of *Charrua*, for there to be progress, there is a need that they get behind the plow. If the presence of exaggeration in *Ualalapi* was in Damboia's menstruation and another woman's milk that was enough to feed several villages, in *Orgia dos loucos* it is in sweat. For example, in the ironic story "O prémio," the sweat from a woman in labor overflows the room and runs up the walls. The future of Mozambique cannot be left to itself or be spoken of only in dreams and ideas.

CRITICAL RECEPTION

In 1990 *Ualalapi* won the Grande Prémio de Ficção Narrative (Grand Prize for narrative fiction) in Mozambique and was reissued by a Portuguese publishing house. *Orgia dos loucos*, published by the Associação de Escritores Moçambicanos, is more difficult to access and has received little notice. *Ualalapi* has provoked considerable discussion, though as yet very little published scholarship. In a brief article on *Ualalapi*, João de Melo calls the book "uma viagem crepuscular e algo apocalíptico ao tempo e ao mito daquele que reinou sobre as terras e as gentes de Gaza" (a twilight journey and apocalyptic of the time and myth of the one who reigned over the land and people of Gaza). Referring to Khosa's colleagues, some of the poets from *Charrua*, Lusophone scholar Russell G. Hamilton calls them "Audacious Young Poets" (*Research in African Literature* 26.1 [Spring 1995]: 85–96), though a member of *Charrua* is cited in Medina's collection as angrily opposed to being categorized as "jovens" (young).

Undoubtedly scholarship will increase as Lusophone African literature in general continues to enter the mainstream of literary and postcolonial discourse. For example, it is useful to consider Khosa's writing in terms of Gayatri Spivak's notion of the "subaltern." Following Khosa's own suggestion on the influence of Gabriel García Marquez, scholars may begin to examine the comparisons and contrasts with magic realism in general. Taking up the cue cited at the beginning, critics will undoubtedly also begin to study *Ualalapi* in terms of theories that dismantle the distinctions between literature and history, which Khosa, as a historian, plays with. Ungulani Ba Ka Khosa is still an actively engaged author, and there is likely more to come.

BIBLIOGRAPHY

Works by Ungulani Ba Ka Khosa

"Damboia" (excerpt from *Ualalapi*). Trans. David Brookshaw. *Literary* Review 38.4 (Summer 1995): 606–613.
Orgia dos loucos. Karingana 13. Maputo: Associação de Escritores Moçambicanos, 1990.
Ualalapi. Colecção Início 6. Maputo: Associação de Escritores Moçambicanos, 1987. New Edition. Uma Terra Sem Amos 50. Lisboa: Caminho, 1990.

Selected Sources on Ungulani Ba Ka Khosa

Ba Ka Khosa, Ungulani. Interview. By Ilídio Rocha. *Jornal de Letras, Artes, & Ideias* 11.466 (June 11, 1991): 5–6.
———. Interview. By Patrick Chabal. *Vozes Moçambicanas*. Lisboa: Vega, 1994. 309–15.
Chabal, Patrick. *Vozes Moçambicanas*. Lisboa: Vega, 1994.
———, ed. *The Post-Colonial Literature of Lusophone Africa*. Evanston, IL: Northwestern University Press, 1996.
Costa, Daniel da, and Fátima Mendonça, organizers. "Qu'est-ce que la littérature mozambicaine?" (a roundtable with Eduardo White, Ungulani Ba Ka Khosa, Armando Artur, and Leite de Vasconcelos). *Littérature du Mozambique*. Paris: Notre Librairie, 1993. 77–81.
Melo, João de. "*Ualalapi* e a literatura moçambicana." *Jornal de Letras, Artes, & Ideias* 11.469 (July 2, 1991): 13.
Medina, Cremilda de Araújo. "Primeira abordagem. Nas praias do Índico." *Sonha Mamana África*. São Paulo. Edições Epopeia, 1987. 21–29.

JARED BANKS

ELLEN KUZWAYO (1914–   )

BIOGRAPHY

Ellen Kuzwayo, the only daughter of Phillip Serasengwe and Emma Mutsi Merafe, was born on June 29, 1914, and grew up on a large family farm, Tshiamelo (Place of goodness), which she inherited in 1930. In 1974 the farm was declared a white area and taken from her by the South African government. This and many other acts of racist violence and violation she and her family experienced prompted Kuzwayo to commit her life to resisting racial discrimination. Simultaneously, however, and in the spirit of what such scholars as Nigerian Chikwenya Okonjo Ogunyemi and African-American Alice Walker have termed womanism, Ellen Kuzwayo has fought against the second-class status of African women living under apartheid. (When applying for her first passport, Kuzwayo was forced to get the permission of her eldest son, himself a minor.)

Called "the mother of Soweto," Kuzwayo was detained without trial for five months in 1978; moved by the resilience of the twelve-and thirteen-year-old girls who sang songs of freedom in adjacent cells, she became known for her care of Soweto's children and her establishment of self-help projects for women. Throughout her life she has striven to retrieve and to create for African peoples a sense of personal and cultural wholeness denied and denuded under apartheid rule. Kuzwayo's efforts have received international recognition and funding; she administered one British trust fund with the help of the Soweto Women's Self Help Coordinating Council, the Black Housewives League, and other women's organizations. The council was renamed the Zamami Soweto Sisters Council; "Zamami," which means "make an effort," encapsulates Kuzwayo's personal and political goal to gain autonomy for African peoples and African women in particular. She has been active in community life and welfare, serving as president of the Black Consumer Union of South Africa and of the Maggie Magaba Trust.

Although Kuzwayo grew up in the country, she has lived most of her life in the explosive urban terrain of Soweto. She has been a schoolteacher, social worker, political activist, writer, mother, and wife. Her parents divorced two years after Ellen's birth, and although she spent the next four years happily ensconced in her grandparents' home, surrounded by the warmth of extended family and community, her family life was saddened by the untimely death of her mother when Ellen was sixteen years old, and by the inexplicable cruelty shown her by her mother's youngest sister, Blanche, with whom she lived at Thaba'Nchu, and who made Ellen's life a misery. Her adult life was similarly saddened by an abusive husband (Kuzwayo, otherwise so forthright in *Call Me Woman*, cannot bring herself to speak of the violence of her marriage to Ernest Moloto, to whom she bore two sons, Everington Matshwene and Justice Bakone). After her 1947 divorce from Moloto, an experience of humiliation exacerbated within apartheid's racist and patriarchal justice system, Kuzwayo met and married Godfrey Kuzwayo, with whom she had a third son, Godfrey.

In her sixties Kuzwayo returned to the University of the Witwatersrand in Johannesburg to study for a higher qualification in social work. She was chosen as Woman of the Year in 1979 by the Johannesburg newspaper the *Star* and was nominated again in 1984.

Kuzwayo came to writing late in life, producing two landmark works. *Call Me Woman*, her 1985 autobiography, called attention to the spirit and successes of South African women, revised Western notions of autobiography by focusing as much attention in her life story on other women's lives as on her own, and, in Nadine Gordimer's words, "Africanised the Western concept of woman." (Kuzwayo, 1985: xi). Her 1990 collection of stories and fables, *Sit Down and Listen*, was born out of Kuzwayo's need to recover her cultural heritage for those generations rent from their families and their cultures by apartheid. She demonstrates remarkable sympathy in her work and in her writing for the frustrations and the militancy of black South African youth struggling against apartheid's inhumanities. She has also helped to make two films, *Awake from Morning* and *Tsiamelo: A Place of Goodness*, both of which have been internationally distributed. She played the part of a skokian (home-brewed beer) queen in the film *Cry the Beloved Country*, a role congruent with Kuzwayo's sympathy for those African women forced into illegal work by their dispossession and disenfranchisement under apartheid. As she says, "It is not easy to live and bring up children in a community robbed of its traditional moral code and values; a community lost between its old heritage and culture and that of its colonists" (Kuzwayo, *Call Me Woman*, 21).

MAJOR WORKS AND THEMES

If Ellen Kuzwayo's collection of simple stories and fables, *Sit Down and Listen*, is an effort to educate Western readers and the children of South Africa about the contemporary urban and rural experience that informs the politics of black South African identities, her autobiography, *Call Me Woman*, attempts more specifically to educate her audience about the politics of African women's identities. As a genre, it represents what Mary Louise Pratt in *Imperial Eyes: Travel Writing and Transculturation* refers to as "autoethnography," a term for lifewriting that seeks to revise, ironize, contest, and confront colonial representations of colonized peoples (7). *Call Me Woman* provides a platform for the presentation of African women's individual and collective contributions to the advancement of African society in South Africa. Both of Kuzwayo's works serve a tutelary function by attempting to provide a context for the stories they tell; they also extend from an oral tradition of storytelling as a means of education. According to Kuzwayo, tradition is meant to ground individual and communal identity and to confer a sense of cultural continuity, belonging, and wholeness to its recipients. This is, therefore, the function of her writing.

An oral tradition informs the structure, style, and method of storytelling and explanation in both works. In *Call Me Woman* Kuzwayo addresses her audience from the first, implicating them as participants in and witnesses to her exploration of the personal and political lives of people enduring the vicissitudes of South African apartheid. Her inclusion of her audience contrives a conversational mode of address in keeping with the collaborative and communal spirit of her "autobiography," in which the story of the individual is indivisible from the stories of her community. Her impulse is at once to correct Western preconceptions of African women as singular, as stereotypical, as victim, and to enable generations of African children (who would otherwise inherit an incomplete history) to understand their place as Africans living within a political, social, and economic context that has ruptured cultural wholeness and continuity.

The story of Ellen Kuzwayo's life is the story of the lives of the women and men of her family, her community, her personal and professional lives, her past, and her present. Revising Western autobiographical tendencies and traditions, in which the focus is usually on the individual, Kuzwayo writes about herself as one among many; her life is relational, communal. She can only tell her story fully if she tells the story of others, for, as an African proverb rather inelegantly translates into English, "A person is a person because of another person." The notion of the self as individual and autonomous is subverted as Kuzwayo's "autobiography"—"autoethnography"—becomes a collection of the biographies of women who have influenced their communities through their spirits of resilience and activism. Writing as a woman and a womanist, Kuzwayo demonstrates how African women negotiate a dialectic of individuality and community; they strive for autonomy within community, revising Western notions of autonomy even as they revise those African traditions that subordinate women. Throughout her autobiography Kuzwayo claims African women's simultaneous imperatives to resist racism alongside their menfolk in the cause of national liberation and to resist all forms of sexism they endure as Africans and as women. Significantly, then, Kuzwayo names herself "Woman" in the title of her autobiography; such an appellation signals, she suggests, a source of great pride. It is enough. It aligns her with all the great women she celebrates in a book that becomes in many ways a roll of honor—a praise song—to the unsung heroines of South Africa. She represents herself as just one of many models of women's strength in the womanist posture of "healing" the wounds and divided consciousnesses of African subjects working toward personal and cultural wholeness for all African peoples. Within the content of her autobiography it becomes apparent that she could well have added "African" to the "woman" of her title; it is African women her work so proudly describes.

Kuzwayo's later work, *Sit Down and Listen*, follows an imperative similar to that evident in *Call Me Woman*; her collection of frequently nonfictional tales extends into textuality an oral tradition of passing on tutelary lessons of experiential history and morality. Often the nonfiction and the fictional accounts derive their source from the immediate community and the experiences of its members; as often, however, the stories have been established in previous generations and have been passed on through repeated telling in a tradition of continuity and rootedness in heritage and local history. For Kuzwayo, the combination of fiction and nonfiction, of symbolic and "realistic" suggestibility, works to create a womanist vision of wholeness, maneuvering between and within the subtleties of cultural continuity and change. As her title so forcefully admonishes, Kuzwayo wants her audience to take the time to "sit down"—to pay attention to what she has to tell them—and "listen." She commands authority and demands respect in her bold and teacherly title. She asks us to imagine that we are engaging in an oral contract, hearing through the text a spoken history and culture, signaling the urgent need for the outside world to listen to those voices muted by apartheid. Her command to listen is issued not only to the outside world, but also to the children of South Africa, the generation she sees as torn from their traditional roots and denied the lessons of their people's pasts. Her work is pedagogical and often didactic, offering an alternative sociological history; the stories are documentaries in which the players and their dramas are drawn from "real life."

The collection reveals the encounter between past and present, tradition and change, orality and literacy, and official history and alternative, personal histories. The stories, told with great flourish, often focus on the pedestrian details that are the stuff of individual lives. They tell the lives of people disenfranchised and legally silenced under apartheid, revealing the politics of division, of economic and social exploitation, of class oppression, of gendered inequities, of cultural invalidation, and of resistance. The stories combine the legendary and the contemporary, the mythic and the quotidian. Kuzwayo becomes the "arranger'' of stories she inherits, stories she creates; she also offers commentary on clusters of stories within the collection. The effect is dialogic; conversations are implicitly established between author and material, between stories that double, pair, shadow, mimic, resonate, and ''speak to'' each other. The structure and style of *Sit Down and Listen* determine ''dialogia'' (Bakhtinian concept), approximating conversation and orality.

The characters of *Sit Down and Listen* are in no way elevated because of their Africanness; indeed, they are seen to be fallible, frequently failing and falling as they attempt to live within the fraught terrain of personal and cultural invalidation. Failings are seen, too, within traditional roles and expectations. In ''One of Many,'' the male protagonist, Mosa, finds himself caught at the crossroads of tradition and Western indifference to and derision of that tradition; such ambivalence characterizes many of the stories. Although many of her characters, the men especially, might appear devoid of moral fabric or community loyalty, Kuzwayo's framing of the tales forbids such easy stereotyping; no matter how seemingly unobtrusively, the racism of apartheid insinuates its Manichean mechanisms into every possible corner of African urban and rural existence, working to unsettle any semblance of African cultural continuity or stability. But African community is not so easily dismantled. As Kuzwayo observes, ''It is something of a miracle that we have managed to retain any vestige of our traditional values'' (*Sit Down and Listen*, 111). Both *Sit Down and Listen* and *Call Me Woman* participate in creating that miracle.

CRITICAL RECEPTION

Although Ellen Kuzwayo has written two major works in her lifetime, she and those who write about her do not consider writing to be her primary work; her community work is the source of her greatest attention and her highest accolades. Indeed, to this date, there is apparently no critical work in print on *Sit Down and Listen*. By contrast, Kuzwayo's autobiography has received significant attention from literary critics interested in women's writing as resistance and in autobiography as a genre; *Call Me Woman* has undoubtedly stretched Western expectations and appreciations of autobiography. In her article ''(In) Continent I-Lands: Blurring the Boundaries between Self and Other in South African Women's Autobiographies,'' Judith Lutge Coullie notes how Kuzwayo's autobiography forces a reappraisal of Western notions of individual identity, of individual ontology; selfhood is communally defined for ''praise-singer'' Ellen Kuzwayo, whose selfhood is predicated upon her relational identity. Not only does Kuzwayo present herself as just one of the victims of apartheid (and, therefore, just one of the heroes in the fight against racism), she defines herself as ''a palimpsest of the innumerable selves of South African Black women'' (140). Julie Phelps Dietche, writing about Kuzwayo, Emma Mashinini, and Caesarina Kona Makhoere, observes how these women's experiences in South African prisons propelled them into speaking out against apartheid, into finding their voices and breaking the tacit silences of disenfranchisement. Imprisonment heightened the urgency to tell the stories of their lives as Africans and as women. In writing, Kuzwayo "defies not only the authorities but also the image of herself as afraid, victimized, silenced, unable to articulate her visions of her self and her people" (64); writing becomes an act of resistance. It is as a resistance writer and a resistance fighter in the lesser-known ranks of community life and work that Ellen Kuzwayo, still living, will be remembered.

BIBLIOGRAPHY

Works by Ellen Kuzwayo

Call Me Woman. Johannesburg: Ravan Press, 1985.
Sit Down and Listen. London: Women's Press, 1990.

Selected Studies of Ellen Kuzwayo

Clayton, Cherry. "Ellen Kuzwayo." *Between the Lines: Interviews with Bessie Head, Sheila Roberts, Ellen Kuzwayo, Miriam Tlali.* Ed. Craig MacKenzie and Cherry Clayton. Grahamstown: National English Literary Museum, 1989. 57–68.
Coullie, Judith Lutge. "(In) Continent I-Lands: Blurring the Boundaries between Self and Other in South African Women's Autobiographies." *Ariel* 27.1 (1996): 133–48.
———. "The Space between Frames: A New Discursive Practice in Ellen Kuzwayo's *Call Me Woman.*" *South African Feminisms: Writing, Theory, and Criticism, 1990–1994.* Ed. M. J. Daymond. New York: Garland, 1996. 131–53.
Davies, Carole Boyce. "Private Selves and Public Spaces: Autobiography and the African Woman Writer." In *Crisscrossing Boundaries in African Literatures, 1986.* Ed. Kenneth Harrow, Jonathan Ngate, and Clarissa Zimra. Washington, D.C.: Three Continents Press and the ALA, 1991. 109–27.
Dietche, Julie Phelps. "Voyaging toward New Freedom: New Voices from South Africa." *Research in African Literatures* 26.1 (1995): 61.
Eko, Ebele O. "The Undaunted Spirit of South African Womanhood: Ellen Kuzwayo's *Call Me Woman.*" *Literature and National Consciousness.* Ed. Ebele Eko, Julius Ogu, and Azubuiko Iboeje. Ibadan, Nigeria: Heinemann, 1989. 233–44.
Elder, Arlene. " 'Who Can Take the Multitude and Lock It in a Cage?': Noemia de Sousa, Micere Mugo, Ellen Kuzwayo: Three African Women's Voices of Resistance." *Matatu: Journal for African Culture and Society* 3.6 (1989): 77–100.
Hollyday, Joyce. "Beacons of Freedom." *Sojourners* 17.11 (1988): 16.
Ibrahim, Huma. "The Autobiographical Content in the Works of South African Women Writers." *Biography: East and West.* Ed. Carol Ramelb. Honolulu: University of Hawaii Press, 1989. 122–26.
Lewis, Desiree. "Myths of Motherhood and Power: The Construction of 'Black Woman' in Literature." *English in Africa* 19.1 (1992): 35–51.

LINDSAY PENTOLFE AEGERTER

ALEX LA GUMA (1925–1985)

BIOGRAPHY

Two factors, both of them intimately associated, account for the sociopolitical and ideologically charged nature of Alex La Guma's fiction: his nurture in Cape Town's notorious and impoverished District Six, and the political activism of his father, Jimmy La Guma. Growing up in Cape Town brought La Guma face to face with the gritty reality of the life of South Africa's dispossessed and victimized people. When he began his career as a writer in 1955 for the *New Age*, a left-wing weekly, he wrote several articles on Cape Town's street life, the matrix from which his first short novel *A Walk in the Night* (1962) sprang. Jimmy La Guma was a militant union organizer, a member of the South African Communist Party, and president of the South African Colored Peoples' Congress. Alex himself became a member of the Communist Party when the Afrikaner Nationalist Party introduced apartheid to South Africa in 1948. His father's relentless struggles against oppression must have shaped and moulded Alex's growing sensibilities; and the son, moreover, must have inherited from the father his unflagging determination to destroy apartheid and restore equality and justice to all South Africans.

Alex La Guma and his wife Blanche paid a high price for their opposition to South Africa's brutal regime. He was one of 156 political leaders arrested and charged with treason in 1956. The trial dragged on for years, and although he was eventually acquitted in 1960, La Guma and his wife suffered several years of continual police harassment, imprisonment, and house arrest after his acquittal. There was, furthermore, an attempt to assassinate him at his home in May 1958. Two of La Guma's searing novels, *A Walk in the Night* (1962) and *And a Threefold Cord* (1964), were written while he was in prison or under house arrest.

In 1966 La Guma and his family went into exile in London, where he served for several years as chairman of the London district of the African National Congress. While in exile he was awarded the first Lotus Prize for Literature by the Afro-Asian Writers Association. In October 1985 La Guma died of a heart attack in Havana, Cuba, where he had lived since 1978 as the Caribbean representative of the ANC.

MAJOR WORKS AND THEMES

The dehumanizing process that South Africa's apartheid system inflicts upon both oppressor and oppressed is a continually recurring theme in Alex La Guma's fiction. All of La Guma's fictional strategies and the imagery he consciously or subconsciously chooses reinforce and enhance this dominant theme. His novels and short stories—for instance, ''Out of Darkness'' (1963) and ''Tattoo Marks and Nails'' (1964) introduce the prison imagery as well as the brutalized and depraved characters later developed in *The Stone Country* (1967)— depict South Africa as an area of spiritual, emotional, and physical incarceration; and the country's nonwhite residents are merely animals to be restrained, hunted down, tortured, and, if necessary, killed. Animal and cave imagery, noticeable in ''Out of Darkness'' and prominent in *And a Threefold Cord*, La Guma's first full-length novel, pervades his fiction. The oppressive bleakness of *And a Threefold Cord*, at the center of which is the horrifying immolation of Freda's children in one of the settlement's shanties, encapsulates the desolation, the despair, and the dehumanizing of South Africa's dispossessed, who have been reduced by apartheid to the status of animals. La Guma's wretched of the earth can aspire only to mere survival, and this is symbolized in Charlie Pauls's rickety house that groans ''like a prisoner on the rack'' (*And a Threefold Cord*, 41), yet survives the relentless, pounding rain with a stubbornness that recalls the defiance of the tortured Elias in *In the Fog of the Seasons' End* (1972).

La Guma's language and carefully chosen symbols reinforce the unrelieved bleakness and futility in the lives of the oppressed. For instance, the black sky is a powerful symbol in La Guma's fiction. In *In the Fog of the Seasons' End* there are strategic references to the oppressive black sky on the morning of the strike that the authorities suppress with brutal force. Several of La Guma's characters, such as Beukes, the ordinary, yet resolutely defiant, resistance worker of *In the Fog of the Seasons' End*, are consumed in the metaphorical darkness of interminable dread. Darkness, furthermore, has the lethal power of a plague in La Guma's work, and it infects and destroys victim and victimizer. Constable Raalt of *A Walk in the Night* is an automaton who hunts down and brutalizes his human prey with the cold and callous indifference one associates with the jungle. Indeed, the theme of predator and prey is prominent in this novella as well as in *The Stone Country*. The human and physical dereliction of *A Walk in the Night* reappears in *In the Fog of the Seasons' End*, where animal imagery and oppressive darkness are succinctly drawn together in several concrete images suggesting human and physical dereliction.

Violence is also pervasive in La Guma's fictional world. When violence is not being perpetrated by the oppressor, it simmers close to the surface in the oppressed. This sense of imminent explosion and brutality is forcefully conveyed by La Guma's emotionally charged prose in *A Walk in the Night* and *Time of the Butcherbird* (1979), for example. Hatred and violence grow like a fetus in the bellies of the embittered Willieboy, recently fired from his job, and Shilling Murile, who returns home from jail to take revenge for his murdered brother. La Guma's tendency to juxtapose light and darkness enhances his treatment of violence and hatred. Fog, haze, smoke, and nuances of light and shade are important symbols in La Guma's fiction. These symbols are linked with war and resistance, and La Guma uses them to drive home the brutal reality of the oppressive state, a reality often hidden behind a mask of congeniality. For instance, the benign and avuncular Major of *In the Fog of the Seasons' End* conceals the horror of the South African regime, which he serves, behind a mask of politeness and innocuousness. La Guma, however, often counterpoints appearance and reality. One notices this in his fondness for juxtaposing passages of idyllic pastoralism and the prosaic realities concealed beneath the surface. Thus Elias's Edenic countryside of silence and birdsong hides the destitution and ignorance of the people, just as the prison's beautiful facade conceals the brutality behind the stone walls in *The Stone Country*. In the short story "The Lemon Orchard" (1967) the moonlit, lemon-scented environment is set against the severe punishment the victim is about to receive.

Mask and disguise are important motifs in La Guma's work. Sometimes they take the form of denial or escape from the dehumanizing society. In *In the Fog of the Seasons' End* Tommy's adolescent obsession with ballroom dancing compensates for his depersonalized status in society; and Beatie Adams's apolitical and complacent attitude protects her from the brutalities beyond the safe and comfortable walls of her white employer's house. But La Guma relentlessly exposes the grim reality behind the oppressor's mask. For instance, his focus on the oppressor's eyes is a good deal more than fondness for the close-up detail. He often draws one's attention to the impenetrably cold and hard features of eyes, faces, and skulls. Although the oppressor's mask is always in place, his eyes reveal the true nature of the evil they seek to mask. Behind the mask is an individual who has become a desensitized automaton in the service of an ignoble regime.

La Guma's fictional world, for all its bleakness and moral darkness, is not nihilistic. La Guma's emphasis is not on the personal fulfillment of individual characters; instead, his fiction points to the eventual fulfillment of South Africa's dispossessed peoples. The relentless darkness of *A Walk in the Night*, for example, is relieved by the promise of future retribution and continuing opposition to the regime that is metaphorically conveyed at the end when Joe, one of La Guma's feckless youngsters, hears waves pounding against granite rock. Elias's death by torture in *In the Fog of the Seasons' End* also carries the promise of retribution and regeneration. Elias's defiance is rooted in his recollection of his African ancestors' resistance to white settlers who are now resuscitated in his torturers. The endings of *In the Fog of the Seasons' End* and *And a Threefold Cord* are also charged with regenerative symbols. In the latter, the bleak and negative images are counterpointed by the image of a simple but compelling beauty adamantly asserting itself in the rubbish dump at the edge of the squalid Settlement. Here a solitary carnation stands "like hope blooming in an anguished breast" (*And a Threefold Cord*, 154). The carnation, we may say, resembles Beukes, a simple, unremarkable, but defiant man born of the very grime that would have prevented his conception. The South African bird being released from long captivity is also symbolically conveyed at the end of *And a Threefold Cord* when Charlie Pauls sees through the driving rain a bird suddenly darting from the roofs of the derelict shanties and winging its way skyward. *Time of the Butcherbird* ends with a flourish of images, all of which suggest sterility. La Guma, however, undercuts the drought and searing heat that the imagery emphasizes with a final, telling description of a flight of birds swooping toward a water hole.

La Guma's fiction dramatically demonstrates that apartheid is the original act of violence. Although the violence bred of apartheid has increased since his death in 1985, recent events in South Africa, such as the creation of a multiracial Transitional Executive Council empowered to govern the country until the first nonracial elections in 1994, and the subsequent election of Nelson Mandela as the first black president of South Africa, underscore the prophetic nature of La Guma's work.

CRITICAL RECEPTION

La Guma's fiction has attracted the attention of several commentators, many of whom, not surprisingly, analyze La Guma's work in terms of the author's political ideology. Kathleen Balutansky, J. M. Coetzee, David Rabkin, Abdul JanMohamed, and Emmanuel Ngara are representative. In *The Novels of Alex La Guma: The Representation of a Political Conflict*, Balutansky argues persuasively that La Guma the political activist and La Guma the writer are inseparable. The result of this union is that La Guma chooses an aesthetic that "focuses on the collective experience of oppression and struggle rather than on individual experience" (2). Balutansky reads *Time of the Butcherbird*, La Guma's last novel, as the culmination of this aesthetic since the novel's symbolic ending "structurally counters the reality of Afrikaner oppression" (127). Balutansky, however, is dissatisfied with the subordinate role of women in La Guma's world, which, she claims, is largely masculine (124). Coetzee also stresses the collective experience in La Guma's fiction. In "Man's Fate in the

Novels of Alex La Guma'' Coetzee traces the development of La Guma's themes from the ''aimless revolt of individuals without allies or ideology to the fraternal revolt of men who understand and combat oppression'' (21). Coetzee regards *In the Fog of the Seasons' End* as the culmination of La Guma's sociopolitical themes: the ''new collective resistance,'' he writes, ''is the new protagonist'' (21). Rabkin discusses the role of South African society in La Guma's fiction. Stress falls on ''the moral character'' of this society instead of on ''the personal and moral development of individual characters'' (''La Guma and Reality in South Africa,'' 61). This emphasis, Rabkin argues, distinguishes La Guma's novels from ''the typical procedures of the novel form'' (61). Abdul JanMohamed offers a detailed analysis of La Guma's treatment of the marginal status of disfranchised South Africans in his *Manichean Aesthetics: The Politics of Literature in Colonial Africa*. The structure and style of La Guma's writing, JanMohamed says, ''reflect the spiritual attenuation of life that results from socio-political disfranchisement'' (225), and the novels chronicle ''the effects of the manichean bifurcation imposed by apartheid'' (227). JanMohamed, too, makes much of La Guma's emphasis on the need for a collective resistance to apartheid. In *Art and Ideology in the African Novel: A Study of the Influence of Marxism on African Writing*, Ngara discusses *In the Fog of the Seasons' End* as a dramatization of the struggle of the oppressed proletariat against their oppressors. The novel's implicit theme, Ngara maintains, is the certainty of the successful socialist revolution and the proletariat's victory. This is suggested in the novel's concluding symbol of the sun rising in the east (97). Ngara also discusses La Guma's narrative techniques and use of language. He claims that characters such as Tommy, Bennett, Flotman, and Isaac are ''types,'' and that Beukes and Elias, ''the only developed characters,'' do not match the ''roundness'' of Ousmane's and Ngugi's main characters (92).

Other commentators such as Gerald Moore, Robert Green, and Adewale Maja-Pearce are largely concerned with the literary qualities and techniques of La Guma's fiction. In *Twelve African Writers*, Moore writes perceptively of La Guma's exceptional gift for description and evocation. Although he thinks that La Guma's descriptive passages are ''occasionally overdone'' (115), Moore believes that La Guma achieves his best effects in the novel and not in the short story. He cites, for example, *Time of the Butcherbird*, which he describes as remarkable for its recollection of rural South Africa after thirteen years of exile, as well as ''the poetic interpretation of landscape and action'' (120). Moore also cites *In the Fog of the Seasons' End*, where La Guma has controlled ''the exuberance of his descriptions'' and has replaced his occasional excesses with ''the ironic juxtapositions'' of *The Stone Country* (117).

Neither Robert Green nor Adewale Maja-Pearce shares Moore's tendency to dismiss La Guma's short fiction. Both critics have shed much light on La Guma's skills as a short-story writer. One of La Guma's strengths, Green shows, is his ''selfless management of the narrator's persona, the creation of an authentic voice for each story'' (''Chopin in the Ghetto: The Short Stories of Alex la Guma,'' 7). La Guma's short stories, Green also argues, are powerful evocations of "the brutalizing effect of apartheid . . . and man's ability to survive" (5); and La Guma's fiction emphasizes, furthermore, "the fearful ordinariness" of that brutality (10). In "The Victim as Hero: Alex la Guma's short Stories," Maja-Pearce gently takes Robert Green to task for describing La Guma's stories as "protest writing" (73). Maja-Pearce maintains that the absence of a stable social order in Africa is particularly suited to the short-story form, and she shows that La Guma's short stories explore the lives of the victimized men and women bred of this instability. Although she notes that "in straining for effect" La Guma "sometimes falls into sentimentality" (73), she points to La Guma's gift for understatement, and she compares La Guma's and Hemingway's short stories and finds that La Guma's "victims are almost as inarticulate." However, Maja-Pearce claims that behind La Guma's rage there is a compassion that appears to be "lacking in Hemingway" (71). This compassion "is rooted in his desire to understand rather than judge" black and white, both of whom are prisoners of apartheid (72).

BIBLIOGRAPHY

Works by Alex La Guma

A Walk in the Night and Other Stories. Ibadan: Mbari, 1962.
Quartet. Ed. Richard Rive. London: Crown Publishers, 1963.
And a Threefold Cord. Berlin: Seven Seas, 1964.
The Stone Country. Berlin: Seven Seas, 1967.
Apartheid: A Collection of Writings on South African Racism by South Africans. Ed. Alex La Guma. New York: International, 1971.
In the Fog of the Seasons' End. London: Heinemann, 1972.
A Soviet Journey. Moscow: Progress, 1978.
Time of the Butcherbird. London: Heinemann, 1979.
Memories of Home: The Writings of Alex La Guma. Ed. Cecil Abrahams. Trenton, N.J.: Africa World Press, 1991.

Selected Studies of Alex La Guma

Abrahams, Cecil. *Alex La Guma*. Boston: Twayne, 1985.
Balutansky, Kathleen. *The Novels of Alex La Guma: The Representation of a Political Conflict*. Washington, D.C.: Three Continents Press, 1990.
Barratt, Harold. "South Africa's Dark Night: Metaphor and Symbol in La Guma's Fiction." *Literary Griot* 3.2 (Fall 1991): 28–36.
Chandramohan, B. *A Study in Trans-ethnicity in Modern South Africa: The Writings of Alex La Guma*. Lewiston, N.Y.: Mellen, 1992.
Coetzee, J. M. "Man's Fate in the Novels of Alex La Guma." *Studies in Black Literature* 4 (Winter 1974): 16–23.
Ezeigbo, T. "A Sign of the Times: Alex La Guma's *Time of the Butcherbird*." *Literary Half-Yearly* 32.1 (January 1991): 100–114.

Green, Robert. "Chopin in the Ghetto: The Short Stories of Alex La Guma." *World Literature Written in English* 20 (Spring 1981): 5–16.

JanMohamed, Abdul. *Manichean Aesthetics: The Politics of Literature in Colonial Africa*. Amherst: University of Massachusetts Press, 1983.

Made, Pat, and Beverley Abrahams. *Study Guide to In the Fog of the Seasons' End*. Harare: Baobab Press, 1993.

Maja-Pearce, Adewale. "The Victim as Hero: Alex La Guma's Short Stories." *London Magazine* 24.3 (1984): 71–74.

Moore, Gerald. *Twelve African Writers*. London: Hutchinson, 1980.

Ngara, Emmanuel. *Art and Ideology in the African Novel: A Study of the Influence of Marxism on African Writing*. London: Heinemann, 1985.

Nkosi, Lewis. *Tasks and Masks: Themes and Styles of African Literature*. London: Longman, 1981.

Povey, John F. "The Political Theme in South and West African Novels." *Africa Quarterly* 9 (1969): 33–39.

Rabkin, David. "La Guma and Reality in South Africa." *Journal of Commonwealth Literature* 8 (June 1973): 54–62.

Sougou, Omar. "Literature and Apartheid: Alex La Guma's Fiction." *Bridges* 4 (December 1992): 35–47.

Updike, John. "Shades of Black." *New Yorker* 49 (January 21, 1974): 84–94.

Western, John. *Outcast Cape Town*. Minneapolis: University of Minnesota Press, 1981.

HAROLD BARRATT

CAMARA LAYE (1928–1980)

BIOGRAPHY

The oldest son of a large family, Camara Laye was born in 1928 in Kouroussa, Upper Guinea, into one of the most respected Malinké clans. His father was a goldsmith who, though a practicing Muslim, maintained strong ties with Malinké culture and kept a small black snake in his bed (King, 2). Laye was raised as a Moslem and as a young child attended a Koranic school before continuing his education in a school established by the French.

As a child, he went through the traditional initiations of Malinké culture, including the ritual of Kondén Diara (the ceremony of lions) and ritual circumcision, references to which reappear in his first novel, *L'enfant noir* (*The African Child*). Indeed, the happy childhood described in *L'enfant noir*, ignorant of the impingement of European culture on African traditions, seems to have been much Laye's own.

After finishing the course of study at his town's French school, Laye attended a vocational school in Conakry, Guinea's capital, where he was separated from his family for the first time. In Conakry, he met Marie Lorifo, who would later become his wife. He did quite well in school, receiving a first in his mechanical aptitude examination and earning a scholarship to allow him to continue his studies in Paris. In 1947, at age nineteen, Laye left for Paris, where he would remain until 1956. There he studied in Argenteuil at the Central School of Automobile Engineering, gaining certification as a mechanic. When his scholarship expired after the first year, Laye chose to remain in France. He worked at the Simca auto-assembly plant doing odd jobs, meanwhile attending night school and working to pass his baccalaureate. Many of his experiences as a student in Paris reappear in *Dramouss* (*A Dream of Africa*), his third novel.

In 1953, while working on his degree, he published *L'enfant noir*. The book was written in an effort to battle his homesickness for his native land while living in Paris. It is highly autobiographical, consisting of a sort of act of memory, an attempt to bring himself into contact with Guinea again: "I was writing as one dreams; I was remembering; I was writing for the pleasure of it" (quoted in Lee, 14). With Negritude poets such as Léopold Senghor and Aimé Césaire active in France and with the continuing publication of *La Présence Africaine* (starting in 1947), the intellectual scene in France was favorable for African writers. *L'enfant noir* was well received as a portrait of African life and as a literary work. The novel was awarded the Prix Charles Veillon. The same year Laye arranged for Marie to come to Paris, where he married her. The following year he published a book that many consider his best, *Le regard du roi* (translated as *The Radiance of the King*), which made him a celebrity both in France and in Africa.

In 1956, dissatisfied with the materialistic side of French life, Laye left France and returned to Africa, first to Dahomey (present-day Benin) and after that to Ghana. When Guinea became an independent republic in 1958, Laye returned to his homeland to participate in the nation's reorganization. He was made the first ambassador to Ghana and helped Guinea obtain aid from Ghana when France cut off assistance (aid was restored in 1959). He served in a number of posts outside of the country before returning to Conakry to take charge of the Department of Economic Agreements. From 1963 to 1965 he served as the associate director of the National Institute of Research and Documentation, where he began to gather material on the oral traditions of his area from the griots (the griots are genealogists and storytellers, the keepers of knowledge). Here can be found the beginnings of his sessions with the griot Babou Condé, and his gathering of material for his last book, *Le maître de la parole* (translated as *The Guardian of the Word*). He also wrote weekly radio plays for Radio-Conakry, which were broadcast every Sunday morning, one of which reappeared in different form in *Dramouss* as "the Griot's tale."

In 1963 Laye participated in a two-part conference on African literature held at the University of Dakar in Senegal and at Fourah Bay College in Sierra Leone, where he read two important papers. His last years in Guinea were difficult. He was imprisoned for a brief period of time and for several years was practically under house arrest. When Guinea severed diplomatic ties with France in 1965, and Sekou Touré's regime swung closer to dictatorship, Camara Laye and his family obtained permission to leave the country on the pretext of travelling for health reasons. He never returned. He took with him the manuscript of his third novel, *Dramouss*, which was published in 1966 in Paris. In this novel, he speaks of his disenchantment with Touré and the revolution.

He settled in Senegal with his family, where he was given a position as a research fellow at the Institut Fondamental d'Afrique Noire, but it was not a lucrative one. His finances strained, he found it increasingly difficult to support his wife and seven children. In Senegal, as part of his assignment, he continued to work with oral traditions, travelling in a Land-Rover through the country to listen to griots tell their stories.

Several years after his arrival in Senegal, his wife Marie received a cable stating that her father, who was very ill and who had just been released from prison, was desperate to see her before his death. Despite Laye's opposition, she chose to fly back to Guinea. At the airport she was arrested and imprisoned for seven years. Laye, left alone to care for seven children, took a second wife, Ramtoulaye Kanté, by whom he had three more children.

By 1971 Laye had written a novel called *L'Exil* (*Exile*). Besides attacking the Guinean regime, the book contained sensitive political material whose release might have been harmful to Laye and his family, particularly to his imprisoned first wife. For this reason, he was advised against publishing the novel and chose not to. During this period he was actively involved in the movement opposing Sekou Touré and was in contact with liberation groups in France, Africa, and the United States.

In 1975 Laye became ill with a kidney infection and was hospitalized. He needed to go to Paris for specialized treatment if he was to survive, but did not have the money to do so. Reine Carducci, the wife of the Italian ambassador to Senegal, became aware of his situation and launched an international campaign to raise funds to pay for his medical expenses. Plon reprinted Laye's work in conjunction with the campaign, and sufficient money was raised in royalties and donations that he was able to go to Paris for treatment.

In 1977 Marie was released from jail after pressure from Laye's publisher and from Reine Carducci. Unwilling to accept Laye's second wife, Marie filed for divorce. The following year Laye published his last work, *Le maître de la parole*, which is a retelling of a Mali epic, the *Soundiata*, as told to Laye by the master griot Babou Condé. In the following year the book received a prize from the French Academy. He was in the process of gathering folktales for children when his kidney infection flared up again. He died in exile in 1980 in Dakar at the age of fifty-two.

MAJOR WORKS AND THEMES

Despite his refusal to make his literature overtly political, Laye was quite politically active. He worked in the Guinean government for a time, but then opposed what he saw as its move toward dictatorship, even struggling to bring the regime down. For Laye, literature and politics were largely separate fields— indeed, the book written while his wife was imprisoned, *Le maître de la parole*, is the least political of all his books, turning away from contemporary life and back to traditional stories.

The Guardian of the Word suggests an interest in traditional epic that is less evident, but still present, in his earlier work. Indeed, several of the projects Laye began but never completed involved continuing the epic tradition. Among these, he wrote most of a modern epic whose central character was President Houphouët-Boigny of the Ivory Coast. He also considered composing with a griot the saga of the Réssemblement Démocratique Africain (Lee, 13), an organization that worked for African emancipation and unity. Laye was interested not only in the traditional narratives, but in the way these traditional narratives could be used to give meaning and power to contemporary life.

Of his four works, *L'enfant noir (The African Child)* has been the most widely read. It and *Dramouss* are essentially autobiographical works, drawing quite strongly on the author's experiences in Africa and France. *L'enfant noir* is the story of Fatoman, an African child with an upbringing similar to Laye's. The book explores the mysteries of childhood, the wonder of the simple events that Fatoman experiences as a child without fully understanding them, a wonder that he hopes to regain through his narrative evocation of his youth. *L'enfant noir* is also a celebration of Malinké culture and tradition and includes moments in which this culture is actively practiced in ways that seem to contradict Western rational thinking. Fatoman's father, for instance, converses with a snake, and his mother is respected as a benevolent witch. Both mother and father serve as representatives of a life outside of Western culture. Rather than trying to oppose the traditional world to the new world of Western culture and technology, Laye writes almost as if the impingement of Africa by the Western world was not occurring. He is not interested in the clash of cultures, but in the celebration of a single culture. This was the reason for the book's popularity, but also grounds for resentment by other African authors, some of whom felt that the book was idyllic and insufficiently engaged.

Laye's second book, *Le regard du roi (The Radiance of the King)*, is more consciously a novel than is *L'enfant noir*. It confronts mystical and philosophical issues through a quest that might be read as an allegory of the human condition. In *L'enfant noir*, Africa is a source of comfort to the child, even if he does not fully understand all that goes on around him. In *Le regard du roi*, however, Africa has become for Clarence, the white protagonist, a sort of code. Everything seems to be happening just beyond his perception, everybody seems to be laughing but him. Whereas the child of *L'enfant noir* finds himself easing slowly into the unfamiliar European world, with no real idea of the ramifications of this move, Clarence the European is thrown into Africa without skills and without knowledge, his only desire being to serve the king. The king, however, seems an inaccessible figure. The novel becomes a quest, leading Clarence through roundabout paths to finally realize his goal of serving the king.

In many respects, the novel is similar to the novels of Kafka, particularly *The Trial*—Clarence and Joseph K. seem to occupy similar worlds, both being lost in them. However, the character of Clarence is not angst-ridden as is Joseph K., not representative of what European literature then considered the modern condition. In addition, Clarence's quest succeeds, whereas none of Kafka's characters seem able to penetrate the law. There is a level of hope not present in Kafka: as Laye says, "Contrarily to Kafka and his characters, I have never felt isolated nor abandoned in this spiritual world'' (quoted in Lee, 46). Though the world is perhaps absurd, it is not a world of resentment or angst.

In *Dramouss* (*A Dream of Africa*), Laye continues the story of Fatoman, the protagonist of *L'enfant noir*, as he arrives in Guinea to visit his family after six years in France. On his first day in Conakry, his uncle informs him that they have taken care of the formalities for his marriage to his girlfriend, Mimie, whom he has not seen since he left Guinea, and the two are married on the spot. Much of the novel revolves around Fatoman's readjustment to his relationship with Mimie and, in a larger sense, to his relationship with Africa.

Generally considered Laye's least successful novel, *Dramouss* explores many complex issues, without sufficiently developing any of them. The novel presents the problems faced by African students in France as well as the difficulties in readjusting to life in Africa on their return. The question of how to reconcile African and European culture, which plays a major part in much of Laye's work, is nowhere more evident than in *Dramouss*. We see both cultures through the eyes of Fatoman, and we experience his growing appreciation for both. In typical fashion, Laye acknowledges the good that the French had done in Guinea, refusing to blame all the problems of Guinea on foreign intervention. This refusal to blame the French stems from Laye's confidence in the power of traditional African culture to take care of the continent's own problems. Near the end of the novel, Laye juxtaposes a griot's story and a political meeting. Fatoman comes to consider that the traditional songs and stories of Malinké culture will benefit the country much more than the roads and buildings that the politicians promise.

Dramouss is highly critical of the political situation that existed in Guinea at the time of its appearance. It accuses the political parties of impatience, violence, and insufficient attention to traditional culture and society. At this time, Sekou Touré's regime was becoming increasingly repressive and violent, and Laye attempted to present this to an audience that knew little of what was actually happening in Guinea.

Despite the focus on political evils, *Dramouss* is not an entirely pessimistic novel. Fatoman at the end of the novel has the chance to converse in a dream with the snake to which his father talks in *L'enfant noir*. This snake, named Dramouss, has the power to reveal the future. In the dream, Dramouss rescues Fatoman from a prison where he is being held for no reason and where he is about to be put to death. After his rescue, a black lion, a symbol of traditional culture, breaks apart the repressive regime, bringing peace to Guinea.

Laye's final work, *Le maître de la parole* (*The Guardian of the Word*), is in fact a translation of the *Soundiata*, an ancient Mali epic, based on a transcription Laye made of the story, as told to him by the griot Babou Condé. The culmination of many years of work collecting stories and recording the songs of griots across much of West Africa, *Le maître de la parole* is an evocative blend of story and song, history and art. Laye always had a strong link through his family to traditional Malinké culture, and he felt the need to preserve these songs and epic stories before they were lost forever. Yet it would be wrong to see this book as only a transcription of an ancient tale, for it is infused throughout with Laye's own concerns, and it is clear that for him the tale is not a dead one—it is as applicable to contemporary Africa as it was to traditional Africa. In the introduction to the epic, Laye discusses the importance of both physical and spiritual needs, but his primary concerns here, as in all his work, are spiritual and emotional, and he dedicates this retelling of the *Soundiata* to the "African soul." For Laye, this story and, more importantly, the telling of the story have a tangible, magical power.

Soundiata, the hero of the tale, was the first emperor of Mali. He reigned from 1230 to 1255 A.D. *Le maître de la parole* recounts his birth, his eventual exile, his rise to power, and his victorious return to his native land. The book spends most of its time in the early part of the hero's life, with his life as a child. It maintains the idiosyncrasies of oral presentation, including frequent songs and narrative intrusions. It is perhaps most profitably read aloud.

CRITICAL RECEPTION

Laye's critical reception has varied and has often been vastly different in Europe and Africa. *L'enfant noir*, which won the Prix Charles Veillon, was well received both in France and Africa, although some African reviewers felt that it was not sufficiently committed to politics. For European readers, the book appealed because it provided an inner glimpse of an African child's daily life and revealed African ritual from an insider's perspective. For African writers and critics such as Mongo Beti, however, the book seemed to lack commitment and depth and seemed to be a deliberate refusal to confront the problem of Africa's collision with Europe.

Le regard du roi, which is now generally acknowledged as Laye's finest book, received a similar reception. While it was well received by French critics, African critics approached the book with less enthusiasm. Mongi Beti again attacked Laye for his politics, and to his voice was added that of playwright Wole Soyinka, who attacked Laye for what he saw as a weak plagiarization of Kafka. More recent African criticism, however, has come to see the novel as spiritually and philosophically very rich, and as sharing certain projects and ideas with Negritude (Jahn, 35–38). Even Soyinka, in more recent writings, seems to have taken a more positive view of the novel.

Dramouss, which has more of a political dimension than *L'enfant noir*, has lost much of the aesthetic strength of the first novel. Its reception was mixed. Its artistic qualities, critics felt, were secondary to its political content. Although critics in Africa had encouraged Laye toward a more active political stand earlier, they did not seem fully willing to support him when he in fact took one.

Le maître de la parole received the Prix de l'Académie Française. The book received quite respectful reviews in both Africa and Europe. However, while Laye's first two books have received a good amount of critical attention, his last book has been almost passed over. Perhaps this is in part due to its being a transcription and translation: critics are less willing to think of it as an original work, as a strong part of Laye's canon.

Laye's reception in English has been complicated by James Kirkup's translations of his work. These translations, despite their poetic qualities, are often inaccurate and occasionally omit whole sentences and paragraphs. Certain scenes and sections are toned down or heightened or modified, according to Kirkup's personal preferences and according to his beliefs about what African literature should be. Apparently colonization can take place on the page as well as in life (discussed in King, 103–7).

Though he wrote only four novels, Camara Laye is likely to be remembered as an important contributor to French-African literature. His first two works continue to be actively read and respected, and because of their aesthetic strengths, they promise to be read for a long time to come.

BIBLIOGRAPHY

Works by Camara Laye

L'enfant noir. Paris: Plon, 1953. Translated by James Kirkup as *The African Child*. New York: Farrar, Straus and Giroux, 1969.

Le regard du roi. Paris: Plon, 1954. Translated by James Kirkup as *The Radiance of the King*. New York: Collier, 1971.

"Et demain?" *Présence Africaine* 14–15 (1957): 290–95.

"Les yeux de la statue." *Présence Africaine* 13 (1957): 102–10.

Dramouss. Paris: Plon, 1966. Translated by James Kirkup as *A Dream of Africa*. New York: Collier, 1971.

"The Black Man and Art." *African Arts* 4 (1970): 58–59.

Le maître de la parole. Paris: Plon, 1978. Translated by James Kirkup as *The Guardian of the Word*. London: Collins, 1980.

Studies of Camara Laye

Achiriga, J. J. "*L'Enfant noir* and *Le Regard du roi*." *La révolte des romanciers noirs de langue française*. Ottawa: Naaman, 1973. 32–65.

Jahn, J. "Camara Laye: An Interpretation." *Black Orpheus* 6 (1959): 35–38.

King, Adèle. *The Writings of Camara Laye*. London: Heinemann, 1980.

Larson, Charles R. "Assimilated Negritude: Camara Laye's *Le Regard du roi*." *The Emergence of African Fiction*. Bloomington: Indiana University Press, 1972. 167–226.

Lee, Sonia. *Camara Laye*. Boston: Twayne, 1984.

Moore, Gerald. "Camara Laye: The Aesthetic Vision." *Twelve African Writers*. Bloomington: Indiana University Press, 1980. 85–104.

BRIAN EVENSON AND DAVID BEUS

DORIS LESSING (1919–   )

BIOGRAPHY

Although Doris Lessing was actually born in Persia and has lived in England since 1949, she is considered an African author because the twenty-five years that she spent growing up on a small farm in what was then Southern Rhodesia had such an impact on her writing. African critic Anthony J. Chennells notes that she is one of only two "settler novelists" included in the 1987 *Tabex Encyclopedia Zimbabwe* (Sprague, *In Pursuit*, 17). Lessing is described by American critic Judith Gardiner as a "colonial in exile" whose work is characterized by "a fruitful unsettledness that makes . . . [her both an] inheritor . . . and [an] antagonist . . . to imperialism. . . . The English literary tradition is the reassuring heritage of a mother tongue, but it is also somewhat alien" (13).

Lessing is marked not only by the colonial's ambiguous relationship to the English literary tradition but also by the landscape of Africa that creates a unique perspective on humankind. Lessing says in the introduction to *African Stories*:

I believe that the chief gift from Africa to writers, white and black, is the continent itself, its presence which for some people is like an old fever, latent always in their blood; or like an old wound throbbing in the bones as the air changes. That is not a place to visit unless one chooses to be an exile ever afterwards from an inexplicable majestic silence lying just over the border of memory or of thought. Africa gives you the knowledge that man is a small creature, among other creatures, in a large landscape. (6)

It is thus not only her novels that are literally set in Africa, such as *Children of Violence* series or *The Golden Notebook*, but her later works as well that are influenced by the land of her upbringing. Lessing's interests in Jungian thought, alternative consciousnesses, and Sufism that pervade her "inner space fiction" could well be the result of her search for the "majestic silence lying just over the border of memory." The insight that a human being is "a small creature, among other creatures, in a large landscape" pervades Lessing's "outer space fiction," her *Canopus in Argos: Archives*. Her 1992 book *African Laughter* is an account of her return visits to her homeland after years of being a "prohibited immigrant." The first volume of her autobiography, *Under My Skin*, which covers the years from her birth to her departure for England in 1949, was published in 1994.

Doris Lessing was born on October 22, 1919, in Kermanshah, Persia (now Iran), the eldest child of Alfred Cook Taylor and Maude McVeagh Taylor. Lessing's parents met in a hospital during World War I where Maude McVeagh nursed Alfred Taylor after his leg was amputated. Lessing said to Roberta Rubenstein in 1977 that both her parents were "acutely neurotic people": "My father was done in by the [F]irst [W]orld [W]ar, from which he never really recovered, and my mother had what is known as an unfortunate upbringing, her mother dying when she was three or so, and she never got over that" (Rubenstein, 177). Alfred Taylor worked as a clerk for the Imperial Bank of Persia, but when Doris was five, they left for Rhodesia. Lessing explains the move in an essay entitled "My Father" in *A Small Personal Voice*: "I am sure it was true he wanted to leave Persia because of 'the corruption.' But it was also because he was already unconsciously longing . . . [to] let go into the dreamlogged personality that was waiting for him" (89–90). With their life savings the Taylors bought a farm several hundred miles south of the Zambezi River and a hundred miles west of Mozambique. Alfred Taylor was an unsuccessful farmer and his wife was embittered by their poverty, but Doris and her younger brother Harry valued their childhood freedom to roam the bush around their farm.

Both children were sent away from the farm for their education. Harry was sent to Ruzawi School, and Doris to a Dominican convent school in Salisbury. In *African Laughter* Lessing says:

The Convent was what [my mother] . . . had to have for me. Like Ruzawi it was a snobbish choice. To me it was a dark oppressive place full of women loaded with their black and white serge robes who smelled bad when it was hot. I knew it was a bad place, but not how bad, until I was grown up. I was there for five years and it did me harm: I am still learning how much harm. (25)

At thirteen Lessing transferred to Girls' High School in Salisbury, but she left a year later. Her formal education ended at age fourteen. Like her heroine Martha Quest, Lessing read extensively on her own, particularly nineteenth-century novels.

At sixteen Lessing went to work for the telephone company and then for some attorneys in Salisbury. In 1939 she married Frank Wisdom and had two children, Jean and John. She used that marriage as a basis for her portrayal of

Martha Quest's marriage to Douglas Knowell in *A Proper Marriage*. She divorced Frank Wisdom after four years, and he kept custody of their children. Lessing then became active in a Marxist group. She explains that in Africa the "Communist party had an enormous effect on politics because it ignored the color bar. In the Communist party white and black people worked together on the basis of equality" (*A Small Personal Voice*, 74; Ingersoll, *Doris Lessing*, 16). Although the Communist Party was formally banned in Southern Rhodesia, the members of Lessing's group called themselves Communists, and Lessing incorporated some of their experiences in several of her novels. In 1945 she married Gottfried Lessing, a half-Jewish East German who had escaped the Nazis and come to Rhodesia but was nevertheless interned for six weeks in a prison camp. He was the model for Anton Hesse in *A Ripple from the Storm* and for Willi Rodde in *The Golden Notebook*, whom Lessing describes as being "the emotional centre of our sub-group [of Communists] . . . because of his absolute certainty that he was right. He was a master of dialectic . . . [but he] despised people who allowed their lives to be disturbed by personal emotions" (Bantam edition, 71, 73). In 1947 their son, Peter Lessing, was born, and two years later they divorced.

In 1949 Doris Lessing left for London with Peter and the manuscript of her first novel, *The Grass Is Singing*. Gottfried Lessing returned to East Germany, where he later became commissar of trade. Lessing's "documentary," *In Pursuit of the English*, describes her life in the early 1950s in a working-class district of London as she struggled to support herself and establish her name as a writer. Lessing continued to be active in politics and march against the atom bomb, as she describes in *The Four-gated City*, but she grew increasingly disillusioned with the Communist Party in England even before Khrushchev's denunciation of Stalin and the invasion of Hungary in 1956. At that point she left the party. She still, however, was labeled a "prohibited immigrant" in Rhodesia because of the criticism of colonialism in her novels. Although she managed to visit Rhodesia once in 1956, which she wrote about in *Going Home*, she was not to return again until 1982.

In the 1950s Lessing became established as a writer, publishing not only *The Grass Is Singing*, which was made into a movie, but also a volume of short stories, *This Was the Old Chief's Country*, a Marxist novel, *Retreat to Innocence*, and the first four volumes of *Children of Violence*, which she described as "a study of the individual conscience in its relations with the collective" (*A Small Personal Voice*, 14). In pursuing her interest in the individual mind as well as the collective, Lessing underwent Jungian analysis and then studied Sufism with Idries Shah. Her Jungian therapist appeared as "Mother Sugar" in *The Golden Notebook*, and Sufism influenced many of her later novels. Lessing also became friends with the radical psychoanalyst R. D. Laing. His ideas about schizophrenia influenced *Briefing for a Descent into Hell* and other novels in which she analyzes mental breakdowns. Lessing was embraced by feminists upon the publication of *The Golden Notebook* in 1962, but she felt uncomfortable with the label. She says in a Preface to *The Golden Notebook* written in 1971, "I don't think that Women's Liberation will change much . . . because it is already clear that the whole world is being shaken into a new pattern by the cataclysms we are living through: . . . if we do get through . . . the aims of Women's Liberation will look very small and quaint" (Bantam edition, viii–ix).

By the 1970s Lessing achieved international recognition. She won the Prix Medici in 1976. By the 1980s her works had been translated into many languages. In 1982 she won the Shakespeare Prize of the West German Hamburger Stiftung and the Austrian State Prize for European Literature. In 1987 she received the Palermo Prize and the Premio Internazionale Mondello. She traveled extensively during the 1980s to America, Europe, Africa, and Asia. She has been nominated several times for the Nobel Prize.

During the 1980s she wrote her series of science-fiction novels, *Canopus in Argos: Archives*, but she interrupted this series in 1983 by writing two books pseudonymously as Jane Somers. She kept a London setting for two subsequent novels, *The Good Terrorist* and *The Fifth Child*, and her latest volume of short stories, *London Observed* (U.S. title, *The Real Thing*). Her recent book *African Laughter* chronicles four visits to Zimbabwe, in 1982, just after the war, and in 1988, 1989, and 1992. In *African Laughter* Lessing mixes memories of her childhood in the bush with analysis of current political situations and descriptions of her work with African women's writing projects, and she again affirms that the basis for all her work is her African experience: "Every writer has a myth country. This does not have to be childhood . . . my myth [was] the bush I was brought up in, the old house built of earth and grass, the lands around the hill, the animals, the birds. Myth does not mean something untrue, but a concentration of truth" (35). This theme will probably be expanded in the autobiography that Lessing is currently writing. She also has plans for a sixth volume of the *Canopus in Argos: Archives* series, set on the evil planet, Shammat.

MAJOR WORKS AND THEMES

Lessing's eighteen novels, six nonfiction works, and many short stories span continents and even galaxies in their setting and range in style from the realism of her early works to the surrealism of her descriptions of madness to the science fiction of her recent works, but all her writings focus on the issue of difference. The nature of the difference may vary from racial and national difference to class, gender, or age difference and even to species difference, but the awareness of issues of power, control, and exploitation that she saw as a child in colonial Rhodesia has marked all her work.

Lessing's first novel, *The Grass Is Singing*, focuses on racial difference in the story of the murder of a white farm woman, Mary Turner, by her black servant, Moses. The novel links a Marxist analysis of poverty and colonialism with a study of Mary's mental breakdown. In its concentration on the character of Mary, the novel is an indictment of white colonial society and attitudes. Moses is primarily a symbol of the exploitation of black Africans; his motivations are not given. There is a short flashback of Mary's impoverished childhood and violent father, but most of the novel describes her life with her husband, Dick Turner, who is a weak man and an unsuccessful farmer. With no antidote to loneliness and poverty, Mary slowly disintegrates. Her handsome servant, Moses, whom she had once whipped across the face, shows her kindness and finally becomes her caretaker. This reversal of roles causes alarm to other white settlers in the area, and their neighbor decides to buy the Turner farm and send over an assistant to help Dick Turner manage it. When Mary Turner sees the young assistant, she tries to order Moses to leave. Mary collapses into insanity and is murdered by Moses, who then waits passively for the police. The novel's title is taken from T. S. Eliot's "The Wasteland," and the poem's tone echoes throughout this bleak portrait of the wasteland of white colonialism.

Lessing's next two novels, *Martha Quest* (1952) and *A Proper Marriage* (1954), move away from the detachment of *The Grass Is Singing* to form the beginning of a bildungsroman of five novels, *Children of Violence*, the first four of which are set in Lessing's fictional African colony, Zambesia. These five novels draw upon Lessing's own life for many of their situations, including Martha Quest's childhood on the veld, her two marriages, her involvement in the Communist Party, and her emigration to London. They portray a broad spectrum of both white colonial life in Africa and mid-twentieth-century life in London. Motifs that run throughout the series are the veld, the city, and the house. In the first novel, Martha Quest is a young girl who loves the veld, the African landscape, but is desperately trying to escape the parochial white colonial culture and her controlling mother. She has an apocalyptic vision of a noble, four-square city, a just city, whose inhabitants live together without racial, ethnic, and national division. She searches for that city, trying first an affair with a young Jewish boy, Adolph King, to prove to the white "Sports Club Crowd" that she is not as narrow as they. That relationship dissolves, and she tries a conventional marriage with Douglas Knowell, which she finds no more satisfying. *A Proper Marriage* describes the stultifying existence of young married couples in a colonial town in the 1940s. One day Martha looks out her window to see a revolving ferris wheel at a distant fair. She suddenly sees her life as nothing but an endless repetition of colonial existence, of her mother's life, and decides to leave Knowell and her child. *A Proper Marriage* is acclaimed by feminists both for its portrayal of the potentially stifling qualities of conventional marriage and for its vivid naturalistic scenes of childbirth.

Lessing took a break from *Children of Violence* in 1956 to write not only the account of her return to Rhodesia, *Going Home*, but also a novel set in London, *Retreat to Innocence*. This novel explores difference in an affair between a young, apolitical English girl and an older, exiled Czechoslovakian Communist. Although Lessing has said that she is dissatisfied with this novel, it was a chance to explore the political themes that became dominant in *A Ripple from the Storm* and *Landlocked*, the next two novels in the *Children of Violence series*. Both novels portray the activities of a Communist group in wartime "Zambesia." Lessing describes the intense idealism of people like Martha who are looking for an alternative to colonialism and fascism, but she also critiques political group dynamics. These novels include Martha's second marriage to an East German Communist, Anton Hesse, and later her intense and transforming affair with Thomas Stern, a Polish Jew and refugee, who travels to Israel to fight for the emerging state, but later dies of a fever in an African village.

Lessing's most famous novel, *The Golden Notebook* (1962), was acclaimed worldwide, especially by feminists. Issues of difference, particularly those in contemporary politics, in colonial wartime Africa, and in the lives of women writers, are embedded in its experimental, almost "postmodern" structure. The novel has five sections. Each section is introduced by an episode entitled "Free Women" and then followed by episodes from each of four differently colored notebooks. The final section is entitled "The Golden Notebook." The "Free Women" episodes focus on the lives of Anna Wulf and her friend Molly Jacobs in contemporary London, where Anna and her young daughter Janet share a flat with Molly and her troubled teenage son Tommy. The Black Notebook discusses Anna's professional life as a writer, such as dinners with television producers, her successful novel of an interracial affair in Africa, and the source of that novel in her memories of wartime years in Africa. The Red Notebook discusses Anna's work as a volunteer editor for the Communist Party and her growing disillusionment, particularly with the party's rigid criteria of social realism for fiction. The Yellow Notebook is a novel within a novel. It is Anna's story about two women, Ella and Julia, who parallel Anna and Molly, and Ella's affair with a doctor, Paul Tanner, who parallels Anna's lover Michael in "Free Women." The Blue Notebook is shaped like a diary with references to Anna's sessions with "Mother Sugar," her Jungian therapist, newspaper clippings from the 1950s on political events, and ideas for stories. "The Golden Notebook" recounts Anna's affair with an American writer, Saul Green, who is based on Lessing's friend Clancy Sigel. Lessing explores the lessons to be learned from temporary madness as both Saul and then Anna descend into their respective madnesses and potentially work through their writers' blocks. (Lessing explored this theme again in *Play with a Tiger*.) The novel ends with one last section of "Free Women" in which Anna and Molly continue with their lives in London.

In 1969 Lessing published the last novel in *Children of Violence* series, *The Four-gated City*. This novel describes Martha Quest's experiences in postwar London. The novel is a brilliant portrayal of a city from a female colonial's point of view. When Martha rides past Trafalgar Square and Nelson's Column, she does not identify with Britain's past; in fact, she thinks of "the haphazard insignificance of . . . [Trafalgar Square], and the babyish statue" and laughs to think that this "is the hub of the Empire" (22). Martha becomes a secretary for Mark Coldridge and eventually runs his household and raises his children because his wife Lynda, who lives in the basement, is mentally ill. The symbolism of the house becomes particularly important in this novel, especially as Martha goes down into the basement and enters Lynda's psyche to learn about the deep places of the human mind. Martha experiments with inducing madness in herself and recognizes that like Lynda, she has psychic gifts. The novel proper ends in 1968 as Mark and his new wife plan to move to Tunisia to build an ideal city, but an apocalyptic appendix is added that is set in the future after an environmental or nuclear disaster has destroyed much of the world. Because of their telepathic gifts Lynda and Martha are able to save a few people who were living in Britain. One of them is a young African boy, Joseph Batts, whom Martha manages to send to Mark's son Francis in Nairobi. Although Martha, Lynda, and Mark all die by the end of the novel, there is some hope that Joseph, who also has psychic gifts, may survive and rebuild civilization.

Lessing's next three novels, which she calls "inner space fiction," develop the analysis of madness that Lessing began to explore in *The Four-gated City*. In *Briefing for a Descent into Hell* (1971), Lessing explores the visions of Charles Watkins, who is a mental patient suffering from amnesia. Watkins's dreams include travel to strange deserted cities where he sees Jungian archetypal creatures. Draine notes that Lessing moves away from realism in this novel into the didactic form of an "apologue," which emphasizes a rhetorical message rather than the representation of experience (106–7). Even though the structures of *The Golden Notebook* and *The Four-gated City* are experimental, their style remains realistic. Lessing's "inner space fiction" thus represents a new direction in her technique. *The Summer before the Dark* (1973) contains some of the same analysis of madness, but it is more popular among readers because it returns to some of Lessing's feminist themes and is more realistic in style. Kate Brown is a bourgeois British woman whose children have grown up and whose husband is unfaithful. The external experiences of an impressive job as a translator and an affair in Spain with a younger man do not resolve her "midlife crisis." When Kate is forced by illness and madness to look inside, however, she begins to learn about herself. She has a recurrent dream of a seal that she must return to the ocean. After Kate manages to finish her dream and save the seal, she goes back to her family but leaves her hair undyed, a small symbol of her new encounter with aging and illness. The last novel in this group, *The Memoirs of a Survivor* (1974), begins where *The Four-gated City* ended, in a city that is disintegrating. Services are collapsing and gangs of youth rove the city streets. The unnamed narrator begins to see visions in one of the walls of her flat where at times she relives parts of her own childhood and at other times she sees archetypal gardens and magic spaces. Sufi thought merges with Jungian thought in her visions. As the outer reality gets worse, the narrator manages literally to walk through the wall into the inner reality and take with her the young girl, Emily, whom she has been taking care of, Emily's boyfriend, Gerald, one of the gang leaders, and Emily's strange cat/dog animal. In this novel Lessing clearly moves away from realism into a visionary mode. In 1981 *The Memoirs of a Survivor* was made into a film by David Gladwell.

Even though readers had become used to Lessing's departure from realism, no one was prepared for Lessing's venture into outer space in *Canopus in Argos: Archives*. In these five novels, issues of colonialism and imperialism are projected onto a galactic scale where the good forces of Canopus battle the evil forces of Shammat to try to bring about an evolution of beings on "Shikasta," a symbol for earth. As Carey Kaplan notes, it is disturbing for readers used to Lessing's stern critique of imperialism in her early novels to see a good "imperialism" in Canopus, but Kaplan suggests that since it "is unlikely that Lessing has become a racist . . . she may very well be an ageist. That is, the Canopeans have all the virtues associated with age: experience, wisdom, aloofness from emotional hysteria, long-sightedness" (Kaplan and Rose, *Doris Lessing*, 155). The first volume, *Re: Colonised Planet 5, Shikasta* (1979), is a veiled history of the earth, originally called Rohanda and now in its failing years called Shikasta, as reported by Johor, a Canopean agent. The novel ends, as did *The Four-gated City*, with a worldwide holocaust. The second volume, *The Marriages between Zones Three, Four, and Five* (1980), shifts format from the dry reports of an agent to a fable that is influenced by Sufi mysticism and evolving levels of consciousness. Queen Al.Ith of Zone Three, which is a calm matriarchy, is forced by "the Providers" to marry Ben Ata of the militaristic and masculine Zone Four. This is no simple marriage of opposites, however, for no sooner have Al.Ith and Ben Ata worked through their mutual distrust than Ben Ata is ordered to marry the savage Queen Vahshi of Zone Five. Al.Ith journeys to higher consciousness in the airy realm of Zone Two.

The Sirian Experiments (1981) returns to the style of *Shikasta* and is narrated by a Sirian agent, Ambien II. The Sirians are also colonizers of Shikasta, but unlike the Canopeans, their methods are sometimes flawed. Ambien journeys throughout "Shikastian" history, experiencing the dangers of an Aztec-like civilization with human sacrifice and a fundamentalist Muslim civilization where she must conceal herself in a heavy black garment. Lessing says of Ambien in the preface:

I have created a female bureaucrat who is dry, just, dutiful, efficient, deluded about her own nature . . . a social scientist. I could like Ambien better than I do. Some of her preoccupations are of course mine. The chief one is the nature of the group mind, the collective minds we are all part of, though we are seldom prepared to acknowledge this. (ix)

Volume 4, *The Making of the Representative for Planet 8* (1982), pursues the creation of a collective mind in the story of the death of Planet 8 in an ice age. The inhabitants were to be taken to Rohanda, but when Rohanda degenerated into Shikasta, the space lift became impossible. The inhabitants fight bravely against the ravages of ice and cold, but cannot survive. Several of them finally go off into the mountains and leave their physical nature behind to merge into a single consciousness, "the representative" of Planet 8. The novel ends in mysticism, but the suffering and deprivation described are very real. The composer Philip Glass collaborated with Lessing to make an opera of this novel in 1988.

Lessing says in a long afterward to *The Making of the Representative for Planet 8* that she was influenced in her writing of it and *The Sirian Experiments* by accounts of the Antarctic explorations of Robert Falcon Scott, who had been a great hero to her parents. Lessing marvels about the way his reputation has changed over the years, linking it to changing historical viewpoints and her own political experiences about Africa:

I was one of the handful of people who in the early fifties tried to get journalists, members of Parliament, politicians to see that things were not well in southern Africa. To say we were talking about criminally oppressive tyrannies was then not possible. . . . We were treated with tolerant amusement . . . dismissed as wrong-headed. . . . Inside ten years the idea that what was going on in southern Africa—in South Africa and Southern Rhodesia—should at least be examined, was a respectable view. (127)

Although Lessing is using a galactic geography in these works, she clearly intends parallels with imperialism in Africa and colonial politics.

The fifth novel in the series, *Documents Relating to the Sentimental Agents in the Volyen Empire* (1983), is a short satire on political rhetoric, both Western and Marxist. Canopean agent Klorathy writes about the problems he has with a young agent, Incent, and a colonial administrator, Grice, who both get involved in galactic politics only to succumb to "Attacks of Rhetoric." Lessing parallels this fictional critique of rigid group thought and political rhetoric in the Massey lectures she gave in Canada in 1985, published as *Prisons We Choose to Live Inside*.

Just as she interrupted the *Children of Violence* series to write *The Golden Notebook*, so also Lessing interrupted the *Canopus in Argos* series to write two pseudonymous books as Jane Somers. Although she claims that she did this partly to test the publishing industry, she also acknowledges that the change in name gave her a way to escape that "kind of dryness, like a conscience that monitors Doris Lessing" (Preface, *The Diaries of Jane Somers*, viii). It allowed Lessing to go back to realist fiction and explore the other side of aging. In *The Diary of a Good Neighbour* a successful publisher, Janna Somers, befriends an aging working-class woman, Maudie Fowler, and with her goes through all the physical experiences of illness and dying. In the second novel, Janna takes care of her disturbed niece, Kate, and falls in love with Richard Curtis. They joyfully wander the streets and parks of London, but they both have too many responsibilities to have an affair. Nonetheless, as Jane Somers, Lessing is optimistic that class and age and gender barriers can be crossed.

In her next two realistic novels published under her own name, Lessing is not so optimistic. *The Good Terrorist* (1985) describes a group of angry young people living in a London squat. Alice Mellings is a thirty-six-year-old "hippie" who joins them and makes the squat livable but only facilitates a bombing. Alice is a good housekeeper, but she cannot prevent the waste of young lives. In *The Fifth Child* (1988) issues of difference and violence enter the structure of the traditional family when Ben Lovatt is born. Ben, who is described as "a Neanderthal" and a "throwback," is a violent child who kills family pets and finally joins a roving gang. In spite of the problems he creates, his mother, Harriet, cannot institutionalize him and allow him to be maltreated. In this disturbing novel Lessing illustrates that the human potential for violence lies not in our rhetoric but in our genes. The scariest kinds of difference lie within.

Lessing's most recent novel, *Love Again*, set in England and France, is more benign in tone. It picks up the themes of *The Diaries of Jane Somers* in looking at age, love, and loss. It folds the theatrical imagery tied with the city in the Jane Somers novels into the plot as a group of theater people write a play about a nineteenth-century Creole woman, Julie Vairon, who moved to France from Martinique and became a talented artist and composer living in isolation in a small village. Lessing combines love stories in the present day with nineteenth-century love stories. Lessing also explores familiar themes of race and exile that run through many of her novels.

CRITICAL RECEPTION

There is no doubt that Doris Lessing is one of the major literary figures of the second half of the twentieth century. Her international reputation is secure. Sprague's *In Pursuit of Doris Lessing* describes the different nuances of that reputation in nine nations: Zimbabwe, South Africa, England, the United States, Canada, France, Germany, Spain, and the USSR. Lessing is most popular in the United States, where there have been annual panels on her at the Modern Language Association Convention since 1971 (with a hiatus in 1979). Kaplan and Rose summarize MLA papers through 1985 in *Doris Lessing: The Alchemy of Survival*. The critical journals *Contemporary Literature* and *World Literature Written in English* both had special issues on her in 1973, and *Modern Fiction Studies* had one in 1980. The *Doris Lessing Newsletter*, which Lessing says embarrasses her but which is extremely useful for scholars, has been published continually since 1976. The 1993 MLA International Bibliography lists 358 entries on Lessing for a ten-year period. Worldwide there are a number of dissertations written on her every year, which are listed periodically in the newsletter. Lessing's most popular work is *The Golden Notebook*, which Sprague says has sold over one million copies (*In Pursuit*, 2). It was "canonized" by the MLA in its inclusion in the Approaches to Teaching World Literature series (Kaplan and Rose, 1989) and has been discussed in almost every significant work of feminist criticism since Elaine Showalter's *A Literature of Their Own* in 1977. Not only *The Golden Notebook* but many of Lessing's works are both taught in universities and appreciated by ordinary readers worldwide. She is an extraordinary figure whose search for a just human society inspires all her many readers.

BIBLIOGRAPHY

Works by Doris Lessing

African Laughter: Four Visits to Zimbabwe. New York and London: HarperCollins, 1992.

African Stories (a collection of all her stories set in Africa). London: Michael Joseph, 1964; New York: Simon and Schuster, 1965.

Briefing for a Descent into Hell. London: Jonathan Cape, 1971; New York: Knopf, 1975.

Collected Stories. 2 volumes. London: Jonathan Cape, 1978. Republished as *Stories.* 1 volume. New York: Knopf, 1978.

The Diaries of Jane Somers. New York: Knopf, 1984. Originally published by Jane Somers as *The Diary of a Good Neighbor* and *If the Old Could.* . . . London: Michael Joseph, 1983–84; New York: Knopf, 1983–84.

Documents Relating to the Sentimental Agents in the Volyen Empire (*Canopus in Argos: Archives,* vol. 5). London: Jonathan Cape, 1983: New York: Knopf, 1983.

The Doris Lessing Reader. New York: Knopf, 1988; London: Jonathan Cape, 1989. (The British edition has different selections from the American one.)

''Each His Own Wilderness.'' *New English Dramatists, Three Plays.* Ed. Martin Browne. Harmondsworth, Middlesex: Penguin, 1959.

The Fifth Child. London: Jonathan Cape, 1988; New York: Knopf, 1988.

Five: Short Novels. London: Michael Joseph, 1953.

The Four-gated City (*Children of Violence,* vol. 5). London: MacGibbon and Kee, 1969; New York: Knopf, 1969.

Fourteen Poems. Northwood, Middlesex: Scorpion Press, 1959.

Going Home. London: Michael Joseph, 1957. Rev. ed. New York: Ballantine, 1968.

The Golden Notebook. London: Michael Joseph, 1962; New York: Simon and Schuster, 1962, and Bantam, 1973.

The Good Terrorist. London: Jonathan Cape, 1985; New York: Knopf, 1985.

The Grass Is Singing. London: Michael Joseph, 1950; New York: Crowell, 1950.

The Habit of Loving (short stories). London: MacGibbon and Kee, 1957; New York: Crowell, 1957.

In Pursuit of the English: A Documentary. London: MacGibbon and Kee, 1960; New York: Simon and Schuster, 1961.

Landlocked (*Children of Violence,* vol. 4). London: MacGibbon and Kee, 1965; New York: Simon and Schuster, 1966.

Love Again. New York: HarperCollins, 1995.

The Making of the Representative for Planet 8 (*Canopus in Argos: Archives,* vol. 4). London: Jonathan Cape, 1982; New York: Knopf, 1982.

A Man and Two Women (short stories). London: MacGibbon and Kee, 1963; New York: Simon and Schuster, 1963.

The Marriages between Zones Three, Four, and Five (*Canopus in Argos: Archives,* vol. 2). London: Jonathan Cape, 1980; New York: Knopf, 1980.

Martha Quest (*Children of Violence*, vol. 1). London: Michael Joseph, 1952; New York: Simon and Schuster, 1964.

The Memoirs of a Survivor. London: Octagon Press, 1974; New York: Knopf, 1975.

Particularly Cats (autobiographical essay). London: Michael Joseph, 1967; New York: Simon and Schuster, 1967.

Play with a Tiger: A Play in Three Acts. London: Michael Joseph, 1962. Also in *Plays by and about Women*. Ed. Victoria Sullivan and James Hatch. New York: Random House, 1973. 210–75.

Prisons We Choose to Live Inside (Essays). London: Jonathan Cape, 1987; New York: Harper and Row, 1987.

A Proper Marriage (*Children of Violence*, vol. 2). London: Michael Joseph, 1954; New York: Simon and Schuster, 1964.

Re: Colonised Planet 5, Shikasta (*Canopus in Argos: Archives*, vol. 1). London: Jonathan Cape, 1979; New York: Knopf, 1979.

The Real Thing: Stories and Sketches. New York: HarperCollins, 1992. British title, *London Observed*. London: Jonathan Cape, 1991.

Retreat to Innocence. London: Michael Joseph, 1956; New York: Prometheus, 1957.

A Ripple from the Storm (*Children of Violence*, vol. 3). London: Michael Joseph, 1958; New York: Simon and Schuster, 1966.

The Sirian Experiments (*Canopus in Argos: Archives*, vol. 3). London: Jonathan Cape, 1981; New York: Knopf, 1981.

A Small Personal Voice (essays). Ed. Paul Schlueter. New York: Knopf, 1974; London: HarperCollins, 1994.

The Summer before the Dark. London: Jonathan Cape, 1973; New York: Knopf, 1973.

The Temptation of Jack Orkney (short stories). New York: Knopf, 1972. British title, *The Story of a Non-marrying Man and Other Stories*. London: Jonathan Cape, 1972.

This Was the Old Chief's Country (short stories). London: Michael Joseph, 1951; New York: Crowell, 1952.

Under My Skin: Volume One of My Autobiography, to 1949. New York: HarperCollins, 1994.

The Wind Blows Away Our Words (commentary on Afghanistan). London: Picador, 1987; New York: Random House, 1987.

Selected Studies of Doris Lessing

Bertelson, Eve, ed. *Doris Lessing*. Johannesburg: McGraw-Hill, 1985.

Brewster, Dorothy. *Doris Lessing*. New York: Twayne, 1965.

Cederstrom, Lorelei. *Fine-tuning the Feminine Psyche: Jungian Patterns in the Novels of Doris Lessing*. New York: Peter Lang, 1990.

The Doris Lessing Newsletter. Ed. Ruth Saxton, Mills College, Oakland, Calif. Ongoing, twice a year. Volumes 1–16 (1976–present).

Drabble, Margaret. "Doris Lessing: Cassandra in a World under Siege." *Ramparts* 10 (1972): 50–54. Reprinted in *Critical Essays on Doris Lessing*. Ed. Claire Sprague and Virginia Tiger. Boston: G.K. Hall, 1986.

Draine, Betsy. *Substance under Pressure: Artistic Coherence and Evolving Form in the Novels of Doris Lessing*. Madison: University of Wisconsin Press, 1983.

Fahim, Shadia S. *Doris Lessing and Sufi Equilibrium*. London: Macmillan, 1994.

Fishburn, Katherine. *Transforming the World: The Art of Doris Lessing's Science Fiction*. Westport, Conn.: Greenwood Press, 1983.

Gardiner, Judith Kegan. *Rhys, Stead, Lessing, and the Politics of Empathy*. Bloomington: University of Indiana Press, 1989.

Greene, Gayle. *Doris Lessing: The Poetics of Change*. Ann Arbor: University of Michigan Press, 1994.

Hardin, Nancy. "The Sufi Teaching Story and Doris Lessing." *Twentieth Century Literature* 23 (1977): 314–26. See related essay by Hardin in *Doris Lessing: Critical Studies*. Ed. Annis Pratt and L. S. Dembo. Madison: University of Wisconsin Press, 1974.

Ingersoll, Earl G., ed. *Doris Lessing: Conversations*. Princeton, NJ: Ontario Review Press, 1994.

Kaplan, Carey, and Ellen Cronan Rose, eds. *Approaches to Teaching Doris Lessing's The Golden Notebook*. New York: Modern Language Association, 1989.

———, eds. *Doris Lessing: The Alchemy of Survival*. Athens: Ohio State University Press, 1988.

King, Jeannette. *Doris Lessing*. London: Edward Arnold, 1989.

Knapp, Mona. *Doris Lessing*. New York: Frederick Ungar, 1984.

Pichanik, J., A. J. Chennells, and L. B. Rix. *Rhodesian Literature in English: A Bibliography (1890–1975)*. Gwelo, Zimbabwe: Mambo Press, 1977.

Pickering, Jean. *Understanding Doris Lessing*. Columbia: University of South Carolina Press, 1990.

Pratt, Annis, and L. S. Dembo, eds. *Doris Lessing: Critical Studies*. Madison: University of Wisconsin Press, 1974.

Rose, Ellen Cronan. *The Tree outside Your Window: Doris Lessing's Children of Violence*. Hanover, N.H.: University Press of England, 1976.

Rubenstein, Roberta. *The Novelistic Vision of Doris Lessing: Breaking the Forms of Consciousness*. Urbana: University of Illinois Press, 1979.

Sage, Lorna. *Doris Lessing*. London: Methuen, 1983.

Saxton, Ruth, and Jean Tobin, eds. *Breaking the Mold: Female Identity, Consciousness, and Form in the Fiction of Virginia Woolf and Doris Lessing*. New York: St. Martin's Press, 1994.

Schlueter, Paul. *The Novels of Doris Lessing*. Carbondale: Southern Illinois University Press, 1973.

Seligman, Dee. *Doris Lessing: An Annotated Bibliography of Criticism*. Westport, Conn.: Greenwood Press, 1981.

Singleton, Mary Ann. *The City and the Veld: The Fiction of Doris Lessing*. Lewisburg, Pa.: Bucknell University Press, 1977.

Sizemore, Christine W. *A Female Vision of the City: London in the Novels of Five British Women*. Knoxville: University of Tennessee Press, 1989.

Sprague, Claire, ed. *In Pursuit of Doris Lessing: Nine Nations Reading*. New York: St. Martin's Press, 1990.

———. *Rereading Doris Lessing: Narrative Patterns of Doubling and Repetition*. Chapel Hill: University of North Carolina Press, 1987.

Sprague, Claire, and Virginia Tiger, eds. *Critical Essays on Doris Lessing*. Boston: G.K. Hall, 1986.

Taylor, Jenny, ed. *Notebooks/Memoirs/Archives: Reading and Rereading Doris Lessing*. Boston: Routledge and Kegan Paul, 1982.

Thorpe, Michael. *Doris Lessing's Africa*. London: Evans Brothers, 1978.

Vlastos, Marion. ''Doris Lessing and R. D. Laing: Psychopolitics and Prophecy.'' *PMLA* 91.2 (March 1976): 245–58. Reprinted in *Critical Essays on Doris Lessing*. Ed. Claire Sprague and Virginia Tiger. Boston: G.K. Hall, 1986.

Whittaker, Ruth. *Doris Lessing*. New York: St. Martin's Press, 1988.

CHRISTINE W. SIZEMORE

MUTHONI LIKIMANI (1926–   )

BIOGRAPHY

Muthoni Likimani was born and brought up at Kahuhia Mission, Murang'a District, Kenya. Her early life as the daughter of one of the first Kenyan Anglican church ministers, Rev. Levi GochanJa, was influential on her development as a writer, particularly in her first novel, *They Shall Be Chastised*.

As an education student in England, Muthoni Likimani became involved in educational broadcasting and advertising. This led to an interesting and varied career that Muthoni Likimani continues to combine with writing. One of the first women to become a program producer at the Kenyan Broadcasting Commission, now the Voice of Kenya, Muthoni Likimani was responsible for women's and children's programs. She is well known in Kenya as "Shangazi" in the children's program of this name and acted the part of the wife in *Mlevi*, the first Swahili film.

Muthoni Likimani's career as a writer began with the publication of letters and articles in local newspapers. Although she wrote from a very early age, it was not until she was encouraged by a Trinidadian broadcaster that she attempted to publish her work. Married to a doctor who moved frequently when her children were very young, Muthoni Likimani found it difficult to write regularly. As a mother and grandmother, she has had to develop a strict routine to allow herself time to write, usually very early in the morning.

Living through difficult periods of Kenyan history has been a major influence on Muthoni Likimani's life. *Passbook Number F. 47927: Women and Mau Mau in Kenya*, Muthoni Likimani's fictionalized accounts of women's stories of Mau Mau, are based on her own observations and the experiences other women have shared with her.

Muthoni Likimani has an active interest in women's issues and has represented Kenya at various international and United Nations seminars. This is reflected in most of her writing, particularly her collection of monologues in verse, *What Does a Man Want?*, where women try to reconcile the demands of men, marriage, and work. In her present career as managing director of Noni's Publicity, an advertising and promotion business in Nairobi, Muthoni Likimani has continued to emphasize the role of women in Kenya with the publication of *Women of Kenya: In the Decade of Development* for the United Nations Conference for Women held in Nairobi in 1985.

MAJOR WORKS AND THEMES

In her first novel, *They Shall Be Chastised*, Muthoni Likimani explores the impact of Western Christian religions on traditional Kikuyu social structures. The conflict between traditional Kenyan cultures and increasing Westernization is a major theme in all her later works.

A humorous collection of free-verse monologues, *What Does a Man Want?* concentrates on the conflicts between women and men in Kenya's changing society. The contradictions between being thought too young and inexperienced or older and less attractive than younger women and between being too caring (read "possessive") or not caring enough are considered in a lighthearted tone. These international experiences of women in relationships are balanced by specific experiences encountered by many African women: the problems of polygamy, the pressures of the extended family, and the divisions between women who work in the country while their husbands work in the city.

Muthoni Likimani is as critical of women's position in traditional Kenyan societies as she is of their changing roles in more Westernized, urban environments. This is most clearly developed in the monologues of characters with cross-cultural relationships. The English woman married to a Kenyan man has as many problems as the Kenyan woman with an English husband who moves to a new life in his country.

Beneath the humorous surface, the real pain of individual characters is clear. They are often deeply aware of the contradictions in their situation, but are trapped by their belief that it is their responsibility to change. In their search for the magic formula that will maintain their difficult relationships, the characters unwittingly warn that there are no answers to these contradictions and that fundamental changes to the basic structures of society are the only means to real change.

In her later works, Muthoni Likimani continues to concentrate on the role of women in society. *Women of Kenya: In the Decade of Development* is a who's who of important and influential Kenyan women. Produced for the United Nations Women's Conference held in Nairobi in 1985, it outlines the importance of women in a wide range of roles from farming to politics. By its nature, *Women of Kenya* is limited to key individuals and a very general outline of the role of women. *Passbook Number F. 47927: Women and Mau Mau in Kenya* is Muthoni Likimani's first international publication. In a series of fictionalized accounts of women's experiences of Mau Mau, Muthoni Likimani rewrites history to include the role of women, which has been largely excluded from historical accounts. The accounts are based on Muthoni Likimani's own experience and observations of family and friends.

In writing *Passbook Number F. 47927*, Muthoni Likimani compares her role as a writer to that of a freedom fighter (James, 60). The characters in her stories are representative of the many women who contributed to the struggle for independence in a wide variety of ways, clearly demonstrating the value of the various roles of women in Mau Mau. Muthoni Likimani celebrates the daring and courage of women who provide information, shelter, and supplies of food and weapons as well as those who fight alongside other freedom fighters in the forests.

The difficulties of women during Mau Mau and their strategies for coping are dramatized in *Passbook Number F. 42927*. Inflexible curfews and forced communal labor cause particular hardships for women, as is portrayed in the situation of the harsh interrogation of Nyambura, who breaks curfew to help her neighbor give birth (Kariokor Location 83). Muthoni Likimani's characters show a strong sense of community, surviving the most difficult circumstances by working together and sharing essential tasks.

Passbook Number F. 42927 can be usefully compared to other accounts of African women's roles in revolutions and struggles for independence. *Mothers of the Revolution*, edited by Irene Staunton, which tells the stories of Zimbabwean women in their own words, has more similarities to Muthoni Likinani's work than the historical fiction written about the Nigerian civil war by Buchi Emecheta and Flora Nwapa. In Ngugi wa Thiong'o and Micere Githae Mugo's *The Trial of Dedan Kimathi*, the role of women is presented as relatively minor. Their concern with "issues" (James, 42) is similar to Muthoni Likimani's, although she chooses to centralize the position of women in society.

CRITICAL RECEPTION

In her introduction to *Passbook Number F. 42927: Women and Mau Mau in Kenya*, Jean O'Barr discusses Muthoni Likimani's work in some detail. Concentrating on *What Does a Man Want?*, O'Barr points out that "women's roles are discussed in terms of whether and how women are social beings in their own right or whether they 'need a man' to be considered whole" (31). This is expanded on in her later article, "Feminist Issues in the Fiction of Kenya's Women Writers." In particular, O'Barr discusses the conflicts between a successful career and social pressures to " 'capture' a man" (66) and "the lack of self-worth and personal gain associated with women's struggle for a 'respected' position in the work force" (65).

The significance of *Passbook Number F. 42927* as a rewriting of history to include women's history is discussed by O'Barr in her "Introductory Essay." She notes that "*Passbook Number F. 42927* both affirms the place of women in Mau Mau as it has been previously described by men, and extends the analysis of women's involvement by documenting the diverse motivations women had and the numerous tasks they undertook" (30). A comparison is made between the role of women in Mau Mau and other nationalist movements.

Adeola James places Muthoni Likimani clearly in the context of her role as an African woman writer through her interview in *In Their Own Voices: African Women Writers Talk*. The interesting link between *Passbook Number F. 42927* and Ngugi wa Thiong'o and Micere Githae Mugo's play *The Trial of Dedan Kimathi* is mentioned, and the influence of West African literature on Muthoni Likimani's writing is discussed. In particular, Muthoni Likimani shows an interest in "books that deal with issues" (62), and in her own writing these issues involve writing about society from a woman's point of view (59).

BIBLIOGRAPHY

Works by Muthoni Likimani

They Shall Be Chastised. Nairobi: East African Literature Bureau, 1974.
What Does a Man Want? Nairobi: Kenya Literature Bureau, 1974.
Passbook Number F. 42927: Women and Mau Mau in Kenya. Women in Society. Basingstoke and London: Macmillan, 1985.
Women of Kenya: In the Decade of Development. Nairobi: Noni's Publicity, 1985.

Studies of Muthoni Likimani

James, Adeola. "Muthoni Likimani." *In Their Own Voices: African Women Writers Talk*. Studies in African Literature. London: James Currey; Portsmouth, N.H.: Heinemann, 1990. 58–62.
O'Barr, Jean F. "Feminist Issues in the Fiction of Kenya's Women Writers." *African Literature Today* 15 (1987): 55–70.
———. "Introductory Essay." *Passbook Number F. 42927: Women and Mau Mau in Kenya*. Muthoni Likimani. Women in Society. Basingstoke and London: Macmillan, 1985.

MAXINE BEAHAN

DAMBUDZO MARECHERA
(1952–1987)

BIOGRAPHY

Dambudzo Marechera, one of the most controversial and irreverent writers that Zimbabwe has ever had, was born in 1952 in Vengere township, near Rusape, into a troubled family. When he was eleven, his father was killed in a car accident, leaving the family without sufficient means of support. Soon evicted, along with his mother and his eight siblings, he struggled to survive in the harsh world of the ghetto. He ran in gangs, got his meals out of garbage cans, and suffered the abuse of white schoolboys. These early experiences in the ghetto established the ground for his subsequent fiction.

With the death of his father, Marechera developed a stammer. The frustration of this handicap resurfaces in his fiction in characters' inability to articulate their thoughts and feelings. He attended different mission schools until 1972, when he entered the University of Rhodesia to study English literature. While in university, he was politically active, at one time conducting a solo protest march against the government of Ian Smith. In 1973 he, along with other students, was kicked out of the university for protesting racial discrimination on campus.

Harassed by police, he finally fled to Botswana and from there to England, to Oxford University, where he was admitted to New College on scholarship. After several troubled years at Oxford, Marechera was given the option of either submitting to voluntary psychiatric treatment or of being expelled. He chose the latter. From 1976 to 1978 he lived a rootless life in London, without either a permanent home or a permanent position, struggling to make ends meet through freelance writing. In 1977 his first book, *The House of Hunger* (1978), was accepted by James Currey at Heinemann. During the same year, he spent three months in jail for illegal possession of marijuana, narrowly escaping deportation.

In 1979 Marechera served as a somewhat unruly writer-in-residence at the University of Sheffield. *The House of Hunger*, which had appeared a year earlier, was awarded the Guardian fiction prize. During the award ceremony, in lieu of a formal speech, Marechera chose to hurl plates at the chandelier.

From 1980 to 1981 Marechera lived by writing articles, stories, and reviews, his income supplemented by writing grants from the Arts Council. His second book, a novel, *Black Sunlight*, appeared in 1980.

In 1982 Marechera returned to Zimbabwe to help with Christ Austin's filming of *The House of Hunger*. Quickly quarreling with Austin, Marechera left the project. He wrote a third book, *Mindblast* (1984), an anthology of shorter work, while sleeping on park benches. As disillusioned with Mugabe's Zimbabwe as he had been with Smith's Rhodesia, Marechera turned toward an increasingly violent nihilism. He spent his last few years as he had spent many others—as a wanderer, sleeping on other people's floors. In 1987, at the age of thirty-five, he died of an AIDS-related lung collapse.

MAJOR WORKS AND THEMES

Marechera's international reputation rests on his first two books, *The House of Hunger* and *Black Sunlight*. In addition, published in Zimbabwe are two other major works, *Mindblast* and *The Black Insider*, as well as a handful of additional poems and stories. All of these works are highly biographical, dealing with rootless, confused, and insecure characters similar to Marechera himself. They also deal nihilistically with the more squalid aspects of African life, depicting characters struggling against poverty, abuse, and oppression of the strongest kind. Much of Marechera's fiction draws on his childhood in the ghetto. He also constructs his fiction from the political turmoil of Rhodesia/Zimbabwe, mirroring this turmoil in the inner turmoil of his personae.

Marechera culls from other writers to assemble a style all his own. A great admirer of American beat writers, Marechera also draws on African and European writing. His few public essays and speeches refer both to African and European writers, without trying to displace either tradition. He is interested in good writing of all varieties. At the same time, Marechera recognizes the need to transform language into something immediately relevant to his own experience. As he suggests in *Dambudzo Marechera, 4 June 1952*, "For a black writer, the language is very racist; you have to have harrowing fights and hair-raising panga duels with the language before you can make it do all that you want it to do. . . . This may mean discarding grammar, throwing syntax out, subverting images from within, beating the drum and cymbals of rhythm, developing torture chambers of irony and sarcasm, gas ovens of limitless black resonance" (*Dambudzo Marechera, 4 June 1952*, 7–8). The result is a style both sharp and eccentric, a unique English that is undeniably African.

The House of Hunger (1978), his strongest book, is a collection of stories focusing primarily on a black township. "House of Hunger," the opening novella, concerns a man's hopeless attempt to wriggle out of the violent township in which he envisions his oncoming destruction. "The Slow Sound of His Feet" is a dreamlike exploration of stuttering and incest. Many of the stories are unredemptive; all are vivid in language and beautiful in their complex and often lyrical manipulations of English sentences.

Black Sunlight (1980) is perhaps more experimental, but no less powerful. Its attitudes might be summarized by a sentence late in the book: "We are like matches being systematically scratched alight and put out in a dark and confined room" (113). Marechera offers here a surrealized view of revolution, in which the political transformations taking place in Zimbabwe are satirized and are blended with the transformations within the self. The narrative is fragmented through a "drugged" narrative style that is both disturbing and structurally complex. For Marechera, politics is always on some level personal and eccentric.

In *Black Sunlight* and the subsequent *Mindblast*, Marechera's nihilism reaches an extreme. A poem included in *Mindblast* suggests that he is "against everything" except "blind impulse." What separates Marechera from other nihilists, however, is a continued sense of political involvement and an unwillingness to accept solipsism as a viable solution. Indeed, Marechera must be seen as an odd sort of postcolonialist. He participates in both African and European traditions, yet despises his participation in both. He has an equal revulsion for both, occupying a sort of Hegelian "unhappy consciousness" in which lies an inverted postcolonialism, the negative equivalent of other writers' affirmation. In his writing style, on the other hand, he is a great appropriator, incorporating both European and African style, constructing his own language.

Mindblast (1984) consists of three political, satirical plays, two semiautobiographical stories that are not among Marechera's best, a collection of reasonably competent poetry, and a memoir of Marechera's wandering through Harare as he attempts to get together another book. The memoir is the strength of the book, possessing an originality that the other selections are short on.

The Black Insider (1990) is an early short novel published only posthumously, the volume being filled out by several uncollected stories and poems. It served as the basis for *Black Sunlight* and contains many similarities to the latter, though very few of the strengths. It is a more realistic analysis of the Zimbabwean rise to independence, its characters eventually destroyed in their fight. Useful as an artifact for those interested in Marechera, it has less literary value than the other work.

A theme that keeps returning in Marechera's work is the struggle of the African with his environment. Though the environment shifts as we move from one work to another, it remains dark and unpromising. Africa's strongest nihilist, Marechera is also a social satirist of the first water and an elegant manipulator of language.

CRITICAL RECEPTION

Marechera's critical reception has been admirably chronicled by Flora Veit-Wild in her annotated bibliography of Marechera and in her source book. *The House of Hunger*, which won the Guardian fiction prize, received a strong reception. It was highly praised by reviewers as notable as Angela Carter and Doris Lessing. Marechera was seen as a writer of surprising talent and great promise, among the best of African writers. *The House of Hunger* is the only one of Marechera's books, as of this writing, to have been released by an American press. African reviewers, however, while acknowledging Marechera's talent, did not approve of his nihilism, one reviewer referring to it as "alien to Africa—a continent of hope and realizable dreams" (Veit-Wild, "Annotated Bibliography," 126).

Black Sunlight did not receive nearly as strong praise. Initially banned in Zimbabwe for obscenity and blasphemy, the book was seen by many as excessive and incomprehensible. It was published by Heinemann despite several indifferent and negative readers' reports. Though acknowledged by many as a strong effort, it was also seen by many Africans as a sellout to European artistic tendencies. In Africa it was criticized, as had been *The House of Hunger*, for presenting a nihilistic view of conditions in Africa.

While the international reception has varied, Marechera's work has always had a harsher reception in Africa than abroad. He is not easy to fit into a political box. He was irreverent, sometimes childish, often disturbing. He was as likely to vent his spleen in one direction as another and to do so at the wrong moments in indiscreet ways, which made him a dangerous political ally. Though liberal, Marechera was seen as a little bit of an embarrassment by progressive groups. Marechera was involved in the same struggles as other African writers, but did not recite the party line.

Mindblast, *The Black Insider*, and a recent collection of Marechera's poems, *Cemetery of the Mind* (1992), have been published only in Zimbabwe, where Marechera seems to have a constant, though not excessively large, readership. It is clear that Marechera's best work appeared with his first two books, and that it is upon these that his reputation must rest.

BIBLIOGRAPHY

Works by Dambudzo Marechera

The House of Hunger. London: Heinemann, 1978.
Black Sunlight. London: Heinemann, 1980.
Mindblast, or the Definitive Buddy. Harare: College Press, 1984.
"The African Writer's Experience of European Literature." *Zambezia* 14.2 (1987): 99–105.
"Soyinka, Dostoyevsky: The Writer on Trial for His Time." *Zambezia* 14.2 (1987): 106–12.

The Black Insider. Harare: Baobab Books, 1990.
Cemetery of the Mind: Collected Poems of Dambudzo Marechera. Harare: Baobab
    Books, 1992.

Studies of Dambudzo Marechera

Caute, D. "Marechera and the Colonel—A Zimbabwean Writer and the Claims of the
    State." *The Espionage of Saints: Two Essays on Silence and the State.* London:
    Hamilton, 1986.
Foster, Kevin. "Soul Food for the Starving: Dambudzo Marechera's *House of Hunger.*"
    Journal of Commonwealth Literature 27.1 (1992): 58–70.
Veit-Wild, Flora. "Dambudzo Marechera: A Preliminary Annotated Bibliography."
    Zambezia 14.2 (1987): 121–29.
———. *Dambudzo Marechera: A Sourcebook on His Life and Work.* New York: Hans
    Zell, 1992.
———, ed. *Dambudzo Marechera, 4 June 1952–18 August 1987: Pictures, Poems,
    Prose, Tributes.* Harare: Baobab Books, 1988.

BRIAN EVENSON

MICERE M. GITHAE MUGO (1942–   )

BIOGRAPHY

Micere M. Githae Mugo, mother and guardian of Mumbi Mugo and Njeri Mugo, was born in Kerugoya, Kenya. Upon completing her primary and secondary education, Mugo attended the University of East Africa, Makerere Campus, in Uganda, where she received her bachelor's degree with honors in 1966. In 1967 she took courses at the Nairobi Campus of the University of East Africa and received a postgraduate diploma education. She later enrolled at the University of New Brunswick, Canada, where she attained a master's and a Ph.D. degree in literature between 1971 and 1973.

Mugo's professional experience covers a very wide spectrum. She taught language and literature at Kaaga Girls' High School from 1967 to 1969. From 1967 to 1968 she was deputy headmistress at Alliance Girls' School and headmistress of Kabare Girls' High School from 1968 to 1969. She later taught at a teachers' training college for one year as a lecturer in curriculum and pedagogics. She started teaching at Nairobi University in 1973 and taught until 1982, becoming dean of the Faculty of Arts (incorporating the humanities and social sciences) from 1980 to 1982. At the university, Mugo was associated with the radical intellectual wing that was critical of Kenyan government repression and its violation of human rights and individual freedom. She was among the leading advocates of greater academic freedom at the university and a more democratic and more open society in the country at large. As a result she, among others, became a constant target of political harassment by successive Kenyan governments, leading eventually to her exile in 1982.

Prior to coming to the United States in 1991, Mugo worked as an associate professor of English at the University of Zimbabwe, where she also headed the

English Unit of the Department of Curriculum and Arts Education. During her stay in Zimbabwe, she received Zimbabwean citizenship. Currently she is a professor at Syracuse University in the Department of African American Studies.

During her tenure as a professor at the University of Nairobi, she was one of the prominent and active academics in a campaign waged against the Eurocentric orientation of literature curriculum at the primary, secondary, and tertiary levels of the educational structure. Hitherto, the curriculum had emphasized the teaching of European literature at the expense of African literature, but the efforts of these academics ultimately transformed the curriculum by giving prominence to African writers and led to the introduction of oral literature as an integral part of the literature curriculum. In her battle against the hegemony of Eurocentrism, Mugo has also attempted to reveal European writers' biases against the Kenyan people in the way they documented history; her discussion of Elspeth Huxley in *Visions of Africa* belongs to this critical tendency. Mugo questions the "authenticity" and "accuracy" of Kenyan historical accounts written from a European point of view, as will be illustrated in *The Trial of Dedan Kimathi*. In her collection of poems, *Daughter of My People Sing*, she also addresses the need to raise people's consciousness regarding their own culture and modes of expression that had been nullified almost to the level of extinction.

Like many African writers, Mugo writes about her own people's experience during the period ranging from the pre-colonial to the post-colonial era. Her major goals have been to redefine the history of the people and to promote cultural liberation in an attempt to revitalize aspects of the African tradition systematically being zapped by the Western mode. This is accomplished through her mimeograph series on *Orature and Human Rights* published in Lesotho and in some of her works she coedited with Shimmer Chinodya like *Chimurenga Book I, Chimurenga Book II, Young Voices, By the Fireside, Imicabango, Nhetembo*, and *Sadza Rangu Riri Kupi*, published in Harare, Zimbabwe. In other words, Mugo has made attempts through her works to break away from cultural imperialism by promoting cultural awareness among Kenyan people and Africans in general.

MAJOR WORKS AND THEMES

Visions of Africa is a thought-provoking evaluation and interpretation of a variety of contributions toward the African literary canon by Elspeth Huxley, Margaret Laurence, Chinua Achebe, and Ngugi wa Thiong'o mapped against the sociopolitical background upon which they are set. Although all these authors hold different visions of Africa, their differences set the premise for Mugo's analysis. Mugo's major task in this text was not to attempt to harmonize these writers' visions of Africa but rather to scrutinize their completeness and authenticity.

Huxley's visions of the Gikuyu people of Kenya are seen as depersonalizing and stereotyping. Her portrayal of the people reveals her limited understanding of the people and is attributed to her interest in examining the natural scene that seemed to appeal to her. She views Africans as people devoid of the creative impulse. Huxley's perception of Africa is thus indicative of the colonial mentality that emphasizes African people's inferiority in comparison to whites.

Chinua Achebe's vision of Africa is described as a form of his self-discovery and the self-discovery of his own people during the pre-colonial and colonial periods. He writes about his people interacting with one another, struggling to survive and, at the same time, to combat colonialism as their new enemy. Achebe's vision of Africa decries the violence inflicted upon his people by European colonialists and attempts to deconstruct the myth that Africans are lazy and ignorant. He in fact depicts his people as intelligent, vigorous, dignified, and purposeful.

Margaret Laurence's vision of the Ghana scene shows individuals struggling to free themselves from oppressive conditions that inhibit them from progress. Laurence's strongest contribution to the African literary canon is her emphasis on a people's quest and search for freedom and self-expression at the individual and political level. Laurence's vision of Africa is one of liberation; this is a concern of most post-colonial African writers. She abhors colonialism and stresses the need for men and women to free themselves from the strangleholds of colonialism. Laurence condemns and loathes the exploitation of one human being by another, whether it be for political expediency or personal benefits.

Ngugi wa Thiong'o's vision of Africa is depicted as one of concern, commitment, and representation of the Gikuyu traditional world, to redefine and to raise the social consciousness of the "masses" that have to combat the encroachment of the colonial forces and mentality. To articulate these concerns, Ngugi probes into the myths, legends, and history as a means of re-creating the scene of the people missing in Huxley's works. Ngugi understands the African peasants and their problems, land being the most central. *Visions of Africa* is one of Mugo's powerful texts in which images of Africans, held by both European writers, Huxley and Laurence, and African writers, Achebe and Ngugi, are articulated.

The Trial of Dedan Kimathi, a play Mugo coauthored with Ngugi wa Thiong'o, is a modulation of the oral-tradition format of representing and redefining history. It is a powerful play that shows a people's collective need to combat imperialism in order to stop their exploitation and the pillage and plunder of their land.

In *The Trial of Dedan Kimathi*, Mugo and Ngugi question the accuracy of documented historical accounts of the Mau Mau freedom fighters, especially the role of Kimathi in the movement. The question of accuracy posed in this play can be visualized as a political statement, radicalizing the ongoing debate among modern Kenyan scholars in post-colonial Kenya on the boundaries between fact and fiction. As has been noted in other works, the Mau Mau freedom fighters had often been described as insane individuals without a vision of the concerns and needs of the people. In this play, however, this assessment is seen merely as a projection of imperialistic views held by Europeans of African activists. Mugo and Ngugi make a conscious effort to confront, nullify, and transcend Western misrepresentation of Kenya's history by revisiting the actual anticolonial struggles waged by Kenyan peasants and workers in their effort to combat forces of colonialism.

The basic plot line of the play portrays the British colonialists' preparations to try Kimathi, attempts by the people to rescue him, and the cowardly decision by the colonialists to execute him. Amidst these plots are other themes and motifs woven into its structure that can be perceived as an affirmation of the general struggles undertaken by many African people faced with the destructive elements of colonialism and the resilience and role of cultural consciousness in this struggle.

At the onset of the play, the atmosphere is tense. The nationalistic agenda of the people is made visible in their solidarity efforts to overcome oppression as they come face to face with the colonial forces who believe that tension in the country will be resolved if Kimathi is hanged. From the writers' point of view, the organized forces of the people, indicative of their collective entity, must not be perceived as agents of terror but as a strong testimony of togetherness.

The central theme of the play is a class struggle of Kenyan peasants against agents of colonial exploitation. We encounter people from a broad spectrum: the local men in the name of soldiers who have joined forces with the enemy, the proponents of change, both men and women, and the young boys and girls who are also subjected to oppression. Both women and children play a significant role in personalizing the events in the play; the fight between the boy and the girl at the beginning of the play makes the people's struggle realistic and of current concern for the people. The Woman in the play bemoans the disintegration of family units as she reflects on the divide-and-conquer politics of colonialism.

Therefore, the history—enacted from oral stories—utilized by Mugo and Ngugi in this play presents a particular truism upon which the play is centered. Both Mugo and Ngugi function as agents of change by trying to mobilize people to be active participants in the redefinition of Kimathi's history. The collective motif of a people recognizing their oppressor and making a conscious effort to overcome the oppression is the basis for redefining history in the play as a major struggle in post-colonial Kenya.

Daughter of My People Sing is a collection of poems whose unifying theme is liberation from cultural imperialism that emphasized Western poetic modes at the expense of the African oral tradition. In this text Mugo taps into the rich oral tradition of her society to express the attitudes of her people based on her personal experiences. She breaks away from academic colonialism by redefining her cultural roots. In the text she rejects the myth that oral communities could not deliver poetry in songs, dance, recitation, and performance. In name-calling and wedding ceremonies, songs are used as a powerful testament of the rich idiomatic expressions of the people. Songs, dances, and recitation as artistic media of expression utilized in *Daughter of My People Sing* are a reaffirmation of a people's culture and collective experience.

The need to redefine her people's cultural heritage and identity leads Mugo to readapt songs central in the African traditional lifestyle as a means of holding onto the cultural identity of her people that is somewhat diminishing in the contemporary society. To achieve this goal, Mugo revisits her childhood memories in order to give her poems substance. Her poem "Where Are Those Songs?" poses the dilemma faced by many Kenyan intellectuals as they witness a rape of the people's cultural norms and practices as they get replaced by the Western practices.

The atrocities of colonialism and imperialism are vividly depicted in "Digging Our Grave," sending countless chills to our mind as Mugo sadly laments the loss of "brotherhood." The agonizing sorrow of mothers crying to have their children spared by those in power reveals the moral decay of the society.

Complementary to directness of expression, Mugo's collection aims at popularizing the African verse as a means of advancing her political sentiments of liberation in a global sense. In "From a Zulu Mother's Diary" and "Rhodesia," the emasculation of the African male, reducing him to a servant, is focal in addressing the question of liberation. The ultimate revolutionary significance of Mugo's politics of liberation should be sought in its proximity to the actual struggle of the people against exploitation. The glimpse of hope for African people is subsumed in Mugo's prophetic voice in the metaphor of the "Locust Retreating." The directness in Mugo's prophecy calls for the national liberation of her people.

The Long Illness of Ex-Chief Kiti is a heartbreaking play in which the impact of colonialism on African societies and the family structure is highlighted. One notes Mugo's other significant purpose in her writings, namely, the examination of the sufferings of her people as a result of colonialism.

Mugo's political ideology of cultural and political liberation takes on a different angle. There is a strong urgency for individuals to liberate their mind as we observe with horror how characters like Mata and Kiti are still struggling to nurse the wounds inflicted upon them by imperialism. The divide-and-rule policy undertaken by the British colonial administrators is seen to have had an adverse effect on the relationships between fathers and sons and between brothers and sisters in the play. Mata, Kiti's son, who was a revolutionary in the struggle against the exploitation of the people under the hands of European imperialism, suffers much mental anguish. He rejects his father for joining hands with the enemy and does not seek any kind of reconciliation with him. For Mata, the wounds of the Mau Mau movement had not ended. Unfortunately for Kiti, who was perceived as an agent of destruction by his own people, his support of the Europeans during the inception of the Mau Mau movement completely destroyed him. He was not only rejected by his own son, but was also imprisoned by the people who had caused him the loss of his family.

In the context of post-colonial Kenya, Kiti is an epitome of the many Kenyan peasants who were left with scars too deep to heal as a constant painful reminder of the wounds of colonialization. Mugo writes sympathetically and sensitively about people's struggle and suffering in their effort to survive painful experiences of colonialism. Although there are diverse methods of healing the wounds, some people resort to fruitless nursing of negative bitterness, indulge in escapism so as to evade the past distress, and, ultimately, direct positive anger toward personal and communal failures while looking ahead to an era of reconstruction. Kiti, left all alone and wounded, is physically and psychologically sick due to his inability to deal with the deep scars inflicted upon him by his oppressors. Therefore, he directs his anger toward himself and his family members. Mata, on the other hand, indulges himself in drinking as an escape mechanism to deal with his wounds.

The Long Illness of Ex-Chief Kiti contains remarkable portraits of quasi-illiterate Kenyan peasants who are struggling to hold onto their culture, but also realizing that the forces they have to combat are stringent. The theme of family warfare woven in this play projects the inner turmoil among family members and at the same time re-creates the dilemma people still face in contemporary Kenya in trying to re-create traditional and cultural practices. The play not only shows the disintegration of the family unit but also presents the moral decay of society that has been transformed into the man-eat-man phenomenon, a baggage attributed to the legacy of colonialism.

CRITICAL RECEPTION

In the introduction to *Daughter of My People Sing*, Njuguna Mugo writes of Mugo's dedication to rejuvenate her cultural heritage through her poetry. Njuguna Mugo notes that poetry for Mugo became a "means of reflecting upon, fathoming deeper into questions such as: 'Who am I? Who are my people? Where are they? What are they? What possibilities exist for us? Shall we witness perpetuation and rebirth or shall ours remain the fate of the parrot?' " (ix). These questions form the nucleus of Mugo's assessment of the Kenyan experience in post-colonial Kenya. Njuguna Mugo also cautions that for Mugo to adequately answer these questions, she had to refrain from borrowing idioms and metaphors from her Western education that repressed her creativity. Her adaptation of the African songs that she understood and that came to her naturally was an effective way to redeem the African verse.

In her introduction to *The Long Illness of Ex-Chief Kiti*, written afterwards, Mugo explicitly indicates her goal in writing the play to be a revisit of Kenyan peasants who had been involved in the liberation war and to answer the questions: Had the war of liberation really ended? Could the gashes and the deep wounds furrowed by the experience of colonization be seen as healed, or were the ugly scars left a permanent symbolic reminder that the enemy had hit so deep that he would remain with us for a long time? In essence, how had Kenyans responded to the war of liberation? In her assessment of the play later, Mugo is very apologetic due to her failure to "confront the more controversial and politically unpalatable issue of land" that could not fit within the framework of the play. She would also have made an effort to redeem Mata, a character in the play, whose only means to deal with the scars of colonialism is drinking alcohol.

In "Historical Reconstruction and Class Struggle in Anti-imperialist Drama: *The Trial of Dedan Kimathi* and *I Will Marry When I Want*," Chidi Amuta maintains that *The Trial of Dedan Kimathi* "must be understood as a dramatization of [the] process of historical reconstruction and rehabilitation" (157). Mugo and Ngugi also note in their introduction that "there was no single historical work written by a Kenyan telling the grandeur of the heroic resistance of Kenyan people fighting foreign forces of exploitation and domination." Both Mugo and Ngugi's debt to their own people was to ensure that there was an "accurate" account of the positive contributions made by Kenyan activists in the liberation movement who had otherwise received a negative portrayal in colonial Kenya.

BIBLIOGRAPHY

Works by Micere M. Githae Mugo

Daughter of My People Sing. Nairobi: Kenya Literature Bureau, 1976.
The Long Illness of Ex-Chief Kiti. Nairobi: East African Literature Bureau, 1976.
Mugo, Micere Githae, and Ngũgĩ Thiong'o. *The Trial of Dedan Kimathi.* Nairobi: Heinemann, 1976.
Visions of Africa. Nairobi: Kenya Literature Bureau, 1978.

Studies of Micere M. Githae Mugo

Amuta, Chidi. "Historical Reconstruction and Class Struggle in Anti-imperialist Drama: *The Trial of Dedan Kimathi* and *I Will Marry When I Want.*" *The Theory of African Literature: Implications for Practical Literature.* London: Institute for African Alternatives Zed Books, 1989.

JUDITH IMALI ABALA

PETER NAZARETH (1940–   )

BIOGRAPHY

Peter Nazareth belongs to what has come to be known as the "first generation" of Anglophone fiction writers from East Africa. A contemporary and schoolmate of Ngugi wa Thiong'o, Jonathan Kariara, Rebecca Njau, David Rubadiri, and other pioneers of East African literature, Nazareth studied at Makerere University in the late 1950s, when it was the leading higher-education institution in sub-Saharan Africa. For five years he served as an editor of *Penpoint*, Makerere's literary magazine, and he was a regular contributor to the early editions of *Transition* and other East African literary journals. Today, Nazareth is best known as a critic, novelist, and educator, and although his personal and professional paths have taken him far afield since his early days—from Uganda to Leeds and Yale, and eventually to the University of Iowa—his work is best understood as being rooted in that early East African milieu.

Peter Nazareth is obsessed with genealogies—of cultures, of ideas, and of influences—and with the limits and possibilities that they create. In his creative and his critical works alike, Nazareth is an inveterate comparatist, exploring and tracing the interactions between and across cultural boundaries, embracing such diverse figures as D. H. Lawrence, Joseph Conrad, Ishmael Reed, and Elvis Presley, in addition to a host of postcolonial writers.

Nazareth's personal history suggests why he might be interested in the complexities of genealogy, since it constitutes a classic example of the rootlessness, border crossing, fragmented identity, and cultural hybridity that typify what has come to be described as the "postcolonial condition." Born in Kampala, Uganda, on April 27, 1940, Nazareth grew up and studied there, eventually working as a civil servant in the country's post-independence administrations.

His parents both hailed from the former Portuguese colony of Goa, although his mother's side of the family had settled in Malaysia. The ambiguity of Goan identity in the East African setting, which implies cultural difference from the majority African population as well as from other Asian groups in the region, features prominently in his short works as well as his novels. Today, Nazareth is variously hailed as a Ugandan writer, as a writer of the "Indian diaspora," as an African of Goan origin, or as a Goan from Africa—all of these being identities that he readily claims.

Nazareth obtained a degree from the English honors program at Makerere University College in 1962 and went on to complete a postgraduate diploma in English studies at Leeds University. On returning to Uganda, he worked for seven years in the Ministry of Finance, until 1973, when he left to take a fellowship at Yale University that had been awarded on the strength of his first novel, *In a Brown Mantle*. This was the time of the general expulsion of Asians from Uganda by the Idi Amin regime, an event that his novel prophesied, and Nazareth never returned there. He moved to the University of Iowa as honorary fellow in the International Writing Program (IWP) and visiting lecturer in the Afro-American Studies Program, where he has been ever since; he is currently professor of English and Afro-American World Studies and advisor to the IWP.

MAJOR WORKS AND THEMES

In his creative and critical works alike, Peter Nazareth demonstrates an inveterate urge to explore origins, connections, and influences. The genealogy of ideas, particularly as they cross over from the metropoles to the colonial setting and back again, are favorite topics. This was already apparent in his postgraduate dissertation, where Nazareth revisited the work of Joseph Conrad at the urging of his colleague and fellow Leeds student, Ngugi wa Thiong'o. Nazareth took the opportunity to explore the Conradian legacy further at the University of Iowa, where he began teaching courses that specifically examine the phenomenon of "Conrad and his descendants," those Third World writers who had been influenced by him. In fact, Nazareth has claimed, "*influence* is too mild a word for the impact Conrad has had on the Third World, that is, the world colonized by Europeans, both in texts and in real life" ("Conrad's Descendants," 101).

A Conradian legacy might be found in Nazareth's own creative works, particularly his novels. His first, *In a Brown Mantle*, is about the betrayal in East Africa of preindependence ideals. Joseph D'Souza is a Lord Jim figure who eventually jumps from what has become for him a ship of sinking political prospects in the loosely fictional nation of Damibia. Exiled in London, living a cold and lonely life, he reexamines his past, and as a way of exorcising the ghosts of history he takes up his pen. As a Goan in a Uganda-like setting, D'Souza has to come to terms with a multitude of personal and communal failures in the effort to create an egalitarian postcolonial society. His involvement in politics comes to a premature end when he betrays his own ethical code and flees to England. The problem, it becomes clear, is that both D'Souza and his political mentor, Robert Kyeyune, are willing to use questionable means to achieve what would otherwise be laudable ends, relying on coercion, deception, and corruption. By contrast, those who maintain high ethical standards—such as Pius Cota, a Goan politician in a neighboring country who is an obvious reference to the Kenyan socialist Pio Gama Pinto—end up assassinated. The result is a legacy of political corruption and ethnic discord in Damibia/Uganda.

If *In a Brown Mantle* presaged general problems in Uganda, *The General Is Up* takes a more direct look at how the drastic policies of a dictator—the General—affect individuals and communities. Again the setting is the Goan community in Damibia. This time it is David D'Costa, a civil servant in the Ministry of Information, who is forced to come to terms with the society in which he grew up, but that suddenly rejects him. Nazareth's narrative is filled with an appreciation for the ironies of identity formation. When, shortly after Damibian independence, David D'Costa decides to take citizenship, it means renouncing his British citizenship:

There had been no problem, so it seemed. He went to a local magistrate and renounced his allegiance to the Queen of England. Then he immediately swore his allegiance to the Head of State of the new nation, who was the Queen of England. That had struck him as odd, but the ways of bureaucrats were strange. (43)

Eventually, D'Costa reluctantly leaves the country following the General's edict giving Asians until "the next moon" to depart or face the consequences.

The death of the General in a dramatic shoot-out closes the story—except that Nazareth adds an intriguing epilogue. Set in the United States and told from the perspective of an American motorist, the narrator describes an encounter with a distraught hitchhiker calling himself Ronald D'Cruz, who leaves with him the draft of a novel entitled *Spiralling: The General Is Up*. Nazareth is of course drawing on the time-worn trope of the found manuscript, but the narrator's closing reference to his own Lebanese heritage reinforces the novel's focus on cultural identity and the search for a society in which tolerance and coexistence are possible.

At first glance, Peter Nazareth's course on Elvis Presley—which he began teaching at the University of Iowa in the spring of 1992, and which generated international attention as well as considerable controversy—represents a radically new direction. In fact, it is yet another example of Nazareth's genealogical explorations. The course, "American Popular Arts: Elvis as Anthology," examines the way in which Elvis responded to and revised music and images from various traditions, creating a "popular" set of songs and images that in fact overlay issues that have much in common with postcolonial questions. Nazareth himself started listening to Elvis in Uganda in the 1950s, even making him the topic of an honors essay in 1959.

In the process of tracing genealogies and influences, Nazareth is interested not only in how they have been transferred and passively accepted; rather, he is intrigued by the ways that those who inherit these genealogies and influences can rework and reshape the legacy in new ways. It is not merely a case of "the Empire writing back," to use the common formulation, but of incorporating as part of the critical task an examination of how traditions are modified for new contexts. For Nazareth, the signifier of this function is the figure of the trickster, a stock character in various African literary traditions. Nazareth is interested in how entire texts function as tricksters, making subversive readings available, although not too obviously. The Trickster Tradition, by Nazareth's account, offers an alternative to the Great Tradition. Conrad, for example, uses trickster techniques in *Heart of Darkness*, writing at the zenith of the British Empire a story that reveals the horror and emptiness of the imperial experience. Nazareth's most recent book, *In the Trickster Tradition*, juxtaposes the works of Andrew Salkey, Francis Ebejer, and Ishmael Reed, arguing that the three have created trickster texts.

CRITICAL RECEPTION

Because his novels were published by regional presses, because of his more recent interests in comparative studies and unorthodox topics such as Elvis Presley, and because of the slippery issue of how to classify him as a writer, Peter Nazareth's creative works have not, as John Scheckter has noted, been treated in any major critical studies, being rather included as part of regional or continental surveys of postcolonial writing. This may change with the new edition of *The General Is Up* by a Canadian publishing house.

The challenge of interpreting Nazareth's work is certainly compounded by the slippery question of his cultural identity. Hans Zell's first edition of *A Reader's Guide to African Literature*, for example, lists Nazareth as a Ugandan writer—but with a question mark that is mentioned in the 1983 edition. Charles Irby highlights his Goan background, while Scheckter's overview is included in a volume on writers of the Indian diaspora.

Peter Nazareth's writing has been published around the world and translated into ten languages. The bibliography includes a selection of the most representative and accessible of his works.

BIBLIOGRAPHY

Works by Peter Nazareth

Fiction

"The Confessor." *Short Story International* 20 (1981): 151–57.
"Eccentric Ferns." *Short Story International* 19 (1980): 127–32.

The General Is Up. Calcutta: Writers Workshop, 1984. Reprint. Toronto: TSAR Books, 1991.

In a Brown Mantle. Nairobi: East African Literature Bureau, 1972.

"The Institute." *Dhana* 4.1 (1974): 65–69.

"Moneyman." *An Anthology of East African Short Stories.* Ed. Valerie Kibera. Nairobi: Longman, 1988. 116–21.

"Rosie's Theme." *Literary Review* 29 (Summer 1986): 496–506.

Two Radio Plays. Nairobi: East African Literature Bureau, 1976. "The Hospital" and "X" were originally produced for the British Broadcasting Corporation African Service.

Literary Criticism

An African View of Literature. Evanston: Northwestern University Press, 1974. First published as *Literature and Society in Modern Africa.* Nairobi: East African Literature Bureau 1972 (reprinted by Kenya Literature Bureau, 1980).

Editor, *African Writing Today.* Special issue of *Pacific Quarterly Moana* 6.3–4 (July–October 1981).

"Bibliyongraphy, or Six Tabans in Search of an Author." *The Writing of East and Central Africa.* Ed. G. D. Killam. London: Heinemann, 1984. 159–76.

"Conrad's Descendants." *Conradiana* 22.2 (Summer 1990).

Editor, *Goan Literature: A Modern Reader.* Special issue of *Journal of South Asian Literature* 18.1 (Winter–Spring 1983).

In the Trickster Tradition: The Novels of Andrew Salkey, Francis Ebejer, and Ishmael Reed. London: Bogle L'Ouverture Press, 1994.

"Second Homecoming: Multiple Ngugis in *Petals of Blood.*" *Marxism and African Literature.* Ed. Georg M. Gugelberger. Trenton, NJ: Africa World Press, 1985. 118–29.

"Survive the Peace: Cyprian Ekwensi as a Political Novelist." *Marxism and African Literature.* Ed. Georg M. Gugelberger. Trenton, NJ: Africa World Press, 1985. 165–77.

The Third World Writer: His Social Responsibility. Nairobi: Kenya Literature Bureau, 1978.

"Waiting for Amin: Two Decades of Ugandan Literature." *The Writing of East and Central Africa.* Ed. G. D. Killam. London: Heinemann, 1984. 7–35.

Studies of Peter Nazareth

Dathorne, O. R. *African Literature in the Twentieth Century.* Minneapolis: University of Minnesota Press, 1975.

Elder, Arlene A. "Indian Writing in East and South Africa: Multiple Approaches to Colonialism and Apartheid." *Reworlding: The Literature of the Indian Diaspora.* Ed. Emmanuel Nelson. Westport, CT: Greenwood Press, 1992. 115–39.

Irby, Charles C. "Goan Literature from Peter Nazareth: An Interview." *Explorations in Ethnic Studies* 8.1 (January 1985): 1–12.

Scheckter, John. "Peter Nazareth." *Writers of the Indian Diaspora: A Bio-Bibliographical Critical Sourcebook.* Ed. Emmanuel S. Nelson. Westport, CT: Greenwood Press, 1993.

Thumboo, Edwin. "A Conversation between Peter Nazareth and Edwin Thumboo on Transformations of Oral Cultures in the Third World." *Pacific Quarterly Moana* 7.2 (1982): 93–101.

Tucker, Martin. "Peter Nazareth." *Literary Exile in the Twentieth Century.* Ed. Martin Tucker. Westport, CT: Greenwood Press, 1991. 508–10.

Zell, Hans. *A Reader's Guide to African Literature.* London: Heinemann, 1972; *A New Reader's Guide to African Literature.* London: Heinemann, 1983.

J. ROGER KURTZ

NGŨGĨ WA THIONG'O (1938–   )

BIOGRAPHY

Ngũgĩ wa Thiong'o was born the fifth child of the third of his father's four wives; he had twenty-seven siblings. The family lived in Kamiriithu Village, twelve miles northeast of Nairobi, Kenya. His father, Thiong'o wa Nducu, was a peasant farmer dispossessed by the British Imperial Land Act of 1915 and therefore forced to become a squatter on property meted out to one of the few native Africans who had profited from the act. His father's condition was similar to that of most of the Kikuyu with whom Ngũgĩ grew up.

In 1947 his parents separated, and in that same year, at the age of nine, Ngũgĩ attended the mission-run school at Kamaandura. After two years he transferred to Maanguu Karinga school. This was part of the Independent Schools Movement run by native Kenyans, and instruction was in Gikuyu. In 1954, however, the government took over control of the school and made English the medium of instruction.

From 1955 till 1959 he attended Alliance High School in Kikuyu, a bit closer to Nairobi. It was run by a consortium of the various Protestant denominations in Kenya and was the first secondary school specifically for Africans. Ngũgĩ was the first from his area of the country to attend.

Early in his adolescence several events took place that had a defining effect on Ngũgĩ's life. In 1953 he underwent the initiation ceremony of circumcision. The following year his stepbrother was shot dead and his older brother joined the Mau Mau. His mother was subsequently tortured. In 1955 his village was destroyed as part of the anti–Mau Mau campaign. Meanwhile, at Alliance High School he was gaining an impressive familiarity with the Bible. The combination of these events strongly affected his novels: while his family was not Christian,

Ngũgĩ himself was devoutly Christian at one time. He published his earliest work as James Ngũgĩ. He later explicitly rejected Christianity, but its implicit message of liberation, coupled with the colonizing impulses of many of its exponents, inspired Ngũgĩ's later employment of biblical themes against the British and neocolonial Kenyans.

In 1959 he entered Makerere University College in Kampala, Uganda (then affiliated with London University), and in 1964 he graduated with an Upper Second Degree in Honors English (having written on Joseph Conrad). In 1961 he had married, and over the next seventeen years his wife, Nyambura, gave birth to six children. In 1961 he also wrote the first version of *The River Between*, and between 1961 and 1964 he became a columnist for *Sunday Post, Daily Nation*, and *Sunday Nation*. During his school years he participated actively in student publications, as well, including *Penpoint* and *Makererean*. In 1962 his play *The Black Hermit* was produced in Kampala, and he wrote *Weep Not, Child*.

In 1964 Ngũgĩ went to Leeds University on a British Council scholarship and wrote on the theme of alienation in the novels of the West Indian George Lamming; he did not, however, complete his master's thesis. While there he also encountered the writings of Marx, Engels, and Frantz Fanon. Their influence is apparent in *A Grain of Wheat*, which he wrote at Leeds.

In 1967 Ngũgĩ returned to Kenya and became a special lecturer in English at Nairobi University, but after just two years in this position he resigned in protest over the administration's failure to adequately safeguard academic freedom. He had grown disillusioned, in any case, with the syllabus and had proposed a greater emphasis on African literature. He was not the only one who had such ideas, and many of his suggestions in this area were soon implemented. In 1971 he returned to the university, but even then the core of his argument, which had been to establish at the heart of the department the study of the historic continuity of African rather than British literary culture, was not fully accepted. Since 1971, though, the department's thinking has in fact moved more decisively in Ngũgĩ's direction.

From the time that he began at Leeds University Ngũgĩ has traveled extensively, giving papers at conferences throughout the world and becoming well known as a spokesman for African literature and Gikuyu, in particular. He has also been a visiting professor at many universities. In 1970, for example, he taught in the United States at Northwestern University; in 1984, at the University of Bayreuth and the University of Auckland, New Zealand; and at Yale in the spring of 1989, 1990, 1991, and 1992. He has also taught at Smith and at Amherst. He has, in an ironic way, been Kenya's gift to the world.

While away from Nairobi in 1969 and 1970 he was writing *Homecoming*, and in late 1970 he began *Petals of Blood*. He finished the latter in September 1975 while staying at a guesthouse in Yalta provided by the Soviet Writers Union. In 1973 he became the acting head of the newly named Department of Literature at the University of Nairobi. He had been the first African in the

English Department and was now the first African to head a department in the university. But troubles were on their way.

In 1974 he began writing the play *The Trial of Dedan Kimathi*. The play was performed in 1976 by the Kenya National Theatre. In that same year Ngũgĩ chaired the cultural committee of the Kamiriithu Community Educational and Cultural Centre (KCECC), a collective that oversaw a very successful literacy program. From these experiences Ngũgĩ wrote the play *I Will Marry When I Want* at the end of the year. At the same time he began the novel *Caitaani Mutharaba-ini*, initially in English; he soon changed his mind and wrote it in Gikuyu.

The following year, 1976, he officially changed his name from James Ngũgĩ to Ngũgĩ wa Thiong'o, and worked on the script for the play *Ngaahika Ndeenda*. In 1977 he published *Petals of Blood*. Both works were seen as highly controversial, and the play's license for performance was quickly withdrawn. At the end of December 1977 Daniel arap Moi, then vice-president and minister for home affairs, ordered Ngũgĩ detained in Kamiti Maximum Security Prison. He was released one year later, following protests around the world by various literary groups and by Amnesty International. While in prison Ngũgĩ wrote *Caitaani Mutharaba-ini* (later translated as *Devil on the Cross*) on toilet paper and began *Detained*.

After his release he and his family were subjected to frequent harassment. While working on a revision of the written Gikuyu language in a study group in Nairobi, he continued giving speeches abroad, in London, Denmark, Japan, and elsewhere. In 1980 both *Caitaani Mutharaba-ini* and *Ngaahika Ndeenda* were published, and *Detained* was published the following year. They increased his international reputation but confirmed the government's hostility toward the writer. In 1981 *The Trial of Dedan Kimathi* was presented in Kiswahili (as *Mzalendo Kimathi*) at the University of Nairobi.

In 1982 the government became more vigilant in its opposition, denying permission for the performance of Ngũgĩ's *Maitu Njugira* (*Mother Sing for Me*) and destroying the public theatre run by the KCECC. Upon hearing of his imminent arrest in June, Ngũgĩ extended the series of lectures he was giving outside the country. He helped form the Committee for the Release of Political Prisoners in Kenya and in 1987 became the chairman of Umoja, a consortium of dissident Kenyans. In 1990 he presented the first Arthur Ravenscroft Lecture at Leeds University. Since the fall of 1992 he has been a professor of comparative literature and performance studies at New York University. In that year he presented one of the Dunning Trust Lectures at Queens University, Kingston, Canada, and the commencement speech at Choate Rosemary Hall. His exile continues.

MAJOR WORKS AND THEMES

Ngũgĩ is a novelist, dramatist, essayist, short-story writer, journalist, and critic. Throughout the development of his career as a writer, his abiding principal theme has been the struggle of the common people of Kenya to come to terms with the effects on their culture of colonialism and the neocolonialism that followed. In the second half of his career he has signaled to the larger world community his decision to make the Kikuyu his first audience, generally writing first in Gikuyu, then translating the work—often into Kiswahili first, and then into English.

The Mau Mau war took place between 1952 and 1958 and touched Ngũgĩ's family intimately. When he began his first novels, therefore, he became the war's chronicler in fiction. *Weep Not, Child* was his first published novel, but he wrote *The River Between* before this. Each of these early novels is a *Bildungsroman*, and each has a protagonist with hopes for messianic deliverance from the country's problems.

The River Between is told in the third person through the eyes of an omniscient narrator. It is set in the late 1920s and 1930s and portrays an allegorical opposition between Christianity and the earlier Kikuyu culture. The community situated on the ridge of Makuyu comes to represent the Christian believers who reject the earlier ways as evil; the community on the ridge of Kameno, on the other hand, is the home of the protagonist, Waiyaki, and had been the home of his ancestor, the Kikuyu prophet Mugo wa Kibiro.

Waiyaki's father, Chege, sees the advantages of Western knowledge, but sees its dangers as well. He encourages Waiyaki to become a student in the missionaries' schools, but warns him not to be won over to their ways. Another member of Chege's generation, on the other hand, represents those who are sincere converts to Christianity: Joshua, in fact, wishes to transform his society by bringing more Kikuyu to the waters of baptism. Waiyaki and Joshua's two daughters, Muthoni and Nyambura, prefer to avoid such rigid dichotomies. In the course of the novel they seek to combine the two cultures.

For Waiyaki, this synthesis is to take the form of a revelation, in which he learns as a child that he is to assume a messianic role, acquire Western knowledge, and then unite his people (the book was originally entitled *The Black Messiah*). He begins this task by resigning from the Christian school and starting an independent Kikuyu school. Muthoni's attempt to combine the two worlds ends tragically. As a Christian, she has been forbidden to undergo female circumcision, but as a Kikuyu this is a necessary rite of initiation into womanhood. She therefore defies her father and goes ahead with the ceremony. Her consequent death ironically pushes the two factions farther apart. Waiyaki, meanwhile, supports the Kiama, a secret society that wishes to maintain Kikuyu culture and lands. But he himself is symbolically torn apart when he falls in love with the Christian Nyambura (Muthoni's sister), who is rejected by the Kiama because she refuses circumcision. She, in turn, rejects Waiyaki's offer of marriage, though she loves him, and instead supports her father.

Another member of Chege's generation, Kabonyi, is the leader of the Kiama faction, and he turns the group against Waiyaki. He usurps Waiyaki's role as prophet and charges the younger man with betrayal of Kikuyu customs. He further plans to lead an attack on the Christians, forcibly circumcising them and burning their huts. Waiyaki warns Joshua, and the Kiama completely abandon him. At this point Nyambura consents to the marriage proposal and is consequently rejected by her father, as her sister had been.

As the Christians prepare for Christmas and the traditional Kikuyus prepare for the circumcision ritual, Waiyaki addresses both groups. He speaks near the Honia, the river between these two communities; its name, ironically, means "regeneration." He has recognized (but too late), he tells the people, that education will not be enough: some political activity to regain Kikuyu lands will be needed. But Kabonyi interrupts by demanding that Waiyaki denounce the "unclean" Nyambura. When he refuses, the Kiama faction arrests the couple.

Among the typical themes announced by this novel and appearing in much that followed were, first, the need for action rather than well-meaning ideals, and, second, the persistence of self-defeating infighting among the Kikuyu and, by extension, among many colonized peoples. By a variation in the point of view in the novel, Ngũgĩ also begins his exploration of the different sorts of psychological damage that colonialism has left behind.

Weep Not, Child, though published before *The River Between*, is a chronological extension of the history of the Kikuyu begun in the book we have just discussed. *Weep Not, Child* focuses on the period about fifteen years after the close of *The River Between*, the events at the end of World War II. It looks at the causes of the Mau Mau war and is the most autobiographical of the novels.

The protagonist, Njoroge, is a young man much like Waiyaki. His family and his father, Ngotho, make sacrifices so that he can get an education, and the village itself sees him as its representative in the educational enterprise that will initiate it into the knowledge of the Western world. Naturally enough, Njoroge internalizes this deputation and begins to envision himself as something of a potential messiah for his people, a combination of the Kikuyu myths and the biblical hopes he is imbibing at school.

Howlands, an English settler, has expropriated Ngotho's lands, though, and the reality of the home situation becomes increasingly desperate and demeaning for Njoroge's family. His father is eventually castrated and tortured to death; his brothers meet similar fates. Howlands's own son is subsequently killed. Meanwhile, as in *The River Between*, there are various views taken of the English by the Kikuyu. Ngotho's contemporary, Jacobo, cooperates with them and is subsequently rewarded with wealth. Again, as in *The River Between*, there is a generational conflict with Romeo-and-Juliet overtones: Njoroge falls in love with Mwihaki, Jacobo's daughter.

But the real story in the novel is the decay of Njoroge's sense of self and his respect for his role in society. He remains, basically, a passive observer of the disintegration around him and takes a defensive stance toward his responsibilities as a member of a collapsing community. To be a messiah in such a world would be too painful, and he finds no adequate outlet for the idealistic dreams that had shaped his childhood. He unsuccessfully attempts suicide. The book suggests that this is one option for the Kikuyu people; the Mau Mau war is another. Neither is without ambiguity.

There is a marked advance in sophistication after these two novels, both in technique and in theme. In subsequent work Ngũgĩ shows a clearer understanding of the complexities of the postcolonial situation and the politics and economics of exploitation. The thinking of Frantz Fanon and others gives his next novel a sharper bite.

Kenya became independent in 1963. *A Grain of Wheat* is set in the last five days before the enactment of this independence. As in *Weep Not, Child*, it rehearses the events of the Mau Mau war, principally through retrospective narration, and demonstrates the ambivalence with which the people look forward to the future. The earlier books had portrayed the personal anguish of anticolonial action or inaction, but had implicitly held out hope for some sort of messianic figure leading the people to independence. Now the emphasis shifts to the community itself and to the interchange among its members. It is difficult to speak, therefore, of any individual as the book's protagonist: the people themselves are the protagonist, and they are a complex blend of qualities. The personal ambiguities of *The River Between* and *Weep Not, Child* are now distributed among five principal characters: Mumbi, Gikonyo, Karanja, Mugo, and Kihika. Each progresses or regresses in the course of the novel, or resists change and demonstrates the dangers of inactivity. An affirmation of community is valorized; complicity with neocolonialism is condemned.

On one level the plot is a detective story, a search for the individual who has betrayed a Mau Mau leader, Kihika. But on a deeper level Ngũgĩ is orchestrating an interior search for the various motives of those who participated in the war. In gradually revealing to the reader the history of the participation of his characters, Ngũgĩ demonstrates that all of them are important to the larger group's resuscitation: qualities that are ignored in an individual at one stage of the community's development, or are demeaned, may at a later stage be called to the fore as precisely what is needed. His is an organic view of group interchange.

The title suggests one of Ngũgĩ's continuing themes: the people's tie to the soil. Its biblical allusion also suggests the self-sacrificial nature that must be part of the community's efforts to rebuild (''unless a grain of wheat die''). Mugo seems to embody the older notion of personal messiahship espoused by Njoroge and Waiyaki, but Kihika speaks of Ngũgĩ's newer sense of shared sacrifice and leadership. While intolerant of the misuse of power, Ngũgĩ shows compassion even for those who have betrayed the community if they move forward toward honesty and generosity. He encourages the move from isolation to communality.

The story takes place in the village of Thabai, which has been destroyed in the war. Among the advances in Ngũgĩ's style is his use of irony in this book: Thabai has chosen Mugo to be its new mayor, not knowing that he had earlier betrayed the patriot Kihika. But Mugo grows in the office. His mirror image, Karanja, moved in the opposite direction, however, and supported the colonial police force. There is irony here, as well: he takes this reactionary step to be near the woman he loves, Mumbi, who had been imprisoned. This is an essentially selfish and self-deluded act, especially since Mumbi loves Gikonyo, and the community rejects Karanja.

The complex web of relationships in this novel is a thematic demonstration of the newer politics of responsibility that Ngũgĩ brought to the writing of the book. Kihika became a patriot, a fighter, by leaving his pregnant lover behind; Gikonyo, on the other hand, does everything he can to return to the relationships the war had forced him to abandon. When he does return, however, he discovers that Mumbi is soon to have not his child, but Karanja's. Ngũgĩ is not interested in blame, but in providing a symbol for the community as a family of mutually dependent relationships. The novel's closing also offers the hope of a burgeoning harvest for the new nation.

Petals of Blood takes the next chronological step, focusing on the neocolonial culture that succeeded independence. The harvest forecast in *A Grain of Wheat* is here characterized as bitter indeed. Again, the plot centers around a cast of characters, each of whom responds variously to the challenges of national independence. The principal focus, however, seems to be Munira, another of Ngũgĩ's characters who prefers to sit on the fence, to remain isolated rather than commit himself to the struggle on one side or the other. His progress toward a markedly neocolonial rejection of native aspirations serves to highlight the nobility of many of the other characters around him, flawed though they also are. He seems to embody the same subjective preoccupations that crippled Karanja in *A Grain of Wheat*.

The novel is set up as an investigation into the murder of three Kenyans who have profited from neocolonialism: Kimeria, Chui, and Mzigo. They represented the institutions of the new society, the businessmen, school administrators, clerics, and legislators. They are, perhaps, too insistently venal to be fully believable characters, but they provide plenty of opportunity for Ngũgĩ to demonstrate the hollow nature of capitalism and the insensitivity of its processes.

Their counterparts are Karega, Wanja, and Abdullah. We see Karega find a voice for his progressively radicalized political Marxist views and become insistent upon the role the community must play in its own regeneration. We observe the forces that lead Wanja to prostitution, forces that offer her few alternatives to the self-defensive posture that shapes her life under the new system. We further recognize the degradation of Abdullah from his former glory as a Mau Mau warrior to his present life as a near beggar.

The story is told in the most interesting way, through a series of flashbacks occasioned by the police investigation. Ngũgĩ is careful in the slow drip of plot details, and it is not until the closing pages that the murder mystery is solved. But the real investigation, one that has been forecast in his earlier novels, is into the complex characters and their motivations. The plot details and relationships among characters have been compared to Dickens; the exploration of motivation may remind the reader of Dostoyevsky.

The community itself plays a major role in the development of the plot, and the characters serve principally as stereotypical members of the larger group. Most significant are the villagers of Ilmorog and their decision to march on parliament to present their grievances. Ngũgĩ suggests that their inevitable disillusionment does not defeat them: the murder, in fact, demonstrates the self-consuming nature of those dedicated to positions of neocolonial power. Instead, the novel ends on a hopeful note similar to that in *A Grain of Wheat*. Wanja is about to have Abdullah's child, and the community that truly signifies hope for Kenya is to continue. But this is a tempered hope, at best, since the powers of neocolonialism continue to usurp the rightful powers of the people themselves. The result is a diminishment of the nation and the aggrandizement of the few.

Devil on the Cross is another stylistic step forward for Ngũgĩ, though it is a step some do not welcome. This is his first novel written in Gikuyu and then translated into English. This process reflects his recognition that his first audience of choice is the people of Kenya, especially those who do not read English. The book is, some say, more clearly didactic than its predecessors. If that is true, it can also be said that it is daring in other ways. It attempts to maintain two styles of narration, one quite realistic, and the other a form of magical realism.

The target of the novel is, again, unbridled capitalism, but Ngũgĩ has also underscored the problems of sexism in a neocolonial society. The setting is Ilmorog, as in *Petals of Blood*, and in the most memorable section the story pits the lowly citizens against an assemblage of thieves of various sorts, representatives of powerful international interests. This latter group has gathered in a cave for a feast in which they vie for the title of greatest thief. The ordinary people, who have not been invited, have run afoul of the law by protesting this imposition from outside. The violence of earlier novels is here somewhat stylized, but presented as inherent in this form of industrialization.

The tale is told as if by a balladeer and centers on Wariinga, a woman who kills her former lover (whose son she had hoped to marry). The echoes of the story of Wanja are obvious. As in earlier novels, there is also a contrast between this character, who grows away from bourgeois notions of class and privilege and assumes an active role in changing society, and a character like Gatuiria, who shrinks before the dangerous possibilities of choice.

This is the first of Ngũgĩ's novels in which laughter is used as a forceful weapon against his intended targets. But the revolutionary rhetoric that accompanies it is, if anything, even fiercer. Since the book is first addressed to the suffering poor, its incitement to rise up and overthrow unjust masters demonstrates his apparent conviction that a simple reform of the colonizer's institutions will not suffice to empower the people and bring lasting reform to the operations of the country. Far from urging the poor to a greater idealism, Ngũgĩ now places the emphasis on finding pragmatic routes to change, such as the organization of trade unions. This is the lesson he has his characters learn. As he has demonstrated in several novels, the middle class tends to follow its own interests; their opportunism plays into the hands of the elite overseers. Thus the poor must assume the responsibility for change.

The stark dichotomy is partially explained by the circumstances in which *Devil on the Cross* was composed. Ngũgĩ began it just before his arrest in 1977 and continued the writing in prison. He tried to conceal it by writing on toilet paper, but it was soon confiscated. It was returned to him in three weeks' time, and he continued the novel and began his prison memoir, *Detained*. The consequent novel strips away much of the trimmings of traditional novels and presents the drama in bold, surreal figures.

Ngũgĩ has one collection of short stories, *Secret Lives and Other Stories*, and a good number of plays: *The Black Hermit; This Time Tomorrow: Three Plays* (including, as well, *The Rebels* and *The Wound in My Heart*); *The Trial of Dedan Kimathi; Ngaahika Ndeenda* (*I Will Marry When I Want*); *Maitu Njugira* (*Mother Sing For Me*); and *Matigari ma Njiruungi*. The first of the plays, *The Black Hermit*, was written at the time that Ngũgĩ was changing his mind regarding the greatest besetting problem in Kenya, and it shows his ambivalence. He had thought that tribalism was the greatest threat, but soon came to regard capitalism and its neocolonial minions to be more significant. *The Trial of Dedan Kimathi*, which Micere Mugo coauthored, is of greater significance and demonstrates Ngũgĩ's commitment to theatre as a form of politics rather than high art. It tells the story of the great Mau Mau hero and the temptations he undergoes from neocolonial forces to give up the struggle for the liberation of the people. The play and those that follow it embody Ngũgĩ's decision to bring his vision to the large mass of people in Kenya who might not read his novels. He endorses a theatre that is not restricted to performance within buildings. This became more insistent in *Ngaahika Ndeenda*, presented in Gikuyu and loudly proclaiming the injustices of neocolonialism. Its production resulted in his imprisonment.

Ngũgĩ's concern that he reach a local audience, and his lifelong concern with education, resulted in his stories for children: *Njamba Nene na Mbaathi i Mathagu, Bathitoora ya Njamba Nene*, and *Njamba Nene na Chibu King'ang'i*. His nonfiction collections include *Homecoming: Essays on African and Caribbean Literature, Culture, and Politics; Writers in Politics; Detained: A Writer's Prison Diary; Barrel of a Pen: Resistance to Repression in Neocolonial Kenya; Decolonising the Mind: The Politics of Language in African Literature; Writing against Neocolonialism*; and *Moving the Centre: The Struggle for Cultural Freedoms*.

As in the plays, so in the prose essays Ngũgĩ persistently applies the political test to art, demanding in the *Homecoming* essays that literature be judged in terms of its effect on the society from which it springs. *Writers in Politics* documents the development of Ngũgĩ's thinking during the 1970s, when he says he stopped being a teacher and became a student at the feet of Kenyan peasants and workers. *Decolonising the Mind* offers a vigorous and sustained explanation of the importance of national languages and the production of national literatures in that language. To do otherwise, argues Ngũgĩ, is to remain complicit in the colonizer's view of the world. *Moving the Centre* argues for the freeing of Kenyan culture from Eurocentrism, colonial legacies, and racism.

CRITICAL RECEPTION

Ngũgĩ wa Thiong'o is seen today as the most important writer from East Africa and one of the three best-known Anglophone African authors; his novels have been translated into more than fourteen languages. A consistent antagonist to neocolonial interests, he is considered by many to be the most significant contemporary writer from the African continent. As we have noted, he would no longer consider himself an Anglophone author: English has become his third language, after Gikuyu and Kiswahili. This commitment to the principle of national culture helps explain both his importance for the African continent and the entire Third World and the ongoing controversy that surrounds him.

That Ngũgĩ has taken such a public stand for literature in native languages is doubly significant, since his *Weep Not, Child* was the first novel written in English to be published by an East African. In 1966 the book went on to win first place for Anglophone novel at the first World Festival of Negro Arts in Dakar, which was awarded by a jury headed by Langston Hughes. This was not his first award, nor was it by any means his last. *The Black Messiah*, which he later revised as *The River Between*, had won first place in the English-language section of the novel-writing competition sponsored by the East African Literature Bureau in 1961.

In 1973 he received the Lotus Prize in Literature at the fifth Afro-Asian Writers Conference in Khazakhstan. In 1981 his novel *Caitaani Mutharaba-ini* (*Devil on the Cross*) received Special Commendation in the Noma Award for Publishing in Africa. His children's story *Njamba Nene na Mbaathi i Mathagu* received the same commendation two years later. He has won the East African Novel Prize and in 1991 received the Paul Robeson Award for Artistic Excellence, Political Conscience, and Integrity.

In his own view, perhaps, his greatest award might be his exile, a clear demonstration that his writing is having an immediate impact. His use of literature for clearly political purposes is the aspect of his writing that meets with negative criticism from some quarters of the academy. Ngũgĩ remains unrepentant and unconvinced by the argument that this is all well and good as long as the rhetoric does not overwhelm the art. As with any ''committed'' writer, he attempts ''to harness the 'laws' of art to the dictates of his own conscience'' (Cook and Okenimkpe, 243).

Ngũgĩ's prose is praised because ''at its best [it] is never far removed from poetry'' (Larson, 122). Others attribute this to the influence of biblical rhythms, beyond the many direct quotations. But some have spoken of his ''apparent stylistic ineptitude,'' suggesting that ''quite a number of his sentences seem not only clumsy, but grammatically wrong'' (Palmer, 9). Such critics complain that ''the real problem with Ngũgĩ's language is that one is constantly irritated by its naïvety and extreme simplicity'' (Palmer, 10). Others counter that as the neocolonial reality has deepened, "Ngũgĩ's style has evolved away from Biblical simplicity" (Nazareth, 252).

Ngũgĩ's characteristic themes have met with various responses, most of them positive. Regarding *A Grain of Wheat*, Nadine Gordimer remarks that it is extremely interesting because it brings a "new" theme to African literature: "the effects on a people of the changes brought about in themselves by the demands of a bloody and bitter struggle for independence" (Gordimer, 226). His religious concerns prompt some to describe Ngũgĩ's work as "the best account yet of how Christianity not only gnawed away at tribal values (the standard charge against it), but how it actually resonated with deep elements in the hearts of the people" (Roscoe, 171).

His powers of characterization are praised as "second to none in Africa" (Roscoe, 190). Larson speaks of his use of the "lyrical collective consciousness" (138) and impressionism, which he describes as "the internal rendering of his character's emotional reactions to the external world" (155). But he comes under attack when didacticism prompts him to present stereotypical mouthpieces for philosophical positions (Nkosi, 334–45).

As others have recognized, however, Ngũgĩ is fully aware that his plays and novels at times become openly rhetorical. He insists, in fact, that they must be; as his own political thinking has clarified and he has increasingly put his talents in the service of change for the common man and woman, his narrative voice has become more urgent. Thus in *Devil on the Cross* "the artistry lies first in laying bare social evils which normally lie snugly concealed by rationalizations and apologia . . . and secondly, in lending to revolutionary idealism a new plausibility and human warmth" (Cook and Okenimkpe, 242).

BIBLIOGRAPHY

Works by Ngũgĩ wa Thiong'o

"Address by Ngũgĩ wa Thiong'o at the Opening of the 6th International Book Fair of Radical and Third World Books at the Camden Centre, London, March 1987." *7th International Book Fair of Radical Black and Third World Books* (program). London: International Book Fair of Radical Black and Third World Books, 1988. 4–5.

Barrel of a Pen: Resistance to Oppression in Neocolonial Kenya. London and Port of Spain: New Beacon Books; Trenton, NJ: Africa World Press, 1983.

The Black Hermit. Kampala: Makerere University Press, 1963; London: Heinemann, 1968.

Caitaani Mutharaba-ini. Nairobi: Heinemann Kenya, 1980. (Translated as *Devil on the Cross.*)

Decolonising the Mind: The Politics of Language in African Literature. London: James Currey; Nairobi: Heinemann Kenya; Portsmouth, NH: Heinemann; Harare: Zimbabwe Publishing House, 1986.

Detained: A Writer's Prison Diary. London: Heinemann, 1981.

Devil on the Cross. Trans. from the Gikuyu. London: Heinemann Educational Books, 1982.

Education for a National Culture. Harare: Zimbabwe Publishing House, 1981.

"The Fig Tree." *Penpoint* 9 (December 1960): 3–9.

A Grain of Wheat. London: Heinemann, 1967. Rev. ed. London: Heinemann, 1986.

Homecoming: Essays on African and Caribbean Literature, Culture, and Politics. London: Heinemann, 1972.

"I Try Witchcraft." *AHS Magazine* (Alliance High School, Kikuyu) September 1957: 21–22.

I Will Marry When I Want (with Ngũgĩ wa Mirii). Trans. from the Gikuyu by the authors. London: Heinemann Educational Books, 1982.

"An Interview with Ngũgĩ." *Weekly Review* January 9, 1978: 9–12.

"An Interview with Ngũgĩ wa Thiong'o." In *Talking with African Writers: Interviews with African Poets, Playwrights, and Novelists*. Ed. Jane Wilkinson. London: James Currey; Portsmouth, NH: Heinemann, 1992.

Maitu Njugira (Mother Sing for Me), play in script. Mimeographed material.

Matigari. Trans. into English by Wangui wa Goro. Oxford: Heinemann, 1989; Trenton, NJ: Africa World Press, 1996.

Matigari ma Njiruungi. Nairobi: Heinemann Kenya, 1986.

Moving the Centre: The Struggle for Cultural Freedoms. London: James Currey; Nairobi: EAEP; Portsmouth, NH: Heinemann, 1993.

Ngaahika Ndeenda (with Ngũgĩ wa Mirii). (Translated as *I Will Marry When I Want*.) Nairobi: Heinemann Kenya, 1980.

Njamba Nene and the Flying Bus (Njamba Nene na Mbaathi i Malhagu). Nairobi: Heinemann, 1986.

Njamba Nene and the Cruel Chief (Njamba Nena na Chibu King'ang'i). Adventures of Njamba Nene 3. Trans. Wangui wa Goro. Illustrations by Emmanuel Kariuki. Nairobi: Heinemann Kenya, 1988.

Njamba Nene's Pistol (Bathitoora ya Njamba Nene). Adventures of Njamba Nene 2. Trans. Wangui wa Goro. Illustrations by Emmanuel Kariuki. Nairobi: Heinemann Kenya, 1986.

"On Writing in Gikuyu." *Research in African Literatures* 16.2 (1985): 151–56.

Petals of Blood. London: Heinemann, 1977; New York: E. P. Dutton, 1978.

"The Rebels." *Penpoint* 11 (October 1961): 59–69.

The River Between. London: Heinemann, 1965.

Secret Lives. London: Heinemann, 1976.

This Time Tomorrow. Nairobi: EALB, [1970? 1971?]. Reprint. Nairobi: Kenya Literature Bureau, 1982.

"This Wound in My Heart." *Penpoint* 13 (October 1962): 23–29.

"The Trench: An Extract from an Unpublished Novel [*Grain*]." *Africa: Tradition and Change*. Ed. Ime Ikiddeh; assistant ed. James Ngugi. Leeds University Union Africa Week. Leeds University, 1965. 25–29.

The Trial of Dedan Kimathi (with Micere Githae Mugo). London: Heinemann, 1976.

"Voluntary Service Camp." *AHS Magazine* (Alliance High School, Kikuyu) September 1958: 29–30.

Weep Not, Child. London: Heinemann, 1964.

Writers in Politics. London: Heinemann, 1981.

Writing against Neo-Colonialism. Wembley: Vita Books, 1986.

Studies of Ngũgĩ wa Thiong'o

Amuka, Peter. *"Kenyan Oral Literature: Ngũgĩ wa Thiong'o Fiction and His Search for a Voice."* Diss. 1986, UCLA.

Bailey, Diana. *Ngũgĩ wa Thiong'o, The River Between: A Critical View.* Ed. Yolande Cantu. London: Collins in Association with British Council, 1985.

Bardolph, Jacqueline. *Ngũgĩ wa Thiong'o: L'homme et l'oeuvre.* Paris: Présence Africaine, 1991.

Bjorkman, Ingrid. *Mother, Sing For Me: People's Theatre in Kenya.* London; Atlantic Highlands, NJ: Zed, 1989.

Brown, David Maughan. *Land, Freedom, and Fiction: History and Ideology in Kenya.* London: Zed Books, 1985.

Cancel, Robert. "Nadine Gordimer Meets Ngũgĩ wa Thiong'o: Text into Film in Oral History." *Research in African Literatures* 26.3 (1995): 36–48.

Cantalupo, Charles, ed. *Ngũgĩ wa Thiong'o: Text and Contexts.* Trenton, NJ: Africa World Press, 1995.

———. *The World of Ngũgĩ wa Thiong'o.* Trenton, NJ: Africa World Press, 1995.

Cook, David, and Michael Okenimkpe. *Ngũgĩ wa Thiong'o: An Exploration of His Writings.* London: Heinemann, 1983.

Drame, Kandioura. *The Novel as Transformation Myth: A Study of the Novels of Mongo Beti and Ngũgĩ wa Thiong'o.* Syracuse: Maxwell School of Citizenship and Public Affairs, Syracuse University, 1990.

Gordimer, Nadine. Review of *A Grain of Wheat. Michigan Quarterly Review* (Fall 1970): 226.

Gugler, Josef. "How Ngũgĩ wa Thiong'o Shifted from Class Analysis to a Neocolonialist Perspective." *Journal of Modern African Studies* 32.2 (1994): 329–39.

Harris, Michael T. *Outsiders and Insiders: Perspectives of Third World Culture in British and Post-colonial Fiction.* New York: Peter Lang, 1994.

Indrasena Reddy, K. *The Novels of Achebe and Ngũgĩ: A Study in the Dialectics of Commitment.* New Delhi: Prestige Books, 1994.

Kessler, K. "Rewriting History in Fiction: Elements of Postmodernism in Ngũgĩ wa Thiong'o's Later Novels." *Ariel* 25.2 (1994): 75–90.

Kiiru, Muchugu. *Ngũgĩ wa Thiong'o's A Grain of Wheat.* Nairobi: Heinemann Kenya, 1985.

Killiam, G. D. *An Introduction to the Writings of Ngũgĩ.* London: Heinemann, 1980.

———, ed. *Critical Perspectives on Ngũgĩ wa Thiong'o.* Washington, DC: Three Continents Press, 1984.

Larson, Charles R. *The Emergence of African Fiction.* Bloomington: Indiana University Press, 1972.

Loflin, Christine. "Ngũgĩ wa Thiong'o's Visions of Africa." *Research in African Literatures* 26.4 (1995): 76–93.

Mazama, Ama. "The Relevance of Ngũgĩ wa Thiong'o for the Afrocentric Quest." *Western Journal of Black Studies* 18.4 (1994): 211–20.

Meyer, Herta. *"Justice for the Oppressed—": The Political Dimension in the Language Use of Ngũgĩ wa Thiong'o.* Essen: Verlag Die Blaue Eule, 1991.

Narang, Hamish. *Politics as Fiction: The Novels of Ngũgĩ wa Thiong'o.* New Delhi: Creative Books, 1995.

Nazareth, Peter. "The Social Responsibility of the East African Writer." *Iowa Review* 7.2–3 (1976): 249–62.

Nkosi, Lewis. "A Voice from Detention." *West Africa* 3162 (February 20, 1978): 334–35.

Nwankwo, Chimalum Moses. *The Works of Ngũgĩ wa Thiong'o: Towards the Kingdom of Woman and Man.* Ikeja: Longman Nigeria, 1992.

Palmer, Eustace. *An Introduction to the African Novel.* London: Heinemann, 1976 (1972).

Parker, Michael, and Roger Starkey, eds. *Postcolonial Literatures: Achebe, Ngũgĩ, Desai, Walcott.* New York: St. Martin's Press, 1995.

Robson, Clifford B. *Ngũgĩ wa Thiong'o.* London: Macmillan, 1979.

Roscoe, Adrian. *Uhuru's Fire: African Literature East to South.* Cambridge: Cambridge University Press, 1977.

Sicherman, Carol. *Bibliography of Ngũgĩ wa Thiong'o: Primary and Secondary Sources, 1957–1987.* Oxford: Hans Zell, 1989.

———. "Ngũgĩ wa Thiong'o and the Writing of Kenyan History." *Research in African Literatures* 20.3 (1989): 347–70.

———. *Ngũgĩ wa Thiong'o: The Making of a Rebel: A Source Book in Kenyan Literature and Resistance.* London: Hans Zell, 1990.

Tsabedze, Clara. *African Independence from Francophone and Anglophone Voices: A Comparative Study of the Post-independence Novels of Ngũgĩ and Sembene.* New York: Peter Lang, 1994.

JOHN C. HAWLEY

LEWIS NKOSI (1936–   )

BIOGRAPHY

Journalist, critic, playwright, and novelist, Lewis Nkosi was born in 1936 in Durban, Natal, South Africa, and educated in public schools in Zululand. In 1955 he launched a career in journalism as editor of a Zulu-English weekly called the *Ilanga LaseNatal* (Natal Sun), and in the following year he joined the staff of South Africa's popular *Drum* magazine. While working for *Drum* as chief reporter and later for the *Post*, Nkosi lived in a ghetto in Johannesburg, a city that he has described as being totally without an inner life; he believes that this intellectual, emotional, and moral ennui, exemplified in South African city life, is responsible for the country's inability to produce a substantial body of literature.

In 1961–62 Nkosi was awarded a Nieman Fellowship in Journalism for a year's study at Harvard University. For his acceptance of the fellowship, South Africa issued him a one-way permit out of his native country, barring any future return. Since leaving for Cambridge, Massachusetts, in 1961, Lewis Nkosi has been a writer in exile, and his works were not allowed to be published or quoted in his homeland.

Upon completion of his studies at Harvard, Nkosi lived in the United States and London for many years, traveling widely, working for radio and television as well as for newspapers and magazines. As a journalist, his numerous outspoken—and often controversial—articles have appeared in the *New Yorker*, the *London Observer*, the *Spectator*, the *Guardian*, the *New Statesman*, *Africa Report*, and *Black Orpheus*, among others. He was literary editor of the *New African* in London and in 1964 served as moderator and interviewer for the "African Writers of Today" series on television. *Home and Exile*, Nkosi's first collection of essays and articles, was published in London in 1964 and received an award at the Dakar World Festival of Negro Arts. The following year *The Rhythm of Violence*, his play set in Johannesburg, was also published in England; it is reported to be the first play to be written and published in English by a black South African since 1936. The Ethiope Publishing Company in Nigeria produced his next collection of essays, *The Transplanted Heart*, in 1975, and Longman published *Tasks and Masks: Themes and Styles of African Literature* in 1981. Nkosi has written some short fiction; his first novel, *Mating Birds*, was published in 1986. Lewis Nkosi, though exiled from his home country, has returned to Africa and teaches literature at the University of Zambia.

MAJOR WORKS AND THEMES

Since South Africa issued Nkosi a one-way permit to leave his home country for America in 1961, the writer has been, in certain ways, defined by his status as an exile. It is possible that the distance has accorded him a clearer vision, as he has developed into one of the most outspoken commentators on virtually every aspect of African life and literature. He is today recognized as one of Africa's leading literary critics, though he is also a fledgling fiction writer.

In his earliest collection of essays, *Home and Exile*, Nkosi clearly articulates the dominant theme of his critical writings, which is to identify the nature and history of indigenous African literature. In answering the question what is African literature? he remarks on an ironic consequence of the colonial experience: the linking of the various peoples of Africa, the spirit of rebellion providing them with a common language and consciousness (117). In his readings of African literature, he focuses on two elements as essential to the understanding of it: (1) the perception and representation of native society and (2) the reflection of a desire for sociopolitical change. *Home and Exile* contains provocative essays that are divided into three sections—"Home," "Exile," and "Literary"—in which he directs his keen eye upon a wide range of subjects, including apartheid, identity, sex, and the law in South Africa in the first group; New York, Paris, jazz, and writing in exile in the second; and various aspects of African literature in the third. He identifies the functioning of apartheid as "a daily exercise in the absurd" (25), describes the decade of the fifties, the last he spent in South Africa, as "fabulous" (3), and then proceeds to convey his lively impressions of the countries that he inhabited or visited as an exile. In the last and longest section, Nkosi critically evaluates both African and black American writing and captures the spirit of colonialism in a single line of Defoe's *Robinson Crusoe*, where Friday is instructed to address Crusoe as "Master" instead of by name (156).

His play, *The Rhythm of Violence*, is set in Johannesburg of the early sixties and revolves around the planting of a bomb in the midst of a white rally in the City Hall by a group of left-wing Boer, English, and African students who are trying to defy the racial prejudices of the oppressive apartheid regime. Complications arise as love blooms between a black boy, Tula, brother of the leader of the student opposition group, and a white girl, Sarie, whose father is expected to attend the rally. Tula informs Sarie of the plot, but arrives too late at the City Hall, which is completely destroyed; he is killed in front of the building. Sarie finds her father and sweetheart both dead; her grief at discovering Tula's slain body leads to the arrest of the plotters as well as herself. Sarie's is a story of loss and doom, but in the midst of the melee, a real as well as symbolic act of freedom and revenge is accomplished. The play was first performed in Nigeria in 1965 and at its best moments manages to capture the essence of the helpless rebellion of the blacks and their white allies against the oppression of apartheid. In a short story, "The Prisoner," published in *African Writing Today*, Nkosi imagines a dramatic overturning of the strictly hierarchical status quo between a black servant and his white master. Another short story by Nkosi, "Potgieter's Castle," is collected in *Come Back, Africa!*; both anthologies were published in the late sixties.

Primarily a journalist, essayist, and critic, Nkosi has received greater and wider acclaim for his nonfictional writings. *The Transplanted Heart*, a collection of twenty essays on art, politics, and travel, was published in Nigeria. *Tasks and Masks: Themes and Styles of African Literature* concentrates on the subject he has long known and studied, considering various aspects of African writing in thoughtful detail. In separate chapters, Nkosi analyzes modern African poetry, drama, and the novel, outlining the development of African writing since the impact of colonialism. In his critiques, he often returns to the peculiar problem of South African literature, a writing that he believes is defined by struggle and conflict, protest, commitment, and explanation. From the South African writer— and he himself is one—Nkosi believes that the world demands not merely art but a sociopolitical commitment to render more than the superficial meaning of a scene (76).

One of the aspects of apartheid life in South Africa that had early engaged Nkosi's attention was the strange interface between sexual behavior and the law, and his caustic pronouncements on the subject are recorded in an essay in *Home and Exile*, where he points out the irony of prohibitive laws for interracial sexual contact, which the whites apparently found appalling anyway (38). He lyrically describes the tragedy of black/white relations in South Africa as islands in a vast and tumultous ocean, "where between these islands billowing tides of confused sexual feelings often rise and threaten to overflow" (37). In *Mating Birds*, the fictional counterpart to his essays and articles on the subject, Nkosi holds up these tides for closer examination as he traces the growing sexual desire of a white woman (Veronica) and a black man (Sibiya) for each other on a segregated Durban beach, and the evolution of their extraordinary affair (if one may call it that) conducted entirely in silence at a symbolic physical distance from each other; at the point when this desire is finally being consummated, Veronica charges Sibiya with rape and has the black offender sentenced to death. The book is the black man's last testament, a plea for social justice from a prison cell where he awaits his execution.

CRITICAL RECEPTION

There is no doubt that Nkosi is today considered a major African critic and essayist, and his work is widely published, read, and acclaimed. His keen perception of political events in South Africa and their repercussions on the country's social and literary life is particularly appreciated. His first offerings as playwright and novelist, however, provoked mixed reactions. *The Rhythm of Violence* has been criticized for its contrived dialogue and lack of discipline; it has been called "hysterical." *Mating Birds*—which was widely reviewed in newspapers, magazines, and journals for the general reader and has begun to receive attention from students of African fiction—though praised for its tackling of a difficult and sensitive subject with compelling intensity, is also seen as a flawed work of art. Henry Louis Gates, Jr., in a review of the novel for the *New York Times Book Review*, comments: "This novel's great literary achievement—its vivid depiction of obsession—leads inevitably to its great flaw. . . . The ambiguities created by [Sibiya's] own troubled story prevent the liberation that he and the readers eagerly seek. . . . Perhaps Mr. Nkosi has created more ambivalence of motive than he wished or than is politically comfortable for blacks in a segregated South Africa" (3). Nevertheless, Nkosi's sincerity and passion for his subjects—primarily apartheid, African writing, travel, exile, and the arts—as made apparent in his controversial fiction and nonfiction alike, have situated him among the more important contemporary African writers.

BIBLIOGRAPHY

Works by Lewis Nkosi

Drama

The Rhythm of Violence. London: Oxford University Press, 1964.

Collections of Essays

Home and Exile and Other Selections. London and New York: Longman, 1965.
The Transplanted Heart. Lagos, Nigeria: Ethiope Publishing, 1975.
Tasks and Masks: Themes and Styles of African Literature. London: Longman, 1981.

Short Stories

"The Prisoner." *African Writing Today*. Ed. E. Mphahlele. Penguin, 1967.
"Potgieter's Castle." *Come Back, Africa!* Ed. H. L. Shore and M. Shore-Bos. International Publishers, 1968.

Novel

Mating Birds. New York: Harper and Row, 1986.

Articles

"The Forbidden Dialogue" (on race relations in South Africa). *UNESCO Courier* May–June 1986: 15.
"The South African Writer's Tale" (on possibilities of a book boycott). *New Statesman* 112 (October 10, 1986): 27.
"A Voice from Detention," *West Africa* 3162 (February 20, 1978): 334–35.

Studies of Lewis Nkosi

Ashcroft, Bill, Gareth Griffiths, and Helen Tiffin. "Colonialism and Silence: Lewis Nkosi's *Mating Birds*." *The Empire Writes Back: Theory and Practice in Postcolonial Literatures*. London and New York: Routledge, 1989. 83–87.
Gates, Henry Louis, Jr. "The Power of Her Sex, the Power of Her Race" (book review). *New York Times Book Review* May 18, 1986: 3.
Hanley, Lynne. "Writing across the Color Bar: Apartheid and Desire." *Massachusetts Review* 32.4 (Winter 1991–92): 495–506.
Packer, George. "Reports from the Inside" (book review). *Nation* 243 (November 22, 1986): 570.

BRINDA BOSE

FLORA NWAPA (1931–1993)

BIOGRAPHY

Flora Nwapa was born in 1931 in Oguta, eastern Nigeria, and died October 16, 1993, in Enugu, Nigeria. She was educated at the University of Ibadan, receiving her B.A. in 1957, and also earned a degree in education from the University of Edinburgh (1958). Nwapa was the education officer in Calabar in 1959 and taught English and geography at Queen's School in Enugu from 1959 until 1962. From 1962 to 1964 she was an administration officer at the University of Lagos. She also worked for the Ministries of Health, Education, and Welfare; Lands, Survey, and Urban Development; and Establishments. She was the managing director of both Tana Press, which publishes adult fiction, and Flora Nwapa and Co., publishing children's fiction, in Enugu, Nigeria. She was married to Gogo Nwakuche, an industrialist. They had three children.

MAJOR WORKS AND THEMES

Flora Nwapa's first novel, *Efuru*, was published in 1966, the first novel published by a Nigerian woman and the first novel in English by an African woman writer. It was followed by *Idu* (1970). Each of these novels has an eponymous heroine, struggling with the issue of childlessness in Igbo society. In her first novel, Nwapa's heroine Efuru is a strong, beautiful woman, but she has trouble conceiving a child. When she does have a baby, the child dies of a fever. After two unhappy marriages, Efuru finally leaves her second husband and, at the end of the novel, has dedicated herself to the lady of the lake, Uhamiri, a goddess who has no children but is beautiful, wealthy, and wise, like Efuru herself. Nwapa's second novel, *Idu*, is also concerned with the issue of motherhood. In

Idu, the dialogic style established in *Efuru* is even more central to the novel's thematic concerns. Through talk, the characters reassess and evaluate experience and fit individual occurrences into the social narrative.

Her next publication was a collection of stories, *This Is Lagos and Other Stories* (1971). These stories anticipate some of the changes in her narrative style that appear in *One Is Enough* (1981) and *Women Are Different* (1986). No longer does she show the subtlety of long conversations; her urban characters don't offer kola nut to one another, nor do they observe the formalities of greeting, with elaborate inquiries after one another's families. In these stories, the urban environment is also shown as debilitating and destructive to the lives of women.

Never Again (1975), a short novel, is set in the Igbo area of Nigeria during the Biafran War. *Wives at War and Other Stories* (1980) also focuses on the period of the Biafran War, emphasizing women's self-sacrifice and survival skills.

In *One Is Enough* (1981) and *Women Are Different* (1986), Nwapa moves her setting to urban Nigeria and widens her critique of Nigerian society to reveal the inadequacies and corruption of politicians and civil servants. In *One Is Enough*, Amaka becomes economically independent, but cynically uses her sexual favors as a way to obtain business contracts. In *Women Are Different*, Nwapa develops the stories of Rose, Comfort, Dora, and Agnes as they try to balance their education, marriage, careers, and children. Nwapa employs a different style in this work, using less conversation and more exposition, as she follows her characters through the decades.

Nwapa has also published a collection of poems, *Cassava Song and Rice Song* (1986), and several works for children, of which *Mammywater* (1979) is the most important. *Mammywater* is a retelling of the Igbo folktale of the lady of the lake. In this story, Soko, a young girl, is taken by Mammywater to her home at the bottom of the lake. Soko's brother, Deke, is determined to go after her. Deke finds Mammywater and pleads with both Mammywater and Urashi, the spirit of the river, to release his sister. Impressed by his humility, the spirits agree. The story emphasizes family loyalty, politeness, and respect for elders—it is Deke's behavior with both an old woman ashore and with the two spirits that results in his sister's release. In this story, Nwapa provides a vision of the lady of the lake that complements the description of Uhamiri in *Efuru*. She also provides a moral tale for Nigerian children based on Igbo cultural traditions.

At the time of her death, Nwapa had completed a manuscript of *The Lake Goddess*, her final novel, which will be published by Africa World Press.

CRITICAL RECEPTION

Most criticism of Nwapa's works has focused on the early novels, *Efuru* and *Idu*. Lloyd Brown argues that the titles of *Efuru* and *Idu* are misleading, suggesting that these will be novels about individual heroines, like *Madame Bovary*.

Rather, Brown sees these heroines as the centers of a web of relationships, the focus of the community's attention and concern.

The style of *Efuru* also sets it apart from traditional Western novels through its extraordinary use of dialogue. Elleke Boehmer calls Nwapa's style "a highly verbalised collective women's biography" (12). Most of the novel consists of conversations, primarily between women, gossiping, commiserating with each other, and suggesting strategies for overcoming problems. Maryse Condé, in her early article "Three Female Writers in Modern Africa," feels that the gossipy nature of the dialogue creates "a disturbing picture of narrowmindedness, superstition, malevolence, greed and fear" (136). Yet Efuru lives within a community of women who support each other. Most important is Ajanupu, her mother-in-law's sister, who offers her advice on childcare, relationships, and trade. Through these conversations, Nwapa reveals Igbo social values and how women themselves accept, reject, or revise these mores in pursuit of their own goals.

Unlike Chinua Achebe's *Things Fall Apart, Efuru* takes place in a community where there is little Western influence. Susan Andrade, in her reassessment of the importance of *Efuru,* argues that the heroine's choice of independence and her proud, intelligent character reveal an indigenous African feminism, not based on Western values. *Efuru* also emphasizes what *Things Fall Apart* elides—the day-to-day life of women with other women. Andrade sees *Efuru* as establishing the beginning of a female literary tradition in Nigeria. In this novel Nwapa begins a dialogue that is taken up by other African women writers about the limitations that the glorification of motherhood creates for African women; Buchi Emecheta's novel *The Joys of Motherhood* gets its title from the last paragraph of *Efuru.*

Nwapa's second novel, *Idu,* also focuses on motherhood. The plot of the novel, especially Idu's choice to die after her husband's death rather than live to take care of her child, has been critiqued as "contrived and artistically invalid" by Oladele Taiwo, but Ernest Emenyonu has praised it, claiming that it is consistent with Nwapa's representation of Igbo culture: "Even among the Igbo, the love between two individuals can be such that one cannot die without the other" ("Who Does Flora Nwapa Write For?", 30).

In Nwapa's collection of short stories, titled *This Is Lagos and Other Stories,* Nwapa's descriptive style is sparce, with the bare minimum of character description and setting. Lloyd Brown's appreciative evaluation of her method in these stories asserts that she uses the chaos of the urban environment, symbolized by the traffic jam, to reveal the confusions and misfortunes of city life. The entire collection is pervaded by a sense of tragedy, and the accidents and calamities that befall her characters seem inevitable. Brown shows that Nwapa's stories use an accumulative story line, building from simple statements and descriptions to the final catastrophe with a series of escalating conflicts. Her choice of the short story is suited to her topic, giving glimpses of the complexity of urban life, rather than trying to form these different story lines into a single artistic whole. The separateness of the stories reflects the isolation and chaos of urban life, and Brown argues that the terseness of her language reflects the "thinness of spirit and that limited humaneness which the stories themselves attribute to the society as a whole" (134).

Never Again (1975), Nwapa's war novel, is compared by Femi Ojo-Ade to Buchi Emecheta's *Destination Biafra*. Ojo-Ade sees Nwapa's narrative as rejecting war altogether, while Emecheta's affirms the Biafran side of the struggle. Nwapa's heroine, Kate, while initially believing in the Biafran cause, ends struggling simply to survive. Similarly, in *Wives at War and Other Stories*, Nwapa's characters emphasize family ties, friendship, and self-sacrifice. The women, Ojo-Ade argues, look beyond the battlefield to the need to rebuild the community once the war is over.

While Katherine Frank sees Amaka, the protagonist of Nwapa's next novel, *One Is Enough*, as a Western-style feminist ("Women without Men"), Jane Bryce-Okunlola claims that Amaka's values are pragmatic and conventional. In Nwapa's other urban novel, *Women Are Different*, the difficulties of the four women protagonists' lives have been linked by Chikwenye Ogunyemi to the postcolonial predicament: "Communities emerging from Fanonic, colonial violence suffer withdrawal symptoms, the characteristic postcolonial traumatic syndrome. Inertia, chaos, and disorientation set in, and these ephemeral disruptive forces must run their course for healing and progress to take place" ("Introduction," 6). In both of these novels, Ogunyemi sees Nwapa as "salting the wound," exposing corruption in order to heal it.

In addition to these works, Flora Nwapa has written a book of poetry, *Cassava Song and Rice Song* (1986), and several works for children, including *Emeka—Driver's Guard* (1972) and *Mammywater* (1979). These children's books were written after Nwapa saw the paucity of books her children were able to find in the bookstores, and were a driving force in Nwapa's decision to set up her publishing house for children's literature, Flora Nwapa & Co. Some recent critical studies on her children's literature include Ezenwa-Ohaeto's "The Child Figures and Childhood Symbolism in Flora Nwapa's Children's Fiction" and Patricia Emenyonu's "The Role of Contemporary Female Nigerian Writers in the Education of Nigerian Youth."

Nwapa's works have started to get new critical attention, as evidenced by the essays on Nwapa in *Motherlands: Black Women's Writing from Africa, the Caribbean, and South Asia* and comparisons of Nwapa to other African women writers by Susan Andrade, Gay Wilentz, Florence Stratton, and others. Africa World Press has recently come out with new editions of her novels and the two collections of short stories, *This Is Lagos* and *Wives at War*, and is planning to publish her posthumous novel *The Lake Goddess*. Initially overlooked in most studies of African writing in the sixties and seventies, she is now seen as the forerunner of a whole generation of African women writers.

In volume 26 of *Research in African Literatures* (Summer 1995), devoted to Nwapa, several critics link a reevaluation of Nwapa's work to a reevaluation of Western feminist theory and postcolonial theory. For example, Obioma Nnaemeka sees Nwapa's work as undoing the dichotomy of tradition and modernity. Nnaemeka strongly critiques Katherine Frank's reading of Efuru's independence of character as a "modern" aspect of the novel. Rather, Nnaemeka points out that within Igbo culture itself, there is a well-established tradition of negotiation and debate within the limits of traditional society. Efuru's ability to find a place for herself as a successful yet childless woman within her society is not a Western innovation, but a revelation of the room for difference within Igbo culture, as shown by the proverb "Let the kite perch and let the eagle perch." The traditional grounds for Efuru's independence are underscored by her religious devotion to the lady of the lake, Uhamiri. Nnaemeka's article, along with Chikwenye Ogunyemi's in the same volume, insists on the need to see both the effects of global capitalism and imperialism and the specific local effects of indigenous African cultures. Their work on Nwapa and Marie Umeh's article on Nwapa's last novel, *The Lake Goddess*, resist readings that try to fit Nwapa's work within pre-existing frameworks of Western feminism or cultural studies. Rather, an African feminism or womanism should be based on the real social and economic situation of women in Africa, which is markedly different from the socioeconomic position of most white, middle-class Western feminists. All three emphasize the figure of the Lake Goddess that runs through Nwapa's works as a symbol of the potential for an African-based feminist or womanist theory which does not reject but rather builds from the foundations of traditional culture.

These approaches to Nwapa share some characteristics of recent postcolonial feminist studies, such as *Scattered Hegemonies*, edited by Inderpal Grewal and Caren Kaplan. While acknowledging the role of global capitalism and imperialism in postcolonial nations, Grewal and Kaplan's essays also analyze the specific local cultural, economic, and historical conditions that are essential for the understanding of postcolonial cultural texts. Rather than identifying postcolonial commonalities, these essays and the recent essays on Nwapa emphasize how global politics are transformed, reworked and reimagined at the local level, reaffirming the vitality and flexibility of indigenous cultures' response to Westernization and imperialism. Studies such as Nnaemeka's, Ogunyemi's and Umeh's clarify the specific Igbo modalities of Nwapa's texts and reveal the sophistication and integrity of Nwapa's vision of African women's lives.

BIBLIOGRAPHY

Works by Flora Nwapa

Efuru. London: Heinemann, 1966.
"My Spoons Are Finished." *Présence Africaine* 63 (1967): 227–35.
Idu. London: Heinemann, 1970.
This Is Lagos and Other Stories. London: Heinemann, 1971.
"The Campaigner." *The Insider: Stories of War and Peace from Nigeria*. Ed. Chinua Achebe. Enugu: Nwankwo-Ifejika Publishers, 1971. 73–78.

Reprinted in *African Rhythms: Selected Stories and Poems*. Ed. Charlotte Brooks. New
    York: Washington Square Press, 1974. 136–55.
Emeka—Driver's Guard. Modern English Readers Series, Grade E. London: University
    of London Press, 1972.
Never Again. Enugu: Tana Press, 1975.
"Women in African Politics." *Africa Woman* 1 (1978): 35–36.
Mammywater. Enugu: F. Nwapa, 1979.
The Adventures of Deke. Enugu: Tana Press, 1980.
Wives at War and Other Stories. Enugu: Tana Press, 1980.
One Is Enough. Enugu: Tana Press, 1981.
Cassava Song and Rice Song. Enugu: Tana Press, 1986.
Women Are Different. Enugu: Tana Press, 1986.
The Lake Goddess. Africa World Press, forthcoming.

Studies of Flora Nwapa

Aidoo, Ama Ata. "These Days [III]—A Letter to Flora Nwapa." *Research in African
    Literatures* 26.2 (Summer 1995): 17–21.
Andrade, Susan Z. "Rewriting History, Motherhood, and Rebellion: Naming an African
    Women's Tradition." *Research in African Literatures* 20.2 (Summer 1990): 91–
    110.
Asanbe, Joseph. "Context of Writer and Audience: Nwapa and Emecheta." *LARES* 6–
    7 (1984–85): 186–96.
Banyiwa-Horne, Nana. "African Womanhood: The Contrasting Perspectives of Flora
    Nwapa's *Efuru* and Elechi Amadi's *The Concubine*." *Ngambika: Studies of
    Women in African Literature*. Ed. Carole Boyce Davies and Anne Adams Graves.
    Trenton, NJ: Africa World Press, 1986. 119–29.
Bazin, Nancy Topping. "Weight of Custom, Signs of Change: Feminism in the Literature
    of African Women." *World Literature Written in English* 25.2 (1985) : 183–97.
Berrian, Brenda F. "African Women as Seen in the Works of Flora Nwapa and Ama
    Ata Aidoo." *College Language Association Journal* 25.3 (March 1982): 331–39.
———. "The Reinvention of Woman through Conversations and Humor in Flora
    Nwapa's *One Is Enough*." *Research in African Literatures* 26.2 (Summer 1995):
    53–67.
Boehmer, Elleke. "Stories of Women and Mothers: Gender and Nationalism in the Early
    Fiction of Flora Nwapa." *Motherlands: Black Women's Writing from Africa, the
    Caribbean, and South Asia*. Ed. Susheila Nasta. London: The Women's Press
    Ltd., 1991; New Brunswick, NJ: Rutgers University Press, 1992. 3–23.
Brown, Lloyd W. *Women Writers in Black Africa*. Westport, CT: Greenwood Press, 1981.
Bryce-Okunlola, Jane. "Motherhood as a Metaphor for Creativity in Three African
    Women's Novels: Flora Nwapa, Rebeka Njau, and Bessie Head." *Motherlands:
    Black Women's Writing from Africa, the Caribbean, and South Asia*. Ed. Susheila
    Nasta. New Brunswick, NJ: Rutgers University Press, 1992. 200–218.
Busia, Abena. "A Tribute from the President of the ALA." *ALA Bulletin* 20.1 (1994):
    7.
Chukwuma, Helen. "Nigerian Female Authors, 1970 to the Present." *Matatu* (Frankfurt)
    1.2 (1987): 23–42.

Condé, Maryse. "Three Female Writers in Modern Africa: Flora Nwapa, Ama Ata Aidoo, and Grace Ogot." *Présence Africaine* 82 (1972): 132–43.

Coulon, Virginia. "Women at War: Nigerian Women Writers and the Civil War." *Commonwealth Essays and Studies* 13.1 (1990): 1–12.

Davies, Carole Boyce. "Motherhood in the Works of Male and Female Igbo Writers: Achebe, Emecheta, Nwapa, and Nzekwu." *Ngambika: Studies of Women in African Literature.* Ed. Carole Boyce Davies and Anne Adams Graves. Trenton, NJ: Africa World Press, 1986. 241–56.

Egejuru, Phanuel. "Flora, Onyiba Nwanyi." *ALA Bulletin* 20.1 (1994): 16–17.

Emenyonu, Ernest. "Flora Nwapa: A Pioneer African Female Voice Is Silenced." *ALA Bulletin* 20.1 (1994): 10–11.

———. "The Nigerian Civil War and the Nigerian Novel: The Writer as Historical Witness." *Studies on the Nigerian Novel.* Ibadan: Heinemann, 1991. 89–105.

———. Review of *Efuru. Ba Shiru* 1.1 (1970): 58–62.

———. "Who Does Flora Nwapa Write For?" *African Literature Today* 7 (1975): 28–33.

Emenyonu, Patricia T. "The Role of Contemporary Female Nigerian Writers in the Education of Nigerian Youth." *Literary Criterion* 23. 1–2 (1988): 216–21.

Ezeigbo, Theodora A. "Traditional Women's Institutions in Igbo Society: Implications for the Igbo Female Writer." *African Languages and Cultures* 3.2 (1990): 149–65.

Ezenwa-Ohaeto. "The Child Figures and Childhood Symbolism in Flora Nwapa's Children's Fiction." *Research in African Literatures* 26.2 (Summer 1995): 68–79.

———. "The Notion of Fulfillment in Flora Nwapa's *Women Are Different.*" *Neohelicon* (Budapest) 19.1 (1992): 323–33.

Frank, Katherine. "Feminist Criticism and the African Novel." *African Literature Today* 14 (1984): 34–48.

———. "Women without Men: The Feminist Novel in Africa." *African Literature Today* 15 (1987): 14–34.

Ikonné, Chidi. "The Folk Roots of Flora Nwapa's Early Novels." *African Literature Today* 18 (1992): 96–104.

———. "The Society and Woman's Quest for Selfhood in Flora Nwapa's Early Novels." *Kunapipi* 6.1 (1984): 68–78.

James, Adeola A. Review of *Idu. African Literature Today* 5 (1971): 150–53.

Jell-Bahlsen, Sabine. "The Concept of Mammywater in Flora Nwapa's Novels." *Research in African Literatures* 26.2 (Summer 1995): 68–79.

Maja-Pearce, Adewale. "Flora Nwapa's *Efuru*: A Study in Misplaced Hostility." *World Literature Written in English* 25 (1985): 10–15.

Mojola, Yemi I. "The Works of Flora Nwapa." *Nigerian Female Writers: A Critical Perspective.* Ed. Henrietta Otukunefor and Obiageli Nwodo. Lagos: Malthouse Press, 1989. 19–29.

Nandakumar, Prema. "An Image of African Womanhood: A Study of Flora Nwapa's *Efuru.*" *Africa Quarterly* 11 (1967): 136–46.

Ngcobo, Lauretta. "Black African Women Writers." *Cambridge Journal of Education* 14.3 (1984): 16–21.

Nnaemeka, Obioma. "Feminism, Rebellious Women, and Cultural Boundaries: Rereading Flora Nwapa and Her Compatriots." *Research in African Literatures* 26.2 (Summer 1995): 80–113.

———. "From Orality to Writing: African Women Writers and the (Re) Inscription of Womanhood." *Research in African Literatures* 25.4 (1994): 137–57.

Nwankwo, Chimalum. "The Igbo Word in Flora Nwapa's Craft." *Research in African Literatures* 26.2 (Summer 1995): 42–52.

Ogundipe-Leslie, Omolara. "Dirge to Flora Nwapa." *ALA Bulletin* 20.1 (1994): 14–15.

Ogunyemi, Chikwenye Okonjo. "Introduction: The Invalid, Dea(r)th, and the Author: The Case of Flora Nwapa, *aka* Professor (Mrs.) Flora Nwazanzuruahu Nwakuche." *Research in African Literatures* 26.2 (Summer 1995): 1–16.

———. "Womanism: The Dynamics of the Contemporary Black Female Novel in English." *Signs: Journal of Women in Culture and Society* 11.1 (1985): 63–80.

Ojo-Ade, Femi. "Women and the Nigerian Civil War: Buchi Emecheta and Flora Nwapa." *Etudes Germano-Africaines* 6 (1988): 75–86.

Ola, V. U. "Flora Nwapa and the Art of the Novel." *Medium and Message* (Calabar) 1 (1981): 91–111.

Oladeji, Niyi. "Women in the Nigerian Novel: Two Novelists' Attitudes to Nigerian Womanhood." *Marang* 4 (1983): 35–46.

Perry, Alison. "Meeting Flora Nwapa" (interview). *West Africa* 18 (June 1984): 1262.

Petersen, Kirsten Holst. "Unpopular Opinions: Some African Women Writers." *Kunapipi* 7.2–3 (1985): 107–20. Reprinted in *A Double Colonization: Colonial and Post-colonial Women's Writing*. Ed. Kirsten Holst Peterson and Anna Rutherford. Mundelstrop, Denmark: Dangaroo, 1986. 107–20.

Sample, Maxine. "In Another Life: The Refugee Phenomenon in Two Novels of the Nigerian Civil War." *Modern Fiction Studies* 37.3 (1991): 445–54.

Schueb, Harold. "Two African Women." *Revue des Langues Vivantes* 37.5 (1971): 545–58.

Stratton, Florence. *Contemporary African Literature and the Politics of Gender*. New York: Routledge, 1994. 80–130.

Taiwo, Oladele. *Female Novelists of Modern Africa*. New York: St. Martin's Press, 1985.

Umeh, Marie. "Finale: Signifyin' the Griottes: Flora Nwapa's Legacy of (Re)Vision and Voice." *Research in African Literatures* 26.2 (Summer 1995): 114–23.

———. "A Tribute to Flora Nwapa." *ALA Bulletin* 20.1 (1994): 8–9.

Wilentz, Gay. *Binding Cultures: Black Women Writers in Africa and the Diaspora*. Bloomington: Indiana University Press, 1992. 3–19.

———. "Flora Nwapa, 1931–1993." *Women's Review of Books* 11.6 (1994): 8.

———. "The Individual Voice in the Communal Chorus: The Possibility of Choice in Flora Nwapa." *ACLALS Bulletin* 7.4 (1986): 30–36.

CHRISTINE LOFLIN

MOLARA OGUNDIPE-LESLIE (1941–)

BIOGRAPHY

Molara Ogundipe-Leslie, one of Nigeria's leading scholars in women's studies and women-in-development studies, was born in Ogun State. Her parents, the late Right Rev. L. M. Ogundipe and Chief Mrs. Grace Tayo Ogundipe, were among the earliest Nigerian Christian converts, and so she had an early exposure to Western education. Taught early by her mother, an elementary-school teacher, Ogundipe-Leslie later attended the then University College at Ibadan, from which she graduated with a First Class Honors degree in English in 1963. The years a little before and after Nigeria's independence, which took place in 1960, saw great changes in the lives of Nigerians. It was during her undergraduate years at Ibadan at this time that Ogundipe-Leslie found her voice as a writer. The English Department at the time, under the leadership of two prominent scholars, Molly Mahood and Ulli Beier, became a center of creativity. It launched the Mbari Artists and Writers Club and gave support to the *Horn*, a student poetry and criticism magazine founded by J. P. Clark, in which Clark himself as well as other major figures—Abiola Irele, Wole Soyinka, and Christopher Okigbo—who were later to give direction to literary creativity in Nigeria also made their debut as writers. She participated actively in the Mbari Artists and Writers Club and wrote poetry and criticism for the *Horn*. Her student publications reveal her nuanced attitude to the events of that time and laid a solid foundation for her long struggle for women's rights and her commitment to the dual tasks of theoretical work and practical action in advocacy.

After teaching for many years at the University of Ibadan, she became head of the Department of English at Ogun State University in Nigeria before joining the editorial team of the Nigerian Guardian group of magazines in 1986. In

1985 her published poetry was collected under the title *Sew the Old Days and Other Poems* and released in Nigeria. Ten years later, in 1995, a volume of her essays was issued in the United States, entitled *Recreating Ourselves*. Recently, she has lived and worked in Canada and the United States, where she has held the New Jersey Chair in Women's Studies, an endowed prestigious chair at Rutgers, and is now chair of Women's Studies at Indiana University–Purdue University at Fort Wayne.

MAJOR WORKS AND THEMES

Scholars have examined the critical work of Molara Ogundipe-Leslie, but her poetry has not been studied in detail. Her poetry is significant for the way it set a new standard for Nigerian women's poetry in its frankness, in its quiet tone, in its range of coverage of women's issues, and in its imagistic power. While other female poets such as Ifi Amadiume in "Bitter Voice of the Masses" (*Passion Waves*, London: Karnak House, 1985) and Catherine Acholonu in "Going Home" have shown concern about the plight of the ordinary Nigerians without displaying any distinctly feminist voice, Ogundipe-Leslie covers the whole gamut of the experience of being female in a male-dominated society. For the first time, a woman bares her soul in an honest fashion about many agonizing areas of experience, which women had hitherto suffered in silence. In the aptly titled poem "ageing woman," for example, Ogundipe-Leslie defies decorum and meditates openly on ageing. In that poem, which is a subtle evocation of the anguish ageing causes women, she underlines her attraction to the themes of women's liberation from male domination. She resents the situation whereby men adore women only when they are young, viewing them primarily as objects for the satisfaction of male sexual appetites. If the attraction women hold for men did not decline as they aged, that is, if men did not see women in the light of their sexual needs but took them in their own right, women would not have to worry so bitterly about ageing. In addressing this topic, her aim is to change the men's self-centered and exploitative attitude toward their womenfolk.

Ogundipe-Leslie favors an arrangement whereby males would regard their female counterparts primarily as human beings, as their partners in nation building. Thus in another poem, "Letter to a Loved Comrade: A Prose Poem," she works to demolish the patriarchal prejudices that negate equality, such as the men's prejudiced beliefs about women's destructive nature. In this engaging poem, all her images are made up of women's bodily functions, which she uses tellingly to impress the view of the significant role women play as the essence of life.

Reversing the negative images of women painted by men, she presents womanhood as a life-giving force and points to the blood a woman sheds while in labor as the ultimate sacrifice one can pay for humanity. She presents the woman's life-giving role as a challenge to men and urges them to redirect toward more positive goals of nation building "the tremors" women's "might" sends through "the stoutest hearts of men" (25). This poem is unique in the way it presents the dreaded process of menstruation in a positive light; it is probably the first feminist poem in Nigeria to imbue the menstrual cycle with progressive images.

While persuading men to refrain from the atrocities they commit against their female companions, Ogundipe-Leslie also performs for her fellow womenfolk the role of a teacher who offers these marginalized entities in society wisdom, radicalizing them so that they can take positive control of their own lives. For the success of this endeavor, she feverishly revisits the tradition of the exploitation, subjugation, and betrayal that women have been subjected to by men. Here her authority derives far less from any novelty of the experiences she describes than from the vigorous images with which she moves her audience of fellow women toward greater awareness of their lot.

Ogundipe-Leslie writes with great insight and patriotism about exploited women in Nigeria, and the real mark of her greatness as a poet is that she approaches universal subjects through a firm engagement with the local, making the everyday experiences of Nigerian women the main focus of her poems. This rootedness in the local and particular explains the reason that in "Yoruba Love," for example, she still deems it relevant to warn young ladies to beware of the antics of the sweet-talking love swindler who is ever ready to dishonor them, even though the cause of women's liberation may appear to have advanced beyond such concerns outside the Nigerian shores, particularly in the West. This poem is very significant from the vantage point of its style. Because the poet knows that if her message is to sink deeply into the audience, it must be expressed using their idiom, she conveys it through the adynation symbol in proverbial usage, which is a favorite rhetorical device among Africans. In "Adynation Symbols in Proverbs: A Few Fragmentary Remarks" (*Proverbium* 15 [1970]), Ronald Grambo has perceptively described adynation symbols as "symbols of impossibility" used to "designate tasks that are impossible to do, such as to pour water by means of a sieve or to make ropes of sand" (45). By conveying the promises the male lover makes in hyperbolic terms, using the adynation symbols in her poem, Ogundipe-Leslie underlines how unrealistic they are.

Among Africans, in general, and the Yoruba, in particular, proverbs are key ingredients that enhance communication, and Bernth Lindfors and Oyekan Owomoyela, who have carried out extensive research on them, have confirmed in *Yoruba Proverbs: Translation and Annotation* (Athens: Ohio University Center for International Studies, African Program, 1973) that in Yoruba land proverbs are "the horses of speech" (1). By conveying the lover's hyperbolic promises in such sarcastic terms, Ogundipe-Leslie is playing the role of the patriotic artist who serves as a guardian of her society's tribal customs by attempting to preserve the chastity of the female members of the group.

In another poem, "Trickster Love," where the poet depicts unflattering images of man as a greedy beast who always shirks the responsibility that should go along with his sexual indulgences, her message is one of rejection of male chauvinism. Through this method, she confirms her determination to bring about the birth of the new woman, who will define her own roles instead of relying on men's undependable sentiments or conscience as the means through which to reverse the existing patterns of relationships. In a context in which women are historically circumscribed to accept the roles carved for them by men, her reasoning is truly revolutionary.

In "When Father Experience Hits with His Hammer," where she uses exceptional force to espouse her image of this new woman, she shows an ability to utilize numerous varied devices. She begins with a pleading tone, urging women to shake off the stereotypical notions of the love they are nursed by in their teens, and the images about "tall, black handsome" men who will satisfy their romantic yearnings (30), capture the utopian fantasies promoted by western films and romantic fiction, which assist in making women fall easy prey to the passionate sensuality of men. She then turns her tone into a bitter attack, damning the women who acquiesce in playing the roles of kitchen hands, mothers, and lovers and have premised their lives on the assumptions that they can get on by seeking to cajole men. By reminding women that no boss will ever willingly give up power, the poet sensitizes them to fight for their rights. On the poem's agenda is the issue of the identity of the woman, and the poet raises it in a very personal way, reiterating the important social roles women must play in the economic, political, and cultural sectors of the nation for patriotic reasons.

Considering Ogundipe-Leslie's perception of the depth of Africa's crisis—the leadership problems, wars and tribal conflicts, poverty, colonial and neo-colonial dominations, and so forth—it is not surprising that she conceptualizes the involvement of all the aggregate human resources a people can boast of as the best approach to nation building. This is not necessarily a matter of her Marxist leanings, contrary to what Maduakor would have us believe, but a matter of her frank realism. In this context, the chief interest of "Song at the African Middle Class" lies in the way it enables the poet to raise haunting and searching questions about the identity of Africa's new political messiahs and the possible direction from which they will come. Grave disappointments had followed the short-lived political activism that threw up Africa's radical leaders of the likes of Samora Machel and Agostinho Neto, leading to widespread disillusionment on the continent regarding the prospects for revolutionary leadership. For Ogundipe-Leslie, on the contrary, the very fact that these leaders could emerge at all is itself the source of hope that Africa will once again see the birth of new saviors. Therefore, she enjoins the African middle class to borrow a leaf from their past and rise up to their political responsibility by taking over control of their countries so that they can meet the needs of their people through raising their standards of living. The lilting melody of her lines and the cool rhetorical questions she raises register the dreams of freedom the poet has for her society.

When she turns specifically to the Nigerian situation, she enlists the entire citizenry to come to terms with the reality of social injustice embedded in the fabric of their national life. She encourages everyone—male and female—to keep faith with a social duty, and her language combines a calm wish with an open request for social revolution. Through her use of moral outrage and the binary images that contrast the abject poverty of the majority with the rank affluence of a few of Nigeria's populace, she realizes her aim to bring about a positive change in the life of her nation by sensitizing the oppressed to redress their destitution. Her other pieces, "A harsh beauty must be . . . Today" and "tendril love of Africa," derive their significance from the images of tenderness with which they address the womenfolk, coaxing them out of their traditional docility and the appropriate behavior men conceive for them, so that they can join the forefront of the national struggle alongside their male counterparts.

Ogundipe-Leslie weaves romantic longing as intertexts into her political arguments, and in many of her poems she employs the multidimensional nature of love as a vehicle for enlarging the reader's sense of her patriotic devotion to her country. By skillfully employing various different graphic forms to conceptualize the complex ways that love manifests itself, she enlarges our understanding of the idea of love beyond the traditional associations of erotic fantasies. In "In song of fear: for rachel," for example, she utilizes a cryptic analogy in which she visualizes love as a force that applies new bursts of energy and restores life to a tired body. Love, the poem makes clear, is a life-transforming event; as such, it is "only the chicken's heart . . . pounding" (40). The image of the chicken's heart effectively presents love as an active agent. But in "descriptions for love," the picture is that of a brittle object that must be handled with care. This poem employs a complex array of images in presenting love in all its paradoxical nature: a phenomenon that is both animate and inanimate, and a force that not only binds but also separates individuals. In "Mating Cry," where she presents love as a healing balm that explodes the barriers between a man and a woman, helping them to understand one another fully through sexual self-surrender to each other, she waxes imagistic. The poem is a call for lovers to energize themselves with love's potent force. In the compact two-line poem "haiku for isis," she strives for an ultimate means of expression when she articulates love as a "child's two year foot" (53), a kind of creative revelation which gives a pleasure comparable to the satisfaction that a well-executed poem gives to a composer. Probably the most revolutionary articulation of the phenomenon of love in the whole modern African poetry, the piece gives poetic conceptualization to a viewpoint that many ordinary women have always had in regarding childbirth as a triumph that epitomizes the ultimate fulfillment of all love endeavors. In fact, the stark radical analogical philosophy that it conveys speaks to genuine talent.

The quality of Ogundipe-Leslie's verse is considerable. She was there from the very beginning when modern Nigerian literature was born at Ibadan, and she has continued with dedication to be heard since then. *Sew the Old Days* offers a rare opportunity for people interested in literary history to have a view of the feminist aspirations that were at the very foundation of modern literary imagination in Nigeria.

CRITICAL RECEPTION

It could well be that Ogundipe-Leslie's poetry has been excluded from critical discourse because it does not fall neatly within the conventional male-defined notions of commitment. Examples of these male definitions of commitment can be found in the book *The Theory of African Literature: Implications for Practical Criticism* (London: Zed Books, 1989) by the Nigerian radical critic Chidi Amuta, who foregrounds the neocolonial situation under which all African and "Third World" writers inevitably live and work, and who warns that all writers in their milieu must contribute toward the socioeconomic, cultural, racial, and political liberation of their people or be condemned into limbo:

In the African world, this historical necessity, in which the poet as a man of culture devotes his art and life to the pursuit of justice and freedom, has become part of the very legitimacy of the poetic undertaking. To be a significant poet in Africa at a time like this is to stand up and be counted in the struggle against foreign domination and class and racial injustice. (177)

Amuta recognizes that many poets all over the world habitually pitch their tent with "the people in their struggle for justice and humane existence." He himself cites poets as "diverse in nationality and outlook" as Christopher Caudwell, John Cornford, Louis Aragon, Christopher Okigbo, Maxim Gorky, and Dennis Brutus among those who have "dedicated their art and sometimes their lives to the pursuit of freedom" (177). But for him, the situation of the African writers is unique in its urgency, which demands exceptional commitment. It is obvious that Amuta upholds a simplistic view of commitment. Because commitment for a woman poet like Ogundipe-Leslie is not simply a matter of literary resistance "against foreign domination and class and racial injustice"—though it is that too—but, more importantly, a concern to "tell about being a woman; secondly, to describe reality from a woman's view, a woman's perspective" (Ogundipe-Leslie, "The Woman Writer," 5), it is not surprising that Amuta excludes her from his incredibly patriarchal study.

So far, the only extended discussion of her poetry is Obi Maduakor's 1989 essay, which obviously was written before the 1985 publication of Ogundipe-Leslie's collection. Maduakor notes correctly the tone of enlightened restraint, doubt, and the quiet ego that dominates Ogundipe-Leslie's poetry, in contrast to the haughtiness, defiance, bravado, melodramatic posturing, and suspenseful comedy of Catherine Acholonu. The problem Maduakor faced is that he conducted his study when Acholonu had already brought out her two books of poems. At the time, Ogundipe-Leslie's collection was still being awaited, and so the critic had to base his evaluation on only six of her poems published in journals and magazines—a small corpus that could not do justice to the poet.

BIBLIOGRAPHY

Works by Molara Ogundipe-Leslie

Sew the Old Days and Other Poems. Ibadan: Evans, 1985.
"The Woman Writer and Her Commitment." *Women in African Literature Today* 15. Ed. Eldred Jones, Eustace Palmer, and Marjorie Jones. London: James Currey; Trenton, N.J.: Africa World Press, 1987. 5–13.
Recreating Ourselves: African Women and Critical Transformations. Trenton, N.J.: Africa World Press, 1995.

Study of Molara Ogundipe-Leslie

Maduakor, Obi. "Female Voices in Poetry: Catherine Acholonu and Molara Ogundipe-Leslie." *Nigerian Female Writers.* Ed. Henrietta Otokunefo and Obiageli Nwodo. Lagos: Malthouse Press, 1989. 75–91.

ODE S. OGEDE

GABRIEL OKARA (1921–   )

BIOGRAPHY

Gabriel Imomotimi Gbaingbain Okara was born in April 1921 in Bumodi, in the Ijaw district of the Delta region, Nigeria. He attended Government College at Umuahia, Nigeria (1935–40), and later studied journalism at Northwestern University in the United States (1956–59). He has taken up various positions in his lifetime: teacher, printer, and bookbinder at Lagos and Enugu, setting up the Government Press, principal information officer for Eastern Nigerian Government Service, general manager of Rivers State Newspaper and Television Corporation, and commissioner for information and broadcasting for the government of the State of Rivers. Presently, he is with the Rivers State Council for Arts and Culture, Port Harcourt, Nigeria.

Okara's literary repute rests on poetry written mainly in the fifties and collected in *The Fisherman's Invocation* (1978) and on one novel, *The Voice* (1964). His first poems were published in the first issue of *Black Orpheus* in 1957. His poem "Call of the River Nun" won the Commonwealth Joint Poetry Award in 1979. Many of his poems in manuscript form were lost during the movements of people following the Nigerian Civil War. In the 1980s Okara published a group of ten poems that appeared in *Black Orpheus* and a few in *Kiabara*.

MAJOR WORKS AND THEMES

Gabriel Okara's collection of poems written in the fifties, *The Fisherman's Invocation*, is striking in its defiance of spirit in the "protest" mode, but also in its affirmation of "the value of the movements of the communal African soul'' (Echeruo, 31). In an interview recorded at the Fifth Annual Festival of the Arts in Ife on December 1, 1972, and collected by Bernth Lindfors, Okara observes that the poem ''The Fisherman's Invocation,'' like *The Voice*, is ''about independence'' (43). Departing from the derivative poetry of the forties and fifties, based on the British Victorian poetic structure and meter, Okara wrote in free verse. Echeruo sums up the prevailing theme in Okara's later poetry as ''the travails of the individual soul as it responds to the world of the outside'' (31). An enduring concern in a number of Okara's poems is the wholeness of human experience and of truth at particular junctures of historical time.

At the interface of communal Africa and colonial Europe is a complex world that Okara explores. Okara delineates the predicament of people inhabiting this world that he examines through ironic and often symbolic reflections on the cultural impact of colonization. He is concerned not merely with external changes but with internal transformations. This theme is best expressed through the shock effect created by Okara's use of Ijaw structures and idioms along with English vocabulary. Evoking an African orality in written European language, Okara consciously foregrounds both the tensions and the new commitments that emerge with creating a new African nation in post-independence times. These are the ''teaching moments'' when ''speaking things'' (words) and ''happening things'' (events) (*The Voice*) must be joined in meaningful ways.

In the first poem of the collection, ''The Fisherman's Invocation,'' the conflict between past and present, tradition and modernity, and African and European is expressed in images of the ''Back'' and the ''Front.'' In a dialogue between two fishermen, Okara invokes the birth of the ''Child-Front'' out of the dead Back, accompanied by the sound of drums. Out of the rupture and chaos ''inside'' is forged the ''fireball Front'' that must be tempered, shaped, and molded with ''mystic touch.'' Affirming the ritualistic forms of African communal participation in time and space through ''circular drums,'' ''circular dances,'' and ''circular songs,'' Okara moves to a somber reflection on the artistic and nationalistic predicament of learning to ''sing half familiar half strange songs'' (15).

''The Call of the River Nun'' is one of Okara's most anthologized poems. In this highly symbolic poem, the call of the river could signify several experiential levels of renewing self in historic time and geographical location. The actual river of his hometown being referred to emerges from the ''hills of Enugu, the Ibo city where Okara was working when he wrote the poem'' (Gingell, 286). Symbolically, the river signifies a link with childhood, a renewal of the past, and also a clear direction in times of confusion. Through symbolism, repetition of words, internal rhymes, and the use of a speaking voice, Okara captures the complex nuances of the internal struggle to articulate the individual's and the nation's dilemma at the crossroads of the colonial and the post-colonial nexus.

Advocating the need for commitment and action in ''Once upon a Time,'' Okara also testifies to the necessity of reevaluating and relearning in order to erase the internalization of the colonizer's ''ice-block'' ways. In ''You Laughed and Laughed and Laughed," the colonizer's mockery and contemptuous disparagement of indigenous African culture and worldview are confronted and ultimately silenced by the warmth of the native's "fire" laughter.

"Piano and Drums" most effectively posits the ravaging impact of the colonial imposition of cultural hierarchy. While the European hears the sounds of the piano in a fairly calm manner, these very sounds imply the violent ways in which the African has been distanced from the "jungle drums," the reference points of his cultural values and beliefs. However, the native still responds to the "mystic rhythm" and is therefore not a completely lost figure.

Further exposing the self-defeating ways in which colonization works on the body, mind, and soul of the native, in poems such as "The Mystic Drum," "One Night at Victoria Beach," "To Paveba," "Expendable Name," and "Sunday," Okara offers a psychic-mystical recipe for healing and renewing the self through keeping the "inside" alive. It is in the "inside" that one can nurture the spirit of full growth and power. In "Spirit of the Wind" and "Revolt of the Gods," Okara invokes the revival of faith in African forms of worship and mysticism. Obi Maduakor refers to Okara as "the poet of the mystic inside." Commenting on the unique quality in Okara's poetry, Maduakor observes:

Part of Okara's mysticism is the poet's retreat into what he calls the "inside." The word *inside* is not a mere poetic conceit with Okara. It is a *real* geographic location existing inside the poet's inner world and psyche. Inside is the poet's inner being, his true self, the spiritual self that is the real man. (41)

Besides the poems collected in *The Fisherman's Invocation*, Okara published a group of ten poems in *Black Orpheus* in 1983, besides a couple in *Kiabara* in 1980. These poems were written in the seventies and reflect Okara's despair and sense of loss as he comments on the postwar Nigerian society. In poems like "Fantasy," "The Precipice," and "Morbidity," Okara observes the very social and psychic ruptures that Frantz Fanon talks about in *The Wretched of the Earth*, particularly with regard to the social pathology and psychological parasitism of the colonial world. Fear, Okara observes, has made the so-called free native entrapped within the masks of self that alienate him from nature and his own community, "estranged by complex humanity" ("Smiling Morning," 6).

Okara's novel *The Voice*, written as a parable and a quest narrative, explores the political and social resonances of an individual's search for the spiritual self. Okolo's quest begins with a question to the townspeople of Amatu, asking them if they have *it*. Chief Izongo and the Elders, representing the people of Amatu, are too full of hatred, greed, and fear to answer this question. Tuere, the witch, the only sympathizer of Okolo in the beginning, is ostracized by the people of Amatu, but she is the only one who has a "strong inside." She warns Okolo about the "bad footsteps coming out of people's insides" (30). Within the colonial context, the people's fears are defined in political terms. Izongo represents the neocolonial who uses rhetoric to merely "toe the party line." One of his advisors, Abadi, has cultivated the art of white man's diplomacy and uses it against his own people. After Okolo's return from banishment, Abadi allows Okolo and Tuere to speak their grievances, but only as a strategy of "letting off steam" (121).

Okolo's exile from Amatu and his journey to Sologa exemplify not only the trials and tribulations that he must undergo but also the complex ways in which people have closed their "insides." Ready to condemn Okolo for a wrong he did not commit, that is seducing a bride-to-be, the mother-in-law and the towns-people of Sologa reveal their narrow-minded, corrupt minds. Further incidents confirm to Okolo that Sologa is ruled by the dictatorial Big One who uses spies, the "listeners," to capture Okolo as soon as he lands on Sologa. Okolo is labeled "mental" by the white supervisor of the "listeners" and is ordered to be taken to the asylum. Sologa proves to be no better than Amatu, and Okolo decides to return to Amatu.

Okolo's return marks a shift in the possible outcome of his revolutionary ideas. While most of the people accept Izongo and the Elders as their leader, there are stirrings of dissension. Ukele, "the cripple," an outcast like Tuere, has already joined Okolo's cause. A messenger with empty feet, as opposed to the one with black shoes (the wearing of shoes could symbolize the native's susceptibility to the white man's materialism), questions the political corruption ("bad money") as well as the value of the white man's education ("their book learning" as opposed to "earth knowledge") (91–94). In the final phase of the narrative, the revolutionary spirit is taking birth. Even as Okolo and Tuere are forced to leave town and eventually are drowned, Ukele's words stay with us: "Your spoken words will not die" (127).

The Voice is powerful in its philosophical, mystical, and political messages. The quest for *it* encompasses the search for the nameless, perhaps the meaning of life, one's purpose, even perhaps a need to believe in something or someone. As Okolo ruminates on his journey back to Amuta, "What is he himself trying to reach? For him it has no name. Names bring divisions and divisions, strife. So let it be without a name; let it be nameless" (12). Okolo not only pursues the search for *it*, he pays the price for keeping it uncorrupted. Okara's message for post-independence Nigeria is in the form of a parable, "teaching words," "straight words" instead of "crooked words" because words have power; they grow and "take root," as Tuere suggests (96).

CRITICAL RECEPTION

Okara's works, especially *The Voice*, have received much attention but sur-prisingly little substantive critical analysis. Critics have tended to react strongly, either favoring Okara's linguistic experimentation or not. I will focus on some of the more substantive criticism that has provided an insight into the programmatic underpinnings of his works.

Early responses to Okara's poetry, especially "The Fisherman's Invocation," with its linguistic experimentation, were mainly negative or mildly appreciative. John Pepper Clark (1970) denounced Okara's "The Fisherman's Invocation" as a "real disaster" (55). K. E. Senanu and T. Vincent (1976) critiqued the same poem as "Okara's worst poem, of embarrassingly uneven quality, with only short spurts of brilliance" (48). Ken Goodwin (1982) also notes that the conclusion of the poem is a "disappointing outcome," attributing this flaw to the "surrealistic superimposition of images," which creates "incongruity" (149). However, Goodwin further examines Okara as a "modern poet" who emerged out of the sensibilities of the more derivative poetry of the forties in West Africa. Okara incorporated elements of Negritude poetry, romantic imagery, surrealism, and dramatic dialogue, along with the modernist preoccupation with language and form. Goodwin discusses at some length Okara's "war poems," praising Okara's "control of rhetorical form" (150). He also commends Okara for his "powerful lyrics" and the performative features of his poetry (153).

Obi Maduakor, responding to the paucity of critical scholarship on Okara in his article "Gabriel Okara: Poet of the Mystic Inside" (1987), sets out to assess the reasons for the neglect of Okara's works and carefully document the unique qualities of Okara's poetry through clarifying his Ijaw-centered worldview that underlies his mysticism. Maduakor traces Okara's connections to the "political developments in his society" and the expression of this connection in the "public voice" poems or "Nigerian Civil War poems" (43) However, Maduakor notes, these messages may often be obscured because Okara shrouds them in mystery. He assesses "The Fisherman's Invocation" as a poem "about the birth of a nation," even as *The Voice* is "concerned with Nigeria's attainment of the status of political independence" (43). He further analyzes "The Revolt of the Gods," in which allegorical figures, the Young God (young officers) and the Old God (seasoned statesmen), debate issues of power, control, and guidance. Maduakor notes that the political message in this poem "indicts the military leadership in both Biafra and Nigeria during the civil war" (44).

Viney Kirpal in "The Structure of the Modern Nigerian Novel and the National Consciousness" (1988), responding to critics who consider the "loosely coordinated inner structure" in modern Nigerian novels as a weakness, accounts for the viability and necessity of this structure in the works of Achebe, Soyinka, Ekwensi, Aluko, and Okara. The nonlinear narrative and plot construction, in Kirpal's view, "create a step-by-step expansion of meaning and apprehension" (48).

Claudio Gorlier in "The Haunted House of National Literature: Individual Malaise and Communal Plight in the Making of a Literary Discourse in A. K. Armah's Novels and G. Okara's *The Voice*" (1989) identifies in Okolo's quest the "mapping-out of a terrain" that involves "a process of factual and mental rediscovery" (16). This rediscovery takes place both on the linguistic and ideological levels. Commenting on Okara's "symbiotic process" through "linguistic readjustment," Gorlier focuses on how this process "nullifies the dichotomy between spoken and written language" (19). On the ideological plane, Okolo's search for *it*, in Gorlier's view, is "reinstating a system of values, a *lebenswelt* repudiated, concealed or even suppressed by the political *elite*" (19). Gorlier identifies two phases in this search, an "inner-directed movement, a mental process towards self-knowledge" and an "outer-directed movement . . . [which] develops a political significance" (19–20). Gorlier identifies some crucial steps in the revolutionary process: defying of political taboos, discovery of truth as a revolutionary weapon, establishing a "relationship with the community," and sharing the "search with the 'masses,' " as well as creating solidarity with the "marginalized" of the society. These steps are reminiscent of the stages Frantz Fanon outlines with regard to revolutionary leadership in *The Wretched of the Earth*. Noting the links between Ayi Kwei Armah's novels and Okara's work, Gorlier argues that they are "specular to a quite different society, hence the manifold tension, in the writers' response to a mobile society, in the recovery and the reassessment of local cultural originality urged by Frantz Fanon, in a radical overhauling of the narrative medium" (22).

Patrick Scott in "Gabriel Okara's *The Voice*: The Non-Ijo Reader and the Pragmatics of Translingualism" (1990) provides an interesting stance on "the relation between African authors and the colonial linguistic legacy" by examining the text's "translingual features" (75). Departing from customary privileging of the author or text, Scott privileges an "aesthetic that is reader-based (an aesthetic of effect and interaction)" (75). He provides the sociolinguistic background to Okara's use of Ijo before delineating a structural analysis of the nature, impact, and consequences of translingualism in *The Voice*. He also suggests approaches to reading translingualism. While some critics have referred to these strategies as odd or perverse, Scott examines Okara's use of "mixed register" as creating the effect of parody and satire. Scott suggests a reader-text interactive approach so that non-Ijo readers (both in and outside Nigeria) can actively understand that in Okara's text the meaning relies on "the constant interplay between Ijo patterns and English expectations" (84). The "interactionist" or " 'serial reinterpretative' approach to translingualism," as Scott argues, has "greater justification in Okara's actual linguistic background," which is multidialectical and multilingual.

Michael J. C. Echeruo's tribute to Okara on his seventieth birth anniversary (1991) identifies the links between Okara's poetry and narrative writing, as well as developments in his vision. Echeruo recollects Okara's reading of "The Fisherman's Invocation" in 1967 at the University of Nigeria, Nsukka, as a "memorable event" (31). Commenting on his "incantatory voice," "an Ijo poetic manner," and "the short lines and impromptu caesuras," Echeruo highlights the performative features of Okara's poetry. He also evaluates *The Voice*, taking it beyond the genre limits of "tragedy" by casting his message "in the idiom of expressive black arts of song and dance" (33).

Okara's work needs a longer, more sustained study, by itself and in relation to other postcolonial African writers. His thematic preoccupations and stylistic innovations also provide starting points for theoretical articulations regarding nation formation and fragmentation, African writing, and dystopic narratives, as well as aesthetic and political imperatives within postcolonial conditions.

BIBLIOGRAPHY

Works by Gabriel Okara

"African Speech . . . English Language." *Transition* 3 (1963): 15–16. Reprinted in *African Writers on African Writing*. Ed. G. D. Killam. Evanston: Northwestern University Press, 1973. 137–39.
"The Dancer." *Kiabara* 3.2 (1980): 81.
The Fisherman's Invocation. London: Heinemann, 1978.
"Morbidity." *Black Orpheus* 5.1 (1983): 3.
"River Nun 2." *Kiabara* 3.2 (1980): 83.
"Smiling Morning." *Black Orpheus* 5.1 (1983): 6.
The Voice. New York: Africana Publishing Co., 1970 (1964).

Selected Studies of Gabriel Okara

Beckmann, Susan. Review. "Gabriel Okara, *The Fisherman's Invocation*." *World Literature Written in English* 20.2 (Autumn 1981): 230–35.
Clark, John Pepper. "Themes of African Poetry of English Expression." *The Example of Shakespeare*. London: Longman, 1970. 29–60.
Echeruo, Michael J. C. "Gabriel Okara at 70." *ALA Bulletin* 17.3 (Summer 1991): 30–36. Also appeared as "Gabriel Okara: A Poet and His Seasons." *World Literature Today* 66.3 (Summer 1992): 452–57.
Gingell, S. A. "His River's Complex Course: Reflections on Past, Present, and Future in the Poetry of Gabriel Okara." *World Literature Written in English* 23.2 (Spring 1984): 284–97.
Goodwin, Ken. "Gabriel Okara." *Understanding African Poetry: A Study of Ten Poets*. London: Heinemann, 1982. 142–53.
Gorlier, Claudio. "The Haunted House of National Literature: Individual Malaise and Communal Plight in the Making of a Literary Discourse in A. A. Armah's Novels and G. Okara's *The Voice*." *Literature and National Consciousness*. Ed. Ebele Eko, Julius Ogu, and Azubuike Iloeje. Ibadan, Nigeria: Heinemann Educational, 1989. 14–25.
King, Bruce, ed. *Introduction to Nigerian Literature*. New York: Africana Publishing Corp., 1972 (1971).
Kirpal, Viney. "The Structure of the Modern Nigerian Novel and the National Consciousness." *Modern Fiction Studies* 34.1 (Spring 1988): 45–54.

Lindfors, Bernth. "Interview with Gabriel Okara." *Dem-Say: Interviews with English Nigerian Writers*. Austin: African and Afro-American Studies and Research Center, University of Texas, 1974. 41–47.

Maduakor, Obi. "Gabriel Okara: Poet of the Mystic Inside." *World Literature Today* 61.1 (Winter 1987): 41–45.

Ngara, Emmanuel. *Stylistic Criticism and the African Novel*. London: Heinemann, 1982.

Obiechina, Emmanuel. *Culture, Tradition, and Society in the West African Novel*. Cambridge: Cambridge University Press, 1975.

Palmer, Eustace. *An Introduction to the African Novel: A Critical Study of Twelve Books by Chinua Achebe, James Ngugi, Camara Laye, Elechi Amadi, Ayi Kwei Armah, Mongo Beti, and Gabriel Okara*. New York: Africana Publishing Corp., 1972.

Scott, Patrick. "Gabriel Okara's *The Voice*: The Non-Ijo Reader and the Pragmatics of Translingualism." *Research in African Literatures* 21.3 (Fall 1990): 75–88.

Senanu, K. E., and T. Vincent, eds. *A Selection of African Poetry*. London: Longman, 1976.

Thumboo, Edwin. "Language as Power: Gabriel Okara's *The Voice* as a Paradigm." *World Englishes* 5.2–3 (1986): 249–64.

PUSHPA NAIDU PAREKH

CHRISTOPHER IFEANYICHUKWU OKIGBO (1932–1967)

BIOGRAPHY

Christopher Okigbo, the man Chinua Achebe called "the finest Nigerian poet of his generation," was born in Ojoto in the Onitsha province of what was then eastern Nigeria (Achebe and Okafor, viii). Okigbo was the fourth child of a Roman Catholic Ibo primary-school teacher, James Okigbo. Christopher Okigbo was a man of many talents and wide-ranging interests in literature, math, music, and Latin. A bright and successful student, he joined the University of Ibadan in 1951 for a degree in medicine. He changed his major to classics and graduated in 1956. He held a series of jobs including that of Latin teacher, librarian, and special representative of Cambridge University Press in Ibadan. He married Sefi in 1963 and had a daughter, Ibrahimat. The political upheaval in Nigeria of 1966 drew Okigbo into it, and he enlisted in the Biafran army and was made a major by special commission. He was killed in the war during a battle near Nsukka. Okigbo is remembered by friends as an intelligent, talented, passionate, and idealistic man. His untimely death deprived Nigeria of one of its most talented poets.

MAJOR WORKS AND THEMES

During his days as a student at the University of Ibadan, Okigbo published his first poems in the *Horn*, a student literary journal edited by another student and poet, J. P. Clark. However, it was only after he graduated that he discovered that poetry was his calling. Okigbo remarked, "The turning point came in December 1958, when I knew that I couldn't be anything else than a poet" (quoted in *Collected Poems*, xii). Between 1957 and 1968, he published his work in many literary journals, such as *Transition* and *Black Orpheus*. He also published several collections of his poetry, including *Heavensgate* (1962), *Limits* (1964), and *Labyrinths* (1971). *Labyrinths*, published posthumously, was a selection he put together himself, but it does not include all his poems. In 1986 Heinemann published *Collected Poems* (with an introduction by Adewale Maja-Pearce), which at this time represents the most comprehensive collection of his poetry.

Okigbo's poetry is complex and allusive and often eludes the first-time reader. As a poet, Okigbo has been compared to T. S. Eliot and Ezra Pound. Although his work is influenced by modernism, it is innovative and not derivative. He blends Western and African traditions in his poetry. For instance, the *Heavensgate* sequence invokes the Ibo goddess of the water, Idoto, and incorporates Christian mythology as the narrator seeks his spiritual identity. This fusion of Western and traditional motifs is quite typical of many postcolonial African writers, including Achebe, Soyinka, and Ngugi. Okigbo's poetry draws from a wide variety of sources: Ibo myth and beliefs, Christianity, Virgil, Nigerian music and rhythms, and English and American modernist poets. In an interview with Dennis Duerden and Cosmo Pieterse, Okigbo commented that the modern African poet is a product of a complex culture who gives voice to its values. He contended that trying to separate the indigenous from the foreign in this cultural system leads to artificiality (*Collected Poems*, xviii). In using Western ideas, Okigbo's poetry does not passively accept the impact of the colonial educational system that violently imposed foreign values on the indigenous cultures. In *Heavensgate*, his protagonist explores this troubled relationship between indigenous values and the Christian values of the colonizer. As a poet, Okigbo attempts to transcend these opposing cultural forces through his poetry.

The speaker in Okigbo's poetry is often a figure who is on a quest for his spiritual self. In an early sequence of poems called "Four Canzones," the speaker is an exile who seeks to retrieve the innocence of his childhood. In the process of his evolution, the speaker rejects the urban values of Lagos and returns to the village of his birth. In the final canzone, the speaker finds his peace. One critic argues that all of Okigbo's poetry is one elaborate poem that "transmutes all experiences into ceremony" (Dathorne, 79). In combining personal narrative, cultural experience, and a spiritual quest, the corpus of Okigbo's poetry reads like the spiritual autobiography of the poet who seeks his own voice as well as the voice of his people.

Okigbo's poetry also indicates the evolution of the poet's political views. In his last sequence of poems, *Path of Thunder: Poems Prophesying War*, he dons the role of a town crier and comments on the failure of government, the corruption of the politicians, and neocolonial economic and political exploitation. The poems lament the loss of a political dream. This last sequence of poems is perhaps Okigbo's most overtly political, and the poet attempts to write about the people behind the myths and rituals. The growing interest in experiences indicates an evolution in Okigbo's thinking regarding myth as the mode of expressing collective experience. The poet/speaker in *Path of Thunder* reveals a new Okigbo; unfortunately for us, he died young and Nigeria lost a promising writer.

CRITICAL RECEPTION

Okigbo's poetry has generated much scholarly attention. Much of the criticism explores the complex web of allusions and tries to explicate difficult passages. Many critics are also intrigued by the complexity of Okigbo's craft. One of the early book-length studies of Okigbo's work is Sunday Onozie's *Christopher Okigbo: Creative Rhetoric* (1972). An outstanding critic, Onozie examines the influences on Okigbo's poetry and focuses on his complex use of myth as both "privileged religious mode of cognition" and an affective and evaluative totem in a specific cultural context (1). The evolution of critical responses to Okigbo's work is well represented by a collection of essays, *Critical Perspectives on Christopher Okigbo*, edited by Donatus Ibe Nwoga. This collection excerpts criticism on the major works as well as some valuable interviews. In addition, this work includes a comprehensive bibliography of Okigbo's work and the scholarship on his poetry.

Okigbo's life and work have also influenced creative works. Ali A. Mazrui's novel of ideas, *The Trial of Christopher Okigbo* (1971), examines Okigbo's commitment to the Biafran ideal and its impact on his integrity as a poet. Another creative volume that critically examines the man and the poet is a collection of memorial poems edited by Chinua Achebe and Dubem Okafor that is provocatively titled *Don't Let Him Die* (1978). Both these works of "creative criticism" offer unique perspectives on Okigbo.

BIBLIOGRAPHY

Works by Christopher Ifeanyichukwu Okigbo

Heavensgate. Ibadan: Mbari, 1962.
Limits. Ibadan: Mbari, 1964.
Labyrinths with Path of Thunder. London: Heinemann, 1971; New York: Africana, 1971.
Collected Poems. London: Heinemann, 1986.

Selected Studies of Christopher Ifeanyichukwu Okigbo

Achebe, Chinua, and Dubem Okafor, eds. *Don't Let Him Die*. Enugu: Fourth Dimension, 1978.
Azuonye, Chukwuma. " 'I, Okigbo, Town-Crier': The Transition from Mythopoeic Symbolism to a Revolutionary Aesthetic in *Path of Thunder*." *The Gong and the Flute: African Literary Development and Celebration*. Ed. Kalu Ogbaa. Westport, CT: Greenwood Press, 1994. 19–36.
Dathorne, O. R. "African Literature IV: Ritual and Ceremony in Okigbo's Poetry." *Journal of Commonwealth Literature* 5 (1968): 79–91.

Mazrui, Ali A. *The Trial of Christopher Okigbo*. London: Heinemann, 1971.

Nazombe, Anthony I. M. "The Labyrinth as a Ritual Initiation Pattern in Christopher Okigbo's 'Labyrinths.' " *Journal of Humanities* 2 (1990): 63–87.

Nwoga, Donatus Ibe, ed. *Critical Perspectives on Christopher Okigbo*. Washington, D.C.: Three Continents Press, 1984.

Onozie, Sunday O. *Christopher Okigbo: Creative Rhetoric*. New York: Africana, 1972.

Woodroffe, Noel. "Songs of Thunder: The Biafran War in the Poetry of Chinua Achebe and Christopher Okigbo." *Commonwealth Essays and Studies* 10.2 (1988): 80–97.

NALINI IYER

BEN OKRI (1959–)

BIOGRAPHY

Ben Okri was born in 1959 in Lagos, Nigeria. He attended Urhobo College, Warri, for a few years and later continued his education privately in Lagos. Okri claims that his childhood has significantly influenced his writing, yet he has not shared many details about his childhood because he believes that it is best explored in his fiction. Instead of providing autobiographical details, Okri prefers to talk about how reading has influenced his writing. He started by reading African, classical, and European myths, and he continued reading from his father's library of the western classics. Noting many strong similarities between these diverse cultural traditions, Okri developed a worldview that combines African and European traditions. His reading also inspired him to begin writing stories and essays while he was still in secondary school. Later he failed to get a place at a Nigerian university, so he took a job at a paint store and started publishing his writing in Nigerian women's journals and evening papers. By the time he turned eighteen, he had completed his first novel, *Flowers and Shadows*, and moved to England, where he attended the University of Essex. He continues to live, read, and write in London.

MAJOR WORKS AND THEMES

Between 1980 and 1995 Ben Okri published eight works: five novels, two collections of short stories, and a volume of poetry. In each of these works, he returns to a consistent repertoire of common postcolonial themes. In particular, he critiques the ubiquity of corruption and violence in contemporary Nigeria, creates a voice for the poorest and most powerless members of African society, and explores the ongoing cultural confrontation between foreign and indigenous traditions in postcolonial Africa. Since these fundamental postcolonial issues have been repeatedly explored by many postcolonial writers, it is difficult to argue that Okri's works inaugurate new themes for African literature. As soon as one turns away from issues of thematic content and begins looking at issues of literary form, however, one notices that Okri's works immediately depart from the ordinary, predictable, and routine. Each of his works of fiction demonstrates a remarkable sense of formal experimentation, and each work progressively extends his creative exploration of multiple literary styles, genres, and traditions. Each time he revisits these common postcolonial themes, therefore, he finds extraordinary new ways to express them with greater insight, imagination, and complexity. Taken together, Okri's fiction represents one of the most significant explorations of literary form in the canon of postcolonial African literature.

Okri's works can be roughly categorized according to three phases, each of which is marked by radical shifts in genre, style, and narrative strategy. Okri's first two works, *Flowers and Shadows* and *The Landscapes Within*, blend the conventions of realism and modernism to explore the effects of modernization on urban Nigeria. In *Flowers and Shadows*, he depicts the coming of age of Jeffia Okwe, an idealistic young Nigerian who aspires to be a teacher. Over the course of the novel, Jeffia struggles to retain his youthful idealism in the face of modern society's complex demands. He looks for familial intimacy in a home where business obsessions keep his absent father chained to the firm, and he seeks justice among legions of petty bureaucrats who are constantly trying to improve upon the colonial arts of corruption and hypocrisy. Along the way, Jeffia wanders through lust, love, and the other common attractions of youth.

Jeffia's path toward adulthood is fairly straightforward, but Okri enlivens his description of it with several stylistic twists. In particular, he uses Nigerian dialects to express his characters' different social classes, he makes numerous references to art and painting to reflect on the nature and function of art, and he frequently slips into stream-of-consciousness associations or surrealistic dream images to reveal the inner workings of his characters' different worldviews. Thus Okri effectively combines the conventions of the European *Bildungsroman*, or coming-of-age novel, with Nigerian English dialects and modernist narrative strategies to explore a modern, postcolonial context. Consequently, *Flowers and Shadows* has many similarities with other postcolonial versions of the *Bildungsroman* such as Chinua Achebe's *Things Fall Apart* or Salman Rushdie's *Midnight's Children*. In many ways, it can be read as a retelling of the conflicts found in *Things Fall Apart* from an urban perspective. Consequently, it focuses on Nigeria's confrontation with the modern social, political, and existential conditions that have followed in the wake of colonialism rather than focusing on the original confrontation between colonizer and colonized. Okri presents a state in which things continue to fall apart, but his idealistic young hero arrives at a more hopeful resolution than Okonkwo's tragic demise.

In *The Landscapes Within*, Okri continues to develop a comparable mixture of realistic narration and modernist stream of consciousness as he explores the inner life of a young Nigerian painter named Omovo. The biggest difference between *Flowers and Shadows* and *The Landscapes Within*, however, is that *The Landscapes Within* makes the philosophical exploration of aesthetics more central to its narrative. By making his youthful protagonist an artist, Okri extends the generic conventions of the *Bildungsroman* toward those of the *Künstlerroman*, which traces the aesthetic maturation of a young artist. Much like James Joyce's youthful artist, Stephen Dedalus, Okri's artist, Omovo, uses art as a way of creating order and meaning in a fragmenting world. Living the life of a lonely, uncompromising artist who is often at odds with his society, Omovo develops the detached observation and creative expression required of the artist. His aesthetic development culminates in a painting titled *Scumscape*, which portrays the miserable conditions of Nigeria's urban poor, but the painting is quickly censored and confiscated because of its powerful social criticism. Both Omovo's *Scumscape* and its censorship demonstrate how Okri adapts the conventions of the European *Künstlerroman* to fit his own postcolonial context. Instead of describing some abstract theory of beauty, Okri's philosophical reflections on art emphasize the political dimensions of artistic production and destruction in a newly independent nation struggling to free itself from the quicksand of neocolonial authoritarianism. In *The Landscapes Within*, therefore, Okri not only reinterprets the *Künstlerroman* from a postcolonial perspective, but he also subtly redirects postcolonial African literature by implicitly arguing that aesthetic responses to colonialism are as necessary as political ones. In this sense, *The Landscapes Within* resembles other postcolonial variations on the *Künstlerroman* such as Wilson Harris's *Da Silva da Silva's Cultivated Wilderness* or Janet Frame's *To the Island*. Both of Okri's first two novels follow a similar narrative strategy of creatively adapting European novelistic conventions to explore postcolonial issues. However, *The Landscapes Within* additionally expands the scope of postcolonial African literature by augmenting its political engagement of social realism with the kind of aesthetic engagement found in many modernist texts.

Okri's next two works, *Incidents at the Shrine* and *Stars of the New Curfew*, mark a new phase in his artistic development. This second phase can be identified by two significant changes. First, Okri begins writing short stories instead of novels; second, he starts experimenting more with African narrative techniques. Okri himself has drawn attention to the importance of his shift to writing short stories by suggesting that writing short stories is an apprenticeship for writing novels. The short story provides an ideal opportunity for an author to perfect his or her mastery of plot, dialogue, and style. This sort of aesthetic development can be seen clearly in the enormous difference between the quality of the two novels that Okri wrote before his short stories and the quality of the third novel, *The Famished Road*, which he wrote after his short stories. More important, these collections of short stories mark a turning point in Okri's aesthetic development because they increasingly use African narrative techniques as an essential aspect of their narrative strategy. *Stars of the New Curfew* particularly develops the rich imagination, complex mythical imagery, and episodic adventures that are also found in works like Amos Tutuola's *The Palm-Wine Drinkard*, Gabriel Okara's *The Voice*, or D. O. Fagunwa's Yoruba novels. This effort to create literary forms modeled after the narrative strategies of African oral traditions continues another important aspect of contemporary postcolonial African writing because it attempts to engage postcolonial aesthetic forms as well as postcolonial sociopolitical issues. By redirecting his experimental energy toward an exploration of African models rather than European ones, Okri prepared himself for a new stage of aesthetic development.

The rest of Okri's novels combine aspects from his two previous literary phases to produce a unique and complex narrative strategy. Okri's most important novel to date, *The Famished Road*, and its sequel, *Songs of Enchantment*, brilliantly demonstrate Okri's ability to combine the techniques of realism, modernism, and African oral traditions. In these two novels, Okri describes the adventures of Azaro, an *abiku* spirit-child who equally possesses a spiritual and an earthly dimension. An *abiku* is a child who has had a hard time deciding that it wants to be born into a mortal existence, so it keeps coming and going between this world and the spirit world until it finally decides which world it wants to embrace. Usually a child is deemed an *abiku* when it is born to a woman who has had repeated miscarriages or children who die at a young age. The child who finally survives is called an *abiku* because it is believed to be the same spirit that tried to be born as the other children. Such reluctant spirits become *abiku* spirit-children when they finally develop the will to choose life, so parents often perform rituals or do special favors to persuade the *abiku* child to choose this life over its spirit life.

Like Okri's previous novels, these later novels also explore the consciousness of a child protagonist as he progresses toward maturity. The dualistic spiritual-physical nature of Okri's *abiku* hero, however, completely alters the trajectory of the *Bildungsroman*. Since Azaro has a dual nature, he must progress through both earthly and mythical realms so he can mature metaphysically as well as socially. Consequently, Okri greatly extends the narrative action of his later fiction to include mythical journeys, intense dreams, and other African rituals or rites of passage. By extending the scope of the novel to include mythical dimensions, Okri participates in another redirection that is characteristic of contemporary postcolonial literature: he effectively redirects his narrative strategy to minimize the significance of the colonial master and maximize the experiences of the postcolonial subject. Instead of focusing on the colonial destruction of traditional African societies and cultures, therefore, he draws attention to their survival, albeit a precarious survival often lived on the threshold between life and death. Even though Okri remains keenly aware of the tragic destruction that colonialism continues to impose on traditional African societies, he refuses to let his characters admit defeat. He rejects the claim that colonialism has conquered, is conquering, or ever will conquer the deeper mysteries of the African spirit. By making his protagonist an *abiku* spirit-child who chooses to live, Okri suggests that the African spirit can survive the seemingly endless cycles of colonial and neocolonial violence by choosing to reconcile its spiritual and physical dimensions. Similarly, Azaro's father defeats multiple colonial and neocolonial aggressors in a series of mythic battles that mix mythical solemnity with folkloric bravado. Azaro's mother also aids the survival of her family and community through her less spectacular, but more lasting, character traits: courage, perseverance, hard work, and common sense. Of course, there are also other characters who do not fare so well. Madame Koto, the purveyor of the local, Westernized bar, degenerates with each of her increasingly corrupt political and economic deals. Ade, another *abiku* spirit-child, chooses to return to the spirit world rather than endure the rigors of mortality; and Jeremiah, an idealistic young journalistic photographer, is so regularly harassed by political thugs that he fades into the background and only pops out for sporadic moments to take a few photos before recommencing his perpetual journey from hiding place to hiding place. Thus Okri faces the many possibilities presented by the postcolonial condition, but he seems to side with the characters who maintain an idealistic, spiritual perspective in spite of their difficulties.

In order to narrate such a journey, Okri fuses his earlier realist and modernist style with the mythical style that he developed in *Stars of the New Curfew*. This mixing of realism with myth and folklore creates a powerful dialogue between European and African literary traditions as it seeks to extend the possibilities of both traditions. Thus Okri extends his engagement of postcolonial issues to the realm of aesthetics by demonstrating that African aesthetic sensibilities, cultural traditions, and narrative strategies will not allow themselves to be colonized by the literary norms of the colonial center. In some significant sense, therefore, the mature experimentation in Okri's later fiction represents a movement for cultural independence that parallels and complements the movements for political independence that swept the postcolonial world during the 1960s and 1970s. Okri's later fiction also exemplifies what Homi K. Bhabha describes as a postcolonial aesthetic of cultural hybridity because it explores the liminal border between diverse cultural traditions. In *The Famished Road*, Okri displays his own mastery of realism, modernism, and African mythical traditions, thereby demonstrating that these diverse cultural traditions can coexist within new hybrid forms. Henry Louis Gates, Jr., has accurately described Okri's unique style as "engagingly lyrical and intriguingly postmodern" (3). *The Famished Road* is clearly a literary tour de force that will soon become a classic of twentieth-century fiction.

Since *Songs of Enchantment* is a sequel of sorts to *The Famished Road*, the themes and techniques used in *The Famished Road* generally carry over into *Songs of Enchantment* as well. The primary difference between *Songs of Enchantment* and *The Famished Road* is that *Songs of Enchantment*'s narrative structure is simpler and more rigorously edited. Consequently, *Songs of Enchantment* is easier to read and understand, but at times this ease of access is paid for by a reduction in lyrical grandeur and philosophical complexity. Nevertheless, Okri's characters undergo many subtle changes and reevaluations in the second novel, and these reevaluations are integral to Okri's Afrocentric and mythopoetic worldview. They demonstrate how openness and transformation are central to both Okri's political agenda and his aesthetic experimentation. In imagining the history of Africa in terms of a mythical road that must always be kept open and characters who are always changing, Okri suggests that the survival and development of the human spirit require a continual openness to new possibilities. Similarly, Okri's radically experimental style promotes an equivalent openness for African aesthetics. Consequently, even though there are significant continuities between *The Famished Road* and *Songs of Enchantment*, the sentient reader must be very careful not to reduce *Songs of Enchantment* to a mere continuation of or sequel to *The Famished Road*. If *Songs of Enchantment* is a sequel, then it is a sequel in the sense that it keeps looking for new possibilities rather than in the sense that it follows the same trajectory as its predecessor.

Okri's latest novel, *Astonishing the Gods*, continues to develop the same kind of spiritual, mythical vision and lyrical aesthetic that Okri develops in *The Famished Road* and *Songs of Enchantment*. Unfortunately, however, it lacks much of the political engagement, experimental energy, and complexity found in Okri's previous novels: its characters are less developed, its narrative structure seems more amorphous than complex, and its mythical vision fails to develop the same intensity because it is not as counterbalanced with a realistic dimension. Nevertheless, even though Okri's latest works seem to suggest that his talent is waning, it seems unlikely that he will simply continue to produce simplified versions of his best work. Instead, it seems more likely that Okri is simply in a transitional period preparing the next evolution of his style. Okri is a fiercely intense writer who is still very young, and one should expect that *The Famished Road* will not be his last monumental work. Hopefully, it will not even be his best.

Always exploring new aesthetic possibilities, Okri has also published a volume of poetry titled *An African Elegy*. Throughout these poems, Okri meditates on various aspects of the human condition: love, solitude, pain, death, faith. In treating these themes, he moves seamlessly between philosophical reflection and the description of intimate details of everyday life. His rich lyrical voice once again demonstrates his ability to continually explore new literary forms, and his intense personal vision creates an atmosphere that is spiritual without being sentimental.

CRITICAL RECEPTION

Ben Okri is quickly becoming one of the most acclaimed African writers of his generation, and his significant contribution to African literature has been recognized by both African and European critics. In an interview with Alastair Niven, Chinua Achebe suggested that the torch of Nigerian literature was currently being passed on from his generation to a new, younger generation of African writers. When asked to explain who represented this new generation, Achebe mentioned Ben Okri specifically. Achebe's tribute to Okri, therefore, not only draws attention to Okri's extraordinary talent, but it also signals the emergence of a younger generation of writers who are charting new directions for African literature. Okri clearly belongs in the vanguard of this generation, and his innovative literary experimentations have drawn increasing international attention to contemporary African literature. In the past few years, Okri has received numerous international literary awards, including the Commonwealth Writers' Prize for Africa, the Chianti Rufino-Antico Fattore International Literary Prize, the *Paris Review* Aga Khan Prize for Fiction, the Premio Grinzane Cavour, and the prestigious Booker Prize.

In particular, critics have praised Okri for his ability to creatively experiment with new literary forms. Even though Okri's earlier novels are not nearly as experimental as his later ones, critics like Ayo Mamudu and Abioseh Michael Porter have shown that they develop unorthodox narrative strategies that attempt to break from the tradition of social realism, which has dominated the African novel ever since it was first used by Chinua Achebe. Consequently, critics emphasize Okri's use of modernist conventions and make frequent comparisons between his first two novels and James Joyce's *A Portrait of the Artist as a Young Man*. While their comparisons with modernism are certainly valid, Okri's restrained use of stream of consciousness and his exploration of familial relations probably bear more similarities to Virginia Woolf's subtler modernist style than to Joyce's more aggressive experimentation. It is not until *The Famished Road* that Okri's writing really takes on the kind of epic grandeur, philosophical depth, and sustained experimentation found in Joyce.

Okri's middle works, *Incidents at the Shrine* and *Stars of the New Curfew*, have received less critical attention even though they represent a crucial phase in Okri's development as an writer. In the future, more critical attention needs to be given to these short stories in order to show how they create a bridge between Okri's earlier and later styles. In particular, greater critical analysis of *Stars of the New Curfew* would show more clearly how Okri has developed a uniquely African sense of postmodernism that derives from a creative extension of African folklore rather than being a derivative imitation of foreign postmodernist techniques. A few critics have begun this process, but there is still much more that needs to be done. For example, Alastair Niven's analysis of a short story from *Incidents at the Shrine* draws attention to Okri's increased mastery of narrative forms, and David Richard's and T. J. Cribb's essays show how *Stars of the New Curfew* explores more African narrative forms. Nevertheless, all three studies are partially flawed in their conclusions. Niven's study critiques Okri for not following the tradition of Achebe, but what is interesting about Okri's work is precisely the fact that it seeks to explore new directions. To try to hold Okri to the standard of Achebe is to misunderstand how his fiction inaugurates new aesthetic issues that require new criteria of critical evaluation. Richard's essay comes closer to the mark by emphasizing how Okri's fiction explores new post-colonial issues, yet it reinscribes these postcolonial concerns too quickly within Western debates about postmodernity, so it fails to adequately develop the African roots of Okri's new style. Cribb's essay more carefully develops Okri's relationship to the tradition of Tutuola and the Yoruba novel, but it simply needs to go farther. Future critics would be wise to follow up on Cribb's essay and systematically develop the relationships between Okri and Tutuola to better understand how African traditions function in Okri's fiction.

Most of the critical analysis of Okri's fiction has focused on *The Famished Road*, which is unquestionably Okri's most important work so far. *The Famished Road* is clearly a literary tour de force that virtually defines the vanguard of contemporary African literature. There is something of a critical irony here that bears mentioning. Gerald Moore once claimed that Tutuola's style was a dead end for African literature because it would not be imitated. *The Famished Road*, however, has turned Tutuola's so-called dead end into the catalyst for exploring new aesthetic directions based on a broader understanding of African folklore and less dependent on its imitation of the European novel. The powerfully unique style that Okri develops in *The Famished Road* has made Okri's work very difficult to categorize, though most critics describes it as an example of magical realism because it fuses a realistic narrative with a mythical one. For example, Olatubosun Ogunsanwo compares it to Gabriel García Marquez's *One Hundred Years of Solitude*, and Jacqueline Bardolph compares it to Salman Rushdie's *Midnight's Children*. Certainly there is validity to these comparisons, as evidenced by Okri's fusion of realism and myth, bold imagination, use of exaggeration and hyperbole, detailed description of uncanny events, and explorations of liminal zones and continually transforming characters. Nevertheless, Okri has tried to keep his work from being simplistically labeled as magical realism. In particular, he emphasizes that he is not trying to create a world of magic and myth that exists next to the real world as much as he is trying to extend our sense of the real world itself to include myths and magical events within it. If future critics want to continue reading *The Famished Road* as a work of magical realism, they would be wise to pay more attention to Okri's comments and, at the very least, take the realistic dimensions of the work as seriously as the magical ones. Ideally, they should take Okri's comments a step further to see the magical events as an African form of realism in which the magical world is part of the real world.

The second label that critics have attached to *The Famished Road* is postmodern. In particular, John C. Hawley argues that Okri's works are postmodern because they mix genres, cross cultural boundaries, and intertextually parody both African and European traditions. Olatubosun Ogunsanwo also argues that *The Famished Road* is postmodern because of its postmodern sense of intertextual parody. Both critics further emphasize that Okri's postmodern sensibilities derive from African as well as European sources. Ogunsanwo explains how *The Famished Road* is a parody of African myths and literature, and Hawley shows how its organizing principle derives from the widespread Nigerian belief in *abiku* spirit-children. These critics demonstrate that Okri does not present us with an either/or situation: his narrative strategies are not *either* imitations of postmodern magical realism *or* sequels to Tutuola's *The Palm-Wine Drinkard*. Rather, they bring both traditions together into a creative dialogue that reworks the one as much as the other. Consequently, if future critics want to read *The Famished Road* as a postmodern work, they need to be much clearer about how its use of African narrative strategies and its exploration of African political issues develop a unique sense of postmodernism. Critics who are interested in looking at the postmodern condition from this genuinely cross-cultural postcolonial perspective will need to return to *The Famished Road* repeatedly to unravel its many-layered mysteries. The key to understanding both Okri's use of magical realism and his use of postmodernism, therefore, is to read his works in the context of the Nigerian oral and literary traditions from which they develop.

BIBLIOGRAPHY

Works by Ben Okri

Flowers and Shadows. London: Longman, 1980.
The Landscapes Within. London: Longman, 1981.
Incidents at the Shrine. London: Heinemann, 1986.
Stars of the New Curfew. New York: Viking Penguin, 1989.
An African Elegy. London: Jonathan Cape, 1992.
The Famished Road. New York: Doubleday/Talese, 1992.
Songs of Enchantment. New York: Doubleday/Talese, 1993.
Astonishing the Gods. London: Phoenix House, 1995.

Selected Studies of Ben Okri

Bardolph, Jacqueline. "Azaro, Saleem, and Askar: Brothers in Allegory." *Commonwealth Essays and Studies* 15.1 (1992): 45–51.
Bruckner, Thomas. "Ben Okri: Vom Erbluhen der Verwesung im Verborgenen der Geschichte." *Beitrage zur afrikanischen Sprach- und Literaturwissenschaft*. Ed. Wilhelm J. G. Mohlig. Koln: Koppe, 1993.
Cribb, T. J. "Transformations in the Fiction of Ben Okri." *From Commonwealth to Postcolonial*. Ed. Anna Rutherford. Sydney: Dangaroo Press, 1992. 145–51.

Garnier, Xavier. "L'invisible dans *The Famished Road* de Ben Okri." *Commonwealth Essays and Studies* 15.2 (1993): 50–57.

Gates, Henry Louis, Jr. "Between the Living and the Unborn." *New York Times Book Review* June 28, 1992: 3, 20.

Hawley, John C. "Ben Okri's Spirit-Child: Abiku Migration and Postmodernity." *Research in African Literatures* 26.1 (1995): 20–29.

Houpt, Simon. "Ben Okri: *The Landscapes Within.*" *African Literature Association Bulletin* 18.3 (1992): 37–39.

Lemus, Silvia. "La Escritura, el Box y Nietzsche: Una Entravista con Ben Okri, un Fabulador que Muerde." *Nexos* July 1995: 55–63.

Mamudu, Ayo. "Portrait of a Young Artist in Ben Okri's *The Landscapes Within.*" *Commonwealth Essays and Studies* 13.2 (1991): 85–91.

Niven, Alastair. "Achebe and Okri: Contrasts in the Response to Civil War."*Short Fiction in the New Literatures in English*. Ed. Jacqueline Bardolph. Nice: Faculté des Lettres et Sciences Humaines, 1989. 277–85.

Nnolim, Charles E. "Ben Okri: Writer as Artist." *Approaches to the African Novel: Essays in Analysis*. London: Saros, 1992. 173–89.

———. "The Time Is out of Joint: Ben Okri as a Social Critic." *Commonwealth Novel in English* 6.1–2 (1993): 61–68.

Ogunsanwo, Olatubosun. "Intertextuality and Post-colonial Literature in Ben Okri's *The Famished Road.*" *Research in African Literatures* 26.1 (1995): 30–39.

Porter, Abioseh Michael. "Ben Okri's *The Landscapes Within*: A Metaphor for Personal and National Development." *World Literature Written in English* 28.2 (1988): 203–10.

Richards, David. " 'A History of Interruptions': Dislocated Mimesis in the Writings of Neil Bissoondath and Ben Okri." *From Commonwealth to Post-colonial*. Ed. Anna Rutherford. Sydney: Dangaroo Press, 1992. 74–82.

Ross, Jean W. "Contemporary Authors Interview." *Contemporary Authors*. Ed. Donna Olendorf. Vol. 138. Detroit, Mich.: Gale Research, 1993. 337–41.

Wilkinson, Jane. "Ben Okri." *Talking with African Writers*. Ed. Jane Wilkinson. London: Heinemann, 1991. 76–89.

ROBERT BENNETT

FEMI OSOFISAN (1946–   )

BIOGRAPHY

The generation born in the late 1940s in Nigeria came to young maturity in the late 1960s, just as the hopes expressed at the 1960 independence celebrations had collapsed into civil war. For Femi Osofisan, who was in his midteens when Wole Soyinka's *A Dance of the Forests* first sounded a warning about overly romantic constructions of history (1960), there was available a new theatrical tradition established in English, attempting for the first time to try to speak to the complexity of a new multilingual, multicultural nation and essentially decolonizing the colonial tongue. English, of course, is not the first language of Nigerians, but it is often a useful language, helping to provide internal communication across sometimes bitter ethnic divisions. However, it cannot appeal to those who do not speak English or do not choose to engage with it, usually the masses. English-language theatre in Nigeria tends to be a middle-class or intellectual cultural activity and also of course opens a window of communication with the wider world.

Femi Osofisan has sought to bring together aspects of the theatrical traditions of his own Yoruba people and of European theatre, most notably Brechtian strategies for provoking thoughtful response to social issues in the audience. Contradiction lies at the heart of creativity, and Osofisan's intellectual positions and his writing often exhibit conscious and therefore productive contradiction, most evident in the ways in which he structures debate into his plays. For example, he is both socialist and cut off from the masses in Nigeria by his use of English and his intellectual training, which makes him cosmopolitan and international. He utilizes Yoruba tradition but in the service of opening up political dialogue that suggests the possibility of dramatic social change and undermines conservatism and elitism. English-language drama in Nigeria is essentially verbal, despite using music and dance, as opposed to, say, Yoruba folk opera, which is musical drama.

Of course, Nobel laureate Wole Soyinka also brought Yoruba tradition, the medium of English, and whatever he found of use in theatre together. Osofisan is heir to Soyinka's pioneering spirit in Nigerian drama, but has also followed very much his own star. He is less evidently a wordsmith than Soyinka, though his plays generally have good, effective dialogue. More than Soyinka, he experiments with surprises that involve the audience in shaping the play itself.

Like Soyinka, Osofisan was born in the Yoruba region of Nigeria and obtained his first degree from the University of Ibadan, the premier Nigerian university at the time both graduated but also primarily a Yoruba institution. From Ibadan he received, therefore, both a solid grounding in international (though primarily British colonial) influences and a strong reinforcement of Yoruba identity. Both dramatists spent some formative years abroad after their first degrees, Soyinka in England and Osofisan in France. Both began to write plays early. Osofisan produced his first play and saw it performed the year he graduated with his B.A. from Ibadan (*A Restless Run of Locusts*, performed 1969). Osofisan went on to get his doctorate, on the origins of drama in West Africa, from the University of Ibadan in 1974. Like Soyinka, he has pursued many different kinds of writing, mainly plays, but also journalism, literary criticism, fiction, and poetry, and also like Soyinka, he has directed his own plays. However, Osofisan has developed his own style of theatre and has largely rejected the mythopoetic style of Soyinka, though the relation between his work and Soyinka's has often been discussed. He needed to find his own space and not simply be influenced by Soyinka's enormously important work, and this he has done.

He was interested in theatre from a young age. He was born in Erunwon, in the then Western Region of Nigeria, and lost his father as a young baby. He traces his political convictions, that is, his radical socialism, to the experience of poverty that the loss of his father brought him and his subsequent identification with the ordinary people of Nigeria. But his own achievements and the help of his extended family took him to the University of Ibadan and to a career as dramatist and academic. From primary school he acted in plays, eventually also directing and writing them. He regards production as a chance to finalize the written script, as do many dramatists, and often revises during or after the first production

Osofisan has done a great deal as writer, theatre practitioner, academic, journalist, and social activist. He is presently professor of theatre arts at the University of Ibadan. He has written and directed his own plays since the late 1960s, as well as contributing articles and monographs on Nigerian literature and society and making television programs. He has always regarded literature as being essentially political, and his work as a whole is a contribution to the political as well as the cultural and intellectual life of his society.

MAJOR WORKS AND THEMES

Osofisan's commitment to social change in Nigeria has been evident since his earliest writing. He criticizes tradition as romantic escapism, as when he said that J. P. Clark constructs tradition as "atemporal, ahistorical . . . idealised, exotic and mythical" ("Trail of Ozidi," 36). But he himself finds ways to use myth and tradition, for example, in his fine play *Morountodun* (1982), in the service of progressive ideas. He well represents a significant number of his generation of Nigerian writers who accept neither nativist conceptions of an ideal African past nor naïve enthusiasms about Western influence, a generation that has seen both colonialism and postcolonialism and has few illusions about either.

Though he wrote first, in his earliest plays, as a social realist, Osofisan has gradually come to develop a unique blend of theatrical styles. He has often utilized his own versions of the Brechtian "A" effect, bringing the audience into the performance in dramatic ways, sometimes even to determine the resolution of a given work. But he draws also on popular Nigerian theatrical and cultural elements, such as song and dance, riddling, evident role playing, and storytelling, and of course he portrays in dialogue the verbal skills for which the Yoruba are justly famous.

The overall purpose of this theatrical eclecticism is to produce a theatre that causes the audience to think through social and political choices and to accept surprise and change. *Who's Afraid of Solarin?* (1978), a rewriting of Nikolai Gogol's intelligent farce about government corruption, *The Inspector General* (1836), celebrates Dr. Tai Solarin, who was public complaints commissioner during the Osabanjo government in Nigeria in the 1970s. But his major themes and concerns can be understood from three representative plays: *The Chattering and the Song* (1977), *Mourountodun* (1982), and the recent *Esu and the Vagabond Minstrels* (1991).

In each play, songs are important. Osofisan has spoken about how writing songs helped him past certain problems in rehearsing an early version of *The Chattering and the Song* (interview with Elaine Savory, 1983). He believes that theatre should be "ad hoc," that is, the writing emerges through the production process. The plot in these plays is less important than the theatrical process, by which the audience participates in determining meaning. The final stage direction in *The Chattering and the Song* is "The play does NOT end" (56). Instead, the audience joins in the Farmer's Anthem begun by actors no longer in costume. In both this play and *Morountodun*, there is a play within a play, and in *Esu and the Vagabond Minstrels*, a debate among actors as members of the audience "rewrites" the end: of course, this is contrived but contributes a dramatic expression of the importance of the audience's involvement in the performance. Indeed, Redio remarks, "Today the play's going to end differently," and the Old Man replies, "And have you told the author about it!" Sin Sin goes on, "Let him watch, like everybody else" (69).

Also in each of the three plays, historical, supernatural, or mythic elements in Nigerian culture that have powerful reverberations in contemporary society are cleverly dislocated from the possibility of being reactionary and are used to further creative rethinking of the priorities of the day. In *The Chattering and the Song*, the Farmer's Rebellion in Agbekoya (1968–69) against taxation is an important backdrop against which middle-class friends of a soon-to-be-married couple playfully explore their own relationships and come to enact the corruptions of a nineteenth-century Yoruba court. Eventually, the affianced couple is betrayed by a spy of the government who arrests them because they have been involved in politics. The complex interweaving of political, social, and personal elements in this play offers encouragement to the audience to affect history by being both knowing and critical. Similarly, in *Morountodun*, the old legend of Moremi, who saved her people by marrying the Ibo king and betraying him for her people, is rewritten when Titubi, her modern counterpart, spies for the government against the farmers in the 1968 revolt. Titubi, unlike her real-life model, who successfully undermined the farmers' movement, rethinks her position and joins the farmers. In *Esu and the Vagabond Minstrels*, Esu, the Yoruba god who presides over misunderstandings, transformations, and contradictions, who carries the will of the gods to man, and who celebrates multiple interpretations of experience, appears at crossroads, with which he is especially associated, in disguise. He offers a group of poor performers a chance at quick wealth if they can each satisfy a serious human need. In the end, after each finds someone to help, only one has responded to the need with personal risk and without thinking of possible returns on this investment. Esu takes the audience's advice before turning this outcome upside down and rewarding the virtuous one. Then his own existence is denied in the final song of the play: human nature, not an external force like a god, will be the source of change. Osofisan thus once again uses tradition as a vehicle for forcing the audience into direct confrontation with its own collective morality. He calls this play a fertility rite; in the sense that it attempts to make conscious and perhaps rewrite a cultural narrative of the audience, this can be understood as a code for releasing creative energies.

Once upon Four Robbers (1980) is the first in the series of plays in which *Esu and the Vagabond Minstrels* is the second. Each takes a folkloric theme, that of a group of people given extraordinary choice in a state of crisis by some unexpected agency. Osofisan notes in his preface to *Esu* that each play has Orunmila, "ever the repository of wisdom and symbol of reconciliation and replenishment" (vi), and thus a sign that the plays are entertainments, intended to please. *Once upon Four Robbers* examines the idea that social injustice breeds violence and that the audience, the people of Nigeria, must make a decision as to what to do to restructure society so as to prevent criminal behavior. Their choice otherwise is graphically enacted by the play: their votes decide on the ending, which is either toleration of onstage executions of the criminals or that the freed thieves attack and rob other actors and then threaten the audience.

Theatre is a paradox: often international, it is also always deeply engaged with local issues. Osofisan's plays, like those of Soyinka but often more so, require a certain knowledge of Nigerian culture and history that ought to be easily and usually acquired by educated people everywhere. Osofisan has begun to attach glossaries and translations to the plays to help the non-Yoruba reader. Howard University Press is preparing to publish a collection of his plays that will make his plays more easily available in America. Whether he utilizes Nigerian tradition or European theatricality, (for example, Beckett's influence can be seen in *Oriki of a Grasshopper*, 1986), Osofisan's plays tackle difficult questions about the nature of political conviction and action in a complex time.

CRITICAL RECEPTION

So far, though there are numerous articles on Osofisan's work, serious interest has mainly been confined to Nigerian critics. An important part of this attention comes from the group of radical literary theorists, critics, and writers such as Biodun Jeyifo and Niyi Osundare, who share Osofisan's social views. Jeyifo remarks (1985), however, that Osofisan's *The Chattering and the Song* is so indirectly ideological that the Farmer's Anthem can seem tacked on to the end. Jeyifo has also seen that there is a danger that overt experiments in theatrical eclecticism can founder by privileging form over meaning.

Tess Onwueme (1988) has written on Osofisan's presentation of women characters. Gender issues are not nearly as central in his work as class issues, however, though he can sometimes write a good part for a woman, as in *Morountodun, The Chattering and the Song*, and *Esu and the Vagabond Minstrels*.

There have been a number of essays on Osofisan's use of ritual and on the relation of his work to that of Soyinka, even on his contribution to literary criticism. Olu Obafemi (1982), however, comments astutely on Osofisan's attempts to combine theatrically elements of tradition, music, and role playing with political agendas, but is concerned that there may be too much of an ideological directive. Sandra Richards (May 1987, August 1987, 1993) has done excellent work in bringing Osofisan to the notice of America, and no doubt now that his plays have begun to be occasionally performed in the United States and Howard University is about to publish a collection of his plays, interest will extend outside Nigeria.

Richard has also written the only book-length study of Osofisan's plays and theatrical practice. Although African theatre and drama as a whole is a relatively neglected field, it is clear that Osofisan is increasingly recognized as an important writer and director, still only in midcareer and producing new work. He has already contributed significantly to postcolonial African drama and theatre. He creates theatre that is politically aware and always supportive of the independent human spirit, of people who stand apart from established, privileged ideologies and think their way through, avoiding simplicities, to intelligent support of the oppressed.

BIBLIOGRAPHY

Works by Femi Osofisan

Published Plays

First production date and place follow the publication details in parentheses.

A Restless Run of Locusts. Ibadan: Onobonoje, 1969 (Akure, 1970).

The Chattering and the Song. Ibadan: Ibadan University Press, 1977 (Ibadan: University of Ibadan Theatre, 1976). Translated into French as *La frame et la chaine. Peuples Noirs, Peuples Africaines* 13: 90–118; 14: 133–157; 15: 163–171.

Who's Afraid of Solarin? Ibadan: Scholars, 1978 (Ibadan: University of Ibadan Theatre, 1977; translated into Yoruba as "Yeepa Slarin Nbo," Ibadan: University of Ibadan Theatre, 1988).

Once upon Four Robbers. Ibadan: BIO Educational Services, 1980 (Ibadan: University of Ibadan Theatre, 1978).

Morountodun and Other Plays. Ikeja: Longman Nigeria, 1982 (*Morountodun*, Ibadan: University of Ibadan Theatre, 1979; revised, Ibadan: Kakaun Sela Kompany, 1980; *No More The Wasted Breed*, Ibadan: BCOS TV, 1982; *Red Is the Freedom Road*, as *You Have Lost Your Fine Face*, Ibadan: University of Ibadan, 1969).

Farewell to a Cannibal Rage. Ibadan: Evans, 1986 (As *Night Is When the Sun Rises*, Ibadan, 1970; Ibadan: University of Ibadan Theatre, 1978; revised version, Benin City: University of Benin Theatre, 1984).

Midnight Hotel. Ibadan: Evans, 1986 (Ibadan Kakaun Sela Kompany, 1982).

Two One-Act Plays. Ibadan: New Horn, 1986 (*Oriki of a Grasshopper*, Ibadan: University of Ibadan Theatre, 1982; revised version, Benin City: University of Benin Theatre, 1985; *Altine's Wrath*, Ibadan TV, 1982; Benin City: University of Benin Theatre, 1984).

Another Raft. Lagos: Malthouse, 1988 (Ibadan: University of Benin Theatre, 1984).

Birthdays Are Not for Dying and Other Plays. Lagos: Malthouse, 1990 (*Birthdays Are Not For Dying*, Ibadan: University of Ibadan Theatre, 1980; *Fires Die and Burn Hard*, Ibadan, 1980; *The Inspector and the Hero*, Ibadan, 1980).

Esu and the Vagabond Minstrels. Ibadan: New Horn, 1991; Howard University Press, forthcoming with *Morountodun, Birthdays Are Not For Dying*, and *Oriki of a Grasshopper* (Benin City: University of Benin Theatre, 1984; revised, Ife: University of Ife Theatre, 1985).

Aringindin and the Night Watchmen. Ibadan: Heinemann, 1992 (Ibadan: University of Ibadan Theatre, 1988).

Yungba-Yungba and the Dance Contest. Ibadan: Heinemann, 1993 (Ibadan: University of Ibadan Theatre, 1990).

Unpublished Plays

"Oduduwa, Don't Go" (Ibadan, 1967).
"The Engagement" (St. Louis African Studies Association, 1991).

Selected Other Works

Kolera Kolej (fiction). Ibadan: New Horn, 1975.
"Criticism and the Sixteen Palmnuts: The Role of Critics in an Age of Illiteracy." *Ch'Indaba* 3.19 (October–December 1977): 6–12.

"Tiger on Stage: Wole Soyinka and the Nigerian Theatre." *Theatre in Africa.* Ed. Oyin Ogunba and Abiola Irele. Ibadan: Ibadan University Press, 1978. 151–75.

"The Trail of Ozidi: Review of J. P. Clark's *The Ozidi Saga.*" *Positive Review* 1.3 (1979): 36–40.

"Anubis Resurgent: Chaos and Political Vision in Recent Literature." *West African Studies in Modern Language Teaching and Research.* Ed. Ayo Banjo, Conrad-Benedict Brann, and Henri Evans. Lagos: National Language Centre, 1981. 185–98.

"Domestication of an Opiate: Western Parasthetics and the Growth of the Ekwensi Tradition." *Positive Review* 4 (January–February 1981): 1–12.

"Ritual and the Revolutionary Ethos: The Humanist Dilemma in Contemporary Nigerian Theatre." *Okike* 22 (September 1982): 72–81.

"Drama and the New Exotic: The Paradox of Form in Contemporary Theatre." *African Theatre Review* 1 (April 1983): 76–85.

"Beyond Translation: Comparatavist Look at Tragic Paradigms and Dramaturgy of Ola Rotimi and Wole Soyinka." Ife: University of Ife Monographs on Literature and Criticism, 3rd series, 1 (1985): 40.

"The Alternative Tradition: A Survey of Nigerian Literature After the War." *European Language Writing in Sub-Saharan Africa.* Ed. Albert S. Gerard. Budapest: Akademiai Kiado, 1986. II, 781–98.

"The Place of Theatre in the Cultural Development of Nigeria." *Cultural Development and Nation Building.* Ed. O. Unoh. Ibadan: Spectrum Books, 1986.

"Wonderland and Orality of Prose: A Comparative Study of Rabelais, Joyce, and Tutuola." Femi Osofisan and Bayo Williams, *The Genre of Prose Fiction: Two Complementary Views.* Ife: University of Ife Monographs on Literature and Criticism, 4th series, 3 (1986): 1–60.

"The Author as Sociologist: Cultural Obstacles to the Development of Literature in Nigeria." *Contemporary Nigerian Literature: A Retrospective and Prospective Exploration.* Ed. Biodun Jeyifo. Lagos: Nigeria Magazine Publications, 1987.

Minted Coins (poems under pseudonym Okinba Launko). Ibadan: Heinemann, 1987.

Cordelia (fiction under pseudonym Okinba Launko). Lagos: Malthouse Press, 1989.

"And After the Wasted Breed? Responses to History and Wole Soyinka's Dramaturgy." *On Stage.* Ed. Ulla Schild. Göttingen, Germany: Mainzer Institut, 1982.

Dream Seeker on Divining Chain (poems under pseudonym Okinba Launko). Ibadan: Kraft Books, 1993.

Selected Studies of Femi Osofisan

Awodiya, Muyiwa. "Femi Osofisan's Theatre." *Perspective on Nigerian Literature, 1700 to the Present.* Ed. Yemi Ogunbiyi. Lagos: Lagos Guardian, 1988. 223–27.

Balogun, F. Odun. "*Kolera Kolej*: A Surrealistic Political Satire." *Africana Journal* 12 (October–December 1981): 323–32.

Bamidele, Lanrele. "The Poet of the Theatre: Osofisan's Experiment with Form and Technique." *New Literary Review* 4 (January 1986): 82–90.

Bamikunle, Aderemi. "Nigerian Playwrights and Nigerian Myths: A Look at Soyinka, Osofisan, and Sowande's Plays". *Critical Theory and African Literature.* Ed. R. Vanamali, Emelia Oko, and Azubike Ileoje. Ibadan: Heinemann, 1987. 121–31.

Egharevba, Chris. "The Carrier Ritual as Medium of Vision in Nigerian Drama: The Examples of Soyinka and Osofisan." *Critical Theory and African Literature*. Ed. R. Vanamili, Emelia Oko, and Azubike Ileoje. Ibadan: Heinemann, 1987. 25–36.

Iji, Eddie. "The Mythic Imagination and Heroic Archetypes: From Moremi Myth to Osofisan's *Mourountodun.*" *Critical Theory and African Literature*. Ed. R. Vanamili, Emelia Oko, and Azubike Ileoje. Ibadan: Heinemann, 1987. 81–98.

Jeyifo, Biodun. "Femi Osofisan as Literary Critic and Theorist." *Perspectives on Nigerian Literature, 1700 to the Present*. Ed. Yemi Ogunbiyi. Lagos: Lagos Guardian, 1988. 228–32.

———. "Theatrical Analogues of the Second Republic: Osofisan's *Midnight Hotel.*" *West Africa* 3398 (September 20, 1982): 2406–10.

———. *The Truthful Lie: Essays in a Sociology of African Drama*. London: New Beacon, 1985. 51–54, 82.

Johnson, Rotimi. "Revolutionary Consciousness and Commitment in Osofisan's *Minted Coins.*" *Neohelicon* 17.2 (1990): 157–68.

Julyor, Chinyere. "Creating New Awareness through Shock Drama." *Nigerian Theatre Journal* 1.1 (1984): 9–15.

Ofeimun, Odia. "Criticism as Homicide: A Reply to Femi Osofisan's 'Literacy as Suicide.' " *Afriscope* 7.

———. "Revolutionary Aesthetics in Nigerian Theatre." *African Literature Today* 12 (1982): 118–36.

Olaogun, Modupe O. "Parables in the Theatre: A Brief Study of Femi Osofisan's Plays." *Okike* 27–28 (March 1988): 43–55.

Onwueme, Tess Akaeke. "Osofisan's New Hero: Woman as Agents of Social Reconstruction." *Sage* 5 (Summer 1988): 25–28.

Osundare, Niyi. "Social Message of a Nigerian Dramatist." *West Africa* January 28, 1980: 147–50.

Richards, Sandra. *Ancient Songs Set Ablaze: The Theatre of Femi Osofisan*. Washington, D.C.: Howard University Press, 1996.

———. "Femi Osofisan." *Twentieth-Century Caribbean and Black African Writers*. Ed. Bernth Lindfors and Reinhard Sander. *Dictionary of Literary Biography*. vol. 125. Detroit: Gale Research, 1993. 243–250.

———. "Nigerian Independence Onstage: Responses from 'Second Generation' Playwrights." *Theatre Journal* 39 (May 1987): 215–27.

———. "Towards a Populist Nigerian Theatre: The Plays of Femi Osofisan." *New Theatre Quarterly* 3 (August 1987): 280–88.

———. "Wasn't Brecht an African Writer? Parallels with Contemporary Nigerian Drama."*Brecht Yearbook* (1989): 168–83.

ELAINE SAVORY*

---

*Elaine Savory used to write as Elaine Savory Fido.

FERDINAND OYONO (1929–   )

BIOGRAPHY

Ferdinand Oyono was born on September 14, 1929, in the village of N'Goulé-makong, southeast Cameroon, among the forests and cocoa plantations that he uses as a backdrop for his novels. His father, Oyono Etoa Jean, a respected tribal leader determined to escape illiteracy, was first educated in German. Later, when France took over the colony, he reenrolled to pursue an education in French, embarking upon a career in colonial administration in 1923. Ferdinand Oyono's mother, Mvodo Belinga Agnès, the daughter of a well-known chief, was just as illustrious as her baptized but polygamous husband. Unlike him, she was a devout, practicing Catholic and left the family home upon the arrival of the second wife, working as a seamstress in order to bring up Ferdinand and his younger sister, Mfoumou Elisabeth. Oyono's primary school years were checkered with failure. They were undoubtedly marked both by the presence of a pious and affectionately dominant mother, who was supported by the local priests in her rejection of traditional ways, and by further exposure to the Catholic faith when he was a chorister and houseboy at the Catholic mission. Such experiences later became fuel for the anticlerical fire of his novels.

In addition to the urban milieu Oyono knew when growing up with his mother in Ebolowa, he experienced a cosmopolitan lifestyle during holiday times spent with his father, who worked all over the country. In 1950, after Oyono finally obtained a brilliant result for his Primary School Certificate, his father dispatched him to France to complete his secondary education. He remained there to study law and political science at the Sorbonne, using his spare time to write his first novel, *Une vie de boy*, and to sketch out his second, *Le vieux nègre et la médaille*, both violently critical of colonialism and published in 1956 within a month of each other. It was these writings, judged "subversive" under the Loi-cadre of Gaston Deferre and sent by Oyono to his father in Cameroon, that ended the latter's career in colonial administration. While studying to become a lawyer, Oyono acted on the stage of the Alliance Française, exhibiting great talent in Louis Sapin's play *Papa Bon Dieu*, but stagefright cut short his acting career. A year later, in 1959, when strolling around the Latin Quarter with a white woman, he experienced brutal racism firsthand: he was assaulted and stabbed while indifferent passersby looked on. In 1960 his third novel, *Chemin d'Europe*, was published, the same year that he embarked upon a successful diplomatic career, representing Cameroon at the United Nations and as ambassador in Liberia, the Benelux countries, France, Italy, Tunisia, Morocco, and Algeria. He is presently the Cameroonian housing minister. Since 1960 Oyono's pen has run dry. Although the titles for a short story (*Un lépreux sur une tombe*) and a fourth novel (*Le pandémonium*) were announced in the 1960s, the reading public still awaits more from this master of satire. Oyono's silence remains a mystery that he refuses to unveil. Critics postulate various explanations: was his writing so linked to the liberation movement that it became redundant once Cameroon obtained independence in January 1960? Have Oyono's creative energies run dry with his involvement in Cameroonian bureaucracy? Does he, like certain other African writers of his generation, impose self-censorship in the face of the multiple problems of his now-independent country?

MAJOR WORKS AND THEMES

Like many other anticolonial African writers of his generation, Oyono can be viewed as a descendant of Negritude. Oyono's literary production is limited to three thought-provoking and highly entertaining novels. Main themes are common to all three, but with evolution in the form of a shift in emphasis. *Une vie de boy* purports to be the diary of Joseph Toundi, a young Cameroonian who dies in Equatorial Guinea, where he has fled after being brutally assaulted by the prison authorities in his own country. The diary traces Toundi's contact with the white man from the time when he flees his father's wrath and takes refuge at the Catholic Mission under the protection of Father Gilbert to his employment as the Commandant's houseboy. His innocent infatuation with the latter's wife and his discovery of her adultery prove his undoing, as the whites rally round to keep their dignity intact and happily seize upon him as a scapegoat. It is the tale of the dashed hopes of a naïve young African whose initial belief in the goodness of the white man is shattered as he witnesses religious hypocrisy, physical brutality, and moral turpitude. Death is the price the young hero pays for demythologizing the colonizer.

Le vieux nègre et la médaille is equally satirical, this time at the expense of the naïveté of Meka, an old man who is honored by French colonial authorities for services rendered to France: two sons killed in the war and his lands donated to the church. This novel recounts a series of comic mishaps. Meka's pathetic attempt to acquire suitable clothing for the occasion enables Oyono to portray Greek tradesmen as exploiters in league with colonial power, a recurrent theme with the author. The description of the ceremony, when Meka waits under the punishing sun, squeezed into his shoes and desperate to relieve himself, followed by the reception, reveals another prominent theme: the white man's hypocrisy with his talk of friendship but his refusal to consummate it. Drunk, drenched by the storm, and his medal lost, Meka is picked up by a police patrol. After the ignominy of a night spent in jail, his release and return to his native village are symbolic: freed from his belief in a possible harmonious relationship with the colonizer, he goes back to traditional ways.

Chemin d'Europe revisits all the main themes of the earlier novels concerning the pernicious effects of colonialism: geographical and social segregation between the black and white sectors of the community, the unhappy alliance between the colonial authorities and the Catholic church, with the latter promoting subservience by threats of hellfire or promises of a place in paradise, the physical cruelty and moral depravity of the white bosses hiding behind a facade of social correctness but who, in their own country, would amount to nothing. The African who believes that he must be assimilated into the world of the whites in order to succeed provides the main thrust for *Chemin d'Europe*. The young hero, Aki Barnabas, reports his early work experiences and frustrated attempts to get to France for a better education and self-advancement. In the final chapter, success is assured at a price in keeping with the hypocrisy fostered by the colonial regime: a fake religious conversion. Oyono's African heroes pay dearly for living in the world of the white colonizer: material, physical, or spiritual loss or death of themselves or their loved ones. The hallmark of this writing is Oyono's acid wit. His characters are often little more than caricatures, skillfully sketched with a satirical touch that leaves the reader vacillating between laughter and tears. Romans à thèse, these novels bear witness to a particular historical era in their exposure of the elements that make up capricious imperialism. The white colonials are vividly painted in their true colors and come under Oyono's merciless scrutiny. Yet he composes a melody in counterpoint: his fellow countrymen do not escape his critical gaze, for they allow themselves to be duped. In evolutionary terms, perhaps the denouement of *Chemin d'Europe* suggests the author's answer for adapting successfully to the white man's world: become like him by exploiting all available resources, even if this means selling one's soul.

CRITICAL RECEPTION

It was not long after Oyono's novels were published that academics recognized their place in the development of the African novel written in French and their stylistic merit. In *Littérature négro-africaine d'expression française: Le mouvement littéraire contemporain dans l'Afrique noire* (Paris: L'École, 1966),

Robert Pageard acknowledges the importance of Oyono's work for the antico-lonialist cause. Jacques Chevrier, in an extensive reference work *Littérature négre, Afrique, Antilles, Madagascar* (Paris: Armand Colin, 1974), analyzes the author's successful didacticism and the cynical irony of his texts. In another competent overview of Negro-African novels in French, *African Literature in French* (Cambridge University Press, 1976), Dorothy Blair hails Oyono as an apostle of Negritude for his earthy realism. In addition to such mainstream reference works, journal articles and postgraduate research have concentrated on the didactic and anticolonial nature of Oyono's writings, autobiographical elements, and the author's gift for ironic humor. The latter years of the 1980s and the 1990s have seen little scholarship devoted to Oyono, probably because his novels are deemed to be limited to their sociohistorical context. However, much remains to be said on their universality and Oyono's consummate mastery of satire.

BIBLIOGRAPHY

Works by Ferdinand Oyono

Une vie de boy. Paris: Julliard, 1956.
Le vieux nègre et la médaille. Paris: Julliard, 1956.
Chemin d'Europe. Paris: Julliard, 1960.

Studies of Ferdinand Oyono

Battestini, Monique, and Simon Battestini. *Ferdinand Oyono, écrivain camerounais.* Paris: Nathan, 1964.
Battestini, Simon. "L'humour chez Ferdinand Oyono." *Actes du Colloque sur la littérature africaine.* Dakar: Publications de la Faculté des Lettres et des Sciences Humaines, 1965. 161–75.
Chevrier, Jacques. *Littérature nègre, Afrique, Antilles, Madagascar.* Paris: Armand Colin, 1974.
————. *Profil d'une oeuvre: Une vie de boy.* Paris: Hatier, 1977.
Diop, David. "Une vie de nègre, *Le vieux nègre et la médaille.*" *Présence Africaine* 11 (1956): 60–65.
Edongo, Menye Hubert. "Le nègre et la ville dans l'oeuvre de Ferdinand Oyono." Mémoire de D.E.S., University of Yaoundé, 1973.
Everson, Vanessa. "Ferdinand et Marianne: Les amours interdites." *Afriques imaginaires: Regards réciproques et discours littéraires.* Paris: L'Harmattan, 1995. 217–28.
Flannigan, Arthur. " 'The Eye of the Witch': Non-verbal Communication and the Exercise of Power in *Une vie de boy.*" *French Review* 56 (1982–83): 51–63.
Kuitche, Gabriel. "Aspect du langage dans l'oeuvre de Ferdinand Oyono." Mémoire de D.E.S., University of Yaoundé, 1971.
Minyono-Nkodo, Mathieu-François. *La dialectique de l'initiation à la vie dans les romans de Ferdinand Oyono.* Yaoundé: Erlac, Université de Yaoundé, 1972.

————. "Essais sur les structures littéraires des romans de Ferdinand Oyono." Diss. University of Montpellier, 1973.

————. *Le monde romanesque de Ferdinand Oyono ou pour une esthétique de la décadence*. Dakar: Les Nouvelles Éditions Africaines, 1979.

————. *Le vieux nègre et la médaille de Ferdinand Oyono, profil d'une oeuvre*. Yaoundé: Erlac, University of Yaoundé, 1972.

Moore, Gerald. "Ferdinand Oyono et la tragi-comédie coloniale." *Présence Africaine* 46 (1963): 221–33.

Nguele, Amagou Philippe. "Ferdinand Oyono: Survivance théâtrale dans un univers romanesque." Mémoire de maîtrise, University of Yaoundé, 1973.

Oke, O. "Ferdinand Oyono's 'Houseboy' and Gustave Flaubert's 'Un coeur simple.'" *Black Orpheus* (December 1971): 127–37.

Ongoyongo, Bosiomo Marie. "Humour et tragédie chez Ferdinand Oyono." Mémoire de maîtrise, University of Paris–Nanterre, 1972.

Owona, Mimboe Jérôme. "Ferdinand Oyono: L'homme et l'oeuvre." Mémoire de D.E.S., University of Yaoundé, 1974.

Pageard, Robert. *Littérature négro-africiane d'expression française: Le mouvement Littéraire contemporain dans l'Afrique noire*. Paris: L'École, 1966.

VANESSA EVERSON

ESSOP PATEL (1943–   )

BIOGRAPHY

Essop Patel was born in Germiston, South Africa, in 1943. His grandfather came from India to South Africa when he was thirteen. His schooling started in a racially mixed location known as "Jamtown" that was later destroyed. At the age of nine, Patel witnessed a defiance campaign against this destruction that caused him to become politicized. In high school Patel recognized that racial hierarchy was a construct that he could not escape in South Africa. In 1962 he went to England, where he stayed for eleven years. During this period he first worked in different jobs in London before he finally took an honors degree in law. In London he came to know people from different parts of the world and had contact with South African exiles, among them Nat Nakasa. After returning to South Africa in 1973, Patel took a postgraduate degree at the University of the Witwatersrand. He is now a practicing advocate in Johannesburg. He is married and has two children.

Patel started writing poems when he was in London. Before his first collection of poems, *They Came at Dawn*, came out in 1980, some of his poems had already been published in the *Classic, New Classic, Staffrider*, and *Ophir*. The Afrika Cultural Centre published his second collection of poetry, *Fragments in the Sun*, along with the performance script of *The Mountain of Volcano*, which was a coproduction with Bhekizizwe Peterson and Benjy Francis. It was performed at the Third World and Radical Book Fair in London in 1985, as we can learn from his interview in *Talking with African Writers* (Wilkinson, 165–66). The Africa Cultural Centre regarded its task to be one of supporting committed art in order to raise the consciousness of the community as an alternative to the tourist art of the apartheid regime. *The Bullet and the Bronze Lady* (1987) is Patel's third volume of poetry and includes some earlier poems that he left out of the two other collections.

MAJOR WORKS AND THEMES

In the first collection of Patel's poetry there is an all-pervading melancholy that is expressed through the representation of pain and suffering. The first poem, "Notes from a Cell," describes the "empty stare," monotony, dejection, and loneliness of imprisonment. Repeatedly Patel uses the word "prison" to point to the situation that in a "prison country," the power structure functions only with control and surveillance, as the title poem also suggests. There is no scope for privacy, no time to hide banned literature away. In *Fragments in the Sun* he voices the permanent fear of the threat of being dragged naked out of one's home. This trauma of the knock at the door becomes very vivid in the poem "Tormentors of Our Dreams" in *The Bullet and the Bronze Lady*. Here poetry is banned: a reason for a subversive silence. There is no freedom of expression. In the poem "On the Steps" (*They Came at Dawn*), he observes that the artist's instrument is damaged while they have put him in a prison.

Children are radicalized even from their birth, as we read in the poem "Revolution is . . ." (*The Bullet and the Bronze Lady*). The images of the maiming and killing of marching children with clenched fists, as in the poem "Black Recollection," are repeated in his poetry. But this marching has a cause; it is for freedom, and at the same time it is a demonstration of Black Consciousness, as we can see in "Telepoem the News" (*They Came at Dawn*). For Patel, poetry has to represent the way from suffering to revolt. Global suffering, according to him, calls for the solidarity of all people. The cry for freedom will bring humanity all over the world together. It will spread like fire to all continents. In *Fragments in the Sun* the metaphors of fire, flame, and volcano express the rage of the people, and the metaphor of storm represents their revolution. Patel believes that suffering is unavoidable to achieve freedom. But at the same time the conviction persists that the suffering will end with freedom. There is an impatience for the "new dawn," a metaphor he uses very frequently. Thus he talks of the "dawning of new tomorrow" in "Sometimes/Tomorrow" (*They Came at Dawn*) and is convinced that the future is beautiful and colorful. It is a part of Patel's philosophy of human consciousness that goes beyond the slogan that black is beautiful and reaches hands to everyone, irrespective of race, as we read in the poem "Give Your Hand to Every Hand" (*The Bullet and the Bronze Lady*). The frontiers do not have to exist in the ideal world of which he dreams.

In describing the solidarity among people all over the world, he can be political and yet at the same time very tender. So the same Patel who complains that there is no country for the dispossessed writes of flower power because love binds people irrespective of color. This love can be ideological but also erotic, which was a punishable offence according to the Immorality Act in South Africa—an absurdity in a country where so many races live together. Several of his poems try to expose this absurdity, one of which is "Miriam of Bengal," which depicts the fate of a princess who is snatched from her own country and sold at the Cape. She was hanged because she was discovered making love with a white man—the first recorded case of the Immorality Act. Equally fascinating is Patel's description of the ecstasy of forbidden love in "Sonnet for Hester Jansz," in which a white woman was imprisoned for committing adultery with her black slave. It will appear in the forthcoming collection *Stain Glass Images*.

Patel's poetry is very often a mixture of lyrical and political elements, as in the poem "On the Green Hill" from *The Bullet and the Bronze Lady*, which expresses the anticipation of a new age. There is a romantic, soft tone in "Country Girl and Lotus Flower." His love poems demonstrate his capacity to represent those universal aspects of life that exist beyond all colors, borders, and times. They can be sometimes surcharged with feelings or be very melancholy where they depict the fear of survival. However, they can also be very playful, as can be seen in the poem "Kisslip" (*The Bullet and the Bronze Lady*) and in the title poem of *Stain Glass Images*, which simultaneously show his capacity to play with words. In *The Bullet and the Bronze Lady*, Patel uses the regional slang to write a number of satirical poems about a naïve Afrikaner girl who sees the world through her own categories of racial compartmentalization. In his interview, edited by Wilkinson, Patel talks about his fascination for regional patois and points to his intention to make poetry come alive by developing the patois and to experiment with the English language that stems from the grass roots (164–65). Similarly, Patel considers it to be of the utmost importance that poetry should not lose its ties with the people. In the poem "Where Have the Poets Gone?" (*The Bullet and the Bronze Lady*), he criticizes the apolitical literature confined to academic circles as opposed to the literature for the people. In the essay "The Historical Role of Poetry in the South African Liberation Struggle," he describes the parallel development of the political resistance of the people and that of resistance literature. Here he points out that a committed poet is a people's poet, and a people's poet has a solidarity with people's struggle for democratic and human values (257–58). However, he does not like to be labeled as a protest poet, for literature cannot leave out the personal aspects of life, like love or feelings of desperation in moments of loneliness, as he delineates in the poem "The Bronze Lady," the story of a deserted woman. His last volume, *Stain Glass Images*, consists of poems of magical realism, as he himself points out in the notes to his book. Here we find postmodern elements of intertextuality, time, and spacelessness, as in the poem, "Tempest," and surreal elements, as in the poem "Dancing Priest," in addition to the bizarre presentation of the history of slavery as a theatre on the stage that is the world, as in "Slave Auction Movie."

CRITICAL RECEPTION

The critical response to Patel's literature is not as yet very widespread, although he has become quite well known in the literary circles of Commonwealth literature. In the foreword to Patel's volume of poetry *They Came at Dawn*, James Matthews talks of him as a promising writer. In his Introduction to *Soweto Poetry*, Chapman maintains that Patel's poetry also shows a "Soweto stylistic sensibility" (18). In "A Vision of Order," Ursula Barnett points to the manner in which Patel stresses the need for a "rallying-spirit," among the people of color in his conception of Black Consciousness (79).

BIBLIOGRAPHY

Works by Essop Patel

The Bullet and the Bronze Lady. Johannesburg: Skotaville Publishers, 1987.
Fragments in the Sun. Johannesburg: Afrika Cultural Centre, 1985.
"The Historical Role of Poetry in the South African Liberation Struggle." *Crisis and Conflict: Essays on South African Literature*. Ed. G. Davis. Essen: Die Blaue Eule, 1990. 247–259.
Stain Glass Images. To be published.
They Came at Dawn. Athlone: Blac Publishing House, 1980.
Ed. *The World of Nat Nakasa*. Johannesburg: Ravan, 1975.

Studies of Essop Patel

Barnett, Ursula A. *A Vision of Order: A Study of Black South African Literature in English (1914–1980)*. London: Sinclair Browne, 1983.
Chapman, Michael, ed. "Introduction." *Soweto Poetry*. Johannesburg: McGraw-Hill, 1982. 11–23.
Matthews, James. "Foreword to 'They Came at Dawn'." *Soweto Poetry*. Ed. Michael Chapman. Johannesburg: McGraw-Hill, 1982. 88.
Wilkinson, Jane, ed. "Essop Patel." *Talking with African Writers: Interviews with African Poets, Playwrights, and Novelists*. London: James Currey, 1990. 159–172.

JOGAMAYA BAYER

ALAN PATON (1903–1988)

BIOGRAPHY

Alan Stewart Paton was born on January 11, 1903, in Pietermaritzburg, Natal, South Africa. He was the eldest of the four children (Alan, Atholl, Eunice, and Ailsa) of James and Eunice Paton, a thrifty couple whose Christadelphian influences later found resonance in the compassionate prose of their progeny. James Paton, who came from Glasgow, Scotland, was given to lapses into sullen, violent moods when he would beat his sons. Paton left home hating his father, but in later years acknowledged that this emotion had abated.

Although neither of his parents was highly educated, Paton was introduced to the magic of reading at an early age. His father's tastes were austere, but his mother had a more relaxed view, and Paton had access to her meagre library containing Ethel M. Dell, Ruby Ayres, Jeffrey Farnol, Rafael Sabatini, and, of course, the Bible. Later Paton read the classic writings of Walter Scott, Charles Dickens, and Robert Louis Stevenson, as well as Shakespeare, Milton, Coleridge, Keats, Shelley, Byron, Browning, and the war poet Rupert Brooke.

But it was the country that wove its magic on him, and it was especially the Ixopo area, in Natal, that enthralled him. He was appointed to the Ixopo High School in 1925—an appointment resisted at first—and here he fell in love for the first time, with Dorrie Lusted, a married woman. Their relationship was strictly platonic, although her husband, Bernard, divined Paton's infatuation with her. Bernard Lusted died in the same year, and after a suitable period of mourning, Paton was able to declare his love for Dorrie, a love that is palpable in all his writing about her. Their relationship culminated in their marriage on July 2, 1928, and lasted till Dorrie's death on October 23, 1967. On January 30, 1969, Paton married his secretary, Anne Hopkins, a divorcée; their marriage lasted till the end of Paton's life.

Paton's biography would not be complete without reference to his role in the Liberal Party of South Africa. He joined the party in 1953 as its vice-president and was elected chairman of the renamed South African Liberal Party in 1956. The aims of the party were to foster a society of political tolerance, justice and fairness, and freedom and equality. However, it is clear that Paton had no political ambitions and that he was acting on the impulses of the other great compulsion in his life, religious faith. It is in his intensely personal religion that Paton found hope for the future of his troubled land. In 1968 the South African Liberal Party was declared illegal for its nonracial membership and became defunct. Alan Paton died at 5:10 A.M. on April 12, 1988, a son of Africa, a writer who gave to that continent, and to the world, a vision of the people and the impulses moving those people who inhabit the southern tip of Africa.

MAJOR WORKS AND THEMES

Paton admitted to the influence of the Old Testament and the story of the Crucifixion on his life and his writings. From this religious source he derived his strongly developed sense of fairness, justice, and humanity and his compassion for those unfortunates who found themselves engulfed by the South African penal system.

In his works, Paton has an awareness of the human capacity for goodness and evil, and a view that it is present in equal amounts in man. For example, Stephen Kumalo in *Cry, the Beloved Country* (1948) has a propensity toward vanity and is not above exacting revenge on those who have harmed him. The novel's central theme is the disintegration of traditional influences on African youth, especially as they migrate from the rural areas toward the cities. The city has often been depicted as a corrupting agent in a young person's life, but in *Cry, the Beloved Country* it is more than a catalyst; instead, it is the cause of the destruction of the societal fabric.

Too Late the Phalarope (1953) is an interesting interplay of historical fact with individual fiction. The novel relates the effect of the Nationalist Party's obsession with racial purity, specifically Afrikaner purity. It is not whites in general who stand to be condemned, but those who have allied themselves to the idolatrous concept of total segregation of the races. The underlying theme of the novel is the inability of man to forgive and yet his expectation that God *must* forgive *his* transgressions. However, it is not love that moves the protagonist, Pieter van Vlaanderen, to enter into a liaison with the black girl, Stephanie. Rather, it is the culmination of a number of extraneous factors, such as sexual deprivation within his marriage; and so the exploitation of the girl is juxtaposed to the inhumanity of social conditions in the country.

Ah, But Your Land Is Beautiful (1981) is overshadowed by the period from 1948—when the Nationalist Party was voted into office—to 1958, the year of Dr. Hendrik Verwoerd's inauguration as prime minister of South Africa. The novel reveals the effect of apartheid laws on the citizens of the country as it documents the inexorable erosion of the human soul in the enactment of racialist ideology. The Christianity of the country is satirized and shown to be based on false premises. People who have opposed apartheid and who have sided with its victims become victims themselves and flee the country. The doctrine of racial purity and the prohibition of miscegenation are also savaged by the novelist.

Paton's autobiographical *Towards the Mountain* (1980) and his two biographies, *Hofmeyr* (1964), republished as *South African Tragedy: The Life and Times of Jan Hofmeyr* (1965), and *Apartheid and the Archbishop* (1973), reflect his vision of the challenge posed to Christian principles by the political aberration called "apartheid." Paton writes revealingly about himself in these autobiographies, admitting to his failings and modestly referring to his strengths. It is here that we find the philosophical foundation for his opposition to apartheid as well as the parochial pronouncements of his fellow English-speaking countrymen. These themes are also contained in his later *Journey Continued: An Autobiography* (1988).

In a collection of his shorter writings, *Knocking on the Door* (1975), edited and selected by Colin Gardner, Paton's hopes and fears for the political dispensation in South Africa are once again adumbrated. In this collection of essays, the concerns Paton had as headmaster at a reformatory are shown to have developed into his acclaimed *Cry, the Beloved Country*, as Gardner points out (Introduction, xi). It is in this collection that we find the poignant verse "To a Small Boy Who Died at Diepkloof Reformatory," written in 1949, a heartfelt outpouring of grief for a life needlessly lost.

The prevailing themes in *Debbie Go Home* (1961)—published as *Tales from a Troubled Land* (1961) in the United States—concern the Diepkloof Reformatory. Here death comes lingeringly or swiftly, deliberately or vicariously. Still, Paton is concerned with the reform of the inmates of the institution, a reform that has to start with the broader society beyond the walls and fences of Diepk-loof. This concern Paton also expressed in his essays on penal reform. The play *Sponono* (1965), written with Krishna Shah, is an extension of three of the short stories found in *Debbie Go Home*, with the characters becoming eloquent commentators on the process of reform.

CRITICAL RECEPTION

In the revised edition of his *Alan Paton*, Edward Callan makes a useful synopsis of Paton's major works as well as of some of his shorter writings. Paton's literary reputation is founded mainly on the reception accorded *Cry, the Beloved Country*, although the story underpinning the "deeper themes and contrasts," Callan finds, "is a very simple one" (28). The novel is not without its faults, however, having been considered too sentimental by some critics, while others have mentioned that although it derives much of its power from the lyricism of the Zulu, the linguistic errors in the translation from the Zulu language are distracting to the informed reader. The generation of black youths since 1970, too, does not find the novel sufficiently realistic. This does not detract from the novel's power, and the reader becomes engrossed in the human tragedy and the inexorable nature of events in the book, based as it is on the social inequities and iniquities of the prevailing South African political ideology.

Too Late the Phalarope (1953) manages to imbue the theme of miscegenation—which so often degenerates into a mere pejorative reflection of relationships with overtones of master/subject—with a sense of Greek tragedy and the inevitability and inexorability of its conclusion. But in Greek tragedy, the future lies beyond the bounds of the text, and in her unpublished dissertation, "The Influence of Religious Traditions on the Life and Work of Alan Paton" (1987), Karen Smith finds that hope lies at the core of the novel: "Out of the disaster that exists around us, there comes hope" (91). Sheridan Baker (1960) finds the novel "vaguely familiar and slightly gratuitous" (153), albeit a "wonderful study of guilt" (153).

Ah, But Your Land Is Beautiful continues, to a degree, the themes explored in *Cry, the Beloved Country*. Although the novel follows more than a quarter of a century after the writing of *Too Late the Phalarope*, critics have been almost unanimous in praising it, contending that it reflects the sustained power of Paton's writing. Written as "faction," the novel retraces the coming to power of the Nationalist Party and the events following this aberration. Paton addresses the forced removal of people from Sophiatown and the passive resistance campaign, a campaign that foreshadowed the eventual Soweto uprising of 1976, its very antithesis. Paton attempts to imbue his characters with a humanity not expected of them. In this novel, for example, we meet the supposedly obdurate Afrikaner who contravenes the infamous Immorality Act (a law prohibiting sexual liaisons between black and white). There are other Afrikaners, too, who are led by their consciences and not by rules and regulations promulgated by a faceless, monolithic parliament.

The progression of development in Paton's work is evident. From a "colonial" base, the development toward a post-colonial literature emerges but is never fully realized. This, one feels, is a result of his disappointingly meagre contribution to the genre.

BIBLIOGRAPHY

Works by Alan Paton

Novels

Cry, the Beloved Country. New York: Charles Scribner's Sons, 1948.
Cry, the Beloved Country: A Story of Comfort in Desolation. London: Jonathan Cape, 1948.
Too Late the Phalarope. New York: Charles Scribner's Sons, 1953.
Ah, But Your Land Is Beautiful. New York: Charles Scribner's Sons, 1981.

Short Stories

Debbie Go Home. London: Jonathan Cape, 1961.
Tales from a Troubled Land. New York: Charles Scribner's Sons, 1961.

Plays

Lost in the Stars (with Maxwell Anderson). New York: Sloane Associates, 1950.
Sponono (with Krishna Shah). New York: Charles Scribner's Sons, 1965.

Biographies

Hofmeyr. Cape Town: Oxford University Press, 1964.
South African Tragedy: The Life and Times of Jan Hofmeyr. New York: Charles Scrib-
     ner's Sons, 1965.
*Apartheid and the Archbishop: The Life and Times of Geoffrey Clayton, Archbishop of
     Cape Town.* Cape Town: David Philip, 1973; New York: Charles Scribner's Sons,
     1973.

Autobiographies

For You Departed. New York: Charles Scribner's Sons, 1969.
Kontaktion for You Departed. London: Jonathan Cape, 1969.
Towards the Mountain: An Autobiography. New York: Charles Scribner's Sons, 1980;
     London: Jonathan Cape, 1981.
Journey Continued: An Autobiography. Cape Town: David Philip, 1988.

Collected Writings

Knocking on the Door: Shorter Writings. Ed. C. Gardner. Cape Town: David Philip,
     1975.

Studies of Alan Paton

Alexander, Peter. *Alan Paton: A Biography.* Oxford: Oxford University Press, 1994.
Baker, Sheridan. "Paton's Late Phalarope." *English Studies in Africa* 3.2 (1960): 152–
     159.
Bentel, Lea. *Alan Paton: A Bibliography.* Johannesburg: University of the Witwatersrand,
     1969.
Callan, Edward. *Alan Paton.* Rev. ed. Boston: Twayne Publishers, 1982.
Fuller, Edmund. *Books with the Man behind Them.* New York: Random House, 1962.
Smith, Karen. *The Influence of Religious Traditions on the Life and Work of Alan Paton.*
     Unpublished Diss. University of South Africa, Pretoria, 1987.

JO E. NEL

OKOT P'BITEK (1931–1982)

BIOGRAPHY

Okot p'Bitek was born in Gulu, northern Uganda, where he attended local primary school and Gulu High School before enrolling at Kings College, Budo, for his early university training. An impressive athlete, he first visited Britain in 1956 as a member of the Ugandan national soccer team and availed himself of the opportunity to study. He obtained a Certificate of Education at Bristol University and then a law degree at the University of Wales at Aberystwyth. Finally he obtained a B.Litt. in social anthropology at Oxford University in 1963. He later earned a D.Phil. in religion from the latter university. On his return to Uganda he lectured in social anthropology at the University College at Makerere. His deep interest in Acoli culture was evident throughout his career. He later acknowledged the influence of his mother, a singer and composer, in developing and encouraging an early love of Acoli creative forms. He himself was an accomplished dancer and drummer. In an article on Acoli folk tales, p'Bitek explained that the Acoli had no professional storytellers, and everyone present at a session was expected to relate tales—thus cultivating the young writer's penchant for self-expression and oratory. He founded the Annual Festival of African Arts in Gulu and served as director of the National Theatre and Cultural Centre in Kampala, Uganda. He was an active proponent of the need to practice and celebrate African culture in both these capacities.

Never one to shy away from controversy, he alienated himself from his own government by his public pronouncements and as a result voluntarily moved to Kenya, where he organized the Art Festival in Kisumu in 1968. In 1969 he was once again on the move, to the University of Iowa, where he spent a year as a fellow of the International Writing Program. Back in Kenya in 1971, he took the position of senior research fellow at the Institute of African Studies and part-time lecturer in sociology and literature at the University of Nairobi. He would be based in Kenya for the rest of his life (as, indeed, were a number of Ugandan writers).

He was of a generation that had been steeped in "traditional" culture and social organization (pre-colonial) and had experienced the transition of its societies into Western-based economic and cultural entities. While their cultural worldview had been formed by their ethnic environment, their education was foreign (British) and imparted by expatriates. With independence, along with other East African academics and writers, he was faced with the urgent question of whether to define the emergent post-colonial societies, the African, and the African worldview in terms of an ethnic group—in his case the Acoli (sometimes referred to as Lwo or Luo); in terms of Western culture; or as a symbiosis of both. P'Bitek himself believed in the primacy and value of ethnic culture and that this could be preserved in the "new society," and he was suspicious of those who adopted foreign ideas without question.

MAJOR WORKS AND THEMES

P'Bitek's first creative work was written, fittingly, in Acoli, a novel entitled *Lak Tar Miyo Kinyero Wi Lobo* (Are Your Teeth White? If So, Smile!) that was published in 1953. The impact and circulation of this novel was limited to Acoli (or Luo) speakers. It was not, therefore, until he wrote the "poetic-novel" *Wer pa Lawino*, which he personally translated into English under the title *Song of Lawino: A Lament* in 1966, that he was to burst onto the literary scene. Until this time, East African writers in English had produced works that conformed closely to British literary aesthetics and that lacked a distinctively regional quality. P'Bitek's work was initially startling because he effectively appropriated the English language to convey ideas and a sensitivity inspired and nurtured by Acoli oral tradition. More than this, the poem was a lively defense of Acoli traditional culture and customs as opposed to the infiltrating British culture. To do this, p'Bitek employed a "village" woman, Lawino, as the custodian and spokesperson for Acoli tradition, and her husband, Ocol, as representative of the Westernized, alienated, educated, middle-class, African intellectual. Although he was to refer to the work as "translated from the Acoli by the author who has thus clipped a bit of the eagle's wings and rendered the sharp edges of the warrior's sword rusty and blunt, and also murdered rhythm and rhyme," p'Bitek had introduced a brilliantly original new form into world literatures in English. He had also set the political tone that would mark all his works, as an unapologetic cultural nationalist and a spokesperson for the downtrodden.

He was to continue to delight his readership in this poetic vein. *Song of Ocol* (1970) is Ocol's rejoinder to Lawino's song and a spirited defense of Western values and social organization as superior to their African counterpart. *Two Songs (Song of Prisoner, Song of Malaya)* was published in 1971. *Song of*

Prisoner was apparently inspired by the assassination of the popular Kenyan politician Tom Mboya. It is an unrelenting attack on the political injustices rampant in Africa following independence and perpetuated by unprincipled leadership elites. The solutions p'Bitek puts forward remain constant, namely, traditional families and social organization as the only hope for future generations in Africa. *Song of Malaya* (Prostitute) reveals and satirizes the hypocritical moral standards espoused by patriarchal society in Africa today concerning sexual and social matters. This volume, dedicated to Patrice Lumumba, was awarded the inaugural Kenyatta Prize for Literature in 1972.

P'Bitek produced two critical translations of Acoli orature: *Horn of my Love* (1974), a collection of Acoli oral poetry; and *Hare and Hornbill* (1978), a collection of Acoli folktales and short stories. Academically p'Bitek devoted his energies to uncovering and clarifying misconceptions concerning African social organization, beliefs, culture, and customs propounded by regional and foreign academics who used Western-derived concepts. In the pages of *Transition*, a journal published at Makerere, to which he was a frequent contributor, he expressed views on aspects of anthropological, sociological, philosophical, and literary studies in, and on, Africa. He published three major academic studies: *Religion of the Central Luo* (1971); *African Religions in Western Scholarship* (1972); and *Africa's Cultural Revolution* (1973).

CRITICAL RECEPTION

The publication of *Song of Lawino* ushered in a new and exciting literary movement. Writers who had not appreciated the possibilities of experimentation with aspects of their cultural tradition in producing contemporary works now found their voice. These included Taban lo Liyong and Okello Oculi. It is not surprising that such an important work raised its fair share of controversy. Critics, while acknowledging the beauty of the work and the innovation it had introduced, raised questions centered around thematic and contextual concerns. Locally, some felt that the attacks on the "modern" African as comically unable to evolve with the changing times were unwarranted, while the representation of "village" life was unduly unsophisticated. Foreign critics bristled at the assessment of Western infiltration in Africa. Later, womanist critics questioned the figures of Lawino and Clementina—the stereotypical representation of the sophisticated city girl—as misleading embodiments of a male view of the state of "noble womanhood" used to symbolize an African culture that had never existed.

P'Bitek's academic endeavors excited as much controversy. His Afrocentric approach was criticized for a lack of awareness of the value of applying traditional Western theories as tools for understanding the African situation—criticism p'Bitek responded to vigorously in the pages of *Transition* and elsewhere. Critics today consider both his literary and academic contribution to African scholarship to have been revolutionary, and an impressive (and growing) list of theses and studies on the author and his craft bear witness to his genius.

BIBLIOGRAPHY

Works by Okot p'Bitek

Song of Lawino: A Lament. Nairobi: East African Publishing House, 1966.
Wer pa Lawino. Nairobi: East African Publishing House, 1969.
Song of Ocol. Nairobi: East African Publishing House, 1970.
Religion of the Central Luo. Nairobi: East African Literature Bureau, 1971.
Two Songs (Songs of Prisoner, Song of Malaya). Nairobi: East African Publishing House, 1971.
African Religions in Western Scholarship. Nairobi: East African Literature Bureau, 1972.
Africa's Cultural Revolution. Nairobi: Macmillan Books for Africa, 1973.
Horn of My Love. London: Heinemann Educational Books, 1974.
Hare and Hornbill. London: Heinemann Educational Books, 1978.

Selected Studies of Okot p'Bitek

Asein, S. O. "Okot p'Bitek: Literature and Cultural Revolution." *Journal of African Studies* 5.3 (1978): 357–72.
Gathungu, Maina. "Okot p'Bitek: Writer, Singer, Culturizer." *Standpoints on African Literature*. Ed. C. L. Wanjala. Nairobi: East African Literature Bureau, 1973.
Heron, George A. *The Poetry of Okot p'Bitek*. London: Heinemann, 1976.
Ngũgĩ Thiong'o wa. *Homecoming: Essays on African and Caribbean Literature, Culture, and Politics*. London: Heinemann, 1972.
Ofuani, Ogo A. "Okot p'Bitek: A Checklist of Works and Criticism." *Review of African Literatures* 16.3 (1985): 370–83.
Roscoe, Adrian. *Uhuru's Fire: African Literature East to South*. Cambridge: Cambridge University Press, 1977.
Smiley, Tamara Masonetta. "The Function of Symbolic Language in the Songs of Okot p'Bitek." M. A. thesis Howard University, 1976.
Wanambisi, Monica Nalyaka. *Thought and Technique in the Poetry of Okot p'Bitek*. New York: Vantage Press, 1984.

AWUOR AYODO

JEAN-JOSEPH RABEARIVELO
(1901–1937)

BIOGRAPHY

It is appropriate to begin an account of Jean-Joseph Rabearivelo's life not with his own birth date, but with another date that was in a sense to define the boundaries of his personal investigations in life: October 1, 1895, the date of the final surrender of the Malagasy armed forces to the French, signalling the effective onset of French colonial rule in Madagascar. Less than a decade after this turning point in Malagasy history, Rabearivelo was born in Madagascar's capital city, Antananarivo. He spent his entire life in and around this city, whose occupation by the French testified to the larger subjugation of the nation. He grew among a people not yet fully accustomed to the daily indignities of colonial rule and whose memories of recently lost independence remained vivid. But the remembrance of defeat at the hands of a foreign army was just as vivid, so that the notion of political independence seemed irreversibly associated with Malagasy pre-colonial history, something to be recalled rather than a future possibility to be anticipated.

Rabearivelo was an only child and was related through his mother to the royalty of the largest Malagasy ethnic group, the Merina people. However, by the time he was born, the family's resources had been seriously depleted, and the family lived in relative poverty. Ostensibly, the loss of slaves following the abolition of slavery by the French colonial administration accounted for the pauperization of most of the Merina royalty, and this may have provided an early source of dissatisfaction with colonialism for Rabearivelo. At any rate, he found himself at the lower rungs of the social ladder struggling to regain a status of some respectability.

Rabearivelo commenced his education in Catholic schools, where he probably learned the French language. He continued later in public schools, from which he was expelled at fourteen for indiscipline. His education did not cease as a result of this incident; rather, he persisted in studying after leaving school and in due course acquired a wide culture and familiarity with the classics of Western civilization. He worked at minor jobs until 1923, when he began to work as a proofreader in a printing press owned by a French *colon*. He was to spend his entire life at this poorly paid job.

The exact circumstances that oriented Rabearivelo toward a lifetime of creative writing remain unclear, although he began to write from the moment he left school. It is not impossible that as a member of a newly disinherited social group, he sought social ascendancy through a profession also held in honor by the conquerors—that of the writer. Indeed, he developed a considerable obsession with the persona of the writer, and not being content with writing alone, he went so far as to model his lifestyle on the real and imaginary reputations of some notable figures of Western literary experience, such as Baudelaire and Casanova.

In order to nurture his vocation as a writer, he maintained relationships with the French literary establishment in Madagascar. These acquaintances included a French magistrate, Pierre Camo, in whose literary journal Rabearivelo's first poems were published. He likewise cultivated friendships with the leading Malagasy-language writers of his time while retaining equal familiarity with Malagasy orature. These diverse influences left their mark on his writing so that throughout his career he wrote, at times alternately and later concurrently, in both French and Malagasy. His varied literary culture, embracing both the new and the traditional, both the French and the Malagasy, both the written and the oral, and his attempts to reconcile them in his writing set him apart from all other writers in colonial Madagascar.

He was able to publish three volumes of poetry in French in the 1920s with the material assistance of his French friends. In the early 1930s he launched his own transient French literary journal, *Capricorne*. In addition, he published three other collections of poetry, two plays, a book on criticism, and two historical texts. At the same time, he regularly contributed articles to journals in Madagascar, in neighboring Mauritius, and in Europe. His stature as the best-known Malagasy writer of that period was consecrated by his acceptance in 1931 into the Académie malgache, an institution founded by the French to provide intellectual leadership on the model of the Académie française.

His publications in French represented only one dimension of his writing. He was likewise prolific in Malagasy, playing a prominent part in a Malagasy literary revival known as the *Mitady ny Very* between 1931 and 1934. His participation consisted of translations of European poetry into Malagasy as evidence that the Malagasy language did not lack any of the resources exploited by European writers. This unusual contribution to a movement urging Malagasy writers to renew contact with traditional sources of inspiration confirms Rabearivelo in the role of mediator between cultures that was to become his preferred stance in his later years.

His literary successes provided little remuneration, while his addiction to the epicurean lifestyle placed further strain on the limited resources available to himself and his family. Harassed by his creditors, unable to secure a higher-paying job with the colonial administration, and refused a much-desired trip to France by the government, he committed suicide in 1937.

MAJOR WORKS AND THEMES

The themes and concerns of Rabearivelo's writing are best understood in the light of the peculiar literary climate of colonial Madagascar. Compared to other sub-Saharan French African colonies, a thriving written literary culture flourished and in fact anteceded colonialism in Madagascar. British missionaries introduced roman script in the nineteenth century, while the pre-colonial Malagasy government provided extensive support for its dissemination and actually decreed compulsory primary education for Malagasy children in 1876. Thus, by the onset of colonial rule, Madagascar had produced more than one generation of Malagasy citizens literate in their own language. Most significantly, writing became a new emblem of Malagasy nationhood since the government itself had espoused the cause of literacy. Interest in written literature in particular continued to grow after the imposition of colonial rule, to the extent of sustaining a large number of Malagasy-language journals specializing in literary matters.

However, colonial rule did generate widespread malaise among the ranks of Malagasy writers. This uneasiness proceeded specifically from fears about the uncertain status of the Malagasy language under a government committed to the advancement of the French language in Madagascar. A decree proscribing the use of Malagasy for instruction in schools underscored the colonial administration's determination to dethrone the Malagasy language. The imprisonment of several leading Malagasy-language writers between 1916 and 1920, accused of involvement with a nationalist movement seeking greater autonomy, dealt a further blow to Malagasy-language writing. Notwithstanding discouragements, several Malagasy writers did continue to write in the Malagasy language. They produced a literature that was increasingly marginalized, with almost no access to publication in book form, and whose existence was barely tolerated by the colonial authorities.

Rabearivelo's major contribution to Malagasy literature was the realization that in a colonized Madagascar, the content and form of ''Malagasy literature'' could not remain as it had been previously. Before Rabearivelo, the term ''Malagasy literature'' had always been understood to refer exclusively to literature in the Malagasy language, while all texts written in French were considered to belong to French literature irrespective of the place of origin of the author. But such ''Malagasy literature'' had now been relegated to a negligible presence in its own homeland. To counter this development, Rabearivelo proposed a new definition of "Malagasy literature" that would incorporate and recognize French-language texts composed by the Malagasy, since only French-language texts could aspire to the vocation of literature in colonial Madagascar. In this fashion, Rabearivelo sought to give expression to the henceforth inevitably hybrid and multicultural character of colonized culture.

Such Malagasy literatures in French were differentiated from the metropolitan category principally through their affirmation of an acute consciousness of "Otherness." The allied themes of cultural displacement, alienation, and exile would further serve Rabearivelo in his elaboration of a non-French French-language literature. In his early collections of poetry, *La coupe de cendres, Sylves,* and *Volumes,* he laments the condition of one who has become an exile on native soil, for he is obliged to speak of the native land in a foreign tongue. The purported "exile" of the Malagasy who immigrated to the uninhabited island from diverse locations, and who therefore are "foreigners" on Malagasy soil, becomes a paradigm for the colonial condition. Images of transplanted trees seeking to be deeper rooted in the nation's soil further contrast with aspirations for flight and distance from the native land, providing the setting for the poet's pondering of the contradiction inherent in the fact of proclaiming commitment to the native land in a foreign language.

Rabearivelo's early works show respect for the rules of classical French prosody, with strict adherence to rhyme schemes, the alexandrine, and the sonnet. The most accomplished of these early works—in terms of mastery of the chosen model—is *Chants pour Abéone.* Even though it was published in 1936, it belongs with his earlier works composed in the 1920s. This collection explores in greater depth the motif of the journey away from the native land and the absence of home that inspires the poet to a greater love for the homeland. The state of alienation occasioned by colonialism thus acquires positive valuation as exile paradoxically results in a greater yearning for and attachment to the native land.

Rabearivelo also produced three prose works, none of which was published in his lifetime. *Un conte de la nuit,* a short story, recounts a tragic personal experience, the death of his youngest daughter. The other two works, *L'aube rouge* and *L'interférence,* are works of historical fiction, focusing on the moment of encounter between the French and the Malagasy that leads to colonial rule. *L'interférence* has now been published and narrates the misfortunes that befall several generations of a Malagasy noble family, weakened initially by the advent of Christianity and eventually destroyed by the military defeat that ushers in colonialism. Rabearivelo's purposes in his historical texts are manifestly directed toward a rewriting of the official French discourse justifying colonialism. Hence the Malagasy here are not savages, but highly civilized, and they are victims, not beneficiaries, of colonialism. The explicit criticism contained in these prose texts may explain why they were not published during Rabearivelo's lifetime.

Rabearivelo wrote two plays in the 1930s, *Imaitsoanala, fille d'oiseau* and *Aux portes de la ville.* In contrast to his unpublishable prose and his increasingly hermetic poetry, drama provided an avenue for instant gratification and renown. However, the immediacy of performance created other constraints. Thus these plays intended for a French-language audience refrained from any reference to colonialism and concentrated on the depiction of Malagasy traditions. The novelty for the audience resided particularly in the presentation of Malagasy rituals and folklore in the French language. Like his later poetry, both plays exist in bilingual (French and Malagasy) versions, though only the French version was published at the time.

Rabearivelo's best-known works of poetry, *Presque-songes* and *Traduit de la nuit*, articulate his resolution of the problem of alienation faced by the colonized writer. His early works in French had been described as and subtitled translations from the Malagasy in order to subordinate the French to so-called Malagasy originals, but there was little evidence to support this claim. *Presque-songes* and *Traduit de la nuit* were real translations, for they existed in both French and Malagasy versions in a manner making it almost impossible to determine the original version conclusively. In so doing, Rabearivelo makes the French version, the only version published in his lifetime, tributary to the Malagasy version, thus subverting the intentions of a system that obliged him to write in a foreign language in order to be published. *Traduit de la nuit*, translated into English as *Translations from the Night*, presents an ethereal world peopled by evanescent bodies in perpetual mutation. Night itself is in constant flux since it must give way to day. This unceasing cycle of change alludes to the condition of the colonized, in whose life the category of place has become variable and unstable, and whose identity is now an amalgam of shifting cultures in uneasy truce.

Barriers to publication functioned as a covert form of censorship for certain kinds of texts in colonial Madagascar. For example, none of Rabearivelo's Malagasy-language works or his more critical French-language works were published in his lifetime. Only in recent years has the Malagasy government begun to publish some of these Malagasy-language manuscripts. His final collection of poetry in French, also published posthumously, underlines Rabearivelo's conception of the role of the colonized writer. *Vieilles chansons des pays d'Imerina* is a translation of a genre of traditional Malagasy poetry, the *hainteny*, into French. The *hainteny* are dialogic love poems traditionally recited in word duels. Rabearivelo's commitment to making these exemplars of Malagasy orature available in French demonstrates his conviction that in a colonial environment, the pre-colonial culture survives and subsists mostly in translation.

CRITICAL RECEPTION

Rabearivelo's works continue to suffer from the insularity of his origins that he tried so desperately to transcend. Furthermore, several of his works published in the 1920s are out of print and totally unavailable. Nonetheless, he is the only Malagasy author who has received considerable attention outside Madagascar.

Although Léopold Senghor included several of Rabearivelo's poems in the *Anthologie de la nouvelle poésie nègre et malgache*, the seminal anthology embodying the aspirations of the Negritude movement, most critics have stressed that though inspired by similar questions, Rabearivelo remains an iconoclastic author whose writing is not directly correlated to the Negritude movement. Rambeloson-Rapiera describes him as "a man of his times" (7), in other words, of the colonial period, but his poems have been generally discussed in isolation with little reference to the specific colonial factors that engendered his work. Thanks, however, to the early articles by Robert Boudry, Rabearivelo's biographer, the personal details of Rabearivelo's life are well known.

Moradewun Adejunmobi (1994, 1995, 1996), however, rejects the critical trend toward perpetuating Rabearivelo's isolation, demonstrating the extent to which, in terms of strategies and concerns, Rabearivelo's writing merits the postcolonial description. Clive Wake observes that Rabearivelo's work anticipates the achievements of the Negritude movement and also identifies various influences on Rabearivelo, including those of the French symbolists, the surrealists, and the Malagasy *hainteny*. Clive Wake and John Reed in their introduction to the major translation of Rabearivelo's poetry into English again emphasize the impact of the symbolists on Rabearivelo's life and poetry.

Jean-Louis Joubert contests the supposed affiliation between Rabearivelo and the surrealists and attributes the change in style and tone of Rabearivelo's mature poetry to the influence of the polysemic tradition of Malagasy orature. Several other critics, including Joubert (1969, 1979, 1989), Ulli Beier (1967), Albert Gérard (1977), Adejunmobi (1996), Marie-Christine Rochmann (1988), and Jonathan Ngate (1988), have attempted to characterize and elucidate Rabearivelo's unusual imagery, especially in his later works.

Rakotozafy examines Rabearivelo's theory and practice of translation in an attempt to determine his original language of composition. Andrianjafy posits that Rabearivelo's prose draws from the French romantic and realist modes, while noting the importance of racial determinism in his depiction of Malagasy resistance to colonialism.

BIBLIOGRAPHY

Works by Jean-Joseph Rabearivelo

La coupe de cendres. Tananarive: G. Pitot de la Beaujardiere, 1924.
Sylves. Tananarive: Imprimerie de l'Imerina, 1927.
Volumes. Tananarive: Imprimerie de l'Imerina, 1928.
Presque-songes. Tananarive: Imprimerie de l'Imerina, 1934.
Imaitsoanala, fille d'oiseau. Tananarive: Imprimerie Officielle, 1935.
Traduit de la nuit. Tunis: Éditions Mirages, 1935.
Aux portes de la ville. Tananarive: Imprimerie Officielle, 1936.
Chants pour Abeone. Tananarive: Éditions Henri Vidalie, 1936.

Lova. Antananarivo: Imprimerie Volamahitsy, 1957.

Stances oubliées. Antananarivo: Imprimerie Liva, 1959.

Presque-songes, Traduit de la nuit. Antananarivo: Friends of the author, 1960.

24 Poems. Trans. Gerald Moore and Ulli Beier. Ibadan: Mbari Press, 1962.

Amboara poezia sy tononkalo malagasy. Tananarive: Editions Madagasikara, 1965.

Vieilles chansons des pays d'Imerina. Tananarive: Editions Madprint, 1974.

Translations from the Night. Trans. John Reed and Clive Wake. London: Heinemann, 1975.

L'interférence suivi d'Un conte de la nuit. Paris: Hatier, 1987.

Irene Ralima. Antananarivo: Imprimerie Nationale, 1987.

Eo ambavahadim-boahitra. Antananarivo: Imprimerie Nationale, 1988.

Imaitsoanala, zana-borona. Antananarivo: Imprimerie Nationale, 1988.

Resy harany. Antananarivo: Imprimerie Nationale, 1988.

Poèmes. Paris: Éditions Hatier, 1989.

Studies of Jean-Joseph Rabearivelo

Adejunmobi, Moradewun. "African Language Writing and Writers: A Case Study of Jean-Joseph Rabearivelo and Ny Avana in Madagascar." *African Languages and Cultures* 7.1 (1994): 1–18.

———. "History and Ideology in Rabearivelo's Prose Works." *Canadian Journal of African Studies* 28.2 (1995): 219–235.

———. *J. J. Rabearivelo, Literature, and Lingua Franca in Colonial Madagascar*. New York: Peter Lang. 1996.

———. "The Multiple Dimensions of Night in the Poetry of Jean-Joseph Rabearivelo." *Review of English and Literature Studies* 2.1 (1985): 1–16.

Andrianjafy, Danielle. "Jean-Joseph Rabearivelo, auteur d'une oeuvre romanesque inédite." *Jean-Joseph Rabearivelo, cet inconnu*. Marseille: Actes Sud, 1989.

Beier, Ulli. "Rabearivelo." *Introduction to African Literature*. London: Longman, 1967.

Boudry, Robert. "Jean-Joseph Rabearivelo, poète malgache." *Revue de Madagascar* January 1939: 29–44.

———. "La mort tragique d'un poète." *Mercure de France* September 1938: 532–549.

Gérard, Albert. "J-J Rabearivelo." *Etudes de littérature africaine francophone*. Dakar: Nouvelles Éditions Africaines, 1977.

Joubert, Jean-Joseph. "Jean-Joseph Rabearivelo et l'enigme." *Jean-Joseph Rabearivelo, cet inconnu*. Marseilles: Actes Sud, 1989.

———. "Jean-Joseph Rabearivelo, poète surréaliste?" *Itineraires* (1979): 84–87.

———. "Sur quelques poèmes de Jean-Joseph Rabearivelo: Essai d'interprétation." *Annales de l'Université de Madagascar: Lettres et Sciences Humaines* 10 (1969): 75–84.

Ngate, Jonathan. "Lire le poème traduit de la nuit: Jean-Joseph Rabearivelo au présent." *ALA Bulletin* 14.3 (1988): 30–34.

Rakotozafy, Mathilde. "Jean-Joseph Rabearivelo, cet inconnu." *Jean-Joseph Rabearivelo, cet inconnu*. Marseille: Actes Sud, 1989.

Rambeloson-Rapiera, Jeannine. "Présence de Jean-Joseph Rabearivelo." *Notre Librairie* 109 (1992): 6–10.

Rochmann, Marie-Christine. "Jean-Joseph Rabearivelo: Poète de la mort." *Présence Africaine* 145 (1988): 165–172.
Wake, Clive. "Jean-Joseph Rabearivelo—A Poet before Negritude." *The Critical Evaluation of African Literature*. Ed. Edgar Wright. London: Heinemann, 1973.

MORADEWUN A. ADEJUNMOBI

TIJAN SALLAH (1958–   )

BIOGRAPHY

The Gambia has yet again produced another genius for the literary world. Tijan M. Sallah, an economist currently working for the World Bank, has emerged in the last ten years as a strong contender for poet laureate of The Gambia, following in the footsteps of Lenrie Peters.

Tijan Sallah, a Gambian, was born in Serrekunda, where he spent his formative years attending both elementary and Koranic schools, learning firsthand in the Koranic schools the art of reciting poetic verses and the rudiments of being a capable student. As a student at Saint Augustine's High School, Sallah was exposed to what he calls "serious Western Literature," which comprises the so-called canonical/master texts. When he entered this world of the English language and literature, he discovered a whole new world of ideas, feelings, people, and culture. Its symbolization differed greatly from that of Africa and its languages. Reading Shakespeare, Swift, Chaucer, Shelley, and other great "masters," he discovered a symbolization totally different from his own, in which Western culture was strongly etched. This fact Sallah attributes to the strong European influence on Gambian writers.

Armed with this discovery, while not abandoning his study of Western literature, he moved somewhat in his focus to the study of literature written about and by African people, which led to the most intellectually stimulating influence of his academic life, the whole body of African Literature. Discovering Achebe and the Negritude writers, whom he credits as partially influencing his writing about The Gambia, Sallah found an entirely new symbolization in which African writers explored through symbols the effects of a language and culture that had been oppressively imposed upon a people of a different language and culture.

This, coupled with encouragement from Reverend Father Joseph Gough, started Sallah on the path to literary production. Gough's ability to spot Sallah's talent led to his first publication, a poem entitled "The African Redeemer" in *Sunu Kibaro*, a Saint Augustine's High School student publication. This poem, written as a tribute to the late Kwame Nkrumah, former president of Ghana, showed Sallah's early consciousness of the importance of using Africa, and Gambia in particular, as his poetic landscape. Words like "maybe someday you will be the Gambia's great writer, and students will be reading your works in the Moore and Beier anthology" from Father Gough boosted Sallah's self-confidence despite his skepticism about making it big as a writer. Though Gough was a central figure, he was not the only person who influenced Sallah to write, as he remembers Marcel Thomasi, Sait Touray, Father Murphy, Gambian writer and poet Lenrie Peters, whose unfailing criticisms made Sallah clarify his style, and Bemba Tambedou, who gave him due publicity on his radio program in the late 1970s titled "Writers of The Gambia."

Sallah's interest in literature allowed him in a sense to explore new worlds from his own home, in a country far removed from much of what he was reading. That interest, along with disciplined study and hard work, took him to the United States of America, where he attended Rabun Gap Nacoochee High School, Georgia. During his one-year stint at Rabun Gap, Sallah edited the student newspaper, the *Silent Runner*, studied under the American poet H. L. Brunt, and published his first poem in America, "Worm Eaters," in the *Atlanta Gazette* of February 17, 1978.

Now well on his way as a writer, Sallah was awarded a scholarship to Berea College as a result of extraordinary academic achievements at Rabun Gap, where he received the award "outstanding proficiency in American history and journalism." At Berea College Sallah's love for writing continued, but his love for economics prevailed, as he decided to read economics and business. This, however, did not mean that Sallah abandoned his literary endeavors. He served as editor of three campus publications, tutored writing, was named most outstanding student of the year, and received the Senior Economics Award and the coveted Berea Francis S. Hutchins Award in Literature. To cap it all, his first book of poems, *When Africa Was a Young Woman*, was published. The publication of his new book brought him instant celebrity status. The book received critical acclaim in various publications and was reviewed over the BBC. It was during this time that American literary critic Charles Larson stated, "There is little question about Sallah's talent."

A scholar, Sallah decided on continuing his education, taking up graduate work in economics at Virginia Polytechnic Institute (Virginia Tech). Virginia Tech proved to have the right ethos for his interests when he started *Kaleidoscope*, a student publication, and became its first editor. By this time he had become a frequent contributor to various journals, magazines, and other publications, notably *Okike, West Africa, Présence Africaine, Poet, Kentucky Poetry Review, Callaloo*, and *Appalachian Heritage*.

On receiving his M.A. and Ph.D. from Virginia Tech, Sallah embarked on a teaching career that parallels his writing career. As a professor of economics, he has taught at Kutztown University in Pennsylvania and North Carolina A&T State University in Greensboro.

In recent years, Sallah has decided to bring his two passions together at the World Bank: As one of 30 men and women selected by the World Bank for its young professionals program out of 2,800 applicants, Tijan plans to wed economics and literature to "help him see the human side of raw numbers." He hopes to give economic development "not only a statistical face, but a human face." He posits that "people who make policies shouldn't be people who sit in Washington and read numbers," and his project at the bank hopes in some sense to place "the human being at the centre of the economic drama." This ability of Sallah to write about human affiliation through actual observation makes him an asset for the World Bank. "They were impressed with my ability to combine economics, which tends to be lean and dry, and literature, which tends to be humanistic. I think economics deals with the head and literature with the heart. The fully integrated person, and the fully integrated society, must be able to merge the head with the heart" (Interview with Tijan Sallah).

Tijan Sallah is definitely a Gambian who is a "fully integrated person." An economist, writer, poet, essayist, he is someone who deserves more critical attention than book reviews as his works become part of the mainstream masterworks and become canonized. He was honored in 1984 with an honorary doctorate of letters by the World Academy of Arts and Culture in Taipei, Taiwan.

MAJOR WORKS AND THEMES

As a writer, Sallah has in recent years published six books and several articles and has entries in numerous anthologies. In *Before the New Earth, When Africa Was a Young Woman*, and *Koraland*, Sallah uses The Gambia as his landscape, depicting Gambian life and experience with seriousness and humor at the same time. In *Dreams of Dusty Roads*, Sallah divides his poems into three parts, Roots (Africa), Branches (America), and Dream-Clouds (in the mind). As the different sections suggest, the three themes, as the author himself puts it, deal with his "experiences in the Gambia, the U.S., . . . metaphysical experiences with the mystical." This collection is a retrospective that provides a guide to the future. This is definitely a book that will fit under the definition of postcolonial, immigrant literature, as it deals with issues of identity tied in closely with the politics of location. The emphasis in the latter part of the book is on mysticism and the workings of the mind of a person pondering about life with angst, but also with some form of resolution, very much based on spirituality.

Sallah's book on the Wolof people of Senegambia, titled *Wolof*, is a "brief" synopsis that introduces the reader to Wolof people, their beliefs, their society, their culture, their politics, and their worldview. It provides basic information on the Wolof that would help create an informed reading of Wolof literature. *New Poets of West Africa* was published in 1995. Sallah serves both as editor and contributor to this monumental work that introduces readers to contemporary West African poets.

Sallah's books have received mostly favorable reviews from literary critics. David Dorsey, writing for *World Literature Today*, states, "Sallah's poems are strong and welcome additions to the accessible corpus of Senegambian verse in English." Ezenwa-Ohaeto likewise notes in *The African Guardian* that Sallah's short stories "are highly influenced by the poetic qualities of Tijan Sallah's talent. This young Gambian, whose works have appeared in international journals and books, shows promise of growing into a remarkable writer." Ojaide Tanure, in his review of Sallah's poetry, gives him high marks for creativity and workmanship. He said that in *Dreams of Dusty Roads* "Tijan Sallah has matured into a master word magician." Nazareth, Larson and Jagne echo the same views about Tijan Sallah's writing in their reviews of his work. Harold Waters gave an unfavorable review to Sallah's latest book, which is one that he edits. He had problems with some of the selections in the book. This, however, does not take away from the importance of the book. The only person to do a comprehensive article on Tijan Sallah is Samuel Baity Garren. Garren explores the different movements in Sallah's works, oscillating between fiction and poetry and his effectiveness as an author who uses both genres. Garren is also impressed with Sallah's use of language and imagery in constructing a postcolonial identity. Postcolonialism is central to Sallah's writings and his critics are aware of this.

BIBLIOGRAPHY

Works by Tijan Sallah

When Africa Was a Young Woman. Calcutta, India: Writers' Workshop, 1980.
Before the New Earth. Calcutta, India: Writers' Workshop, 1988.
Koraland. Washington, D.C.: Three Continents Press, 1989.
Dreams of Dusty Roads: New Poems. Washington, D.C.: Three Continents Press, 1993.
New Poets of West Africa. Nigeria: Malthouse Press, 1995.
Wolof: The Heritage Library of African Peoples. New York: Rosen Publishing Group, 1996.

Studies of Tijan Sallah

Dorsey, David. "Tijan M. Sallah Koraland." *World Literature Today* 64.1 (winter 1990): 177–78.
Ezenwa-Ohaeto. "For a New Earth." *The African Guardian* May 22, 1989, 35.
———. "A Poetic Journey into Experience." *Daily Times* Wednesday, August 15, 1990, 10.

Garren, Samuel Baity. "Exile and Return: The Poetry and Fiction of Tijan Sallah."
    Wasafiri 15 (spring 1992): 9–14.
Jagne, Siga Fatima. "A Poet in His Own Right." *Gambia Weekly*, no. 33 (August 17,
    1990).
Larson, Charles. "Writing from the Third World." *World Literature Today* 55.1 (winter
    1981): 57–58.
Nazareth, Peter. "Gambia—*Before the New Earth*." *World Literature Today* 63.3 (sum-
    mer 1989): 521–22.
Qaide, Tanure. "Gambia—*Dreams of Dusty Roads* by Tijan M. Sallah." *World Liter-
    ature Today* 68.1 (winter 1994): 188.
Waters, Harold. "New Poets of Africa." *World Literature Today* 70.3 (summer 1996):
    746.

SIGA FATIMA JAGNE

OLIVE SCHREINER (1855–1920)

BIOGRAPHY

Olive Emilie Albertina Schreiner was born in Wittebergen, in present-day Lesotho, on March 24, 1855. Her parents, Gottlob Schreiner and Rebecca Lyndall, were missionaries who had been sent out from England; the father was originally of German extraction. Critics have noted the significance of the fact that Schreiner used her mother's maiden name as the first name of the heroine in her most famous novel, *The Story of an African Farm*. Schreiner grew up in the Cape Colony of South Africa and had a precocious childhood, much like those enjoyed by the heroines of her two major novels. In her midteenage years, she began to be involved in intellectual debates, which provoked her permanent repudiation of her parents' Christianity. In 1874 she began to write seriously, beginning all her major works, including *From Man to Man*, which remained unfinished at her death. Continuing an ambitious program of reading and self-discovery, she also gradually saved money for a trip to England, which finally occurred in 1881. Here she submitted *The Story of an African Farm* to publishers; it was accepted by Chapman and Hall in 1883. The novel proved tremendously popular and brought Schreiner wide friendship and acceptance in various maverick and freethinking circles, which included figures such as the sexologist Havelock Ellis and the socialist and homosexual activist Edward Carpenter. Schreiner, as a person as well as an artist, was from here on of two worlds: the advanced and trendy world of symbolist London as well as the provincial and stultifying colonial milieu of South Africa, which nonetheless remained the homeland of Schreiner's heart.

After a few abortive romances, Schreiner settled down and married Samuel Cronwright, an understanding gentleman ostrich farmer who went so far as to take Schreiner's surname when they wed in 1894. Schreiner and Cronwright-Schreiner, as he came to be known, had an understanding if not necessarily passionate relationship. Schreiner became pregnant several times, but each time her pregnancy ended in a miscarriage. Although Schreiner continued to work on her two other novels and published important short, allegorical stories, she devoted most of her time to social and political journalism. She developed an odd and intense friendship and antagonism with the great imperialist Cecil Rhodes, admiring his drive and energy but loathing his racism and aggressiveness. In 1897 Schreiner wrote *Trooper Peter Halket of Mashonaland*, her most direct protest against the segregationist and racist policies advocated by Rhodes.

Schreiner's political role reached a peak with the outbreak of the Boer War in 1899. As an English-speaking Boer sympathizer of half-German descent, Schreiner was ideally placed to interpret the conflict for the rest of the world. As a result of her position, she was placed under martial law in 1900, and her house was later burnt down in one of the battles. After the war, in the new situation of a politically unified but racially ethnic and divided South Africa, Schreiner embarked upon *Woman and Labour*, her most comprehensive statement on issues of gender, and began the great, unfinished work of attempting to complete her most ambitious project, *From Man to Man*. This work, though, was only published in incomplete form after her death, as was true of her novel *Undine* as well. With the onset of World War I, Schreiner once again resumed her pacifist activities. This time, though, they lacked the vigor and the local knowledge that had made her earlier activism so prominent. During the last years of her life, Schreiner's vigor and creativity lagged, and she became increasingly despondent. She died on December 10, 1920, of heart failure, leaving her greatest work incomplete, yet having founded, against all odds, an Anglophone literary tradition in southern Africa.

MAJOR WORKS AND THEMES

Olive Schreiner has long been accorded a peripheral place in Anglophone literary history. In the 1990s, though, she is emerging as a major woman writer of the late nineteenth century. Combining an eloquent, ambitious, and visionary style with a keen awareness of the political and moral tragedies afflicting her native South Africa, Schreiner is perhaps the most important of all the early women writers in the various white settler colonies of the British Empire.

The Story of an African Farm (1883) seemed to many readers to have sprung out of nowhere; for such an ambitious, complex, symbolic work to have emerged out of a thinly established colony on the utter periphery of the English-speaking world defied the usual precepts of literary history. One of the themes of the book, indeed, is the extreme isolation and parochialism of the characters. Lyndall and Waldo grow up together as children among a group of simple, culturally impoverished people; yet they both possess striking, unusual imaginations and intellects. The gap between the abstract, surreal, and philosophical imaginings of Lyndall and Waldo and the comical foibles and intrigues of characters such as the Boer farmwoman Tant' Sannie and the rogue and imposter Bonaparte Blenkins helps account for the novel's wild and fascinating combination of local color and transcendental allegory.

Lyndall is one of the most complex heroines in all of nineteenth-century fiction, and the most emblematic of Schreiner's representations of womanhood. Fiercely independent and totally unwilling to be absorbed into a domestic economy in the manner of her marriage-bound cousin and playmate Em, Lyndall possesses a creativity and indomitable energy that does not even register on the extremely rigid map of gender roles characterizing the colonial society in which she matures. Prompted by her rebellion against domestic norms, she flees the farm and seeks a male soulmate outside marriage; but this effort ends in tragedy as she dies in childbirth.

Gregory Rose, a friendly aesthete from England, is there to attend Lyndall in her last moments of suffering, and he is there (in order to gain access to her) dressed as a woman—an indication of his notable androgyny, expressed both in his name and in his attitudes. Schreiner uses Gregory's character to point to the arbitrary nature of gender boundaries and to implicitly argue for a liberation of individual temperaments and desires from the constraints of social propriety. Gregory also represents European aestheticism as it impacts upon the African continent; his refinement and sensitivity stand in utter contrast to the bleak declarativeness of the karroo around him.

It is not Gregory, though, but the homegrown and rough-hewn Waldo who represents the true center of the aesthetic in the novel. A ''natural'' artist, who in his carvings expresses all the pent-up creativity that the repressiveness of his surroundings discourages, Waldo lacks Lyndall's hardiness and develops an almost symbiotic dependence on her, to be shattered by Lyndall's early death. After this calamity, Waldo himself slowly wastes away, dying sadly but almost unobtrusively at the end of the book. Waldo is at the center of the book's theoretical musings. Near the middle of the book, he meets a stranger who recounts an allegory that has long been the most famous set piece of Schreiner's novel. It is of a hunter who searches all his life for the truth, only to find that it exceeds his grasp. Finally, as he is about to die, he sees one white feather descend, a pure though fragile token of art. He then dies, having at once yearned for the truth and witnessed that, if there is such a thing, it is passing and ephemeral.

It can be argued, though, that it is no one individual who is at the center of *The Story of an African Farm*, but the landscape itself, with its veldts and karroos previously unknown to European writing. Schreiner portrays the dislocation attendant on the gap between cultural expectation and territorial reality inherent in the European settlement of Africa. The Europeans at once value the exoticism of Africa as a cultural and rhetorical Other, yet expect to create near duplications of their original homelands in the new societies. Schreiner's interest in landscape also manifests an ecological and environmental concern; her characters, though not determined by the landscape, do define themselves in relation to it in a way that is deeper than just romantic spectatorship.

For all the success of *The Story of an African Farm*, Schreiner did not live to complete another novel. During the following decade, much of her best work was in her short allegories, partially collected in *Dream Life and Real Life* (1893). One of these, "The Policy in Favor of Protection—," is a notable depiction of the ironies and dilemmas surrounding the postcolonial condition. A successful, self-sufficient female journalist harbors a secret love for a man of her acquaintance, but she nonetheless encourages a younger woman to try to win his heart, even though she knows that her far greater intellectual and emotional depth makes her a superior candidate. The older woman's self-renunciation is given a deliberately political parallel as it is compared to the policy of trade protectionism that advocates of the "imperial preference" wanted to give to such white settler British colonies as South Africa and Australia. Schreiner searchingly diagnoses the intersection of personal and political interests in the lives of her protagonist; for her, even the most agonizingly private dilemma is fraught with public implications, and, correspondingly, no measure of the political situation of the subjects of European imperialism can be adequate without taking stock of private, interior feelings and sensations.

Another political allegory of Schreiner's was *Trooper Peter Halket of Mashonaland* (1897). Using the convention of Jesus coming back to Earth to upbraid his errant would-be followers (much as Dostoyevsky had done in the Grand Inquisitor parable in *The Brothers Karamazov*), Schreiner graphically demonstrates the inherent evil and injustice of racism and shows that it is in utter contrast to the ideals of advanced European culture so often used to justify visions of white supremacism. Schreiner is often accused of neglecting the racial inequalities in South Africa, but in *Trooper Peter Halket of Mashonaland* she makes a searing indictment of white racism during the era of imperialism, the Boer War, and after. That this story is so often criticized as "didactic" by white male critics only shows how Schreiner's sensibility was far in advance of the critical pieties of the early and middle twentieth century.

In *Woman and Labour* (1911) Schreiner continued her assertive exploration of her own feminine identity by calling for the fashioning of a constructive role for women in contemporary society. Women, Schreiner insisted, were neither to be simple adornments for their husband's careers and reputations nor minimum-wage laborers called into the economy for supplementary purposes. Women were to be accorded a station where they could contribute to the society according to their abilities without compromising their crucial and, for Schreiner, important role in raising children, which Schreiner nonetheless insisted should in no way compromise their necessary and urgent social emancipation.

Schreiner's most popular work will always be *The Story of an African Farm*, but the posthumously published *From Man to Man* (1927) is by far her most ambitious work. Much as in "The Policy in Favor of Protection—," the governing dynamic here is the relationship between two women, one of whom is a few years older than the other. Rebekah is a committed intellectual, a woman of genius, who like Lyndall finds the people around her (particularly the men) inadequate to the quality of her character and the intensity of her vision. Bertie is a more intuitive and carefree sort whom Rebekah often feels she needs to protect and shepherd even as she envies the younger woman's carefree spontaneity. The book begins with a novella-length set piece, "The Child's Day," which is the most tactile and immediate evocation of a child's inner experience since Wordsworth's *Prelude*. The long second and unfinished part of the book, "The Woman's Day," plays out the fates of Rebekah and Bertie as they are ill treated by a society that views women only as commodities. Bertie enters a whirl of social life in which her impetuous innocence is time after time betrayed. Rebekah enters into a loveless marriage whose emotional poverty leads her to embark upon ambitious speculations on world history and anthropology in the long chapter "Raindrops in the Avenue." With an ambitiousness recalling Hegelian or Darwinistic thought but totally lacking their tendency toward white supremacism, Rebekah recounts the rise and fall of empires and the nature of the various races of man, all the while insisting on the possibility of human progress and improvement and the equality of all human peoples. Even as we admire the philosophical sweep of Rebekah's vision, we are reminded that Rebekah is a woman, an individual, who goes about her domestic responsibilities even as she thinks such visionary thoughts, and is herself only part of a two-person drama in which Bertie also represents aspects of contemporary womanhood Schreiner deemed it valuable to depict. The tragic ending of the book—Bertie dies, and Rebekah is left always unfulfilled, though adamantly surviving—illustrates the precept that, as one of the book's chapter titles reminds us, "no ideal can be gained by a coup d'état." But, as always, Schreiner argues eloquently on behalf of future hope and liberation.

CRITICAL RECEPTION

From the beginning, Schreiner's work has been at the heart of the tradition of white South African literature in English it helped initiate. Her unique vision of the South African landscape and its harsh, obdurate beauty told white South Africans that there was something to be cherished and nurtured in their own physical environment. Her ability to chronicle local manners influenced such later writers as Pauline Smith and H. C. Bosman. More broadly, her vision of a tolerant and pluralistic South Africa where the rights of the African majority were respected served as a beacon for white liberal South Africans, a demonstration that their culture was not totally racist, that it possessed a redeeming, reformist, and humane margin that hopefully would one day wrest the stage from the racist propaganda of apartheid, which English-speaking South Africans saw, rightly or wrongly, as predominantly a project of Afrikaans-speaking whites. Thus English-speaking white South African intellectuals, of whom a prominent recent example was Guy Butler, saw Schreiner as both a fully ac-

complished imaginative writer who could hold her own with the best the metropolitan culture of Europe could produce, and a South African political
visionary who offered a healing vision for that country's land and its people.
More radical whites, such as Ruth First, Schreiner's most recent biographer,
who was also a militant African National Congress activist, turned to Schreiner
in light of her unflinchingly antiracist attitudes.

As J. M. Coetzee pointed out, however, in his 1989 book *White Writing*, the
liberal white tradition in South Africa has its limitations, among them an excessive sense of self-entitlement and a patronizing attitude toward the black
Africans they sought to liberate. Coetzee points out that whatever Schreiner's
love of the African landscape, her natural vistas are unpeopled: there is little
sense of the black African population that in actuality existed all around her. In
the wake of the dismantling of apartheid after 1990 and the election of a multiracial and democratic government led by President Nelson Mandela in 1994,
the South African literary establishment has recognized the need to concentrate
on the study of black writers, and thus Schreiner's reputation has for the moment
taken a back seat. Yet it could be argued that Schreiner is of pivotal importance
for the idea of an African postcolonial feminist literature. Her ability to find
hidden political echoes in the richness and pathos of her characters' spiritual
and psychological experience and her portrayal of the indissolubly linked pre-
dicaments of the personal and political that characterize women's lives then as
now were crucial precedents for the work of such black Southern African writers
as the Botswanan (South African–born) Bessie Head and the Zimbabwean Tsitsi
Dangarembga.

Schreiner's critical reputation was initially very high in England, and she was
regarded as a woman of genius and a harbinger of the spirit of the age. After
her death, though, the male-dominated and intermittently downright misogynistic canonizing machine of modernism denigrated Schreiner, as it did seemingly
every recent woman novelist other than Virginia Woolf, for alleged sentimentality, long-windedness, formal shapelessness, and idealism. The traits that made
Schreiner out-of-date in the 1940s, however, have made her very relevant at the
turn of the twenty-first century, and Schreiner's international reputation has
never been higher. Part of this is due to the way the poststructuralist rehabilitation of allegory has replaced the modernist exaltation of symbol and made
Schreiner, the master allegorist, seem a rhetorical pioneer. But Schreiner's renewed popularity is primarily due to feminist criticism. In the comprehensive
revival of long-neglected international Anglophone women's fiction, Schreiner's
work has finally received its due. Her exploration of the psychology and politics
of gender and her grasp of the fluidity of gender categories has been fore-
grounded in recent treatments of her work, and she has been explicitly linked
to English ''New Woman'' novelists of the 1890s, such as Mary Cholmondeley
and George Egerton, and also to other white women authors residing in Africa.
Schreiner's intellectual complexity enables her to be a source of feminist theory
and not just an object of its analysis. The next step, perhaps, would be for the

feminist and postcolonial insights on Schreiner's work to be fully integrated with each other; but that is a task for Schreiner criticism in the years ahead.

BIBLIOGRAPHY

Selected Works by Olive Schreiner

The Story of an African Farm. London: Chapman and Hall, 1883.
Dream Life and Real Life. London: Unwin, 1893.
Trooper Peter Halket of Mashonaland. London: Unwin, 1897.
Woman and Labour. London, Unwin, 1911.
From Man to Man. London: Unwin, 1927.
Undine. London: Unwin, 1929.

Selected Studies of Olive Schreiner

Berkman, Joyce Avrich. *The Healing Imagination of Olive Schreiner*. Amherst: University of Massachusetts Press, 1989.

Chrisman, Laura. "Allegory, Feminist Thought, and the *Dream* of Olive Schreiner." *Prose Studies* 13.1 (1990): 126–50.

———. "Empire, Race, and Feminism at the Fin de Siècle: The Works of George Egerton and Olive Schreiner." *Cultural Politics at the Fin de Siècle*. Ed. Sally Ledger and Scott McCracken. New York: Cambridge University Press, 1995.

Clayton, Cherry, ed. *Olive Schreiner*. Johannesburg: McGraw-Hill, 1983.

Coetzee, J. M. *White Writing: On the Culture of Letters in South Africa*. New Haven: Yale University Press, 1989.

Cronwright-Schreiner, Samuel. *The Life of Olive Schreiner*. London: Unwin, 1924.

First, Ruth, and Ann Scott. *Olive Schreiner*. London: André Deutsch, 1980.

Horton, Susan R. *Difficult Women, Artful Lives: Olive Schreiner and Isak Dinesan, in and out of Africa*. Baltimore: Johns Hopkins University Press, 1995.

Monsman, Gerald. *Olive Schreiner's Fiction: Landscape and Power*. New Brunswick: Rutgers University Press, 1991.

Rive, Richard, ed. *Olive Schreiner Letters*. Oxford: Oxford University Press, 1988.

Smith, Malvern Van Wyk, and Don MacLennan, eds. *Olive Schreiner and After*. Cape Town: D. Philip, 1983.

Thurman, Howard. Introduction to *A Track to the Water's Edge: The Olive Schreiner Reader*. New York: Harper, 1973.

NICHOLAS BIRNS

LEÏLA SEBBAR (1941–   )

BIOGRAPHY

Leïla Sebbar was born on November 19, 1941, in Aflou to an Algerian father who was a primary-school teacher and a French mother "from France," as the author frequently stresses in interviews, making her different from an Algerian-born French person. She was not a "Pied noir" and consequently did not display the predictable range of colonial and racist attitudes to be found in most of the French population born in Algeria. She left Algeria in 1958, four years before the proclamation of independence, and completed her studies in France, where she became a teacher, following in her father's footsteps. She has been living in Paris for more than twenty years, where she first became very much involved in the intellectual circle of Jean-Paul Sartre and Simone de Beauvoir. Her first works were published by *Les Temps Modernes* in the seventies when the famous Sartrian review was at its peak. Her first publication was an essay that bears witness to Sartre's influence. It is related to a field that the philosopher explored in the late forties in a study called "Orphée noir" and is called "Le mythe du bon nègre au XVIIème siècle." De Beauvoir's influence is no less strong and can be seen in the feminist orientation that Leïla Sebbar soon developed in essays like "On tue les petites filles" and also "Si je parle la langue de ma mère," the latter also published in the review directed by Sartre. The feminist inspiration remained the main component of Sebbar's literary work as she moved gradually to fictional creation, devoting herself to writing mainly novels, with occasional short stories. In the eighties she became an important figure in what was called, maybe not very appropriately in her case, "Beur" literature. She is presently continuing her career as a novelist, producing a new novel every two or three years under the banner of Stock editions.

MAJOR WORKS AND THEMES

The academic interest in analysis and interpretation of aspects of the African colonial myth that kept Sebbar's attention at the beginning of her writing was quickly abandoned for another theme that became and still remains the central preoccupation of the writer: the condition of the immigrant North African family. After several articles and studies related to Algeria (among these were *On tue les petites filles*, 1978, and *Des femmes dans la maison*, 1981), she published *Fatima ou les Algériennes au square* in 1981. Classified as a "récit," the text is inspired by a sociological study that Sebbar turned into a collection of stories of immigrant children. One central child, Dalila, remembers tales and memories heard from her mother and her friends talking at the square in a low-class immigrant suburb where their uprooted families have been forced to settle. This first important semifictional work already contains most of the themes that Sebbar developed later: multiplicity of characters all related to each other through one main heroine, the immigrants' homesickness, and the discomfort of their ill-adapted offspring. As mentioned by Christiane Achour in her attempt to list Algerian literary production in French, the "liberation of feminine speech inside immigration" is another distinctive feature of this book.

The novel that followed in 1981 may be considered as the starting point of her career as a "Beur" writer, though her belonging to this movement might be very rightly contested. The name "Beur" comes from the slang talked by the new generation descending from immigrant families, born in France, educated there, ignorant of their parents' culture. Ill at ease both with Algerian and French backgrounds, these young people try to survive by developing their own cultural values, the main one being their own language. This language was soon adopted by the whole of French youth. It was named "verlan" and consisted in pronouncing words backwards. "Beur" is therefore an approximate reversal of "Arabe" and was used to refer to second-generation immigrants. *Shérazade, 17 ans, brune, frisée, les yeux verts* is related to the "Beur" culture since it tells the story of the young daughter of Algerian immigrants who was born and raised in France and who tries to use and escape from what the France of the eighties rather meanly allows her. She treasures what she remembers of her holidays in a distant and idealized Algeria to which she is determined to return; this is the land of her grandfather. However, whether this belongs to "Beur" literature is very contestable since Sebbar adopts in her portrayal of this milieu the very same sociological approach she followed for her previous novel (*Fatima ou les Algériennes au square*). She collected information on the rebellious youth she describes; her characters speak its language, its slang, with a certain awkwardness. Their behavior and their thought processes remain essentially existential. The cultural interest of her heroes is directly derived from Sartre and de Beauvoir's way of thinking in the years after the war and into the seventies. Therefore, their way of life is somehow rather artificial. This group of marginalized young people squatting together flirts with the world of drugs, prostitution, fashion, and advertising that is used as an appealing background for the young reader but that is a far cry from reality. The action has very little to do with the universe in which immigrants must fight daily. Shérazade's "mal de vivre" is not far from the blues of Sagan's characters. In her attempt to actualize her work Sebbar seems to lose part of the sincerity shown in her first publications.

Nevertheless, the trilogy on Shérazade (two other novels followed the first one: *Les carnets de Shérazade*, 1985, and *Le fou de Shérazade*, 1991), shows the consistent strength of Sebbar's interest for her heroine and her surroundings. It develops along what should be considered as the central theme of her literature, the "crossing"—a theme that is also to be found at the heart of another novel, *Le chinois vert d'Afrique* (1984). The young boy hero of this book, as indicated by the title, is a mixture of several cultural and racial backgrounds. His slit eyes are inherited from his Vietnamese grandmother, and his curly hair comes from his Algerian grandfather. The same crossing is also at work in the tastes, the cultures, and the interchanges of most of the characters evolving around Shérazade. Indeed, she tries to absorb as much as she can from each new experience she comes across. This is obviously the most successful part of Sebbar's writing. She manages to extract all the rich excitement coming from the newborn cross-culture that does not seem to know boundaries. This unlimited interest mirrors the scope of Sebbar's output. A writer of philosophical and historical essays, as already mentioned, and of short stories and novels, she has also taken part in collective works, several of which are dedicated to photography: *Génération Métisse* (1988), *Femmes des hauts-plateaux* (1990), and *Marseille, Marseilles* (1992). These collective works all deal with Sebbar's main preoccupations: Algeria, "crossing," and immigration. They are therefore an intimate component of her work as a writer.

After the trilogy, Sebbar seemed to need a renewal of inspiration; hence the publication of a completely new type of novel in 1993, *Le silence des rives*. All the apparent veneer of modernism at work in the writing centered on Shérazade has given way to a more lyrical inspiration. If women have always been at the core of her creation, this novel inaugurates what could be a more original way of portraying and supporting them. Sebbar still makes use of the technique of multiple characters, but it is the language itself that has changed. The story takes place mainly in Algeria, where women are confined to sterile waiting for the improbable return of their men. Death is a recurrent theme, symbolically embodied in a trinity of three body-washers who may represent the Parcae. On the other side of the sea, in exile, a man is also waiting for his death, deprived of the support of his loved ones. Sebbar has abandoned the imitation of youth's way of talking; her style is highly poetic, rich in images and emotions. *Le silence des rives* is like a parable on exile and memory. Her evocation of Algerian death rites, far from being a concession to exoticism, has a universal meaning irrespective of age, culture, or race.

CRITICAL RECEPTION

Very few studies have been undertaken on Leïla Sebbar. There is one short description of her work up to 1982 in the *Dictionnaire des auteurs maghrébins de langue française* by Jean Déjeux, published in 1984, and a more important detailed account of her writing in the *Dictionnaire des oeuvres algériennes en langue française*, edited by Christiane Achour in 1990. She is also frequently mentioned in articles on ''Beur'' literature and appears briefly in several other studies on the literature of the Maghreb. She is usually referred to as a writer of novels and essays on immigration.

BIBLIOGRAPHY

Works by Leïla Sebbar

Essays

''Le mythe du bon nègre au XVIIIème siècle.'' *Les Temps Modernes* July-August-September 1974.
''Melle Lili ou l'ordre des poupées.'' *Les Temps Modernes* May 1976.
''Une femme . . . Un homme . . . et deux docteurs, autopsie d'une émission.'' *Esprit* Septembre 1977.
On tue les petites filles. Paris: Stock 2, 1978.
Le pédophile et la maman. Paris: Stock 2, 1980.

Récits

Fatima ou les Algériennes au square. Paris: Stock, 1981.
Parle mon fils parle à ta mère. Paris: Stock, 1984.

Fiction

''Elle, c'est ma maman.'' *Les Cahiers du GRIF* September 1977.
''La petite, elle restait dans son lit.'' *Les Temps Modernes* February 1978.
''Si je parle la langue de ma mère.'' *Les Temps Modernes* February 1978.

Short Stories

''Tu ne téléphones plus.'' *Sorcière* 17 (1979).
''Jeanne et Saïd.'' *Rendez-vous à Aulnay* (1982).
''L'explosion.'' *Paris-Dakar—autres nouvelles*. Paris: Souffles, 1987.
La négresse à l'enfant. Paris: Syros-Alternatives, 1990.

Novels

Shérazade, 17 ans, brune, frisée, les yeux verts. Paris: Stock, 1982.
Le chinois vert d'Afrique. Paris: Stock, 1984.
Les carnets de Shérazade. Paris: Stock, 1985.
J. H. cherche âme-soeur. Paris: Stock, 1987.

Le fou de Shérazade. Paris: Stock, 1991.
Le silence des rives. Paris: Stock, 1993.

Albums in Collaboration

Des femmes dans la maison, anatomie de la vie domestique. Paris: Nathan, 1981.
Génération métisse: Photographies d'Amadou Gaye. Paris: Syros-Alternatives, 1988.
Femmes des hauts-plateaux, Algérie 1960. Photographies de Marc Garanger. Paris: La
     Boîte à Documents, 1990.
Marseille, Marseilles. Photographies d'Yves Jeanmougin. Marseille: Éditions Paren-
     thèses, 1992.

Correspondence

Lettres parisiennes, autopsie de l'exil. With Nancy Huston. Paris: Barrault, 1986.

Studies of Leïla Sebbar

Achour, Christiane, ed. *Dictionnaire des oeuvres algériennes en langue française*. Paris:
     L'Harmattan, 1990. 85, 108, 208, 291, 312, 414, 415, 514.
Déjeux, Jean. *Dictionnaire des auteurs maghrébins de langue française*. Paris: Karthala,
     1984. 191.

S. D. MÉNAGER

LÉOPOLD SÉDAR SENGHOR (1906–   )

BIOGRAPHY

Léopold Sédar Senghor was born in 1906 in Joal, in the heart of Sererland, about seventy miles south of Dakar, the present-day capital of Senegal. His father Diogoye was of noble descent and was very wealthy. His mother belonged to a less wealthy family. As a child, Senghor lived in a relatively cohesive social environment. Later on, in his poetry, Senghor would refer to his early childhood as "Le Royaume de l'enfance" ("The kingdom of childhood").

Since Serer society is based on matrilineality, the young Léopold spent the first seven years of his life in Djilor (further south of Joal) with his mother and maternal uncles and aunts while the father remained in Joal. In Djilor, Senghor enjoyed the richness and sociability of his extended family: maternal uncles and aunts, maternal grandparents, cousins, and other relatives. There is, however, a peculiarity in Senghor's childhood in that he barely spent time with his father. The latter had many wives and two scores of children; furthermore, all his time was taken by his trade and commercial activities.

At the age of twelve, Senghor left Djilor and returned to Joal in order to attend the Catholic mission school of Ngazobil, near Joal. Besides learning systematic education, Senghor was exposed to Catholicism and catechism. It is ironic that young Léopold was sent to white school by his father as a form of punishment for his wanderings in the fields with shepherds and cows; besides, his mother staunchly opposed her young son's attending school; yet this was the man who would later become one of the most prominent poets writing in French as well as a graduate of the famous Sorbonne university in Paris. Besides the influence of the maternal clan on Senghor, Helène Senghor (wife of René

Senghor, Léopold's older half-brother) had a decisive influence in the intellectual shaping, formation, and maturation of Léopold Senghor.

If instruction at the Ngazobil mission school was at a rudimentary level, Senghor was going to be academically challenged when he moved at age seventeen (1923) to Dakar for secondary education at the Libermann Seminary, another mission school. The Libermann Seminary was to prepare Senghor for the priesthood, but his religious vocation would soon wither away. Senghor did not get along with one of the fathers at the seminary (Father Lalouse). Senghor considered the latter to be racist, paternalistic, and condescending vis-à-vis the black pupils. Thus Senghor left the Libermann Seminary for the Lycée Van Vollenhoven, where he finished his secondary-school education and obtained the prestigious *baccalauréat* diploma in 1928, the diploma that is the key that opens the doors of the university.

In 1928 Senghor arrived in Paris and started attending lectures at the Sorbonne. He was advised by one of his professors to leave the Sorbonne and go to Lycée Louis-le-grand, an elite secondary school; Senghor followed the advice. In that lycée, Senghor prepared a tough academic competition that allows the successful student to enter the much-coveted and prestigious École Normale Supérieure. As a student, Senghor often visited with Blaise Diagne, a well-known and respected man from Senegal, the first African member of the French Chamber of Deputies (Assemblée Nationale). Diagne was also a role model as well as a symbol of success of a Negro man among whites, the latter being supposedly "superior" and more "civilized" than the former. Diagne became Senghor's patron in Paris.

In Paris, Senghor discovered the French poets and writers who would later have an influence on his writings: Maurice Barrés, Claudel, Rimbaud, Valéry, Baudelaire, Verlaine, and Mallarmé. Like Claudel, Senghor was a devout Catholic and went to mass every Sunday. In 1931 Senghor graduated from the Lycée Louis-le-grand. He did not make it to the École Normale Supérieure and consequently enrolled at the Sorbonne, taking literature courses in order to become a high-school (lycée) teacher. At the Sorbonne, Senghor prepared for the *agrégation* degree in grammar, a degree no African had obtained yet. Senghor was going to be the first black African *agrégé* of grammar. In 1931 Senghor met another student freshly arrived from Martinique, Aimé Césaire. The idea, concept, and philosophy of Negritude would flower out of that encounter. It was also at Louis-le-grand that Senghor met a fellow classmate, Georges Pompidou, who later became president of France.

In 1932, thanks to Blaise Diagne's intervention, Senghor was granted French citizenship, the latter being the key that opens the doors of the French civil service. Senghor failed twice the *agrégation* exam. If having French citizenship is a blessing, the other side of the coin is that that citizenship also carries the duty of compulsory military service. After having written many letters to the administration, Senghor was sent back to Paris in a regiment of colonial infantry, instead of staying in Verdun, in the east of France, where he had been sent in the first place. Thus, while in the military in Paris, he prepared for his exam at the same time. In 1935, after a third try, Senghor finally became an *agrégé* of the University of Paris–Sorbonne in grammar.

In 1935 Senghor published his first article in a student publication, *L'Étudiant noir*. Senghor also showed a keen interest in ethnography and linguistics. He found inspiration in the works of the French scholar and colonial administrator Maurice Delafosse as well as in the works of Leo Frobenius, the German anthropologist and ethnographer. The two European scholars were the first ones to make a serious study of African history and culture and thereby promoted the idea that Africans have a complex and sophisticated culture of their own and had created magnificent empires such as those of Mali, Ghana, and Songhay. That same year Senghor moved to the city of Tours and took up a teaching position in a lycée.

The year 1937 marked Senghor's entry into politics and his moving into the public spotlight. He made two important speeches, one in Dakar and the other one in Paris, thus catching the eye of important people, Africans and French alike. The next significant year in Senghor's life was 1939. That year, with the beginning of World War II, he was drafted again and served in the regiment of colonial infantry. He was captured by the Germans as a prisoner of war and spent eighteen months in a camp.

The end of World War II also witnessed a quickening of the decolonization process. In 1945 Senghor and Lamine Guèye, a Senegalese lawyer, both were elected to represent the French African colonies under the umbrella of the Overseas Territories of France at the French parliament. Both Senghor and Guèye were allied with the French socialists (SFIO) even though, in his student days in the 1930's, Senghor had flirted with the French Communist Party (PCF), along with Césaire. However, Senghor switched sides by becoming a member of the SFIO socialist party, headed by the French political leader Léon Blum. In order to be elected deputy, Senghor had to come back to Senegal in order to campaign. Because of Senghor and Guèye's persuasion, a draft constitution was written at the National Assembly in Paris that allowed the creation of the French Union in which Africans were represented at the parliament on the basis of equality and free consent. In 1948, with Senghor's help, Alioune Diop, another Senegalese intellectual living in Paris at that time, created *Présence Africaine*, a cultural journal with prominent French intellectuals such as André Gide, Albert Camus, and Jean-Paul Sartre serving on the advisory board.

Some meaningful events of the time, such as a popular demonstration in Madagascar in 1947 that ended in a bloody repression carried out by the French colonial authorities, and the wars in Indochina and Algeria, all had had an impact on Senghor's political thinking and actions and, by the same token, had modified his attitude and allegiance toward France. In 1947 Senghor broke with Guèye and ceased living under the latter's shadow. Senghor created a new political party, BDS (Bloc Démocratique Sénégalais). From 1948 to 1960 Senghor became a master politician and was well respected. Along the same lines, he became the voice and supporter of the Senegalese peasantry and countryside, as opposed to Guèye, who always and exclusively defended the interests of the city dwellers of the Four Communes of Dakar, Saint-Louis, Gorée, and Rufisque. Only people who were born in these Four Communes were French citizens.

In 1948 Senghor married Ginette Eboué, the daughter of Félix Eboué, the prominent Guyanese colonial administrator who was a one-time governor of French Equatorial Africa. Senghor had two children from that marriage, which ended in divorce. In 1960 Senegal gained its independence from France, and Senghor became its first president up to 1980. In 1962–63 he had some serious conflicts of power with his prime minister Mamadou Dia, another well-known Senegalese politician. The latter ended up in prison, and Senghor remained the sole captain at the helm of the Senegal ship. In 1980 Senghor voluntarily left the presidency and was replaced by his long-time prime minister, Abdou Diouf. This was unique in the annals of the young history of modern Africa, for post-colonial African presidents usually either die in power or end up on the firing line or in military coups d'état. The ultimate consecration for Senghor came in 1983 when he was elected to the Académie française and became "an immortal." Since leaving the presidency, Senghor has shared his time between Paris, Normandy (where his second French wife is originally from), and Dakar. He travels around the world and gives lectures and presentations on his poetic work.

MAJOR WORKS AND THEMES

When the name Senghor is invoked, what comes first to mind is his poetry. Senghor is considered one of the greatest poets of all times writing in French. Three epochs deserve to be delineated in a chronological fashion; moreover, these three periods are overall clearly reflected in Senghor's poetry.

The first collections of poems (*Chants d'ombre*, 1945; *Hosties noires*, 1948) deal with the themes of exile and nostalgia. Senghor found himself in Paris right after having finished high school in Dakar. His new environment is at best alien to him and at worst hostile. The weather is gray, cold, rainy, and snowy, and the European people lack warmth, all of this being the opposite of his native Africa, where the sun shines all the time and the people burst with warmth, vitality, and smiles. At the same time, one can detect a certain paradox in the poet's early life in Paris, for if on the one hand Senghor is homesick and nostalgic for his native Joal and Senegal, on the other hand he is immersing himself in the rigorous, Cartesian, and European Western way of life. As an example, Senghor was deeply marked and inspired by the work of the Jewish French philosopher Henri Bergson, author of *Les données immédiates de la conscience* (1889). In this book, Bergson rehabilitates the concept of intuition. For Senghor, the Negro is intuitive by essence. He feels everything around him and has an intimate relationship with Nature. Thus Senghor is so grateful to Bergson for having inspired him that he dubbed the year of publication of the French philosopher's book "The Revolution of 1889," bringing into mind or paralleling another famous date in French history, the Revolution of 1789.

The publication of the second collections of poems (*Éthiopiques*, 1956; *Nocturnes*, 1961) coincided with Senghor's full adherence to the decolonization process in Africa. During this period, he was a member of the French parliament. Then there was the aborted Fédération du Mali in 1961 when the newly independent West African neighbors Senegal and Mali (the latter was headed by president Modibo Keïta) decided to unite, thus creating a single republic. That republic, however, did not last. All these events are more or less reflected in these two collections of poetry. Additionally, this period can be considered as a time in which Senghor was opening up to the Other (be it Western, European, or non-African).

Finally, the last collections of poems (*Lettres d'hivernage*, 1973; *Élégies majeures*, 1979) consecrate the poet's coming of age, his maturity. Moreover, in the 1970's Senghor forcefully advocated the idea of the *Civilisation de l'universel*, or what he also terms symbiosis. In this instance, Senghor, or better yet other people, considered that he had fully expounded the concept of Negritude and had meaningfully contributed to the renaissance and rebirth of African and Negro cultures, civilization, and languages, in short, the propagation around the world of the African personality and the affirmation of the dignity of the black person. From now on, the poet considers that the African must move beyond that stage of affirmation; otherwise, there is a risk of ghettoization. Hence the opening up of the African to the rest of the world, also known under the twin dialectical concepts of *Enracinement et Ouverture* (the act of rooting oneself into Africa and into one's culture first and then opening up to the rest of the world, to other ideas, to differences). The ultimate and final stage is a world in which all cultural differences would be erased and there would be only a single civilization for everybody, irrespective of race, nationality, class, creed, gender, or color.

Besides the three groups of collections already specified, another notable collection of poems is *Chants pour Naett* (1949). The poems in this collection are an interplay between music and words, so the poet appeals to traditional African musical instruments in order to support his poetic songs on Africa and its peoples. Senghor's poems have been translated into many languages: Spanish, English, German, Russian, Swedish, Italian, Chinese, Japanese, and others.

Senghor has written many articles and essays for conferences, lectures, seminars, public debates, town meetings, and political conventions in Senegal and around the world. These essays and articles are published in scholarly journals, newspapers, and magazines. Starting in 1961, most of these essays and articles have been regrouped and published by the Parisian publication house Seuil. There are five collections of essays: *Liberté I* (1961), *Liberté II* (1971), *Liberté III* (1977), *Liberté IV* (1983), and the final collection, *Liberté V* (1993).

Senghor has primarily written in three areas of interest: linguistics, politics, and sociology. His interest in linguistics and the study of African languages was aroused while he was a university student in Paris. He then decided to attend the Paris Institute of Ethnology. After passing his *agrégation* examination, Senghor enrolled in a doctoral program at the Sorbonne but never finished writing his dissertation because that time coincided with his entry into politics. Nevertheless, he had composed half of that dissertation, whose topic was the structural and morphological study of the Wolof language. He had also done prior fieldwork for his dissertation in Senegal. Besides Wolof, Senghor also wrote about the Serer language, his native tongue.

The political and sociological essays encompass a vast array of topics, themes, and subjects: Negritude, the French language in Africa, traditional African cultures and societies, pre-colonial Africa, *Francophonie, métissage*, African history, European and French literatures, philosophy, and culture, African music, art, sculpture, dance, painting, poetry, African socialism, and others.

In 1953, together with another Senegalese author, Abdoulaye Sadji, Senghor wrote a children's book that was designed for primary-school children. Most, if not all, Senegalese children who came into the French colonial school system and, after that, to the Senegalese school system after 1953, myself included, have read and enjoyed *La belle histoire de Leuk-le-lièvre*. This book is a reconstruction of traditional tales and folktales that are based primarily on the animal world of the West African savannah and forest.

Senghor is universally known because of the philosophy and concept of Negritude. The idea of Negritude is tied to the very concept of Being, of how the Negro and African perceives being and living on this earth. Thus not only does the poet have to deal with ontological and epistemological problems, but moreover, he wants to bring to the fore the meaning of African cosmogony. Another aspect of Negritude is that it has always been defined (at least at its inception) in contradistinction to Europe. Of course, this situation can be explained because of the European colonization, domination, and subjugation of Africa. It is important to note that the word "Negritude" was coined by Aimé Césaire and was developed and expounded through poetry by Césaire, Léon Damas, and Senghor, but Senghor has been its most ardent defender as well as its best-known ambassador.

The Senghorian concept of Negritude can be understood only in conjunction with another concept: intuition. For Senghor, the Negro is intuitive, whereas the European is more Cartesian, more calculating. This has led the poet to put forward the famous statement "L'émotion est nègre, la raison est héllène" (emotion is Negro, reason is Greek). In spite of this early posturing, Senghor has always avoided overcriticizing European civilization. Rather, he focused more on Africa but occasionally appealed to European ideas, writers, philosophers, art, and culture when they were relevant to his subject. But even though Senghor appealed to Europe for a positive outlook, he likewise vigorously denounced the paternalistic, racist, and condescending attitude of certain European intellectuals and politicians, be they on the right, left, or liberal side of the spectrum.

Senghor's statement about reason and intuition has led to numerous protests and criticism on the part of certain African intellectuals, academics, and writers. I will come back to that reaction in the following section devoted to the critical reception of Senghor's work. The poet has given the following definition of Negritude: "Negritude is the totality of the cultural values of the Black world" (Vaillant, 244). It is worth noting here that Senghor is not solely concerned with Africa. Rather, his conception of Negritude is more inclusive, encompassing the blacks in the diaspora, primarily the Americas. It is also to the point to remind the reader that the Harlem Renaissance in New York City in the 1920's had had an impact on Senghor, Césaire, and Damas as well as on the way in which all three poets have formulated the concept of Negritude. Senghor had discovered and loved the African-American poets of the Harlem Renaissance when he came to Paris. There he had the opportunity to read in French translation and appreciate black poets and writers of the Americas such as Langston Hughes, Claude McKay, Jean Toomer, and Countee Cullen. Senghor also read the works of Alain Locke and W. E. B. Du Bois.

Generally speaking and in a broadsided fashion, Senghor's poetry is wrought around the twin pillars of rhythm and image; other notable features are the poet's chanting and celebration of Africanness and blackness. Throughout his poems, Senghor invites his readers and/or listeners to feel the pulse of ancient and ancestral Africa, to dance to the rhythms of the drums, tom-toms, balafons, koras, xalams, and other traditional musical instruments. Thus Africa is the continent of music, of rhythm, of dance, of joy, of happiness—in other words, of the celebration of life par excellence.

For Senghor, African images are conceived not as something that responds to a calculated and mathematical equation (as in the European sense) but, rather, as analogical and multidimensional symbols. Overall, Senghor captures the idea of fluidity, of plasticity, of movement that one finds within African culture, art, and thought. To that end, we are often reminded that Pablo Picasso was deeply influenced and inspired by African sculpture as well as the French poet André Breton (father of the surrealist movement), just to name these two Europeans. Senghor insists on the fact that all cultures borrow from each other, Europe included. Senghor also likens the poetry of Negritude to jazz, as the latter musical form was invented and developed by African Americans; both art forms share one thing in common: improvisation.

Another equally important theme for Senghor and, for that matter, for all colonized and ex-colonized peoples is the usage of European languages in Africa, and of French in this instance. Why write in French and not, let us say, in Wolof or Serer? According to the poet, responding to such queries, French has a universal appeal, aim, and goal; therefore, it is normal that Africans use it. Furthermore, for Senghor, the usage of French and Senegalese languages should not be formulated in terms of either/or. Still, according to him, if speaking Wolof, Serer, or Pulaar in Senegal is a normal thing, writing in French is also normal. Senghor finds nothing odd about speaking and writing in French. Finally, on the question of the usage of French in Africa, Senghor advocates a bilingual or multilingual policy, which policy can be translated into practical terms as the peaceful coexistence of French and African languages, both sides enriching one another. This idea of enrichment is so dear to Senghor that he considers that anything that is pure (be it a human being, a culture, a race, a language, a society, on whatever) is at once poor. For him, the meeting and mixing of peoples, races, and languages, in short, the act of borrowing and of giving, can only lead to openness of mind, to enrichment. Ultimately, Senghor believes that there will be eventually only one world civilization, a unique and universal one.

A related question to the theme of the usage of the French language in Africa is *Francophonie*. The latter idea was initiated and promoted by Senghor but was encouraged and supported by the various French governments from the early 1970s onward to the late 1980s and to the present. Senghor has tirelessly campaigned and traveled around the world in order to propagate and sell the *Francophonie* idea. But the idea that really undergirds the *Francophonie* project is the defense and preservation of the French language around the world; it was (and still is) felt that French was becoming less and less important in today's world where English is predominant, and other languages, like Spanish, are gaining increasing importance. Consequently, structures were created by countries that have the usage of the French language in common with the backing and blessing of France: Association of Francophone Universities, Association of Francophone Parliaments, Association of Francophone Mayors, and others.

In the area of politics, besides writing and speaking on domestic affairs at home in Senegal, Senghor elaborated some very complex political concepts and a peculiar vision of the world. The case in point is African socialism. For him, socialism is not new to Africans in that the latter have had that way of life since time immemorial through the prism of the communal aspect of life in African societies where the concept of sharing is extremely important. In the 1970's Senghor moved even further away from scientific socialism as conceived by Marx, Engels, and, later on, Lenin. Thus Senghor advocates ''an African re-reading and reappraisal of Marx,'' his famous ''Pour une re-lecture africaine de Marx.'' For Senghor, scientific socialism does not reflect social reality, but rather expresses the personal point of view of its inventors, namely, Marx and Engels. If Africans are already endowed with humanism (or humanness), a quality that makes them open to the rest of the world, what would they need scientific socialism for?

In the last analysis, the main challenge that the concept of Negritude presently faces is whether it is still a relevant concept for Africans. Quite a few people consider that in the days of European arrogance, colonization, and sense of superiority vis-à-vis all the other races on earth, it was vital and indeed necessary to have a concept and a weapon such as Negritude in order to counter the lies, fabrications, misperceptions, and misrepresentations concerning Africa by Europe. However, in postcolonial and independent Africa, Africans do not need anymore to demonstrate to the white man that they are intelligent and that they have a culture and a civilization. To many, those are bygone days; Africans are way beyond that stage of identity affirmation, for the job has been done by the pioneering African (as well as by well-meaning European and Western) intellectuals, historians, and writers from the 1930's to the 1970's.

CRITICAL RECEPTION

Senghor's poetic production has received wide attention all over the world. It is, however, fair to say that Europeans in general, and the French in particular, were the first to enjoy this new and peculiar type of poetic tradition coming from Africa, that is, from the colony, and carrying along an exotic flavor. In the 1930s and 1940s there was not a wide readership in French-speaking Africa that could read and comprehend Senghor as well as the other African writers. Thus the early African literary production was really aimed for the European market. Of course, things have tremendously changed over the last fifty years, for today more Africans have access to the works of Senghor and of the other African writers and poets thanks to education.

Just as in the debate pertaining to the usage and writing in the French language by Africans (instead of their own languages), the same beast lifts its head again; thus the same question is asked: For whom does the African writer write? A complementary and subsidiary matter is formulated in the following fashion: Does the African writer primarily write for an African audience or a foreign (that is, European) one? These questions were more pertinent in the 1930s, for, as I pointed out earlier, in those days, people in Paris and France were more likely to buy the books of Senghor and read his poetry than the people of Senegal. It is then fair to say that the African writer used to write for a European audience during the first half of the twentieth century. Today, more Africans are reading their own writers and poets writing in European languages; equally important is the fact that the African writer and poet have become increasingly universal. The themes that they treat are universal and are equally treated by writers in Europe, Asia, the Americas, and elsewhere, the most common theme being the condition and fate of humans on this earth.

In spite of his success as a poet, Senghor has faced virulent and often hostile attacks and criticism from some African intellectuals; within the African Francophone intellectual and literary circles, Stanislas Adotevi (a philosopher from Benin), Marcien Towa, and Mongo Béti (respectively, a philosopher and a novelist from Cameroon) are the most consistent critics of Senghor and his ideas. On the African Anglophone side, Ezekiel Mphahlele (a writer from South Africa) and the Nobel laureate Wole Soyinka (from Nigeria) have adamantly opposed Senghor. These critics appreciate Senghor's poetry. However, they do not agree with the basic premise upon which the philosophy of Negritude is founded. It is important to note that Senghor's assertions and analytical definition of this concept are open to various interpretations. If, on the one hand, the poet's aim was to counter the white European arrogance and assumptions on the inferiority and savagery of the Negro in general and of the black African in particular, he nonetheless went further by putting in an antinomic fashion Africa and Europe. For Senghor's critics, as far as the poet is rehabilitating, glorifying, and celebrating African cultures and life, that's fine. However, when he asserts that intuition is Negro and that reason is Greek (thus implying that Europe is superior to Africa), he unleashes a storm of protests on the part of his critics.

Senghor considers that he is being unjustly attacked and that he is misunderstood. He said that he based his statement about intuition on the Bergsonian philosophy and concept that stresses the fact that intuition precedes science and discovery. Senghor did not mean in any fashion or way that the Negro was inferior to the white man. All the same, these further developments and corrections on Senghor's part neither abated the attacks nor satisfied his detractors. Because of his political activities, his defense of the French language, and, most of all, his position as president of the Republic of Senegal, the most virulent critics said that Senghor was just a puppet who kept and defended the neocolonial interests and assets of France in Africa. In spite of all these assaults, Senghor maintained and sustained his idea about the very foundation and being of the philosophy of Negritude, just like a captain of a vessel who keeps his boat on course in the middle of a fierce sea storm and high waves.

Senghor was not unanimously applauded in Europe either. Some French intellectuals and thinkers thought that Negritude was plain racism, or better, that it was "a disguised form of black racism." Senghor did not answer to the latter attack coming from the European and French side. It was the French philosopher Jean-Paul Sartre who came to the poet's rescue. Sartre wrote a preface entitled "Orphée noir" to Senghor's *Anthologie de la nouvelle poésie négre et Mangache* (1948); Sartre declared that Negritude was "an antiracist racism."

If we jump back to the 1930's, the first opposition to Senghor's ideas had already occurred during that period. This rift was between Senghor and his West Indian intellectual friends (from Martinique and Guadeloupe) of the Latin Quarter and of the Sorbonne, in particular, Étienne Léro. The latter was a hard-core Communist militant and intellectual. He considered that Senghor's opinions on Negritude and vis-à-vis the anticolonial struggle were too soft. The next rupture was with another Marxist poet and novelist from Haiti, René Depestre. The last anti-Negritude opponent of that epoch was an intellectual from Martinique named René Ménil. Ménil and Léro were friends.

All this indicates that Senghor is accustomed to being criticized. However, he has said that one must distinguish between good and bad critics. He made it a point to answer only to those he considered as being good, relevant, and constructive critics. Later on, during the 1940s, when Senghor definitely returned to Africa, took part in the decolonization process, and became the first president of Senegal, the real debate shifted around the Francophone-Anglophone divide. Africans of the Anglophone part of the continent accused the French-speaking Africans of being too "French," too assimilated to French culture. As an example, they cited Senghor. Again, Senghor responded by saying that one can adhere to the values and culture of France without necessarily becoming French, without being assimilated; one is and remains an African while using the French language and getting the best of French culture.

Finally, one must take into account the fact that for Senghor, all roads lead to poetry. According to him, poetry is the absolute manifestation of human creativity and beauty. Without poetry, there is no life. It has always been that way (since the time humans began expressing themselves artistically), and it will remain like that as long as humans are on this earth.

BIBLIOGRAPHY

Works by Léopold Sédar Senghor

"Les classes nominales en wolof et les substantifs à initiale nasale." *Journal de la Société des africanistes*, 1944.
"L'article conjonctif en wolof." *Journal de la Société des africanistes*, 1945.
Chants d'ombre. Paris: Seuil, 1945.
"L'harmonie vocalique en sérère (dialecte du Dyéguène)" *Journal de la Société des africanistes*, 1945.
Anthologie de la nouvelle poésie nègre et malgache ("Orphée noir" preface by Jean-Paul Sartre). Paris: PUF, 1948.
Hosties noires. Paris: Seuil, 1948.
Chants pour Naett. Paris: Seuil, 1949.
La belle histoire de Leuk-le-lièvre (cowritten with Abdoulaye Sadji). Paris: Hachette, 1953.
Éthiopiques. Paris: Seuil, 1956.
La dialectique du nom-verbe en wolof. Dakar, 1961.
Liberté I: Négritude et humanisme. Paris: Seuil, 1961.
Nocturnes. Paris: Seuil, 1961.
Liberté II: Nation et voie africaine du socialisme. Paris: Seuil, 1971.
Lettres d'hivernage. Paris: Seuil, 1973.
Liberté III: Négritude et civilisation de l'universel. Paris: Seuil, 1977.
Élégies majeures. Paris: Seuil, 1979.
Liberté IV: Socialisme et planification. Paris: Seuil, 1983.
Discours de réception à l'Académie française. Paris: Seuil, 1984.
Poèmes (all of Senghor's poems in one volume). Paris: Seuil, 1984.
Ce que je crois. Paris: Grasset, 1988.
Oeuvre poétique. Paris: Seuil, 1990.
Liberté V: Le Dialogue des cultures. Paris: Seuil, 1993.

Selected Studies of Léopold Sédar Senghor

Aziza, Mohamed. *Léopold Sédar Senghor et la poésie de l'action (entretiens)*. Paris: Stock, 1980.
Badiou, Alain. *La poésie de Senghor*. Paris, France: Vin nouveau, 1957.

Damas, Léon-Gontran. *Poètes d'expression française, 1900–1945*. Paris: Seuil, 1947.

Decaunes, Luc. "Hosties noires." *Cahiers du sud* 292.

Desjeux, Chantal. "La femme dans l'oeuvre de Léopold Sédar Senghor." Diplôme de maîtrise, Paris, 1969.

Éditions Présence Africaine. Hommage à Léopold Sédar Senghor, homme de culture. Paris: Présence africaine, 1976.

Emmanuel, Pierre. *Les jeunes poètes*. Paris, France: Temps présent, 1945.

Grosjean, Jean. *Éthiopiques*. Paris: N.R.F., 1956.

Guibert, Armand. *Léopold Sédar Senghor* (collection Poètes d'aujourd'hui). Paris: Éditions P. Seghers, 1961.

Hymans, Jacques-Louis. *L'élaboration de la pensée de L. S. Senghor, esquisse d'un itinéraire intellectuel*. Paris: Fondation des sciences politiques, 1964.

———. *Léopold Sédar Senghor, an Intellectual Biography*. Edinburgh: Edinburgh University Press, 1971.

Jan, Mohamed, and Rachid Sultan. "Le message du métissage culturel dans la poésie de L. S. Senghor." Mémoire, Université Paul-Valéry, Montpellier, 1973.

Jouanny, Robert. *Les voies du lyrisme dans les "Poèmes" de L. S. Senghor, étude critique*. Genève: Éditions Slatkine, 1986.

Juin, Hubert. "L. S. Senghor." *Combat*, 1956.

Kesteloot, Lilyan. *Les écrivains noirs de langue française: Naissance d'une littérature*. Bruxelles: Université libre de Bruxelles, 1962.

Lambert, Paul. "Léopold Sédar Senghor, poète de l'unité." Mémoire, Université Lovanium, Léopoldville, 1960.

Lebaud, Geneviève. *Senghor ou la poésie du Royaume d'enfance*. Dakar: Nouvelles éditions africaines, 1976.

Leusse, Hubert de. *Léopold Sédar Senghor, l'Africain*. Paris: Hatier, 1967.

Markovitz, Irving Leonard. *Léopold Sédar Senghor and the Politics of Negritude*. New York: Atheneum, 1969.

Milcent, Ernest, and Monique Sordet. *L. S. Senghor et la naissance de l'Afrique moderne* (preface by G. Pompidou). Paris: P. Seghers, 1969.

Ndiaye, Simone. "L'image de la poésie de L. S. Senghor." Mémoire, Université de Dakar, 1960.

Okechukwu, Mezu S. *Léopold Sédar Senghor et la défense et illustration de la civilisation noire*. Paris: Marcel Didier, 1968.

Piquion, René. *Manuel de Négritude*. Port-au-Prince, Haiti: Henri Deschamps, 1965.

Rous, Jean. *Léopold Sédar Senghor: La vie d'un président de l'Afrique nouvelle*. Paris, France: Jean Didier, 1967.

Sartre, Jean-Paul. "Orphée noir." Preface to *Anthologie de la nouvelle poésie nègre et malgache* by L. S. Senghor. Paris: PUF, 1948.

Sénégal d'aujourd'hui. "Numéro spécial: 70ème anniversaire du président Senghor." Dakar, November 1976.

Le Soleil (governmental daily newspaper of Senegal). "Numéro spécial: Colloque sur la négritude." Dakar, May 8, 1971.

Testas, Pierre. *Chants d'ombre*. Paris: L'Université syndicaliste, 1945.

Thomas, Louis-Vincent. *Les idéologies négro-africaines d'aujourd'hui*. Paris, France: Nivet, 1965.

Towa, Marcien. *L. S. Senghor: Négritude ou servitude?* Yaoundé: Clé, 1971.

Vaillant, Janet G. *Black, French, and African: A Life of Léopold Sédar Senghor*. Cambridge, Mass.: Harvard University Press, 1990.
Zuccarelli, François. *Un parti politique africain: L'U.P.S.* France: Éditions R. Pichon and R. Dunand-Auzias, 1970.

SAMBA DIOP

WOLE SOYINKA (1934–   )

BIOGRAPHY

Akinwande Oluwole Soyinka, known as Wole Soyinka or simply as W. S. is a dramatist, poet, novelist, literary critic, theatre director, and sometime actor; a political activist par excellence; the first black Nobel Prize winner for literature; and arguably the most prolific and most distinguished African writer writing in the English language. Four rather untraditional autobiographies to date (one political, three literary) conveniently introduce the reader to the author's cultural background and strong political commitments. Born in colonial Nigeria of well-educated Nigerian parentage, Wole Soyinka has strong-willed and activist roots in his Yoruba lineage and culture that have gestated and informed much of his work in postcolonial Nigeria. He was a precociously individual child whose curiosity for knowledge and acute sensibilities as to the nature of things took him to various schools in his early education, beginning with St. Peter's Primary School in Ake Abeokuta (1938–43), where his father was headmaster, to Abeokuta Grammar School (1944–45), where his maternal uncle, the most revered Rev. A. O. Ransome-Kuti ("Daodu" in *Ake*), was principal, and away from home to Government College in Ibadan (1946–50). He then proceeded to postsecondary education at University College, Ibadan (now the University of Ibadan), the premier institution for higher education in Nigeria under colonial administration; there he spent two years before going on to complete his bachelor's degree in England, majoring with honors in English at the University of Leeds. He was a loner (certainly not in the sense of aloofness or elitist snobbery), bold, self-confident, stubborn, rebellious, yet generous almost to a fault; his individualist traits, many of which were not uncommon in his family, would not only get him into trouble several times in his life, but also create and influence most of the main characters in his works.

Soyinka's eventful creative career spans some forty years to date, beginning with poems and short stories in magazines as a student at the universities he attended. Earlier in his life, before going abroad to study, he had identified himself as an exceptionally gifted child with a versatile aptitude for voracious reading, making up words and stories and writing dramatic sketches for school entertainments and fifteen-minute plays for radio in Nigeria. However, his towering stature as a professional literary giant has been nurtured by several experiences. At Leeds, he studied under distinguished professors and literary figures such as G. Wilson Knight (who acknowledged him as an insightful interpreter of *King Lear*) and the Marxist critic Arnold Kettle; there he was brought into contact with a wide range of classical and modern European and American literature. As he recalled in various interviews, he loved the language and the humanism of Shakespeare, the re-creative and inventive processes of the Greek mythic and ritual theatre, the political satires of Aristophanes, the form and spectacle of Japanese Noh drama, and the versatile and eclectic drive of Spanish and Irish theatre. In England and Europe in the late 1950s, before coming back to Nigeria, he had memorable experiences as a bouncer and barman in nightclubs and as a bricklayer in Holland, incidents that were re-created in early works such as the short story ''A Maverick in the Land of the Dykes,'' published in the *Nigerian Sunday Times* (circa 1959), and the poem ''Telephone Conversation.'' At the Royal Court, a theatre that promoted the young and angry avant-garde playwrights of the 1960s, such as John Osborne, John Arden, Arnold Wesker, Harold Pinter, and Edward Bond, Soyinka participated as a play reader and as actor and writer in the writers' experimental workshop, an experience that significantly gave him a strong sense of what theatre should reflect or provoke, as recalled in the first paragraphs of his Nobel Prize speech. At the Court in 1959, in one of the Sunday-night workshop productions, his first professional one-act, *The Invention*, a humorous but scathing agitprop about apartheid South Africa, along with excerpts from ''The House of Banigeji'' and ''A Dance of the African Forests,'' received its premiere production. Later that year *The Swamp Dwellers* also had its London premiere production, and almost simultaneously in Nigeria this play and *The Lion and the Jewel* were hailed as ''the first performance of African plays'' at the University College Arts Theatre, thereby setting off a welcome wave of exciting indigenous theatrical activities (as opposed to colonial examples and imitations) within the University College community and across the nation.

However, Soyinka's external influences must ultimately be placed against a background of internal and innate influences—the multiplicity of the imposing numinous and cultural forces of his Yoruba ancestry—that have haunted him since childhood. With both sets of influences he would attempt on the one hand to forge a genuine creative unity, and on the other to engage them in a kind of comparatively complex and ritualistic tension to address universal themes. Thus, coming back from Europe to Nigeria in 1959, from the center of the Western powers and cultures (the source of his external influences) that had imposed a colonial bind on his African cultural heritage, coming home to partake, like many of his colleagues, in the mutant heat of preparations for self-rule and independence from those colonial ties, he immediately set out to assess the political realities of change and to put his various ideas into dramatic practice. With a Rockefeller Foundation grant to do research into West African traditional forms of drama, he founded the 1960 Masks, a theatre laboratory he hoped would develop a permanent National Theatre company that would serve as a facility for promoting his researched African forms and works by African writers. The first product of this objective was his own independence-commissioned *A Dance of the Forests*, which launched the company's first production directed by him.

The political turbulence that started to devastate Nigeria and many other newly independent African states during the 1960s impulsed Soyinka's uncompromising activism and outspokenness, in real life and creatively, against neo-colonialism, ethnic nepotism, political partisanship, and corruption. This dangerous, single-handed role and commitment against the first Nigerian civilian government and then the military takeovers that ensued led to his detention and incarceration for almost three years, with no formal charge or sentencing, during the Nigerian civil war against secessionist Biafra, a conflict that he, however, only tried passionately to resolve.

On the other hand, those beginning years of intense political instability and the ones following generated from Soyinka a profusion of creative productivity in a profound effort to give expression to the catastrophic, cataclysmic consequences of the corrupt and corruptive power of postcolonial leadership. Before his detention, he wrote a number of satirical sketches published under the title *Before the Blackout* and produced in a kind of guerilla revues by his new 1964 company, the Orisun Theatre, which replaced the defunct 1960 Masks. In 1965 two radio plays, *The Detainee* and *Camwood on the Leaves*, were produced by the BBC, and *The Road* was given its world premiere production by Joan Littlewood's Theatre Royal on the East End of London as part of the Commonwealth Festival of the Arts. Also within that year was published his first novel, *The Interpreters*, and his first full-length play since *A Dance of the Forests, Kongi's Harvest*, which climaxed his satiric sketches and began his series of plays on corrupt power. Significantly, this play was premiered in Nigeria in front of political dignitaries to apparent satiric effect, especially through an embarrassment he created with the national-anthem-like opening glee of the play. Incidentally, partly because of Soyinka's impeccable portrayal of the character part of Kongi in that first production and the subsequent movie of the play, and partly because of his seemingly ruthless directorial discipline at that period in time, that name has since become attached to its creator as a nickname among his actors, former students, and friends. *Idanre and Other Poems*, which consists of an epic poem and some of the earlier poems published in various journals, completes the works of the period before his solitary confinement.

Inevitably, that very productive period was also one of years in which Soyinka began to gain international focus as an African writer of note. Not only were his strong political views read or heard on the media in Europe and the United States (through, for instance, the London-based Transcription Centre, a Ford Foundation–funded organization specializing in African and Third World political and literary interests), but his creative power was also being acknowledged. In London, after *The Road* at Stratford East, *The Trials of Brother Jero* was produced at Hampstead Theatre Club and *The Lion and the Jewel* at the Royal Court Theatre in 1966, both featuring Femi Euba, a founding member of the 1960 Masks whom Soyinka formally introduced to the stage, and Jumoke Debayo, another Nigerian London-based actress. Among the rave reviews these plays had, Penelope Gilliatt in the *Observer* was quick to compare Soyinka's imaging and power of language to the Irish dramatists, classical and modern, who had for centuries in like manner revitalized the English language. Thus, on account of this initial international acclaim, Soyinka's first brief detention by the civilian police and then the long solitary confinement by the Nigerian military government, from August 1967 to October 1969, did not fail to capture world attention, drawing criticisms from the international press. Well-known writers such as Lillian Hellman, Robert Lowell, Norman Mailer, and William Styron consolidated and sent a strongly written statement to Nigeria protesting its military regime's unconscionable action.

Because of Soyinka's extraordinary will and indefatigably creative fiber, his years of imprisonment seemed to have strengthened rather than obliterated his creativity, even though the writer's life in prison did once or twice come to near extinction—each attempt was brought to light in the outside world just in time before its execution. Rather, every possible writing implement that happened within his bounds in his "sixteen paces by twentythree" cell, materials such as toilet papers, cigarette packets, contraband pencils, and homemade "Soy-ink," became a treasured survival mechanism for his manacled but creative spirit. Consequently, several works, sketched or mentally written during his confinement, focus his state of mind and the catastrophic conditions of his prison experiences. Easily recognized as products of the Nigerian civil war are an autobiographical documentary, *The Man Died*; a book of poems expressing the atrocities of events, *A Shuttle in the Crypt*; a novel based on certain crucial realities of leadership, *Season of Anomy*; and a play, *Madmen and Specialists*, which pessimistically dramatizes the pervasive corruption in structures of power. However, his life continued to be in danger after his release from confinement at the end of the civil war, and he was forced into self-exile first in Britain and then in Ghana. This was primarily because of his controversial exposition of the horrible facts of war and his prison experience in *The Man Died*, which was subsequently banned in Nigeria.

In trying to assess and come to terms with Africa's and indeed the Third

World's all-encompassing sociopolitical problem of postcolonial leadership, Soyinka's creativity has continued to vacillate between the pessimism of frustrated idealism and the optimism of assertive commitment to change; between the hopelessness of the merciless destructive potential of the individual will and the hopefulness of its more compassionate creative counterforce. Such is the complementarity that he has grappled with, in both theory and practice, in his concept of Ogun, the patron god of the creative essence whose combative will forges that creative-destructive will of his human artist-avatars. Soyinka formally formulated his mythopoeic concept within his critical views of African literature and his thoughts on the foundations of Yoruba tragedy in *Myth, Literature, and the African World*. A depth-rich and rather complex work, written during his years in exile (1973–76), it attempted to define more clearly the artistic potential of his principal characters, especially in his later works—characters such as Dionysus in his adaptation of *The Bacchae of Euripides*, Elesin-Oba in *Death and the King's Horseman*, Kamini in *A Play of Giants*, and Shaka in his second epic poem, *Ogun Abibiman*. To further his creative output, his versatility of form and the urgent need to expose the fascism of the second civilian government led Soyinka to explore the resources of film in the sixteen-millimeter *Blues for a Prodigal*, which he wrote and directed in 1984.

Because of the humanism in his extraordinary creative corpus and in his political activism, both of which have striven to shape Africa's postcolonial literature and future, Soyinka has received numerous awards, such as the John Whiting Drama Prize that he shared with Tom Stoppard in 1967 and the Jock Campbell/*New Statesman* award in 1968. He was also the recipient of honorary degrees from various universities, including Yale and Harvard in the United States and Leeds and Montpellier in Europe, all of which were climaxed by his Nobel Prize for Literature in 1986.

Furthermore, Soyinka has been able to combine a substantial academic record with his creative pursuits. Before his imprisonment, he was acting head of the English Department at Lagos University, and afterwards, during his exile between 1973 and 1976, he was visiting professor in the Department of English at the University of Sheffield, the overseas fellow in Churchill College at Cambridge University, and visiting professor at the Institute of African Studies at the University of Ghana in Legon. Coming back to Nigeria after the political controversy over the banned book had subsided, he took up teaching positions at the University of Ife (now Obafemi Awolowo University), first as professor of comparative literature and then as head of the Dramatic Arts Department, a position he finally relinquished in 1983. Since then, he has taken up visiting professorship and lectureship assignments in various universities in Britain and the United States, including his most recent position as visiting scholar at Harvard University and Emory University. Indeed as a man of many parts, he was also, until recently, actively involved as the director of the Road Safety Corps, an organization he created in his unrelenting effort to curb the senseless fatal accidents on Nigerian roads.

Other literary works by Soyinka to date are *Mandela's Earth and Other Poems*, a book of poems dedicated to Nelson Mandela for his rather baffling but instructive survival resilience to years of apartheid's (indeed the world's) oppression, and two sequels to his childhood memoirs in *Ake*—one, *Isara: A Voyage around "Essay,"* focusing on his father's colonial environ, and the other, *Ibadan: The Penkelemes Years*, about the developments that culminated in the political turbulence of the 1960s. There are also three new published plays, *From Zia with Love*, which premiered in Siena, Italy, and *A Scourge of Hyacinths*, first produced by the BBC Radio, in both of which Soyinka uses the now-added epidemic, the drug mafia, to address the parallel perennial problem of Africa's stagnant development, that is, the tyranny and political deadlock since independence from the colonial masters. The third play, *The Beatification of Area Boy*— Soyinka's reaction to the horrifying expulsion by the military regime of a Lagos shanty community—was premiered in Britain at the West Yorkshire Playhouse in Leeds and was brought to the Brooklyn Academy in New York in 1996. His most recent work, whose title speaks for itself, is his impassioned philosophical essay, *The Open Sore of a Continent: A Personal Narrative of the Nigerian Crisis*, published in 1996. At the time of this writing, Soyinka has once again been forced into exile by the present fascist military regime—a genocide-driven power whose daily repressive, insensitive preoccupation is beyond any human logic or imagination. Outside his country, in the United States and Europe, the writer-activist has continued to be the bitterest advocate against this leadership in an effort to expose and oust the persistent arrogance of its reign of terror.

MAJOR WORKS AND THEMES

Soyinka probably would like to be recognized most especially as a dramatist and man of the theatre. He implied that much at the opening of his Nobel Prize acceptance speech (dedicated to Nelson Mandela) as he related back to a moment in the past, in his theatrical beginnings, to inform the crucial political situations of the present world order. This recognition would seem to be justified, considering his gamut of plays, but more especially so because in his drama can be located elements of his other equally important literary forms—the poetry of his language and images, the compelling narrative of the monologues, the descriptive revue-style enactments or flashbacks linking the past with the present, and his manipulation of words and symbols, which are all to be found in most of his plays. Also consistent with the drama are the subjects and themes that are dominant in the fiction and poetry, subjects and themes that encompass the existential man and his sociopolitical world, and that his main characters and Soyinka himself, for that matter, often describe. Within the generality of the subject frame are themes on being, salvation, betrayal, cultural survival, waste, corruption of power, destruction of the human potential, and other topics.

Regarding his microcosmic African world that informs and, directly or indirectly, involves the macrocosmic universe, the cultural man, potentially both creative and destructive, continually pits himself against the inimical forces with which he is inevitably in social contact; it is an encounter in which, in terms of survival, he fatally exposes himself to death, and only his individual combative will can perhaps secure him from emasculation or in fact total extinction. This is the fiber and spirit of which tragic heroes are made, and that also define Soyinka's Ogunian heroes. However, in Soyinka's Yoruba traditional culture, such a total annihilation is not possible since its worldview is based on a cyclical universe consisting of the worlds of the living, the dead, and the unborn, worlds that are viscerally linked with one another through the transitional passage or gulf. It is this unknown abyss, potent with mysteries and knowledge, that man constantly quests to understand, for within it lies man's essences, qualities, and reasons for being. Such is the basis of the Yoruba Ifa-oracle corpus that its priests constantly broach for knowledge about existence on behalf of the individual or the community, god or man. This metaphysical ordering is also the ritual base of plays like *The Swamp Dwellers, The Strong Breed, The Road, The Bacchae of Euripides*, and *Death and the King's Horseman*; the novel *Season of Anomy*; and, of course, the epic poems *Idanre* and *Ogun Abibiman*.

Within this complex network of cultural makeup are variables, and the Yoruba are adept at variables and adaptation. For instance, contact with the white colonial world (or any other world, for that matter) is in itself a positive thing, for it presents other unknown mysteries and knowledge whose numinosity must be probed on the chance that it helps to unveil a metaphysical secret or a better understanding of the Yoruba world and being. History shows that such contacts were welcome among the Yoruba traders and caboceers who were not necessarily threatened by a foreign contact's possible domination of the indigenous culture, and when they were threatened, they fought with subtle strategies. They seemed to be attracted to the contact by its possibility of developing a kind of syncretic knowledge with their culture. At any rate, the kind of identity security implied by the Yoruba attitude may indirectly explain the stubborn proliferation of Yoruba culture and religion in the New World during and after slavery. Also, the Yoruba welcoming spirit, flair for adaptation, and identity assurance may explain Soyinka's innate exhilaration at working within two main cultural mediums to achieve a kind of sumptuous and fertile imagery—such a spirit would seem especially to justify his author's note in *Death and the King's Horseman* downplaying the "colonial thing" as merely incidental to his cultural objective. For it is the Yoruba, or the African by extension, as Soyinka would rather have it, who must ultimately hold himself or herself accountable for any exploitative adaptation of foreign contacts and knowledge, that is, the African as the syncretic "interpreter" of his or her many-sided influences against the sociocultural and political background of the African world. Consequently, the focus of blame and satire essentially underscores the African in political-based works such as *Kongi's Harvest, Opera Wonyosi, Madmen and Specialists, A Play of Giants*, the novel *Season of Anomy*, and the many poems that constitute *A Shuttle in the Crypt*.

In his works, what is made manifest, or what Soyinka dramatizes, is that individual will that tends sometimes to get surfeited with power, destructive power, and that has the potential of annihilating its complementary creative power, just as it devastatingly did in *Madmen and Specialists*, perhaps the only play of its kind and one to which Soyinka himself often refers as his most pessimistic play. For it seems to be the balance of these forces or a quest for it, the balance in the destructive-creative potential, or the destructive presence of one and at least the instinctive view of the creative other in sight, that makes man an "artist" or makes life worth living or dying for. Consequently, the uncertainty of this balance or of its possibility underlies man's conflict with himself, his community, and his society. For instance, in *The Road* the Professor, an artist of metaphysics, albeit a dissembling one, is intoxicated with the symbols of his probings and quest for knowledge about death and restoration, a quest he sometimes falsifies with lucrative and creative manipulation of images (a human erring or trait?). However, in order to feel or receive the much-anticipated restorative process, he has to experience a state of disintegration through a ritual symbol of death—an experience not unlike that realized in the transitional abyss by Ogun ("The Fourth Stage" in *Myth, Literature, and the African World*), who in that sense is the Professor's traditional as opposed to Christian spiritual mentor. In *Death and the King's Horseman*, we see another artist of metaphysics in the nature of Elesin-Oba, who broaches the numinous passage through his art of poetry and dance, an action that is cultural and hereditary and, in that sense, a genuine trait as opposed to the Professor's dissembling character. Yet Elesin too experiences a human failing that limits his individual will, at least until the horror resulting from his failure challenges him to a subsequent action, albeit a little too late.

We realize, however, that as tradition has it, the failing itself has a cosmic and therefore traditional connection. For Ogun, the spiritual god and patron of these artist characters, was similarly limited at a moment in mythic time by his artful capacity to consume palm wine, a wilful act whose generative, superhuman power mistakenly massacred both ally and enemy alike on the battleground. In fact, knowledge of this failing in terms of Ogun may throw some light on a characteristic that sometimes baffles Soyinka's readers about some of his characters. Lone individuals such as Eman in *The Strong Breed*, Daodu in *Kongi's Harvest*, and Ofeyi in *Season of Anomy*, who display a certain individual will and messianic attributes that could force change and save, are nevertheless so incapacitated by many odds that they almost seem to be helplessly (and hopelessly) ineffectual at the end, although some turn round, like Elesin-Oba and Daodu, to effect a last-minute act of will. Some, such as Eman, go on to offer themselves as a sacrificial example, a choice that is, however, pretty much out of their control. The implication here may be deliberate, that these characters, however much they possess an Ogunian temperament, are nevertheless limited by their peculiar weakness within the world in which they live or the situation in which they find themselves, against which their respective combative will is invariably measured. In terms of implicating the world that some of these characters inhabit as consequential to their limitations, Soyinka's life itself comes to mind, with his messianic idealistic attributes that are incapacitated by the status quo. In the sociopolitical conditions of his African world, he has been known to stage several one-man battles against political policies and insensitively corrupt governmental factions, but to no effective avail, the ultimate being his intervention in the Nigerian-Biafran civil war that resulted in his imprisonment for more than two years, exposing him dangerously to near extinction. Such characters would seem to fit the conception of the "dreamer" in a poem of the same title. To fail, however, does not mean to abandon hope, as Soyinka himself often has demonstrated and as he reflected in his Nobel Prize acceptance speech, since the ideas sown by the revolutionary "dreamer" may one day germinate into fruits of change. This perhaps is the ultimate level of sacrifice demanded by Ogun's combative will.

Indeed, the problem with Soyinka's "dreamers" is their seeming ineffectuality and unfulfillment as full-fleshed "Ogun-artists" and therefore their inner conflicts that are caught between the ideal (their ideas) and being human. Asked why he bothers at all with the actions and decisions that obviously expose him dangerously, he explains the tension that occurs at such periods in terms of a raison d'être that certainly recognizes a hopeless pursuit and therefore does not consciously court death, and an unconscious commitment to "profoundly held values" (Gates, interview). The contrasting characteristics assumed by such a conflict are clearly played against one another in *Season of Anomy* in Ofeyi's mind between his values and the Dentist's, and in *The Bacchae of Euripides* between the rational and the irrational in both the characters of Pentheus and Dionysus.

But there are other types of artists in Soyinka's works, artists who potentially display the creative-destructive characteristic but allow their destructive capacity to overshadow their creative instincts. Such are the characters of the Old Man and his son Bero in *Madmen and Specialists*, one an artist of philosophy, and the other that of a kind of mechanistic power, both unconditionally destructive vehicles whose creative potential has been rendered somewhat insensitive and corrupted by their respective intoxication with power. In this play there seems to be no restorative process in sight, and as such it is a very pessimistic play, curiously so from a writer who has always been adamantly optimistic about positive change. Kamini, in *A Play of Giants*, is also such a power-drunk destructive character in a play that is also oppressively pessimistic. However, Soyinka's sympathy for this megalomaniac, perhaps reflective of his bias for the erring but potentially superhuman Ogunian figures, seeps through the satiric strains of the drama. For Kamini's figure is implicitly tableaued against his Western and Eastern as well as, one should add, African counterparts, all complicit and equally guilty terrors roaming loose in the wide world. Undoubtedly Soyinka wishes this play to be a pessimistic replica of *Madmen*, as he implied in his fiftieth-birthday speech, "Reflections of a Member of the Wasted Generation,'' replicated in the introductory notes to the play, which happened at a time when Nigeria faced another political deadlock and was on the verge of another civil war. But the seeming fascination and compassionate softening (if one may call it that) with which Kamini's character is drawn in fact unsparingly directs the satiric lash at the epidemic contagion that affects not one but all levels of interacting political powers and systems.

More important, Soyinka's ''artists'' can be viewed against the political canvas that encompasses various political developments in postcolonial Africa, what Soyinka refers to as ''internal hazards,'' the principal enemy of postindependence Africa. For a dominant theme in his works focuses on the question of leadership and the survival of African traditional culture. Rightly written to celebrate the Nigerian independence in 1960, the award-winning play *A Dance of the Forests*, while it performs the superficial function of celebration with a dance of tribal masks, underscores the assumed freedom with a more crucial concern, the need for unity among the cultic tribes and for a selfless, foresightful builder of nation. These concerns would seem to have some justification in the various events that followed, for instance, the political upheavals that mushroomed with opportunists and wealth hoarders and with power-centered corrupt leadership that facilitated the various changes, from the neocolonial ethnocentric civilian rule to the mindless mechanistic military regime. The history of the past internecine conflicts that devastated past African empires, much of which informed Soyinka's warning in the play, rather than correcting itself, gave new and stronger political reins to the old, feudal characteristics.

With a view to bringing attention to these realities in the 1960s, Soyinka's strategy for corrective measures expresses itself in satire, as situated in several dramatic sketches constituting *Before the Blackout*, and in his first full dissection of African leadership, *Kongi's Harvest*, in which Kongi, a tyrant dictator type, short of being toppled by the powerless indigenous figureheads and the confused, unorganized reforming factions, is nevertheless shocked out of his senses by a victim of his own tyranny. Was Soyinka warning African dictators that their power days were numbered, that they should beware of a revolutionary potential of the people that was not sufficiently ready at that time but would be able to kill once organized? If so, the warning did not seem to cut deeply into any skin; on the other hand, in none of the subsequent plays of Soyinka do we confront any organized force set to accomplish such goals. For instance, in *A Play of Giants* (1984) such a force remains ineffectual and only in the background, and in *From Zia with Love* (1992) the seemingly organized prisoners appear to have merely identified the sociopolitical disease rather than to have attacked it or at least consolidated its cure. In Soyinka's novel, *Season of Anomy* (1973), Ofeyi constructs the ideological potential and the significance of the ''Third Force'' only in his thought process. As for *Opera Wonyosi* (1981), the ''people'' are more inclined to employ the corruption of the state's system to justify their own corrupted action than to eradicate it in general—in the fashion, one might observe, of Brecht's *Threepenny Opera*, one of the plays that inspired

Soyinka's drama. Consequently, *Opera Wonyosi* not only echoes Brecht's ironic materialist thematic line, "Who would not like a peaceable existence? / But this old world is not that kind of place." Its principal character, Macheath, just as Brecht did, also seems to have been favored and exonerated by Soyinka. Nevertheless, the satire, about a totally corrupt society, is noticeable even though it fails to be as biting as it could otherwise have been. Certainly one of satire's employed elements is its ridicule, which, along with its degree of seriousness properly focused, often measures the degree of its satiric bite. *Opera Wonyosi* tends to underplay such a serious edge, just as *Requiem for a Futurologist* does—a light satire on dissembling religious leaders and prophetic charlatans, written in the mode of the Jero plays, but with its satiric edge blunted by its level of witty humor.

Madmen and Specialists, written in 1970, on the other hand, fulfils that satiric intensity and therefore the playwright's objective to dissect, diagnose, and uncompromisingly indict African leadership and its effects on cultural survival— hence Soyinka's own admission of it as his most pessimistic play, correctly so, since the background of the play identifies and recalls the crimes of the Nigerian civil war and its devastating effects on culture, a war that had also buffeted as well as sharpened the creative psyche of the playwright. Thus we have in this play two potentially creative leaders of an African state who, however, have been insanely intoxicated with their attributes, one corrupted by his psychoanalytic restorative philosophy, the other by sociopolitical imperatives that now engage him to proscribe victims of his militaristic espionage as opposed to prescribing curative medicine as a leading researcher and medical doctor. Ritually counterpointing this serious indictment with sardonic ridicule are the mendicants, paradoxically the deformed by-products of war.

The leadership system that Soyinka indicts is a system within systems, Western, African, or Eastern; traditional or modern; religious, spiritual, or scientific; social, political, or economic. For they all have a common factor that is corruptible through time and power; and although new forms appear, they are mere schisms of the old. As such, individualistic assertion and self-expression are doomed, and survival is hopeless. In terms of the recurrent pattern of political deadlock through corrupt, self-serving African leadership, in terms of Soyinka's own prison experiences, in terms of the persistent black-on-black tyranny that sometimes made any honest advocacy against apartheid or racism rather difficult and seemingly cheap, Soyinka saw no discernible bright future for cultural growth.

However, in spite of his correct diagnosis, given the ever-present diabolical stagnancy in the development of African states, it is obvious that Soyinka's overall humanism and faith in the restorative process would not allow him to be definitive with that pessimistic conclusion. The vacillating pattern of hope and despair in his works appears to show a tendency toward pessimism only at desperate moments when he is pushed to the wall and his life and creativity would seem to be hard hit and threatened by certain annihilation. Such a time is probably the present when he remains forced into exile.

In the more fluid narrative medium of *Season of Anomy*, based on dehumanizing experiences that gave *Madmen* its dramatic drive, Soyinka offers a model system of government that is workable in a community called Aiyero, a short form of Aiyetoro (literally, "the progressive world"), the real-life community on which the author bases his model of moral order. The model system could be workable if it survives (the real-life system did not) the infiltrations and corrupting influences of the outside world, more specifically the agents of the capitalistic world of the Cartel. The regenerative peace of Aiyero and its leadership contrasts sharply with the destructive mafiadom of the Cartel, the Africa system that needs to be subverted, but by which method? This is the conflict and dilemma in Ofeyi and implicitly in the author, for they both would rather favor a kind of educative, however limited and limiting, moral discourse and action, as opposed to the brutal although logical violence that the character of the Dentist fervently supports. On second thought the human experience of "man-wrought plagues," in the tragic repetitive pattern of history of the hunter and the hunted and the hunted hunter, compels an inevitable combination of the two approaches, or indeed the hopelessness of either ever achieving complete success. As with most of Soyinka's politically motivated works, the possible closure action is only suggested, but its effectiveness is left hanging, and perhaps justly so, since the future in real life is also harrowingly hanging and seemingly hopeless.

Soyinka's fictional and theatrical world in general seems to be that of men, inhabited by only a few women of substance. Even where the female characters are consciously created strong and appear to possess complex qualities or a potential for heroic action, such as Iriyise in *Season of Anomy*, Simi in *The Interpreters*, Segi in *Kongi's Harvest*, Iyaloja in *Death and the King's Horseman*, or even Rola (Madame Tortoise) in *A Dance of the Forests*, they seem in general to lack the capacity or are not positioned in the role to effect a definitive thematic action on their own. However, the predominance of male characters in these plays is not because of the sometimes misinterpreted attitude of African men by feminist theories, especially in the West, but because of the women's understanding of certain roles of men (in complement to theirs) in culture. For instance, Iyaloja certainly has the power to assert and effect the traditional ethic (demonstrated in the play only after she has exercised wisdom and tolerance to an untraditional indulgence of Elesin-Oba); she is, however, only partially instrumental in the implicit cultural continuity and survival because this is incumbent on Elesin-Oba's family to make manifest. Iriyise, on the other hand, possesses an extraordinary revolutionary impulse, but it is one that she offers and that complements the overall quest for change of Ofeyi; it is one abducted (like Eurydice) or harnessed, which Ofeyi (like Orpheus) journeys into the psyche-underworld to wrestle with and liberate within his central quest.

On the other hand, when women appear in Soyinka's works, they are prominent in terms of essences of womanhood or femininity, in terms of manifestations of the Yoruba goddesses Oya, Yemoja, and Oshun, and as such, in terms of beauty, love, sensual and sensuous power, seminal receptacle for growth, creative matrix, earth mother, market entrepreneur, fertility, man's companion, inspiration, and life giver—all of which express themselves in various fateful and fatal characteristics of humanity. These essences and their manifestations, it seems, are best evoked compellingly through the power of poetry as opposed to drama (apparently Soyinka once attempted but abandoned a drama on "Segi"); consequently, their power seems to thrive in the poetic language of Soyinka's works, and of course in his poems on women (*Idanre and Other Poems*).

In fact, this poetic evocation of women is very much at the heart of Soyinka's mythopoeic language in general, imaging ritual and metaphysical implications for the terrestrial quester and artist into the "chthonic" realm in terms of birth and rebirth, sowing and harvesting, and in terms of seeds, buds, shoots, grains, fibers, earth's colors, initiation, drought, sacrifice, embers, rains, and so on. On the one hand, it is a language that parallels, re-creates, and updates classical myths (Western and African) in heightened modern context and realities, where even common names like Orpheus and Eurydice locate their Yoruba tonal constructs in Ofeyi and Iriyise with an added depth of evocative, cultural significance. On the other hand, it is a language that reminds one of the vast scope of Shakespeare's language, the ritual, narrative, or dramatic arena of which is both complexly local and universal. As such, Soyinka's "mythopoeisis" is also a revitalizing, restorative language in which the medium of the English language is used to explore and transpose the nuances of the African (Yoruba) culture, thus fusing, enriching, transforming, and elevating the English and the Yoruba into a metaphoric unified medium of celebration of the human potential, indeed of the transcendence of postcolonial African literature.

CRITICAL RECEPTION

Earlier in Soyinka's career, his language, although seen as fresh, inventive, and full of promise, was often criticized as obscure, unnecessarily difficult, indulgent, and exotic. A critic of his first professional play, *The Invention* on South Africa's apartheid, found the "humours and the horrors of the situation . . . too easy" and embarrassing, and his images "unusual and unprecise" (*Spectator*, November 6, 1959). Interestingly, the comment strikes a common chord, albeit with different emotional states, with Soyinka's remembered embarrassed reaction: around the same period at the Royal Court, he strongly declined to participate in a workshop performance on account of the limitations of a dramatic text on East Africa's "Mau Mau" created from a Western perspective (Nobel Prize speech). A difference in the two attitudes may be that the English critic reacted to an unfamiliar African text on a subject matter toward which he also probably felt rather indifferent, whereas Soyinka's objection was grounded in his African familiarity with both text and subject matter.

However, the response of the Nigerian critics to the 1960 production of *A*

Dance of the Forests was also not very favorable, summing up the complexities of the play as, like the rather derogatory comment of a Caribbean playwright, Barry Reckord, an example of an "Africana Exotica" (*Transition* November 1963, 7)—which would seem to slight Soyinka's stated theatrical intention of creating "an exciting theatre." In similar vein, an English critic of the 1966 London production of *The Lion and the Jewel* at the Royal Court found the satirical bite of the play "rather too pale and naive for international delectation" (*Plays and Players*, February 1967); but overall, the newspaper reviews of that production were generally very complimentary.

Performances of Soyinka's plays tend to present two distinct critical challenges. In Nigeria, while the acting, as expected, may have been emotionally authentic, the language delivery has been problematic because of its "foreignness," in spite of Soyinka's closeness to Yoruba nuances and images and in spite of the actor's understanding of these cultural subtexts. On the other hand, in the West, especially in North America, it is the mythopoeic images and the nuances that have been difficult to conceive, and that have flawed otherwise technically competent actors, as they have thrown some of the lead actors in his U.S. productions. In either case, Soyinka's language poses demands of orientation, of tuning of the senses to the unfamiliar, a process that has made later critics reevaluate and experience its imaging and power, when well understood and felt, as compelling, provocative, original, and profound. The audiences' and critics' responses to more recent productions have been generally very favorable; an exception is probably a rather politically biased review in the *New York Times* of the otherwise "stunning" Lincoln Center production of *Death and the King's Horseman* in New York (*New York Times* December 11, 1984).

The literary critical arena includes some left-wing radicals, especially among the Nigerian Marxist intellectuals of the 1960s and 1970s. Favoring more the socialist commitments of writers such as Ngũgĩ wa Thiong'o and Sembène Ousmane, and the direct narrative simplicity of writers such as Chinua Achebe, they not only found Soyinka an elitist obscurantist but also considered his vision inconsistent with the revolutionary ideology and materialist historicity of the so-called socialists. Prominently against their argument may be placed Soyinka's own response in a series of articles, notably "Who's Afraid of Elesin-Oba?" in which he attacks and exposes his Marxist critics as pseudocritical, preprogramed neophytes, from whose naïvely upheld intellectual stratum and pontifications he had learnt through experience to dissociate himself. Deconstructing their premises, he legitimizes his position as an artist and reformer whose mythopoeisis is evidently far from opposing reform (since its challenges offer many artistic approaches) but is certainly not bound by any programmatic ideologies. Its essential objective is to re-create realities (cultural or political) through diverse mediums and interrelated forms of art. It is perhaps against this intratextual background of his literary affirmation that Soyinka's artistic development should be measured.

Equally dissociationally trenchant is his position against those who embrace or applaud, and therefore evaluate his work in comparison with the literature of Negritude, which attempts to celebrate the intrinsic beauty that is African and black—a preoccupation and justification that is often far too sentimentally one-sided and narcissistic for Soyinka's constitution. While he critically recognizes the vision of Negritude and the potential of some of its literature, he denounces its contrived and adopted European dialectical premise and Manichean syllogism that formulate the movement's creative ideology (*Myth, Literature, and the African World*). He reiterates, variously in his essays and speeches on the subject, his famous tongue-in-cheek loaded pun on Negritude's self-contemplation of blackness ("negre"), which, like the manifested posture of a "tiger," does not need to proclaim its "tigritude." Overall, his objections would seem to be cast more at the overromantic, sentimental practitioners of Negritude than at the objectives of the movement.

Critics who challenge Soyinka's position tend to use his very weapon of assault to demolish his constructs, questioning the African validity of his own European influences and adoptions, such as the English language and the form and style he uses to create. Soyinka has enthusiastically deflated such objectives, indicating the stupidity of shutting one's creativity from foreign influences that are inevitable anyway, given the present high-tech possibilities of our present mechanized world (Gates, "Interview"). For him, as he has always claimed, the important fact of creativity lies in the re-creative process. In this regard we may observe with him that in his mythopoeisis and what he calls "selective eclecticism," he has tried to imbue the influences with his Africanness, even though his recalcitrant critics, led by Chinweizu and Iheahukuru, have found the mythopoeic process of, for example, *Idanre*, with its god-centered passages, very obscure, unnecessarily made inaccessible, and confusing ("Towards the Decolonization of African Literature").

Given the mutant complexities of the questing mind and the more controlled temper of his recent interviews, it is possible that Soyinka sometimes may have been either misunderstood or taken too seriously, or both. At any rate, whatever his weaknesses as a writer and artist, which a few skeptics have tried to inflame, the recognition of his creative genius nationally and internationally would seem to have clearly overshadowed such shortcomings, perhaps far beyond the artistic or critical imagination of his colleagues. Alongside this merit is his inimitable stature and daring as an uncompromising activist against social injustice, repression, and tyranny, a stature he has maintained to the present day as he engages in exile the totalitarian leadership that terrorizes and is committed to killing any strain of creative impulse. In this regard, he self-demonstrably champions his own concept of the dangerous "chthonic" passage where superior human and god alike, with a combative will, selflessly persists to search for knowledge and direction for the good of all.

BIBLIOGRAPHY

Works by Wole Soyinka

Plays

Before the Blackout. Ibadan, Nigeria: Orisun Acting Editions, 1971.
Camwood on the Leaves. London: Methuen, 1973.
Collected Plays 1 (*A Dance of the Forests, The Swamp Dwellers, The Strong Breed, The Road, The Bacchae of Euripides*). London: Oxford University Press, 1973.
Collected Plays 2 (*The Lion and the Jewel, Kongi's Harvest, The Trials of Brother Jero, Jero's Metamorphosis, Madmen and Specialists*). London: Oxford University Press, 1974.
Death and the King's Horseman. London: Methuen, 1975.
Opera Wonyosi. London: Rex Collings, 1981.
Requiem for a Futurologist. Rex Collings, 1983.
A Play of Giants. London: Methuen, 1984.
From Zia with Love and *A Scourge of Hyacinths*. London: Methuen, 1992.
The Beatification of Area Boy. London: Methuen, 1995.

Film

Blues for a Prodigal. Nigeria: Ewuro Productions, 1984.

Fiction

The Interpreters. London: André Deutsch, 1965.
The Forest of a Thousand Daemons: A Hunter's Saga (translation of *Ogboju Ode Ninu Igbo Irunmole*, by D. O. Fagunwa). London: Nelson, 1968.
Season of Anomy. London: Rex Collings, 1973.

Poetry

Idanre and Other Poems. London: Methuen, 1967.
A Shuttle in the Crypt. London: Collings/Methuen, 1971.
Ogun Abibiman. London and Ibadan: Rex Collings, 1976.
Mandela's Earth. New York: Randon House, 1988.

Nonfiction

The Man Died: Prison Notes of Wole Soyinka. London: Rex Collings, 1972.
Ake: The Years of Childhood. New York: Random House, 1982.
Isara: A Voyage around "Essay." New York: Random House, 1989.
Ibadan: The Penkelemes Years: A Memoir, 1946–1965. London: Methuen, 1994.

Selected Critical Works

"And after the Narcissist?" *African Forum* 1.4 (Spring 1966): 53–64.
"Neo-Tarzanism: The Poetics of Pseudo-Tradition." *Transition* 48 (Accra, Ghana, 1975): 38–44.
Myth, Literature, and the African World. London: Cambridge University Press, 1976.
"Who's Afraid of Elesin-Oba?" University of Ife, Nigeria: Mimeograph, 1977.

The Critic and Society. University of Ife Inaugural Lecture Series, 49 (1980).

"Reflections of a Member of the Wasted Generation." University of Ife Mimeograph, 1984; Introduction to *A Play of Giants* (London: Methuen, 1984).

This Past Must Address Its Present: The 1986 Nobel Lecture. Statements: Occasional Papers of the Phelps-Stokes Fund, no. 3 (March 1988).

The Open Sore of a Continent: A Personal Narrative of the Nigerian Crisis. New York: Oxford University Press, 1996.

Interviews

Euba, Femi. Informal interviews from personal contact.

Gates, Henry L., Jr. "Interview with Wole Soyinka." Monograph. New Haven, CT, December 1984. Excerpts published as "Wole Soyinka: Writing, Africa, and Politics." *New York Times Book Review* June 23, 1985.

Jeyifo, B. "Wole Soyinka: A Transition Interview." *Transition* 42 (Accra, Ghana, 1973): 62–64.

Selected Studies of Wole Soyinka

Chinweizu, Onwuchekwa Jemie, and Madubuike Iheahukwu. "Towards the Decolonization of African Literature." *Transition* 48 (Accra, Ghana, 1975): 29–37, 54, 56–57.

Euba, Femi. *Archetypes, Imprecators, and Victims of Fate: Origins and Developments of Satire in Black Drama*. Westport, CT: Greenwood Press, 1989.

Gates, Henry L., Jr. "Being, the Will, and the Semantics of Death." *Harvard Educational Review* 51.1 (1981): 163–174

Gibbs, James, Keith H. Ketrak, and Henry Louis Gates. *Wole Soyinka: A Bibliography of Primary and Secondary Sources*. Westport, CT: Greenwood Press, 1986.

Jones, Eldred D. *The Writing of Wole Soyinka*. Rev. ed. London: Heinemann, 1983.

July, Robert W. "The Artist Credo: The Political Philosophy of Wole Soyinka." *Journal of Modern African Studies* 19.3 (1981): 477–498.

Maduakor, Obi. *Wole Soyinka: An Introduction to His Writing*. New York and London: Garland Publishing, 1986.

FEMI EUBA

EFUA THEODORA SUTHERLAND (1924–1996)

BIOGRAPHY

Efua Theodora Sutherland, née Efua Theodora Morgue, was born on June 27, 1924, in Cape Coast, Gold Coast. After completing her secondary education at St. Monica's Training College in Ashanti region, she went abroad to Teacher Training College, Homerton College, Cambridge University, where she received her B.A. in education, and also to the School of Oriental and African Studies, University of London. On her return home in 1951, she taught at a couple of institutions, including her alma mater, St. Monica's Training College. She married William Sutherland, an African American, in 1954, and they had three children. Sutherland occupies a unique position as teacher, playwright, and theater director. She was the founding director of experimental theater groups like the Experimental Theatre Players, now the Ghana Drama Studio; founder of the Ghana Society of Writers, now the Writers' Workshop in the Institute of African Studies, University of Ghana, Legon; the creator of Kodzidan (story house), a community theater place in Ekumfi-Atwia; and also founding director of Kusum Agoromba, a touring theater group at the School of Drama, University of Ghana, Legon. Efua Sutherland was also cofounder of *Okyeame*, a literary magazine in Ghana. Her efforts were recognized in the award of an honorary doctorate by the University of Ghana. Outside of the theater, she served as advisor to the president of Ghana, Jerry Rawlings. She was a consultant to the Du Bois Center for African Culture and also worked with the National Commission on Children. Efua Sutherland died in January 1996.

MAJOR WORKS AND THEMES

Efua Sutherland is well known for three of her plays, *Foriwa, Edufa*, and *The Marriage of Anansewa*. Though *Edufa* has been seen as closely related to Euripides' *Alcestis*, her contribution to postcolonial writing lies in the way she draws on both relevant European dramatic forms and the traditional Akan storytelling art called *Anansesem* and its dramatic techniques, including audience participation, to produce plays that are contemporary in theme. This is clearly seen in her play *The Marriage of Anansewa*, whose plot involves Ananse, the trickster in Akan oral narratives, and his scheme as a caring father to secure the most suitable husband for his daughter Anansewa. As in traditional storytelling sessions, the play begins with *mboguo*, musical performances used to break up the narration at intervals or comment on the story. She also makes use of the convention of the Storyteller, an omniscient presence who is involved in the action and who attempts to get the audience to be similarly involved with him. In spite of the humor, there is a serious side to the play. Sutherland sees Ananse as "a kind of Everyman, artistically exaggerated and distorted to serve society as a medium for self-examination." One area for examination is the exploitation of suitors by prospective fathers-in-law like Ananse. Ananse selects four wealthy chiefs, shows them a picture of his marriageable daughter, and without informing each chief that he is competing against three others, invites them to formally ask for his daughter's hand in marriage. Marriage thus becomes a kind of auction where the woman is "sold" to the highest bidder. Another issue raised by this play and the other two major plays is the role of women in contemporary society. Ananse is clearly in charge of the women in this play, including his mother and aunt and Christie Yamoah, a fashionable and educated woman.

In Sutherland's first play, *Foriwa*, women also play a significant role in nation building. Elements of this play first appeared in a short story entitled "New Life in Kyerefaso." Though Foriwa's refusal to marry eligible bachelors is a familiar story in oral prose narratives all over West Africa, Sutherland goes beyond this theme of obeying one's parents in the choice of marriage and looks at a society's outdated ideas about community and society to reinforce the theme of revitalizing traditions to forge a new, more progressive present. The play, which was first performed in Akan in 1962, has been read by some critics as an allegory about the condition of Ghana five years after independence. The line "Kyerefaso has long been asleep," spoken by Labaran, a Hausa from the northern part of the country whose ethnic background contributes to his initial marginalization in society, is supposed to underscore moral apathy and a blind allegiance to tradition that have led to economic problems and physical decay. The Queen Mother has been trying unsuccessfully to awaken the people of Kyerefaso. With the arrival of Labaran, a university graduate who shares the Queen Mother's vision of renewal and revitalization of tradition, and the help of her daughter Foriwa, Kyerefaso is awakened to see that a society cannot be complacent about its past; the rituals and traditions of the past have to find new meaning in the present if society wants to progress. It is significant to note the role played by the Queen Mother and Foriwa in this struggle for change and renewal. Though women are normally considered the caretakers of tradition, these two are not enslaved by it. Foriwa, for example, will not marry just anyone because her friends are married or society expects a woman her age to be married. Indeed, she sees that "the sparkle has died" from the eyes of these friends who are married to unproductive men. Her impending marriage to Labaran will be a "marriage of true minds," two people committed to work together as equals. Their marriage also challenges accepted ethnic barriers. North or south, east or west, people will have to unite to work for the good of their community, and women have a vital role to play in this process.

Sutherland continues to look at women's role in society in her play *Edufa*. Edufa, the "emancipated," Western-educated protagonist, consults a diviner who informs him of his impending death. A selfish individual who is portrayed as having embraced the worst in Western individualism and materialism, he rejects traditional values of family and community and casually asks family members whether they love him well enough to die for him. Without hesitation, his wife Ampoma unselfishly declares her love for him and vicariously accepts his death. Edufa's lack of respect for tradition is also shown in his disrespect of his father Kankam, who attempts to rescue him from the state of moral turpitude. Ampoma, on the other hand, emerges as a morally superior character. Though she lets Edufa know that her approaching death is actually his, she still expresses love for him, symbolized by the gift of waist beads she hangs around his neck. She is also concerned for their children and seeks to be a hospitable hostess to the women who constitute the chorus. She also addresses these women about their role in society. After publicly embracing Edufa, an act that is considered immodest by their society, she speaks against restrictions placed on women: "Women, I hope you don't think me without modesty. . . . The things we would rather encourage lie choking among the weeds of our restrictions. And before we know it, time has eluded us" (146).

Efua Sutherland also places emphasis on passing on oral tradition to children. In her own words, African writers should write for children; thus her work also includes a number of children's plays that are didactic and entertaining.

CRITICAL RECEPTION

On the whole, critics have responded favorably to Sutherland's "journey of discovery" of a modern Ghanaian theater that integrates both Western theatrical devices and traditional drama forms. In his chapter on Sutherland, Lloyd Brown acknowledges her special place in West African theater, with her emphasis on "the integral relationship between the conventions of sexual role-playing and the conventions of dramatic role-playing" (62). Furthermore, he sees her drama, like that of her countrywoman Ama Ata Aidoo, as one that questions and analyzes the meaning of tradition and women's role in society. Michael Etherton, in a segment on Efua Sutherland, praises her as a "playwright of considerable ability and experience" (224). He is impressed by the theatrical qualities of *The Marriage of Anansewa* "with its sophisticated performance devices, inventiveness and skillful integration of music and speech" (224). There are some critics who feel that her emphasis on theatrics undermines theme. Critic Charles Angmor considers the theme of *Edufa* as "specious" and the play on the whole as "not convincing" because of lack of logic and artificial language (181–182).

BIBLIOGRAPHY

Works by Efua Theodora Sutherland

The Roadmakers. Photographs by Willis E. Bell. Accra: Ghana Information Services, 1961.
"Samataase Village." *Okyeame* 1 (1961): 53–58.
"Venture into Theatre." *Okyeame* 1 (1961): 47–48.
Foriwa. Accra: Ghana State Publishing, 1962; Accra: Panther House, 1970.
Playtime in Africa (poems for children). Photographs by Willis E. Bell. New York: Altheneum, 1962.
"You Swore an Oath" (one-act play). *Présence Africaine* 22 (1964): 231–247.
Edufa. London: Longman, 1967; Three Continents, 1970.
Odasani (a play based on *Everyman*). Accra: Anowuo, 1967.
Vulture! Vulture! and Tahinta: Two Rhythm Plays. Accra: Ghana Publishing, 1968.
The Original Bob: The Story of Bob Johnson, Ghana's Ace Comedian. Accra: Anowuo, 1970.
Ananse and the Dwarf Brigade (based on *Alice in Wonderland*). First produced in Cleveland, Karamu House Theatre, February 5, 1971.
"Song of the Fishing Ghosts." Poems: "The Redeemed," "Once upon a Time," "The Dedication," "Song of the Fishing Ghosts." *Messages: Poems from Ghana.* Ed. Kofi Awoonor and G. Adali-Morty. London: Heinemann, 1971.
"Our Songs Are about It." *Ghanaian Writing as Seen by Her Own Writers as Well as by German Authors.* Ed. A. Kayper-Mensah and Horst Wolff. Tübingen: Erdmann, 1972.
Anansegoro: Story-telling Drama in Ghana. Accra: Afram, 1975.
The Marriage of Anansewa. London: Longman, 1975.
Efua Sutherland of Ghana (recording). Washington, D.C.: Voice of America, 1978.
The Voice in the Forest. New York: Philomel, 1983.
The Marriage of Anansewa and Edufa. Harlow, UK: Longman, 1987.
Nyamekye (a collection of speech, drama, and dance and a one-act play).
The Pineapple Child (a fantasy). Unpublished.

Studies of Efua Theodora Sutherland

Amankulor, J. N. "An Interpretation and Analysis of *The Marriage of Anansewa.*" *Okike Educational Supplement* 2 (1980): 149–171.
Angmor, Charles. "Drama in Ghana." *Ghanaian Literatures.* Ed. Richard K. Priebe. Contributions in Afro-American and African Studies 120. New York: Greenwood Press, 1988. 171–186.
Asagba, Austin O. "Storytelling as Experimental Drama: A Study of Efua Sutherland's *The Marriage of Anansewa.*" *Lore and Language* 8.2 (1989): 43–50.

Brown, Lloyd W. *Women Writers in Black Africa*. Westport, Conn: Greenwood Press, 1981. 61–83.

Etherton, Michael. *The Development of African Drama*. New York: Africana Publishing Co., 1982.

Hagan, John C. "Influence of Folklore on *The Marriage of Anansewa*." *Okike* 27–28 (1988): 19–30.

Holloway, Karla F. C. *Moorings and Metaphors: Figures of Culture and Gender in Black Women's Literature*. New Brunswick, NJ: Rutgers University Press, 1992. 142–145, 151–157.

Muhindi, K. "L'apport d'Efua Theodora Sutherland à la dramaturgie contemporaine." *Présence Africaine* 133–134 (1985): 75–85.

Okafor, Chinyere. "J. P. Clark's *The Masquerade* and Efua Sutherland's *Foriwa*." *Commonwealth Essays and Studies* 16.1 (1993): 89–95.

———. "Parallelism versus Influence in African Literature: The Case of Efua Sutherland's *Edufa*." *Kiabara* 3.1 (1980): 113–131.

———. " 'A Woman Is Not a Stone But a Human Being': Vision of Woman in the Plays of Aidoo and Sutherland." *Medium and Message*. Ed. Ernest Emenyonu et al. Calabar, Nigeria: Dept. of English and Literary Studies, University of Calabar, 1981. 165–177.

Pearce, Adetokunbo. "The Didactic Essence of Efua Sutherland's Plays." *Women in African Literature Today* 15 (1987): 71–81.

Talbert, Linda Lee. "Alcestis and Edufa: The Transitional Individual." *World Literature Written in English* 22 (1983): 183–190.

Thies-Torkornoo, Susanne. "Die Rolle der Frau in der afrikanischen Gesellschaft: Eine Betrachtung von Ama Ata Aidoos *Anowa* und Efua T. Sutherlands *Foriwa*." *Matatu* 1 (1987): 53–67.

Utudjian, Elaine Saint-Andre. "Ghana and Nigeria." *Post-Colonial English Drama: Commonwealth Drama since 1960*. New York: St. Martin's Press, 1992.

Wilentz, Gay. *Binding Cultures: Black Women Writers in Africa and the Diaspora*. Bloomington: Indiana University Press, 1992. 20–37.

———. "Writing for the Children: Orature, Tradition, and Community in Efua Sutherland's *Foriwa*." *Research in African Literatures* 19.2 (1988): 182–196.

ADAKU T. ANKUMAH

SONY LABOU TANSI (1947–1995)

BIOGRAPHY

Sony Labou Tansi completed his studies at the École Normale Supérieure in Brazzaville, in the Republic of the Congo. He qualified as a French and English teacher, but after teaching for several years he worked at the Ministry for Scientific Research before devoting his time to writing and to the theater.

Sony Labou Tansi was not only one of the most prolific African writers, but also one of the most strikingly original, creative, and innovative. He published poetry, short stories, plays, and six novels at the prestigious Paris-based publishing house Éditions du Seuil. His work received extensive critical acclaim and several literary prizes, including the Prix Spécial du Festival de la Francophonie in 1979 for *La vie et demie*, the Grand Prix Littéraire de l'Afrique Noire in 1983 for *L'anté-peuple*, and the Palme de la Francophonie in 1985 for *Les sept solitudes de Lorsa Lopez*. He also received a number of awards for his theatrical productions and for his entries in the Best Short Story in the French Language international contest.

From 1979 onwards he directed the Rocadu Zulu Theater Company he had founded; his productions featured regularly beginning in 1983 at the Festival International des Francophonies in Limoges and were also staged in France, as well as in a number of other African and European countries. Sony Labou Tansi became an opposition-party activist in the Mouvement Congolais pour le Développement de la Démocratie Intégrale (MCDDI) as the Congo underwent political transition from a Marxist-Leninist people's republic to a pluralist democracy in 1991. He was elected a deputy for Makélékélé in Brazzaville in 1992; it soon became clear, however, that this involvement in politics exceeded the accepted boundaries of authorial commitment. Sony Labou Tansi's passport was withdrawn by the new government, headed by Pascal Lissouba, and his movements were restricted to his immediate neighborhood. The most disquieting aspect of this was that Sony Labou Tansi was sick at the time and unable to obtain the medical attention he so desperately needed; he died of complications from AIDS on June 14, 1995.

MAJOR WORKS AND THEMES

Sony Labou Tansi's writing relentlessly denounced the oppressive and tyrannical nature of monolithic post-colonial dictatorships. He successfully combined the political and artistic qualities of his writing and refused to subordinate the aesthetic dimension to considerations of content. While political commitment remained an integral part of his work, his primary concern was to ensure that the message articulated did not kill creativity. He sought to break away from his pioneers and to develop his own style, gradually eroding previous literary traditions and distancing himself from earlier anticolonial considerations to turn his attention toward contemporary Africa and examine the challenges it faced as it headed toward the twenty-first century.

One of the most important aspects of this transition was the attempt to redefine the framework of the text and to distance himself from Western literary models, a move characteristic of a number of his contemporaries (Henri Lopes, for example). This particular aspect of his work has led critics to compare his writings to those of certain Latin American authors, in particular the Colombian writer Gabriel García Marquez.

The titles of Sony Labou Tansi's works are particularly revealing and indicative of the radical literary work they designate. Among the most notable, we have *Conscience de tracteur*, *La parenthèse de sang*, *Je soussigné cardiaque*, and *La vie et demie*. These titles compel the reader to ask fundamental questions with regards to their relationship to the text and to reassess their understanding of both the act of reading and of writing. It is thus not surprising that we now find characters who are themselves writers, and through whom Sony Labou Tansi is able to confront a number of issues such as anti-intellectualism, as well as to reflect upon the significance of writing and the expectations of a writer in the post-colonial context.

A further interesting development is the repeated recourse to ''Avertissements'' (Forewords) in several of his novels; these stand as attempts to define his concept of literary writing. *La vie et demie*, for example, is described as ''a fable that sees tomorrow through today's eyes'' (10), while in *Les sept solitudes de Lorsa Lopez*, Sony Labou Tansi writes, ''Art stems from its ability to enable reality to express what it would otherwise have been unable to articulate through its own means or, in any case, that which it ran the risk of consciously passing over in silence'' (11).

The question of language remains of critical concern and importance in discussing post-colonial African literature. Sony Labou Tansi was one of the most outspoken on these issues and always sought to underline the plurality and cultural diversity of those who use the French language today.

Sony Labou Tansi's use of the French language is complex and the result of profound reflection with regard to his historical relationship to it. He claims to "write in French because that is the language in which the people I am a spokesperson for were raped, that is the language in which I myself was raped. I remember my virginity [. . .] I have never had to resort to French, it is the French language which had recourse to me" (see *Equateur*, 30).

Sony Labou Tansi's actual usage of the French language is arguably one of the most original aspects of his work. The radical syntactic and lexical reform has coincided with a modification of traditional narrative linearity. This has manifested itself in the extensive use of neologisms, slang, defiled language, sexual terms, and African and Spanish words. The Congolese author Sylvain Bemba (one of the most important influences in Sony Labou Tansi's literary career) has described some of these practices as "literary recombinations" ("héro" plus "érotique" yields "hérotique") and has described the process as "writing by inventing, and inventing by writing" (*Revue Equateur*, 50). Sony Labou Tansi's use of language is also particularly violent, and he has repeatedly stated that "normal" language would reflect or at least imply a "normal" situation; the extravagance of the political regimes and the horrors perpetrated by a number of post-colonial dictatorships can only be reflected in the extravagance of language. The dismemberment of language and of narrative linearity is thus echoed in the disfigurement of "bodies," and Sony Labou Tansi finds himself compelled to redefine existing language that falls short in describing the present state of affairs.

In the play *La parenthèse de sang*, a tragicomic satire, Sony Labou Tansi depicts the corrupt nature of the military and the arbitrariness of its actions. A group of soldiers descend on the home of the recently deceased Libertashio and proceed to interrogate the mourning family as to his whereabouts. Their mission consists of arresting Libertashio or recovering his remains. The persistent insubordination of officers results in repeated executions; the atmosphere of confusion culminates in a "stagewide" massacre following the news that the "Capitale" has reviewed its policy and is no longer interested in Libertashio.

Another play, *Je soussigné cardiaque*, attacks bureaucracy and the resulting helplessness and powerlessness of the individual in a society whose values have been reduced to power and money. The theme of power dominates *Antoine m'a vendu son destin*, a more recent theatrical production, in which the main protagonist, Antoine, plots to overthrow himself in an attempt to ferret out his enemies. However, when his plan backfires, he ends up behind bars reflecting on his situation. In *Moi, veuve de l'empire*, Sony Labou Tansi denounces, through the reenactment of Julius Caesar's murder, the violence that has become characteristic of contemporary governments.

In his first novel, *La vie et demie*, Sony Labou Tansi takes us to an imaginary country, Katamalanasie, in which we encounter a cannibalistic "Providential

Guide.'' In a gruesome scene, the rebel Martial is literally cut up into pieces, but his spirit refuses to die. His daughter Chaïdana takes on the struggle where he left off and sets out to eliminate one by one the opposition through prostitution and by poisoning them. The tyranny characteristic of some African states is once again the subject of criticism in *L'état honteux*, and with *L'anté-peuple*, Sony Labou Tansi's narrative is no longer anchored in an imaginary setting but rather in contemporary Zaire and Angola. This novel plots the downfall of Dadou, a College Principal, who, like the schoolteacher in *Je soussigné cardiaque*, Mallot, finds himself at one with the corrupt governing authorities. In his fourth novel, *Les sept solitudes de Lorsa Lopez*, Sony Labou Tansi reflects on the role of artistic expression and the ways in which it can compensate for ''history's silence.'' Sony Labou Tansi's framework broadens considerably with *Les yeux du volcan*, but it is now a universal audience that he seeks to warn against the excesses of those who manipulate power; Sony Labou Tansi suggests that people, like the symbolic volcano, will eventually ''erupt.'' *Le commencement des douleurs*, Sony Labou Tansi's last novel, was published posthumously in 1995. The novel continues to expose the repressive nature of postcolonial government authorities, but is a groundbreaking work in that it addresses environmental issues.

CRITICAL RECEPTION

Studies have attempted to formulate a preliminary insight into the postcolonial framework, but have usually failed to identify the idiosyncrasies of the various authors in question (most notably, Séwanou Dabla's *Nouvelles écritures africaines* and Jacques Chevrier's *Littérature nègre*). While revealing similarities between texts and writers, close textual readings highlight instead the remarkable originality of each writer as a constituent part of a rich and diversified literary corpus. Koffi Anyinefa's *Littérature et politique en Afrique noire* stands as the most thorough study of its kind on Sony Labou Tansi. He undertakes close readings of several texts and examines the links between politics and the novel. Jonathan Ngaté's *Francophone African Fiction: Reading a Literary Tradition* includes an excellent analysis of Sony Labou Tansi's novel *L'anté-peuple*. Kenneth W. Harrow's *Thresholds of Change in African Literature: The Emergence of a Tradition* focuses on a number of postcolonial Anglophone and Francophone authors; the last chapter is devoted to Sony Labou Tansi's *La vie et demie*, *Les sept solitudes de Lorsa Lopez*, and *Les yeux du volcan* and situates these novels within the context of post-colonial literary and political discourse.

Sony Labou Tansi's works have received considerable attention in scholarly articles, and reviews of his publications have rarely failed to concur on both the quality and the importance of his work. Bernard Magnier and André Nataf in the review *Notre Librairie* (no. 2, 1982) claimed, ''Upon publication of his first novel, *La Vie et Demie*, Sony Labou Tansi assumed the position of leader which he has not relinquished since.'' Marie-Roger Biloa, in *Jeune Afrique* magazine

(1987), described him "as the most gifted writer of his generation," and Gilles Costaz in *Le Matin* newspaper (no. 3303, October 17–18, 1987) wrote that "one can already say that the Congolese writer Sony Labou Tansi is one of the greatest in the French language today."

Sony Labou Tansi produced works of astounding quality and with remarkable regularity. He assumed a deserved position at the forefront of African literature, and it will be only a matter of time before his work assumes the prominent position it deserves in discourse on post-colonial Africa.

BIBLIOGRAPHY

Works by Sony Labou Tansi

Plays

Conscience de tracteur. Paris: Éditions NEA/CLE, 1979.
Je soussigné cardiaque. Paris: Hatier, 1981.
La parenthèse de sang. Paris: Hatier, 1981.
Antoine m'a vendu son destin. Equateur, no. 1 (October–November 1986).
Moi, veuve de l'empire. Paris: *L'Avant Scène Théâtre*, no. 815 (October 1987).
Le coup de vieux. Paris: Présence Africaine, 1988.
Qui a mangé Madame d'Avoine Bergotha? Paris: Éditions Lansman, 1989.
La résurrection rouge et blanche de Roméo et Juliette. Revue Acteurs, no. 83 (1990).
Une chouette petite vie bien osée. Paris: Éditions Lansman, 1992.

Novels

La vie et demie. Paris: Éditions du Seuil, 1979.
L'état-honteux. Paris: Éditions du Seuil, 1981.
L'anté-peuple. Paris: Éditions du Seuil, 1983.
Les sept solitudes de Lorsa Lopez. Paris: Éditions du Seuil, 1985.
Les yeux du volcan. Paris: Éditions du Seuil, 1988.
Le commencement des douleurs. Paris: Éditions du Seuil, 1995.

Works in Translation

Parentheses of Blood. Trans. Lorraine Alexander Veach. New York: Ubu Repertory Theater Publications, 1985.
The Second Ark. Trans. Richard Miller. New York: Ubu Repertory Theater Publications, 1986.
The Anti-People. Trans. J. A. Underwood. London and New York: Marion Boyars, 1988.

Selected Studies of Sony Labou Tansi

L'Afrique de Sony: Une voix du Congo. Service Image et Initiatives Publicitaires de L'Agip, Agip S.P.A., 1987.
Anyinefa, Koffi. *Littérature et politique en Afrique noire: Socialisme et dictature comme*

thèmes du roman congolais d'expression française. Bayreuth: Bayreuth African Studies 19/20, 1990.

Biloa, Marie-Roger. "Sony Labou Tansi: La passion de la démesure." *Jeune Afrique* 1396 (October 7, 1987): 54–55.

Césaire, Ina. "*La vie et demie.*" *Présence Africaine* 124 (1984): 163–65.

Chemain, Arlette. "Sony Labou Tansi: Affabulation, critique sociale, et ressourcement." *Notre Librairie* 92–93 (1988): 132–33.

Chevrier, Jacques. *Littérature nègre.* Paris: Armand Colin, 1984.

Dabla, Séwanou. *Nouvelles écritures africaines: Romanciers de la seconde génération.* Paris: L'Harmattan, 1986.

Equateur. "*Sony Labou Tansi.*" *Equateur,* no. 1 (October–November 1987).

Hammond, Kenneth. "L'Anté-Peuple." *World Literature Today* 58.2 (Spring 1984): 316.

Harrow, Kenneth W. *Thresholds of Change in African Literature: The Emergence of a Tradition.* Portsmouth, NH: Heinemann, 1994.

Julien, Eileen. "Dominance and Discourse in *La vie et demie,* or How to Do Things with Words." *Research in African Literatures* 20.3 (1989): 371–84.

"Littérature Congolaise." *Notre Librairie* (March–May 1988): 92–93.

Luce, Louise Fiber. "Passages: The Women of Sony Labou Tansi." *French Review* 64.5 (April 1991): 739–46.

Magnier, Bernard, and André Nataf. "Sony Labou Tansi (Congo)." *Notre Librairie* 82 (January–March 1986): 37.

Michelman, Fredric. "*Les Yeux du Volcan.*" *World Literature Today* 64.1 (Winter 1990): 177.

Ngal, Georges. "Les 'tropicalités' de Sony Labou Tansi." *Silex* 23 (1982): 134–43.

Ngaté, Jonathan. *Francophone African Fiction: Reading a Literary Tradition.* Trenton, N.J.: Africa World Press, 1988.

Nkashama, Pius Ngandu. "La mémoire du temps . . . le temps de la mémoire dans le théâtre de Sony Labou Tansi." *Notre Librairie* 102 (July–August 1990): 31–35.

Wisard, François. "Le problème du temps dans *L'Etat honteux* de Sony Labou Tansi." *Cahiers du Cedaf* 1–3 (1987): 83–99.

Yewah, Emmanuel. "Sony Labou Tansi and His Unstable Political Figures." *French Review* 67.1 (October 1993): 93–104.

DOMINIC THOMAS

MOSITI TORONTLE (1964–   )

BIOGRAPHY

Mositi Torontle was born and raised in Francistown, Botswana. She is a graduate of the University of Botswana with a B.A. Hum. (1989) and a teacher by profession. She is actively involved in the Botswana Writers Association, the church, women issues, and singing. *The Victims* was Torontle's first major work. She has published several short stories in the monthly journal *Kutlwano*. She has also published several poems in various journals and books.

MAJOR WORKS AND THEMES

The main theme of *The Victims* is South African labor immigration and its impact on neighboring countries, focusing on Botswana. It is this very theme that foregrounds the intersection of colonialism, apartheid, postindependence, and the daily struggle to survive.

Through focusing on one of the main characters, Mmapula, a struggling woman whose husband is exploited by South Africa's white minority regimes, Torontle amply shows that this is not a unique case, but a regional problem. By recalling past generations and by activating ghosts of the unhappy spirits of the dead, the author further shows that the problem of labor immigration is as old as colonialism in the Southern African region. Almost every family has lost a son, a brother, a husband, or a father who never returned from the South African labor immigration contract with mining industries.

Locating labor immigration within the center of colonialism, the author depicts Mmapula as a survivor and shows that Kgetho, her husband, is not a failure, but a victim of exploitative economic forces beyond his control. All this, however, is achieved without sacrificing the double oppression of gender. Where the whole society has indeed been "shaken, shattered, and scattered," it is the women who stand in the midst of the wreck, trying to piece it all together. Hence the dominance of women characters in this novel not only articulates the author's commitment to feminism, but also depicts the historical situation of Southern Africa. Colonial structures had evicted all men to work in the South African mines, leaving women behind with the responsibility of producing food and raising children. Post-coloniality is, therefore, a reality in *The Victims*. Whether by design or not, the employment of local language, the form of the novel, the multiple identities of the characters, and the reinterpretation of the Bible underline post-colonialism in the novel.

There is an extensive use of Setswana sentences and words, some of which are not translated. This rudely awakens the reader to the fact that this is more than just an English writer. The frequent use of local language may express the inadequacy of the English language to articulate issues specific to the culture. However, this appropriation in itself is an act of resistance against the language of imperialism as well as a denial of the English language as the master language for all people, everywhere.

The attack on English as a language of the oppressor appears twice. First, Dineo, one of the main characters, is depicted as having a psychological problem with switching from Setswana to English. Second, when an old man, who has never learnt or spoken English, begins to speak it under the influence of the Holy Spirit in church, the prophet silences him, declaring, "It was said, they heard them speak their own languages" (61).

While this is a novel, its form cultivates a new way of writing. Torontle employs folktales, singers and songs, letters, poems, stories within stories, and the local naming system to express herself as best as she can. In particular, one finds a sublayer of a song neatly woven into the narrative text. Given that the use of a song is an integral means of expression, protest, resistance, and survival in southern Africa, this is, perhaps, Torontle's most outstanding contribution insofar as integrating local forms of language in the novel is concerned.

One of the impressive ways of integrating local forms of language is the use of the Batswana naming system in the novel. History is not only written in songs of the village, but also in the names of the children. Thus in part 2 Torontle employs an episodic plot to depict how oral colonized societies can write their experiences through naming their children accordingly, such that they bear the history of their people on their bodies. Hence by the time a schoolteacher begins to teach the history of colonialism, labor immigration, and apartheid, the teacher can only activate what is already written in their names and the names of their fathers. Memories are activated, painfully. The history teacher becomes a source of unravelling a text written on the bodies of people. The text written on the body is captured by Thabo, a South African refugee, who says, "I bear on my body the screams and wounds of my dying people" (122).

The author can be highly credited for depicting a post-colonial setting of

Southern Africa with honesty. The multicultural identities of the characters in *The Victims* pronounce it an irreversible post-colonial society. For instance, children listen to their grandmother's tales by the fireside and read *Macbeth* at school; people consult the traditional doctors and go to the hospital; villagers are Christians and venerate their African Ancestors. This is at once a society whose scope has been challenged to a wider vision of life. Thabo, whose experience has been stretched by apartheid violence, dreams of a world where differences of color, gender, political orientation, race, and religion can be celebrated rather than suppressed. He yearns for a day when people can live together without perceiving each other through the eyes of superior and inferior.

Of particular interest also is how the Bible and Christianity are brought to the forefront in two ways: as presented by colonial missionaries to a nonreading society and as reappropriated by it in the postindependence era. The colonial presentation is recalled in the conversion of Kgosi Sechele of Bakwena, who was forced to divorce his wives to be a Christian. Sechele learns to read and discovers that both David and Solomon had many wives, and he immediately questions why the Bakwena people were presented with a different story.

The reappropriation of the Bible, however, is championed by the African Independent Healing churches, which revolted against the discriminative colonial church. Here the Bible has become just another form of local wisdom: it is hardly opened but is retold, dramatized, and mixed with the visions of Batswana Ancestors to encourage people in their struggle to survive. Women in the African Independent Healing church venerate the Dead Ancestors as well as biblical heroines such as Mary Magdalene. Through this creative integration, the patriarchal Christian religion is subverted and supplanted by the inclusive divine worldview of the Batswana people. A feminist discourse is thus neatly woven.

Torontle seizes the historical colonial removal of males from rural areas to develop an astute feminist perspective. Where Jesus would have met the Samaritan woman at the well, a woman meets her. Where male disciples would have been commissioned, a woman is sent to the village. Where a male priest would use prayer for healing, a woman prophet uses prayer, water, and local healing methods.

Women prophets call upon God and the Ancestors to heal the land. Dead women Ancestors are venerated and called upon to protect the endangered men in South African mines; women ghosts direct lost people and sing for their survival all night long; and women try everything to raise up their children and send them to school. One cannot miss that the society is held by these women against all the odds, although this exposes them to double oppression.

In sum, the greatest gift of Torontle's writing is the honesty to confront the multicultural identity of her post-colonial society. She gives no priority to any religion, language, medicine, or history. Rather, she shows how the different cultures have collided and fused, giving birth to something new. No doubt, the struggle of all the characters demonstrates that the answers are not yet found. Nevertheless, the characters are indeed agents of their own situation and circumstances. These characters are neither caught in the regrets of yesterday nor the pains of today, but they continue to map their own destinies as they look beyond the horizons.

CRITICAL RECEPTION

In his review of *The Victims*, Peter Mikwisa, a professor of English literature at the University of Botswana, holds: ''Torontle Mositi's achievement in this novel is the way she has been able to show that although the migrant labor system laid siege to traditional African societies, there were people, like Mmapula and Dineo, who refused to be cowed and destroyed by it. Their heroism and pride as they struggle to be subjects and not pathetic victims of history, are convincing and remain the highlights of the novel for me'' (47).

Although Mikwisa further comments that *The Victims* ''is the first novel by the author who is better known as a poet,'' Torontle is largely an oral poet whose collection of poetry is largely unpublished. In Botswana, where two international publishing houses monopolize the publishing and reading market, which primarily consists of students, the rise of local English writers is often suppressed. Because these houses bring their own published English books, they are hardly eager to publish local writers. English writers, more often than not, have had to sit on their works or self-publish. This has had both negative and positive effects. Negatively, the classics of former colonizers continue to be the main texts of the students; that is, the colonization of the mind still grinds on. Positively, writing in Setswana has been greatly encouraged and is indeed very lively. Since the international publishing houses cannot bring any outside books written in Setswana, the latter have fared much better in getting published.

To return to Torontle's poetry, I find post-coloniality and feminist concerns evident in two of her few published poems, ''Africa'' and ''On Board.'' The former, being one of her earliest poems, largely reflects the sentiments of the struggle for independence in Africa. Torontle likens Africa to a maiden whose virginity has been violated through rape, and a mother whose breasts have been sucked dry—too dry to feed the children she bears. Notable here is that Torontle's concerns focus on the struggle against colonialism rather than gender oppression. She even uses the image of a physically abused woman to describe Africa, an image that is a party to naturalizing the oppression of women.

Yet in one of her latest poem, ''On Board,'' Torontle seems to have come into direct confrontation with her social location of being a ''doubly colonized subject.'' The latter largely reflects the postindependence era, when African women had come to a rude awakening that despite their active participation in the armed struggle against imperialism, they remained patriarchally colonized by their male counterparts. Torontle amply captures this awakening, calling upon her women readers to get on board and make journeys to a different plane of post-colonialism. She explicitly expresses a feminist ecstatic intention of taking off on women's own self-determination as well as to live the dream of freedom against those who have refused to grant them passports.

The Victims, published after both of these poems, addresses the subject of double colonization more forcefully, with a constant replay of patriarchal versus colonial oppression. Mmapula is shown to be oppressed because of her gender, but colonial oppression also affects Kgetho and Tom, who are both alienated from their homes by the South African apartheid regime. In Torontle's constant reevaluation of colonial versus patriarchal oppression, I believe that we get some of the much-needed work in theorizing double colonization.

To conclude, despite the persisting power of former colonizing powers to control what can be written, published, and read, Torontle's work indicates that post-colonial subjects still insist on articulating their discourse of decolonization. Whereas Torontle writes from a position of a historically colonized subject, her gender concerns clearly show that African women writers are already a long way into addressing the issue of double colonization in the post-colonial space.

BIBLIOGRAPHY

Works by Mositi Torontle

"Africa." *Kutlwano* 27 (1989): 34–35.
"No Longer at Ease." *Marang* (University of Botswana English-language journal), (1991): 53.
"Shrouded." *Mokwadi* (University of Botswana writers' workshop journal), (1992): 39.
"On Board." *Songs, Screams, and Pleas*. Gaborone: Mmegi Publishing House, 1993: 8.
The Victims. Gaborone: Botsalano Press, 1993.

Studies of Mositi Torontle

Mikwisa, Peter. Review of *The Victims*. Gaborone: *Mmegi* August 28, 1994: 47.

MUSA W. DUBE

AMOS TUTUOLA (1920–   )

BIOGRAPHY

Amos Tutuola was born to Christian parents in Abeokuta, Nigeria, a cocoa-growing region in southwestern Nigeria. These facts have colored much of his life. His father's income from the cocoa crop was highly erratic. An uncle paid for Amos's tuition at a Salvation Army school. Though the child initially revealed no distinctive scholarly aptitude, his mother arranged for the boy to work as a live-in houseboy for a government clerk in order to ensure that his tuition at an Anglican school was covered by his employer. The subject with which the young Tutuola most demonstrated fascination was the folklore of the citizens of Abeokuta, a region strongly marked by syncretisms of traditional Yoruba and contemporary Christian beliefs.

Upon his father's death in 1939, and without any prospect of a patron to finance his further formal education, Tutuola began trying a number of vocations that all met with disappointment. These included farming, blacksmithing, and messengering for the Nigerian Department of Labor. In spite of passing from one inappropriate post to another, he completed his first full-length book, *The Palm-Wine Drinkard*, in 1946. He married Victoria Alake the following year, and the pair have parented three children. The international success of *The Palm-Wine Drinkard*, published by Faber and Faber and reviewed by Dylan Thomas, was followed by the publication of three other novels during the 1950s, *My Life in a Bush of Ghosts, Simbi and the Satyr of the Dark Jungle*, and *The Brave African Huntress*. These additional publications did nothing to further Tutuola's job opportunities, and he worked as a storekeeper for the Nigerian Broadcasting Corporation throughout many of his most productive years as a writer. Only since 1979 has he found occasional employment commensurate with his talents, being a research fellow at the University of Ife and an associate of the International Writing Program at the University of Iowa. He currently resides in Ibadan, Nigeria.

MAJOR WORKS AND THEMES

There is a remarkable consistency of form throughout Tutuola's books. His books belong clearly to that genre identified by critic Northrop Frye in *Anatomy of Criticism* as "the romance mode of fiction." Romances spotlight a human hero who must engage in a quest, often spiritual and psychological, in order to unearth a core identity. This quest often entails a lengthy and complex journey to another world, often an underworld, where the hero's courage and ingenuity are tested through encounters with supernatural beings and/or humans with miraculous powers. As a result of such encounters, the hero's character is fundamentally transformed, and the adventurer's return home marks the beginning of a new mode of enlightened being for the hero.

The fittingness of this "romance" pattern as a description of Tutuola's art becomes obvious as his plots are summarized. *The Palm-Wine Drinkard* spotlights the quest of a character who enters the underworld ("Deads' Town") in search of his wine tapster. He undergoes numerous physical and mental trials and tribulations at the hands of a demonic fish and bird, a monstrous infant (which grows out of his wife's thumb), and the ghostly madmen of "Unreturnable-Heaven's Town." The consequence of having successfully endured confrontations with these supernatural spirits is a self-knowledge gained by the hero, an awareness catalyzed by an encounter with a beneficent being, "Faithful-Mother." This newly discovered wisdom permits him to instruct his fellow villagers about offering a sacrifice that stops a serious famine.

The hero of *My Life in a Bush of Ghosts* encounters an equally fantastic array of otherworldly beings in an underworld odyssey, including the author's first monster combining the characteristics of a Yoruba folkloric figure with an image of modern Western technology, "the Television-handed Ghostess." There is also an explicit reference to the positive role Christianity plays for ghosts in the underworld, and the suggestion that the hero's Christian faith helped him complete his underworld quest through "the bad bush" and become a person without fear of his mortality.

Simbi and the Satyr of the Dark Jungle and *The Brave African Huntress* continue the theme of the quest romance, substituting heroic women for the adventuresome males found in Tutuola's earlier tales. Another small deviation from Tutuola's earlier books occurs when the heroine of *Simbi and the Satyr of the Dark Jungle* chooses to begin her quest as the result of curiosity about poverty and pain. Heroic figures in the author's earlier books began their quests either through greed (*The Palm-Wine Drinkard*) or accident (*My Life in a Bush of Ghosts*).

While episodes of a hero's terrifying encounters with strange beings in an otherworldly setting occur in *Feather Woman of the Jungle* and *Ajaiyi and His Inherited Poverty*, the object of the heroic quest shifts. The heroes of these books seek wealth rather than spiritual or psychological knowledge. The hero of *Feather Woman of the Jungle* concludes his quest with enormous reserves of gold. A different twist occurs in *Ajaiyi and His Inherited Poverty*, where the hero returns home with a new appreciation of nonmaterial "wealth" along with the awareness that material poverty need no longer be his inescapable fate.

The Witch-Herbalist of the Remote Town finds a hero undergoing his underworld quest in search of a fertility potion for his barren wife from the all-powerful Witch-Herbalist, a direct descendant of the "Faithful-Mother" of *The Palm-Wine Drinkard* and one of many beneficent female spirits in the author's imagination. As a result of the hero not following the instructions about the potion exactly as offered by the Witch-Herbalist, the hero becomes pregnant coterminously with his spouse and undergoes adventures with a water goddess before reentering a conventional male form.

All of Tutuola's books present an oddly timeless world where ancient Yoruba folkloric and religious realities simultaneously exist with Western Christian and scientific realities. The author places modern weapons and electronic devices in underworlds inhabited by eternal ghosts. While no explicit references are given by the author to major events in Africa's colonial and postcolonial history, it is easy to be struck by how the persistently repeated motif of "trial by fire," a passage heroically won by demonstrations of courage, ingenuity, faith, and intensively focused and lengthy labor, speaks to the present political, social, and economic realities of postcolonial Africa.

CRITICAL RECEPTION

Most critics, whether affirming or deriding the value of the author's works, have taken a similar approach to that of Harold R. Collins, the author of the only full-length critical study of Tutuola's art. Collins focuses largely upon Tutuola's imaginative use of the English language and equally imaginative invention of supernatural characters. Collins goes to considerable lengths in presenting the author as a conscious craftsman whose unconventional English syntax, spelling, and punctuation represent an artful technique that assists readers in comprehending the author's imaginary worlds where all conventional rules of order are suspended. This defense of Tutuola's style is a response to the extremely negative tone about Tutuola's "illiteracy" assumed by the majority of Nigeria's literary critics upon the publication of *The Palm-Wine Drinkard*. Perhaps the most detailed linguistic analysis of Tutuola's style is given by A. Afolayan, who identifies Tutuola's language as "Yoruba English," a language possessing Yoruba's deep grammar that nevertheless has many of the surface features of conventional English grammar (Heywood, 50). Agreeing with Collins and Afolayan, critic Oladele Taiwo further defines Tutuola's literary style as one bridging the traditionally oral Yoruba storytelling style with a Western-influenced African literary style. Any critical analysis of Tutuola's style invites considerable speculation since Tutuola's publishers have yet to make public all of the editorial changes introduced by editors who might have been offended by the irregularities of the author's "Yoruba English." Geoffrey Parrinder's introduction to the Grove Press edition of *My Life in a Bush of Ghosts* offers the cryptic statement that "the book has been edited to remove the grosser mistakes, clear up some ambiguities, and curtail some repetition." Since Tutuola is a master of a literary style that valorizes ambiguous characterization and plotting, not to mention repetition, all key characteristics of the ancient Yoruba oral tradition, one wonders how seriously the reader can believe Parrinder's claim that these editorial changes left "the original flavor of the style" intact.

The supernatural pantheon of characters in Tutuola's books—demonic animals and suprahuman and cosmic beings—has invited commentary emphasizing the roots of Tutuola's creativity in traditional Yoruba folklore and in the fables of Yoruba author D. O. Fagunwa, whose *The Forest of a Thousand Demons* bears some resemblance in plot and characters to *My Life in a Bush of Ghosts*. John Coates follows the lead of Collins in reading Tutuola's characters as the archetypes articulated in the psychology of Carl Jung. This critical approach suggests that Tutuola wrote allegories in which fundamental human personality types and emotions were personified. Support for this perspective is offered by the author, who acknowledges the major influence of John Bunyan's *The Pilgrim's Progress* upon his writing (where characters are named "Despair" and "Faithful"). A further confirmation of this Jungian interpretation might be offered by Tutuola's *Pauper, Brawler, and Slanderer*, curiously the only Tutuola book in which the heroic characters undergo no spiritual or psychological transformation as a consequence of a quest. The book's title defines three characters who are less human than pure personality traits personified.

The boldest departure from these dominant directions of stylistic and characterological analysis comes from the Nigerian novelist Chinua Achebe. Rather than focusing upon Tutuola's unconventional English, or upon psychological and spiritual meanings of his ghostly characters, Achebe suggests reading Tutuola as a moralist addressing the economic realities of postcolonial Africa. Without directly addressing the author's professed Christianity, Achebe suggests that *The Palm-Wine Drinkard* be read in light of "the social and ethical question being posed. 'What happens when a man immerses himself in pleasure to the exclusion of all work?'" (102). Achebe writes that Tutuola is "the most moralistic of all Nigerian writers" because Tutuola is concerned that Africans live by a viable work ethic and refuse to become manic "consumers" along lines supported by commercial and political interests in Europe and the United States. Achebe further suggests that Tutuola views poverty as a painful yet vital opportunity for self-knowledge. Contradicting Achebe's interpretation is Adrian Roscoe, who considers Tutuola an "uncommitted" writer, uninterested in material Africa.

BIBLIOGRAPHY

Works by Amos Tutuola

The Palm-Wine Drinkard and His Dead Palm-Wine Tapster in the Deads' Town. London: Faber, 1952; New York: Grove Press, 1953.

My Life in a Bush of Ghosts. New York: Grove Press, 1954. Reprint. London: Faber, 1978.

Simbi and the Satyr of the Dark Jungle. London: Faber, 1955.

The Brave African Huntress. Illustrated by Ben Enwonwu. New York: Grove Press, 1958.

Feather Woman of the Jungle. London: Faber, 1962.

Ajaiyi and His Inherited Poverty. London: Faber, 1967.

The Witch-Herbalist of the Remote Town. London: Faber, 1981.

The Wild Hunter in the Bush of Ghosts (facsimile of manuscript). Edited with an introduction by Bernth Lindfors. Washington, D.C.: Three Continents Press, 1982.

Pauper, Brawler, and Slanderer. London: Faber, 1987.

The Village Witch Doctor and Other Stories. London: Faber, 1990.

Selected Studies of Amos Tutuola

Achebe, Chinua. *Hope and Impediments*. Garden City, N.Y.: Doubleday, 1988.

Afolayan, A. "Language and Sources of Amos Tutuola." Ed. Christopher Haywood. *Perspectives on African Literature*, 49–63.

Coates, John. "The Inward Journey of the Palm-wine Drinkard." *African Literature Today* 11 (1980): 122–29.

Collins, Harold R. *Amos Tutuola*. New York: Twayne Publishers, 1969.

Heywood, Christopher, ed. *Perspectives on African Literature: Selections from the Proceedings of the Conference on African Literature Held at the University of Ife, 1968*. New York: African Publishing Corporation, 1971.

Lindfors, Bernth, ed. *Critical Perspectives on Amos Tutuola*. Washington, D.C.: Three Continents Press, 1975.

Moore, Gerald. *Seven African Writers*. New York: Oxford University Press, 1962.

Obiechina, Emmanuel R. *Language and Theme: Essays in African Literature*. Washington, D.C.: Howard University Press, 1970.

Roscoe, Andrian A. *Mother Is Gold: A Study in West African Literature*. New York: Cambridge University Press, 1971.

Taiwo, Oladele. *Culture and the Nigerian Novel*. New York: St. Martin's Press, 1976.

NORMAN WEINSTEIN

SELECTED BIBLIOGRAPHY

Abdalla, Raqiya Haji Dualeh. *Sisters in Affliction: Circumcision and Infibulation of Women in Africa*. London: Zed Press, 1982.

Abrahams, Cecil, ed. *The Tragic Life: Bessie Head and Literature in Southern Africa*. Trenton, N.J.: Africa World Press, 1990.

Abrash, Barbara, ed. *Black African Literature in English since 1952: Works and Criticism*. New York: Johnson Reprint Corp., 1967.

Achebe, Chinua. *Hopes and Impediments*. London: Heinemann, 1988.

Afshar, Haleh. "GHANA: To Be a Woman." *Sisterhood Is Global*. Ed. Robin Morgan. New York: Anchor Press/Doubleday, 1984. 258–265.

———. *Women, State, and Ideology: Studies from African and Asia*. Basingstoke, Hampshire: Macmillan, 1987.

Allen, Jeffner. *The Thinking Muse: Feminism and Modern French Philosophy*. Bloomington: Indiana University Press, 1989.

Althusser, Louis. *Lenin and Philosophy*. Translated from the French by Ben Brewster. New York: Monthly Review Press, 1971.

Amadiume, Ifi. *Male Daughters, Female Husbands: Gender and Sex in an African Society*. London: Zed Books, 1987.

Angoff, Charles, and John Povey, eds. *African Writing Today*. New York: Manyland Books, 1969.

Anozie, Sunday O. *Structural Models and African Poetics: Towards a Pragmatic Theory of Literature*. London: Routledge and Kegan Paul, 1981.

Anzaldúa, Gloria. *Borderlands/La Frontera: The New Mestiza*. San Francisco: Spinsters/Aunt Lute, 1987.

Appiah, Kwame Anthony. *In My Father's House: Africa in the Philosophy of Culture*. New York: Oxford University Press, 1992.

———. "Structures on Structures: The Prospects for a Structuralist Poetics of African Fiction." In Henry Gates, ed. *Black Literature and Literary Theory*. New York: Routledge. 127–150.

Ashcroft, Bill, Gareth Griffiths, and Helen Tiffin. *The Empire Writes Back: Theory and Practice in Post-colonial Literatures*. London: Routledge, 1989.

Auffret, Séverine. *Des couteaux contre des femmes*. Paris: Des femmes, 1982.

Bâ, Amadou Hampaté. *Vie et enseignement de Tierno Bokar: La sage de Bandiagara*. Paris: Seuil, 1980.

Badran, Margot, and Miriam Cooke, eds. *Opening the Gates: A Century of Arab Feminist Writing*. Bloomington: Indiana University Press, 1990.

Baker, Houston A., Jr., ed. *Reading Black: Essays in the Criticism of African, Caribbean, and Black American Literature*. Ithaca, N.Y.: Cornell University Press, 1976.

Banham, Martin, Errol Hill, and George Woodyard, eds. *The Cambridge Guide to African and Caribbean Theatre*. Cambridge: Cambridge University Press, 1994.

Barber, Karin. "African-Language Literature and Postcolonial Criticism." *Research in African Literatures* 26.4 (Winter 1995): 3–30.

Bay, Edna G., ed. *Women and Work in Africa*. Boulder, Colo.: Westview Press, 1982.

Bell, Roseann P., Bettye J. Parker, and Beverly Guy-Sheftall, eds. *Sturdy Black Bridges: Visions of Black Women in Literature*. Garden City, N.Y.: Anchor Press Doubleday, 1979.

Beneria, Lourdes, eds. *The Sexual Division of Labor in Rural Societies*. New York: Praeger, 1982.

Bernstein, Hilda Watts. *For Their Triumphs and for Their Tears: Women in Apartheid South Africa*. Rev. and enl. ed. London: International Defence and Aid Fund for Southern Africa, 1985.

Berrian, Brenda. *Bibliography of African Women Writers and Journalists*. Washington, D.C.: Three Continents Press, 1985.

Bettelheim, Charles. *Planification et croissance accélérée*. Paris: FM/Petite Collection Maspero, 1967.

Bhabha, Homi. *The Location of Culture*. London: Routledge, 1994.

———, ed. *Nation and Narration*. London: Routledge, 1990.

———. "Remembering Fanon: Self, Psyche, and the Colonial Condition." *Colonial Discourse and Postcolonial Theory: A Reader*. Ed. Patrick Williams and Laura Chrisman. New York: Columbia University Press, 1994. 112–123. Originally appeared as Foreword to Frantz Fanon's *Black Skin, White Masks*. London: Pluto Press, 1986. vii–xxi.

Blair, Dorothy. *African Literature in French*. Cambridge: Cambridge University Press, 1976.

Borgomano, Madeleine. *Voix et visages de femmes, dans les livres écrits par des femmes en Afrique francophone*. Abidjan: CEDA, 1989.

Boserup, Ester. *Woman's Role in Economic Development*. New York: St. Martin's Press, 1970.

Bowie, Fiona, Deborah Kirkwood, and Shirley Andener. *Women and Missions: Past and Present: Anthropological and Historical Perceptions*. Providence, R.I.: Berg, 1993.

Breckenridge, Carol A., and Peter van der Veer, eds. *Orientalism and the Postcolonial Predicament*. Philadelphia: University of Pennsylvania Press, 1993.

Brown, Ella. "Reactions to Western Values as Reflected in African Novels." *Phylon: The Atlanta University Review of Race and Culture* 48.3 (Fall 1987): 216–228.

Brown, Lloyd W. *Women Writers in Black Africa*. Westport, Conn.: Greenwood Press, 1981.

Brown, Susan, Isabel Hofmeyr, and Susan Rosenberg, eds. *Lip from Southern African Women*. Johannesburg: Ravan Press, 1983.

Bruner, Charlotte, ed. *The Heinemann Book of African Women's Writing*. Oxford: Heinemann, 1983.

———, ed. *Unwinding Threads: Writing by Women in Africa*. London: Heinemann, 1983.

Bullwinkle, Davis. *African Women, a General Bibliography, 1976–1985*. New York: Greenwood Press, 1989.

———. *Women of Northern, Western, and Central Africa: A Bibliography, 1976–1985*. New York: Greenwood Press, 1989.

Burness, Don. *Wanasema: Conversations with African Writers*. Athens: Ohio University Monographs in International Studies, Africa Series, no. 46, 1985.

Busia, Abena. "But Caliban and Ariel Are Still Both Male: On African Colonial Discourse and the Unvoiced Female." In *Crisscrossing Boundaries in African Literature*. Ed. Kenneth W. Harrow, Jonathan Ngate, and Clarisse Zimra. Annual Selected Papers of the ALA, 1986/12. Washington, D.C.: Three Continents Press, African Literature Association, 1991. 129–140.

———. *Daughters of Africa: An International Anthology of Words and Writings by Women of African Descent from the Ancient Egyptian to the Present*. New York: Pantheon Books, 1992.

Butler, Judith. *Gender Trouble: Feminism and the Subversion of Identity*. London: Routledge, 1990.

Cabral, Amilcar. *Return to the Source*. New York: Monthly Review Press, 1973.

Callaway, Barbara, and Lucy Creevey. *The Heritage of Islam: Women, Religion, and Politics in West Africa*. Boulder, Colo.: Lynne Rienner, 1994.

Carby, Hazel. *Reconstructing Womanhood: The Emergence of the Afro-American Woman Novelist*. New York: Oxford University Press, 1987.

Césaire, Aimé. *Discourse on Colonialism*. New York: Monthly Review Press, 1972.

Cham, Mbye B. "Contemporary Society and the Female Imagination: A Study of the Novels of Mariama Ba." *African Literature Today* 15 (1987): 89–101.

———. "The Female Condition in Africa: A Literary Exploration by Mariama Bâ." *Current Bibliography on African Affairs* 17.1 (1984–85): 29–52.

Chaudhury, Kanishka. "Theoretical Confrontations in the Study of Postcolonial Literature." *Modern Fiction Studies* 37.3 (1991): 610–612.

Christian, Barbara. "The Race for Theory." *Cultural Critique* 6 (Spring 1987): 51–63.

Cixous, Hélène. *"Coming to Writing" and Other Essays*. Cambridge, Mass.: Harvard University Press, 1991.

Clausen, Jeanette, and Sara Friedrichsmeyer, eds. *Women in German Yearbook 9: Feminist Studies in German Literature and Culture*. Lincoln: University of Nebraska Press, 1992.

Clayton, Cherry. "White Writing and Postcolonial Politics." *Ariel* 25.4 (October 1994): 153–167.

Collins, Patricia Hill. *Black Feminist Thought: Knowledge, Consciousness, and the Politics of Empowerment*. London: Routledge, 1991.

Coquery-Vidrovitch, Catherine. *L'histoire des femmes en Afrique*. Paris: L'Harmattan, 1987.

Cummings, Mary Lou. *Surviving without Romance: African Women Tell Their Stories*. Scottdale, Pa.: Herald Press, 1991.

Cutrufelli, Maria Rosa. *Women of Africa: Roots of Oppression*. London: Zed Press, 1983.

Daly, Mary. *Gyn/Ecology: The Metaethics of Radical Feminism*. Boston: Beacon Press, 1978.

Dathorne, O. R. *African Literature in the Twentieth Century*. Minneapolis: University of Minnesota Press, 1975.

Davies, Carole Boyce. *Black Women, Writing, and Identity: Migrations of the Subject*. London: Routledge, 1994.

————. "Private Selves and Public Spheres: Autobiography and the African Woman Writer." In Kenneth Harrow, Jonathan Ngate, Clarisse Zimra, eds., *Crisscrossing Boundaries in African Literature*. Annual Selected Papers of the ALA, 1986/12. 109–127.

Davies, Carole Boyce, and Elaine Savory Fido. "African Women Writers. Toward a Literary History." *A History of Twentieth-Century of African Literatures* Ed. Oyekan Owomoyela. Lincoln: University of Nebraska Press, 1993. 311–346.

Davies, Carole Boyce, and Anne Graves, Adams eds. *Ngambika: Studies of Women in African Literature*. Trenton, N.J.: Africa World Press, 1986.

Davies, Carole Boyce, and Molara Ogundipe-Leslie, eds. *Black Women's Diasporas: Writing New Worlds*. London: Pluto Press, 1994.

de Lauretis, Teresa. *Feminist Studies/Critical Studies*. Bloomington: Indiana University Press, 1986.

Deniel, Raymond. *Femmes des villes africaines*. Abidjan: Inades, 1985.

Desalmand, Paul. *L'emancipation de la femme en Afrique et dans le monde: Textes et documents*. Abidjan: Les Nouvelles éditions africaines, 1981.

Dieng, M. "Code de la famille du Sénégal: Les dessous anti-islamiques." *Le Militant Musulman* 5 (1994): 13–14.

Diop, Abdoulaye Bara. *La société Wolof: Tradition et changement: Les systèmes d'inégalité et de domination*. Dakar: Karthala, 1981.

Diop, Cheikh Anta. *L'Afrique noire précoloniale*. Paris: Présence Africaine, 1960.

Diop, Fatimatou Zahra, and Fatoumata Sow. "Le code de la famille: Une arme pour la libération des femmes." *Fippu* 2 (1989): 8–9.

Dolan, Catherine S. "Gender and the Colonial Mission in Africa." Thesis (M.A.) State University of New York at Binghamton, Anthropology Department, 1992.

Egejuru, Phanuel. "Who Is the Audience of Modern African Literature?" *Obsidian: Black Literature in Review* 5.1–2 (1979): 53.

Ekong, Julia Meryl. *Bridewealth, Women, and Reproduction in Sub-Saharan Africa: A Theoretical Overview*. Bonn: Holos, 1992.

Fanon, Frantz. *Black Skin, White Masks*. New York: Grove Press, 1967.

————. *Toward the African Revolution* New York: Grove Press, 1988 (c 1967).

————. *The Wretched of the Earth*. New York: Grove Press, 1968 (c 1963).

Fetzer, Glenn W. "Women's Search for Voice and the Problem of Knowing in the Novels of Mariama Bâ." *College Language Association Journal* 35.1 (September 1991): 31–41.

Flewellen, Elinor C. "Assertiveness vs. Submissiveness in Selected Works by African Women Writers." *Ba Shiru: A Journal of African Languages and Literature* 12.2 (1985): 3–18.

Foucault, Michel. *The History of Sexuality: Volume 1: An Introduction*. Translated from the French by Robert Hurley. New York: Pantheon, 1978.

———. *The Use of Pleasure: Volume 2 of The History of Sexuality*. Translated from the French by Robert Hurley. New York: Pantheon Books, 1985.

Freire, Paulo. *Pedagogy of the Oppressed*. New York: Herder and Herder, 1970.

Gates, Henry Louis, Jr., ed. *Black Literature and Literary Theory*. New York: Methuen, 1984.

———. "Literature, Theory, and Commitment." In *Crisscrossing Boundaries in African Literature*. Ed. Kenneth W. Harrow, Jonathan Ngate, and Clarisse Zimra. Annual Selected papers of the ALA, 1986/12. Washington, D.C.: Three Continents Press, African Literature Association, 1991. 59–64.

———. *The Signifying Monkey: A Theory of African-American Literary Criticism*. Oxford: Oxford University Press, 1988.

Gérard, Albert S. *African Language Literatures: An Introduction to the Literary History of Sub-Saharan Africa*. Washington, D.C.: Three Continents Press, 1981.

Goodwin, June. *Cry Amandla! South African Women and the Question of Power*. New York: Africana Pub. Co., 1984.

Gover, Daniel. "The Fairytale and the Nightmare." *The Tragic Life: Bessie Head and Literature in Southern Africa*. Ed. Cecil Abrahams. Trenton, N.J.: Africa World Press, 1990.

Gray, John, ed. *Black Theatre and Performance: A Pan-African Bibliography*. New York: Greenwood Press, 1986.

Gugelberger, Georg, ed. *Marxism and African Literature*. Trenton, N.J.: Africa World Press, 1986.

Gurnah, Abdulrazak, ed. *Essays on African Writing: A Re-evaluation*. Oxford: Heinemann, 1993.

Hafkin, Nancy J. *Women and Development in Africa: An Annotated Bibliography*. Addis Ababa: United Nations Economic Commission for Africa, 1977.

Hafkin, Nancy J., and Edna G. Bay, eds. *Women in Africa: Studies in Social and Economic Change*. Stanford, Calif.: Stanford University Press, 1976.

Harasym, Sarah, ed. *The Post-colonial Critic: Interviews, Strategies, Dialogues*. New York: Routledge, 1990.

Haraway, Donna J. *Simians, Cyborgs, and Women: The Reinvention of Nature*. New York: Routledge, 1991.

Harrison, Nancy. *Winnie Mandela: Mother of a Nation*. London: Gollancz, 1985.

Harrow, Kenneth W., ed. *Faces of Islam in African Literature*. London: J. Currey, 1991.

———, ed. *Thresholds of Change in African Literature: The Emergence of a Tradition*. Portsmouth, N.H.: Heinemann, 1994.

Harrow, Kenneth W., Jonathan Ngate, and Clarisse Zimra, eds. *Crisscrossing Boundaries in African Literatures*. Annual Selected Papers of the ALA, 1986/12. Washington, D.C.: Three Continents Press, African Literature Association, 1991.

Hay, Margaret Jean, and Sharon Stichter, eds. *African Women South of the Sahara*. London: Longman, 1984.

Hennessy, Rosemary. *Materialist Feminism and the Politics of Discourse*. London: Routledge, 1993.

Heywood, Christopher. *Perspectives on African Literature*. New York: Africana, 1971.

Al-Hibri, Azizah, and Marian Young, eds. *Women and Islam*. Oxford: Pergamon Press, 1982.

Hicks, Diane Emily. *Border Writing: The Multidimensional Text*. Minneapolis: University of Minnesota Press, 1991.

Hoare, Quintin, and Geoffrey N. Smith, eds. *Selections from the Prison Notebooks of Antonio Gramsci*. New York: International Publishers, 1971.

Holloway, Karla F. C. *Moorings and Metaphors: Figures of Culture and Gender in Black Women's Literature*. New Brunswick: Rutgers University Press, 1992.

hooks, bell. *Black Looks: Race and Representation*. Boston: South End Press, 1992.

Horn, Peter. *Writing My Reading: Essays on Literary Politics in South Africa*. Amsterdam: Rodopi, 1994.

Hull, Gloria T., Patricia Bell-Scott, and Barbara Smith, eds. *All the Women Are White, All the Blacks Are Men, But Some of Us Are Brave*. Old Westbury, N.Y.: Feminist Press, 1982.

Hume, David. *Philosophical Works*. Boston: Little, Brown, 1854.

Innes, C. L. "Mothers or Sisters? Identity, Discourse, and Audience in the Writing of Ama Ata Aidoo and Mariama Ba." *Motherlands: Black Women's Writing from Africa, the Caribbean, and South Asia*. Ed. Susheila Nasta. New Brunswick: Rutgers University Press, 1992. 129–151.

Irele, Abiola. *The African Experience in Literature and Ideology*. London: Heinemann, 1981.

———. "The Criticism of Modern African Literature." *Perspectives on African Literature*. Ed. Christopher Heywood. New York: Africana, 1971. 9–30.

Irigaray, Luce. *This Sex Which Is Not One*. Trans. Catherine Porter. Ithaca, N.Y.: Cornell University Press, 1985.

Ivan-Smith, Edda. *Women in Sub-Saharan Africa*. London: Minority Rights Group, 1988.

Izevbaye, D. S. "Shifting Bases: The Present Practice of African Criticism." *Research in African Literatures* 21.1 (1990): 127–136.

Jaccard, Anny-Claire. "Les visages de l'Islam chez Mariama Bâ et Aminata Sow Fall." *Nouvelles du Sud* 6 (1986–87): 171–182.

James, Adeola, ed. *In Their Own Voices: African Women Writers Talk*. London: J. Currey; Portsmouth, N.H.: Heinemann, 1990.

James, Stanlie, and Abena Busia, eds. *Theorizing Black Feminisms: The Visionary Pragmatism of Black Women*. London: Routledge, 1993.

Jameson, Fredric. *Marxism and Form: Twentieth-Century Dialectical Theories of Literature*. Princeton: Princeton University Press, 1971.

Jeyifo, Biodun. "Determinations of Remembering: Post-colonial Fictional Genealogies of Colonialism in Africa." *Stanford Literature Review* 10.1–2 (Spring/Fall 1993): 99–116.

———. "The Nature of Things: Arrested Decolonization and Critical Theory." *Research in African Literatures* 21.1 (1990): 33–47.

Jinadu, L. Adele. *Fanon: In Search of the African Revolution*. Enugu: Fourth Dimension Publishing Co., 1980.

Jones, Eldred Durosimi, Eustace Palmer, and Marjorie Jones, eds. *Women in African Literature Today*. London: James Currey, 1987.

Joubert, Jean-Louis. "Francophonie et littérature francophone dans le monde nègro-africaine." *Moderna Sprak* 88.2 (1994): 175–181.

Kalu, Anthonia. "Those Left Out in the Rain: African Literary Theory and the Re-invention of the African Woman." *African Studies Review* 37.2 (September 1994): 13–75.

Katrak, Ketu H. "Decolonizing Culture: Toward a Theory for Postcolonial Women's Texts." *Modern Fiction Studies* 35.1 (1989): 157–179.

Kemp, Yakini. "Romantic Love and the Individual in Novels by Mariama Bâ, Buchi Emecheta, and Bessie Head." *Obsidian II: Black Literature in Review*. 3.3 (1988): 1–16.

Khatibi, Abdelkebir. "Literary Nationalism and Internationalism." In *Faces of Islam in African Literature*. Ed. Kenneth W. Harrow. London: J. Curry, 1991. 3–10.

King, Bruce, ed. *Introduction to Nigerian Literature*. New York: Africana Publishing Corp., 1972 (1971).

Knipp, Thomas. "Politics and Aesthetics: The Theory of Literature and the Practice of Poetry in West Africa." In *Thresholds of Change in African Literature: The Emergence of a Tradition*. Ed. Kenneth W. Harrow. Portsmouth, NH: Heinemann, 1994. 171–180.

La Blanc, Michael L., ed. *Contemporary Black Biography*. Detroit and London: Gale Research, 1992.

Laclau, Ernesto, and Chantal Mouffe. *Hegemony and Socialist Strategy: Towards a Radical Democratic Politics*. London: Verso, 1985.

Lapchick, Richard Edward, and Stephanie Urdang. *Oppression and Resistance: The Struggle of Women in Southern Africa*. Westport, Conn.: Greenwood Press, 1982.

Larrier, Renee. "Correspondance et creation littéraire: Mariama Bâ's *Une Si Longue Lettre*." *French Review: Journal of the American Association of Teachers of French* 64.5 (1991): 747–753.

Lee, Sonia. "Le theme du bonheur chez les romancières de l'Afrique occidentale." *Présence Francophone: Revue Internationale de Langue et de Littérature* 29 (1986): 91–103.

Lemaire, Charles François Alexandre. *Africaines, contribution à l'histoire de la femme en Afrique*. Microform. Bruxelles, Impr. Scientifique, 1897.

Lindfors, Bernth. *Comparative Approaches to African Literatures*. Amsterdam: Rodopi, 1994.

Lindfors, Bernth, and Reinhard Sander, eds. *Twentieth-Century Caribbean and Black African Writers*. First and Second Series. Detroit: Gale Research, 1992, 1993.

Lipman, Beata. *We Make Freedom: Women in South Africa*. London: Pandora Press, 1984.

Little, Kenneth Lindsay. *The Sociology of Urban Women's Image in African Literature*. Totowa, N.J.: Rowman and Littlefield, 1980.

Lorde, Audre. *Sister Outsider: Essay and Speeches*. Trumansburg, N.Y.: Crossing Press, 1984.

Loth, Heinrich. *Woman in Ancient Africa*. Westport, Conn.: L. Hill and Co., 1987.

Mabuza, Lindiwe. *One Never Knows: An Anthology of Black South African Women Writers in Exile*. Braamfontein: Skotaville Publishers, 1989.

Mackenzie, Craig, and Cherry Clayton, eds. *Between the Lines: Interviews With Bessie Head, Sheila Roberts, Ellen Kuzwayo, Miriam Tlali*. Grahamstown: National English Literary Museum, 1989.

Magona, Sindiwe. *Forced to Grow*. London: Women's Press, 1992.

Mani, Lata. "Multiple Mediations: Feminist Scholarship in the Age of Multinational Reception." *Inscriptions* 1989: 1–23.

Markovitz, Irving Leonard, ed. *Studies in Power and Class in Africa*. New York: Oxford University Press, 1987.

Masaba, Rev. D. T. "The Alpha and Omega of the Ancient Days." *Decision* (San Diego) November 1991.

Mazrui, Ali. "The Black Woman and the Problem of Gender: Trials, Triumphs, and Challenges." 1991 Guardian Lecture, Lagos, Nigeria. Reprinted as "The Black Woman and the Problem of Gender: African Perspective." *Research in African Literatures* 24 (Spring 1993): 87–112. With a reply from Omolara Ogundipe-Leslie.

Mbaye d'Enerville, Annette. *Femmes africaines: Propos recueillis par Annette Mbaye d'Enerville sur les thèmes de femmes et société: Suivi de Une si longue lettre par Mariama Bâ: Avec cinq compositions de Gnagna Diène.* Romorantin: Éditions Martinsart, 1982.

Meaney, Gerardine. *(Un)Like Subjects: Women, Theory, Fiction.* London: Routledge, 1993.

Meena, Ruth, ed. *Gender in Southern Africa: Conceptual and Theoretical Issues.* Harare: SAPES Books, 1992.

Memmi, Albert. *The Colonizer and the Colonized.* Boston: Beacon Press, 1967.

Mernissi, Fatima. *Beyond the Veil: Male-Female Dynamics in a Modern Muslim Society.* Cambridge: Schenkman, 1975.

Miller, Christopher. *Blank Darkness: Africanist Discourse in French.* Chicago: University of Chicago Press, 1985.

———. *Theories of Africans: Francophone Literature and Anthropology in Africa.* Chicago: University of Chicago Press, 1990.

Milolo, Kembe. *L'image de la femme chez les romancières de l'Afrique noire francophone.* Fribourg, Suisse: Éditions universitaires, 1986.

Minh-ha, Trinh T. *Woman, Native, Other: Writing Postcoloniality and Feminism.* Bloomington: Indiana University Press, 1989.

Mishra, Vijay, and Bob Hodge. "What Is PostColonialism?" Ed. Patrick Williams and Laura Chrisman. New York: Columbia University Press, 1994. 276–290. Originally appeared in *Textual Practice* 5.3 (1991): 399–414.

Mohanty, Chandra. "Under Western Eyes: Feminist Scholarship and Colonial Discourse." *Third World Women and the Politics of Feminism.* Ed. Chandra Talpade Mohanty, Ann Russo, and Lourdes Torres. Bloomington: Indiana University Press, 1991. 1–47. First Published in *Boundary 2* 12.3–13.1 (Spring/Fall 1984): 333–358.

Mohanty, Chandra Talpade, Ann Russo, and Lourdes Torres, eds. *Third World Women and the Politics of Feminism.* Bloomington: Indiana University Press, 1991.

Moi, Toril. *Sexual/Textual Politics: Feminist Literary Theory.* London: Methuen, 1985.

Moraga, Cherrie. *Loving in the War Years: Lo que nunca paso por sus labios.* Boston: South End Press, 1983.

Moraga, Cherrie, and Gloria Anzaldua, eds. *This Bridge Called My Back: Writings by Radical Women of Color.* Watertown, Mass.: Persephone Press, 1981.

Moser, Gerald, and Manuel Ferreira. *A New Bibliography of the Lusophone Literatures of Africa.* Oxford: Zell, 1993.

Moya, Lily Patience. *Not Either an Experimental Doll: The Separate Worlds of Three South African Women.* London: Women's Press, 1987.

Mudimbe, V. Y. *The Invention of Africa: Gnosis, Philosophy, and the Order of Knowledge.* Bloomington: Indiana University Press, 1988.

Mulokozi, Mugyabuso M. "A Survey of Swahili Literature: 1970–1988." *Africa Focus* 8.1 (1992): 49–61.

Nasta, Susheila, ed. *Motherlands: Black Women's Writing from Africa, the Caribbean, and South Asia.* New Brunswick: Rutgers University Press, 1992.

Nelson, Cary, and Lawrence Grossberg, eds. *Marxism and the Interpretation of Culture.* Urbana: University of Illinois Press, 1988.

Ngũgĩ wa Thiong'o. *Decolonizing the Mind: The Politics of Language in African Literature.* London: Heinemann, 1986.

————. *Moving the Centre: The Struggle for Cultural Freedoms.* London: Heinemann, 1993.

Niang, Sada. "Modes de contextualisation dans *Une si longue lettre* et *L'appel des arènes.*" *Literary Griot* 4.1–2 (Spring/Fall, 1992): 111–125.

Nietzsche, Friedrich. *Beyond Good and Evil: Prelude to a Philosophy of the Future.* Trans. Helen Zimmern. New York: Russell and Russell, 1964.

Njoku, John E. Eberegbulam. *The World of the African Woman.* Metuchen, N.J.: Scarecrow Press, 1980.

Nnaemeka, Obioma. "From Orality to Writing: African Women Writers and the (Re)Inscription of Womanhood." *Research in African Literatures* 25.4 (Winter 1994): 137–157.

Nwanosike, Eugene O. *Women and Rural Development: A Select and Partially Annotated Bibliography.* Douala, Cameroon: International Association Pan African Institute Development. West Africa, 1984.

Obbo, Christine. *African Women: Their Struggle for Economic Independence.* London: Zed Press, 1980.

Ofosu-Appiah, L. H., ed. *Dictionary of African Biography.* New York: Reference Publications, 1977.

Ogundipe-Leslie, Molara. "African Women, Culture, and Another Development." *Theorizing Black Feminisms: The Visionary Pragmatism of Black Women.* Ed. Stanlie James and Abena Busia. London: Routledge, 1993.

————. "The Female Writer and Her Commitment." *Women in African Literature Today.* Ed. Eldred Durosimi Jones, Eustace Palmer and Marjorie Jones. London: James Currey, 1987.

Ogunyemi, Chikwenye O. *Africa Wo/Man Palava: The Nigerian Novel by Women.* Chicago: University of Chicago Press, 1996.

Okpewho, Isidore. "Understanding African Marriage: Towards a Convergence of Literature and Sociology." *Transformations of African Marriage.* Ed. David Parkin and David Nyamwaya. Manchester: Manchester University Press, 1987.

Oliver, Caroline. *Western Women in Colonial Africa.* Westport, Conn.: Greenwood Press, 1982.

Omotoso, Kole. *Achebe or Soyinka? A Study in Contrasts.* Oxford: Zell, 1994.

Ong, Aihwa. "Colonialism and Modernity: Feminist Representations of Women in Non-Western Societies." *Inscriptions* 3.4 (1991): 79–93.

Onwuanibe, Richard C. *A Critique of Revolutionary Humanism: Frantz Fanon.* St. Louis: Warren H. Green, 1983.

Osagie, Iyunolu Folayan. "Technologies of Myth and the Inscription of Subjectivity: Reading Bessie Head's *A Question of Power* and Toni Morrison's *Beloved*" Diss. Cornell University, 1992.

Owomoyela, Oyekan, ed. *A History of Twentieth-Century African Literatures.* Lincoln: University of Nebraska Press, 1993.

Pala, Achola O., and Madina Ly. *La femme africaine dans la société précoloniale*. Paris: UNESCO, 1979.

Parpart, Jane L., and Kathleen A. Staudt, eds. *Women and the State in Africa*. Boulder, Colo.: L. Rienner Publishers, 1989.

Parry, Benita. "Problems in Current Theories of Colonial Discourse." *Oxford Literary Review* 9.1–2 (1987): 27–57.

Paulme, Denise, ed. *Women of Tropical Africa*. Trans. H. M. Wright. Berkeley: University of California Press, 1963.

Pauwels, Randall L. "Swahili Literature and History in the Post-structuralist Era." *International Journal of African Historical Studies* 25.2 (1992): 261–283.

Phillips, Maggi. "Engaging Dreams: Alternative Perspectives on Flora Nwapa, Buchi Emecheta, Ama Ata Aidoo, Bessie Head, and Tsitsi Dangarembga's Writing." *Research in African Literatures* 25.4 (Winter 1994): 89–103.

Pratt, Mary Louise. *Imperial Eyes: Travel Writing and Transculturation*. London and New York: Routledge, 1992.

Qunta, Christine N., ed. *Women in Southern Africa*. London: Allison and Busby, 1987.

Reyes, Angelita. "Crossing the Bridge: The Great Mother in Selected Novels of Toni Morrison, Paule Marshall, Simone Schwarz-Bart, and Mariama Bâ." Unpublished Dissertation, Wisconsin, 1985.

Rich, Adrienne. *Of Woman Born: Motherhood as Experience and Institution*. New York: Norton, 1976.

Robertson, Claire, and Iris Berger, eds. *Women and Class in Africa*. New York: Africana Pub. Co., 1986.

Robinson, Ronald, John Gallagher, and Alice Denny. *Africa and the Victorians: The Official Mind of Imperialism*. 2nd ed. Basingstoke, Hampshire, and London: Macmillan, 1981.

Romero, Patricia W., ed. *Life Histories of African Women*. London: Ashfield Press, 1988.

Rubin, Martin. *Sarah Gertrude Millin: A South African Life*. Johannesburg: Donker, 1977.

Saadawi, Nawal El. *The Hidden Face of Eve: Women in the Arab World*. London: Zed Press, 1980.

Sacks, Karen. *Sisters and Wives: The Past and Future of Sexual Equality*. Westport, Conn.: Greenwood Press, 1979.

Said, Edward. *Culture and Imperialism*. New York: Alfred A. Knopf, 1993.

———. "Literature, Theory, and Commitment." In *Crisscrossing Boundaries in African Literatures*. Ed. Kenneth W. Harrow, Jonathan Ngate, and Clarisse Zimra. Annual Selected Papers of the ALA, Washington, D.C.: Three Continents Press, African Literature Association, 1991.

Sample, Maxine. "The Representation of Space in Selected Works by Bessie Head, Buchi Emecheta, and Flora Nwapa." Diss. Emory University, 1990.

Sanderson, Lilian Passmore. *Against the Mutilation of Women: The Struggle to End Unnecessary Suffering*. London: Ithaca Press, 1981.

Sandoval, Chela. "U.S. Third World Feminism: The Theory and Method of Oppositional Consciousness in the Postmodern World." *Genders* 10 (Spring 1991): 1–24.

Schild, Ulla, ed. *Jaw-bones and Umbilical Cords: A Selection of Papers Presented at the 3rd Janheinz Jahn Symposium 1979 and the 4th Janheinz Jahn Symposium 1982*. Berlin: D. Reimer, 1985.

Schipper, Mineke, ed. *Unheard Words: Women and Literature in Africa, the Arab World,*

Asia, the Caribbean, and Latin America. Trans. Barbara Potter Fasting. London;
New York: Allison and Busby, 1985.

Scobie, Alastair. *Women of Africa*. London: Cassell, 1960.

Sherwood, Marika. *Women under the Sun: African Women in Politics and Production:
A Bibliography, 1982–5*. London: Institute for African Alternatives, 1988.

Slomski, Genevieve. "Dialogue in the Discourse: A Study of Revolt in Selected Fiction
by African Women." *Dissertation Abstracts International* 47.5 (November 1986):
1721A.

Smith, Valerie. "Black Feminist Theory and the Representation of the Other." *Changing
Our Own Words: Essays on Criticism, Theory, and Writing by Black Women*. Ed.
Cheryl Wall. New Brunswick: Rutgers University Press, 1989. 38–57.

Spillers, Hortense J. "Mama's Baby, Papa's Maybe: An American Grammar Book."
Diacritics 17.2 (Summer 1987): 65–81.

Spivak, Gayatri Chakravorty. "The Burden of English." *Orientalism and the Postcolonial Predicament*. Ed. Carol A. Breckenridge and Peter van der Veer. Philadelphia: University of Pennsylvania Press, 1993. 134–157.

———. "Can the Subaltern Speak?" *Marxism and the Interpretation of Culture*. Ed.
Cary Nelson and Lawrence Grossberg. Urbana: University of Illinois Press, 1988.
271–313.

———. "Literature, Theory, and Commitment." In *Crisscrossing Boundaries in African
Literatures*. Ed. Kenneth W. Harrow, Jonathan Ngate, and Clarisse Zimra. Annual
Selected Papers of the ALA, Washington, D.C.: Three Continents Press, African
Literature Association, 1991.

———. "The Politics of Interpretations." *In Other Worlds: Essays in Cultural Politics*.
London: Routledge, 1988.

Staunton, Cheryl Antoinette. "Three Senegalese Women Novelists: A Study of Tem-
poral/Spatial Structures." Diss. George Washington University, 1986.

Steady, Filomina Chioma. *The Black Woman Cross-culturally*. Cambridge, Mass.:
Schenkman, 1981.

Stevenson, Catherine Barnes. *Victorian Women Travel Writers in Africa*. Boston: Twayne
Publishers, 1982.

Stichter, Sharon, and Jane L. Parpart. *Patriarchy and Class: African Women in the Home
and the Workforce*. Boulder, Colo.: Westview Press, 1988.

Stratton, Florence. *Contemporary African Literature and the Politics of Gender*. London
and New York: Routledge, 1994.

———. "The Shallow Grave: Archetypes of Female Experience in African Fiction."
Research in African Literatures 19.1 (Summer 1988): 143–169.

Stringer, Susan. "Cultural Conflict in the Novels of Two African Writers, Mariama Bâ
and Aminata Sow Fall." *SAGE: A Scholarly Journal on Black Women* 5 supp.
(1988): 36–41.

Suleri, Sara. "Woman Skin Deep: Feminism and the Postcolonial Condition." Ed. Patrick Williams and Laura Chrisman. New York: Columbia University Press, 1994.
244–256. Originally appeared in *Critical* Inquiry 18 (Summer 1992): 756–769.

Swanepoel, C. F., ed. *Comparative Literature and African Literatures*. Pretoria: Via Afrika, 1993.

Taiwo, Oladele. *Female Novelists in Modern Africa*. New York: St. Martin's Press, 1985
(1984).

Terborg-Penn, Rosalyn, Sharon Harley, and Andrea Benton Rushing, eds. *Women in*

Africa and the African Diaspora. Washington, D.C.: Howard University Press, 1987.

Thiam, Awa. *Speak Out, Black Sisters: Feminism and Oppression in Black Africa.* Translation of *La parole aux négresses.* London: Pluto, 1986.

Tiffin, Chris, and Alan Lawson, eds. *De-scribing Empire: Postcolonialism and Textuality.* London: Routledge, 1994.

Touré, Sekou. "The Political Leader as the Representative of a Culture." Speech. Rome, Italy, 1959.

Tucker, Robert, ed. *The Marx-Engels Reader.* New York: Norton, 1972.

Udenta, Vedenta O. *Revolutionary Aesthetics and the African Literary Process.* Enugu, Nigeria: Fourth Dimension, 1993.

Umeh, Marie, ed. *Emerging Perspectives on Buchi Emecheta.* Trenton, N.J.: Africa World Press, 1996.

Van Sertima, Ivan, ed. *Black Women in Antiquity.* New Brunswick, N.J.; London: Transaction Books, 1988.

Veit-Wild, Flora. *Teachers, Preachers, Non-Believers: A Social History of Zimbabwean Literature.* London: Zell, 1992.

———. "Women Writing about the Things That Move Them: Interview with Tsitsi Dangarembga." *Black Women's Writings': Crossing the Boundries.* Ed. Carole Boyce Davies. Frankfurt: Matatu, 1989.

Wachege, P. N. *African Women Liberation: A Man's Perspective.* Kiambu, Kenya: P. N. Wachege, 1992.

Walker, Alice. *Possessing the Secret of Joy.* New York: Harcourt Brace Jovanovich.

Walker, Alice, and Pratibha Parmar. *Warrior Marks: Female Genital Mutilation and the Sexual Blinding of Women.* New York: Harcourt Brace, 1993.

Walker, Cherryl. *Women and Resistance in South Africa.* London: Onyx Press, 1982.

Walker, Margaret. "On Being Female, Black, and Free." *The Writer on Her Work.* Ed. Janet Stenburg. New York: W. W. Norton and Co., 1980. 101.

Ware, Helen Ruth Elizabeth, ed. *Women, Education, and Modernization of the Family in West Africa.* Canberra: Dept. of Demography, Australian National University; Miami: Distributed by Australian National University Press, 1981.

Warner-Vieyra, Myriam. *Juletane.* Trans. Betty Wilson. London: Heinemann, 1987.

Weed, Elizabeth, ed. *Coming to Terms: Feminism, Theory, Politics.* New York: Routledge, 1989.

Weedon, Chris. *Feminist Practice and Poststructuralist Theory.* Oxford: Basil Blackwell, 1987.

Weixlmann, Joe, and Houston A. Baker, Jr., eds. *Black Feminist Criticism and Critical Theory.* Greenwood, F.L.: Penkeville, 1988.

West, Cornel. "Marxist Theory and the Specificity of Afro-American Oppression." *Marxism and the Interpretation of Culture.* Ed. Cary Nelson and Lawrence Grossberg. Urbana: University of Illinois Press, 1988. 17–33.

Westley, David. "A Select Bibliography of South African Autobiography." *Biography* 17.3 (Summer 1994): 268–280.

White, Jonathan, ed. *Recasting the World: Writing after Colonialism.* Baltimore: Johns Hopkins University Press, 1993.

Wilentz, Gay Alden. *Binding Cultures: Black Women Writers in Africa and the Diaspora.* Bloomington: Indiana University Press, 1992.

Wilkinson, Jane, ed. *Talking with African Writers: Interviews with African Poets, Playwrights, and Novelists*. London: James Currey, 1992 (1990).

Williams, Eric. *Capitalism and Slavery*. New York: Perigee Books, 1944.

Williams, Patrick, and Laura Chrisman. *Colonial Discourse and Post-colonial Theory: A Reader*. New York: Columbia University Press, 1994.

Zahar, Renate. *Colonialism and Alienation*. Trans. Willfried F. Feuser. Benin City: Ethiope Publishing Co., 1974.

Zell, Hans M., Carol Bundy, and Virginia Coulon, ed. *A New Reader's Guide to African Literature*. 2nd edition. New York: Africana, 1983.

Zongo, Opportune. *Women's Voices on Africa: A Century of Travel Writings*. New York: M. Wiener, 1992.

INDEX

Abrahams, Cecil, 215

Achebe, Chinua, xvi, xxiv, 8, 16, **19–31**, 37, 42, 50–51, 106, 158, 223, 235, 306–8, 330–31, 339, 341, 343, 356, 359–63, 365, 370, 373, 408, 451, 474–75; *Anthills of the Savannah*, xvi, 25; *Arrow of God*, 23–24; *Beware, Soul Brother*, 25; *Chike and the River*, 27; *Don't Let Him Die*, 362; *The Drum*, 27; *The Flute*, 27; *Girls at War and Other Stories*, 26; *Hopes and Impediments*, 26, 477; *A Man of the People*, xvi, 24–25, 223; *Morning Yet on Creation Day*, 19–21, 23, 26, 28, 51; *No Longer at Ease*, 23, 235; "The Novelist as Teacher," 20; *Okike: An African Journal of New Writing*, 20; *Things Fall Apart*, 19–24, 27–28, 339, 365; *The Trouble with Nigeria*, 26; *Uwa ndi Igbo: A Journal of Igbo Life and Culture*, 20

Acholonu, Catherine, 346, 350

Activism, 91, 207, 263–64, 271, 308, 311, 348, 375, 413–14, 418, 443. *See also* Politics, activism

Acts: British Imperial Land Act, 318; Immorality Act, xxviii, 185, 338, 394; Suppression of Communism Act, 85. *See also* Colonial, laws

African: aesthetics, 54–56, 89–90, 165, 271–72, 281, 357–58, 366–69, 371; childhood, 27, 38, 217, 225, 228, 255, 262–64, 275–81, 283–88, 309, 322, 340, 364, 425, 443; countries, xiii, 24, 191, 396, 400–402, 404, 408–10, 413, 425–49, 434; culture and experience, x, xxiii, 23–25, 27, 32, 34, 46, 41, 42, 50, 53–55, 60, 107–8, 113, 115, 118, 120, 125–26, 131–32, 136, 145, 149–58, 191, 207, 210, 213, 224–25, 262–67, 275–80, 285, 319, 353–54, 364–71, 397–98, 427, 429–31, 440, 447, 449, 468; diaspora, 2, 33, 36, 165; empires, 447; feminism, x–xi, xv–xxiii, xvii–xxix, 1–17, 35–36, 42, 60–63, 68–74, 81–83, 122, 126–28, 139–43, 149–63, 172–74, 179, 287, 291–95, 298–99, 339–42, 345–51, 418–20, 456–59, 469–70, 477–89 (*see also* Arab culture, feminists; Black, women; Womanism); identity, 36, 48–49, 53, 126–27, 136; immigrants, 77–79, 242, 246, 283–84, 421, 466; language, xiii, xiv, 49, 111–13, 130–33, 136–37, 139, 171 (*see also* Anglophone; Ethnic Africans; Francophone literature; Indigenous Africans; Women, writers and writing); leaders/leadership, 119, 151–55, 172, 189, 222, 224, 230, 233, 338, 348, 417, 427, 447–48; literature, ix–xi, xiii–xv, xxix, 1–17, 24, 49–50, 120, 152, 157–58, 171, 258–60, 276, 281, 299, 319, 333–34, 370–72, 441, 463–74; Marxist analysis of, 286; past, 33, 79; politics, 10, 33–35, 46–49, 56, 77, 108, 223; psyche, 9, 223; readers, 82; and segregation, 384; society, xxi, xxiv, 10, 47, 60, 73, 77, 150–51, 156, 158, 171–72, 225, 230, 235, 264, 285, 310, 365, 367–68; spirituality, mysticism and African traditional religions, 52–58, 352–55, 468; traditions and values, xxi, xxvi, 7, 10, 32, 34–36, 40, 42, 49–50, 53–56, 61, 77–78, 80, 143, 167, 173, 208, 212, 223, 235, 265, 275, 280, 302, 306, 308–11, 338, 361, 367–72, 378; women, xv, 33–36, 42, 60–74, 76–83, 120–21, 131–33, 151–52, 156, 158, 171–72, 188–200, 231, 261–63, 285, 296–99, 308, 340–41, 468–70 (*see also* African, feminism); worldview, xxiv, 158, 210, 364, 444, 469–70; writers/ing, ix–xxviii, 1–17, 215 (*see also* African, literature; Women, writers and writing)

African-American, 2, 27, 54–56, 89–90, 144, 165, 173, 188, 262, 271–72, 281, 340, 358, 366–69, 371. *See also* American; Black

Aidoo, Ama Ata, xvii, xviii, xxvi, 11–12, 16, **32–39**, 53, 58, 217, 219; *Anowa*, 32, 34; *Changes*, 35–36; *The Dilemma of a Ghost*, 32–33; *No Sweetness Here*, 32, 34; *Our Sister Killjoy*, 32, 34–37; *Someone Talking to Sometime*, 32, 35

Alienation, 184, 188, 192, 218–19, 235, 254, 403–4, 470; from country/culture, 403, 470; linguistic, 143; literature of, 102; from others (*see* Self, and other); from self, 23, 203 (*see also* Self); spiritual, 55

Algeria, xviii, xxviii, 46, 48, 98, 135, 241, 243, 247, 249, 383, 420–24, 427

Alkali, Zaynab, xxii, **40–44**; *The Cobwebs*, 42; "Das eigene Lieben" (The Survivor), 42; "Feminism," 42; "Haus des Schreckens" (House of Horror), 42; "Salzlose Asche" (Saltless Ash), 42; *The Stillborn*, xxii, 40–43; *The Virtuous Woman*, 41

Allan, Tuzyline Jita, *Womanist and Feminist Aesthetics*, 155

Amadiume, Ifi, 6, 346

American, 173, 378, 410; criticism of, 107; culture, 213; influence, xxviii, 96, 314, 361; imperialism, ix

Amuta, Chidi, 89–90, 350; *The Theory of African Literature*, 350

Andrade, Susan, 340

Anglophone, xiii, 20, 56, 312, 327, 331, 414, 418, 434, 463; and Francophone voices, 331

Angola, 4, 194, 463

Anyinefa Koffi, 463

Anzaldua, Gloria, xxvi

Apartheid, xix, 56, 85–91, 145, 183, 188–91, 195, 201, 207, 262–73, 335–36, 387, 393, 443, 448, 450, 466–68, 470; and anti-apartheid, 85–88, 190–96, 393; condemnation of, xx, 80, 188, 268, 393; and desire, 336; immoral construct of, 195; injustices of, xvi–xvii, 85, 89, 265, 273; laws, 85, 184, 392; oppressions of, 333–34, 443; and post-apartheid, xxv, 87, 90, 196; regime, 333; resistance to, 190; society, 208; system of, xix, xvvii, 207, 263, 269, 417. *See also* Women, and Apartheid

Appiah, Kwame Anthony, xxvi

Arabic culture, xviii, xxviii, 98, 101–2, 123, 136–37, 248 (*see also* Islam; Koran; Maghreb); feminists, 102; language and literature, 176, 253; women, 99, 102–4, 253; writers, xiv, 96–104, 253 (*see also* African, literature)

Armah, Ayi Kwei, xv, xvi, **45–51**, 53, 132, 146, 357, 359; *The Beautyful Ones Are Not Yet Born*, xv, 46–47, 50, 74; "The Festival Syndrome," 49; *Fragments*, 45–50; *The Healers*, 49–50;

468; and morality, 119; and mythology, 361; and wedding, 121

Circumcision and clitoridectomy, 78; female, 321; male, 318

City dwellers, 100, 119, 236; *Female Vision of the City*, 294. *See also* Metropolitan

Cixous, Hélène, 7, 16

Clark-Bekederemo, J. P., xvi, **105–10**, 345, 356, 360, 376; *America, Their America*, 106–7; *The Bikoroa plays*, 106, 108; *Casualities*, 106, 108–9; *A Decade of Tongues*, 106; *The Example of Shakespeare*, 106; *Mandela and Other Poems*, 109; *Ozidi*, 106–9; *The Ozidi Saga*, 106; *Poems*, 105, 107; *A Reed in the Tide*, 106–7; *Song of a Goat*, 105, 107, 109; *State of the Union*, 108–9; *Three Plays*, 106; *The Wives' Revolt*, 106

Class, xx, xxi, 1, 7, 53, 120, 150, 178, 214, 325, 330, 348, 350, 374, 378; barriers and differences, 120, 202, 238, 285, 290; exploitation and oppression, 238, 265, 272; and immigration, 421; privileges, 42, 47, 192; ruling, 124, 223; structure, 236; struggle, 308, 311; taboos, 206; tensions, 210; and war, 223, 238

Cobham, Rhonda, 156, 179

Coetzee, J. M., 188, 199, 271–73, 418–19; *White Writing*, 418–19

Colonialism, ix–x, xxii, xxiv, xxv, xxvii, 1–17, 22–23, 33–34, 45, 49, 52–54, 61, 73, 111–13, 119–20, 130–32, 135–43, 145, 175–78, 189–90, 258, 285–90, 307–11, 313, 316, 319, 322, 333, 336, 353–55, 366–68, 374, 383–84, 394, 400–403, 421, 426, 431, 438, 440, 443–54, 466 (*see also* Acts; Apartheid; Imperialism); analysis of, 235; and anticolonialism, 107, 122, 133, 308, 323, 383, 385, 434, 461 (*see also* British, colonialism); and bureaucracy, 100, 314, 383, 462 (*see also* Capitalism); and colonization, 286, 469; conceptions, 124; conditions, ix, 77–78, 313, 403, 438, 467; and conflict, 222, 263;

criticism of, xvi, 107, 243, 284, 307, 439; and cultural and economic dominance, 10, 52, 54–55, 367, 403; double, 131, 135, 196, 344, 469–70; and education, xxi, 52, 59, 223, 361; European, ix, xvi, 4, 107, 400, 444; evils of, xxiii, 131, 440; experience, xv, 33, 120, 190; and exploitation, xvi, 2; and the feminine, 218 (*see also* French, colonization); and hegemony, 136; hypocrisy, 384; influence of, 321, 403; injustices of, 77, 129–30, 235, 263; Italian, 175; language legacy, 113; laws, 86, 90, 190, 334 (*see also* Acts; Apartheid, laws); and masculinism, ix; mental/ity, 42, 243, 307, 469; and mimicry, 121; moral failure of, 190; and nationalism (*see also* Nationalism and Nationalists); oppression, xiv, 35, 76, 236, 270, 308, 470; orientaiton to, 195 (*see also* orientalism; Patriarchy); period of, 68, 123, 131, 136, 177–78, 222, 259, 306–7, 405; and postcolonialism, 1–17, 353, 366–68, 371, 394, 410–11, 419, 432, 467 (*see also* Postcolonialism); and the psyche, 223; psychological effect of, 107, 322, 354; resistance to, xxviii (*see also* Resistance); and sexuality, 190; and the Sharpeville Massacre, 85; and slave trade/slavery, 131, 166, 389, 400; trauma, 132; university of, 223, 354; violence, 183, 340, 368 (*see also* Wars; White)

Colonized subject, ix, 4, 7, 12, 122, 130, 223, 264, 365–66, 430, 432; condition of, 404; pathology of, 121

Colonizer, 175, 178, 353–54, 361, 365, 384; attitudes towards and portrayal of Africans, 223, 259, 307, 354; culture and religion of, 224; demythologizing, 383; and education, 469; language of, 132, 137; world view of, 4, 326

Coltrane, John, 144

Communist party, 284, 286–87, 427

Congo, 144, 146, 460–65

Conrad, Joseph, 27, 313; *Heart of Darkness*, 27

ABOUT THE CONTRIBUTORS

JUDITH IMALI ABALA is an assistant professor in English at Ohio Dominican College. A citizen of Kenya, she earned her doctorate from Ohio State University. She has taught courses in Swahili language and literature, black studies, philosophy in contemporary African literature, and culture and language. A creative writer herself, she has conducted field research on oral narratives in Kenya.

MORADEWUN A. ADEJUNMOBI has worked at the University of Ibadan in Nigeria, the Centre d'études d'Afrique noire in Bordeaux, France, and at the University of Botswana in southern Africa. At present, she teaches in the African-American and African Studies program at the University of California in Davis, from where she continues to carry out research on African literature in European languages. She is the author of a book-length study of Madagascar's most famous writer, entitled *JJ Rabearivelo, Literature, and Lingua Franca in Colonial Madagascar.*

LINDSAY PENTOLFE AEGERTER, assistant professor in the Department of English at the University of North Carolina, Wilmington, teaches postcolonial, Third World, multicultural, and women's literature, with a special emphasis on African, African-American, and Caribbean women's literature. Originally from Zimbabwe, she returns home each summer to extend her research into African women's writing and to attend the Zimbabwe Women Writers workshops. She has published work on Zimbabwean writer Tsitsi Dangarembga, on pedagogies of postcolonial literature, and on her theoretical principles of the dialectic of autonomy and community, the matrix of identity, and the politics of location.

ADAKU T. ANKUMAH is an assistant professor of English at Tuskegee University, Tuskegee, Alabama. Her current research interest is female writers from Africa.

AWUOR AYODO, who passed away in the summer of 1996, was completing her Ph.D. in comparative literature, focusing on the "Storytelling Tradition of Black Women in Africa, the Caribbean, and the United States," at the University of Illinois at Urbana-Champaign. Her article "Definitions of the Self in Luo Women's Orature" appeared in the *Review of African Literatures* (1994). Her short story "Workday" was published in *The Heinemann Book of African Women's Writing* (1993).

JARED BANKS is a doctoral student in African languages and literature at the University of Wisconsin–Madison, specializing in Lusophone African literature. He has also done research on mythology, film, and the Yoruba language and culture, both in Africa and the diaspora. He was recently awarded the Fulbright IIE for research in Mozambique.

HAROLD BARRATT is professor of English at the University College of Cape Breton, Sydney, Nova Scotia, Canada, and has served as coordinator of the English Sub-Department and chair of the Department of Languages, Letters, and Communication. He is the coeditor of Frank Collymore's *The Man Who Loved Attending Funerals and Other Stories*. Among his numerous publications are entries in the *Dictionary of Literary Biography, Reworlding: The Literature of the Indian Diaspora*, and *Writers of the Indian Diaspora: A Bio-bibliographical Critical Sourcebook*. He is also completing a collection of essays, *August Prelude: A West Indian in Cape Breton*.

JOGAMAYA BAYER, born in India, based in Germany, is an independent scholar. Her published articles, mainly on Indian literature in English, have included an entry in *Writers of the Indian Diaspora*.

MAXINE BEAHAN is a doctoral student at Stirling University, Scotland, working on a Ph.D. in feminist theory and East and West African writers. She is currently engaged in social work with Home-Start voluntary agency, offering support for families with young children.

ROBERT BENNETT is a graduate student in English at the University of California at Santa Barbara. He received a B.A. in philosophy and an M.A. in English from Brigham Young University. His master's thesis is titled "Wilson Harris' Caribbean Carnival: Trickster Discourse as a Postcolonial, Postmodern Narrative Strategy." His primary research interests include the postcolonial literature, literary theory, and general trends in twentieth-century literature.

DAVID BEUS is a doctoral student in comparative literature at the University of North Carolina, Chapel Hill, specializing in eighteenth-century literature and contemporary African literature. One aspect of the eighteenth century that interests him in particular is African-European relations.

EMEVWO BIAKOLO was born in the Delta State, Nigeria, and studied in the University of Ibadan, obtaining a Ph.D. in English in 1988. Currently he teaches African poetry and oral literature at the University of Botswana, Gaborone. He has published a collection of poems, *Ravages and Solaces* (1994). Another collection, *Strides of the Night*, and an edited selection of conference papers, *Critical Currents and African Literature*, are in press.

ALMA JEAN BILLINGSLEA-BROWN is an assistant professor in English at Spelman College. She teaches black women writers, the African diaspora, and seminars on African-American literature, Folklore, and black aesthetics. She has conducted research on African literature at the University of Ghana, Legon, and is currently working on a study entitled "Crossing Borders: Folklore and Contemporary African-American Women's Fiction and Visual Art."

NICHOLAS BIRNS teaches at the New School for Social Research, New York, and is the book review editor of the journal *Antipodes: A North American Journal of Australian Literature*. He has published in *Arizona Quarterly* and *Studies in Romanticism*.

BRINDA BOSE is a doctoral student at Boston University, Boston, working on gender, race, and silence in modern and postcolonial literature and on issues of influence, repetition and revision. She has published essays in *And the Birds Began to Sing: Religion and Literature in Post-Colonial Cultures* (1996) and *Bharati Mukherjee: Critical Perspectives* (1993).

HEMA CHARI is an assistant professor at California State University, Los Angeles, and teaches postcolonial literature and theory, modern British literature, and film. Her essay "Decentered on the (A) isle of the Postcolonial: *My Beautiful Laundrette, Sammy and Rosie Get Laid*, and *Madame Souzatska*" appeared in *Spectator* (Spring 1989). Several essays on nation, gender, immigrant, and diasporic issues are forthcoming. She is also working on a book, *Fabulous Artificer and the Forked Tongue of the Postcolonial Reality*.

ELENI COUNDOURIOTIS is an assistant professor in the Department of English at the University of Connecticut, Storrs. She obtained her Ph.D. in English and comparative literature from Columbia University in 1992. Her article on Bessie Head, "Authority and Invention in the Fiction of Bessie Head" appeared in *Research in African Literatures* (1996). She is also working on a book project derived from her dissertation, *Realism as Historical Method*, in which she is expanding the treatment of African literature and broadening the theoretical scope of the project.

CAROLE BOYCE DAVIES is a professor of English and director of African-New World studies at Florida International University, Miami, Florida. She has taught in the Department of English and African-American Studies and Comparative Literature at the State University of New York at Binghamton. Among her numerous publications are *Ngambika: Studies of Women in African Literature* (coedited with Anne Adams Graves, 1986), *Out of the Kumbla: Caribbean Women and Literature* (coedited with Elaine Savory Fido, 1990), "Private Selves and Public Spaces: Autobiography and the African Woman Writer," *College Language Association Journal* (1991), and *Black Women, Writing, and Identity: Migrations of the Subject* (1994).

SAMBA DIOP earned his Ph.D. at the University of California, Berkeley. He is presently an assistant professor of French at Harvard University. He has taught at the State University of New York at Buffalo. His publications include *The Oral History and Literature of the Wolof People of Waalo, Northern Senegal* and articles on the African novel in French and English, African oral literatures and traditions, and African cinema.

SAMUEL A. DSEAGU is a senior lecturer and head of the Department of English at the University of Ghana, Legon. His publications include "The Form of Asante Folk Tales," *Universitas* (1988); "The Influence of Folklore Techniques on Form of the African Novel," *New Literary History* (1992); and "Ghana Television Drama as a Reflection of Government Opinion," *Research Review* (1992).

MUSA W. DUBE is a lecturer in the University of Botswana. She was on study leave at Vanderbilt University. She teaches New Testament in the Department of Theology and Religion. Her interests are feminist, literary, and postcolonial interpretations of the Bible. She has published a number of articles on religion.

FEMI EUBA was born in Lagos, Nigeria. He trained as an actor in England at the Rose Bruford College of Speech and Drama in Kent. He received an M.F.A. in playwriting and an M.A. in Afro-American studies at Yale University and a Ph.D. in literature at the University of Ife in Nigeria. He has had professional theatre experience as actor, playwright, and director in England, Nigeria, and the United States. He currently teaches playwriting, acting, and directing, as well as black drama and theatre, at Louisiana State University. He also directs a play production annually for LSU Theatre.

BRIAN EVENSON teaches at the Department of English, Oklahoma State University, Stillwater. He received his doctorate in English literature from the University of Washington. He has published essays and reviews in numerous journals, among which are "Heterotopia and Negativity in Beckett's *Molly(s)*" in *Symposium: A Quarterly Journal in Modern Foreign Language* (1992) and

"Zimbabwe's Beat Generation: Dambudzo Marechera and African Literature" (review) in *Exquisite Corpse* (1992). He has also translated Edouard Maunick's *Ensoleille Vif* from the French-African (with David Beus) (1992).

VANESSA EVERSON has been lecturing in French language and literature, with special responsibility for courses on Ferdinand Oyono, at the Pietermaritzburg campus of the University of Natal since 1987. She has presented papers at international conferences and has published articles on the Cameroonian author.

JOHN C. HAWLEY is associate professor of English at Santa Clara University. He is the editor of *Cross-Addressing: Resistance Literature and Cultural Borders* (1996) and of *Writing the Nation: Self and Country in the Post-colonial Imagination* (1996). He has written on South African literature, Buchi Emecheta, Ben Okri, Mongo Beti, Nuruddin Farah, Driss Chraïbi, and others.

HILDEGARD HOELLER received her doctorate from Rutgers University. She is an assistant professor in the Department of Arts and Humanities at Babson College, Massachusetts. She was a preceptor in the Expository Writing Program at Harvard University. Her fields of interest are American fiction, feminist criticism, genre studies, composition, and African literature. She has published "The Unpeaceful Voices of African Women Writers," *MAWA Review* (1993), and other articles in journals such as *South Carolina Review* and *Names*.

NALINI IYER received her Ph.D. in English from Purdue University. She is currently assistant professor of English at Seattle University, where she teaches postcolonial literature and British literature. At present, she is revising her dissertation on British women writers and imperialism.

SIGA FATIMA JAGNE is at present the executive director of the Women's Bureau with ADCO Development Services and Associates in the Gambia. She has served as an assistant professor in comparative literature in the English Department at Spelman College, Atlanta, and has taught African literature, the African diaspora and the world, literary theory and criticism, women's studies, and other courses. She received her Ph.D. from the State University of New York at Binghamton, focusing on feminist studies and African women's literature, particularly Mariama Bâ and Bessie Head. Her research interests are numerous and include immigration, women in academia, and oral performance poetry.

J. ROGER KURTZ is assistant professor of English at SUNY College at Brockport. He is the author of *Urban Obsessions, Urban Fears: An Introduction to the Kenyan Novel* (1998).

ANNE E. LESSICK-XIAO is currently completing her Ph.D. in the Department of African Languages and Literature at the University of Wisconsin–Madison. Her dissertation grew out of a Fulbright predissertation grant to the Congo in 1989–90 and focuses on selected works by Jean Malonga, Sylvain Bemba, and Sony Labou Tansi. An ESL/EFL and Swahili instructor for the last fifteen years, she is active in both foreign-language pedagogy and literary criticism.

CHRISTINE LOFLIN is an assistant professor of English at Grinnell College. Her Ph.D. from the University of Wisconsin–Madison focused on ''Race, Nationalism, and Colonialism in the African Landscape.'' Her review of *A People's Voice: Black South African Writing in the Twentieth Century* is forthcoming in *Africa Today*. Her article on Ngugi wa Thiong'o was recently published in *Research in African Literatures*.

CAROL P. MARSH-LOCKETT is assistant professor of English at Georgia State University in Atlanta, where she teaches courses in seventeenth-century English literature, African-American literature, and Caribbean literature. She has published essays and reviews in *CLA Journal, Dictionary of Literary Biography, Fifty Caribbean Writers*, and *Encyclopedia of Post-colonial Literatures in English*. She was the guest editor of *Decolonising Caribbean Literature* (*Studies in the Literary Imagination* 26.2, 1993) and has forthcoming publications in *New Critical Perspectives on Ben Johnson* and *The Oxford Companion to African American Literature*.

CRAIG W. MCLUCKIE was educated in Scotland and Canada; he teaches English literature at Okanagan University College in Canada. His criticism on African and Scottish literatures has been published internationally.

LISA MCNEE, a candidate for the Ph.D. in comparative literature at Indiana University, is writing a dissertation on Senegalese women's autobiographical discourses under the direction of Eileen Julien.

SORAYA MÉKERTA, a native of Algeria, is an assistant professor in French, Francophone literature, film, and the African diaspora and the world. She received her Ph.D. from the University of Minnesota. Her research interests span postcolonialism, neocolonialism, immigration, and North African studies.

S. D. MÉNAGER teaches in the Department of French, University of Natal, Pietermaritzburg.

JO E. NEL was born in Mufulira, Zambia, and studied in South Africa. Specializing in modern British drama, he has published on Shakespeare and has reviewed a number of books, especially those pertaining to South African literature. Authors reviewed include Nadine Gordimer, Vusi Mavimbene, Peter Horn, Gillian Slovo, and Don Mattera.

EMMANUEL S. NELSON is a professor of English at the State University of New York at Cortland. Among the several books that he has edited are *Connections: Essays on Black Literatures* (1988), *Reworlding: The Literature of the Indian Diaspora* (Greenwood, 1992), *Writers of the Indian Diaspora: A Bio-bibliographical Critical Sourcebook* (Greenwood, 1993), and *Bharati Mukherjee: Critical Perspectives* (1993).

JULIANA MAKUCHI NFAH-ABBENYI is an assistant professor of English and postcolonial literatures at the University of Southern Mississippi. She holds a licence ès lettres bilingues, a maîtrise, and a doctorat in Negro-African literature from the University of Yaounde (Cameroon) and a Ph.D. in comparative literature from McGill University (Montreal). She has researched oral and written literatures from Africa and the African diaspora, with emphasis on folktales and women's writing. She has published in journals such as *Canadian Women's Studies* and *Comparative Literature in Canada* as well as essay chapters. Her book *Gender in African Women's Writing: Identity, Sexuality, and Difference* is forthcoming.

ODE S. OGEDE is a professor of African literature, oral and written, at Ahmadu Bello University, Zaria, Nigeria. He has been on leave, teaching in the United States at the University of Pennsylvania (1994–95), Lincoln University (1995–96), and at North Carolina Central University (1996–97). His forthcoming books on African literature are *Torrent of Songs* and *The Shaping Vision of Achebe and Armah: Language, Narrative, and Metaphors in Modern African Literature.*

CHINYERE GRACE OKAFOR is the head of the Department of English and Literature, University of Benin, Benin City, Nigeria. She has published, among other articles, an article on Efua Sutherland in *Kiabara: Journal of the Humanities.*

IYUNOLU FOLAYAN OSAGIE is assistant professor of English at Pennsylvania State University, teaching American literature, postcolonial and Third World literature and theory, and African, Caribbean, and African-American women's literature. She completed her Ph.D. dissertation at Cornell University on Bessie Head's *A Question of Power* and Toni Morrison's *Beloved.* She has published in *African American Review* and has book and article manuscripts in progress.

PUSHPA NAIDU PAREKH is assistant professor of comparative literature in the English Department, Spelman College, Atlanta. She teaches postcolonial literature, women in non-Western literatures, African literature, the African diaspora and the world, British literature, and immigrant women's literature. She has published chapters and articles on postcolonial, immigrant, and American writers. Her book *Response to Failure* on British poets is forthcoming.

LYNNE DUMONT ROGERS recently finished her Ph.D. in comparative literature from the University of Connecticut, Storrs. Her dissertation is a Kristevean reading of selected works of Moroccan writers Tahar Ben Jelloun and Mohammed Khaïr-Eddine and the Spanish writer Juan Goytisolo. She is currently continuing her research on the Maghreb and Arab novel.

ELAINE SAVORY teaches at the New School for Social Research, New York City. She has taught at universities in Ghana, Nigeria, and the West Indies and has written extensively on Caribbean and African literatures, especially on theatre and drama, poetry, and women's writing. She has coedited with Carole Boyce Davies *Out of the Kumbla: Caribbean and Women Literature* (1990). Her first volume of poems, *flame tree time*, was published in Jamaica (1993). Presently, she is completing a study of Jean Rhys, her second volume of poems, *gingerbread house*, and a volume of personal essays.

CHRISTINE W. SIZEMORE is a professor of English at Spelman College, Atlanta, where she has taught for seventeen years. She published a book entitled *A Female Vision of the City: London in the Novels of Five British Women* (1989) and has recently published on Buchi Emecheta and Virginia Woolf.

DOMINIC THOMAS is one of the founders of the United Kingdom–based Association for the Study of African and Caribbean Literatures in French (ASCLF). After teaching at the University College, London, and Middlesex University, he recently completed his doctoral dissertation at Yale University, entitled "New Writing for New Times: Nationalism in Congolese Literature." He also directed Sony Labou Tansi's *La parenthèse de sang* in England in 1989. He is currently W. M. Scholl Assistant Professor of French and Francophone Studies at the University of Notre Dame and is working on Francophone sub-Saharan theatre and on the relationship between African authors and the post-colonial political elite.

MARIE UMEH teaches literature of the African world, Western literature, and writing composition in the Department of English at John Jay College of Criminal Justice, the City University of New York. She is the former chairperson of the English Department at Anambra State College of Education in Awka, Anambra State, Nigeria, where she taught African and American literatures for seven years. She has published extensively on Buchi Emecheta in various journals and books and is the editor of the anthology *Emerging Perspectives on Buchi Emecheta* (1996).

MARY B. VOGL is completing her Ph.D. in French literature at Indiana University. Her dissertation is entitled "Picturing the Maghreb: Orientalism, Photography, and Representation in Contemporary Francophone Texts." Her forthcoming publications include essays on Hanan El Shayk and Alifa Rifaat in

The Encyclopedia of Literary Translation and an essay in *La Présence de l'Autre dans la littérature francophone*.

NORMAN WEINSTEIN is a writer and educator with expertise in special program development in the arts and humanities. His areas of focus include poetry, therapeutic uses of texts with the elderly, and the literary and musical forms of Africa and the African diaspora. His several book and article publications span creative writing (poetry) and literary and music criticism, for example, *Nigredo* (1982), *Gertrude Stein and the Literature of the Modern Consciousness* (1970), and *A Night in Tunisia: Imaginings of Africa in Jazz* (1992). He currently resides on the outskirts (Abeokuta edge) of Ibadan, Nigeria.